Praise for the First Edition

An enjoyable and important read. Highly recommended!

—David Barkol, Microsoft

An instant classic! The only book you need to learn and master Angular 2 and TypeScript.

—David DiMaria, MapQuest

Excellent! The purpose of this book is not knowledge but action.

—Irach Ilish Ramos Hernandez, Groupaxis

Shows you how to leverage the combined power of TypeScript and Angular 2, with all the best practices baked in.

—Sébastien Nichele, Pacifica

This book helps a newbie gain a firm grasp of the span of technologies in the Angular 2 ecosystem, and as such it's a go-to resource for those just getting started.

—Jeremy Bryan, Software Architect, CACI International

A great, comprehensive coverage of Angular 2, easy to follow with a plethora of helpful examples.

—Polina Keselman, Principal Java developer

Angular Development with Typescript

SECOND EDITION

YAKOV FAIN
ANTON MOISEEV

MANNING
SHELTER ISLAND

For online information and ordering of this and other Manning books, please visit www.manning.com. The publisher offers discounts on this book when ordered in quantity. For more information, please contact

Special Sales Department
Manning Publications Co.
20 Baldwin Road
PO Box 761
Shelter Island, NY 11964
Email: orders@manning.com

Manning Publications Co.
20 Baldwin Road
PO Box 761
Shelter Island, NY 11964

Development editor: Kristen Watterson
Technical development editor: Doug Warren
Review editor: Aleksandar Dragosavljević
Project manager: Vincent Nordhaus
Copy editor: Corbin Collins
Proofreader: Katie Tennant
Technical proofreader: Keith Webster
Typesetter: Dottie Marsico
Cover designer: Marija Tudor

ISBN 9781617295348
Printed and bound by CPI Group (UK) Ltd, Croydon, CR0 4YY
1 2 3 4 5 6 7 8 9 10 – SP – 23 22 21 20 19 18

brief contents

contents

preface

Our quest for a good JavaScript framework started about five years ago. One of our largest projects was written using the Apache Flex framework (formerly Adobe Flex). Flex is an excellent framework for developing web UIs, but it requires Flash Player, which isn't in favor anymore.

After trying several pilot JavaScript projects, we noticed a substantial drop in our developers' productivity. A task that required one day in Flex and ActionScript would need three days in other JavaScript frameworks, including AngularJS. The main reasons were the lack of types in JavaScript, poor IDE support, and the absence of compiler support.

After switching to Angular and TypeScript, we can confirm that it's the most productive way of developing mid- to large-size web applications that can run in any modern browser, as well as on mobile platforms.

These are the main reasons we believe that Angular and TypeScript are the right tools for developing web applications:

- *Clean separation of UI and app logic.* There's a clean separation between the code that renders the UI and the code that implements application logic. The UI doesn't have to be rendered in HTML, and there are already products that support native UI rendering for iOS and Android.
- *Modularization.* There's a simple mechanism for modularizing applications with support for the lazy loading of modules.
- *Navigation.* The router supports complex navigation scenarios in single-page applications.

- *Loose coupling.* Dependency injection gives you a clean way to implement loose coupling between components and services. Binding and events allow you to create reusable and loosely coupled components.
- *Component lifecycle.* Each component goes through a well-defined lifecycle, and hooks for intercepting important component events are available for application developers.
- *Change detection.* An automatic (and fast) change-detection mechanism spares you from the need to manually force UI updates while providing you a way to fine-tune this process.
- *No callback hell.* Angular comes with the RxJS library, which allows you to arrange subscription-based processing of asynchronous data, eliminating callback hell.
- *Forms and validation.* Support for forms and custom validation is well designed. You can create forms either by adding directives to form elements in the template or programmatically.
- *Testing.* Unit and end-to-end testing are well supported, and you can integrate tests into your automated build process.
- *Tooling.* Angular is well supported by IDEs. The TypeScript code analyzer warns you about errors as you type. Angular CLI quickly generates a new project and various artifacts (such as components and services), comes with a web server, and performs dev and prod builds, sparing developers from dealing with configuration scripts.
- *Concise code.* Using TypeScript classes and interfaces makes your code concise and easy to read and write.
- *Compilers.* The TypeScript code can be compiled into ES3, ES5, or the latest versions of JavaScript. Ahead-of-time compilation of app templates makes the initial app rendering faster and eliminates the need to package the Angular compiler with your app.
- *Server-side rendering.* Angular Universal turns your app into HTML in an offline build step that can be used for server-side rendering, which in turn greatly improves indexing by search engines and SEO.
- *Modern-looking UI components.* Angular Material offers more than 35 well-designed UI components.

As you can see from this list, Angular comes with the batteries included.

From a project-management perspective, Angular is appealing, because there are already more than a million AngularJS developers, and most of them will switch to Angular. Having a large pool of workers with specific skills is an important consideration for selecting a technology for new projects. Besides, there are more than 15 million Java and .NET developers, combined, and many of them will find the syntax of TypeScript a lot more appealing than JavaScript because of its support for classes, interfaces, generics, annotations, class member variables, and private and public variables, not to mention its helpful compiler and solid support from familiar IDEs. New major releases of Angular are published semiannually, and the upgrades from one release to another go smoothly.

Writing the first edition of this book was difficult, because we started with early alpha versions of the framework, which were changing quite frequently. Now, the framework is stable, and after three years of real-world development and running countless workshops, we understand and can explain the Angular framework a lot better. We do encourage you to buy this second edition of the book even if you already own the first one.

acknowledgments

Yakov would like to thank his best friend Sammy for creating a warm and cozy environment while Yakov was working on this book. Unfortunately, Sammy can't talk, but he loves Yakov and all family members. Sammy's breed is Mini Golden Retriever. Special thanks go to all the people who enrolled in our workshop and provided valuable feedback.

Anton would like to thank the authors and contributors to the open source projects used in this book. Without the numerous hours they regularly dedicate to the projects, constant work to grow, and support communities, the book won't be possible. He's also grateful to Yakov Fain and Manning Publications for giving him the opportunity to coauthor this book, and to his family for being patient while he was working on the book.

We would both like to thank Keith Webster for his work on this book. In addition, the authors would like to thank the following people for reviewing the book: Alain Couniot, Alberto Acerbis, Angel Ramon Rodriguez, Dennis Sellinger, Desmond Horsley, Javier Mercado, Joseph Hunt, Kunal Jaggi, Michael Angelo, Mike Jensen, Peter Lawrence, Rahul Rai, Rudi Steinbach, and Ruslan Verbelchuk.

about this book

Although Angular applications can be developed in JavaScript, using TypeScript is a lot more productive. The framework itself was developed in TypeScript, and in this book we use TypeScript for all the code examples. Chapter 1 has a section titled "Why develop in TypeScript and not in JavaScript?" where we explain our reasons for selecting this language.

Who should read this book

Both authors are practitioners, and we wrote this book for practitioners. Not only do we explain the features of the framework using basic code samples, but we also gradually build a single-page online auction application in the course of this book.

While working both editions of this book, we ran multiple workshops using the code samples from the book. This allowed us to get early (and overwhelmingly positive) feedback about the book's content. We really hope that you'll enjoy the process of learning Angular with this book.

Our early drafts had chapters on ECMAScript and TypeScript at the start of the book, but several reviewers suggested we move this material to the appendixes so readers could start learning about Angular sooner. We made this change, but if you aren't already familiar with the syntax of ECMAScript and TypeScript, looking through appendixes A and B first will make it easier to reason about the code samples in the book.

Starting from chapter 6, we use reactive programming and observable streams, which are offered by the RxJS library described in appendix D. If you are new to reactive programming, we suggest you go through appendix D after reading the first five chapters.

Where to get the source code

This book contains many examples of source code both in numbered listings and in-line with normal text. In both cases, source code is formatted in a `fixed-width font like this` to separate it from ordinary text. Sometimes code is also **`in bold`** to highlight code that has changed from previous steps in the chapter, such as when a new feature adds to an existing line of code.

In many cases, the original source code has been reformatted; we've added line breaks and reworked indentation to accommodate the available page space in the book. In rare cases, even this was not enough, and listings include line-continuation markers (➥). Additionally, comments in the source code have often been removed from the listings when the code is described in the text. Code annotations accompany many of the listings, highlighting important concepts.

We maintain a GitHub repository with the source code at https://github.com/Farata/angulartypescript. Angular keeps evolving, and we may update the code samples after the book is printed.

How this book is organized

This section provides a brief overview of the book's content.

Chapter 1 starts with a high-level overview of the Angular architecture, and then we'll introduce you to Angular CLI—the tool that will generate a new Angular project in less than a minute so you can see the first app running right away. We'll discuss different ways of compiling Angular projects. Finally, we'll introduce a sample ngAuction application that you'll be developing with us starting from chapter 2.

Chapter 2 will get you familiar with the main artifacts of Angular: components, services, directives, pipes and modules. At the end of chapter 2, we provide detailed instructions on creating the first version of the sample ngAuction app. From this point on, most chapters end with a hands-on section where you'll be working on this sample online auction, gradually adding new features or even doing a complete rewrite.

Chapter 3 introduces the Angular router, used to arrange client-side navigation in a single-page app. You'll learn how to configure routes and how to pass parameters between them. You'll also see how to create component hierarchies where both parents and children have their own routes.

Chapter 4 covers more-advanced router features. You'll learn how to protect routes and create components with multiple router outlets. We'll show you how to use the router for loading your app modules lazily (on demand). At the end of this chapter, you'll continue working on ngAuction under our guidance.

Chapter 5 is about dependency injection (DI). We'll start with an overview of DI as a design pattern, explaining the benefits of having a framework to create and inject object instances. You'll learn the roles of providers and injectors and how to easily swap the object being injected if need be. At the end of this chapter, you'll make a small facelift to ngAuction using the Angular Material library of UI components.

Chapter 6 is about working with observable streams of data, and prior to reading this chapter, you need to become familiar with the basics of the RxJS library covered in appendix D. We'll start by showing you how to treat events with observables. Then you'll see various Angular APIs that offer ready-to-use observable streams. You'll also learn how to discard unwanted HTTP requests with the RxJS `switchMap` operator.

Chapter 7 introduces the Flex Layout library that will allow you to design UI layouts that adapt to the width of user devices. You'll also see how to use the `ObservableMedia` service that allows you to apply different CSS depending on the screen size. At the end of this chapter, we'll start rewriting ngAuction from scratch using the Angular Material and Flex Layout libraries.

Chapter 8 is about arranging intercomponent communications in a loosely coupled manner. You'll learn about the input and output properties of Angular components and see how two components can communicate without knowing about each other, via a common parent or an injectable service.

Chapter 9 includes an overview of the component lifecycle and the change detection mechanism. At the end of the chapter, we'll add a product view to ngAuction.

Chapter 10 will get you familiar with the Angular Forms API. You'll learn the difference between the template-driven and reactive forms. You'll see how to access form data entered by the user as well as update forms programmatically.

Chapter 11 continues coverage of the Forms API. Here you'll learn how to validate form data. You'll learn how to create and use built-in custom validators for both template-driven and reactive forms. Finally, we'll add a search form to ngAuction so the user can search for products. You'll have a chance to apply the concepts from chapters 10 and 11 in practice.

Chapter 12 is about communicating with web servers using HTTP. Angular offers an `HttpClient` service with a rich API. You'll see how to issue GET and POST requests and intercept all HTTP requests and responses to implement cross-cutting concerns. As an additional bonus, you'll learn how to write web servers using Node and Express frameworks. We'll use these servers so Angular clients have someone to talk to, and show you how to write scripts for deploying Angular apps under web servers.

Chapter 13 explains how to write Angular applications that communicate with the server using the WebSocket protocol, which is an efficient and low-overhead way of communication. One of the most valuable features of WebSocket communications is that the server can initiate pushing data to the client when an important event happens, without waiting for the client to request the data. You'll see a practical use of WebSocket communication in our ngAuction, which implements bidding notifications over WebSockets. The new version of ngAuction comes as two separate projects—one with client-side code and another with server code.

Chapter 14 is about testing. We'll introduce you to unit testing with Jasmine and end-to-end testing with Protractor. We'll also show you how to test the search workflow in ngAuction with Protractor.

Chapter 15 is about maintaining app state in Redux style using the ngrx library. It starts with explaining the principles of Redux, and then you'll see how ngrx implements these principles in Angular apps. The chapter ends with a code review of the final version of ngAuction, which uses ngrx for state management.

This book comes with four appendixes. They cover a new syntax of ECMAScript, TypeScript, basics of the Node package manager (npm), and the library of RxJS extensions.

Appendix A contains an overview of the syntax introduced in ECMAScript 6, 7, and 8. You'll learn how to use classes, fat-arrow functions, spread and rest operators, what destructuring is, and how to write asynchronous code as if it's synchronous with the help of the `async-await` keywords. At the time of this writing, ECMAScript 6 is supported by most of the major web browsers.

Appendix B is an overview of the syntax of TypeScript, which is a superset of JavaScript. TypeScript will increase your productivity when creating JavaScript apps. Not only will you learn how to write classes, interfaces, and generics, but also how to compile TypeScript code into JavaScript that can be deployed in all web browsers today.

Appendix C is a brief overview of the npm and Yarn package managers, which are used to install JavaScript packages, libraries, and frameworks on developer machines. You'll understand how project dependencies are configured in the package.json file and what semantic versioning is about.

Appendix D is an introduction to RxJS, a popular library of reactive extensions. You'll learn the roles of observables, observers, and subscribers and how to compose RxJS operators to handle data streams in a functional way. While the RxJS library can be used with any JavaScript app, it's a crucial part of the Angular framework, so understanding the main concepts of RxJS is a must.

Book forum

Purchase of *Angular Development with Typescript, Second Edition* includes free access to a private web forum run by Manning Publications where you can make comments about the book, ask technical questions, and receive help from the authors and from other users. To access the forum, go to https://forums.manning.com/forums/angular-development-with-typescript-2E. You can also learn more about Manning's forums and the rules of conduct at https://forums.manning.com/forums/about.

Manning's commitment to our readers is to provide a venue where a meaningful dialogue between individual readers and between readers and authors can take place. It is not a commitment to any specific amount of participation on the part of the authors, whose contribution to the forum remains voluntary (and unpaid). We suggest you try asking them some challenging questions lest their interest stray! The forum and the archives of previous discussions will be accessible from the publisher's website as long as the book is in print.

about the authors

Yakov Fain works for Farata Systems, an IT consulting boutique, where he helps various clients with their Angular-related projects. Yakov is a Java Champion, and he has authored multiple books on software development. He has written more than a thousand blogs at yakovfain.com. Although most of his books are printed, his *Java Programming for Kids, Parents, and Grandparents* is available for free download in several languages at http://myflex.org/books/java4kids/java4kids.htm. His Twitter handle is @yfain.

Anton Moiseev is a lead software developer at SuranceBay. He's been developing enterprise applications for more than a decade with Java and .NET technologies. He has a solid background and strong focus on web technologies, implementing best practices to make the frontend work seamlessly with the backend. He has taught a number of training sessions on AngularJS and Angular frameworks. His Twitter handle is @antonmoiseev.

about the cover illustration

The illustration on the cover of *Angular Development with TypeScript, Second Edition* is taken from the 1805 edition of Sylvain Maréchal's four-volume compendium of regional dress customs. This book was first published in Paris in 1788, one year before the French Revolution. Each illustration is colored by hand. This figure, captioned "Le Tuteur" or "The Tutor," is just one of many figures in Maréchal's collection. Their diversity speaks vividly of the uniqueness and individuality of the world's towns and regions just 200 years ago. This was a time when the dress codes of two regions separated by a few dozen miles identified people uniquely as belonging to one or the other. The collection brings to life a sense of the isolation and distance of that period and of every other historic period—except our own hyperkinetic present.

Dress codes have changed since then, and the diversity by region, so rich at the time, has faded away. It is now often hard to tell the inhabitant of one continent from another. Perhaps we have traded cultural diversity for a more varied personal life—certainly for a more varied and fast-paced technological life.

We at Manning celebrate the inventiveness, the initiative, and the fun of the computer business with book covers based on the rich diversity of regional life two centuries ago, brought back to life by Maréchal's pictures.

1 Introducing Angular

This chapter covers

- A high-level overview of the Angular framework
- Generating a new project with Angular CLI
- Getting started with Angular modules and components
- Introducing the sample application ngAuction

Angular is an open source JavaScript framework maintained by Google. It's a complete rewrite of its popular predecessor, AngularJS. The first version of Angular was released in September 2016 under the name Angular 2. Shortly after, the digit *2* was removed from the name, and now it's just *Angular*. Twice a year, the Angular team make major releases of this framework. Future releases will include new features, perform better, and generate smaller code bundles, but the architecture of the framework most likely will remain the same.

Angular applications can be developed in JavaScript (using the syntax of ECMAScript 5 or later versions) or TypeScript. In this book, we use TypeScript; we explain our reasons for this in appendix B.

NOTE In this book, we expect you to know the syntax of JavaScript and HTML and to understand what web applications consist of. We also assume that you know what CSS is. If you're not familiar with the syntax of

TypeScript and the latest versions of ECMAScript, we suggest you read appendixes A and B first, and then continue reading from this chapter on. If you're new to developing using Node.js tooling, read appendix C.

NOTE All code samples in this book are tested with Angular 6 and should work with Angular 7 without any changes. You can download the code samples from https://github.com/Farata/angulartypescript. We provide instructions on how to run each code sample starting in chapter 2.

This chapter begins with a brief overview of the Angular framework. Then we'll start coding—we'll generate our first project using the Angular CLI tool. Finally, we'll introduce the sample application ngAuction that you'll build while reading this book.

1.1 Why select Angular for web development?

Web developers use different JavaScript frameworks and libraries, and the most popular are Angular, React, and Vue.js. You can find lots of articles and blog posts comparing them, but such comparisons aren't justified, because React and Vue.js are libraries that don't offer a full solution for developing and deploying a complete web application, whereas Angular does offer that full solution.

If you pick React or Vue.js for your project, you'll also need to select other products that support routing, dependency injection, forms, bundling and deploying the app, and more. In the end, your app will consist of multiple libraries and tools picked by a senior developer or an architect. If this developer decides to leave the project, finding a replacement won't be easy because the new hire may not be familiar with all the libraries and tools used in the project.

The Angular framework is a platform that includes all you need for developing and deploying a web app, batteries included. Replacing one Angular developer with another is easy, as long as the new person knows Angular.

From a technical perspective, we like Angular because it's a feature-complete framework that you can use to do the following right out of the box:

- Generate a new single-page web app in seconds using Angular CLI
- Create a web app that consists of a set of components that can communicate with each other in a loosely coupled manner
- Arrange the client-side navigation using the powerful router
- Inject and easily replace *services*, classes where you implement data communication or other business logic
- Arrange state management via injectable singleton services
- Cleanly separate the UI and business logic
- Modularize your app so only the core functionality is loaded on app startup, and other modules are loaded on demand
- Creating modern-looking UIs using the Angular Material library

- Implement reactive programming where your app components don't pull data that may not be ready yet, but subscribe to a data source and get notifications when data is available

Having said that, we need to admit that there is one advantage that React and Vue.js have over Angular. Although Angular is a good fit for creating single-page apps, where the entire app is developed in this framework, the code written in React and Vue.js can be included into any web app, regardless of what other frameworks were used for development of any single-page or multipage web app.

This advantage will disappear when the Angular team releases a new module currently known as `@angular/elements` (see https://github.com/angular/angular/tree/master/packages/elements). Then you'll be able to package your Angular components as custom elements (see https://developer.mozilla.org/en-US/docs/Web/Web_Components/Custom_Elements) that can be embedded into any existing web app written in JavaScript, with or without any other libraries.

1.2 Why develop in TypeScript and not in JavaScript?

You may be wondering, why not develop in JavaScript? Why do we need to use another programming language if JavaScript is already a language? You wouldn't find articles about additional languages for developing Java or C# applications, would you?

The reason is that developing in JavaScript isn't overly productive. Say a function expects a `string` value as an argument, but the developer mistakenly invokes it by passing a numeric value. With JavaScript, this error can be caught only at runtime. Java or C# compilers won't even compile code that has mismatching types, but JavaScript is a dynamically typed language and the type of a variable can be changed during runtime.

Although JavaScript engines do a decent job of guessing the types of variables by their values, development tools have a limited ability to help you without knowing the types. In mid- and large-size applications, this JavaScript shortcoming lowers the productivity of software developers.

On larger projects, good IDE context-sensitive help and support for refactoring are important. Renaming all occurrences of a variable or function name in statically typed languages is done by IDEs in a split second, but this isn't the case in JavaScript, which doesn't support types. If you make a mistake in a function or a variable name, it's displayed in red. If you pass the wrong number of parameters (or wrong types) to a function, again, the errors are displayed in red. IDEs also offer great context-sensitive help. TypeScript code can be refactored by IDEs.

TypeScript follows the latest ECMAScript specifications and adds to them types, interfaces, decorators, class member variables (fields), generics, enums, the keywords `public`, `protected`, and `private`, and more. Check the TypeScript roadmap on GitHub at https://github.com/Microsoft/TypeScript/wiki/Roadmap to see what's coming in future releases of TypeScript.

TypeScript interfaces allow you to declare custom types. Interfaces help prevent compile-time errors caused by using objects of the wrong type in your application.

The generated JavaScript code is easy to read and looks like hand-written code. The Angular framework itself is written in TypeScript, and most of the code samples in the Angular documentation (see https://angular.io), articles, and blogs are use TypeScript. In 2018, a Stack Overflow developer survey (https://insights.stackoverflow.com/survey/2018) showed TypeScript as the fourth-most-loved language. If you prefer to see more scientific proof that TypeScript is more productive compared to JavaScript, read the study "To Type or Not to Type: Quantifying Detectable Bugs in JavaScript," (Zheng Gao et al., ICSE 2017) available at http://earlbarr.com/publications/typestudy.pdf.

From the authors' real-world experience

We work for a company, Farata Systems, that over the years developed pretty complex software using the Adobe Flex (currently Apache Flex) framework. Flex is a productive framework built on top of the strongly typed, compiled ActionScript language, and the applications are deployed in the Flash Player browser plugin (a virtual machine).

When the web community started moving away from using browser plugins, we spent two years trying to find a replacement for the Flex framework. We experimented with different JavaScript-based frameworks, but the productivity of our developers seriously suffered. Finally, we saw a light at the end of the tunnel with a combination of the TypeScript language, the Angular framework, and the Angular Material UI library.

1.3 Overview of Angular

Angular is a component-based framework, and any Angular app is a tree of components (think views). Each view is represented by instances of component classes. An Angular app has one root component, which may have child components. Each child component may have its own children, and so on.

Imagine you need to rewrite the Twitter app in Angular. You could take a prototype from your web designer and start by splitting it into components, as shown in figure 1.1. The top-level component with the thick border encompasses multiple child components. In the middle, you can see a New Tweet component above two instances of the Tweet component, which in turn has child components for reply, retweet, like, and direct messaging.

A parent component can pass data to its child by binding the values to the child's component property. A child component has no knowledge of where the data came from. A child component can pass data to its parent (without knowing who the parent is) by emitting events. This architecture makes components self-contained and reusable.

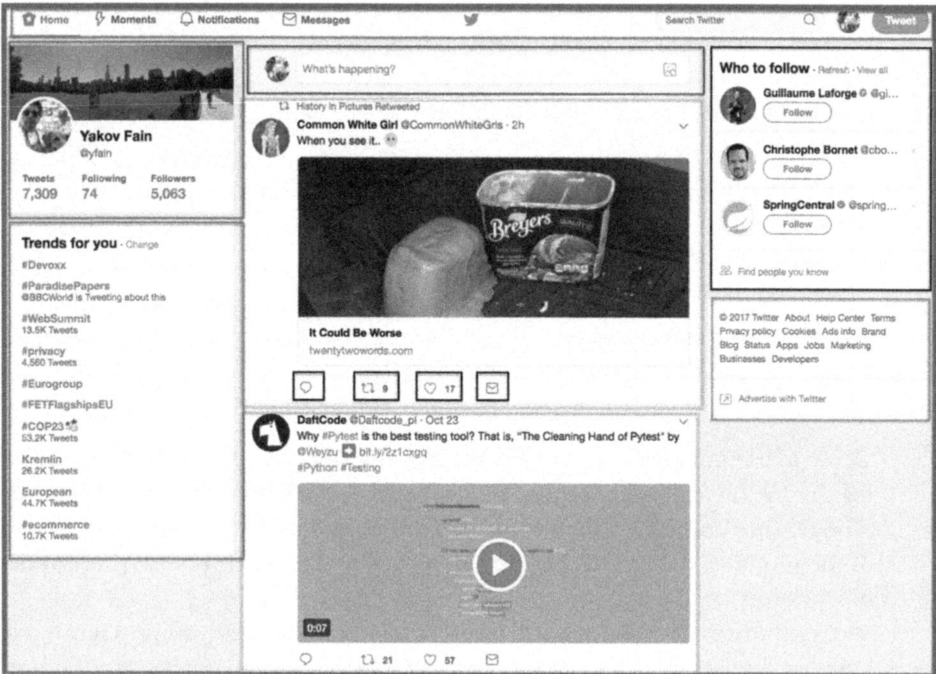

Figure 1.1 Splitting a prototype into components

When writing in TypeScript, a *component* is a class annotated with a decorator, `@Component()`, where you specify the component's UI (we explain decorators in section B.10, "Decorators," in appendix B).

```
@Component({
    ...
}
export class AppComponent {
    ...
})
```

Most of the business logic of your app is implemented in services, which are classes without a UI. Angular will create instances of your service classes and will inject them into your components. Your component may depend on services, and your services may depend on other services. A *service* is a class that implements some business logic. Angular injects services into your components or other services using the dependency injection (DI) mechanism we talk about in chapter 5.

Components are grouped into Angular modules. A *module* is a class decorated with `@NgModule()`. A typical Angular module is a small class that has an empty body, unless you want to write code that manually bootstraps the application—for example, if an app includes a legacy AngularJS app. The `@NgModule()` decorator lists all components and other artifacts (services, directives, and so on) that should be included in this module. The following listing shows an example.

Listing 1.1 A module with one component

```
@NgModule({
  declarations: [
    AppComponent          <-- Declares that AppComponent belongs to this module
  ],
  imports: [
    BrowserModule
  ],
  bootstrap: [AppComponent]   <-- Declares that AppComponent is a root component
})
export class AppModule { }
```

To write a minimalistic Angular app, you can create one `AppComponent` and list it in the `declarations` and `bootstrap` properties of `@NgModule()`. A typical module lists several components, and the root component is specified in the `bootstrap` property of the module. Listing 1.1 also lists `BrowserModule`, which is a must for apps that run in a browser.

Components are the centerpiece of the Angular architecture. Figure 1.2 shows a high-level diagram of a sample Angular application that consists of four components and two services, all packaged inside a module. Angular injects its `HttpClient` service into your app's `Service1`, which in turn is injected into the `GrandChild1` component.

The HTML template of each component is inlined either inside the component (the `template` property of `@Component()`) or in the file referenced from the component using the `templateUrl` property. The latter option offers a clean separation between the code and the UI. The same applies to styling components. You can either

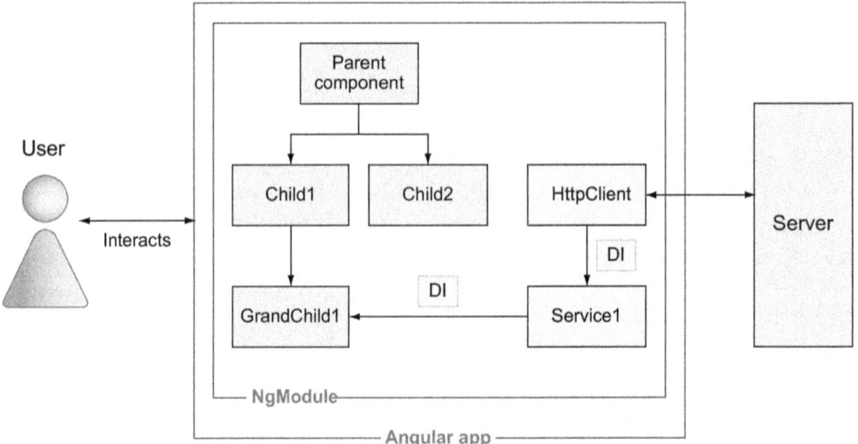

Figure 1.2 Sample architecture of an Angular app

inline the styles using the `styles` property, or provide the location of your CSS file(s) in `styleURLs`. The following listing shows the structure of some search component.

Listing 1.2 Structure of a sample component

```
@Component({
  selector: 'app-search',
   templateUrl: './search.component.html',
   styleUrls: ['./search.component.css']
 })
export class SearchComponent {
  // Component's properties and methods go here
}
```

Other components' templates can use the tag <app-search>.

The template's code is in this file.

The component's styles are in this file (there could be more than one).

The value in the `selector` property defines the name of the tag that can be used in the other component's template. For example, the root app component can include a child search component, as in the following listing.

Listing 1.3 Using the search component in the app component

```
@Component({
  selector: 'app-root',
  template: `<div>
              <app-search></app-search>
             </div>`,
  styleUrls: ['./app.component.css'],
})
export class AppComponent {
    ...
}
```

The UI of the AppComponent includes the UI of the SearchComponent.

Listing 1.3 uses an inline template. Note the use of the backtick symbols instead of quotes for a multiline template (see section A.3 in appendix A).

The Angular framework is a great fit for developing single-page applications (SPAs), where the entire browser's page is not being refreshed and only a certain portion of the page (view) may be replacing another as the user navigates through your app. Such client-side navigation is arranged with the help of the Angular router. If you want to allocate an area within a component's UI for rendering its child components, you use a special tag, `<router-outlet>`. For example, on app start, you may display the home component in this outlet, and if the user clicks the Products link, the outlet content will be replaced by the product component.

To arrange navigation within a child component, you can allocate the `<router-outlet>` area in the child as well. Chapters 3 and 4 explain how the router works.

UI components for Angular apps

The Angular team has released a library of UI components called Angular Material (see https://material.angular.io). At the time of this writing, it has more than 30 well-designed UI components based on the Material Design guidelines (see https://material.io/guidelines). We recommend using Angular Material components in your projects, and if you need more components in addition to Angular Material, use one of the third-party libraries like PrimeNG, Kendo UI, DevExtreme, or others. You can also use the popular Bootstrap library with Angular applications, and we show how to do this in the ngAuction example in chapter 2. Starting in chapter 7, you'll rewrite ngAuction, replacing Bootstrap components with Angular Material components.

Angular for mobile devices

Angular's rendering engine is a separate module, which allows third-party vendors to create their own rendering engine that targets non-browser-based platforms. The TypeScript portion of the components remains the same, but the content of the `template` property of the `@Component` decorator may contain XML or another language for rendering native components.

For example, you can write a component's template using XML tags from the NativeScript framework, which serves as a bridge between JavaScript and native iOS and Android UI components. Another custom UI renderer allows you to use Angular with React Native, which is an alternative way of creating native (not hybrid) UIs for iOS and Android.

We stated earlier that a new Angular app can be generated in seconds. Let's see how the Angular CLI tool does it.

1.4 Introducing Angular CLI

Angular CLI is a tool for managing Angular projects throughout the entire life-cycle of an application. It serves as a code generator that greatly simplifies the process of new-project creation as well as the process of generating new components, services, and routes in an existing app. You can also use Angular CLI for building code bundles for development and production deployment. Angular CLI will not only generate a boilerplate project for you, it will also install Angular framework and all its dependencies.

Angular CLI has become a de facto way of starting new Angular projects. You'll install Angular CLI using the package manager npm. If you're not familiar with package managers, read appendix C. To install Angular CLI globally on your computer so it can be used for multiple projects, run the following command in the Terminal window:

```
npm install @angular/cli -g
```

After the installation is complete, Angular CLI is ready to generate a new Angular project.

1.4.1 Generating a new Angular project

CLI stands for *command-line interface*, and after installing Angular CLI, you can run the `ng` command from the Terminal window. Angular CLI understands many command-line options, and you can see all of them by running the `ng help` command . You'll start by generating a new Angular project with the `ng new` command. Create a new project called hello-cli:

```
ng new hello-cli
```

This command will create a directory, hello-cli, and will generate a project with one module, one component, and all required configuration files including the package.json file, which includes all project dependencies (see appendix C for details). After generating these files, Angular CLI will start npm to install all dependencies specified in package.json. When this command completes, you'll see a new directory, hello-cli, as shown in figure 1.3.

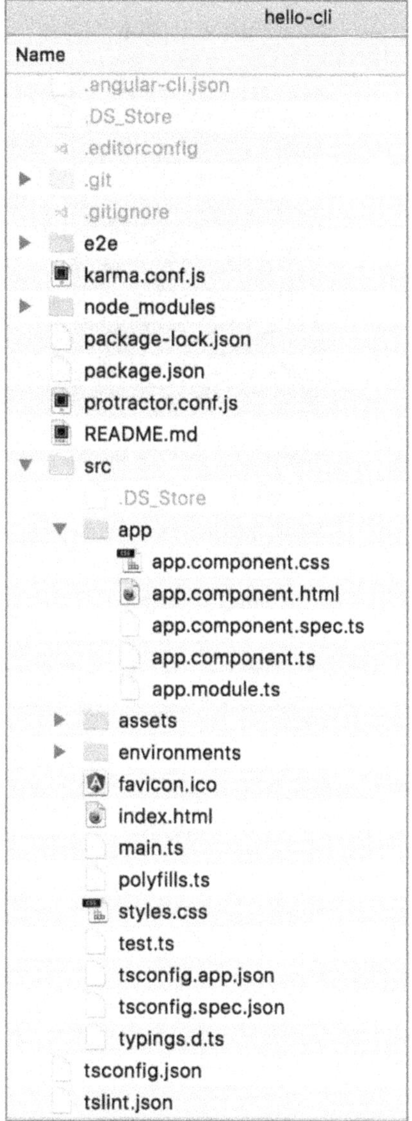

Figure 1.3 A newly generated Angular project

TIP Say you have an Angular 5 project and want to switch to the latest version of Angular. You don't need to modify dependencies in the package.json file manually. Run the `ng update` command, and all dependencies in package.json will be updated, assuming you have the latest version of Angular CLI installed. The process of updating your apps from one Angular version to another is described at https://update.angular.io.

We'll review the content of the hello-cli directory in chapter 2, but let's build and run this project. In the Terminal window, change to the hello-cli directory and run the following command:

```
ng serve
```

Angular CLI will spend about 10–15 seconds to compile TypeScript into JavaScript and build the application bundles. Then Angular CLI will start its dev server, ready to serve this app on port 4200. Your terminal output may look like figure 1.4.

```
/Users/yfain11/hello-cli
MacBook-Pro-8:hello-cli yfain11$ ng serve
** NG Live Development Server is listening on localhost:4200, open your browser
on http://localhost:4200/ **
Date: 2017-11-02T10:11:19.984Z
Hash: 6a0410d7576a15d5375e
Time: 5746ms
chunk {inline} inline.bundle.js (inline) 5.79 kB [entry] [rendered]
chunk {main} main.bundle.js (main) 20.2 kB [initial] [rendered]
chunk {polyfills} polyfills.bundle.js (polyfills) 548 kB [initial] [rendered]
chunk {styles} styles.bundle.js (styles) 33.5 kB [initial] [rendered]
chunk {vendor} vendor.bundle.js (vendor) 7.02 MB [initial] [rendered]

webpack: Compiled successfully.
```

Figure 1.4 Building the bundles with `ng serve`

Now, point your Web browser at http://localhost:4200, and you'll see the landing page of your app, as shown in figure 1.5.

Congratulations! You created, configured, built, and ran your first Angular app without writing a single line of code!

The `ng serve` command builds the bundles in memory without generating files. While working on the project, you run `ng serve` once, and then keep working on

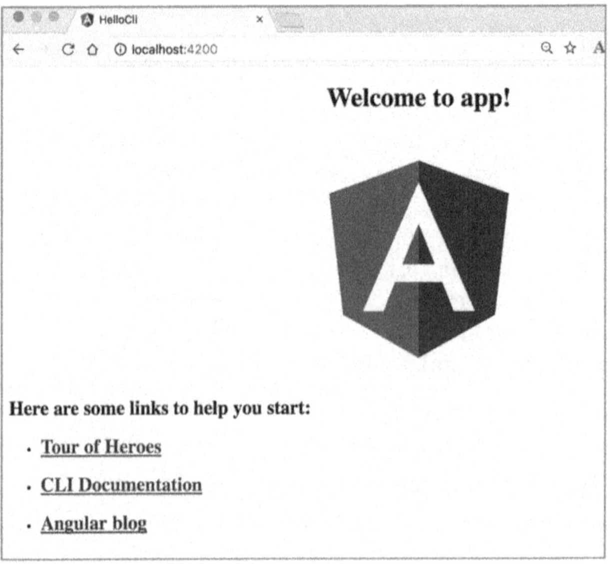

Figure 1.5 Running the app in the browser

your code. Every time you modify and save a file, Angular CLI will rebuild the bundles in memory (it takes a couple of seconds), and you'll see the results of your code modifications right away. The following JavaScript bundles were generated:

- inline.bundle.js is a file used by the Webpack loader to load other files.
- main.bundle.js includes your own code (components, services, and so on).
- polyfills.bundle.js includes polyfills needed by Angular so it can run in older browsers.
- styles.bundle.js includes CSS styles from your app.
- vendor.bundle.js includes the code of the Angular framework and its dependencies.

For each bundle, Angular CLI generates a source map file to allow debugging the original TypeScript, even though the browser will run the generated JavaScript. Don't be scared by the large size of vendor.bundle.js—it's a dev build, and the size will be substantially reduced when you build the production bundles.

Webpack and Angular CLI

Currently, Angular CLI uses Webpack (see http://webpack.js.org) to build the bundles and `webpack-dev-server` to serve the app. When you run `ng serve`, Angular CLI runs `webpack-dev-server`. Starting with Angular 7, Angular CLI offers an option to use Bazel for bundling. After the initial project build, if a developer continues working on the project, Bazel can rebuild the bundles a lot faster than Webpack.

Some useful options of ng new

When you generate a new project with the `ng new` command, you can specify an option that can change what's being generated. If you don't want to generate a separate CSS file for the application component styles, specify the inline-style option:

```
ng new hello-cli --inline-style
```

If you don't want to generate a separate HTML file for the application component template, use the inline-template option:

```
ng new hello-cli --inline-template
```

If you don't want to generate a file for unit tests, use the skip-tests option:

```
ng new hello-cli --skip-tests
```

If you're planning to implement navigation in your app, use the routing option to generate an additional module where you'll configure routes:

```
ng new hello-cli --routing
```

For the complete list of available options, run the `ng help new` command or read the Angular CLI Wiki page at https://github.com/angular/angular-cli/wiki.

1.4.2 Development and production builds

The `ng serve` command bundled the app in memory but didn't generate files and didn't optimize your Hello CLI application. You'll use the `ng build` command for file generation, but now let's start discussing bundle-size optimization and two modes of compilation.

Open the Network tab in the dev tools of your browser and you'll see that the browser had to load several megabytes of code to render this simple app. In dev mode, the size of the app is not a concern, because you run the server locally, and it takes the browser a little more than a second to load this app, as shown in figure 1.6.

Name	Status	Type	Initiator	Size	Time
polyfills.bun...	200	script	0	536 KB	
styles.bundl...	200	script	0	33.0 KB	
vendor.bun...	200	script	0	6.7 MB	
main.bundl...	200	script	0	20.0 KB	
data:image/...	200	svg+...	platfor...	(from memory cache)	
ng-validate.js	200	script	content...	(from disk cache)	
info?t=1509...	200	xhr	zone.js:...	368 B	
websocket	101	web...	sockjs.j...	0 B	
backend.js	200	script	content...	(from disk cache)	

Figure 1.6 Running the non-optimized app

Now visualize a user with a mobile device browsing the internet over a regular 3G connection. It'll take 20 seconds to load the same Hello CLI app. Many people can't tolerate waiting 20 seconds for any app except Facebook (30% of the earth's population lives on Facebook). You need to reduce the size of the bundles before going live.

Applying the `--prod` option while building the bundles will produce much smaller bundles (as shown in figure 1.6) by optimizing your code. It'll rename your variables as single letters, remove comments and empty lines, and remove the majority of the unused code. Another piece of code that can be removed from app bundles is the Angular compiler. Yes, the `ng serve` command included the compiler into the vendor .bundle.js. But how are you going to remove the Angular compiler from your deployed app when you build it for production?

1.5 JIT vs. AOT compilation

Let's revisit the code of app.component.html. For the most part, it consists of standard HTML tags, but there's one line that browsers won't understand:

```
Welcome to {{title}}!
```

These double curly braces represent binding a value into a string in Angular, but this line has to be compiled by the Angular compiler (it's called `ngc`) to replace the binding with something that browsers understand. A component template can include other Angular-specific syntax (for example, structural directives `*ngIf` and `*ngFor`) that needs to be compiled before asking the browser to render the template.

When you run the `ng serve` command, the template compilation is performed inside the browser. After the browser loads your app bundles, the Angular compiler (packaged inside vendor.bundle.js) performs the compilation of the templates from main.bundle.js. This is called *just-in-time* (JIT) compilation. This term means that the compilation happens when the bundles arrive at the browser.

The drawbacks of JIT compilation include the following:

- There's an interval of time between loading bundles and rendering the UI. This time is spent on JIT compilation. For a small app like Hello CLI, this time is minimal, but in real-world apps, JIT compilation can take a couple of seconds, so the user needs to wait longer before seeing your app.
- The Angular compiler has to be included in vendor.bundle.js, which adds to the size of your app.

Using JIT compilation in production is discouraged, and you want templates to be precompiled into JavaScript before the bundles are created. This is what *ahead-of-time* (AOT) compilation is about.

The advantages of AOT compilation are as follows:

- The browser can render the UI as soon as your app is loaded. There's no need to wait for code compilation.
- The `ngc` compiler isn't included in vendor.bundle.js, and the resulting size of your app might be smaller.

Why use the word *might* and not *will*? Removing the `ngc` compiler from the bundles should always result in smaller app size, right? Not always. The compiled templates are larger than those that use a concise Angular syntax. The size of Hello CLI will definitely be smaller, as there's only one line to compile. But in larger apps with lots of views, the compiled templates may increase the size of your app so that it's even larger than the JIT-compiled app with `ngc` included in the bundle. You should use the AOT mode anyway, because the user will see the initial landing page of your app sooner.

NOTE You may be surprised by seeing `ngc` compiler errors in an app that was compiling fine with `tsc`. The reason is that AOT requires your code to be statically analyzable. For example, you can't use the keyword `private` with properties that are used in the template, and no default exports are allowed. Fix the errors reported by the ngc compiler and enjoy the benefits of AOT compilation.

No matter whether you choose JIT or AOT compilation, at some point you'll decide to do an optimized production build. How do you do this?

1.5.1 Creating bundles with the –prod option

When you build bundles with the `--prod` option, Angular CLI performs code optimization and AOT compilation. See it in action by running the following command in your Hello CLI project:

```
ng serve --prod
```

Open the app in your browser and check the Network tab, as shown in figure 1.7. Now the size of the same app is only 108 KB gzipped.

Expand the column with the bundle sizes—the dev server even did the gzip compression for you. The filenames of the bundles include a hash code of each bundle. Angular CLI calculates a new hash code on each production build to prevent browsers from using the cached version if a new app version is deployed in prod.

Shouldn't you always use AOT? Ideally, you should unless you use some third-party JavaScript libraries that produce errors during AOT compilation. If you run into this problem, turn AOT compilation off by building the bundles with the following command:

```
ng serve --prod --aot false
```

Figure 1.8 shows that both the size and the load time increased compared to the AOT-compiled app in figure 1.7.

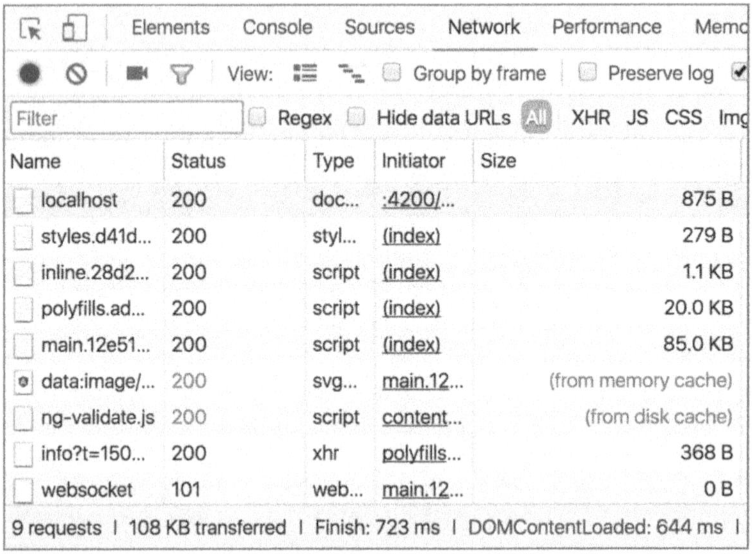

Elements Console Sources Network Performance Memo

View: Group by frame Preserve log

Filter Regex Hide data URLs All XHR JS CSS Img

Name	Status	Type	Initiator	Size
localhost	200	doc...	:4200/...	875 B
styles.d41d...	200	styl...	(index)	279 B
inline.28d2...	200	script	(index)	1.1 KB
polyfills.ad...	200	script	(index)	20.0 KB
main.12e51...	200	script	(index)	85.0 KB
data:image/...	200	svg...	main.12...	(from memory cache)
ng-validate.js	200	script	content...	(from disk cache)
info?t=150...	200	xhr	polyfills...	368 B
websocket	101	web...	main.12...	0 B

9 requests | 108 KB transferred | Finish: 723 ms | DOMContentLoaded: 644 ms |

Figure 1.7 Running the optimized app with AOT

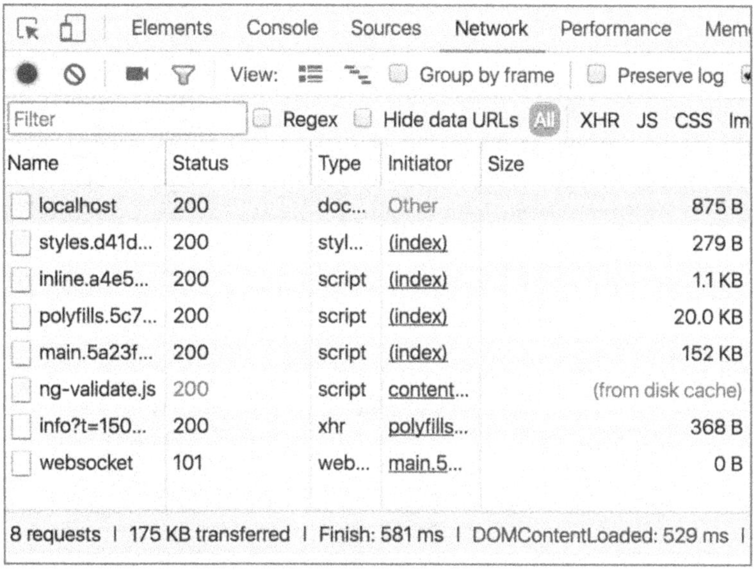

Elements Console Sources Network Performance Mem

View: Group by frame Preserve log

Filter Regex Hide data URLs All XHR JS CSS Im

Name	Status	Type	Initiator	Size
localhost	200	doc...	Other	875 B
styles.d41d...	200	styl...	(index)	279 B
inline.a4e5...	200	script	(index)	1.1 KB
polyfills.5c7...	200	script	(index)	20.0 KB
main.5a23f...	200	script	(index)	152 KB
ng-validate.js	200	script	content...	(from disk cache)
info?t=150...	200	xhr	polyfills...	368 B
websocket	101	web...	main.5...	0 B

8 requests | 175 KB transferred | Finish: 581 ms | DOMContentLoaded: 529 ms |

Figure 1.8 Running the optimized app without AOT

1.5.2 *Generating bundles on the disk*

You were using the `ng serve` command, which was building the bundles in memory. When you're ready to generate production files, use the `ng build` command instead. The `ng build` command generates files in the dist directory (by default), but the bundle sizes won't be optimized.

With `ng build --prod`, the generated files will be optimized but not compressed, so you'd need to apply the gzip compression to the bundles afterward. We'll go over the process of building production bundles and deploying the app on the Node.js server in section 12.5.3 of chapter 12.

After the files are built in the dist directory, you can copy them to whatever web server you use. Read the product documentation for your web server, and if you know where to deploy an index.html file in your server, this would be the place for the Angular app bundles as well.

The goal of this section was to get you started with Angular CLI, and we'll continue its coverage in chapter 2. The first generated app is rather simple and doesn't illustrate all the features of Angular; the next section will give you some ideas of how things are done in Angular.

1.6 *Introducing the sample ngAuction app*

To make this book more practical, we start every chapter by showing you small applications that illustrate Angular syntax or techniques, and at the end of most of the chapters you'll use the new concepts in a working application. You'll see how components and services are combined into a working application.

Imagine an online auction (let's call it ngAuction) where people can browse and search for products. When the results are displayed, the user can select a product and bid on it. The information on the latest bids will be pushed by the server to all users subscribed to such notifications.

The functionality of browsing, searching, and placing bids will be implemented by making requests to the RESTful endpoints, implemented in the server developed with Node.js. The server will use WebSockets to push notifications about the user's bid and about the bids placed by other users. Figure 1.9 depicts sample workflows for ngAuction.

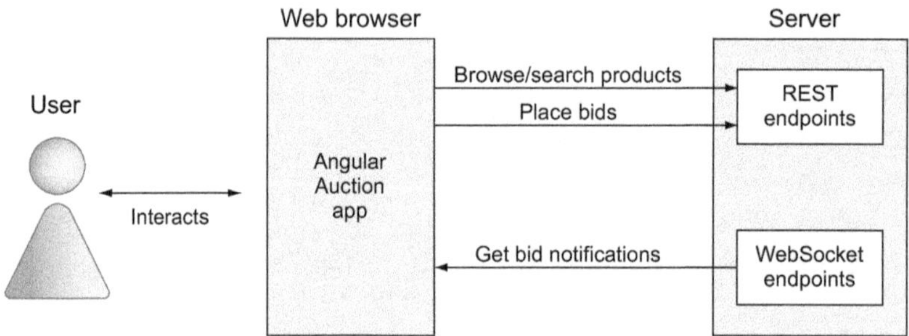

Figure 1.9 The ngAuction workflows

Figure 1.10 shows how the first version of the ngAuction home page will be rendered on desktop computers. Initially, you'll use gray placeholders instead of product images.

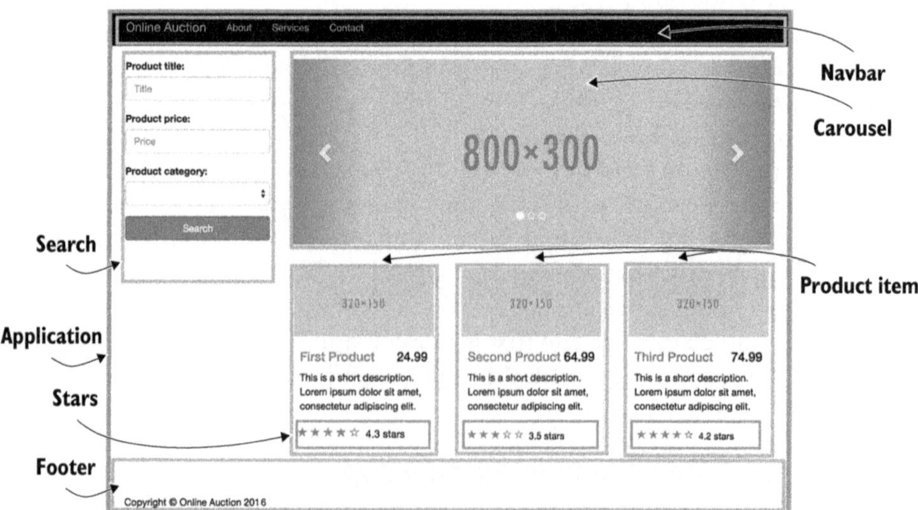

Figure 1.10 The ngAuction home page with highlighted components

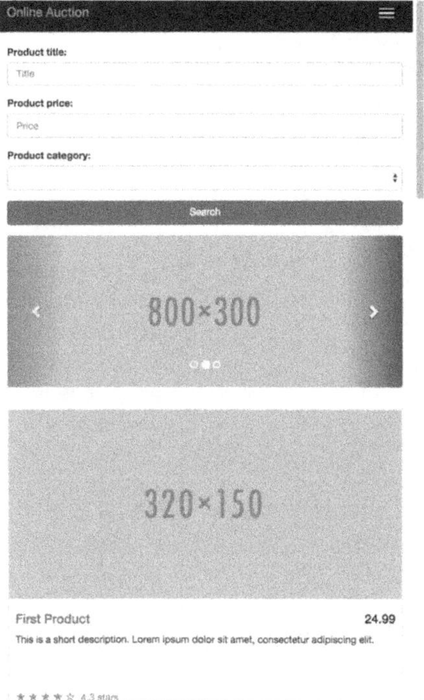

Figure 1.11 The online auction home page on smartphones

You'll use responsive UI components offered by the Bootstrap library (see http://getbootstrap.com), so on mobile devices the home page may be rendered as in figure 1.11.

Starting in chapter 7, you'll redesign ngAuction to completely remove the Bootstrap framework, replacing it with the Angular Material and Flex Layout libraries. The home page of the refactored version of ngAuction will look like figure 1.12.

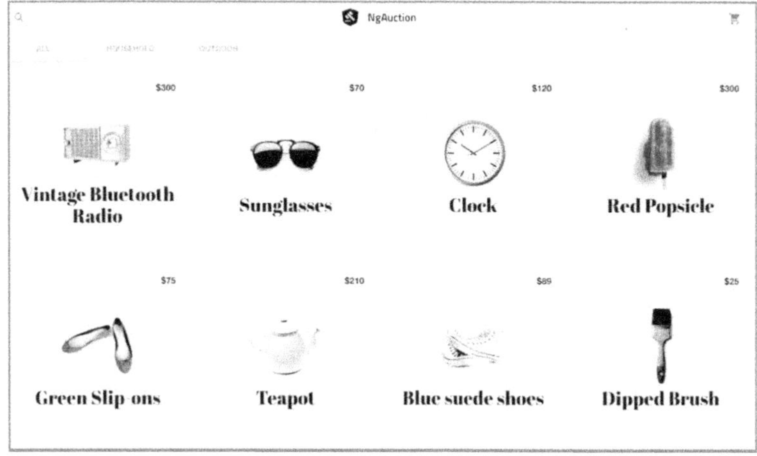

Figure 1.12 The redesigned ngAuction

The development of an Angular application comes down to creating and composing components. In chapter 2 you'll generate this project and its components and services using Angular CLI, and in chapter 7, you'll refactor its code. Figure 1.13 shows the project structure for the ngAuction app.

In chapter 2, you'll start by creating an initial version of the landing page of ngAuction, and in subsequent chapters, you'll keep adding functionality that illustrates various Angular features and techniques

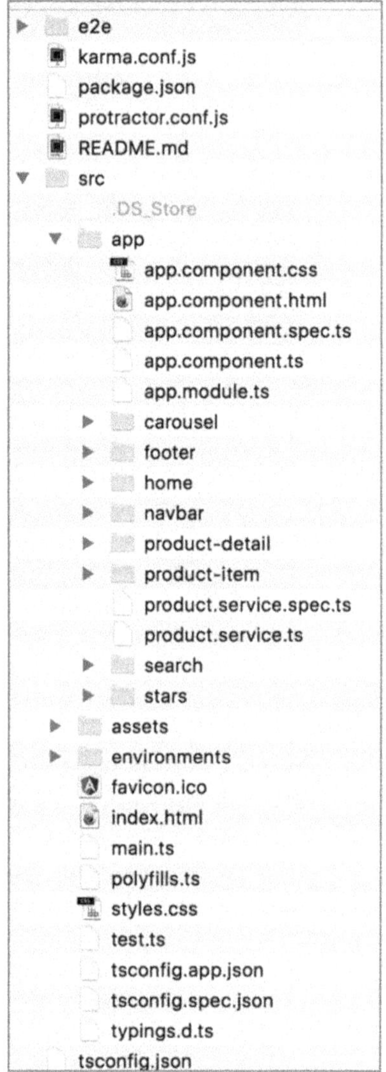

Figure 1.13 The project structure for the online auction app

NOTE We recommend that you develop Angular applications using an IDE like WebStorm (inexpensive) or Visual Studio Code (free). They offer the autocomplete feature, provide convenient search, and have integrated Terminal windows so you can do all your work inside the IDE.

Summary

- Angular applications can be developed in TypeScript or JavaScript.
- Angular is a component-based framework.
- The TypeScript source code has to be transpiled into JavaScript before deployment.
- Angular CLI is a great tool that helps in jump-starting your project. It supports bundling and serving your apps in development and preparing production builds.

2 The main artifacts of an Angular app

This chapter covers

- Understanding components, directives, services, modules, and pipes
- Generating components, directives, services, and routes with Angular CLI
- Looking at Angular data bindings
- Building the first version of the ngAuction app

In this chapter, we'll start by explaining the roles of the main artifacts of Angular applications. We'll introduce you to each one and show how Angular CLI can generate these artifacts. Then we'll do an overview of the Angular CLI configuration file where you can modify your project settings.

After that, we'll discuss how data binding is implemented in Angular. At the end of the chapter, you'll develop the initial version of the ngAuction application that you'll continue working on throughout the book.

2.1 Components

A component, the main artifact of any Angular app, is a class with a view (UI). To turn a class into component, you need to decorate it with the `@Component()` decorator. A component can consist of one or more files—for example, a file with the extension .ts with the component class, a .css file with styles, an .html file with a template, and a .spec.ts file with test code for the component.

You don't have to split the code of each component into these files. For example, you can have a component in just one file with inline styles and templates and no files with tests. No matter how many files will represent your component, they all should be located in the same directory.

Any component belongs to exactly one module of an app, and you have to include the name of the component's class into the `declarations` property of the `@NgModule()` decorator in the module file. In chapter 1, we already had an `AppComponent` listed in the `AppModule`.

> **The ng generate command of Angular CLI**
>
> Even after generating a new project, you can keep using Angular CLI for generating artifacts by using the `ng generate` command or its alias `ng g`. Here are some options you can use with the `ng g` command:
>
> - `ng g c`—Generates a new component.
> - `ng g s`—Generates a new service.
> - `ng g d`—Generates a new directive.
> - `ng g m`—Generates a new module.
> - `ng g application`—Generates a new app within the same project. This command was introduced in Angular 6.
> - `ng g library`—Starting with Angular 6, you can generate a library project. This is not an app, but can include services and components as well.
>
> Each of these commands requires an argument, such as the name of the item, to generate. For a complete list of available options and arguments, run the `ng help generate` command or refer to the Angular CLI documentation.
>
> Here are some examples of using the `ng g` command:
>
> - `ng g c product` will generate four files for a new product component in the src/app/product directory and add the `ProductComponent` class to the `declarations` property of `@NgModule`.
> - `ng g c product -is --it --spec false` will generate a single file, product .component.ts, with inlined styles and template and no test in the src/app/product directory, and add `ProductComponent` to the `declarations` property of `@NgModule`.

- `ng g s product` will generate the file product.service.ts containing a class decorated with `@Injectable` and the file product.service.spec.ts in the src/app directory.

`ng g s product -m app.module` will generate the same files as the preceding command and will also add `ProductService` to the `providers` property of `@NgModule`.

Let's add a product component to the Hello CLI project you created in chapter 1 by running the following command in the root directory of that project:

```
ng g c product --is --it --spec false
```

This command will create the src/app/product directory with the product.component .ts file.

Listing 2.1 product.component.ts

```
@Component({
  selector: 'app-product',
  template: `
  <p>
  product Works!      <—— A default text to render
   </p>
  `,
  styles: []
})
export class ProductComponent implements OnInit {     <—— Implementing OnInit requires the ngOnInit() method in the class.

  constructor() { }

  ngOnInit() {}     <—— A lifecycle method
 }
```

The generated `@Component()` decorator has the `app-product` selector, the `template` property with inlined HTML, and the `styles` property for inline CSS. Other components can include your product component in their templates by using the `<app-product>` tag.

The class in listing 2.1 has an empty constructor and one method, `ngOnInit ()`, which is one of the component lifecycle methods. If implemented, `ngOnInit()` is invoked after the code in the constructor. `OnInit` is one of the lifecycle interfaces that require the implementation of `ngOnInit()`. We'll cover a component lifecycle in section 9.2 in chapter 9.

NOTE The `@Component()` decorator has a few more properties that we'll discuss when it comes time to use them. All properties of the `@Component()` decorator are described at https://angular.io/api/core/Component.

Using selector prefixes

The selector of the component in listing 2.1 has the prefix `app-`, which is a default prefix for apps. For library projects, the default prefix is `lib-`. A good practice is to come up with a more specific prefix that would better identify your application. Your project is called Hello CLI, so you may want to give the `hello-` prefix to all your components. To do this, use the `-prefix` option while generating your components:

```
ng g c product -prefix hello
```

That command would generate a component with the `hello-product` selector . An easier way to ensure that all generated components have a specific prefix is to specify the prefix in the file .angular-cli.json (or in angular.json, starting with Angular 6), discussed later in this chapter.

If you open the app.module.ts file, you'll see that `ProductComponent` has been imported and added to the `declarations` section by your `ng g c` command:

```
@NgModule({
  declarations: [
    AppComponent,
    ProductComponent
  ],
  imports: [
    BrowserModule
  ],
  providers: [],
  bootstrap: [AppComponent]
})
export class AppModule { }
```

The newly generated `ProductComponent` class was added to the `declarations` property of `@NgModule()`. We'll keep using components in each chapter of this book so you'll get a chance to learn the various features of Angular components.

What's metadata?

TypeScript decorators allow you to modify the behavior of a class, property, or method (or its arguments) without changing their code by enabling you to provide metadata about the decorated artifact. In general, *metadata* is additional information about data. For example, in an MP3 file, the audio is the data, but the name of the artist, song title, and album cover are metadata. MP3 players include metadata processors that read the metadata and display some of it while playing the song.

In the case of classes, metadata refers to additional information about the class. For example, the `@Component()` decorator tells Angular (the metadata processor) that this is not a regular class, but a component. Angular generates additional JavaScript code based on the information provided in the properties of the `@Component()`

> nsdecorator to turn a class into a UI component. The `@Component()` decorator doesn't change the internals of the decorated class but adds some data describing the class so the Angular compiler can properly generate the final code of the component.
>
> In the case of class properties, the `@Input()` decorator tells Angular that this class property should support binding and be able to receive data from the parent component. You'll learn about the `@Input()` decorator in section 8.2.1 in chapter 8.
>
> Under the hood, a decorator is a function that attaches some data to the decorated element. See section B.10 in appendix B for more details.

A component is a class with a UI, and a service is a class where you implement the business logic of your app. Let's get familiar with services.

2.2 Services

For cleaner code separation, we usually don't use a component for code that fetches or manipulates data. An injectable service is the right place for handling data. A component may depend on one or more services. Chapter 5 covers how dependency injection works in Angular. Here, we'll give you an idea of how services and components work together.

Let's start with generating a service in a shared folder, assuming that this service will be used by multiple components. To ensure that the `providers` property of `@NgModule()` will be updated with the newly generated service, use the following option:

```
ng g s shared/product -m app.module
```

The new file product.service.ts will be generated in the src/app/shared directory:

```
@Injectable()
export class ProductService {
  constructor() { }
}
```

Accordingly, the app.module.ts file will be updated to include the provider for this service:

```
@NgModule({
...
  providers: [ProductService]
})
export class AppModule { }
```

Next, implement some methods in `ProductService` with the required business logic. Note that the generated `ProductService` class is annotated with the `@Injectable()` decorator. To have Angular instantiate and inject this service into any component, add the following argument to the component's constructor:

```
constructor(productService: ProductService){
  // start using the service, e.g. productService.getMyData();
}
```

A service isn't the only artifact without a UI. Directives also don't have their own UI, but they can be attached to the UI of components.

> **What's new in Angular 6**
>
> Starting from Angular 6, the `ng g s` command generates a class with the `Injectable()` decorator:
>
> ```
> @Injectable({
>   providedIn: 'root'
> })
> ```
>
> `providedIn: 'root'` allows you to skip the step of specifying the service in the `providers` property of the `NgModule()` decorator.

2.3 Directives

Think of an Angular directive as an HTML enhancer. Directives allow you to teach an old HTML element new tricks. A *directive* is a class annotated with the `@Directive()` decorator. You'll see the `@Directive()` decorator used in section 11.7 in chapter 11.

A directive can't have its own UI, but can be attached to a component or a regular HTML element to change their visual representation. There are two types of directives in Angular:

- *Structural*—The directive changes the structure of the component's template.
- *Attribute*—The directive changes the behavior or visual representation of an individual component or HTML element.

For example, with the structural `*ngFor` directive, you can iterate through an array (or other collection) and render an HTML element for each item of the array. The following listing uses the `*ngFor` directive to loop through the `products` array and render an `<li>` element for each product (assuming there's an interface or `Product` class with a `title` property).

Listing 2.2 Iterating through products with `*ngFor`

```
@Component({
  selector: 'app-root',
  template: `<h1>All Products</h1>
  <ul>
    <li *ngFor="let product of products">      <-- Renders <li> for each product
      {{product.title}}      <-- Each <li> element shows the product title.
    </li>
  </ul>
  `})
```

```
export class AppComponent {

  products: Product[] = [];     <-- *ngFor iterates through this array.

 // the code to populate products is removed for brevity
}
```

The following element uses the structural `*ngIf` directive to either show or hide the `<mat-error>` element, depending on the return (true or false) of the `hasError()` method, which checks whether the value in a form field `title` has invalid minimum length:

```
<mat-error *ngIf="formModel.hasError('minlength', 'title')" >Enter at least 3
     characters</mat-error>
```

Later in this chapter when we talk about two-way binding, we'll use the attribute `ngModel` directive to bind the value in the `<input>` element to a class variable, `shippingAddress`:

```
<input type='text' placeholder="Enter shipping address"
   [(ngModel)]="shippingAddress">
```

You can create custom attribute directives as well, described in the product documentation at https://angular.io/guide/attribute-directives.

Yet another artifact that doesn't have its own UI but that can transform values in the component template is a pipe.

2.4 Pipes

A *pipe* is a template element that allows you to transform a value into a desired output. A pipe is specified by adding the vertical bar (|) and the pipe name right after the value to be transformed:

```
template: `<p>Your birthday is {{ birthday | date }}</p>`
```

In the preceding example, the value of the `birthday` variable will be transformed into a date of a default format. Angular comes with a number of built-in pipes, and each pipe has a class that implements its functionality (for example, `DatePipe`) as well as the name that you can use in the template (such as `date`):

- An `UpperCasePipe` allows you to convert an input string to uppercase by using `| uppercase` in the template.
- A `LowerCasePipe` allows you to convert an input string to lowercase by using `| lowercase` in the template.
- A `DatePipe` allows you to display a date in different formats by using `| date`.
- A `CurrencyPipe` transforms a number into a desired currency by using `| currency`.
- An `AsyncPipe` unwraps the data from the provided `Observable` stream by using `| async`. You'll see a code sample that uses `async` in section 6.5 in chapter 6.

Some pipes don't require input parameters (such as `uppercase`), and some do (such as `date:'medium'`). You can chain as many pipes as you want. The following code snippet shows how you can display the value of the `birthday` variable in a medium date format and in uppercase (for example, JUN 15, 2001, 9:43:11 PM):

```
template=
  `<p>{{ birthday | date: 'medium' | uppercase}}</p>`
```

As you can see, with literally no coding you can convert a date into the required format as well as show it uppercase (see the date formats in the Angular `DatePipe` documentation, http://mng.bz/78lD).

In addition to predefined pipes, you can create custom pipes that can include code specific to your application. The process of creating custom pipes is described at https://angular.io/guide/pipes. Code samples for this chapter include an app demonstrating a custom pipe that can convert the temperature from Fahrenheit to Celsius and back.

Now you know that your app can include components, services, directives, and pipes. All these artifacts must be declared in your app module(s).

2.5 Modules

An Angular module is a container for a group of related components, services, directives, and pipes. You can think of a module as a package that implements certain functionality from the business domain of your application, such as a shipping or billing module. All elements of a small application can be located in one module (the root module), whereas larger apps may have more than one module (feature modules). All apps must have at least a root module that's bootstrapped during app launch.

From a syntax perspective, an Angular module is a class annotated with the `@NgModule()` decorator. To load the root module on application startup, invoke the `bootstrapModule()` method in the main.ts file of your app:

```
platformBrowserDynamic().bootstrapModule(AppModule);
```

The Angular framework itself is split into modules. Including some of the Angular modules is a must (for example, `@angular/core`), whereas some modules are optional. For example, if you're planning to use the Angular Forms API and make HTTP requests, you should add `@angular/forms` and `@angular/common/http` in your package.json file and should include `FormsModule` and `HttpClientModule` in the root module of your app, as shown in the following listing.

Listing 2.3 A sample root module

```
@NgModule({
  declarations: [
    AppComponent        <-- The only component included in this module
  ],
  imports: [            <-- Other modules that are needed for this app
     BrowserModule,
```

```
    FormsModule,
    HttpClientModule
  ],
  bootstrap: [AppComponent]    <-- The top-level component to be loaded on app startup
})
export class AppModule { }
```

If you decide to split your app into several modules, in addition to the root module you'll need to create *feature modules*, covered next.

2.5.1 Feature modules

An Angular app may consist of a root module and feature modules. You can implement a certain feature of your app (for example, shipping) in a feature module. Whereas the `@NgModule()` decorator of the root module of a web application must include the `BrowserModule`, feature modules include the `CommonModule` instead. Feature modules can be imported by other modules. The `@NgModule()` decorator of feature modules doesn't include the `bootstrap` property, because bootstrapping the entire app is the responsibility of the root module.

The following listing generates a small app called Hello Modules and adds a feature module called `ShippingModule` to it.

Listing 2.4 Generating a project and a feature module

```
ng new hello-modules    <-- Generates a new project called hello-modules
 cd hello-modules
ng g m shipping    <-- Generates a new feature module called shipping
```

This app will have a feature module with the following listing's content in the file src/app/shipping/shipping.module.ts.

Listing 2.5 Generated feature module

```
@NgModule({
  imports: [
    CommonModule    <-- Feature module imports CommonModule instead of the BrowserModule
   ],
  declarations: []
})
export class ShippingModule { }
```

Now let's generate a new shipping component, instructing Angular CLI to include it into `ShippingModule`:

```
ng g c shipping -it -is -m shipping
```

This command generates the file shipping/shipping.component.ts with the decorated class `ShippingComponent` with an inline template and an empty `styles` property. The command also adds it to the declarations section of the ShippingModule. The code for the shipping component is shown in the following listing.

Listing 2.6 Generated shipping component

```
@Component({
  selector: 'app-shipping',
  template: `
  <p>
  shipping Works!   <-- A default template
   </p>
  `,
  styles: []
})
export class ShippingComponent implements OnInit {   <-- Implementing the lifecycle interface OnInit

  constructor() { }

  ngOnInit() {}   <-- This lifecycle hook is invoked after the constructor.
 }
```

Note the selector of the shipping component: app-shipping. You'll be using this name in the template of the AppComponent.

The code for your shipping module will include the shipping component and will look like the following listing.

Listing 2.7 Generated shipping module

```
@NgModule({
  imports: [
    CommonModule
  ],
  declarations: [ShippingComponent]
})
export class ShippingModule { }
```

A feature module may declare its own components and services, but to make all or some of them visible to other modules, you need to export them. In this case, you need to add an exports section to the shipping module so it looks as follows.

Listing 2.8 Exporting a shipping component

```
@NgModule({
  imports: [
    CommonModule
  ],
  declarations: [ShippingComponent],
  exports: [ShippingComponent]   <-- Exporting a component from the module
 })
export class ShippingModule { }
```

External modules will see only those members of the shipping module that were explicitly mentioned in `exports`. The shipping module may include other members, like classes, directives, and pipes. If you don't list them in the `exports` section, these members will remain private to the shipping module and will be hidden from the rest of the app. Now you should include the shipping module in the root module.

Listing 2.9 Adding the shipping module to the root module

```
@NgModule({
  declarations: [
    AppComponent
  ],
  imports: [
    BrowserModule,
    ShippingModule        <-- Adds the shipping module to the root module
   ],
  providers: [],
  bootstrap: [AppComponent]
})
export class AppModule { }
```

To have the browser render the shipping component in the root component, you can add the `<app-shipping>` tag to the template of the `AppComponent`.

Listing 2.10 Adding a shipping component

```
@Component({
  selector: 'app-root',
  template: `
  <h1>Welcome to {{title}}!!</h1>
  <app-shipping></app-shipping>       <-- Adds the ShippingComponent to the root component's template
   `,
  styles: []
})
export class AppComponent {
  title = 'app';
}
```

Run this app with `ng serve` and open the browser at http://localhost:4200. You'll see the window that renders the `AppComponent` from the root module and the `ShippingComponent` from the shipping module, as shown in figure 2.1.

"Welcome to app!!" is the greeting from the `AppComponent` located in the root module, whereas "shipping Works!" comes from the `ShippingComponent` located in your feature module. This was a rather simple example,

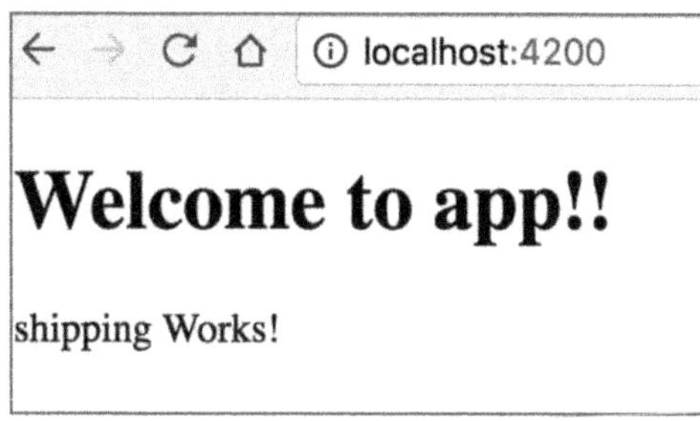

Figure 2.1 Running the two-module app

but it illustrates how you can *modularize* an app so its specific features are located in a separate reusable module and can be developed by a separate developer(s).

Your app modules can be loaded either eagerly on application startup, as was done with the Hello Modules project, or lazily, such as when the user clicks a specific link. In section 4.3 in chapter 4, you'll see a sample app with a module that's lazy loaded.

You know by now that a component consists of TypeScript code and the UI (the template). The next concept to learn is how the code and the UI can be synchronized as the data changes either programmatically or as the result of the user's interaction with the app.

2.6 Understanding data binding

Angular has a mechanism called *data binding* that allows you to keep a component's properties in sync with the view. In this section, we'll explain how data binding works with properties and events.

Angular supports two types of data binding: *unidirectional* (default) and *two-way*. With unidirectional data binding , the data is synchronized in one direction: either from the class member variable (property) to the view or from the view event to the class variable or a method that handles the event. Angular updates the binding during its change detection cycle, explained in section 9.1 in chapter 9.

2.6.1 Binding properties and events

To display a value of a class variable in a template's string, use double curly braces. If a class has a variable called `name`, you can show its value like this:

```
<h1>Hello {{name}}!</h1>
```

This is also known as *interpolation* , and you can use any valid expression inside these double curly braces.

Use square brackets to bind the value from a class variable to a property of an HTML element or an Angular component. The following binds the value of the class variable `isValid` to the `hidden` property of the HTML `<span>` element:

```
<span [hidden]="isValid">This field is required</span>
```

Note that the square brackets are used to the left of the equals sign. If the value of the `isValid` variable is false, the text of the `span` element isn't hidden, and the user will see the message "This field is required." As soon as the value of the `isValid` variable becomes true, the text "This field is required" becomes hidden.

The preceding examples illustrate unidirectional binding from the class variable to the view. The next listings will illustrate the unidirectional binding from the view to a class member, such as a method.

To assign an event-handler function to an event, put the event name in parentheses in the component's template. The following listing shows how to bind the `onClickEvent()` function to the `click` event, and the `onInputEvent()` function to the `input` event.

Listing 2.11 Two events with handlers

```
<button (click)="onClickEvent()">Get Products</button>

<input placeholder="Product name" (input)="onInputEvent()">
```

If the button is clicked, invoke the method onClickEvent().

As soon as the value of the input field changes, invoke the method onInputEvent().

When the event specified in parentheses is triggered, the expression in double quotes is reevaluated. In listing 2.11, the expressions are functions, so they're invoked each time the corresponding event is triggered.

If you're interested in analyzing the properties of the event object, add the `$event` argument to the method handler. In particular, the target `property` of the event object represents the DOM node where the event occurred. The instance of the event object will be available only within the binding scope (that is, in the event-handler method). Figure 2.2 shows how to read the event-binding syntax.

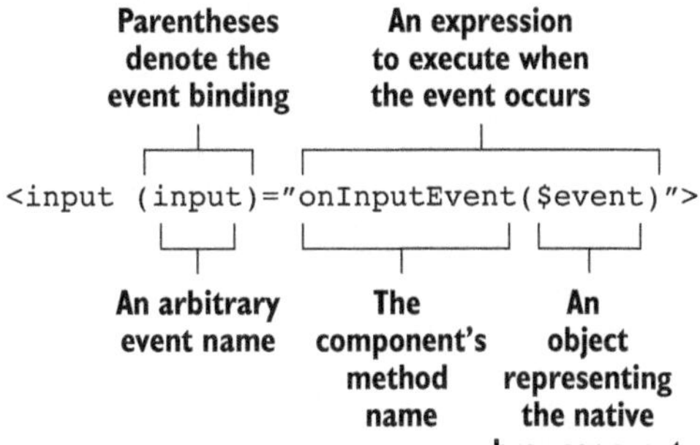

Figure 2.2 Event-binding syntax

The event in parentheses is called the *target of binding*. You can bind functions to any standard DOM events that exist today (see "Event reference" in the Mozilla Developer Network documentation, http://mzl.la/1JcBR22) or that will be introduced in the future.

Parentheses are used for binding to the standard DOM events as well as the custom events of a component. For example, say you have a price-quoter component that can emit a custom event, `lastPrice`. The following code snippet shows how to bind the `lastPrice` event to the class method `priceQuoteHandler()`:

```
<price-quoter (lastPrice)="priceQuoteHandler($event)">?</price-quoter>
```

You'll learn how to create components that emit custom events in chapter 8, section 8.2.2.

2.6.2 One- and two-way data binding in action

Let's run and review two simple apps from the project bindings that come with this chapter. If you use the Angular 5 code samples, the two apps `oneway` and `twoway` are configured by creating two elements in the `apps` array in the file .angular-cli.json. If you use the Angular 6 code samples, these two apps are configured in the file angular.json.

> **Configuring Angular CLI projects**
>
> Prior to Angular 6, the generated projects include the configuration file .angular-cli.json, which allows you to specify where the source code is located, which directory will contain the compiled code, where to find the assets of your project, where the code and styles required by third-party libraries (if any) are, and more. Angular CLI uses properties of this file during generation of the your app artifacts, during builds, and while running tests.
>
> You can find the complete and current description of each config property in the document "Angular CLI Config Schema," available at https://github.com/angular/angular-cli/wiki/angular-cli. You'll use the `apps` config property in this section and the `styles` and `scripts` properties in section 2.7.
>
> Starting in Angular 6, projects are configured in the angular.json file, and its schema is described at https://github.com/angular/angular-cli/wiki/angular-workspace. Now the project is treated as a workspace, which can contain one or more apps and libraries with their own configurations, but all of them share the dependencies located in a single directory: node_modules.

These two apps will be configured similarly—only the app names and the names of the files that boot these apps will differ, as shown in the following listing.

Listing 2.12 Angular 5: Configuring two apps in .angular-cli.json

```
"apps": [
  {
    "name": "oneway",      <-- The name of the first app
     ...
    "main": "main-one-way-binding.ts",      <-- The bootstrap file of the first app
   ...
  },
  {
    "name": "twoway",      <-- The name of the second app
     ...
    "main": "main-two-way-binding.ts",      <-- The bootstrap file of the second app
   ...
  }
  ]
```

Because both apps are located in the same project, you need to run `npm install` once. In Angular 5 and earlier versions, you can bundle and run any of these app by specifying the `--app` option with the `ng serve` or `ng build` command . The file main-one-way-binding.ts contains the code to bootstrap the app module from the directory named one-way, and the file main-two-way-binding.ts bootstraps the app module from the two-way directory of this project.

In Angular 5, if you want to build the bundles in memory and start the dev server with the app configured under the name `oneway`, the following command will do it:

```
ng serve --app oneway
```

NOTE If you use the Angular 6 version of the code samples, the option `--app` is not required: `ng serve oneway`.

If you also want Angular CLI to open the browser to http://localhost:4200, add the `-o` to the preceding command:

```
ng serve --app oneway -o
```

Open the bindings project in your IDE and run the `npm i` command in its Terminal window. After dependencies are installed, run the preceding command to see the one-way sample app in action. It'll render the page as shown in figure 2.3.

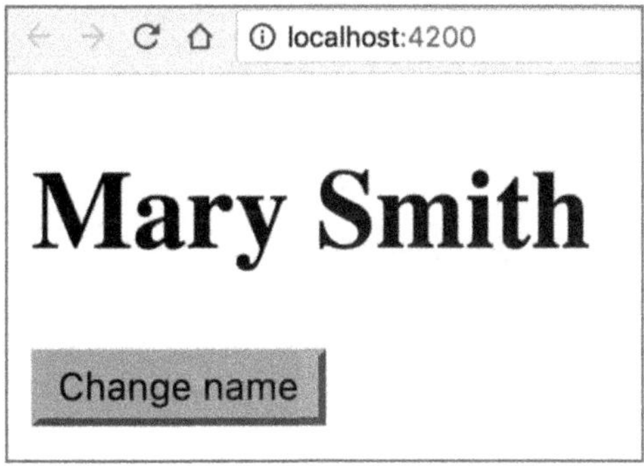

Figure 2.3 Running a one-way binding app

In the Angular 6 version of the code samples, the apps `oneway` and `twoway` are configured in the angular.json file in the `projects` section. The following command will run the `oneway` app, rendering the UI shown in figure 2.3.

```
ng serve oneway
```

The following listing shows the code of the `AppComponent` that rendered this page.

Listing 2.13 The `AppComponent` for the one-way binding sample

```
@Component({
  selector: 'app-root',
  template:`
  <h1>{{name}}</h1>
```

Initially uses a one-way property binding to render the value of the class variable name

```
    <button (click)="changeName()">
    Change name
  </button>
  `
})
export class AppComponent {
  name: string = "Mary Smith";

  changeName() {
  this.name = "Bill Smart";
  }
}
```

A button click updates the value of the variable name to Bill Smart using a one-way event binding to the method changeName().

As soon as the user clicks the button, the `changeName()` method modifies the value of `name`, one-way property binding kicks in, and the new value of the `name` variable will be shown on the page.

Now stop the dev server (Ctrl-C), and run the app configured under the name `twoway`:

```
ng serve --app twoway -o
```

The template of this page has the following HTML tags: `<input>`, `<button>`, and `<p>`. Enter `26 Broadway` in the input field, and you'll see a page like the one shown in figure 2.4.

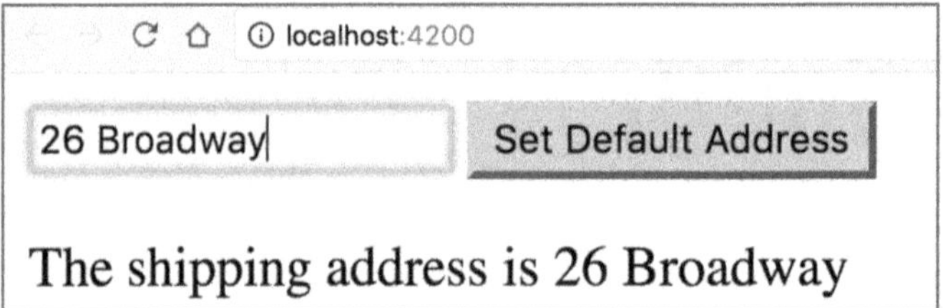

Figure 2.4 Running a two-way binding sample app

The value of the text inside the `<p>` tag changes as soon as the value in the input field changes. If you click the button, the value of the input field and the paragraph will change to `"The shipping address is 123 Main Street"`. In this app, you use two-way binding. The code for the app component is shown in the following listing.

Listing 2.14 A two-way binding sample

```
@Component({
  selector: 'app-root',
  template: `
  <input type='text'
   placeholder="Enter shipping address"
   [(ngModel)]="shippingAddress">

  <button (click)="shippingAddress='123 Main Street'">
  Set Default Address
```

Using ngModel to denote the two-way binding

```
  </button>
   <p>The shipping address is {{shippingAddress}}</p>
  `
})
export class AppComponent {
  shippingAddress: string;
}
```

Updating the value of shippingAddress on click

You bind the value of the input field to the `shippingAddress` variable by using the Angular `ngModel` directive:

```
[(ngModel)]="shippingAddress"
```

Remember, square brackets represent property binding, and parentheses represent event binding. To denote two-way binding, surround a template element's `ngModel` with both square brackets and parentheses. In the preceding code, you instruct Angular to update the `shippingAddress` variable as soon as the value in the input field changes, and update the value of the input field as soon when the value of `shippingAddress` changes. This is what the two-way binding means.

When you were typing `26 Broadway`, the value of the `shippingAddress` variable was changing as well. The click on the button would programmatically change the address to 123 Main Street, and this value is propagated back to the input field.

While reviewing the code of this app located in the two-way directory, note that the app module imports `FormsModule`, required because you use the `ngModel` directive, which is part of the Forms API, covered in chapter 7.

2.7 Hands-on: Getting started with ngAuction

From here on, most chapters will end with a hands-on section containing code review or instructions for developing a certain aspect of the ngAuction app, where people can see a list of featured products, view details for a specific product, perform a product search, and monitor bidding by other users. We'll gradually add code to this application so you can see how different Angular parts fit together. The source code that comes with this book includes the completed version of such hands-on sections in the ngAuction folders of the respective chapters, but we encourage you to try these exercises on your own (source code can be found at https://github.com/Farata/angulartypescript and www.manning.com/books/angular-development-with-typescript-second-edition).

This hands-on exercise contains instructions for developing an initial version of the sample auction introduced in chapter 1. You'll start by generating a new Angular CLI project, and then you'll create the home page, split it into Angular components, and create a service to fetch products.

> **NOTE** The completed version of this exercise is located in the directory chapter2/ngAuction. To run this version of ngAuction, switch to the ngAuction directory, run `npm install`, and start the application by running the `ng serve` command. We assume you have Angular CLI and the npm package manager installed on your computer.

2.7.1 The initial project setup for ngAuction

Let's start the development of ngAuction from scratch. Each section in the hands-on exercise will contain a set of instructions for you to follow so you can develop ngAuction on your own.

Generate a new directory and, using Angular CLI, generate a new project—ngAuction—by running the following command:

```
ng new ngAuction --prefix nga --routing
```

- `ng new`—Generates a new project.
- `--prefix nga`—The generated .angular-cli.json file will have the `prefix` property value `nga` (for ngAuction). The generated app component will have the `nga-root` selector, and all other components that we'll be generating for ngAuction will also have selectors with the prefix `nga-`.
- `--routing`—You'll add navigation to ngAuction in chapter 3. The `--routing` option will generate a boilerplate module for routing support.

Open the newly generated ngAuction directory in your IDE, go to the integrated Terminal view, and run the following command there:

```
ng serve -o
```

This command will build the bundles, start the dev server, and open the browser, which will render the page as in the Hello CLI app shown in chapter 1 in figure 1.5.

In chapters 2, 3, and 5 you'll use the Bootstrap 4 framework (see http://getbootstrap.com) for styling and implementing the responsive web design in ngAuction. The term *responsive web design* (RWD) means that the view layouts can adapt to the screen size of the user's device. Starting in chapter 7, you'll redesign the UI of ngAuction using Angular Material components (see https://material.angular.io) and remove the Bootstrap framework from this project.

Because the Bootstrap library has jQuery and Popper.js as peer dependencies, you need to run the command in the following listing to install them in the ngAuction project.

Listing 2.15 Installing Bootstrap, jQuery, and Popper.js

```
npm i bootstrap jquery popper.js --save-prod
```

> **TIP** If you use npm older than 5.0, use the `--save` option instead of `--save-prod`. In npm 5, there are shortcuts: `-P` for `--save-prod` (default) and `-D` for `--save-dev`.

When you have to use global styles or scripts from an external JavaScript library, you can add them to the .angular-cli.json config file or, starting in Angular 6, to angular.json. In your case, the Bootstrap getting-started guide (see https://getbootstrap.com/docs/4.1/getting-started) instructs you to add bootstrap.min.css to the index .html of the app. But because you're use Angular CLI, you'll add it to the `styles` section in .angular-cli.json, so it looks like this:

```
"styles": [
  "styles.css",
  "../node_modules/bootstrap/dist/css/bootstrap.min.css"
]
```

The Bootstrap documentation also instructs you to add the jQuery js/bootstrap.min.js file, and you'll add it to the `scripts` section in .angular-cli.json as follows:

```
"scripts": [
  "..node_modules/jquery/dist/jquery.min.js",
  "..node_modules/bootstrap/dist/js/bootstrap.min.js"
]
```

> **TIP** When you're running the `ng serve` or `ng build` commands, the preceding scripts will be placed in the scripts.bundle.js file.

2.7.2 Generating components for ngAuction

Your ngAuction app will consist of several Angular components. In the last section, you generated the project with the root app component. Now, you'll generate more components using the command `ng generate component` (or `ng g c`). Run the commands in the following listing in your Terminal window to generate the components shown in figure 1.10 in chapter 1.

Listing 2.16 Generating components for ngAuction

```
ng g c home
ng g c carousel
ng g c footer
ng g c navbar
ng g c product-item
ng g c product-detail
ng g c search
ng g c stars
```

Each of the components in listing 2.12 will be generated in a separate folder. Open app.module.ts, and you'll see that Angular CLI has also added the import statements and declared all of the these components there.

Now you'll generate the product service that will provide the data for ngAuction in the next chapter. Run the following command to generate the product service:

```
ng g s shared/product
```

Add `ProductService` to the `providers` property of `@NgModule()`:

```
@NgModule({
  ...
  providers: [ProductService],
```

```
    ...
})
export class AppModule { }
```

TIP While writing or generating code, you may see that some of your code fragments are marked with red squiggly lines. Hover over these lines to get more information. It may be not a TypeScript compiler error but a TSLint complaint about your coding style. Run the command `ng lint --fix`, and these styling errors could be automatically fixed.

2.7.3 The application component

The application component is the root component of ngAuction and will host all other components. Your app.component.html will include the following elements: navbar at the top, search on the left, the router outlet on the right, and the footer at the bottom. In chapter 3, you'll use the tag `<router-outlet>` to render either the `HomeComponent` or `ProductDetailComponent`, but in the initial version of ngAuction, you'll be rendering only `HomeComponent` there. Replace the content of app.component.html with the following listing.

Listing 2.17 The `AppComponent` template

```
<nga-navbar></nga-navbar>

<div class="container">
  <div class="row">
    <div class="col-md-3">
      <nga-search></nga-search>
    </div>

    <div class="col-md-9">
      <router-outlet></router-outlet>
    </div>
  </div>
</div>

<nga-footer></nga-footer>
```

- The navbar component goes at the top.
- Three columns of the Bootstrap's flex grid are given to the search component.
- Rendering the search component
- Nine columns are given to the router outlet area.
- Router outlet area
- The footer component is rendered at the bottom.

You may see some unfamiliar CSS classes in HTML elements—they all come from the Bootstrap framework. For example, the styles `col-md-3` and `col-md-9` come from the Bootstrap flexible grid layout system, in which the width of the viewport is divided into 12 invisible columns. You can read about the Bootstrap grid system at https://getbootstrap.com/docs/4.0/layout/grid.

Out of the box, the Bootstrap grid supports five tiers for different widths of user devices: `xs`, `sm`, `md`, `lg`, and `xl`. For example, `md` stands for medium devices (992 px (pixels) or more), `lg` is 1200 px or more, and so on. In your app component, you want to allocate three columns in medium or larger viewports to the search component (`<nga-search>`) and nine columns to the `<router-outlet>`.

Since you didn't specify how many columns to allocate to `<nga-search>` if the device is smaller than `md`, the browser will give the entire viewport's width to your search component, and `<router-outlet>` will be rendered under the search. The UI elements of your app component will be laid out differently, depending on the width of the user's screen.

Start the app with `ng serve -o`, and the browser will display a page that looks similar to the page shown in figure 2.5.

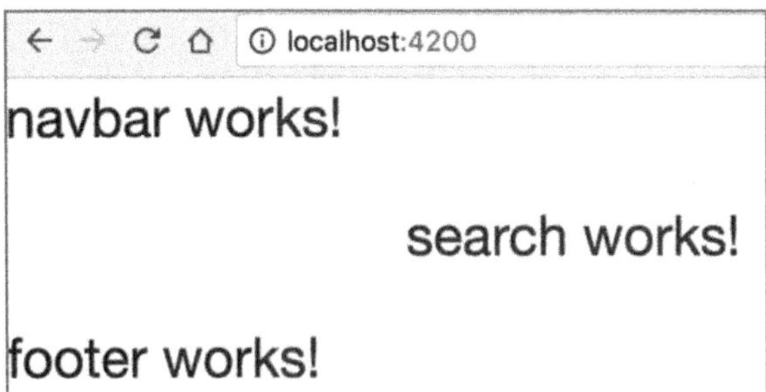

Figure 2.5 Running the first version of ngAuction

This doesn't look like a landing page of an online auction app yet, but at least the app didn't break after you added the Bootstrap framework and generated components and a service. Keep this app running and continue adding code according to the upcoming instructions, and you'll see how it gradually turns into a more usable web page.

2.7.4 *The navbar component*

A typical navigation bar stays at the top of the page, providing the app menu. The Bootstrap framework offers multiple styles for the navigation bar component described at https://getbootstrap.com/docs/4.0/components/navbar. Replace the contents of navbar.component.html with the following listing.

Listing 2.18 The navbar component template

```
<nav class="navbar navbar-expand-lg navbar-light bg-light">    ← Bootstrap's nav component and CSS selectors
  <a class="navbar-brand" [routerLink]="['/']">ngAuction</a>    ← Bootstrap's navbar-brand denotes your auction brand and routes to the default page on click.
  <button class="navbar-toggler" type="button"
   data-toggle="collapse"
   data-target="#navbarSupportedContent"
   aria-controls="navbarSupportedContent"
   aria-expanded="false" aria-label="Toggle navigation>
   <span class="navbar-toggler-icon"></span>
 </button>

 <div class="collapse navbar-collapse"
   id="navbarSupportedContent">    ← Bootstrap's collapsible is rendered as three horizontal bars on small screens.
```

```
    <ul class="navbar-nav mr-auto">
   <li class="nav-item active">
     <a class="nav-link" href="#">Home <span class="sr-
    only">(current)</span></a>
   </li>
   <li class="nav-item">
     <a class="nav-link" href="#">About</a>
   </li>
   <li class="nav-item dropdown">                    <- Services drop-down menu
      <a class="nav-link dropdown-toggle" href="#"
        id="navbarDropdown" role="button"
        data-toggle="dropdown" aria-haspopup="true" aria-expanded="false">
        Services
     </a>
   <div class="dropdown-menu" aria-labelledby="navbarDropdown">
     <a class="dropdown-item" href="#">Find products</a>    <- Drop-down
      <a class="dropdown-item" href="#">Place order</a>       menu items
   <div class="dropdown-divider"></div>
     <a class="dropdown-item" href="#">Pay</a>
   </div>
   </li>
   </ul>
  </div>
</nav>
```

As soon as you save this file, Angular CLI will automatically rebuild the bundles, and your page will look like figure 2.6.

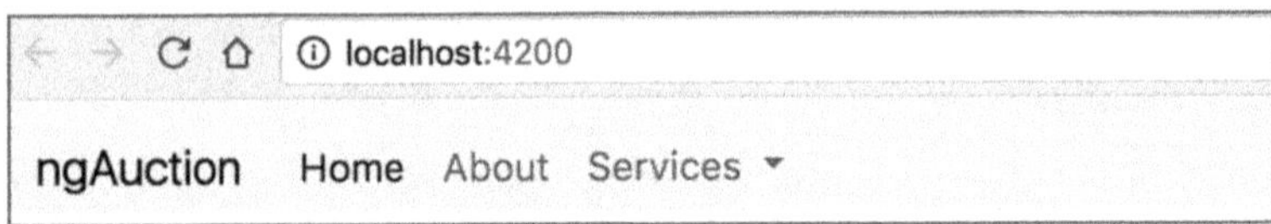

Figure 2.6 Rendering the navbar

What if you don't see the page shown in figure 2.6, and the browser just renders an empty page instead? Any time you see something you don't expect, open Chrome Dev Tools and see if there are any error messages in the Console tab.

Make the width of the browser window small, and the menu will collapse, rendering three horizontal bars on the right, as shown in figure 2.7.

Figure 2.7 Collapsed navbar menu

2.7.5 The search component

Eventually, you'll implement the `SearchComponent` to perform the product search based on the product title, price, or category. But in the initial version of ngAuction, you just want to render the view of the `SearchComponent`. Replace the content of search.component.html to look like the following listing.

Listing 2.19 The search component template

```
<form name="searchForm">
  <div class="form-group">
     <label for="productTitle">Product title:</label>
    <input type="text" id="productTitle"
      placeholder="Title" class="form-control">
   </div>
  <div class="form-group">
    <label for="productPrice">Product price:</label>
    <input id="productPrice"
     name="productPrice" type="number" min="0"
     placeholder="Price" class="form-control">
   </div>
  <div class="form-group">
    <label for="productCategory">Product category:</label>
    <select id="productCategory" class="form-control"></select>
   </div>
  <div class="form-group">
    <button type="submit"
    class="btn btn-primary btn-block">Search</button>
   </div>
</form>
```

All values in class selectors come from the Bootstrap framework.

The rendered app is shown in figure 2.8.

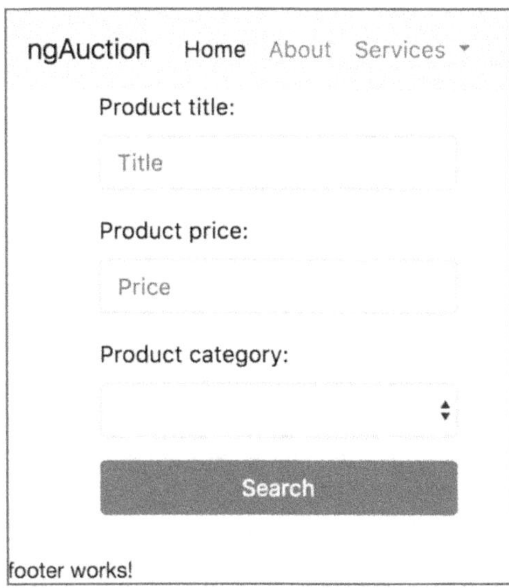

Figure 2.8 Rendering the search component

Now, let's take care of the footer component.

2.7.6 The footer component

Your footer will just display the copyright message. The following listing modifies the content of footer.component.html.

Listing 2.20 The footer component template

```
<div class="container">
  <hr>
  <footer>
   <div class="row">
     <div class="col-lg-12">
       <p>Copyright &copy; ngAuction 2018</p>
     </div>
   </div>
  </footer>
</div>
```

All values in class selectors come from the Bootstrap framework.

Your ngAuction app renders the home page as shown in figure 2.9.

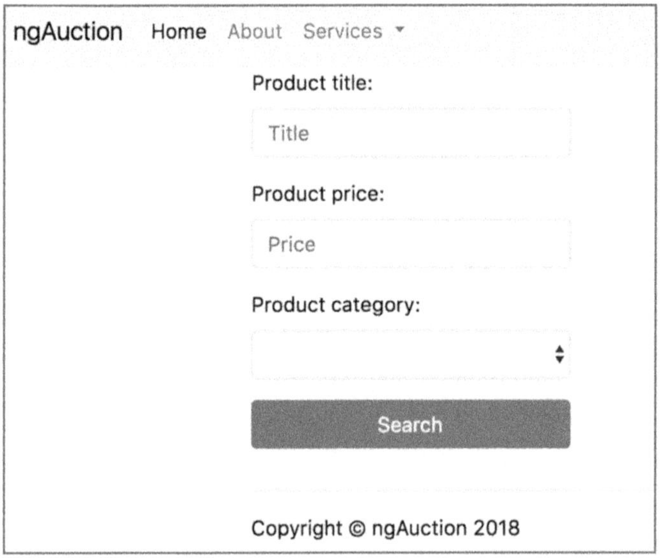

Figure 2.9 Rendering the footer

2.7.7 The carousel component

At the top of the ngAuction landing page, you want to implement a slide show of the featured products. For this, you'll use the carousel component that comes with Bootstrap (see https://getbootstrap.com/docs/4.0/components/carousel). To rotate slides manually, the carousel component includes previous/next controls (little arrows on the sides) and indicators of the current slide (dashes at the bottom).

For simplicity, you'll use gray rectangles instead of actual images. The handy https://placeholder.com service returns gray rectangles of a specified size, and in the carousel, you'll use three 800 x 300 px gray rectangles.

Modify the code of carousel.component.html to look like the following listing.

Listing 2.21 The carousel component template

```
<div id="myCarousel" class="carousel slide" data-ride="carousel">
  <ol class="carousel-indicators">
    <li data-target="#myCarousel" data-slide-to="0" class="active"></li>
    <li data-target="#myCarousel" data-slide-to="1"></li>
    <li data-target="#myCarousel" data-slide-to="2"></li>
  </ol>
  <div class="carousel-inner">
    <div class="carousel-item active">
      <img class="d-block w-100" src="http://placehold.it/800x300">
     </div>
  <div class="carousel-item">
    <img class="d-block w-100" src="http://placehold.it/800x300">
   </div>
  <div class="carousel-item">
    <img class="d-block w-100" src="http://placehold.it/800x300">
   </div>
  </div>
  <a class="carousel-control-prev" href="#myCarousel"
   role="button" data-slide="prev">
     <span class="carousel-control-prev-icon" aria-hidden="true"></span>
    <span class="sr-only">Previous</span>
  </a>
  <a class="carousel-control-next" href="#myCarousel"
   role="button" data-slide="next">
     <span class="carousel-control-next-icon" aria-hidden="true"></span>
    <span class="sr-only">Next</span>
  </a>
</div>
```

The first slide is an 800 x 300 px gray rectangle.

Second slide

Third slide

Clicking the left arrow renders the previous image.

Clicking the right arrow renders the next image.

Now, you need to add some styles to the carousel. Because it's a custom component, you'll add `display: block` to its CSS file. You also want to add some space at the bottom of the carousel so other components won't overlap. To apply these styles to the component itself and not to its internals, you'll use the pseudo class selector `:host` that represents the carousel, in this case. To ensure that the slide images take the entire width of the `<div>` that hosts the carousel, add the following listing's style to the carousel.component.css file.

Listing 2.22 carousel.component.css

```
:host {
    display: block;
    margin-bottom: 10px;
}

img {
  width: 100%;
}
```

- `:host` — Applies styles to the carousel component and not to its internals
- `display: block;` — Displays the component as a block element that takes the entire width
- `margin-bottom: 10px;` — Adds some space below the carousel
- `width: 100%;` — Images should take the entire width of the carousel.

Overriding Bootstrap styles

Most of the Bootstrap framework styles are located in the node_modules/bootstrap/dist/css/bootstrap.css file. If you want to override some of the default styles, see how Bootstrap defines them and decide what you want to change. Then, define the CSS style in your component that matches the selector of the Bootstrap file.

For example, the carousel indicators are rendered as dashes, and the Bootstrap CSS selector `.carousel-indicators li` looks like the following:

```
.carousel-indicators li {
  position: relative;
  -webkit-box-flex: 0;
  -ms-flex: 0 1 auto;
  flex: 0 1 auto;
  width: 30px;
  height: 3px;
  margin-right: 3px;
  margin-left: 3px;
  text-indent: -999px;
  background-color: rgba(255, 255, 255, 0.5);
}
```

If you want to change the indicators from dashes to circles, add the following style to the carousel.component.css:

```
.carousel-indicators li {
  width: 10px;
  height: 10px;
  border-radius: 100%;
}
```

Don't be surprised if, after adding code in the carousel component, the rendering of ngAuction hasn't changed and still looks like figure 2.9. That's because you haven't added the `<nga-carousel>` tag to any parent component yet. You'll add `<nga-carousel>` to the home component, which you'll create next.

2.7.8 *The home component*

The template of your app component includes the `<router-outlet>` area, which, on the `md`-size viewports, will be located to the right of `<nga-search>`. In chapter 3, you'll modify ngAuction to render either the home or the product-detail component in the `<router-outlet>`, but for now, you'll render the home component there. Your home component will host and render the carousel at the top and several products under it.

Modify the content of the generated home.component.html to look like the following listing.

Listing 2.23 The home component template

```
<div class="row carousel-holder">
  <div class="col-md-12">
  <nga-carousel></nga-carousel>
   </div>
</div>
<div class="row">
  We'll render several ProductItem components here
 </div>
```

The carousel goes at the top of the home component.

In chapter 3, you'll replace this text with product-item components.

The first `<div>` hosts the carousel, and the second one displays the text revealing your plans to render several product items there. Still, the UI of your running ngAuction hasn't changed, and you may have guessed that it's because you didn't include the `<nga-home>` tag in your app component. And you won't be doing that. You'll use Angular Router to render `HomeComponent` inside the `<router-outlet>` area.

Chapters 3 and 4 cover the router in detail—for now, you'll just make a small change in the generated app/app-routing.module.ts file, which includes the line in the following listing for route configuration.

Listing 2.24 Configuring routes

```
const routes: Routes = [];
```

Replace the code in the preceding listing with the code in the following one.

Listing 2.25 Mapping an empty path to the home component

```
const routes: Routes = [
  {
  path: '', component: HomeComponent
  }
];
```

This means that if the path after the base URL is empty (the URL of ngAuction has nothing after the port number), render the `HomeComponent`. You'll also need to add an import statement for `HomeComponent` in the app-routing.module.ts file.

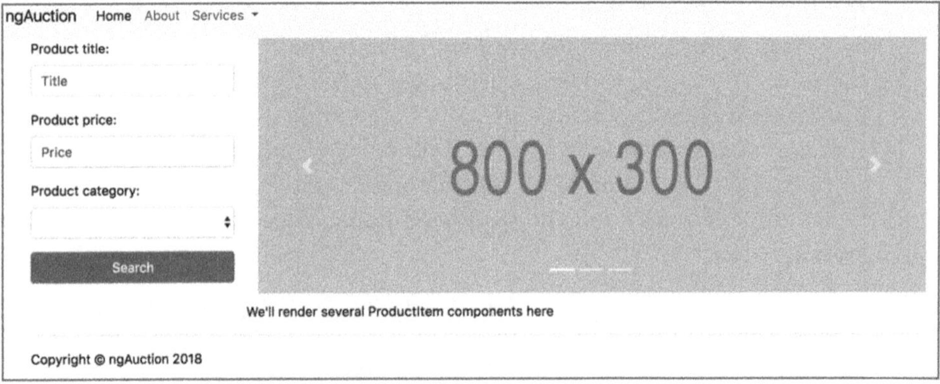

Figure 2.10 Rendering ngAuction with the home component

Now your ngAuction renders as shown in figure 2.10, and the carousel will run a slide show of gray rectangles.

The initial version of ngAuction is ready. You can start reducing the width of the browser window to see how this UI will be rendered on a smaller device. As soon as the window width becomes smaller than 992 pixels (the value of the Bootstrap `md` size), the browser will change the page layout, giving the entire window's width to the search component, and the home component will be rendered under the search. This is responsive web design in action.

Summary

- An Angular application is represented by a hierarchy of components that are packaged into modules.
- Each Angular component contains a template for UI rendering and a class implementing the component's functionality.
- Templates and styles can be either inlined or stored in separate files.
- Angular CLI is a useful tool even after the project has been generated.
- Data binding is a mechanism to keep the UI of the component and the values in the underlying class in sync.
- You can use third-party JavaScript libraries in Angular projects.

3 Router basics

This chapter covers

- Configuring parent and child routes
- Passing data while navigating from one route to another
- Configuring and using child routes

In a single-page application (SPA), the web page won't be reloaded, but its parts may change. You'll want to add navigation to this application so it'll change the content area of the page (known as the *router outlet*) based on the user's actions. The Angular router allows you to configure and implement such navigation without performing a full page reload.

In general, you can think of a *router* as an object responsible for the view state of the application. Every application has one router object, and you need to configure the routes of your app.

In this chapter, we'll discuss the major features of the Angular router, including configuring routes in parent and child components, passing data to routes, and adding router support to the HTML anchor elements.

The ngAuction app now has a home view; you'll add a second view so that if the user clicks the title of a product on the home page, the page's content will change to display the details of the selected product. At any given time, the user will see either the `HomeComponent` or the `ProductDetailComponent` in the `<router-outlet>` area.

3.1 Routing basics

You can think of an SPA as a collection of states, such as home, product detail, and shipping. Each state represents a different view of the same SPA.

Figure 3.1 shows the landing page of the ngAuction app, which has a navigation bar (a component) at the top, a search form (another component) on the left, and a footer (yet another component) at the bottom, and you want these components to remain visible all the time.

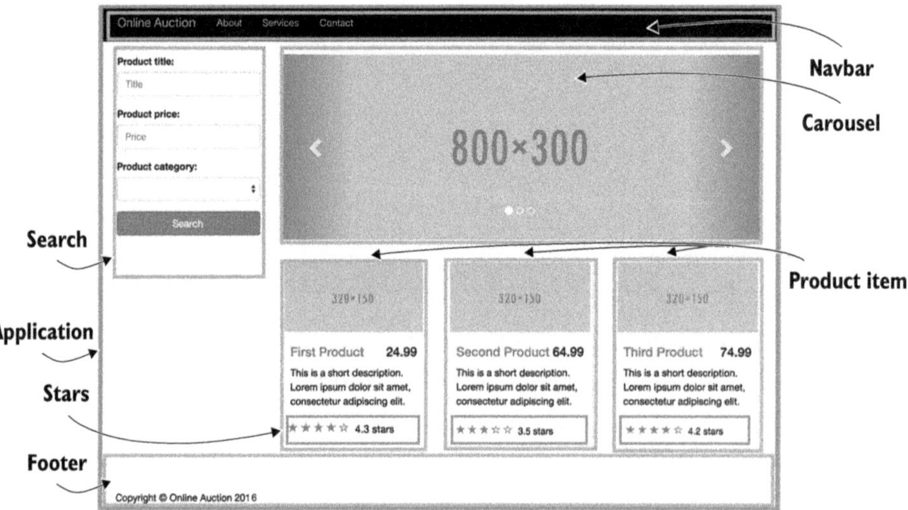

Figure 3.1 Components on the home page of ngAuction

Besides the parts that are always visible, there's a content area (see figure 3.2) that initially will display the `<nga-home>` component and its children but can show other views as well, based on the user's actions. To show other views, you'll need to configure the router so it can display different views in the outlet, replacing one view with another. You'll be assigning a component for each view that you want to display in this area. This content area is represented by the tag `<router-outlet>`.

> **TIP** There can be more than one outlet on the page. We'll cover this in section 4.2 in chapter 4.

The router is responsible for managing client-side navigation, and later in this chapter we provide a high-level overview of the router. In the non-SPA world, site navigation is implemented by a series of requests to a server, which refreshes the entire page by sending the appropriate HTML documents to the browser. With SPAs, the code for rendering components is already on the client (except for the lazy-loading scenarios covered in section 4.3 of chapter 4), and you need to replace one view with another.

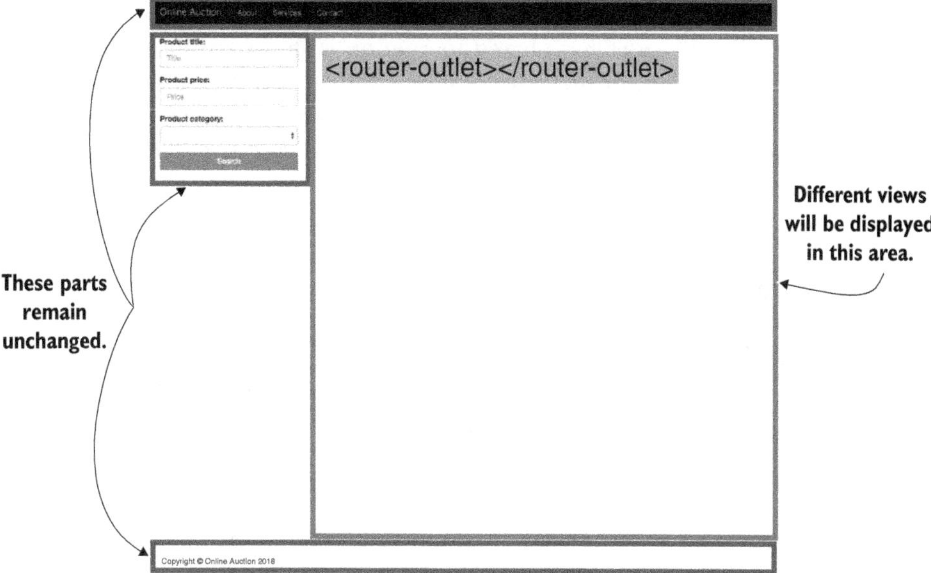

Figure 3.2 Allocating the area for changing views

As the user navigates the application, the app can still make requests to the server to retrieve or send data. Sometimes a view (the combination of the UI code and data) has everything it needs already downloaded to the browser. Other times a view will communicate with the server by issuing AJAX requests or via WebSockets. Each view will have a unique URL shown in the location bar of the browser. We'll discuss that next.

3.2 *Location strategies*

At any given time, the browser's location bar displays the URL of the current view. A URL can contain different parts, or segments. It starts with a protocol followed by a domain name, and it may include a port number. Parameters that need to be passed to the server may follow a question mark (this is true for HTTP `GET` requests), like this: http://mysite.com:8080/auction?someParam=1234.

In a non-SPA, changing any character in the preceding URL results in a new request to the server. In SPAs, you need the ability to modify the URL without forcing the browser to make a server-side request so the application can locate the proper view on the client. Angular offers two location strategies for implementing client-side navigation:

- `HashLocationStrategy`—A hash sign (#) is added to the URL, and the URL segment after the hash uniquely identifies the view to be used as a web page fragment. This strategy works with all browsers, including the old ones.
- `PathLocationStrategy`—This `History` API–based strategy works only in browsers that support HTML5. This is the default location strategy in Angular.

3.2.1 Hash-based navigation

A sample URL that uses hash-based navigation is shown in figure 3.3. Changing any character to the right of the hash sign doesn't cause a direct server-side request but navigates to the view represented by the path (with or without parameters) after the hash. The hash sign serves as a separator between the base URL and the client-side location of the required content.

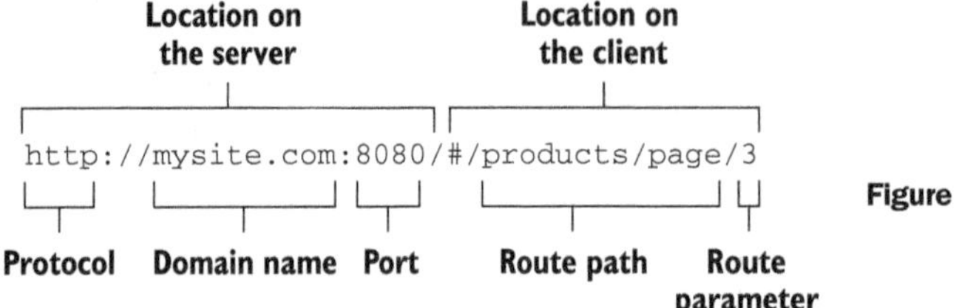

Figure 3.3 Dissecting the URL

Try to navigate an SPA like Gmail and watch the URL. For the Inbox, it looks like this: https://mail.google.com/mail/u/0/#inbox. Now go to the Sent folder, and the hash portion of the URL will change from *inbox* to *sent*. The client-side JavaScript code invokes the necessary functions to display the Sent view. But why does the Gmail app still show you the "Loading . . ." message when you switch to the Sent box? The JavaScript code of the Sent view can still make AJAX requests to the server to get the new data, but it doesn't have to load any additional code, markup, or CSS from the server.

To use hash-based navigation, `@NgModule()` has to include the `providers` value (we discuss providers in the section 5.2 in chapter 5), as shown in the following listing.

Listing 3.1 Using the hash location strategy

```
import {HashLocationStrategy, LocationStrategy} from "@angular/common";
...
@NgModule({
...
  providers:[{provide: LocationStrategy, useClass: HashLocationStrategy}]
 })
```

The provider is needed, so Angular injects the service supporting the hash location strategy.

3.2.2 History API-based navigation

The browser's `History` API allows you to move back and forth through the user's navigation history as well as programmatically manipulate the history stack (see "Manipulating the Browser History" in the Mozilla Developer Network, http://mng .bz/i64G). In particular, the `pushState()` method is used to attach a segment to the base URL as the user navigates your SPA.

Consider the following URL: http://mysite.com:8080/products/page/3 (note the absence of the hash sign). The URL segment *products/page/3* can be pushed (attached) to the base URL programmatically without using the hash tag. If the user navigates from page 3 to 4, the application's code will push the URL segment *products/page/4*, saving the previously visited *products/page/3* in the browser history.

Angular spares you from invoking `pushState()` explicitly—you just need to configure the URL segments and map them to the corresponding components. With the `History` API–based location strategy, you need to tell Angular what to use as a base URL in your application so it can properly append the client-side URL segments. If you want to serve an Angular app on a non-root path, you have to do the following:

- Add the `<base>` tag to the header of index.html, such as `<base href="/mypath">`,or use the `--base-href` option while running `ng build`. Angular CLI–generated projects include `<base href="/">` in index.html.
- Assign a value for the `APP_BASE_HREF` constant in the root module and use it as the `providers` value. The following listing uses / as a base URL, but it can be any URL segment that denotes the end of the base URL.

Listing 3.2 Adding support to a `History`-based API

```
import { APP_BASE_HREF } from '@angular/common';
...
@NgModule({
...
  providers:[{provide: APP_BASE_HREF, useValue: '/mypath'}]
 })
class AppModule { }
```

The provider is needed so the router properly resolves URLs.

`APP_BASE_HREF` affects how the router resolves `routerLink` properties and the `router.navigate()` calls within the app, whereas the `<base href=". . .">` tag affects how the browser resolves URLs when loading static resources like `<link>`, `<script>`, and `<img>` tags.

3.3 The building blocks of client-side navigation

Let's get familiar with the main concepts of implementing client-side navigation using the Angular router. Routes are configured using the `RouterModule`. If your application needs routing, make sure your package.json file includes the dependency `@angular/router`. Angular includes many classes supporting navigation—for example, `Router`, `Route`, `Routes`, `ActivatedRoute`, and others. You configure routes in an array of objects of type `Route`, as in the following listing. Each of the elements in this array is an object of type `Route`.

Listing 3.3 A sample routes configuration

```
const routes: Routes = [
    {path: '',         component: HomeComponent},
    {path: 'product', component: ProductDetailComponent}
];
```

Renders the HomeComponent by default

If the URL contains the product fragment, renders ProductDetailComponent

Because route configuration is done on the module level, you need to let the app module know about the routes in the `@NgModule()` decorator. If you declare routes for the root module, use the `forRoot()` method , for example, as shown in the following listing.

Listing 3.4 Letting the root module know about the routes

```
import { BrowserModule } from '@angular/platform-browser';
import { RouterModule } from '@angular/router';
...
@NgModule({
  imports: [BrowserModule,
            RouterModule.forRoot(routes)],
      ...
})
```

Creates a router module and a service for the app root module

If you generated your app using the Angular CLI command `ng new` with the `--routing` option (as you did in the hands-on section in chapter 2), you'll get a separate file, app-routing.module.ts, where you can configure routes, as illustrated in the next listing.

Listing 3.5 A separate module with route support

```
const routes: Routes = [
   { path: '', component: HomeComponent},
  { path: 'product', component: ProductDetailComponent}
];

@NgModule({
  imports: [RouterModule.forRoot(routes)],
   exports: [RouterModule]
 })
export class AppRoutingModule {}
```

Configures routes

Creates a router module and a service for the app root module

Makes this module accessible from other modules

If you're configuring routes for a feature module (not for the root one), use the `forChild()` method, which also creates a router module but doesn't create the router service (`forRoot()` should have created the service by now), as you can see in the following listing.

Listing 3.6 Creating a router module for a feature module

```
@NgModule({
  imports: [CommonModule,
            RouterModule.forChild(routes)]
      ...
})
export class MyFeatureModule {}
```

Creates a router module but doesn't create the router service

Let's start with a simple app that illustrates routing. Say you want to create a root component that has two links, Home and Product Details, at the top of the page. The application should render either `HomeComponent` or `ProductDetailComponent`, depending on which link the user clicks. `HomeComponent` will render the text "Home Component,"

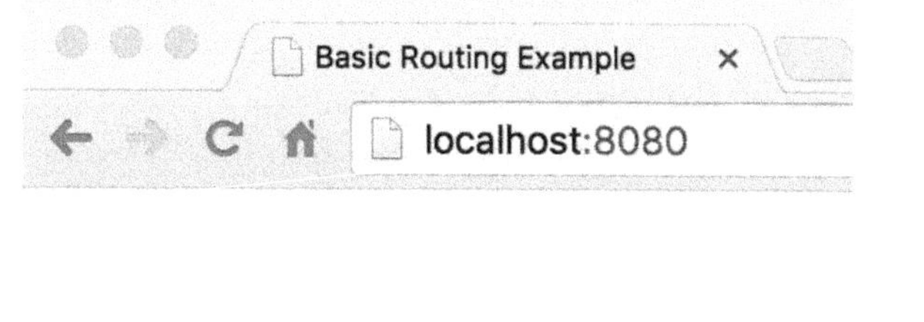

Figure 3.4 Home component rendered with red background

and `ProductDetailComponent` will render "Product Detail Component." Initially the web page should display `HomeComponent`, as shown in figure 3.4.

After the user clicks the Product Details link, the router should display the `ProductDetailComponent`, as shown in figure 3.5.

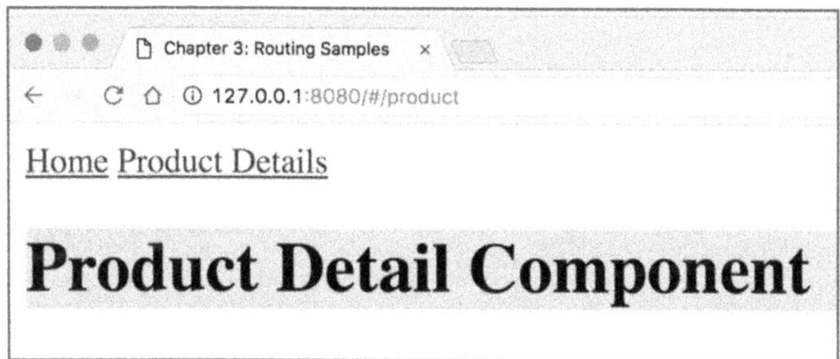

Figure 3.5 Product-detail component rendered with cyan background

You can see how the URLs for these routes look in figures 3.4 and 3.5. The main goal of this basic app is to become familiar with the router, so the components will be very simple, as in the following listing.

Listing 3.7 `HomeComponent`

```
@Component({
    selector: 'home',
    template: '<h1 class="home">Home Component</h1>',
    styles: ['.home {background: red}']})
 export class HomeComponent {}
```

Renders this component with red background

The code of the ProductDetailComponent looks similar, as you can see in the following listing, but instead of red it uses a cyan background.

Listing 3.8 ProductDetailComponent

```
@Component({
    selector: 'product',
    template: '<h1 class="product">Product Detail Component</h1>',
    styles: ['.product {background: cyan}']})
export class ProductDetailComponent {}
```

Renders this component with cyan background

The Routes type is just a collection of the objects of the type defined in the Route interface, as shown in the next listing.

Listing 3.9 Angular's Route interface

```
export interface Route {
    path?: string;
    pathMatch?: string;
    matcher?: UrlMatcher;
    component?: Type<any>;
    redirectTo?: string;
    outlet?: string;
    canActivate?: any[];
    canActivateChild?: any[];
    canDeactivate?: any[];
    canLoad?: any[];
    data?: Data;
    resolve?: ResolveData;
    children?: Routes;
    loadChildren?: LoadChildren;
    runGuardsAndResolvers?: RunGuardsAndResolvers;
}
```

You can pass to the forRoot() or forChild() functions a config object that only has a couple of properties filled in. In the basic app, you use just two properties defined in the Route interface: path and component. We'll do it in a file called app.routing.ts, as in the following listing.

Listing 3.10 app.routing.ts

```
const routes: Routes = [
    {path: '',        component: HomeComponent},
    {path: 'product', component: ProductDetailComponent}
];

export const routing = RouterModule.forRoot(routes);
```

HomeComponent is mapped to a path containing an empty string, which implicitly makes it a default route.

If the URL has the product segment after the base URL, renders the ProductDetail-Component in the router outlet

Invokes forRoot() and exports the router configuration so it can be imported by the root module

The next step is to create a root component that will contain the links for navigating between the home and product-detail views. The following listing shows the root AppComponent located in the app.component.ts file.

Listing 3.11 app.component.ts

```
@Component({
    selector: 'app-root',
    template: `
      <a [routerLink]="['/']">Home</a>    ⊲— Creates a link that binds routerLink to the empty path
       <a [routerLink]="['/product']">Product Details</a>    ⊲— Creates a link that binds routerLink to the path /product
       <router-outlet></router-outlet>    ⊲— The <router-outlet> specifies the area on the page where the router will render the components (one at a time).
     `
})
export class AppComponent {}
```

The square brackets around routerLink denote property binding, while the brackets on the right represent an array with one element (for example, `['/']`). The second anchor tag has the routerLink property bound to the component configured for the /product path. The matched components will be rendered in the area marked with <router-outlet>, which in this app is located below the anchor tags.

None of the components are aware of the router configuration, because it's the module's business, as shown in the following listing.

Listing 3.12 app.module.ts

```
...
import {routing} from './app.routing';    ⊲— Imports the routes configuration

@NgModule({
    imports:        [ BrowserModule,
                      routing ],    ⊲— Adds the routes configuration to @NgModule()
     declarations: [ AppComponent,
                      HomeComponent,
                      ProductDetailComponent],
    providers:[{provide: LocationStrategy, useClass: HashLocationStrategy}],    ⊲— Lets the dependency injection mechanism know that you want HashLocationStrategy
     bootstrap:     [ AppComponent ]
})
class AppModule {}
```

The module's providers property is an array of registered providers (there's just one in this example) for dependency injection, which is covered in chapter 5. At this point, you just need to know that although the default location strategy is PathLocationStrategy, you want Angular to use the HashLocationStrategy class for routing (note the hash sign in the URL in figure 3.5).

In the project router-samples that comes with this chapter, we've configured multiple applications in the .angular-cli.json file. The app described in this section has the name *basic*, and you can run it by entering the following command in your Terminal window:

```
ng serve --app basic -o
```

NOTE In Angular 6, the .angular-cli.json file is renamed angular.json. Also, if you decide to run the Angular 6 version of this app (it comes with the book code samples), the `--app` option isn't needed: `ng serve basic -o`.

TIP Don't forget to run `npm install` in the project router-samples.

In the basic routing code sample, we arranged the navigation using `routerLink` in HTML anchor tags. But what if you need to arrange navigation programmatically without asking the user to click a link?

3.4 Navigating to routes with navigate()

Let's modify the basic code sample to navigate by using the `navigate()` method. You'll add a button that will also navigate to the `ProductDetailComponent`, but this time no HTML anchors will be used.

The following listing reuses the router configuration from the previous section but invokes the `navigate()` method on the `Router` instance that will be injected into the `AppComponent` via its constructor.

Listing 3.13 Using `navigate()`

```
@Component({
  selector: 'app',
  template: `
    <a [routerLink]="['/']">Home</a>
    <a [routerLink]="['/product']">Product Details</a>
    <button (click)="navigateToProductDetail()>Product Details
     </button>
    <router-outlet></router-outlet>
  `
})
class AppComponent {

    constructor(private _router: Router){}

    navigateToProductDetail(){
        this._router.navigate(["/product"]);
    }
}
```

Clicking this button invokes the navigateToProductDetail() method.

Angular will inject the instance of Router into the router variable.

Navigates to the configured product route programmatically

In listing 3.13, the user needs to click a button to go to the product route. But the navigation could be implemented without requiring user actions—just invoke the `navigate()` method from your application code when necessary. For example, you can force the app to navigate to the login route if the user isn't logged in.

By default the address bar of the browser changes as the user navigates with the router. If you don't want to show the URL of the current route, use the `skipLocationChange` directive :

```
<a [routerLink]="['/product']" skipLocationChange>Product Details</a>
```

In this case, the URL remains http:// localhost:4200/#/ even when the user navigates to the `product` route. To achieve the same effect with programmatic navigation, use the following syntax:

```
this._router.navigate(["/product"], {skipLocationChange: true});
```

Handling 404 errors

If the user enters a nonexistent URL in your application, the router won't be able to find a matching route and will print an error message on the browser console, leaving the user to wonder why no navigation is happening. Consider creating an application component that will be displayed whenever the application can't find the matching component.

For example, you could create a component named _404Component and configure it with the wildcard path `**`:

```
[
  {path: '',          component: HomeComponent},
  {path: 'product', component: ProductDetailComponent},
  {path: '**', component: _404Component}
])
```

The wildcard route configuration has to be the last element in the array of routes. The router always treats the wildcard route as a match, so any routes listed after the wildcard route won't be considered.

3.5 Passing data to routes

The basic routing application showed how you can display different components in the router outlet area, but you often need to also pass some data to the component. For example, if the app component shows a list of products and you want to navigate to the product-detail route, you need to pass the product ID to the component that represents the destination route. In this case, you need to add a parameter to the `path` property in the route configuration. In the following listing, you change the configuration of the `product` route to indicate that the `ProductDetailComponent` has to be rendered when the URL segment includes the value after `'product'` (the colon denotes the variable part of the path - `:id`).

Listing 3.14 Routes configuration

```
const routes: Routes = [
    {path: '',          component: HomeComponent},
    {path: 'product/:id', component: ProductDetailComponent}
 ];
```

If the URL contains the fragment product followed by a value, renders ProductDetailComponent and passes the value to it

Accordingly, your app component needs to include the value of the product ID in the `routerLink`to ensure that the value of the product ID will be passed to the `ProductDetailComponent` if the user chooses to go this route. The new version of the app may look like the following listing.

Listing 3.15 app.component.ts

```
@Component({
    selector: 'app-root',
    template: `
        <a [routerLink]="['/']">Home</a>
        <a [routerLink]="['/product', productId]">Product Detail</a>
         <router-outlet></router-outlet>
    `
})
class AppComponent {
  productId = 1234;
 }
```

If the user clicks this link, navigates to the product route, passing the value of productId

Sets the value of the productId property

The second `routerLink` is bound to the two-element array providing the static part of the path /product and the value `/:id` that represents the product ID. The elements of the array build up the path specified in the routes configuration given to the `RouterModule.forRoot()` method. For the product-detail route, Angular will construct the URL segment /product/1234.

To see this app in action, run the following command in your Terminal window:

```
ng serve --app params -o
```

3.5.1 Extracting parameters from ActivatedRoute

If a parent component can pass a parameter to the route, the component that represents the destination route should be able to receive it. Instruct Angular to inject the instance of `ActivatedRoute` to the constructor of the component that represents the destination route. The instance of the `ActivatedRoute` will include the passed parameters, as well as the route's URL segment and other properties. The new version of the component, which renders product detail and is capable of receiving parameters, will be called `ProductDetailComponent`, which will get an object of type `ActivatedRoute` injected into it, as shown in the following listing.

Listing 3.16 `ProductDetailComponentParam`

```
@Component({
  selector: 'product',
  template: `<h1 class="product">Product Detail for Product: {{productID}}</h1>`,
   styles: ['.product {background: cyan}']
})
export class ProductDetailComponent {
  productID: string;

  constructor(route: ActivatedRoute) {
     this.productID = route.snapshot.paramMap.get('id');
   }
}
```

- Displays the received product ID
- The ActivatedRoute object is injected into the constructor of this component.
- Gets the value of the parameter named id and assigns it to the productID class variable, which is used in the template via binding

Figure 3.6 shows how the product-detail view will be rendered in the browser. Note the URL: the router replaced the product/:id path with /product/1234.

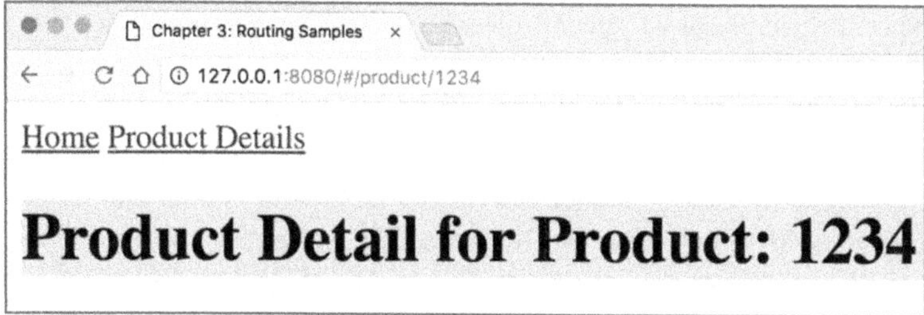

Figure 3.6 The product-detail route received the product ID `1234`.

Passing changing parameters to the route

In this app, you use the property `snapshot` of type `ActivatedRouteSnapshot` to retrieve the parameter's value. The `snapshot` means "one-time deal," and this property is used in scenarios when the parameters passed to the route never change. In your app, it works because the product ID in the parent route never changes and is always `1234`. But if you try to change the URL shown in figure 3.6 manually (for example, make it /product/12345), the `ProductDetailComponent` won't reflect the change in the parameter.

There are scenarios when the parameter value keeps changing after navigating to a route. For example, the `AppComponent` renders a list of products, and the user can select different products. Both `AppComponent` and `ProductDetailComponent` are rendered in the same window. In this case, instead of using the `snapshot` property, you need to subscribe to the `ActivatedRoute.paramMap` property, which will emit a new value each time the user clicks on a different product, for example:

(continued)

```
route.paramMap.subscribe(
  params => this.productID = params.get('id')
);
```

You'll see this example in chapter 6 in section 6.6.

Let's review the steps that Angular performed under the hood to render the main page of the application:

1. Check the content of each `routerLink`.
2. Concatenate the values specified in the array. If an array item is an expression, evaluate this expression (like `productId`). Finally, append the value of `APP_BASE_HREF` in the beginning of the resulting string.
3. The `RouterLink` directive adds the `href` attribute if this directive is attached to an <a> element; otherwise, it just listens to the `click` events.

Figure 3.7 shows a snapshot of the home page of the application with the Chrome Developer Tools panel open. Because the `path` property of the configured home route had an empty string, Angular didn't add anything to the base URL of the page. But the anchor under the Product Details link has already been converted into a regular HTML tag. When the user clicks the Product Details link, the router will attach a hash sign and add /product/1234 to the base URL so that the absolute URL of the product-detail view will become http:// localhost:4200/#/product/1234.

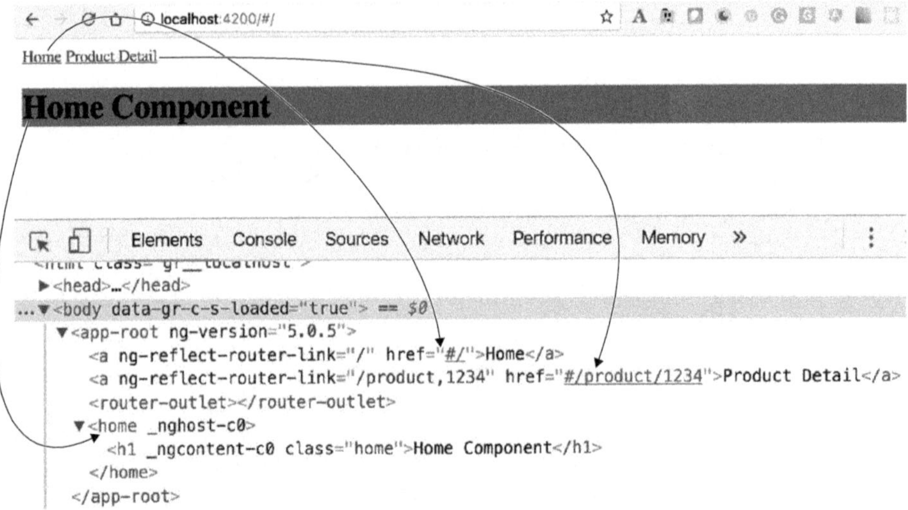

Figure 3.7 Angular-compiled code in the browser

NOTE In this section, you learned how to pass dynamic data to routes—the data that may change during the runtime. Sometimes, you need to pass static data to routes (data that doesn't change). You can pass any arbitrary data to routes by using the `data` property in the routes configuration. You'll see such an example in section 4.3.1 in chapter 4.

Sometimes, you need to pass to a route optional query parameters that are not part of the route configuration. Let's take a look at how to pass query parameters.

3.5.2 Passing query parameters to a route

You can use query parameters (the URL segment after the question mark), as in the following URL: http:// localhost:4200/products?category=sports. Query parameters aren't scoped to a particular route, and if you want to pass them while navigating with the `routerLink`, you can do as follows:

```
<a [routerLink]="['/products']" [queryParams]="{category:'sports'}">?
      Sports products </a>
```

Because query parameters aren't scoped to a particular route and can be accessed by any active route, the route configuration doesn't need to include them:

```
{path: 'products', component: ProductDetailComponent}
```

To pass query parameters using programmatic navigation, you need to have access to the `Router` object. The code could look like the following listing.

Listing 3.17 Injecting and accessing the `Router` object

```
constructor (private router: Router) {}   <-- Injects the Router object

showSportingProducts() {
   this.router.navigate(['/products'],              <-- Invokes navigate() on the Router object
                        {queryParams: {category: 'sports'}});
}
```

In this example, you pass an object with one query parameter; but you can specify multiple parameters as well.

To receive query parameters in the destination component, you'll use the `ActivatedRoute` object again.

Listing 3.18 Receiving query parameters

```
@Component({
  selector: 'product',
  template: `<h1 class="product">Showing products in {{productCategory}}</h1>
     `,
  styles: ['.product {background: cyan}']
})
export class ProductDetailComponent {
  productCategory: string;
```

```
  constructor(route: ActivatedRoute) {
     this.productCategory = route.snapshot.queryParamMap.get('category');
  }
}
```

Extracts the query param named category

To see this code sample in action, run the following command:

```
ng serve --app queryparams -o
```

3.6 Child routes

An Angular application is a tree of components that have parent-child relations. A child component can have its own routes, but all routes are configured outside of any component. Imagine that you want to enable `ProductDetailComponent` (the child of the `AppComponent`) to show either the product description or the seller's info. Moreover, there could be more than one seller of the same product, so you'll need to pass the seller ID to show the details of the seller. The following listing configures routes for the child, `ProductDetailComponent`, by using the `children` property of the `Route`.

Listing 3.19 Configuring child routes

```
const routes: Routes = [
  {path: '',            component: HomeComponent},
  {path: 'product/:id', component: ProductDetailComponent,
    children: [
      {path: '',          component: ProductDescriptionComponent},
      {path: 'seller/:id', component: SellerInfoComponent}
    ]}
];
```

This property configures routes for ProductDetailComponent.

ProductDescriptionComponent there by default.

From ProductDetailComponent, the user can navigate to the SellerInfoComponent.

Here, the `children` property is a part of the configuration of the route with the path product/:id. You pass the product ID while navigating to the `product` route, and then, if the user decides to navigate to the `seller`, you pass the seller ID to the `SellerInfoComponent`.

Figure 3.8 shows how the application will look once the user clicks the Product Details link on the root component, which renders `ProductDetailComponent` (the child), showing `ProductDescriptionComponent` by default, because the latter component was configured for the empty `path` property.

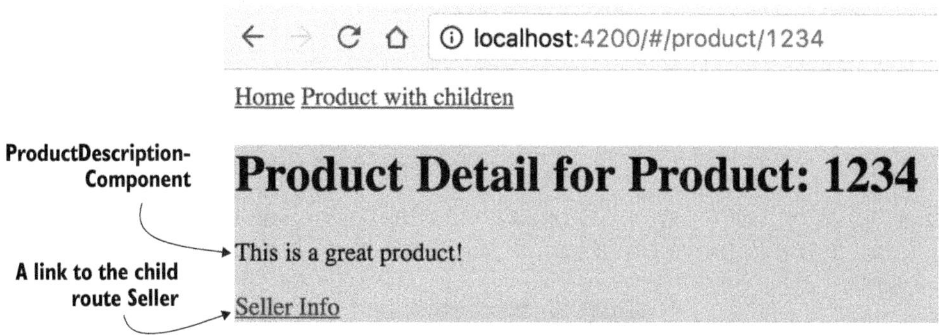

Figure 3.8 The product description route

Figure 3.9 shows the application after the user clicks the Product Details link and then clicks Seller Info.

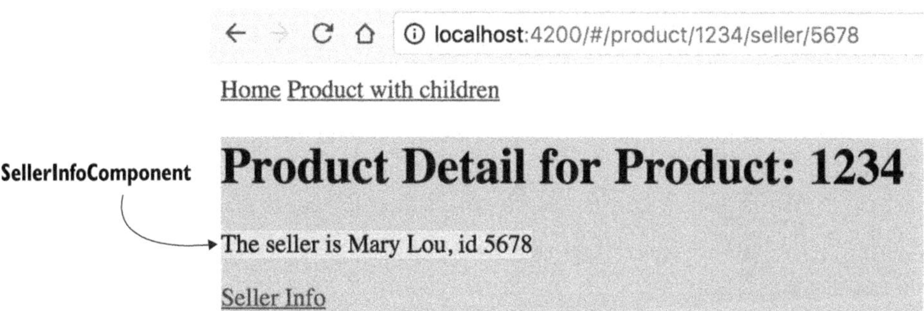

Figure 3.9 The child route renders `SellerInfo`

> **NOTE** If you're reading the electronic version of this book, you'll see that the seller's info is shown on a yellow background. We did this intentionally to discuss the styling of components a bit later in this chapter.

To implement the views shown in figures 3.8 and 3.9, you'll modify `ProductDetailComponent` so it also has two children, `SellerInfoComponent` and `ProductDescriptionComponent`, and its own `<router-outlet>`. Figure 3.10 shows the hierarchy of components that you're going to implement.

The following three listings show the code of the `ProductDetailComponent`, `ProductDescriptionComponent`, and `SellerInfoComponent`. The new version of `ProductDetailComponent` has its own outlet, where it can display either `ProductDescriptionComponent` (the default) or `SellerInfoComponent`.

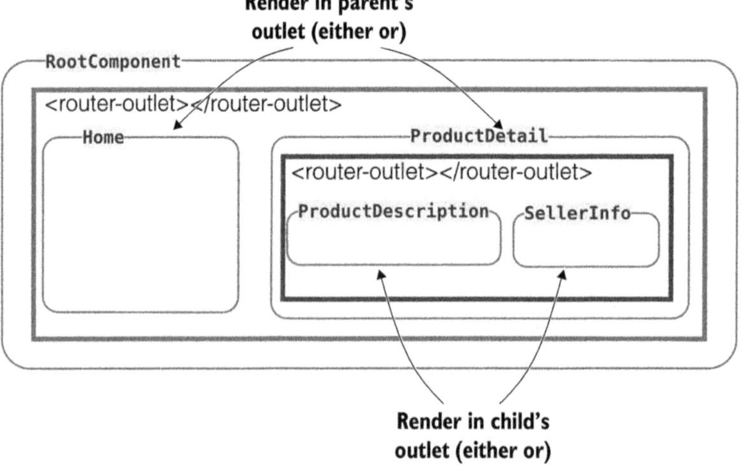

Figure 3.10 The routes hierarchy

Listing 3.20 product.detail.component.ts

```
@Component({
    selector: 'product',
    styles: ['.product {background: cyan}'],
    template: `
      <div class="product">
        <h1>Product Detail for Product: {{productId}}</h1>
        <router-outlet></router-outlet>
         <p><a [routerLink]="['./seller', sellerId]">Seller Info</a></p>
      </div>
    `
})
export class ProductDetailComponent {
  productId: string;
  sellerId = 5678;

  constructor(route: ActivatedRoute) {
    this.productId = route.snapshot.paramMap.get('id');
  }
}
```

ProductDetailComponent allocates its own router-outlet area for rendering its child components one at a time.

When the user clicks this link, Angular adds the /seller/5678 segment to the existing URL and renders SellerInfoComponent.

When the user clicks the Product With Children link, and it has children, the product/1234 segment is added to the URL. The router finds a match to this path in the configuration object and renders the `ProductDetailComponent` in the outlet.

The user navigates to the `ProductDetailComponent`, which by default renders the `ProductDescriptionComponent` as per route configuration. Then, the user clicks the

ⓘ localhost:4200/#/product/1234/seller/5678

Figure 3.11 The URL of the seller component

Seller Info link, and the URL will include the product/1234/seller/5678 segment after the hash sign, as shown in figure 3.11.

The router will find a match in the configuration object and will render `SellerInfoComponent` in the child's `<router-outlet>`. The code of the `ProductDescriptionComponent` is trivial, as you can see in the following listing.

Listing 3.21 product.description.component.ts

```
@Component({
    selector: 'product-description',
    template: '<p>This is a great product!</p>'
})
export class ProductDescriptionComponent {}
```

Because `SellerInfoComponent` expects to receive the seller ID, its constructor needs an argument of type `ActivatedRoute` to get the seller ID, as the following listing shows, and as you did in `ProductDetailComponent`.

Listing 3.22 seller.info.component.ts

```
@Component({
    selector: 'seller',
    template: 'The seller is Mary Lou, id {{sellerID}} ',
    styles: [':host {background: yellow}']    <- A pseudo class :host is used to display the content of this component on a yellow background.
 })
export class SellerInfoComponent {
   sellerID: string;

   constructor(route: ActivatedRoute){    <- Injects the ActivatedRoute object
      this.sellerID = route.snapshot.paramMap.get('id');    <- Gets the value of the passed id and assigns it to sellerID for rendering
   }
}
```

The `:host` pseudo class selector can be used with elements that are created using Shadow DOM (discussed in section 8.5.1 in chapter 8), which provides better encapsulation for components. Although not all web browsers support Shadow DOM yet, Angular emulates Shadow DOM by default. Here, you use `:host` to apply the yellow background color to `SellerInfoComponent`. In the emulated mode, the `:host` selector is transformed into a randomly generated, attribute-based selector, like this:

```
[ng-host-f23ed] {
  background: yellow;
}
```

The attribute (here, `ng-host-f23ed`) is attached to the element that represents the component. Shadow DOM styles of the components aren't merged with the styles of the global DOM, and the IDs of the components' HTML tags won't overlap with the IDs of the DOM.

To run this code sample, enter the following command in the Terminal window of the router-samples project:

```
ng serve --app child -o
```

Deep linking

Deep linking is the ability to create a link to specific content inside a web page rather than to the entire page. In the basic routing applications, you've seen examples of deep linking:

- The URL http://localhost:4200/#/product/1234 links not just to the product-detail page but to a specific view representing the product with an ID of `1234`.
- The URL http://localhost:4200/#/product/1234/seller/5678 links even deeper. It shows the information about the seller with an ID of `5678` that sells the product whose ID is `1234`.

You can easily see deep linking in action by copying the link http:// localhost: 4200/#/product/1234/seller/5678 from the application running in Chrome and pasting it into Firefox or Safari. There is a caveat, though. With `PathLocationStrategy`, when you enter the direct URL of the route in the browser's address bar, it still makes a request to the server, which won't find the resource (and rightly so) named as your route. This will cause a 404 error. Configure your web server to do a redirect to index.html of your app in cases when a requested resource isn't found. This will put your Angular app back in control, and the route will be properly resolved. The Angular CLI development server is already configured for redirects.

Router events

As the user navigates your app, Angular dispatches events, such as `NavigationStart`, `NavigationEnd`, and so on. There are about a dozen router events, and you can intercept any of them if need be. In chapter 6, section 6.6, you'll see an example of using router events to decide when to show and hide the progress bar if the navigation is slow. For debugging purposes, you can log router events in the browser's console by using the `enableTracing` option (it works only in the root module):

```
RouterModule.forRoot(
  routes,
  {enableTracing: true}
)
```

Now that you've learned router basic features, let's see how can you apply them in your ngAuction application.

3.7 Hands-on: Adding navigation to the online auction

NOTE Source code for this chapter can be found at https://github.com/Farata/angulartypescript and www.manning.com/books/angular-development-with-typescript-second-edition.

This hands-on exercise starts where we left off in chapter 2. So far, you've partially implemented the landing page of ngAuction; your goal is to render several product items under the carousel component so the landing page looks as shown in figure 3.12.

The data for this view will be provided by `ProductService`. This hands-on exercise contains instructions for injecting the `ProductService` into the `HomeComponent`. You'll also implement the navigation so that when the user clicks the product title, the `Router` will render the `ProductDetail` component in the `<router-outlet>` area.

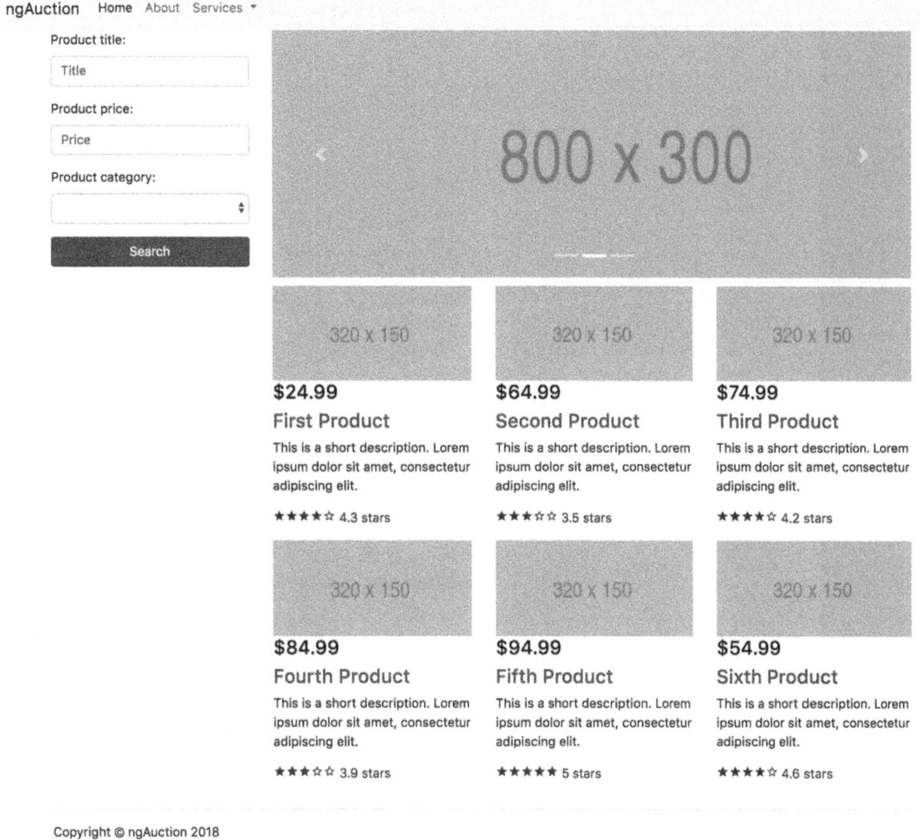

Figure 3.12 The landing page of ngAuction with products

Your `ProductService` will contain hardcoded data about the products. Adding `ProductService` as an argument to the constructor of `HomeComponent` will instruct Angular to instantiate and inject the product object into this component.

As a starting point, you'll use the project in the chapter3/ngAuction folder, which, for the most part, is the same as chapter2/ngAuction with one addition: the shared/product.service.ts file contains the code to provide product data.

To start working on this exercise, open the chapter3/ngAuction folder in your IDE and install the project dependencies by running the `npm install` command.

3.7.1 ProductService

`ProductService` contains hardcoded data about products and the API to retrieve them. Let's review the code in product.service.ts shown in the following listing (we removed the majority of the hardcoded data for brevity).

Listing 3.23 product.service.ts

```
export class Product {                  <-- The Product instances will be
  constructor(                              returned by the methods of
   public id: number,                       ProductService.
   public title: string,
   public price: number,
   public rating: number,
   public description: string,
   public categories: string[]) {
  }
}
                                            The class ProductService
export class ProductService {         <--  offers an API to get products.

  getProducts(): Product[] {                     <-- This method returns all
     return products.map(p => new Product(p.id, p.title,    hardcoded products.
      p.price, p.rating, p.description, p.categories));
  }

  getProductById(productId: number): Product {    <-- This method returns
     return products.find(p => p.id === productId);     one product based on
  }                                                     productId.
}

const products = [          <-- An array with
   {                            hardcoded products
    'id': 0,
    'title': 'First Product',
    'price': 24.99,
    'rating': 4.3,
    'description': 'This is a short description.
    ➥ Lorem ipsum dolor sit amet, consectetur adipiscing elit.',
    'categories': ['electronics', 'hardware']
  },
  {
    'id': 1,
    'title': 'Second Product',
    'price': 64.99,
```

```
    'rating': 3.5,
    'description': 'This is a short description.
    ➥Lorem ipsum dolor sit amet, consectetur adipiscing elit.',
    'categories': ['books']
  }];
  }
```

Shortly, you'll be adding the code that will have Angular create an instance of the `ProductService` class and inject it into `ProductItemComponent` and `ProductDetail-Component` so they can invoke the `getProducts()` and `getProductById()` methods on the service.

3.7.2 ProductItemComponent

Figure 3.13 shows six products, each an instance of `ProductItemComponent`.

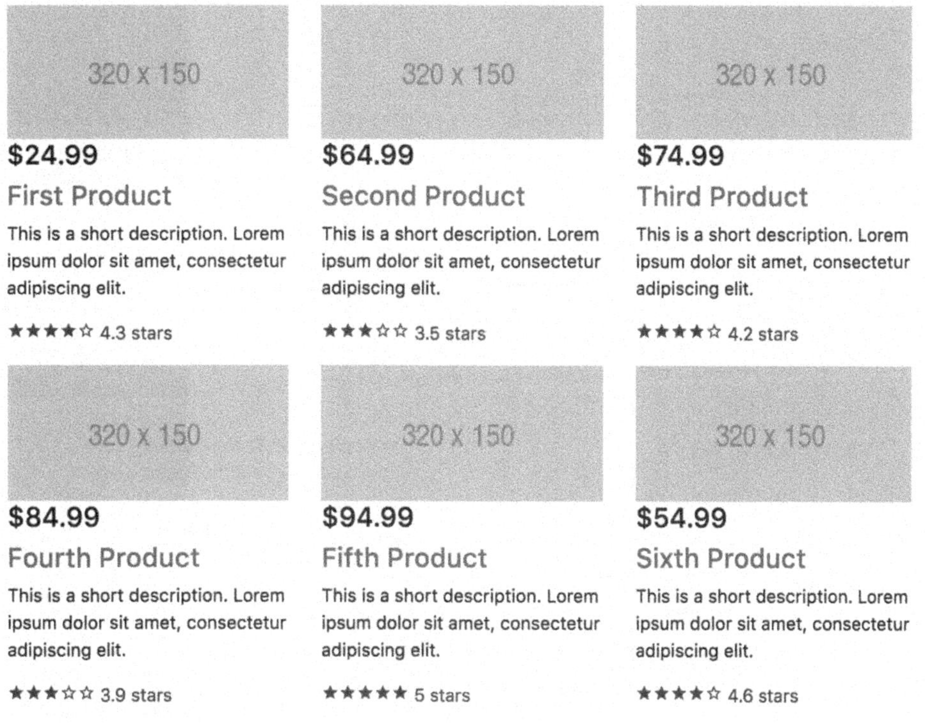

Figure 3.13 Six instances of `ProductItemComponent`

`ProductItemComponent` knows how to render one product based on the product provided by its parent (`HomeComponent`). Modify product-item.component.ts to look like the following listing.

Listing 3.24 product-item.component.ts

```
import {Component, Input} from '@angular/core';
import {Product} from '../shared/product.service';

@Component({
  selector: 'nga-product-item',
  templateUrl: './product-item.component.html',
  styleUrls: ['./product-item.component.css']
})
export class ProductItemComponent {

  @Input() product: Product;        <-- This input property will receive the
 }                                      product from the parent component.
```

The product to render will be given to `ProductItemComponent` via its property `product` decorated with `@Input()`. The `@Input()` properties are described in section 8.2.1. in chapter 8.

Modify product-item.component.html with the content shown in the following listing.

Listing 3.25 product-item.component.html

```
<div class="thumbnail">                                       Applying the currency
  <img src="http://placehold.it/320x150">                     pipe for formatting
  <div class="caption">
    <h4 class="float-right">{{product.price | currency}}</h4>  <--
     <h4><a [routerLink]="['/products', product.id]">{{product.title}}</a> <--
     </h4>                                                    The product title
    <p>{{product.description}}</p>                            becomes
  </div>                                                      a link to navigate to
  <!--  <div class="ratings">      <--                        product details.
     <nga-stars [rating]="product.rating"></nga-stars>
  </div> -->
</div>                      The rating component is commented
                            out and will be added later.
```

Note that you bind the product's `price`, `title`, and `id` properties in the component's template. You also use an Angular built-in pipe, `currency`, for price formatting. For now, you'll keep the `<nga-stars>` component commented out because the code of the `StarsComponent` isn't ready yet. Note that `product.title` is a `routerLink` that will navigate to `ProductDetailComponent` when the user clicks it. The instance of `ProductItemComponent` will be hosted by `HomeComponent`, which you'll update next.

3.7.3 HomeComponent

The home component will

- Use the injected `ProductService` to retrieve all featured products and store them in the `products` array.
- Render the `ProductItemComponent` for each product located in the `products` array.

In section 2.7.8 in chapter 2, you implemented the first version of the `HomeComponent` and added the carousel to its template. Now, you need to modify the constructor to inject the `ProductService` and retrieve the products in the `ngOnInit()` method. Modify the code in home.component.ts to look like the following listing.

Listing 3.26 home.component.ts

```
import {Component, OnInit} from '@angular/core';
import {Product, ProductService} from '../shared/product.service';

@Component({
  selector: 'nga-home',
  templateUrl: './home.component.html',
  styleUrls: ['./home.component.css']
})
export class HomeComponent implements OnInit {

  products: Product[]=[];
  constructor(private productService: ProductService) { }

  ngOnInit() {
     this.products = this.productService.getProducts();
    }
}
```

Injecting the ProductService

Implementing the lifecycle method ngOnInit() that's invoked after the constructor

Using the ProductService to retrieve products

When Angular instantiates `HomeComponent`, it injects the instance of `ProductService`. Because you used the `private` qualifier, the generated JavaScript will have an instance variable, `productService`.

Angular invokes the component lifecycle method `ngOnInit()` after the constructor, and you invoke the `getProducts()` method there. In section 9.2. in chapter 9, we'll discuss the component lifecycle methods, and you'll see why `ngOnInit()` is the right place for fetching data.

Modify home.component.html to loop through the array `products` with the structural directive `*ngFor` and render each product.

Listing 3.27 home.component.html

The carousel component goes on top.

```
<div class="row">
  <div class="col-md-12">
    <nga-carousel></nga-carousel>
   </div>
</div>
<div class="row">
  <div *ngFor="let product of products"
             class="col-sm-4 col-lg-4 col-md-4">
     <nga-product-item [product]="product"></nga-product-item>
   </div>
</div>
```

Iterating through the array products

Allocates four columns of the Bootstrap flexible grid for each component

Rendering the <nga-product-item> component for each product

Each product is represented by the same HTML fragment on the web page. Because there are multiple products, you need to render the same HTML multiple times. The `NgFor` directive is used inside the component template to loop through the list of items in the data collection, rendering HTML markup for each item. In component templates, `*ngFor` represents the `NgFor` directive.

Because the `*ngFor` directive is located inside a `<div>`, each loop iteration will render a `<div>` with the content of the corresponding `<nga-product-item>` inside. To pass an instance of a product to `ProductItemComponent`, you use the square brackets for property binding:

```
<nga-product-item [product]="product">
```

The `[product]` on the left refers to the property named `product` inside the `<nga-product-item>` component, and `product` on the right is a local template variable declared on the fly in the `*ngFor` directive as `let product`.

The Bootstrap's grid styles `class="col-sm-4 col-lg-4 col-md-4"` instruct the browser to split the width of the `<div>` by evenly allocating 4 columns (out of 12) to each product on small, large, and medium devices, as shown in figure 3.14. Try to remove this class, and see how it affects the UI.

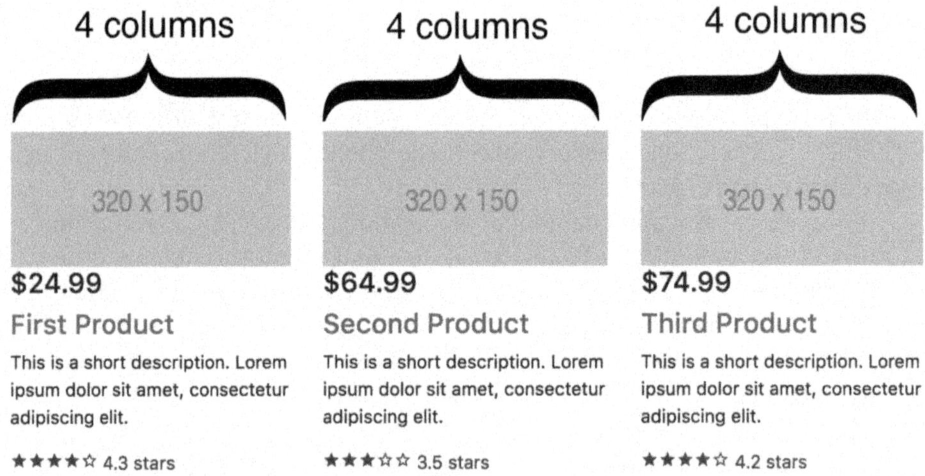

Figure 3.14 Splitting the `<div>` width using Bootstrap grid

Run the `ng serve -o` command , and you'll see six products rendered under the carousel, as shown in figure 3.14, except there won't be any stars with product ratings. We'll take care of the stars next.

3.7.4 StarsComponent

The `StarsComponent` will render stars to display the product rating, as shown in figure 3.15.

Figure 3.15 The `StarsComponent`

On the landing page of ngAuction, the `StarsComponent` will be a child component of `ProductItemComponent`. Eventually, we'll reuse it in the `ProductDetailComponent` as well.

Modify the code of the generated stars.component.ts file to look as follows.

Listing 3.28 stars.component.ts

```
import {Component, Input, OnInit} from '@angular/core';

@Component({
  templateUrl: 'stars.component.html',
  styleUrls: ['./stars.component.css'],
  selector: 'nga-stars'
})
export class StarsComponent implements OnInit {
  @Input() count = 5;
  @Input() rating = 0;
  stars: boolean[] = [];

  ngOnInit() {
     for (let i = 1; i <= this.count; i++) {

      this.stars.push(i > this.rating); // push true or false

    }
  }
}
```

- `@Input() count = 5;` — Decorates the property count with @Input (covered in section 8.1.2 in chapter 8) so the parent component can assign its value using property binding
- `@Input() rating = 0;` — Decorates the property rating with @Input for the same reason
- `stars: boolean[] = [];` — Each element of this array corresponds to a single star.
- `ngOnInit()` — Initializes the stars array with Boolean values based on the rating provided by the parent component

The count property specifies the total number of stars to be rendered. If the parent component doesn't provide the value for this input property, five stars will be rendered by default. The `StarsComponent` can render more or fewer stars if need be. The following listing shows how you can render seven stars.

Listing 3.29 Rendering seven stars

```
<nga-stars [rating]="product.rating"
           [count]="7"></nga-stars>
```

- `[rating]="product.rating"` — Binding the product.rating to the rating input property of the <nga-stars> component
- `[count]="7"` — Binding 7 to the count input property

The elements of the `stars` array with the `false` value represent stars without a color, and those with `true` represent stars filled with color. The `rating` property stores the average product rating that determines how many stars should be filled with color and how many should remain empty.

The Bootstrap 4 framework doesn't include images that render stars. There are several popular libraries of icon fonts out there (Material Design Icons, Font Awesome, Octicons, and so on); we'll use Material Design Icons. To keep them local in the project, install these icons as follows:

```
npm i  material-design-icons
```

Then add these fonts to the `styles` section of the .angular-cli.json file so it looks like the following listing.

Listing 3.30 Styles section of .angular-cli.json

```
"styles": [
  "styles.css",
  "../node_modules/bootstrap/dist/css/bootstrap.min.css",
  "../node_modules/material-icons/css/material-design-icons.min.css"   <-- Adding Material Design Icons
 ]
```

Modify the content of stars.component.html to look like the following listing.

Listing 3.31 stars.component.html

```
<p>
  <span *ngFor="let isEmpty of stars"     <-- Iterates through the Boolean array stars and applies either the filled or empty star
         class="material-icons">     <-- Uses the material-icons style
            {{ isEmpty ? 'star_border' :     <-- A Material Design star filled with color is called star_rate.
                              'star_rate' }}     <-- An empty star style is called star_border.
   </span>
  <span>{{ rating }} stars</span>
</p>
```

Note how you bind either one CSS class or another (double curly brackets). To style the star icon, add the following styles to stars.component.css.

Listing 3.32 stars.component.css

```
:host {
  display: block;
}

.material-icons {     <-- Styles the star icon
   display: inline-block;
  font-size: inherit;
  height: 16px;
  width: 16px;
}
```

The ProductItemComponent will be the parent of the StarsComponent. To make it a child of the ProductItemComponent, uncomment the <div> in the product-item .component.html file created earlier.

Listing 3.33 Adding a <div> with the <nga-stars> component

```
<div class="ratings">
  <nga-stars [rating]="product.rating"></nga-stars>
</div>
```

Makes the stars dark red (see the CSS in the next listing)

Binding the product.rating to the input property of the <nga-stars> component

The CSS selector ratings will be defined in the product-item.component.css file. You'll make the stars dark red and add some padding by using the following listing's style in the product-item.component.css file.

Listing 3.34 product-item.component.css

```
.ratings {
  color: darkred;
}

img {
  width: 100%;
}
```

Setting the color to dark red

Ensures that images won't overlap each other

You add this style to the parent of StarsComponent to be able to pick different star colors in the child component if need be. If another component will need to render stars, you can choose another color there. Now your ProductItemComponent renders ratings for each child product, as shown in figure 3.14.

It's time to implement navigation with the Router.

3.7.5 *ProductDetailComponent*

In chapter 2, you generated the routing module, but it has only one configured route, which renders HomeComponent, as you can see in the following listing.

Listing 3.35 app-routing.module.ts

```
import {NgModule} from '@angular/core';
import {Routes, RouterModule} from '@angular/router';
import {HomeComponent} from "./home/home.component";

const routes: Routes = [
  {
    path: '', component: HomeComponent
  }
];

@NgModule({
  imports: [RouterModule.forRoot(routes)],
```

Configuring a default route

Creating a router module and service for the app root module

```
    exports: [RouterModule]
  })
export class AppRoutingModule { }
```

Reexporting the RouterModule so other modules can access it

You want to add another route so that when the user clicks on the product title in the `ProductItemComponent`, the `Router` replaces `HomeComponent` with `ProductDetailComponent`. During this navigation, you want to pass the ID of the selected product to `ProductDetailComponent`. Modify the routes configuration to look like the following listing, and don't forget to import `ProductDetailComponent`.

Listing 3.36 Configuring a second route

```
const routes: Routes = [
  { path: '', component: HomeComponent},
  { path: 'products/:productId', component: ProductDetailComponent}
 ];
```

Configuring a route for the URL fragments, like products/123

The `ProductDetailComponent` will receive the selected product ID from the parent via the injected `ActivatedRoute` and then make a request to `ProductService` to retrieve product details. Because `ProductDetailComponent` will reuse the instance of `ProductService` that Angular created for you on app startup, add this service to the constructor's arguments. Modify the code in product-detail.component.ts to look like the following listing.

Listing 3.37 product-detail.component.ts

```
import { Component, OnInit } from '@angular/core';
import {Product, ProductService} from '../shared/product.service';
import {ActivatedRoute} from '@angular/router';

@Component({
  selector: 'auction-product-detail',
  templateUrl: './product-detail.component.html',
  styleUrls: ['./product-detail.component.css']
})
export class ProductDetailComponent implements OnInit {

  product: Product;

  constructor(private route: ActivatedRoute,
              private productService: ProductService) { }

  ngOnInit() {
    const prodId: number = parseInt(
                      this.route.snapshot.params['productId']);
     this.product = this.productService.getProductById(prodId);
    }
}
```

Both ActivatedRoute and ProductService are injected into the constructor.

Extracts the parameter productId from the ActivatedRoute

Invokes getProductById() on the service, providing prodId as an argument

The values of the properties of the instance variable `product` will be bound to the component template and rendered by the browser. The template of `ProductDetailComponent` will contain the product image (a gray rectangle) with product price, title, and description.

Modify the content of product-detail.component.html to look like the following listing.

Listing 3.38 product-detail.component.html

```
<div class="thumbnail">
  <img src="http://placehold.it/820x320">
  <div>
    <h4 class="float-right">{{ product.price }}</h4>
     <h4>{{ product.title }}</h4>
     <p>{{ product.description }}</p>
   </div>
  <div class="ratings">
     <p><nga-stars [rating]="product.rating"></nga-stars></p>
   </div>
</div>
```

- Renders the product price on the right
- Renders the product title
- Renders the product description
- Uses the class ratings to render stars in the dark red color
- Renders the StarsComponent with binding on the product rating to the component's property rating

`ProductDetailComponent` also uses <nga-stars>. For a change, let's paint the stars dark green by adding the following listing's style in product-detail.component.css.

Listing 3.39 product-detail.component.css

```
.ratings {
  color: darkgreen;
   padding-left: 10px;
  padding-right: 10px;
}
```

- Sets the star color to dark green

Run the app with `ng serve -o`—the navigation to the product-detail view will work. Click the title of the first product, and the `Router` will create an instance of the `ProductDetailComponent`. The browser will show the product details, as shown in figure 3.16.

Run this app with `ng serve -o` to see the landing page of ngAuction. Note that in the product-detail view, the stars are shown in the dark green color, whereas on the landing page, they're dark red.

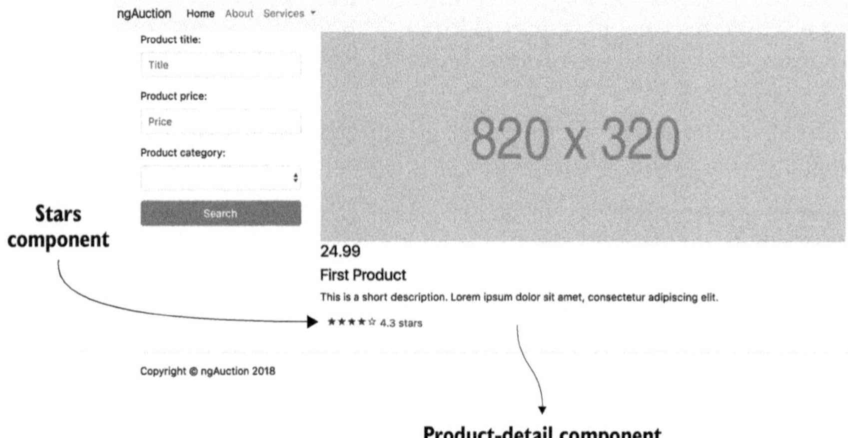

Figure 3.16 Rendering product details

Summary

- You can configure routes in parent and child components.
- You can pass data to routes during navigation.
- During navigation, the router renders components in the area defined by the `<router-outlet>` tag.

4 Router advanced

This chapter covers

- Guarding routes
- Creating components that have multiple router outlets
- Lazy-loading modules

This chapter covers some advanced router features. You'll learn how to use router guards that allow you to restrict access to certain routes, warn the user about unsaved changes, and ensure that important data is retrieved before allowing the user to navigate to a route.

We'll then show you how to create components that have more than one router outlet. Finally, you'll see how to load modules *lazily*—meaning only when the user decides to navigate to certain routes.

This chapter doesn't include the hands-on section for ngAuction. If you're eager to switch from dealing with routing to learning other Angular features, you can skip this chapter and come back to it at a later time.

4.1 Guarding routes

Angular offers several *guard interfaces* that give you a way to mediate navigation to and from a route. Let's say you have a route that only authenticated users can visit.

In other words, you want to guard (protect) the route. Figure 4.1 shows a workflow illustrating how a login guard can protect a route that can be visited only by authenticated users. If the user isn't logged in, the app will render a login view.

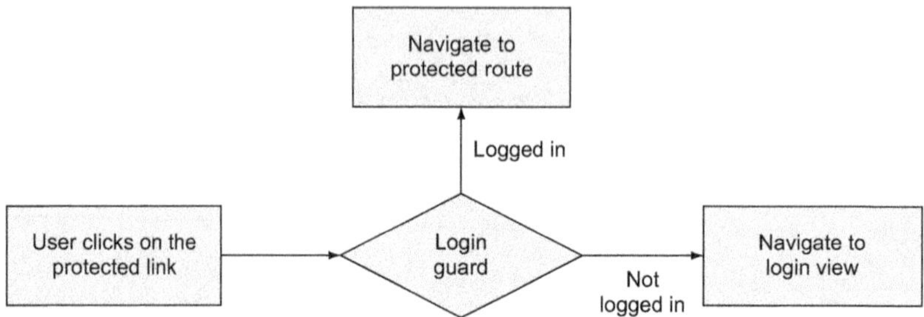

Figure 4.1 A sample login workflow with a guard

Here are some other scenarios where guards can help:

- Open the route only if the user is authenticated and authorized to do so.
- Display a multipart form that consists of several components, and the user is allowed to navigate to the next section of the form only if the data entered in the current section is valid.
- Remind the user about unsaved changes if they try to navigate from the route.
- Allow navigation to the route only after a certain data structure is populated.

These are the guard interfaces:

- `CanActivate` allows or disallows navigation to a route.
- `CanActivateChild` mediates navigation to a child route.
- `CanDeactivate` allows or disallows navigating away from the current route.
- `Resolve` ensures that the required data is retrieved before navigating to a route.
- `CanLoad` allows or disallows lazy-loading modules.

Section 3.3 of chapter 3 mentions that the `Routes` type is an array of items that conforms to the `Route` interface. So far, you've used such properties as `path` and `component` in configuring routes. Now, you'll see how to mediate navigation to or from a route and ensure that certain data is retrieved before navigating to the route. Let's start with adding a guard that'll work when the user wants to navigate to a route.

4.1.1 Implementing the CanActivate guard

Imagine a component with a link that only logged-in users can navigate to. To guard this route, you need to create a new class (for example, `LoginGuard`) that implements the `CanActivate` interface, which declares one method, `canActivate()`. In this method, you implement the validating logic that will return either `trueor` `false`. If canActivate() of the guard returns true, the user can navigate to the route. You need to assign this guard to the property canActivate, as in the following listing.

Listing 4.1 Configuring a route with a canActivate guard

```
const routes: Routes = [
    ...
    {path: 'product',
     component: ProductDetailComponent,
     canActivate: [LoginGuard]}          <-- The LoginGuard will mediate navigation to the ProductDetailComponent.
 ];
```

Because canActivate properties of Route accept an array as a value, you can assign multiple guards if you need to check more than one condition to allow or forbid the navigation.

Let's create a simple app to illustrate how you can protect the product route from users who aren't logged in. To keep the example simple, you won't use an authentication service but will generate the login status randomly. The following class implements the CanActivate interface. The canActivate() function will contain code that returns true or false. If the function returns false (the user isn't logged in), the application won't navigate to the route, will show a warning, and will navigate the user to the login view.

Listing 4.2 login.guard.ts

```
@Injectable()
export class LoginGuard implements CanActivate {

    constructor(private router: Router) {}    <-- Injects the Router object

    canActivate() {
        // A call to the actual login service would go here
        // For now we'll just randomly return true or false

        let loggedIn = Math.random() < 0.5;  <-- Randomly generates the login status

        if (!loggedIn) {                     <-- Conditionally displays a "not logged in" message
            alert("You're not logged in and will be redirected to Login page");
           this.router.navigate(["/login"]);  <-- Redirects to the login page
        }

        return loggedIn;
    }
}
```

This implementation of the canActivate() function will randomly return true or false, emulating the user's logged-in status.

The next step is to use this guard in the router configuration. The following listing shows how the routes could be configured for an app that has home and product-detail routes. The latter is protected by LoginGuard.

Listing 4.3 Configure one of the routes with a guard

```
export const routes: Routes = [
    {path: '',        component: HomeComponent},
    {path: 'login',   component: LoginComponent},
    {path: 'product', component: ProductDetailComponent,
                      canActivate: [LoginGuard]}          <-- Adding a guard to the product route
];
```

Your `LoginComponent` will be pretty simple—it will show the text "Please login here," as shown in the following listing.

Listing 4.4 login.component.ts

```
@Component({
  selector: 'home',
  template: '<h1 class="home">Please login here</h1>',
  styles: ['.home {background: greenyellow}']
})
export class LoginComponent {}
```

Angular will instantiate the `LoginGuard` class using its DI mechanism, but you have to mention this class in the list of providers that are needed for injection to work. Add the name `LoginGuard` to the list of providers in `@NgModule()`.

Listing 4.5 Adding the guard to the module's providers

```
@NgModule({
    imports:      [BrowserModule, RouterModule.forRoot(routes)],
    declarations: [AppComponent, HomeComponent,
                   ProductDetailComponent, LoginComponent],
    providers:    [LoginGuard]      <-- Adds the guard class to the provider's list so Angular can instantiate and inject it
     bootstrap:    [AppComponent]
})
```

The template of your root component will look like the following listing.

Listing 4.6 The `AppComponent`'s template

```
template: `
        <a [routerLink]="['/']">Home</a>
        <a [routerLink]="['/product']">Product Detail</a>
        <a [routerLink]="['/login']">Login</a>       <-- The login page
         <router-outlet></router-outlet>
    `
```

To see this app in action, run the following command:

```
ng serve --app guards -o
```

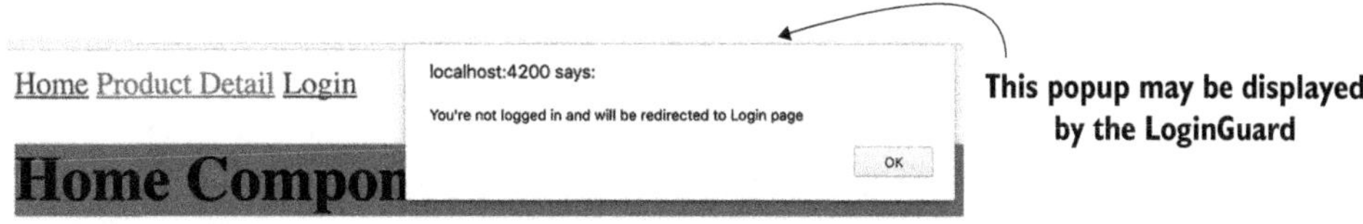

Figure 4.2 Clicking the Product Detail link is guarded

Figure 4.2 shows what happens after the user clicks the Product Detail link, but the `LoginGuard` decides the user isn't logged in.

Clicking OK closes the pop-up window with the warning and navigates to the /login route. In figure 4.2, you implement the `canActivate()` method without providing any arguments to it. But this method can be used with optional parameters:

```
canActivate(destination: ActivatedRouteSnapshot, state: RouterStateSnapshot)
```

The values of `ActivatedRouteSnapshot` and `RouterStateSnapshot` will be injected by Angular automatically, and this may be quite handy if you want to analyze the current state of the router. For example, if you'd like to know the name of the route the user tried to navigate to, this is how you can do it:

```
canActivate(destination: ActivatedRouteSnapshot, state: RouterStateSnapshot)
     {
      console.log(destination.component.name);
   ...
}
```

The `CanActivate` guard controls who gets in, but how you can control whether a user should be allowed to navigate *from* the route? Why do you even need this?

4.1.2 Implementing the CanDeactivate guard

The `CanDeactivate` interface mediates the process of navigating from a route. This guard is quite handy in cases when you want to warn the user that there are some unsaved changes in the view. To illustrate this, you'll update the app from the previous section and add an input field to the `ProductDetailComponent`. If the user enters something in this field and then tries to navigate from this route, your `CanDeactivate` guard will show the "Do you want to save changes" warning, as shown in the following listing.

Listing 4.7 The `ProductDetailComponent` with an input field

```
@Component({
  selector: 'product',
  template: `<h1 class="product">Product Detail Component</h1>
             <input placeholder="Enter your name" type="text"
             [formControl]="name">`,
   styles: ['.product {background: cyan}']
})
```

Binding the variable name to a directive from Forms API

```
export class ProductDetailComponent {
   name: FormControl = new FormControl();     ◁── Creating an instance of
 }                                                  FormControl from Forms API
```

Listing 4.7 uses the Forms API, which is covered in chapters 10 and 11. At this point, it suffices to know that you create an instance of the `FormControl` class and bind it to the <input> element. In your guard, you'll use the `FormControl.dirty` property to know if the user entered anything in the input field. The following listing creates a `UnsavedChangesGuard` class that implements the `CanDeactivate` interface.

Listing 4.8 `UnsavedChangesGuard` implements `CanDeactivate`

```
                                                    Implementing the
                                                    CanDeactivate guard for the
@Injectable()                                       ProductDetailComponent
export class UnsavedChangesGuard
                  implements CanDeactivate<ProductDetailComponent> {   ◁──

──▷ canDeactivate(component: ProductDetailComponent) {

      if (component.name.dirty) {   ◁──
         return window.confirm("You have unsaved changes. Still want to leave?"
       );
      } else {
        return true;                                  Checking whether the
      }                                               content of the input
    }                                                 control has been changed
}
Implementing canDeactivate()
required by the CanDeactivate guard
```

The `CanDeactivate` interface uses a parameterized type, which you specified using TypeScript generics syntax: `<ProductDetailComponent>`. The method `canDeactivate()` can be used with several arguments (see https://angular.io/api/router/CanDeactivate), but you'll just use one: the component to guard.

If the user entered any value in the input field—`if (component.name.dirty)`—you'll show a pop-up window with a warning. You need to make a couple more additions to the app from the previous section. First, add the `CanDeactivate` guard to the routes configuration.

Listing 4.9 Adding `CanDeactivate` and `CanDeactivate` guards to a route

```
const routes: Routes = [
    {path: '',          component: HomeComponent},
    {path: 'login',     component: LoginComponent},            Adding the
    {path: 'product', component: ProductDetailComponent,       LoginGuard to
        canActivate: [LoginGuard],                        ◁──  the product route
         canDeactivate: [UnsavedChangesGuard]}   ◁── Adding the
 ];                                                  UnsavedChangesGuard
                                                     to the product route
```

The next listing includes the new guard in the providers list in the module.

Listing 4.10 Specifying providers for guards

```
@NgModule({
    ...
    providers: [LoginGuard,                    <-- Adding the LoginGuard provider
                UnsavedChangesGuard]           <-- Adding the UnsavedChangesGuard provider
})
```

Run this app (`ng serve --app guards -o`), visit the /product route, and enter something in the input field. Then, try to click another link in the app or the browser's back button. You'll see the message shown in figure 4.3.

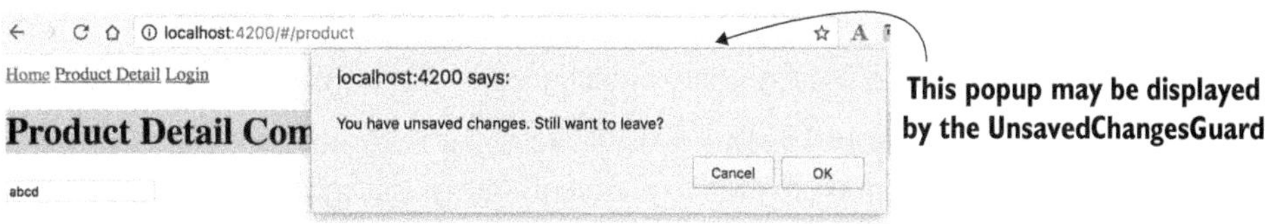

Figure 4.3 Unsaved changes guard in action

Now you know how to control the navigation to and from a route. The next thing is to ensure that the user doesn't navigate to a route too soon, when the data required by the route isn't ready yet.

4.1.3 Implementing the Resolve guard

Let's say you navigate to a product-detail component that makes an HTTP request to retrieve data. The connection is slow, and it takes two seconds to retrieve the data. This means that the user will look at the empty component for two seconds, and then the data will be displayed. That's not a good user experience. What if the server request returns an error? The user will look at the empty component to see the error message after that. That's why it may be a good idea to not even render the component until the required data arrives.

If you want to make sure that by the time the user navigates to a route some data structures are populated, create a `Resolve` guard that allows getting the data *before* the route is activated. A *resolver* is a class that implements the `Resolve` interface. The code in its `resolve()` method loads the required data, and only after the data arrives does the router navigate to the route.

Let's review an app that will have two links: Home and Data. When the user clicks the Data link, it has to render the `DataComponent`, which requires a large chunk of data to be loaded before the user sees this view. To preload the data (a 48 MB JSON file), you'll create a `DataResolver` class that implements the `Resolve` interface. The routes are configured in the following listing.

Listing 4.11 Routes with the resolver

```
const routes: Routes = [
  {path: '',        component: HomeComponent},
  {path: 'mydata', component: DataComponent,
    resolve:{                                    ← Configures the resolve guard for the mydata route
       loadedJsonData: DataResolver    ← Specifies the class that will preload the data
     }
  }
];
```

Note that the HomeComponent has no guards. You've configured the DataResolver only for the route that renders DataComponent. Angular will invoke its resolve() method every time the user navigates to the mydata route. Because you named the property of the resolve object loadedJsonData, you'll be able to access preloaded data in the DataComponent using the ActivatedRoute object, as follows:

```
activatedRoute.snapshot.data['loadedJsonData'];
```

The code of your resolver is shown next. In this code, you use some of the syntax elements that haven't been covered yet, such as @Injectable() (explained in chapter 5), HttpClient (chapter 12), and Observable (appendix D and chapter 6), but we still want to review this code sample because it's about the router.

Listing 4.12 data.resolver.ts

```
@Injectable()      ← Marks this service as injectable
 export class DataResolver implements Resolve<string[]>{

    constructor ( private httpClient: HttpClient){}     ← Injects the HttpClient service to read the data

    resolve(): Observable<string[]>{      ← Implements the resolve() method

      return this.httpClient
                .get<string[]>("./assets/48MB_DATA.json");   ← Reads the data from the file
     }
}
```

Your resolver class is an injectable service that implements the Resolve interface, which requires implementing a single resolve() method that can return an Observable, a Promise, or any arbitrary object.

> **TIP** Because a resolver is a service, you need to declare its *provider* (covered in section 5.2 of chapter 5) in the @NgModule() decorator.

Here, you use the HttpClient service to read the file that contains an array of 360,000 records of random data. The HttpClient.get() method returns an Observable, and so does your resolve() method. Angular generates the code for resolvers that autosubscribes to the observable and stores the emitted data in the ActivatedRoute object.

In the constructor of the `DataComponent`, you extract the data loaded by the resolver and store it in the variable. In this case, you don't display or process the data, because your goal is to show that the resolver loads the data before `DataComponent` is rendered. Figure 4.4 shows the debugger at the breakpoint in the constructor. Note that the data was loaded and is available in the constructor of the `DataComponent`. The UI will be rendered after the code in your constructor completes.

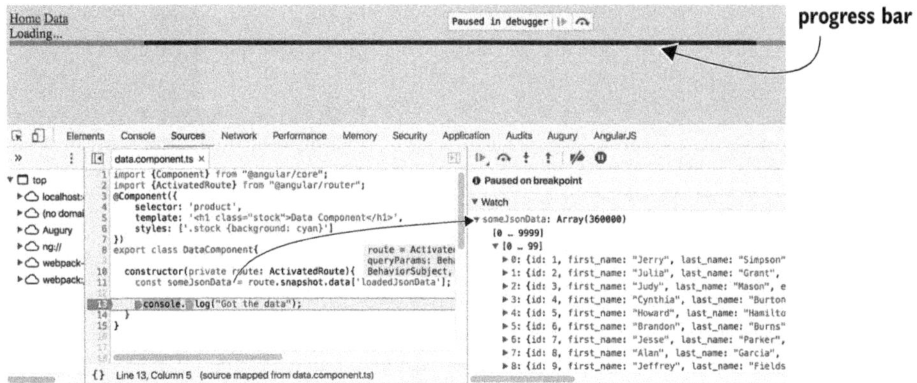

Figure 4.4 The data is loaded.

The source code of this app is located in the directory resolver, and you can see it in action by running `ng serve --app resolver -o`.

Every time you navigate to the `mydata` route, the file will be reloaded and the user will see a progress bar (`mat-progress-bar`) from the Angular Material library of UI components. You'll be introduced to this library in section 5.6 of chapter 5.

The progress bar is used in the template of the `AppComponent`, but how does `AppComponent` know when to start showing the progress bar and when to remove it from the UI? The router triggers events during navigation, such as `NavigationStart`, `NavigationEnd`, and some others. Your `AppComponent` subscribes to these events, and when `NavigationStart` is triggered, the progress bar is displayed, and on `NavigationEnd` it's removed, as shown in the following listing.

Listing 4.13 app.component.ts

```
@Component({
  selector: 'app-root',
  template: `
    <a [routerLink]="['/']">Home</a>
    <a [routerLink]="['mydata']">Data</a>
    <router-outlet></router-outlet>
    <div *ngIf="isNavigating">
       Loading...
      <mat-progress-bar mode="indeterminate"></mat-progress-bar>
    </div>
```

Conditionally shows/hides the progress bar based on the isNavigating flag

```
})
export class AppComponent {

  isNavigating = false;

  constructor (private router: Router){
     this.router.events.subscribe(
       (event) => {
        if (event instanceof NavigationStart){
          this.isNavigating=true;
        }

        if (event instanceof NavigationEnd) {
          this.isNavigating=false;
        }
       }
     );
  }
}
```

- Initially the flag isNavigating is false.
- Injects the Router object
- Subscribes to Router events
- Sets the flag to true if NavigationStart is triggered
- Sets the flag to false if NavigationEnd is triggered

TIP To avoid reading such a large file over and over again, you can cache the data in memory after the first read. If you're interested in seeing how to do this, review the code of another version of the resolver located in the data.resolver2.ts file. That resolver uses an injectable service from data .service.ts, so on subsequent clicks, instead of the file being read, the data is retrieved from the memory cache. Since the data service is a singleton, it'll survive creations and destructions of the `DataComponent` and cached data remains available.

Reloading the active route

You can reload the route that's already active and rerun its guards and resolvers using the configuration `runGuardsAndResolvers` and `onSameUrlNavigation` options.

Say the user visits the `mydata` route and after some time wants to reload the data *in the same route* by clicking the Data link again. The `routes` configuration in the following listing does this by reapplying the guards and resolvers:

```
const routes: Routes = [
  {path: '',          component: HomeComponent},
  {path: 'mydata', component: DataComponent,
    resolve: {
      mydata: DataResolver
    },
    runGuardsAndResolvers: 'always'
  }
];

export const routing = RouterModule.forRoot(routes,
  {onSameUrlNavigation: "reload"}
  );
```

- Runs guards and resolvers always
- Reloads the component when the user navigates to the same route

You can read about the other guards in the product documentation at https://angular.io/guide/router#milestone-5-route-guards.

Now, we'll move on to covering another subject: how to create a view that has more than one <router-outlet>.

4.2 Developing an SPA with multiple router outlets

The directory ngAuction contains the code of ngAuction that implements the functionality described in chapter 3's hands-on section.

So far, in all routing code samples you've used components that have a single tag, <router-outlet>, where Angular renders views based on the configured routes. Now, you'll see how to configure and render views in sibling routes located in the same component. Let's consider a couple of use cases for multi-outlet views:

- Imagine a dashboard-like SPA that has several dedicated areas (outlets), and each area can render more than one component (one at a time). Outlet A can display your stock portfolio, either as a table or as a chart, while outlet B shows either the latest news or an advertisement.
- Say you want to add a chat area to an SPA so the user can communicate with a customer service representative while keeping the current route active as well. You want to add an independent chat route allowing the user to use both routes at the same time and be able to switch from one route to another.

In Angular, you can implement either of those scenarios by having not only a *primary* outlet, but also named *secondary* outlets, which are displayed at the same time as the primary one.

To separate the rendering of components for primary and secondary outlets, you'll need to add yet another <router-outlet> tag , but this outlet must have a name. For example, the following code snippet defines primary and chat outlets:

```
<router-outlet></router-outlet>                         <-- The primary outlet
 <router-outlet name="chat"></router-outlet>            <-- The secondary (named) outlet
```

Figure 4.5 shows an app with two routes opened at the same time after the user clicks the Home link and then the Open Chat link. The left side shows the rendering of HomeComponent in the primary outlet, and the right side shows ChatComponent rendered in a named outlet. Clicking the Close Chat link will remove the content of the named outlet (you add an HTML <input> field to HomeComponent and a <textarea> to ChatComponent so it's easier to see which component has focus when the user switches between the home and chat routes).

Note the parentheses in the URL of the auxiliary route, http:// localhost:4200/#home(aux:chat). Whereas a child route is separated from the parent using the forward slash, an auxiliary route is represented as a URL segment in parentheses. This URL tells you that home and chat are sibling routes.

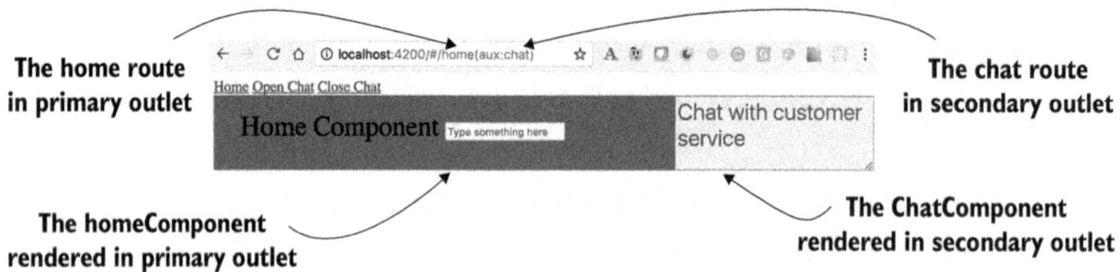

Figure 4.5 Rendering a chat view with a secondary route

The configuration for the chat route specifies the name of the outlet where the `ChatComponent` has to be rendered, shown in the following listing.

Listing 4.14 Configuring routes for two outlets

```
export const routes: Routes = [
  {path: '',  redirectTo: 'home', pathMatch: 'full'},
   {path: 'home', component: HomeComponent},
   {path: 'chat', component: ChatComponent, outlet: "aux"}
 ];
```

- Redirects an empty path to the home route
- If the URL includes home, renders the HomeComponent in the primary outlet
- If the URL includes chat, renders the ChatComponent in the outlet named aux

In this configuration, we wanted to introduce you to the `redirectTo` property. The `HomeComponent` will be rendered in two cases: either by default at the base URL, or if the URL has only the /home segment, as in http:// localhost:4200/home. The `pathMatch: 'full'` means that the client's portion URL must be exactly /, so if you entered the URL http:// localhost:4200/product/home, it wouldn't redirect to `home`.

The template of the app component can look like the following listing.

Listing 4.15 A template of a component that has two outlets

```
template: `
      <a [routerLink]="['']">Home</a>
       <a [routerLink]="['', {outlets: { aux: 'chat'}}]">Open Chat</a>
       <a [routerLink]="[{outlets: { aux: null }}]">Close Chat</a>
       <br/>
      <router-outlet></router-outlet>
       <router-outlet name="aux"></router-outlet>
    `
```

- A link to navigate to a default route in the primary outlet
- A link to navigate to the chat route in the outlet named aux
- A link to remove the outlet named aux from the UI
- This area is allocated for the primary outlet.
- This area is allocated for the secondary outlet named aux.

Note that you have two outlets here: one primary (unnamed) and one secondary (named). When the user clicks the Open Chat link, you instruct Angular to render the component configured for `chat` in the outlet named `aux`. To close a secondary outlet, assign `null` instead of a route name.

If you want to navigate to (or close) the named outlets programmatically, use the `Router.navigate()` method:

```
navigate([{outlets: {aux: 'chat'}}]);
```

To see this app with two router outlets in action, run the following command in the router-samples project:

```
ng serve --app outlets -o
```

There's one more problem the router can help you with. To make the app more responsive, you want to minimize the amount of code that the browser loads to display the landing page of your app. Do you really need to load all the code for each route on application startup?

4.2.1 Lazy-loading modules

Some time ago, one of your authors was working on a website for a European car manufacturer. There was a menu item called "European Delivery" for US citizens, who could fly to the car factory in Europe, pick up their new car there, and spend two weeks driving their own car and enjoying everything that Europe has to offer. After that, the car would be shipped to the United States. Such a trip would cost several thousand dollars, and as you can imagine, not many website visitors would be interested in exploring this option. Then why include the code supporting the menu European Delivery into the landing page of this site, increasing the initial page size?

A better solution would be to create a separate European Delivery module that would be downloaded only if the user clicked the menu item, right? In general, the landing page of a web app should include only the minimal core functionality that must be present when a user visits the site.

Any mid-size or large app should be split into several modules, where each module implements certain functionality (billing, shipping, and so on) and is *lazy-loaded* on demand. In chapter 2, section 2.5.1, you saw an app split into two modules, but both modules were loaded on application startup. In this section, we'll show you how a module can be lazy loaded.

Let's create an app with three links: Home, Product Details, and Luxury Items. Imagine that luxury items have to be processed differently than regular products, and you want to separate this functionality into a feature module called `LuxuryModule`, which will have one component named `LuxuryComponent`. Most users of the app have modest incomes and will rarely click the Luxury Items link, so there's no reason to load the code of the luxury module on application startup. You'll load it *lazily*—only if the user clicks the Luxury Items link. This way of doing things is especially important for mobile apps when they're used in a poor connection area—the code of the root module has to contain only the core functionality. The code of `LuxuryModule` is shown in the following listing.

Listing 4.16 luxury.module.ts

```
@NgModule({
    imports: [CommonModule,
         RouterModule.forChild([
         {path: '', component: LuxuryComponent}
      ])],
    declarations: [LuxuryComponent]
})

export class LuxuryModule {}
```

- Imports CommonModule as required for feature modules
- Configures the default route for this feature module using the forChild() method
- By default, renders its only component, LuxuryComponent

In the next listing, the code of `LuxuryComponent` just displays the text "Luxury Component" on a yellow (suggesting gold) background.

Listing 4.17 luxury.component.ts

```
@Component({
    selector: 'luxury',
    template: `<h1 class="gold">Luxury Component</h1>`,
     styles: ['.gold {background: yellow}']
 })
export class LuxuryComponent {}
```

- Applying the CSS selector gold
- Declaring the CSS selector gold

The code of the root module is shown in the following listing.

Listing 4.18 app.module.ts

```
@NgModule({
  imports: [BrowserModule,
    RouterModule.forRoot([
       {path: '',        component: HomeComponent},
      {path: 'product', component: ProductDetailComponent},
      {path: 'luxury', loadChildren: './luxury.module#LuxuryModule'}
     ])
  ],
  declarations: [AppComponent, HomeComponent, ProductDetailComponent],
  providers:[{provide: LocationStrategy, useClass: HashLocationStrategy}],
  bootstrap: [AppComponent]
})
export class AppModule {}
```

- Configures routes for the root module
- Instead of the property component, uses the loadChildren component for lazy loading

Note that the `imports` section only includes `BrowserModule` and `RouterModule`. The feature module `LuxuryModule` isn't listed here. Also, the root module doesn't mention `LuxuryComponent` in its `declarations` section, because this component isn't a part of the root module. When the router parses the routes configuration from both root and feature modules, it'll properly map the `luxury` path to the `LuxuryComponent` that's declared in the `LuxuryModule`.

Instead of mapping the path to a component, you use the `loadChildren` property,providing the path and the name of the module to be loaded. Note that the value of `loadChildren` isn't a typed module name, but a string. The root module doesn't know about the `LuxuryModule` type; but when the user clicks the Luxury Items link, the loader module will parse this string and load `LuxuryModule` from the luxury .module.ts file shown earlier.

To ensure that the code supporting `LuxuryModule` isn't loaded on app startup, Angular CLI places its code in a separate bundle. In your project router-samples, this app is configured under the name `lazy` in .angular-cli.json. You can build the bundles by running the following command:

```
ng serve --app lazy -o
```

The Terminal window will print the information about the bundles, as shown in the following listing.

Listing 4.19 The bundles built by ng serve

```
chunk {inline} inline.bundle.js (inline)
chunk {luxury.module} luxury.module.chunk.js ()   <-- A separate bundle was built for a lazy-loaded bundle.
 chunk {main} main.bundle.js (main) 33.3 kB
chunk {polyfills} polyfills.bundle.js (polyfills)
chunk {styles} styles.bundle.js (styles)
chunk {vendor} vendor.bundle.js (vendor)
```

The second line shows that your luxury module was placed in a separate bundle named luxury.module.chunk.js.

> **NOTE** When you run `ng build --prod`, the names of the bundles for lazy modules are numbers, not names. In the code sample, the default name of the bundle for the luxury module would be zero followed by a generated hash code, something like 0.0797fe80dbf6edcb363f.chunk.js. If your app had two lazy modules, they would be placed in the bundles with the names starting with 0 and 1, respectively.

If you open the browser at localhost:4200 and check the network tab in dev tools, you won't see this module there. See figure 4.6.

Click the Luxury Items link, and you'll see that the browser made an additional request and downloaded the code of the `LuxuryModule`, as seen at the bottom of figure 4.7. The luxury module has been loaded, and the `LuxuryComponent` has been rendered in the router outlet.

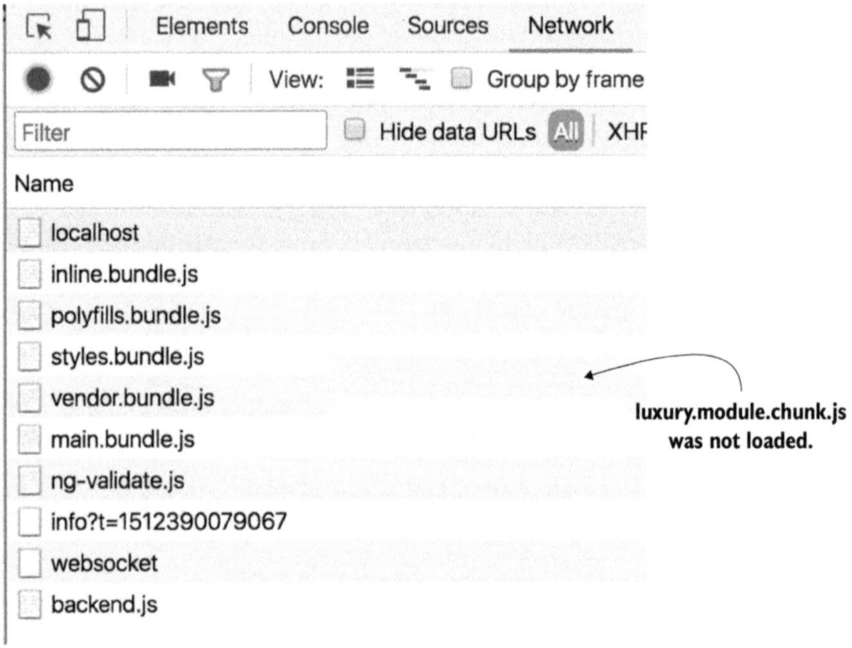

Figure 4.6 Luxury module is not loaded

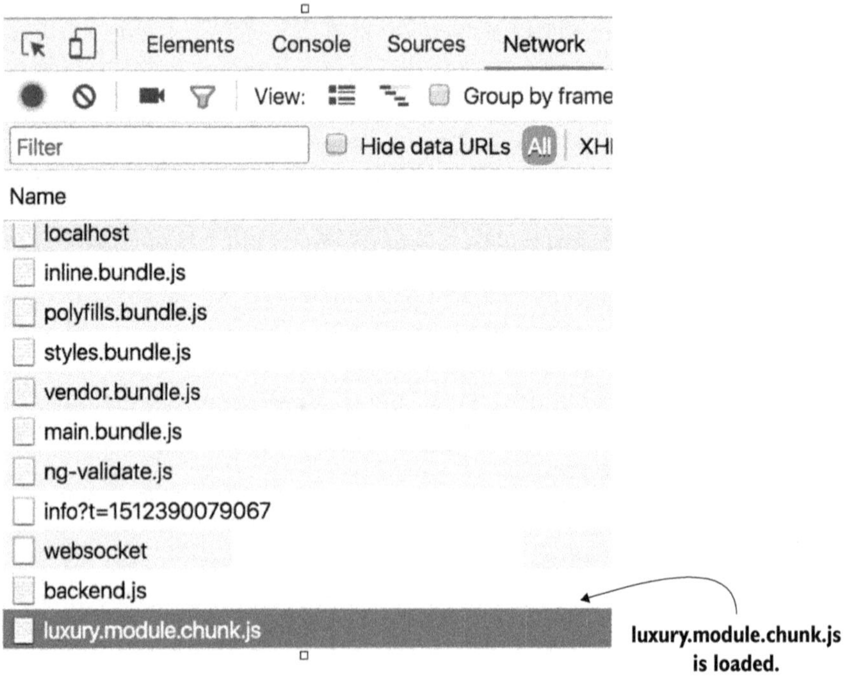

Figure 4.7 Luxury module is loaded after the button click

This simple example didn't substantially reduce the size of the initial download. But architecting large applications using lazy-loading techniques can lower the initial size of the downloadable code by hundreds of kilobytes or more, improving the perceived performance of your application. *Perceived performance* is what the user *thinks* of the performance of your application, and improving it is important, especially when the app is being loaded from a mobile device on a slow network.

On one of our past projects, the manager stated that the landing page of the newly developed web app had to load blazingly fast. We asked, "How fast?" He sent us a link to some app: "As fast as this one." We followed the link and found a nicely styled web page with a menu presented as four large squares. This page did load blazingly fast. After clicking any of the squares, it took more than 10 seconds for the selected module to be lazy loaded. This is perceived performance in action.

> **TIP** Make the root module of your app as small as possible. Split the rest of your app into lazy-loaded modules, and users will praise the performance of your app.

4.2.2 Preloaders

Let's say that after implementing lazy loading, you saved one second on the initial app startup. But when the user clicks the Luxury Items link, they still need to wait this second for the browser to load your luxury module. It would be nice if the user didn't need to wait for that second. With Angular *preloaders*, you can kill two birds with one stone: reduce the initial download time *and* get immediate response while working with lazy-loaded routes.

With Angular preloaders, you can do the following:

- Preload all lazy modules in the background while the user is interacting with your app
- Specify the preloading strategy in the routes configuration
- Implement a custom preloading strategy by creating a class that implements the `PreloadingStrategy` interface

Angular offers a preloading strategy called `PreloadAllModules`, which means that right after your app is loaded, Angular loads all bundles with lazy modules in the background. This doesn't block the application, and the user can continue working with the app without any delays. Adding this preloading strategy as a second argument of `forRoot()` is all it takes, as shown in the following listing.

Listing 4.20 Adding a preloading strategy

```
RouterModule.forRoot([
    {path: '',        component: HomeComponent},
    {path: 'product', component: ProductDetailComponent},
    {path: 'luxury', loadChildren: './luxury.module#LuxuryModule' }
  ],
    {
```

```
  preloadingStrategy: PreloadAllModules    <-- Adding the PreloadAllModules
})                                              preloading strategy
```

After this code change, the network tab will show that luxury.module.chunk.js was also loaded. Large apps may consist of dozens of lazy modules, and you may want to come up with some custom strategy defining which lazy modules should be preloaded and which shouldn't.

Say you have two lazy modules, `LuxuryModule` and `SuperLuxuryModule`, and you want to preload only the first. You can add some Boolean variable (for example, `preloadme: true`) to the configuration of the `luxury` path:

```
{path: 'luxury', loadChildren: './luxury.module#LuxuryModule', data:
➥ {preloadme: true} }
{path: 'luxury', loadChildren: './superluxury.module#SuperLuxuryModule' }
```

Your custom preloader may look like the following listing.

Listing 4.21 A sample custom preloader class

```
@Injectable()
export class CustomPreloadingStrategy implements PreloadingStrategy {    <-- Creates a class implementing the PreloadingStrategy interface

  preload(route: Route,
          load: () => Observable<any>): Observable<any> {    <-- Passes to the preload() method a callback function that returns an Observable
     return (route.data && route.data['preloadme']) ?    <-- Checks the value of the preloadme property on the data object for each route configuration. If it exists and its value is preloadme: true, then invokes the load() callback.
        load(): empty();    <-- No need to preload—returns an empty Observable
  }
}
```

Because `CustomPreloadingStrategy` is an injectable service, you need to add it to the `providers` property of the root module in the `@NgModule` decorator. Don't forget to specify the name of your custom preloader as an argument in the `forRoot()` method.

Summary

- Mediate client-side navigation using guards.
- Create more than one `<router-outlet>` tag in the same component if need be.
- Minimize the initial size of your app by implementing lazy-loading techniques.

5 Dependency injection in Angular

This chapter covers

- Introducing dependency injection as a design pattern
- Understanding how Angular implements DI
- Registering object providers and using injectors
- Adding Angular Material UI components to ngAuction

Chapter 4 discussed the router, and now the ngAuction app knows how to navigate from the home view to the product-detail view. In this chapter, we'll concentrate on how Angular automates the process of creating objects and assembling the application from its building blocks.

An Angular application is a collection of components, directives, and services that may depend on each other. Although each component can explicitly instantiate its dependencies, Angular can do this job using its dependency injection (DI) mechanism.

We'll start this chapter by identifying the problem that DI solves and reviewing the benefits of DI as a software engineering design pattern. Then we'll go over the specifics of how Angular implements the DI pattern using an example `ProductComponent` that depends on a `ProductService`. You'll see how to write an injectable service and how to inject it into another component.

After that, you'll see a sample application that demonstrates how Angular DI allows you to easily replace one component dependency with another by changing just one line of code. At the end of the chapter, we'll go through a hands-on exercise to build the next version of ngAuction, which uses Angular Material UI components.

Design patterns are recommendations for solving certain common tasks. A given design pattern can be implemented differently depending on the software you use. In the first section, we'll briefly introduce two design patterns: dependency injection and inversion of control (IoC).

5.1 The dependency injection pattern

If you've ever written a function that takes an object as an argument, you already wrote a program that instantiates this object and *injects* it into the function. Imagine a fulfillment center that ships products. An application that keeps track of shipped products can create a `Product` object and invoke a function that creates and saves a shipment record:

```
var product = new Product();
createShipment(product);
```

The `createShipment()` function depends on the existence of an instance of the `Product` object, meaning the `createShipment()` function has a dependency: `Product`. But the function itself doesn't know how to create `Product`. The calling script should somehow create and give (think *inject*) this object as an argument to the function.

Technically, you're decoupling the creation of the `Product` object from its use—but both of the preceding lines of code are located in the same script, so it's not real decoupling. If you need to replace `Product` with `MockProduct`, it's a small code change in this simple example.

What if the `createShipment()` function had three dependencies (such as product, shipping company, and fulfillment center), and each of those dependencies had its own dependencies? In that case, creating a different set of objects for the `createShipment()` function would require many more manual code changes. Would it be possible to ask someone to create instances of dependencies (with their dependencies) for you?

This is what the dependency injection pattern is about: if object A depends on an object identified by a token (a unique ID) B, object A won't explicitly use the `new` operator to instantiate the object that B points at. Rather, it will have B *injected* from the operational environment.

Object A just needs to declare, "I need an object known as B; could someone please give it to me?" Object A doesn't request a specific object type (for example, `Product`) but rather delegates the responsibility of what to inject to token B. It seems that object A doesn't want to be in control of creating instances and is ready to let the framework control this process, doesn't it?

> **The inversion of control pattern**
>
> Inversion of control is a more general pattern than DI. Rather than making your application use some API from a framework (or a software container), the framework creates and supplies the objects that the application needs. The IoC pattern can be implemented in different ways, and DI is one of the ways of providing the required objects. Angular plays the role of the IoC container and can provide the required objects according to your component declarations.

5.2 Benefits of DI in Angular apps

Before we explore the syntax of Angular DI implementation, let's look at the benefits of having objects injected versus instantiating them with a `new` operator. Angular offers a mechanism that helps with registering and instantiating component dependencies. In short, DI helps you write code in a loosely coupled way and makes your code more testable and reusable.

> **What is injected in Angular**
>
> In Angular, you inject services or constants. The *services* are instances of TypeScript classes that don't have a UI and just implement the business logic of your app. *Constants* can be any value. Typically, you'll be injecting either Angular services (such as `Router` or `ActivatedRoute`) or your own classes that communicate with servers. You'll see an example of injecting a constant in section 5.6. A service can be injected either in a component or in another service.

5.2.1 Loose coupling and reusability

Say you have a `ProductComponent` that gets product details using the `ProductService` class. Without DI, your `ProductComponent` needs to know how to instantiate the `ProductService` class. This can be done multiple ways such as by using `new`, calling `getInstance()` on a singleton object, or invoking some factory function `createProductService()`. In any case, `ProductComponent` becomes *tightly coupled* with `ProductService`, because replacing `ProductService` with another implementation of this service requires code changes in `ProductComponent`.

If you need to reuse `ProductComponent` in another application that uses a different service to get product details, you must modify the code, as in `productService = new AnotherProductService()`. DI allows you to decouple application components and services by sparing them from knowing how to create their dependencies.

Angular documentation uses the concept of a *token*, which is an arbitrary key representing an object to be injected. You map tokens to values for DI by specifying providers. A *provider* is an instruction to Angular about *how* to create an instance of an object for future injection into a target component, service, or directive. Consider the following listing, a `ProductComponent` example that gets the `ProductService` injected.

Listing 5.1 `ProductService` injected into `ProductComponent`

```
@Component({
  providers: [ProductService]
 })
class ProductComponent {
  product: Product;

  constructor(productService: ProductService) {

     this.product = productService.getProduct();
    }
}
```

- Specifies the ProductService token as a provider for injection
- Injects the object represented by the ProductService token
- Uses the API of the injected object

Often the token name matches the type of the object to be injected, so listing 5.1 is a shorthand for instructing Angular to provide a `ProductService` token using the class of the same name. The long version would look like this: `providers:[{provide: ProductService, useClass: ProductService}]`. You say to Angular, "If you see a class with a constructor that uses the `ProductService` token, inject the instance of the `ProductService` class."

Using the `provide`property of `@Component()` or `@NgModule`, you can map the same token to different values or objects (such as to emulate the functionality of `ProductService` while someone else is developing a real service class).

NOTE You already used the `providers` property in chapter 3, section 3.1.2, but it was defined, not on the component, but on the module level in `@NgModule()`.

Now that you've added the `providers` property to the `@Component()` decorator of `ProductComponent`, Angular's DI module will know that it has to instantiate an object of type `ProductService`.

The next question is, when is the instance of the service created? That depends on the decorator in which you specified the provider for this service. In listing 5.1, you specify the provider inside the `@Component()` decorator . This tells Angular to create an instance of `ProductService` when `ProductComponent` is created. If you specify `ProductService` in the `providers` property inside the `@NgModule()` decorator , then the service instance would be created on the app level as a singleton so all components could reuse it.

`ProductComponent` doesn't need to know which concrete implementation of the `ProductService` type to use—it'll use whatever object is specified as a provider. The reference to the `ProductService` object will be injected via the constructor argument, and there's no need to explicitly instantiate `ProductService` in `ProductComponent`.

Just use it as in listing 5.1, which calls the service method `getProduct()` on the `ProductService` instance magically created by Angular.

If you need to reuse the same `ProductComponent` with a different implementation of the `ProductService` type, change the providers line, as in `providers: [{provide: ProductService, useClass: AnotherProductService}]`. You'll see an example of changing an injectable service in section 5.5. Now Angular will instantiate `AnotherProductService`, but the code of `ProductComponent` that uses `ProductService` doesn't require modification. In this example, using DI increases the reusability of `ProductComponent` and eliminates its tight coupling with `ProductService`.

5.2.2 Testability

DI increases the testability of your components in isolation. You can easily inject mock objects if you want to unit test your code. Say you need to add a login feature to your application. You can create a `LoginComponent` (to render ID and password fields) that uses a `LoginService`, which should connect to a certain authorization server and check the user's privileges. While unit testing your `LoginComponent`, you don't want your tests to fail because the authorization server is down.

In unit testing, we often use mock objects that mimic the behavior of real objects. With a DI framework, you can create a mock object, `MockLoginService`, that doesn't connect to an authorization server but rather has hardcoded access privileges assigned to users with certain ID/password combinations. Using DI, you can write a single line that injects `MockLoginService` into your application's login view without needing to wait until the authorization server is ready. Your tests will get an instance of `MockLoginService` injected into your application's login view (as seen in figure 5.1), and your tests won't fail because of issues that you can't control.

NOTE In the hands-on section of chapter 14, you'll see how to unit test injectable services.

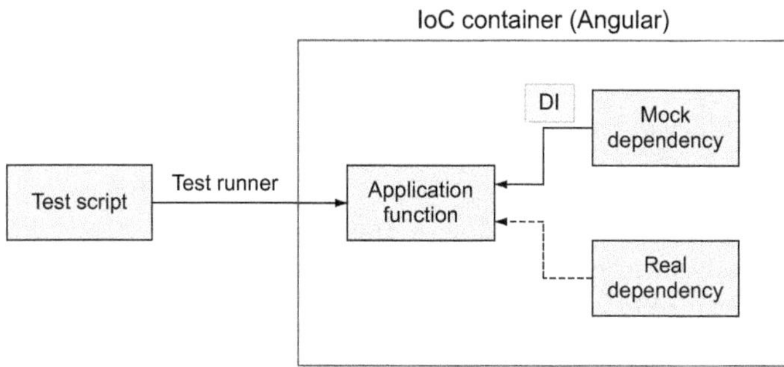

Figure 5.1 DI in testing

5.3 Injectors and providers

Now that you've had a brief introduction to dependency injection as a general, software-engineering design pattern, let's go over the specifics of implementing DI in Angular. In particular, we'll go over such concepts as injectors and providers.

Each component can have an `Injector` instance capable of injecting objects or primitive values into a component. Any Angular application has a root injector available to all of its modules. To let the injector know what to inject, you specify the provider. An injector will inject the object or value specified in the provider into the constructor of a component. Providers allow you to map a custom type (or a token) to a concrete implementation of this type (or value).

> **NOTE** Although eagerly loaded modules don't have their own injectors, a lazy-loaded module has its own subroot injector that's a direct child of the parent's module injector. You'll see an example of injection in a lazy-loaded module in section 5.7.

> **TIP** In Angular, you can inject a service into a class only via its constructor's arguments. If you see a class with a no-argument constructor, it's a guarantee that nothing is injected into this class.

We'll be using `ProductComponent` and `ProductService` in several code samples in this chapter. If your application has a class implementing a particular type (such as `ProductService`), you can specify a provider object for this class on the application level in the `@NgModule()` decorator, like this:

```
@NgModule({
  ...
  providers: [{provide: ProductService, useClass: ProductService}]
})
```

When the token name is the same as the class name, you can use the shorter notation to specify the provider in the module:

```
@NgModule({
  ...
  providers: [ProductService]
})
```

The `providers` line instructs the injector as follows: "When you need to construct an object that has an argument of type `ProductService`, create an instance of the registered class for injection into this object." When Angular instantiates a component that has the `ProductService` token as an argument of the component's constructor, it'll either instantiate and inject `ProductService` or just reuse the existing instance and inject it. In this scenario, we'll have a singleton instance of the service for the entire application.

If you need to inject a different implementation for a particular token, use the longer notation:

```
@NgModule({
  ...
  providers: [{provide: ProductService, useClass: MockProductService}]
})
```

The `providers` property can be specified in the `@Component()` annotation. The short notation of the `ProductService` provider in `@Component()` looks like this:

```
@Component({
  ...
 providers: [ProductService]
})
export class ProductComponent{

    constructor(productService: ProductService) {}
    ...
}
```

You can use the long notation for providers the same way as with modules. If a provider was specified at the component level, Angular will create and inject an instance of `ProductService` during component instantiation.

Thanks to the provider, the injector knows what to inject; now you need to specify *where* to inject the service. With classes, it comes down to declaring a constructor argument specifying the token as its type. The preceding code snippet shows how to inject an object represented by the `ProductService` token. The constructor will remain the same regardless of which concrete implementation of `ProductService` is specified as a provider.

The `providers` property is an array. You can specify multiple providers for different services if need be. Here's an example of a single-element array that specifies the provider object for the `ProductService` token:

```
[{provide: ProductService, useClass: MockProductService}]
```

The `provide` property maps the token to the method of instantiating the injectable object. This example instructs Angular to create an instance of the `MockProductService` class wherever the `ProductService` token is used as a constructor's argument. Angular's injector can use a class or a factory function for instantiation and injection. You can declare a provider using the following properties:

- `useClass`—To map a token to a class, as shown in the preceding example
- `useFactory`—To map a token to a factory function that instantiates objects based on certain criteria
- `useValue`—To map a `string` or a special `InjectionToken` to an arbitrary value (non-class-based injection)

How can you decide which of these properties to use in your code? In the next section, you'll become familiar with the `useClass` property. Section 5.6 illustrates `useFactory` and `useValue`.

5.4 A simple app with Angular DI

Now that you've seen a number of code snippets related to Angular DI, let's build a small application that will bring all the pieces together. This will prepare you to use DI in the ngAuction application.

5.4.1 Injecting a product service

You'll create a simple application that uses `ProductComponent` to render product details and `ProductService` to supply data about the product. If you use the downloadable code that comes with the book, this app is located in the directory di-samples/basic. In this section, you'll build an application that produces the page shown in figure 5.2.

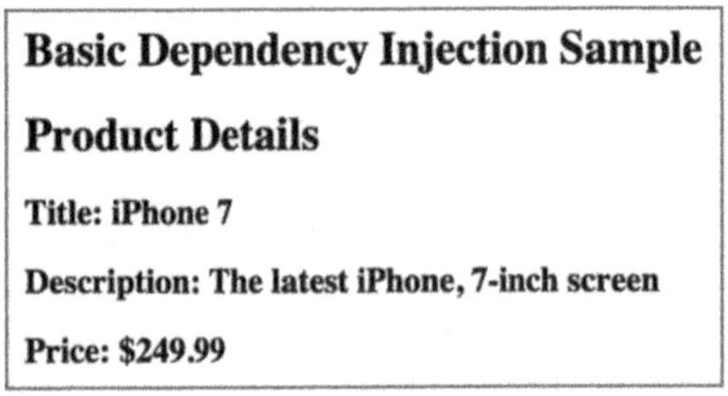

Basic Dependency Injection Sample

Product Details

Title: iPhone 7

Description: The latest iPhone, 7-inch screen

Price: $249.99

Figure 5.2 A sample DI application

`ProductComponent` can request the injection of the `ProductService` object by declaring the constructor argument with a type:

```
constructor(productService: ProductService)
```

Figure 5.3 shows a sample application that uses these components.

The `AppModule` has a root, `AppComponent`, that includes `ProductComponent`, which is dependent on `ProductService`. Note the `import` and `export` statements. The class definition of `ProductService` starts with the `export` statement, to enable other components to access its content.

The `providers` attribute defined on the component level (refer to figure 5.3) instructs Angular to provide an instance of the `ProductService` class when `ProductComponent` is created. `ProductService` may communicate with some server, requesting details for the product selected on the web page, but we'll skip that part for now and concentrate on how this service can be injected into `ProductComponent`. The following listing implements the components from figure 5.3, starting from the root component.

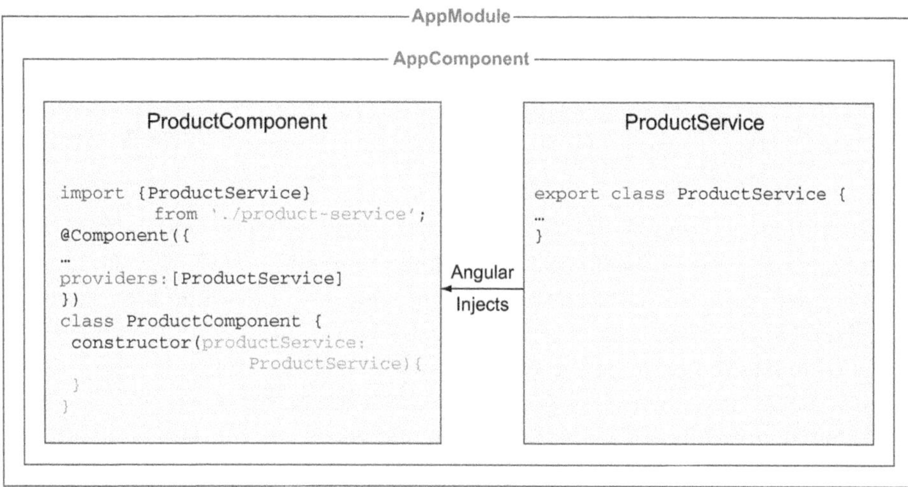

Figure 5.3 Injecting `ProductService` into `ProductComponent`

Listing 5.2 app.component.ts

```
import {Component} from '@angular/core';

@Component({
  selector: 'app-root',
  template: `<h1>Basic Dependency Injection Sample</h1>
             <di-product-page></di-product-page>`
 })
export class AppComponent {}
```

Including the <di-product-page> component into the template

Based on the `<di-product-page>` tag, you can guess that there's a component with the selector having this value. This selector is declared in `ProductComponent`, whose dependency, `ProductService`, is injected via the constructor, as shown in the next listing.

Listing 5.3 product.component.ts

```
import {Component} from '@angular/core';
import {ProductService, Product} from "./product.service";

@Component({
  selector: 'di-product-page',
   template: `<div>
  <h1>Product Details</h1>
  <h2>Title: {{product.title}}</h2>
  <h2>Description: {{product.description}}</h2>
  <h2>Price: \${{product.price}}</h2>
</div>`,
  providers: [ProductService]
 })
```

Specifying the selector of this component

The short notation of the providers property tells the injector to instantiate the ProductService class.

```
export class ProductComponent {
  product: Product;

  constructor(productService: ProductService) {      <-- Angular instantiates ProductService and injects it here.

    this.product = productService.getProduct();
  }
}
```

In listing 5.3, you use the `ProductService` class as a token for a type with the same name, so you use a short notation without the need to explicitly map the `provide` and `useClass` properties. When specifying providers, you separate the token of the injectable object from its implementation. Although in this case, the name of the token is the same as the name of the type—`ProductService`—the code mapped to this token can be located in a class called `ProductService`, `OtherProductService`, or some other name. Replacing one implementation with another comes down to changing the `providers` line.

The constructor of `ProductComponent` invokes `getProduct()` on the service and places a reference to the returned `Product` object in the `product` class variable, which is used in the HTML template. By using double curly braces, you bind the `title`, `description`, and `price` properties of the `Product` class.

The product-service.ts file includes the declaration of two classes: `Product` and `ProductService`, as you can see in the following listing.

Listing 5.4 product-service.ts

```
export class Product {                     <-- The Product class represents a product (a value object). It's used outside of this script, so you export it.
   constructor(
    public id: number,
    public title: string,
    public price: number,
    public description: string) {
  }
}

export class ProductService {

  getProduct(): Product {                  <-- For simplicity, the getProduct() method always returns the same product with hardcoded values.
     return new Product(0, "iPhone 7", 249.99,
           "The latest iPhone, 7-inch screen");
  }
}
```

In a real-world application, the `getProduct()` method would have to get the product information from an external data source, such as by making an HTTP request to a remote server.

To run this example, do `npm install` and run the following command:

```
ng serve --app basic -o
```

The browser will open the window, as shown earlier in figure 5.2. The instance of `ProductService` is injected into `ProductComponent`, which renders product details provided by the service.

In the next section, you'll see a `ProductService` decorated with `@Injectable()`, which is required only when the service itself has its own dependencies. It instructs Angular to generate additional metadata for this service. The `@Injectable()` decorator isn't needed in the example because `ProductService` doesn't have any other dependencies injected into it, and Angular doesn't need additional metadata to inject `ProductService` into components.

An alternative DI syntax with @Inject()

In our example, the provider maps a token to a class, and the syntax for injecting is simple: use the constructor argument's type as a token, and Angular will generate the required metadata for the provided type:

```
constructor(productService: ProductService)
```

There's an alternative and more verbose syntax to specify the token using the decorator `@Inject()`:

```
constructor(@Inject(ProductService) productService)
```

In this case, you don't specify the type of the constructor argument, but use the `@Inject()` decorator to instruct Angular to generate the metadata for the `ProductService`. With class-based injection, you don't need to use this verbose syntax, but there are situations where you have to use `@Inject()`, and we'll discuss this in section 5.6.1.

5.4.2 *Injecting the HttpClient service*

Often, a service will need to make an HTTP request to get necessary data. `ProductComponent` depends on `ProductService`, which is injected using the Angular DI mechanism. If `ProductService` needs to make an HTTP request, it'll have an `HttpClient` object as its own dependency. `ProductService` will need to import the `HttpClient` object for injection; `@NgModule()` must import `HttpClientModule`, which defines `HttpClient` providers. The `ProductService` class should have a constructor for injecting the `HttpClient` object. Figure 5.4 shows `ProductComponent` depending on `ProductService`, which has its own dependency: `HttpClient`.

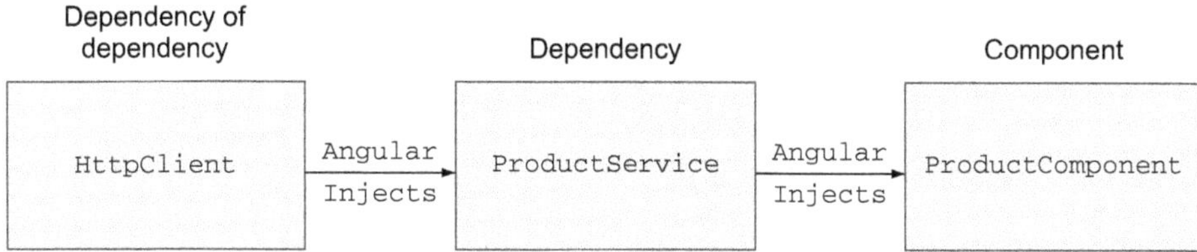

Figure 5.4 A dependency can have its own dependency.

The following listing illustrates the `HttpClient` object's injection into `ProductService` and the retrieval of products from the products.json file.

Listing 5.5 Injecting `HttpClient` into `ProductService`

```
import {HttpClient} from '@angular/common/http';
import {Injectable} from "@angular/core";

@Injectable()
export class ProductService {
    constructor(private http: HttpClient) {     // Injecting HttpClient
       let products = http.get<string>('products.json')     // Using HTTP GET
                      .subscribe(...);     // Subscribing to the result of the HTTP request
     }
```

Because `ProductService` has its own injectable dependency, you need to decorate it with `@Injectable()`. Here, you inject a service into another service. The class constructor is the injection point, but where do you declare the provider for injecting the `HttpClient` type object? All the providers required to inject various flavors of `HttpClient` objects are declared in `HttpClientModule`. You just need to add it to your `AppModule`, as in the following listing.

Listing 5.6 Adding `HttpClientModule`

```
import { HttpClientModule} from '@angular/common/http';     // Imports HttpClientModule in the root module
 ...
@NgModule({
  imports: [
    BrowserModule,
    HttpClientModule     // Adds HttpClientModule to the imports section
   ],
  declarations: [AppComponent],
  bootstrap: [AppComponent]
})
```

NOTE Chapter 12 explains how `HttpClient` works.

Starting in Angular 6, the `@Injectable()` decorator allows you to specify the `provideIn` property, which may spare you from explicit declaration of the provider for the service. The following listing shows how you can instruct Angular to automatically create the module-level provider for `ProductService`.

Listing 5.7 Using `provideIn`

```
@Injectable(
  provideIn: 'root'
)
export class ProductService {
...
}
```

Now that you've seen how to inject an object into a component, let's look at what it takes to replace one implementation of a service with another, using Angular DI.

5.5 Switching injectables made easy

Earlier in this chapter, we stated that the DI pattern allows you to decouple components from their dependencies. In the previous section, you decoupled `ProductComponent` from `ProductService`. Now let's simulate another scenario.

Suppose you've started development with a `ProductService` that should get data from a remote server, but the server's feed isn't ready. Rather than modify the code in `ProductService` to introduce hardcoded data for testing, you'll create another class: `MockProductService`.

To illustrate how easy it is to switch from one service to another, you'll create a small application that uses two instances of `ProductComponent`. Initially, the first one will use `MockProductService` and the second, `ProductService`. Then, with a one-line change, you'll make both of them use the same service. Figure 5.5 shows how the app renders two product components that use different implementations of `ProductService`.

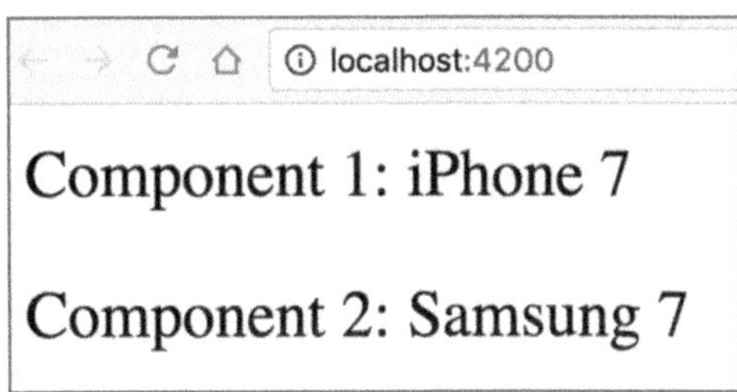

Figure 5.5 Two components and two products

The iPhone 7 product is rendered by `Product1Component`, and the Samsung 7 is rendered by `Product2Component`. This application focuses on switching product services using Angular DI, so we've kept the components and services simple. The app that comes with this chapter has components and services in separate files, but we put all the relevant code in the following listing.

Listing 5.8 Two products and two services

```
// a value object
class Product {
  constructor(public title: string) {}
}

// services
class ProductService {          <-- Bad design
   getProduct(): Product {
    return new Product('iPhone 7');
  }
}

class MockProductService  {     <-- Bad design
```

```
    getProduct(): Product {
     return new Product('Samsung 7');
   }
}

// product components
@Component({
  selector: 'product1',
  template: 'Product 1: {{product.title}}'})
class Product1Component {
  product: Product;

  constructor(private productService: ProductService) {
     this.product = productService.getProduct();
  }
}

@Component({
  selector: 'product2',
  template: 'Product 2: {{product.title}}',
  providers: [{provide: ProductService, useClass: MockProductService}]
 })
class Product2Component {
  product: Product;

  constructor(private productService: ProductService) {
     this.product = productService.getProduct();
  }
}

@Component({
  selector: 'app-root',
  template: `
    <product1></product1>
    <p>
    <product2></product2>
   `
})
class AppComponent {}

@NgModule({
  imports:      [BrowserModule],
  providers:    [ProductService],
   declarations: [AppComponent, Product1Component, Product2Component],
  bootstrap:    [AppComponent]
})
class AppModule { }
```

Since there is no provider declared on this component level, it'll use the app-level provider.

Declares a provider on the component level just for ProductComponent2

ProductComponent2 gets MockProductService because its provider was specified at the component level.

Browser renders two child components of AppComponent

Declares the app-level provider

TIP Listing 5.8 has two lines marked as bad design. Read the sidebar "Program to abstractions" for explanations.

If a component doesn't need a specific `ProductService` implementation, there's no need to explicitly declare a provider for it, as long as a provider was specified at the parent-component level or in `@NgModule()`. In listing 5.8, `Product1Component` doesn't declare its own provider for `ProductService`, and Angular will find one on the application level.

But each component is free to override the `providers` declaration made at the app- or parent-component level, as in `Product2Component`. Each component has its own injector, and during the instantiation of `Product2Component`, this injector will see the component-level provider and will inject `MockProductService`. This injector won't even check whether there's a provider for the same token on the app level.

If you decide that `Product2Component` should get an instance of `ProductService` injected, remove the `providers` line in its `@Component()` decorator.

From now on, wherever the `ProductService` type needs to be injected and no `providers` line is specified on the component level, Angular will instantiate and inject `ProductService`. Running the application after making the preceding change renders the components as shown in figure 5.6.

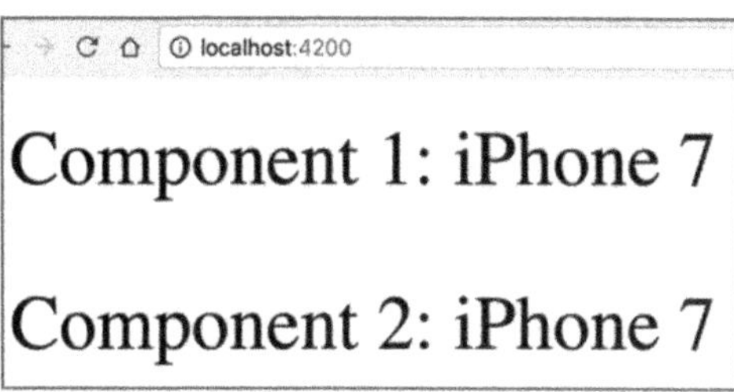

Figure 5.6 Two components and one service

To see this app in action, run the following command:

```
ng serve --app switching -o
```

Imagine that your application had dozens of components using `ProductService`. If each of them instantiated this service with a `new` operator, you'd need to make dozens of code changes. With Angular DI, you're able to switch the service by changing one line in the `providers` declaration.

> **Program to abstractions**
>
> In object-oriented programming, it's recommended to program to interfaces, or *abstractions*. Because the Angular DI module allows you to replace injectable objects, it would be nice if you could declare a `ProductService` interface and specify it as a provider. Then you'd write several concrete classes that implement this interface and switch them in the `providers` declaration as needed.
>
> You can do this in Java, C#, PHP, and other object-oriented languages. The problem is that after transpiling the TypeScript code into JavaScript, the interfaces are removed, because JavaScript doesn't support them. In other words, if `ProductService` were declared as an interface, the following constructor would be wrong, because the JavaScript code wouldn't know anything about `ProductService`:
>
> ```
> constructor(productService: ProductService)
> ```

(continued)

But TypeScript supports abstract classes, which can have some of the methods implemented, and some abstract—declared but not implemented. Then, you'd need to implement some concrete classes that extend the abstract ones and implement all abstract methods. For example, you can have the classes shown here:

```
export abstract class ProductService{          <- Declares an abstract class
   abstract getProduct(): Product;              <- Declares an abstract method
 }

export class MockProductService extends ProductService{     <- Creates the first concrete
   getProduct(): Product {                                      implementation of the
    return new Product('Samsung 7');                            abstract class
  }
}

export class RealProductService extends ProductService{     <- Creates the second
   getProduct(): Product {                                      concrete implementation
    return new Product('iPhone 7');                             of the abstract class
  }
}
```

Note that If your abstract class doesn't implement any methods (as in this case), you could use the keyword `implement` instead of `extend`.

The good news is that you can use the name of the abstract class in the constructors, and during the JavaScript code generation, Angular will use a specific concrete class based on the provider declaration. Having the classes `ProductService`, `MockProductService`, and `RealProductService` declared, as in this sidebar, will allow you to write something like this:

```
@NgModule({
  providers: [{provide: ProductService, useClass: RealProductService}],
   ...
})
export class AppModule { }

@Component({...})
export class Product1Component {
  constructor(productService: ProductService) {...};
  }
}
```

Here, you use an abstraction both in the token and in the constructor's argument. This wasn't the case in listing 5.8, where `ProductService` was a concrete implementation of certain functionality. Replacing the providers works the same way as described earlier, if you decide to switch from one concrete implementation of the service to another.

Here, you use an abstraction both in the token and in the constructor's argument. This wasn't the case in listing 5.8, where `ProductService` was a concrete implementation of certain functionality. Replacing the providers works the same way as described earlier, if you decide to switch from one concrete implementation of the service to another.

In listing 5.8, you declared the `ProductService` and `MockProductService` classes as having methods with the same name, `getProducts()`. If you used the abstract-class approach, the TypeScript compiler would give you an error if you'd tried to implement a concrete class but would miss an implementation of one of the abstract methods. That's why two lines in listing 5.8 are flagged as bad design.

What if your component or module can't map a token to a class but needs to apply some business logic to decide which class to instantiate? Furthermore, what if you want to inject just a primitive value and not an object?

5.6 Declaring providers with useFactory and useValue

In general, factory functions are used when you need to apply some application logic prior to instantiating an object. For example, you may need to decide which object to instantiate, or your object may have a constructor with arguments that you need to initialize before creating an instance. Let's modify the app from the previous section to illustrate the use of factory and value providers.

The following listing shows a modified version of `Product2Component`, which you can find in the factory directory of the di-samples app. It shows how you can write a factory function and use it as a provider for injectors. This factory function creates either `ProductService` or `MockProductService`, based on the `boolean` flag `isProd`, indicating whether to run in a production or dev environment, as shown in the following listing.

Listing 5.9 product.factory.ts

```
export function productServiceFactory (isProd: boolean) {
  if (isProd) {?
    return new ProductService();?
  } else {?
    return new MockProductService();?
  }?
}
```

Injects the value of isProd into the factory function

Instantiates the service based on the value of isProd

You'll use the `useFactory` property to specify the provider for the `ProductService` token. Because this factory requires an argument (a dependency), you need to tell Angular where to get the value for this argument, and you do that using a special property, `deps`, as shown in the following listing.

Listing 5.10 Specifying a factory function as a provider

```
{provide: ProductService,? useFactory: productServiceFactory,
                           deps: ['IS_PROD_ENVIRONMENT']}
```

This function used for instantiating a service

The dependency of this factory function

Here, you instruct Angular to inject a value specified by the `IS_PROD_ENVIRONMENT` token into your factory function. If a factory function has more than one argument, you list the corresponding tokens for them in the `deps` array.

How do you provide a static value for a token represented by a string? You do it by using the `useValue` property. Here's how you can associate the value `true` with the `IS_PROD_ENVIRONMENT` token:

```
{provide: 'IS_PROD_ENVIRONMENT', useValue: true}
```

Note that you map a string token to a hardcoded primitive value, which is not something you'd do in real-world apps. Let's use the environment variables from the environment files generated by Angular CLI in the directory src/environments to find out whether your app runs in dev or production. This directory has two files: environment.prod.ts and environment.ts. Here's the content from environment.prod.ts:

```
export const environment = {
  production: true
};
```

The environment.ts file has similar content but assigns `false` to the `production` environment variable. If you're not using the `--prod` option with `ng serve` or `ng build`, the environment variables defined in environment.ts are available in your app code. When you're building bundles with `--prod`, the variables defined in environment.prod.ts can be used:

```
{provide: 'IS_PROD_ENVIRONMENT', useValue: environment.production}
```

In the environment files you can define as many variables as you need and access them in your application using *dot notation* , as in `environment.myOtherVar`.

The entire code of your app module that uses providers with both `useFactory` and `useValue` is shown in the following listing.

Listing 5.11 Providers with `useFactory` and `useValue`

```
...
import {ProductService} from './product.service';
import {productServiceFactory} from './product.factory';
import {environment} from '../../environments/environment';

@NgModule({
  imports:      [BrowserModule],
  providers: [{provide: ProductService,?
```

```
    useFactory: productServiceFactory,
                                        deps: ['IS_PROD_ENVIRONMENT']},
                {provide: 'IS_PROD_ENVIRONMENT',
                useValue: environment.production}],
  declarations: [AppComponent, Product1Component, Product2Component],
  bootstrap:    [AppComponent]
})
export class AppModule {}
```

Maps the value from the environment file to the IS_PROD_ENVIRONMENT token

Maps the productServiceFactory factory function to the ProductService token

Specifies the argument to be injected into the factory function

You can find the complete code of the app that implements `useFactory` and `useValue` as well as the environment variable `production` in the directory called factory of the di-samples project. First, run this app as follows:

```
ng serve --app factory -o
```

In the dev environment, the factory function provides the `MockProductService`, and the browser renders two components showing Samsungs. Now, run the same app in production mode:

```
ng serve --app factory --prod -o
```

This time, the value of `environment.production` is `true`, the factory provides the `ProductService`, and the browser renders two iPhones.

To recap, a provider can map a token to a class, a factory function, or an arbitrary value to let the injector know which objects or values to inject. The class or factory may have its own dependencies, so the providers should specify all of them. Figure 5.7 illustrates the relationships between the providers and the injectors of the sample app.

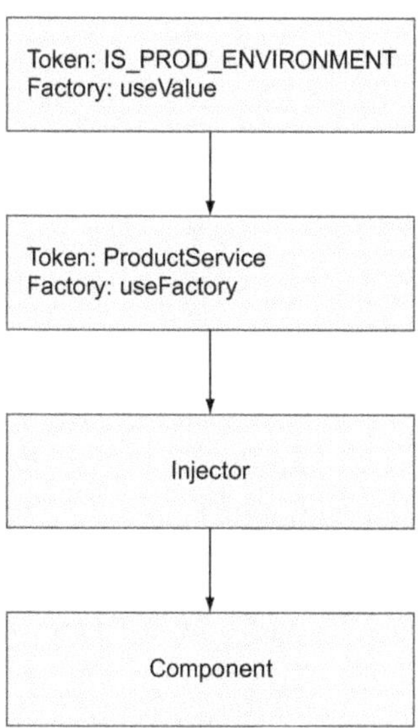

Figure 5.7 Injecting dependencies with dependencies

It's great that you can inject a value into a string token (such as `IS_PROD_ENVIRONMENT`), but this may potentially create a problem. What if your app uses someone else's module that coincidentally also has a token `IS_PROD_ENVIRONMENT` but injects a value with different meaning there? You have a naming conflict here. With JavaScript strings, at any given time there will be only one location in memory allocated for `IS_PROD_ENVIRONMENT`, and you can't be sure what value will be injected into it.

5.6.1 Using InjectionToken

To avoid conflicts caused by using hardcoded strings as tokens, Angular offers an `InjectionToken` class that's preferable to using strings. Imagine that you want to create a component that can get data from different servers (such as dev, production, and QA) and you want to inject the string with the server's URL into a token named `BackendUrl`. Instead of injecting the URL string token, you should create an instance of `InjectionToken`, as shown in the next listing.

Listing 5.12 Using `InjectionToken` instead of a string token

```
import {Component, Inject, InjectionToken} from '@angular/core';

export const BACKEND_URL  = new InjectionToken('BackendUrl');   ◁— Instantiates InjectionToken

@Component({
  selector: 'app-root',
  template: '<h2>The value of BACKEND_URL is {{url}}</h2>',
  providers: [{provide:BACKEND_URL, useValue: 'http://myQAserver.com'}]   ◁— Declares a provider for injecting the value into the token
})
export class AppComponent {
  constructor(@Inject(BACKEND_URL) public url) {}   ◁— Injects http://myQAserver.com into the BACKEND_URL token
}
```

Here, you wrap the string `BackendUrl` into an instance of `InjectionToken`. Then, in the constructor of this component, instead of injecting a vague string type, you inject a `BACKEND_URL` that points at the concrete instance of `InjectionToken`. Even if the code of another module also has `new InjectionToken('BackendUrl')`, it's going to be a different object.

`BACKEND_URL` isn't a type, so you can't specify your instance of `InjectionToken` as a type of the constructor's argument. You'd get a compilation error:

```
constructor(public url: BACKEND_URL)   // error
```

That's why you didn't specify the argument type of the `AppComponent` constructor but used the `@Inject(BACKEND_URL)` decorator instead to let Angular know which object to inject.

> **TIP** You can't inject TypeScript interfaces, because they have no representation in the transpiled JavaScript code.

You know that providers can be defined on the component and module level, and that module-level providers can be used in the entire app. Things get complicated when your app has more than one module. Will the providers declared in the `@NgModule` of a feature module be available in the root module as well, or will they be hidden inside the feature module?

5.6.2 Dependency injection in a modularized app

Every root app module has its own injector. If you split your app into several eagerly loaded feature modules, they'll reuse the injector from the root module, so if you declare a provider for `ProductService` in the root module, any other module can use it in DI.

What if a provider was declared in a feature module—is it available for the app injector? The answer to this question depends on how you load the feature module.

If a module is loaded eagerly, its providers can be used in the entire app, but each lazy-loaded module has its own injector that doesn't expose providers. Providers declared in the `@NgModule()` decorator of a lazy-loaded module are available within such a module, but not to the entire application. Let's consider two different scenarios: one with a lazy-loaded module and another with an eagerly loaded module.

5.7 Providers in lazy-loaded modules

In this section, you'll experiment with the providers declared inside a lazy-loaded module. You'll start with modifying the app from section 4.3 in chapter 4. This time, you'll add an injectable `LuxuryService` and declare its provider in `LuxuryModule`. The `LuxuryService` will look like the following listing.

Listing 5.13 luxury.service.ts

```
import {Injectable} from '@angular/core';

@Injectable()
export class LuxuryService {

  getLuxuryItem() {                    <-- This service has one method.
     return "I'm the Luxury service from lazy module";
  }
}
```

The `LuxuryModule` declares the provider for this service, as shown in the following listing.

Listing 5.14 luxury.module.ts

```
@NgModule({
    ...
    declarations: [LuxuryComponent],      <-- This module has one component.
     providers: [LuxuryService]           <-- Declares a provider for LuxuryService
 })

export class LuxuryModule {}              <-- Exports the module to make it visible in other modules
```

The `LuxuryComponent` will use the service, as shown in the following listing.

Listing 5.15 luxury.component.ts

```
@Component({
    selector: 'luxury',
    template: `<h1 class="gold">Luxury Component</h1>
               The luxury service returned {{luxuryItem}} `,
    styles: ['.gold {background: yellow}']
})
export class LuxuryComponent {
  luxuryItem: string

  constructor(private luxuryService: LuxuryService) {}     <-- Injects the LuxuryService

  ngOnInit() {
    this.luxuryItem = this.luxuryService.getLuxuryItem();    <-- Invokes a method on the LuxuryService
   }
}
```

Remember, the `AppModule` lazy loads the `LuxuryModule`, as you can see in the next listing.

Listing 5.16 The root module

```
@NgModule({
  imports: [ BrowserModule,
    RouterModule.forRoot([
       ...
       {path: 'luxury',
          loadChildren: './lazymodule/luxury.module#LuxuryModule'} ]    <-- Specifies the module in quotes for lazy loading
       )
  ],
  bootstrap: [AppComponent]
})
export class AppModule {}
```

Running this app will lazy load `LuxuryModule`, and `LuxuryComponent` will get `Luxury-Service` injected and will invoke its API.

The following listing tries to inject `LuxuryService` into `HomeComponent` from the root module (both modules belong to the same project).

Listing 5.17 home.component.ts

```
import {Component} from '@angular/core';
import {LuxuryService} from "./lazymodule/luxury.service";

@Component({
  selector: 'home',
  template: '<h1 class="home">Home Component</h1>',
  styles: ['.home {background: red}']
})
export class HomeComponent {

  constructor (luxuryService: LuxuryService) {})    <-- Injects LuxuryService into a component of another module
 }
```

You won't get any compiler errors, but if you run this modified app, you'll get the runtime error "No provider for LuxuryService!" The root module doesn't have access to the providers declared in the lazy-loaded module, which has its own injector.

5.8 Providers in eagerly loaded modules

Let's add a `ShippingModule` to the project described in the previous section, but this one will be loaded eagerly. Similar to `LuxuryModule`, `ShippingModule` will have one component and one injectable service called `ShippingService`. You want to see whether the root module can also use the `ShippingService` whose provider is declared in the eagerly loaded `ShippingModule`, shown in the following listing.

Listing 5.18 shipping.module.ts

```
// imports are omitted for brevity
@NgModule({
  imports: [
    CommonModule,
    RouterModule.forChild([            // Adds a route for a feature module
            {path: 'shipping', component: ShippingComponent}
     ])],
  declarations: [ShippingComponent],
  providers: [ShippingService]
})
export class ShippingModule { }
```

> **TIP** In section 2.5.1 in chapter 2, `ShippingModule` also included `exports: [ShippingComponent]` in the `@NgModule()` decorator. You had to export the `ShippingComponent` there because it was used in the `AppComponent` template located in `AppModule`. In this example, you use `ShippingComponent` only inside `ShippingModule`, so no export is needed.

`ShippingComponent` gets `ShippingService` injected and will invoke its `getShippingItem()` method that returns a hardcoded text, "I'm the shipping service from the shipping module."

Listing 5.19 shipping.component.ts

```
import {Component, OnInit} from '@angular/core';
import {ShippingService} from './shipping.service';

@Component({
  selector: 'app-shipping',
  template: `<h1>Shipping Component</h1>
             The shipping service returned {{shippingItem}}`,
  styles: []
})
export class ShippingComponent implements OnInit {

  shippingItem: string;

  constructor(private shippingService: ShippingService) {}    // Injects ShippingService

  ngOnInit() {
```

```
        this.shippingItem = this.shippingService.getShippingItem();
    }
}
```

Uses ShippingService

Figure 5.8 shows the structure of the project and the content of the root `AppModule`. In line 17, you eagerly load `ShippingModule`, and in line 18, you lazy load `LuxuryModule`.

```
lazy-injector
  lazymodule
    luxury.component.ts
    luxury.module.ts
    luxury.service.ts
  shipping
    shipping.component.ts
    shipping.module.ts
    shipping.service.ts
  app.component.ts
  app.module.ts
  home.component.ts
```

```
1  import { BrowserModule } from '@angular/platform-browser';
2  import { NgModule } from '@angular/core';
3  import { RouterModule} from '@angular/router';
4  import {AppComponent} from './app.component';
5  import {HomeComponent} from './home.component';
6  import {LocationStrategy, HashLocationStrategy} from '@angular/common';
7  import {ShippingModule} from './shipping/shipping.module';
8
9  export function shippingModuleLoader() {
10   return ShippingModule;
11 }
12
13 @NgModule({
14   imports: [ BrowserModule, ShippingModule,
15     RouterModule.forRoot([
16       {path: '',         component: HomeComponent},
17       {path: 'shipping', loadChildren: shippingModuleLoader},
18       {path: 'luxury', loadChildren: './lazymodule/luxury.module#LuxuryModule'} ]
19       )
20   ],
21   declarations: [ AppComponent, HomeComponent],
22   providers: [{provide: LocationStrategy, useClass: HashLocationStrategy}],
23   bootstrap:    [ AppComponent ]
24 })
25 export class AppModule {}
26
```

Figure 5.8 An app module that uses feature modules

> **NOTE** By the time you read this, the function in lines 9–11 may not be needed, and line 17 for eager loading the `ShippingModule` could look like this: `{path: 'shipping', loadChildren: () => ShippingModule}`. But at the time of writing, using a function in line 17 results in errors during the AOT compilation.

To see this app in action, run the following command:

```
ng serve --app lazyinjection -o
```

Clicking the Shipping Details link shows the data returned by the `ShippingService`, as shown in figure 5.9. `ShippingService` was injected into `ShippingComponent` even though you didn't declare the provider for `ShippingService` in the root app module.

This proves the fact that providers of eagerly loaded modules are merged with providers of the root module. In other words, Angular has a single injector for all eagerly loaded modules.

Figure 5.9 Navigating to the shipping module

5.9 Hands-on: Using Angular Material components in ngAuction

> **NOTE** Source code for this chapter can be found at https://github.com/Farata/angulartypescript and www.manning.com/books/angular-development-with-typescript-second-edition.

In the hands-on section of chapter 3, you used DI in ngAuction. You added the `ProductService` provider in `@NgModule()`, and this service was injected into `HomeComponent` and `ProductDetailComponent`. In the final version of `ngAuction`, you'll also inject `ProductService` into `SearchComponent`.

In this section, we won't be focusing on DI but rather introducing you to the Angular Material library of modern-looking UI components. The goal is to replace the HTML elements on the landing page of ngAuction with Angular Material (AM) UI components. You'll still keep the Bootstrap library in this version of ngAuction, but starting in chapter 7, you'll do a complete rewrite of ngAuction so it'll use only AM components.

You'll use ngAuction from chapter 3 as a starting point, gradually replacing HTML elements with their AM counterparts, so the landing page will look as shown in figure 5.10.

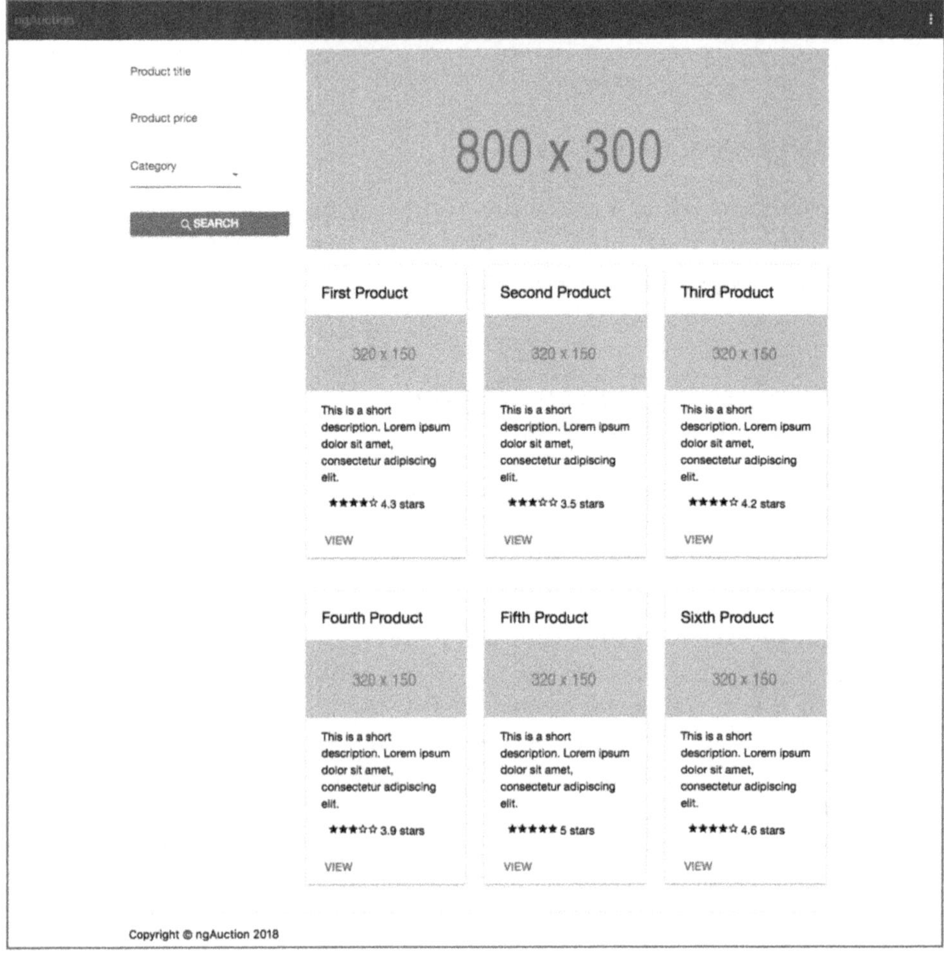

Figure 5.10 ngAuction with Angular Material components

5.9.1 *A brief overview of the Angular Material library*

Angular Material is a library of UI components developed by Google, based on the Material Design guidelines that define the classic principles of good design and consistent user experience (see https://material.io/guidelines). The guidelines provide suggestions for how the UI for a web or mobile app should be designed.

AM offers more than 30 UI components and four prebuilt themes. A *theme* is a collection of palettes, each of which defines different shades of colors that look good when used together (see https://material.io/guidelines/style/color.html), as seen in figure 5.11.

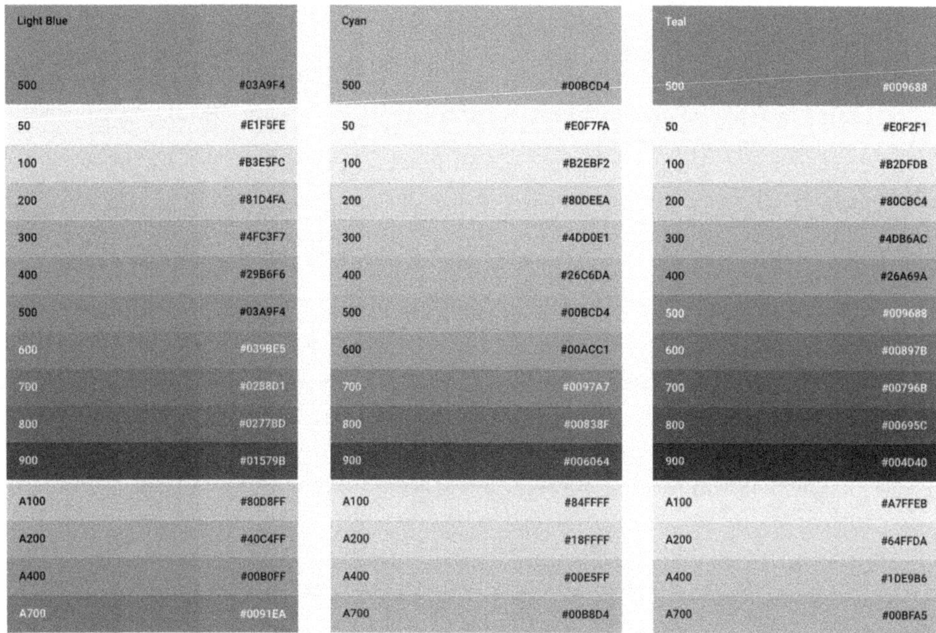

Figure 5.11 Sample Material Design palettes

The color with the number 500 is a *primary* color for the palette. We'll show you how to customize palettes in the hands-on section of chapter 7. At the time of writing, AM comes with four prebuilt themes: `deeppurple-amber`, `indigo-pink`, `pink-bluegrey`, and `purple-green`. One way to add a theme to your app is by using the `<link>` tag in your index.html:

```
<link href="../node_modules/@angular/material/prebuilt-themes/indigo-
     pink.css" rel="stylesheet">?
```

Alternatively, you can add a theme to your global CSS file (styles.css) as follows:

```
@import '~@angular/material/prebuilt-themes/indigo-pink.css';
```

Any app built with AM can specify the following colors for the UI components:

- `primary`—Main colors
- `accent`—Secondary colors
- `warn`—For errors and warnings
- `foreground`—For text and icons
- `background`—For component backgrounds

While styling the UI of your app, for the most part you won't be specifying the color names or codes as it's done in regular CSS. You'll be using one of the preceding keywords.

> **TIP** In the hands-on section of chapter 7, you'll start using the CSS extension SaaS for styling.

The following line shows how to add the AM toolbar component styled with the primary color for whatever theme is specified:

```
<mat-toolbar color="primary"></mat-toolbar>
```

Should you decide to switch to a different theme, there's no need to change the preceding code—the <mat-toolbar> will use the primary color of the newly selected theme.

AM components include input fields, radio buttons, checkboxes, buttons, date picker, toolbar, grid list, data table, and more. For the current list of components, refer to product documentation at https://material.angular.io. Some of the components are added to your component templates as tags, and some as directives. In any case, the AM component names begin with the prefix `mat-`.

The following listing shows how create a toolbar that contains a link and a button with an icon.

Listing 5.20 Creating a toolbar with Angular Material

```
<mat-toolbar color="primary">?                         <-- AM toolbar of primary theme color
   <a [routerLink]="['/']">Home</a>?

  <button mat-icon-button>                             <-- A button with an icon
     <mat-icon>more_vert</mat-icon>                    <-- Places the Google Material icon more_vert on the button
 ?  </button>?
</mat-toolbar>
```

Here, you use two AM tags, <mat-toolbar> and <mat-icon>, and one directive, `mat-icon-button`. Each AM component is packaged in a feature module, and you'll need to import the modules for the required AM components in the `@NgModule()` decorator of your `AppModule`. You'll see how to do this while giving a face lift to your ngAuction.

> **TIP** If you want to build the new version of ngAuction on your computer, copy the directory chapter3/ngAuction into another location, run `npm install` there, and follow the instructions in the next sections.

5.9.2 *Adding the AM library to the project*

First, you need to install three modules required by the AM library by running the following commands in the project root directory:

```
npm i @angular/material @angular/cdk @angular/animations
```

In this version of ngAuction, you'll use the prebuilt `indigo-pink` theme, so replace the content of the styles.css file with this line:

```
@import '~@angular/material/prebuilt-themes/indigo-pink.css';
```

TIP Starting from Angular CLI 6, you can add the AM library to your project with one command: `ng add @angular/material`. This command will install the required packages and modify the code in several files of your app, so you have less typing to do. We didn't use this command here because we want to keep all AM components used in this app in a separate feature module.

5.9.3 Adding a feature module with AM components

AM components are packaged as feature modules, and you should add only those modules that your app needs rather than adding the entire content of the AM library. You can either add the required modules to the root app module or create a separate module and list all required components there.

In this version of ngAuction, you'll keep the UI components for ngAuction in a separate module. Generate a new `AuctionMaterialModule` by running the following command:

```
ng g m AuctionMaterial
```

This command will generate boilerplate of a feature module in the app/auction-material/auction-material.module.ts file. Modify the code of this file to look like the following listing.

Listing 5.21 A feature module for AM UI components

```
import { NgModule } from '@angular/core';
import { CommonModule } from '@angular/common';

import {MatToolbarModule} from '@angular/material/toolbar';
import {MatIconModule} from '@angular/material/icon';
import {MatMenuModule} from '@angular/material/menu';
import {MatButtonModule} from '@angular/material/button';
import {MatInputModule} from '@angular/material/input';
import {MatSelectModule, } from '@angular/material/select';
import {MatCardModule} from '@angular/material/card';
import {MatFormFieldModule} from '@angular/material/form-field';
import {BrowserAnimationsModule}
              from '@angular/platform-browser/animations';

@NgModule({
  imports: [
    CommonModule
  ],
  exports: [
    MatToolbarModule, MatIconModule, MatMenuModule, MatButtonModule,
    MatInputModule, MatSelectModule, MatCardModule,
    MatFormFieldModule, BrowserAnimationsModule
  ]
})
export class AuctionMaterialModule { }
```

Imports only those AM modules that ngAuction needs

This module declares providers for animation services.

This is a feature module, so import the CommonModule.

Reexports the AM modules so they can be used in other modules of ngAuction

Now, open app.module.ts (the root module of ngAuction) and add your `AuctionMaterialModule` feature module to the `imports` property of `@NgModule()`, as you see in the following listing.

Listing 5.22 Adding the AM feature module

```
import {AuctionMaterialModule} from "./auction-material/auction-
     material.module";
...
@NgModule({
  ...
  imports: [
    ...
    AuctionMaterialModule        // Adds the AM feature module to the root one
   ]
  ...
})
```

Now's a good time to build and run ngAuction:

```
ng serve -o
```

You won't see any changes in the ngAuction UI just yet, but keep the dev server running so the appearance of the landing page will gradually change as you add more code in the next sections.

5.9.4 Modifying the appearance of NavbarComponent

The navbar component is a black bar with a menu. You'll start by replacing the existing content of navbar.component.html to use `<mat-toolbar>`, which will eventually contain the menu of the auction. Remove the current content of this file and add an empty toolbar there:

```
<mat-toolbar color="primary"></mat-toolbar>
```

While making changes, keep an eye on the UI of your running ngAuction—it has an empty blue toolbar now. You want the toolbar to contain the link to the home page and a pop-up menu that will be activated by a button click. The button should contain an icon with three vertical dots (see figure 5.14), and the directive `mat-icon-button` turns a regular button into a button that can contain `<mat-icon>`. For the image, you'll use `more_vert`, which is the name of one of the Google material icons available for free at https://material.io/icons.

Add the link and the button by modifying the content of navbar.component.html to match the following listing.

Listing 5.23 Adding a link and an icon button to the toolbar

```
<mat-toolbar color="primary">

<a [routerLink]="['/']">ngAuction</a>        <!-- Adds a link to navigate to a default route -->

<button mat-icon-button >        <!-- Adds a button that looks like three vertical dots -->
```

```
  <mat-icon>more_vert</mat-icon>
</button>

</mat-toolbar>
```

Now the toolbar will look like figure 5.12.

Figure 5.12 A toolbar with a broken icon

You specified the name of the icon `more_vert`, but didn't add Google material icons to index.html. Add the following to the <head> section of index.html:

```
<link href="https://fonts.googleapis.com/icon?family=Material+Icons"
      rel="stylesheet">
```

Now the `more_vert` icon is properly shown on the button, as shown in figure 5.13.

Figure 5.13 A toolbar with a fixed icon

The next step is to push this button to the right side of the toolbar, regardless of screen width. You'll add a `<div>` between the link and the button to fill the space. Add the following style to navbar.component.css:

```
.fill {
  flex: 1;
}
```

By default, the toolbar has the CSS flexbox layout (see https://css-tricks.com/snippets/css/a-guide-to-flexbox). The style `flex:1` translates to "Give the entire width to the HTML element."

Place the `<div>` between the `<a>` and `<button>` tags in navbar.component.html:

```
<div class="fill"></div>
```

Now the button is pushed all the way to the right, as shown in figure 5.14.

Figure 5.14 Pushing the button to the right

At this point, clicking the button doesn't open a menu for two reasons:

- You haven't created a menu yet.
- You haven't linked the menu to the button.

The ngAuction app from chapter 3 had three links: About, Services, and Contacts. Let's turn them into a pop-up menu. Each menu item will have an icon (`<mat-icon>`) and text. In Angular Material, a menu is represented by `<mat-menu>`, which can contain one or more items, such as `<button mat-menu-item>` components.

Add the code in the following listing right after the `</mat-toolbar>` tag in navbar.component.html.

Listing 5.24 Declaring items for a pop-up menu

```
<mat-menu #menu="matMenu">          <—— Uses the AM menu control
   <button mat-menu-item>         <—— First menu item
     <mat-icon>info</mat-icon>
    <span>About</span>
  </button>
  <button mat-menu-item>          <—— Second menu item
     <mat-icon>settings</mat-icon>
    <span>Services</span>
  </button>
  <button mat-menu-item>          <—— Third menu item
     <mat-icon>contacts</mat-icon>
    <span>Contact</span>
  </button>
</mat-menu>
```

Each `<mat-icon>` uses one of the Google Material icons (`info`, `settings`, and `contacts`). Note that you declare a local template variable, `#menu`, to reference this menu and assigned it to the AM `matMenu` directive. In itself, `<mat-menu>` doesn't render anything until it's attached to a component with the `matMenuTriggerFor` directive. To attach this menu to your toolbar button, bind the `menu` template variable to the `matMenuTriggerFor` directive . Update the button to look as follows:

```
<button mat-icon-button [matMenuTriggerFor]="menu">
  <mat-icon>more_vert</mat-icon>
</button>
```

NOTE You can replace `<button>` tags with `<a [routerLink]>` links.

If you click the toolbar button now, it'll show the menu, as shown in figure 5.15.

Figure 5.15 The toolbar menu

5.9.5 *Modifying the SearchComponent UI*

The `SearchComponent` template will contain a form with three controls: a text input, a number input, and a select dropdown, which will be implemented with the `matInput` directives (they should be placed inside `<mat-form-field>`) and `<mat-select>`. To make the Search button stand out, you'll also add a `mat-raised-button` directive and the search icon to this button.

Modify the code in the search.component.html file to look like the following listing.

Listing 5.25 search.component.html

```
<form #f="ngForm">                          ◁ Uses the template-driven Forms API

  <mat-form-field>                          ◁ First form field
     <input matInput
           type="text"
           placeholder="Product title"
           name="title" ngModel>
  </mat-form-field>

  <mat-form-field>      ◁ Second form field
      <input matInput
           type="number"
           placeholder="Product price"
           name="price" ngModel>
  </mat-form-field>

  <mat-form-field>    ◁ Third form field
     <mat-select placeholder="Category" name="category" ngModel>
      <mat-option *ngFor="let c of categories"
                 [value]="c">{{ c }}</mat-option>
    </mat-select>
  </mat-form-field>

  <button mat-raised-button color="accent" type="submit"> ◁ The form's Submit button
     <mat-icon>search</mat-icon>SEARCH
  </button>
</form>
```

The `ngForm` and `ngModel` directives are parts of template-driven forms defined in the `FormModule` (described in section 10.2.1 of chapter 10), and you need to add it to the `@NgModule()` decorator in `AppModule`, as shown in the following listing.

Listing 5.26 Adding support for the Forms API

```
import {FormsModule} from '@angular/forms';

@NgModule({
  ...
  imports: [
   ...
    FormsModule      ◁ Adds support for the template-driven Forms API
   ]
})
```

Let's make sure the UI is properly rendered. For now, on smaller screens, it looks like figure 5.16.

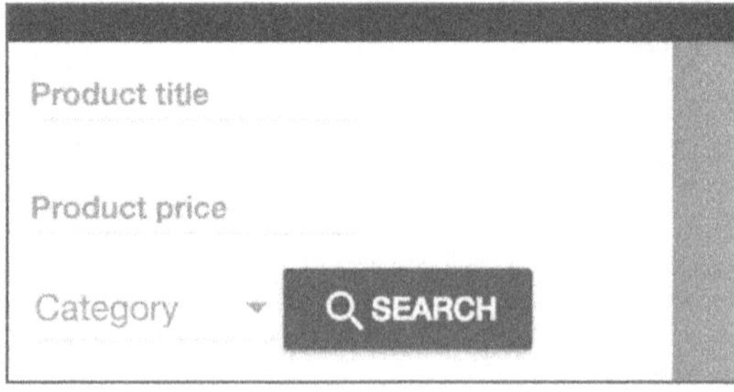

Figure 5.16 The search form with a misaligned button

The `mat-form-field` components and the `mat-select` dropdown should occupy the entire width of the search component. You also want to add more space between the form controls.

Add the styles in the following listing to the search.component.css file.

Listing 5.27 A fragment of search.component.css

```
mat-form-field, mat-select, [mat-raised-button] {
  display: block;
  margin-top: 16px;
  width: 100%;
}
```

`display: block;` tells the browser to render the search component as a standard `<div>`. Now the search form is well aligned, as shown in figure 5.17.

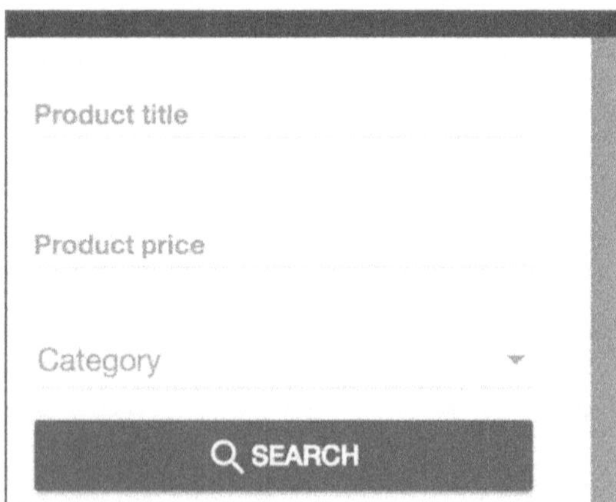

Figure 5.17 The search form

The Search button won't perform search in this version of ngAuction, and the search form won't do input validation either. You'll fix this in section 11.8 in chapter 11 after we discuss the Angular Forms API.

5.9.6 Replacing the carousel with an image

At the time of writing, Angular Material doesn't have a carousel component. In a real-world project, you'd find the carousel component in one of the third-party libraries, such as the PrimeNG library (www.primefaces.org/primeng/#/carousel), but in this version of ngAuction, you'll replace the carousel with a static image.

Replace the content of carousel.component.html with the following code:

```
<img src="http://placehold.it/800x300" alt="Banner">
```

Now the browser shows a gray rectangle in place of the carousel. You could have kept the Bootstrap carousel in place, but it's not worth loading the entire Bootstrap library just for the carousel. The goal is to gradually switch to AM components.

5.9.7 More fixes with spacing

Let's put some space between the toolbar and other components by adding the following style to app.component.css:

```
.container {
  margin-top: 16px;
}
```

Now, add some space between the carousel and product items. Modify the home.component.css file to look like the following code (`display:block` is for rendering this custom component as a `<div>`):

```
:host {
  display: block;
}

auction-carousel {
  margin-bottom: 16px;
}
```

5.9.8 Using mat-card in ProductItemComponent

The next step is to display your products as tiles, and each `<nga-product-item>` will use the `<mat-card>` component. To render each product inside the card, modify the content of the product-item.component.htmlfile to look like the following listing.

Listing 5.28 product-item.component.html

```
<mat-card>                                                    ◁ Defines the content of the AM <mat-card> component
   <mat-card-title>{{ product.title }}</mat-card-title>        ◁ The product title goes on top.
   <img mat-card-image src="http://placehold.it/320x150">      ◁ Product image
   <mat-card-content>
    {{product.description}}                                    ◁ Product description
   </mat-card-content>
  <mat-card-actions>
    <a mat-button color="accent"
```

```
      [routerLink]="['/products', product.id]">VIEW</a>
  </mat-card-actions>
</mat-card>
```

A link to navigate to product details

5.9.9 Adding styles to HomeComponent

Your `HomeComponent` hosts several instances of `ProductItemComponent`. Now let's add more styles to home.component.css so the products are displayed nicely and aligned using the CSS style `flex`. Add the following listing's styles to home.component.css.

Listing 5.29 home.component.css

```
.product-grid {
  display: flex;
   flex-wrap: wrap;
  margin: 0 -8px;
}

nga-product-item {
  margin: 0 8px 16px;
  flex-basis: calc(100% / 3 - 16px);
 }
```

Uses CSS flexbox

Gives one third of the screen width plus a margin to each component

Now the landing page of ngAuction has a more modern look, as shown earlier in figure 5.10. Not only does it look better than the version of ngAuction from chapter 3, but its controls (the search form, the menu) provide fast and animated response to the user's actions. Try to place the focus in one of the search fields, and you'll see how the field prompt moves to the top. The button search also shows a ripple effect.

You didn't change the look of the product-detail page shown in figure 3.16 in chapter 3. See if you can do that on your own. When all standard UI elements are replaced with AM components, you can remove the dependency on the Bootstrap library from both package.json and .angular-cli.json (or from angular.json, if you use Angular 6).

Summary

- Providers register objects for future injection.
- You can declare a provider that uses not only a class, but a function or a primitive value as well.
- Injectors form a hierarchy, and if Angular can't find the provider for the requested type at the component level, it'll try to find it by traversing parent injectors.
- A lazy-loaded module has its own injector, and providers declared inside lazy-loaded modules aren't available in the root module.
- Angular Material offers a set of modern-looking UI components.

6 Reactive programming in Angular

This chapter covers

- Handling events as observables
- Using observables with Angular `Router` and forms
- Using observables in HTTP requests
- Minimizing network load by discarding unwanted HTTP responses

The goal of the first five chapters was to jump-start your application development with Angular. In those chapters, we discussed how to generate a new project from scratch, covering modules, routing, and dependency injection. In this chapter, we'll show you how Angular supports a *reactive* style of programming, in which your app reacts on changes either initiated by the user or by asynchronous events like data arriving from a router, form, or server. You'll learn which Angular APIs support data push and allow you to subscribe to RxJS-based observable data streams.

NOTE If you're not familiar with RxJS library concepts such as observables, observers, operators, and subscriptions, read appendix D before proceeding with this chapter.

Angular offers ready-to-use observables for implementing various scenarios: handling events, subscribing to the route's parameters, checking the status of a form, handling HTTP requests, and more. You'll see some examples of using Angular observables, but each of the following chapters contains reactive code as well.

You may say that any JavaScript app can use event listeners and provide callbacks to handle events, but we'll show you how to treat events as data streams that *push* values to the observers over time. You'll be writing code that *subscribes* to observable event streams and handles them in the observer objects. You'll be able to apply one or more operators to handle an event as it moves to the observer, which isn't possible with the regular event listeners.

> **NOTE** Source code for this chapter can be found at https://github.com/Farata/angulartypescriptand www.manning.com/books/angular-development-with-typescript-second-edition. You can find the code samples used in this section in the directory named observables. Open this directory in your IDE and run `npm install` to install Angular and its dependencies. We provide instructions on how to run code samples when it's required.

Let's start by discussing how to handle events with and without observables.

6.1 Handling events without observables

Each DOM event is represented by the object containing properties describing the event. Angular applications can handle standard DOM events and can emit custom events as well. A handler function for a UI event can be declared with an optional `$event` parameter . With standard DOM events, you can use any functions or properties of the browser's `Event` object (see "Event" in the Mozilla Developer Network documentation, http://mzl.la/1EAG6iw).

In some cases, you won't be interested in reading the event object's properties, such as when the only button on a page is clicked and this is all that matters. In other cases, you may want to know specific information, like what character was entered in the `<input>` field when the `keyup` event was dispatched. The following code listing shows how to handle a DOM `keyup` event and print the value from the input field that emitted this event.

Listing 6.1 Handling the keyup event

```
template:`<input id="stock" (keyup)="onKey($event)">`    ◁ Binds to the keyup event
 ...

onKey(event:any) {
  console.log("You have entered " + event.target.value);    ◁ Event handler method
 }
```

In this code snippet, you care only about one property of the `Event` object: the `target`. By applying *object destructuring* (see section A.9.1 in appendix A), the `onKey()` handler can get the reference to the `target` property on the fly by using curly braces with the function argument:

```
onKey({target}) {
  console.log("You have entered " + target.value);
}
```

If your code dispatches a custom event, it can carry application-specific data, and the event object can be strongly typed (not be `any` type). You'll see how to specify the type of a custom event in listing 8.4 in chapter 8.

A traditional JavaScript application treats a dispatched event as a one-time deal; for example, one click results in one function invocation. Angular offers another approach where you can consider any event as an observable stream of data happening over time. For example, if the user enters several characters in the `<input>` field, each of the characters can be treated as an emission of the observable stream.

You can subscribe to observable events and specify the code to be invoked when each new value is emitted and, optionally, the code for error processing and stream completion. Often you'll specify a number of chained RxJS operators and then invoke the `subscribe()` method.

Why do we even need to apply RxJS operators to events coming from the UI? Let's consider an example that uses event binding to handle multiple `keyup` events as the user types a stock symbol to get its price:

```
<input type='text' (keyup) = "getStockPrice($event)">
```

Isn't this technique good enough for handling multiple events dispatched as the user types? Imagine that the preceding code is used to get a price quote for AAPL stock. After the user types the first `A`, the `getStockPrice()` function will make a request to the server, which will return the price of `A`, if there is such a stock. Then the user enters the second `A`, which results in another server request for the `AA` price quote. The process repeats for `AAP` and `AAPL`.

This isn't what you want. To defer the invocation of `getStockPrice()`, you can place it inside the `setTimeout()` function with, say, a 500-millisecond delay to give the user enough time to type several letters:

```
const stock = document.getElementById("stock");

  stock.addEventListener("keyup", function(event) {
    setTimeout(function() {
      getStockPrice(event);
    }, 500);
  }, false);
```

Don't forget to call `clearTimeout()` and start another timer should the user continue typing in the input field.

How about composing several functions that should preprocess the event before invoking `getStockPrice()`? There's no elegant solution to this. What if the user types slowly, and during the 500-millisecond interval manages only to enter AAP? The first request for AAP goes to the server, and 500 milliseconds later the second request for AAPL is sent. A program can't discard the results of the first HTTP request if the client returns a `Promise` object, and may overload the network with unwanted HTTP responses.

Handling events with RxJS offers you a convenient operator named `debounceTime` that makes the observable emit the next value only if a specified time passes (such as 500 milliseconds) and the data producer (the `<input>` field in our case) doesn't produce new values during this interval. There's no need to clear and re-create the timer. Also, the `switchMap` operator allows easy cancellation of the observable waiting for a pending request (for example, `getStockPrice()`) if the observable emits new values (for example, the user keep typing). What can Angular offer to handle events from an input field with subscribers?

6.2 Turning DOM events into observables

In Angular applications, you can get direct access to any DOM element using a special class, `ElementRef`, and we'll use this feature to illustrate how you can subscribe to events of an arbitrary HTML element. You'll create an app that will subscribe to the `<input>` element where the user inputs the stock symbol to get its price, as discussed in the previous section.

To turn a DOM event into an observable stream, you need to do the following:

1. Get a reference to the DOM object.
2. Create an observable using `Observable.fromEvent()`, providing the reference to the DOM object and the event you want to subscribe to.
3. Subscribe to this observable and handle the events.

In a regular JavaScript app, to get a reference to the DOM element, you use a DOM selector API, `document.querySelector ()`. In Angular, you can use the `@ViewChild()` decorator to get a reference to an element from a component template.

To uniquely identify the template elements, you'll use local template variables that start with the hash symbol. The following code snippet uses the local template variable `#stockSymbol` as an ID of the `<input>` element:

```
<input type="text" #stockSymbol placeholder="Enter stock">
```

If you need to get a reference to the preceding element inside the TypeScript class, you can use the `@ViewChild('stockSymbol')` decorator, and the application in the following listing illustrates how to do that. Note that you import only those RxJS members that you actually use.

Listing 6.2 fromevent/app.component.ts

```
import {AfterViewInit, Component, ElementRef, ViewChild} from '@angular/core';
import {Observable} from "rxjs";
import {debounceTime, map} from 'rxjs/operators';
```

```
@Component({
  selector: "app-root",
  template: `
    <h2>Observable events</h2>
    <input type="text" #stockSymbol placeholder="Enter stock" >
  `
})
export class AppComponent implements AfterViewInit {

  @ViewChild('stockSymbol') myInputField: ElementRef;

  ngAfterViewInit() {

    let keyup$: =
        Observable.fromEvent(this.myInputField.nativeElement, 'keyup');

     let keyupValue$ = keyup$
    .pipe(
       debounceTime(500),
        map(event => event['target'].value))
     .subscribe(stock => this.getStockQuoteFromServer(stock));
  }

    getStockQuoteFromServer(stock: string) {

      console.log(`The price of ${stock} is
➥ ${(100 * Math.random()).toFixed(4)}`);
    }
}
```

Declares the property myInputField that holds a reference to the <input> field

Places the code in the ngAfterViewInit() component lifecycle method

Creates an observable from the keyup event

Waits for a 500 ms pause in the observable's emissions

Converts the DOM event into the target.value property, which has the stock symbol entered by the user

Invokes the getStockQuoteFromServer() method for each value emitted by the observable

Prints the generated random stock price

TIP Starting from Angular 6, instead of `Observable.fromEvent()`, just write `fromEvent()`.

NOTE In listing 6.2, the code to subscribe to events is placed in the `ngAfterViewInit ()` component lifecycle method, which Angular invokes when the component's UI is initialized. You'll learn about component lifecycle methods in section 9.2 in chapter 9.

You can see this code sample in action by running the following command:

```
ng serve --app fromevent -o
```

Open the browser's console and start entering the stock symbol. Depending on the speed of your typing, you'll see one or more messages in the console reporting stock price(s).

It's great that you can turn any DOM event into an observable, but directly accessing the DOM by using `ElementRef` is discouraged, because it may present some security vulnerabilities (see https://angular.io/api/core/ElementRef for details). What's a better way to subscribe to value changes in a DOM object?

6.3 Handling observable events with the Forms API

The Angular Forms API (covered in chapters 10 and 11) offers ready-to-use observables that push notifications about important events that are happening with the entire form or with form control. Here are two examples:

- `valueChanges` —This property is an observable that emits data when the value of the form control is changing.
- `statusChanges` —This property is an observable that emits the validity status of the form control or the entire form. The status changes from valid to invalid or vice versa.

In this section, we'll show you how to use the `valueChanges` property with the HTML `<input>` element.

The `FormControl` class, one of the fundamental blocks of forms processing, represents a form control. By default, whenever the value of the form control changes, the underlying `FormControl` object emits an event through its `valueChanges` property of type `Observable`, and you can subscribe to it.

Let's rewrite the app from the previous section by using the Forms API to subscribe to the `input` event of the `<input>` field and generate stock quotes. The form elements can be bound to component properties via the `formControl` directive, and you'll use it instead of accessing the DOM object directly.

The following listing applies the RxJS `debounceTime`operator prior to invoking `subscribe ()`, instructing the `this.searchInput.valueChanges` observable to emit the data if the user isn't typing anything during 500 milliseconds.

Listing 6.3 formcontrol/app.component.ts

```
import {Component} from '@angular/core';
import {FormControl} from '@angular/forms';
import {debounceTime} from 'rxjs/operators;

@Component({
  selector: 'app-root',
  template: `
       <h2>Observable events from formcontrol</h2>
     <input type="text" placeholder="Enter stock"
            [formControl]="searchInput">          ◁ Links this <input> element to the component property searchInput
  `
})
export class AppComponent {

  searchInput = new FormControl('');

  constructor() {
    this.searchInput.valueChanges             ◁ The valueChanges property is an observable.
       pipe(debounceTime(500))                ◁ Waits for 500 ms of quiet time before emitting the content of the <input> element
       .subscribe(stock => this.getStockQuoteFromServer(stock));   ◁ Subscribes to the observable
  }

  getStockQuoteFromServer(stock: string) {
```

```
    console.log(`The price of ${stock} is ${(100 * Math.random()).toFixed(4)}
     `);
  }
}
```

Your `subscribe()` method provides the `Observer` with one method (no error or stream-completion handlers). Each value from the stream generated by the `searchInput` control is given to the `getStockQuoteFromServer()` method. In a real-world scenario, this method would issue a request to the server (and you'll see such an app in section 6.4), but your method just generates and prints a random stock price.

If you didn't use the `debounceTime` operator, `valueChanges` would be emitting values after each character typed by the user. Figure 6.1 shows what happens after you start this application and enter `AAPL` in the input field.

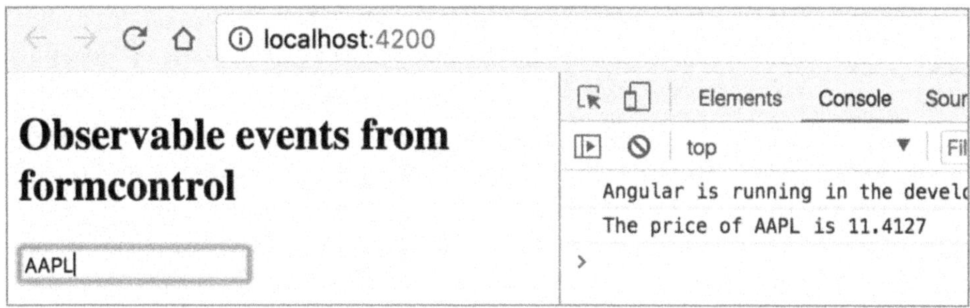

Figure 6.1 Getting the price for AAPL

To see this app in action, run the following command in the Terminal:

```
ng serve --app formcontrol -o
```

> **NOTE** You may argue that you could implement this example in listing 6.3 and figure 6.1 by simply binding to the `change` event, which would be dispatched when the user finished entering the stock symbol and moved the focus out of the input field. This is true, but in many scenarios you'll want an immediate response from the server, such as retrieving and filtering a data collection as the user types.

In listing 6.3, you don't make any network requests to the server for price quotes—you generate random numbers on the user's computer. Even if the user enters a wrong stock symbol, this code sample will invoke `Math.random()`, which has a negligible effect on the application's performance. In a real-world application, the user's typos may generate network requests that introduce delays while returning quotes for mistakenly entered stock symbols. How would you go about discarding the results of unwanted requests?

6.4 Discarding results of unwanted HTTP requests with switchMap

One of the advantages of observables over promises is that observables can be cancelled. In the previous section, we offered one scenario in which a typo might result in a server request that returns unwanted results. Implementing master-detail views is another use case for a request cancellation. Say a user clicks a row in a list of products to see the product details that must be retrieved from the server. Then they change their mind and click another row, which issues another server request; in that case, the results of the pending request should ideally be discarded.

In Angular, HTTP requests return observables. Let's look at how to discard the results of pending HTTP requests by creating an application that issues HTTP requests as the user types in the input field. We'll use two observable streams:

- The observable stream produced by the search `<input>` field
- The observable stream produced by the HTTP requests issued while the user is typing in the search field

For this example, you'll use the free weather service at http://openweathermap.org, which provides an API for making weather requests for cities around the world. To use this service, go to OpenWeatherMap and receive an application ID (`appid`). This service returns the weather information as a JSON-formatted `string`. For example, to get the current temperature in London in Fahrenheit (`units=imperial`), the URL could look like this: http://api.openweathermap.org/data/2.5/find?q=London&units=imperial&appid=12345.

You'll construct the request URL by concatenating the base URL with the entered city name and the application ID. As the user enters the letters of the city name, the code subscribes to the event stream and issues HTTP requests. If a new request is issued before the response from the previous one comes back, the `switchMap` operator (explained in section D.8 in appendix D) cancels and discards the previous inner observable (so the results of the previous HTTP request never reach the browser) and sends the new one to this weather service. This example, shown in the following listing, also uses the `FormControl` directive to generate an observable stream from the input field where the user enters the name of the city.

Listing 6.4 weather/app.component

```
@Component({
  selector: "app-root",
  template: `
    <h2>Observable weather</h2>
    <input type="text" placeholder="Enter city" [formControl]="searchInput">
    <h3>{{weather}}</h3>
  `
})
export class AppComponent implements OnInit{
  private baseWeatherURL = 'http://api.openweathermap.org/data/2.5/weather?q=';
  private urlSuffix: = "&units=imperial&appid=12345";
```

```
  searchInput = new FormControl();
  weather: string;

  constructor(private http: HttpClient) {}

  ngOnInit() {

    this.searchInput.valueChanges
      .pipe(switchMap(city => this.getWeather(city)))
       .subscribe(
        res => {
          this.weather =
            `Current temperature is  ${res['main'].temp}F, ` +
           `humidity: ${res['main'].humidity}%`;
        },
        err => console.log(`Can't get weather. Error code: %s, URL: %s`,
                             err.message, err.url)
      );
  }

  getWeather(city: string): Observable<any> {
     return this.http.get(this.baseWeatherURL + city + this.urlSuffix)
       .pipe(catchError( err => {
          if (err.status === 404){
           console.log(`City ${city} not found`);
           return Observable.empty()}
          })
      );
  }
}
```

Creates the subscription in ngOnInit(), which is invoked after component properties are initialized

The switchMap operator takes the entered value from the input field (the first observable) and passes it to the getWeather() method, which issues the HTTP request to the weather service.

Initializes the weather variable with the info on temperature and humidity

The getWeather() method constructs the URL and defines the HTTP GET request.

Intercepts errors if the user enters a city that doesn't exist

To keep the app running, returns an empty observable in case of 404

TIP Starting from TypeScript 2.7, you need to initialize the class variables either during declaration or in the constructor: for example, `weather = ''`. If you don't want to do this, set the TypeScript compiler's `strictPropertyInitialization` option to `false`.

Note two observables in listing 6.4:

- The `FormControl` directive creates an observable from the input field events (`this.searchInput.valueChanges`).
- `getWeather()` also returns an observable.

We often use the `switchMap` operator when the data generated by the outer observable (the `FormControl`, in this case) is given to the inner observable (the `getWeather()` function): Observable1 -> `switchMap(function)` -> Observable2 -> `subscribe()`.

If Observable1 pushes the new value, but the inner Observable2 hasn't finished yet, Observable2 gets cancelled. We're switching over from the current inner observable to the new one, and the `switchMap` operator unsubscribes from the pending Observable2 and resubscribes again to handle the new value produced by Observable1.

In listing 6.4, if the observable stream from the UI pushes the next value before the observable returned by `getWeather()` has emitted a value, `switchMap` kills the observable from `getWeather()`, gets the new value for the city from the UI, and invokes `getWeather()` again. Cancelling `getWeather()` results in `HttpClient` discarding the results of the pending HTTP request that was slow and didn't complete in time.

The `subscribe()` method has only a callback for handling data coming from the server, where you extract the temperature and humidity from the returned JSON. If the user makes a request to a nonexistent city, the API offered by this weather service returns 404. You intercept and handle this error in the `catchError` operator. Imagine a slow typer who enters `Lo` while trying to find the weather in *London*. The HTTP request for `Lo` goes out, a 404 is returned, and you create an empty observable so the `subscribe()` method will get an empty result, which is not an error.

To run this app, you need to first obtain your own key (it takes one minute) at http://api.openweathermap.org and replace 12345 in the code in listing 6.4 with your own key. Then you can run this app with the following command:

```
ng serve --app weather -o
```

The browser will open the app at http://localhost:4200, rendering a window with a single input field where you can enter the city name. Figure 6.2 shows the network traffic as you type the word *London* on a computer with a fast 200 Mbps internet connection.

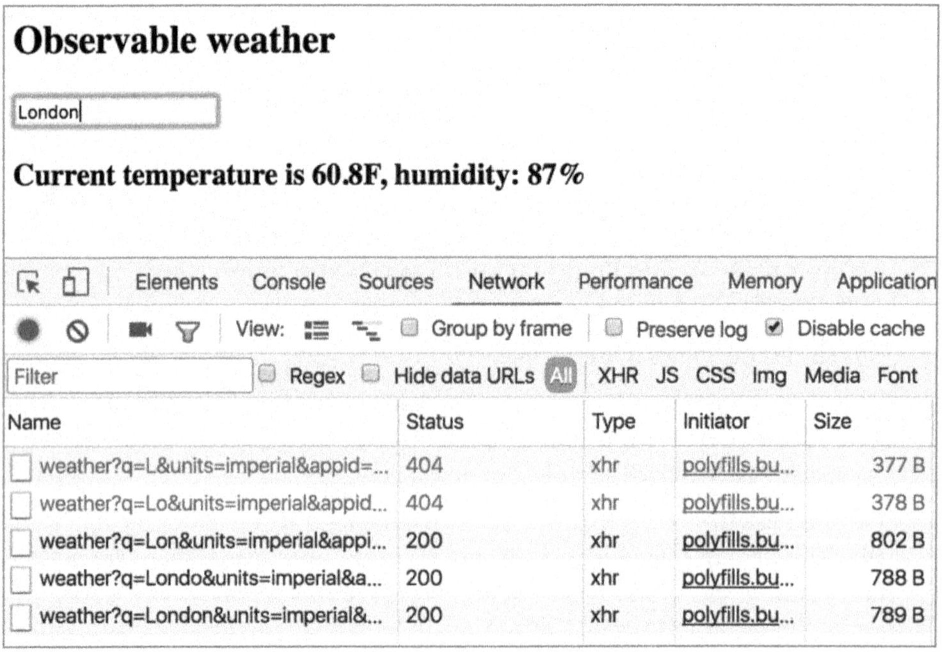

Figure 6.2 Getting weather without throttling

In this case, six HTTP requests were made and returned the HTTP responses. Read the queries in the first two. The requests for the cities `L` and `Lo` came back with 404. But requests for `Lon`, `Lond`, `Londo`, and `London` completed successfully, sending back hundreds of bytes each, unnecessarily congesting the network. Add these bytes up—you'll get 3,134 bytes in total, but users on a fast network wouldn't even notice this.

Now let's emulate a slow network and verify that discarding unwanted results works. On a slow internet connection, each HTTP request takes more than 200 ms to complete, but the user keeps typing, and the responses of the pending HTTP requests should be discarded.

The Network tab of Chrome Developer Tools has a dropdown with selected option Online, which means use the full connection speed. Now, let's emulate a slow connection by selecting the Slow 3G option instead. Retyping the word *London* results in multiple HTTP requests, but the connection is slow now, and the results of pending requests are discarded and never reach the browser, as shown in figure 6.3. Note that this time you get 789 bytes back, which is much better than 3,134.

With very little programming, you save bandwidth by eliminating the need for the browser to handle four HTTP responses for cities you're not interested in and that may not even exist. Just by adding one line with `switchMap`, you accomplish a lot. Indeed, with good frameworks or libraries, you write less code. Angular pipes also allow you to achieve more with less manual coding, and in the next section you'll learn about `AsyncPipe`, which will eliminate the need to make the `subscribe()` call.

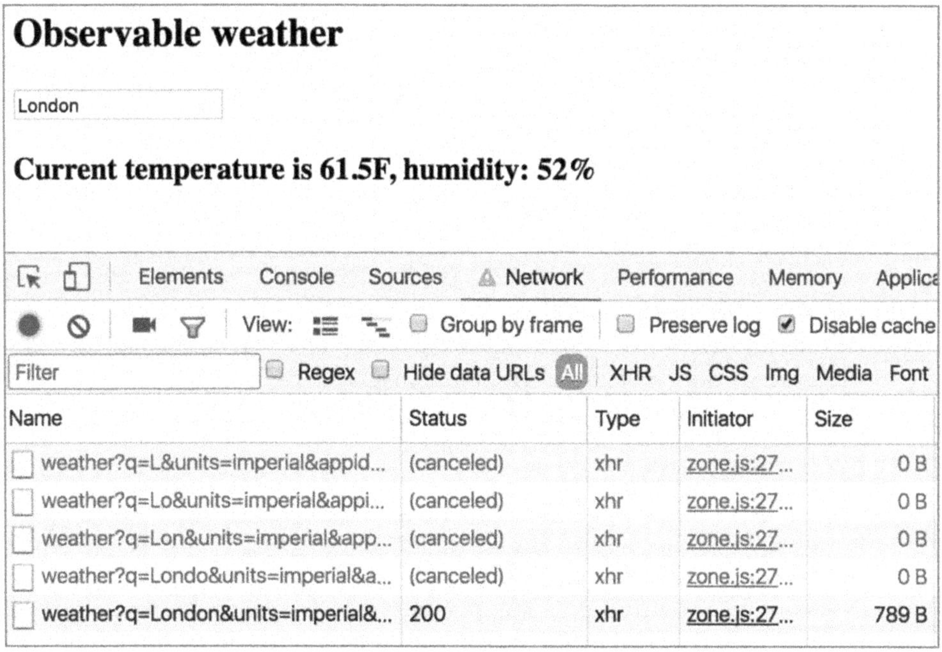

Figure 6.3 Getting weather with throttling

6.5 Using AsyncPipe

Section 2.5 in chapter 2 introduced you to pipes, which are used in a component template and can convert the data right inside the template. For example, a `DatePipe` could convert and display a date in the specified format. A pipe is placed in the template after the vertical bar, for example:

```
<p> Birthday: {{birthday | date: 'medium'}}</p>
```

In this code snippet, `birthday` is a component property of type `Date`. Angular offers an `AsyncPipe` that can take a component property of type `Observable`, autosubscribe to it, and render the result in the template.

The next listing declares a `numbers` variable of type `Observable<number>` and initializes it with an observable that emits a sequential number with an interval of 1 second. The `take(10)` operator will limit the emission to the first 10 numbers.

Listing 6.5 asyncpipe/app.component.ts

```
import {Component} from '@angular/core';
import 'rxjs/add/observable/interval';
import {take} from 'rxjs/operators';
import {Observable} from "rxjs";

@Component({
  selector: "app-root",
  template: `{{numbers$ | async}}`          <- Autosubscribes to observable numbers
 })
export class AppComponent {

  numbers$: Observable<number> =
             Observable.interval(1000)     <- Emits sequential numbers every second
                .pipe(take(10));     <- Takes only 10 numbers from 0 to 9
 }
```

TIP Starting in Angular 6, instead of `Observable.interval()`, just write `interval()`.

As explained in appendix D, to start getting data from an observable, we need to invoke the `subscribe()` method. In listing 6.5, there's no explicit invocation of `subscribe()`, but note the `async` pipe in the template. The `async` pipe autosubscribes to the `numbers` observable and displays the numbers from 0 to 9 as they're being pushed by the observable. To see this example in action, run the following command:

```
ng serve --app asyncpipe -o
```

This was a pretty simple example that never throws any errors. In real-world applications, things happen, and you should add error handling to the observable with the `catch` operator, as you did in the previous section in the weather example.

Now let's consider one more app that uses the `async` pipe. This time, you'll invoke a function that returns an observable array of products, and you'll use the `async` pipe to render its values. This app will use the `ProductService` injectable, whose getProducts() method returns an observable array of the Product objects, as shown in the following listing.

Listing 6.6 asyncpipe-products/product.service.ts

```
import {Injectable} from '@angular/core';
import {Observable} from "rxjs";
import 'rxjs/add/observable/of';

export interface Product {   <—— Defines the Product type
    id: number;
   title: string;
   price: number
}

@Injectable()
export class ProductService {

  products: Product[] = [    <—— Populates the products array
     {id: 0, title: "First Product", price: 24.99},
    {id: 1, title:"Second Product", price: 64.99},
    {id: 2, title:"Third Product", price: 74.99}
  ];

  getProducts(): Observable<Product[]> {

    return Observable.of(this.products);    <—— Turns the products array into an observable
   }
}
```

TIP Starting from Angular 6, instead of Observable.of() just write of().

The next listing shows an app component that gets the ProductService injected and invokes getProducts(), which returns an observable. Note that there's no explicit invocation of subscribe() there—you use the async pipe in the template. In this component, you use Angular's structural directive *ngFor to iterate through products and for each product render the <li> element with the product title and price, as you can see in the following listing.

Listing 6.7 asyncpipe-products/app.component.ts

```
import {Component} from '@angular/core';
import {Product, ProductService} from "./product.service";
import {Observable} from "rxjs";

@Component({
  selector: "app-root",
  template: `
       <ul>
         <li *ngFor="let product of products$ | async">    <—— Iterates through products and pipes them to async for subscription
            {{product.title}} {{product.price}}    <—— Renders the product title and price
          </li>
       </ul>
    `
})
```

```
export class AppComponent {

  products$: Observable<Product[]>;

  constructor(private productService: ProductService) {}

  ngOnInit() {

    this.products$ = this.productService.getProducts();
  }
}
```

Declares the observable products$ using generics syntax for type checking

Assigns the value to products$

It's important to understand that the `getProducts()` function returns an empty observable that hasn't emitted anything yet, and you assign it to the `products$` variable. No data is pushed to this component until you subscribe to `products$`, and the `async` pipe does it in the template.

To see this application in action, run the following command:

```
ng serve --app asyncpipe-products -o
```

Figure 6.4 shows how the browser will render products.

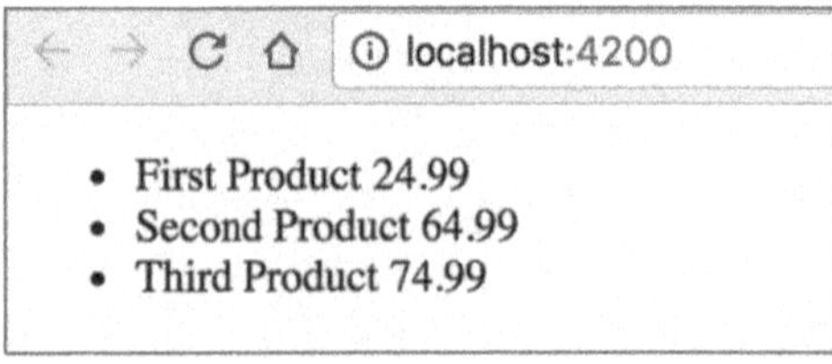

Figure 6.4 Rendering observable products

Since we're talking about pipes, let's apply the Angular built-in `currency` pipe to show the price in US dollars. All it takes is adding the `currency` pipe right after `product.price`:

```
{{product.title}} {{product.price | currency : "USD"}}
```

You can read more about the `currency` pipe and its parameters at https://angular.io/api/common/CurrencyPipe. Figure 6.5 shows how the browser will render products after applying the currency pipe for US dollars.

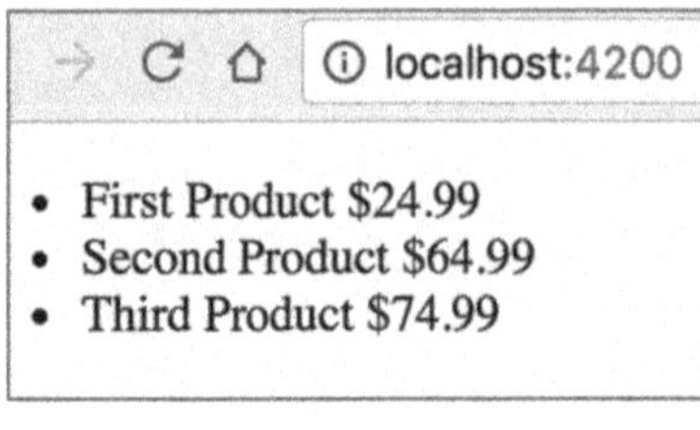

Figure 6.5 Rendering observable products

Using async as

With async pipes , you can use the special syntax `async as` to avoid creating multiple subscriptions in templates. Consider the following code, which creates two subscriptions in a template, assuming that there's an observable `product$`:

```
<div>
  <h4>{{ (product$ | async).price}}</h4>              <-- First subscription
  <p>{{ (product$ | async).description }}</p>  <-- Second subscription
</div>
```

The following code rewrites the previous by creating a local template variable, `product`, which would store the reference to a single subscription and then reuse it in multiple places in the same template:

```
<div *ngIf="product$ | async as product">    <-- Creates a subscription and stores it in the product variable
    <h4>{{ product.price}}</h4>               <-- Uses the subscription called product
    <p>{{ product.description }}</p>
</div>
```

Now let's see where observables can be used during navigation with the router.

6.6 Observables and the router

Angular Router offers you observable properties in various classes. Is there an easy way to find them? The fastest way is to open the type definition file (see appendix B) for the class you're interested in. Usually, IDEs offer you an option on the context (right-click) menu to go to the declaration of the selected class. Let's use the `ActivatedRoute` class as an example and take a look at its declaration. It's located in the router_state.d.ts file (we removed some content for brevity), as shown in the following listing.

Listing 6.8 A fragment from `ActivatedRoute`

```
export declare class ActivatedRoute {
    url: Observable<UrlSegment[]>;
    queryParams: Observable<Params>;
    fragment: Observable<string>;
    data: Observable<Data>;
    snapshot: ActivatedRouteSnapshot;
    ...
    readonly paramMap: Observable<ParamMap>;
    readonly queryParamMap: Observable<ParamMap>;
}
```

In section 3.4 in chapter 3, you injected `ActivatedRoute` into the `ProductDetail-Component` so it could receive the route parameters during navigation. Back then, you used the `snapshot` property of `ActivatedRoute` to get the value from the parent route. This technique works fine if you need to get parameters that never change. But if the parameters in the parent route change over time, you need to subscribe to an observable such as `paramMap`.

Why would the value of the parent's parameter change? Imagine a component that shows a list of products, and when the user selects a product, the app navigates to the route that shows product details. Often, these use cases are called *master-detail communications* .

When the user clicks the product for the first time, the router performs the following steps:

1. Instantiates `ProductDetailComponent`
2. Attaches `ProductDetailComponent` to the DOM object
3. Renders `ProductDetailComponent` in the router outlet
4. Passes the parameter (for example, product ID) to `ProductDetailComponent`

If the user selects another product in the parent's component, the first three steps won't be performed, because `ProductDetailComponent` is already instantiated, attached to the DOM, and rendered by the browser. The router will just pass a newly selected product ID to `ProductDetailComponent`, and that's why subscribing to `paramMap` is the way to go. The following listing implements this scenario, starting from `AppComponent`.

Listing 6.9 master-detail/app.component.ts

```
interface Product {   <— Defines the Product type
   id: number;
  description: string;
}

@Component({
  selector: 'app-root',
  template: `
        <ul style="width: 100px;">
           <li *ngFor="let product of products"
             [class.selected]="product === selectedProduct"
             (click) = onSelect(product)>        <— When the user selects an item, invokes the onSelect() handler
                <span>{{product.id}} {{product.description}} </span>
           </li>
        </ul>

        <router-outlet></router-outlet>
     `,
  styles:[`.selected {background-color: cornflowerblue}`]
})
export class AppComponent {

  selectedProduct: Product;

  products: Product[] = [
    {id: 1, description: "iPhone 7"},
    {id: 2, description: "Samsung 7"},
    {id: 3, description: "MS Lumina"}
  ];
```

```
  constructor(private _router: Router) {}     ◁  Injects the router so you can
                                                 use its navigate() method
  onSelect(prod: Product): void {
    this.selectedProduct = prod;
    this._router.navigate(["/productDetail", prod.id]);   ◁  Navigates to the
  }                                                          productDetail route
}
```

The routes for this app are configured as follows:

```
[
 {path: 'productDetail/:id', component: ProductDetailComponent}
]
```

The `ProductDetailComponent`'s code that subscribes to `paramMap` is shown in the following listing.

Listing 6.10 master-detail/product.detail.component.ts

```
                                                    Embeds the value of
@Component({                                        productId into the header
  selector: 'product',
  template: `<h3 class="product">Details for product id {{productId}}</h3>`,   ◁
   styles: ['.product {background: cyan; width: 200px;} ']
})
export class ProductDetailComponent {

  productId: string;

  constructor(private route: ActivatedRoute) {      Subscribes to the
                                                    paramMap observable
    this.route.paramMap
      .subscribe(      ◁
         params => this.productId = params.get('id'));   ◁
    }
}                                    Extracts the current product id and
                                     assigns it to the productId property
                                     for displaying in the UI
```

Now `ProductDetailComponent` will render the text identifying the current product according to user selections. Figure 6.6 shows how the UI looks after the user selects the second product in the list. To see this app in action, run the following command:

```
ng serve --app master-detail -o
```

In chapter 7, you'll rewrite ngAuction, and you'll see how the `ObservableMedia` class from the Flex Layout library will notify you about changes in the screen size (for example, the user reduces the width of the window). This observable is also quite handy in changing the UI layout based on the viewport width of smaller devices like smartphones and tablets.

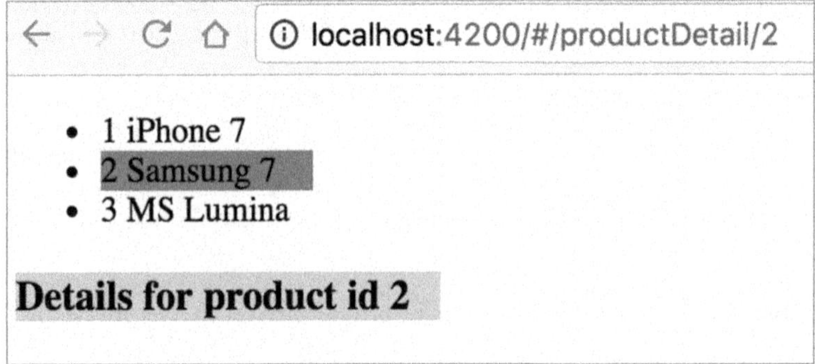

Figure 6.6 Implementing a master-detail scenario

Summary

- Using observable data streams simplifies asynchronous programming. You can subscribe to and unsubscribe from a stream as you need.
- Using the `async` pipe is a preferable way to subscribe to observables.
- The `async` pipe automatically unsubscribes from the observable.
- Using the `switchMap` operator combined with `HttpClient` allows you to easily discard unwanted results of pending HTTP requests.

7 Laying out pages with Flex Layout

This chapter covers

- Implementing responsive web design using the Flex Layout library
- Using the `ObservableMedia` service
- Changing the layout based on the viewport size

When it comes to developing a web app, you need to decide whether you'll have separate apps for desktop and mobile versions or reuse the same code on all devices. The former approach allows you to use the native controls on mobile devices so the UI looks more natural, but you need to maintain separate versions of the code for each app. The latter approach is to use a single code base and implement *responsive web design* (RWD) so the UI layout will adapt to the device screen size.

NOTE The term RWD was coined by Ethan Marcotte in the article "Responsive Web Design," available at http://alistapart.com/article/responsive-web-design.

There's a third approach: in addition to your web application that works on desktops, develop a *hybrid* application, which is a web application that works inside the mobile browser but can invoke the native API of the mobile device too.

In this chapter, you'll see how to make your app look good and be functional on large and small screens using the RWD approach. Chapter 6 covered observables that can push notifications when certain important events happen in your app. Let's see if you can use observables to let you know if the user's screen size changes and change the UI layout based on the width of the viewport of the user's device. Users with smartphones and users with large monitors should see different layouts of the same app.

We'll show you how to use the Flex Layout library for implementing RWD and how to use its `ObservableMedia` service to spare you from writing lots of CSS.

Finally, you'll start rewriting the ngAuction app, illustrating many of the techniques you've learned, with the main goal to remove Bootstrap from the app, using only the Angular Material and Flex Layout libraries.

7.1 Flex Layout and ObservableMedia

Imagine that you've laid out the UI of your application, and it looks great on a user's monitor with a width resolution of 1200 pixels or more. What if the user opens this app on a smartphone with a viewport width of 640 pixels? Depending on the device, it may either render only a part of your app's UI, adding a horizontal bar at the bottom, or scale down the UI so it fits in a small viewport, making the app difficult to use. Or consider another scenario: users with large monitors who reduce the width of their browser window because they need to fit another app on their monitor.

To implement RWD, you can use CSS media queries, represented by the `@media` rule. In the CSS of your app, you can include a set of media queries offering different layouts for various screen widths. The browser constantly checks the current window width, and as soon as the width crosses a *breakpoint* set in the `@media` rules (for example, the width becomes smaller than 640 pixels), a new page layout is applied.

Another way to implement flexible layouts is by using CSS Flexbox with media queries (see http://mng.bz/6B42). The UI of your app is styled as a set of flexible boxes, and if the browser can't fit the Flexbox content horizontally (or vertically), the content is rendered in the next row (or column).

You can also implement RWD with the help of CSS Grid (see http://mng.bz/k29F). Both Flexbox and CSS Grid require a good understanding of `@media` rules.

The Angular Flex Layout library (see https://github.com/angular/flex-layout) is a UI layout engine for implementing RWD without writing media queries in your CSS files. The library provides a set of simple Angular directives that internally apply the rules of the `flexbox` layout and offer you the `ObservableMedia` service that notifies your app about the current width of the viewport on the user's device.

Angular Flex Layout has the following advantages over the standard CSS API:

- It produces cross-browser-compatible CSS.
- It provides an Angular-friendly API for dealing with media queries using directives and observables.

NOTE In this section, we provide a minimal description of the Flex Layout library to get you started quickly. For more details and demos, refer to the Flex Layout documentation at https://github.com/angular/flex-layout/wiki.

The Flex Layout library provides two APIs: static and responsive. The static API allows you to use directives to specify layout attributes for containers and their children. The responsive API enhances static API directives, enabling you to implement RWD so app layouts change for different screen sizes.

7.1.1 *Using Flex Layout directives*

There are two types of directives in the Flex Layout library: one for containers and one for their child elements. A container's directives are used to align its children. Child directives are applied to child elements of a container managed by Flex Layout. With child directives, you can specify the order of each child, the amount of space it takes, and some other properties, as shown in table 7.1.

Table 7.1 Frequently used Flex Layout directives

Directive	Description
Container directives	
`fxLayout`	Instructs the element to use CSS Flexbox for laying out child elements.
`fxLayoutAlign`	Aligns child elements in a particular way (to the left, to the bottom, evenly distribute, and so on). Allowed values depend on the `fxLayout` value attached to the same container element—see Angular Flex Layout documentation.
`fxLayoutGap`	Controls space between child elements.
Child directives	
`fxFlex`	Controls the amount of space a child element takes within the parent container.
`fxFlexAlign`	Allows selectively changing a child's alignment within the parent container prescribed by the `fxLayoutAlign` directive.
`fxFlexOrder`	Allows changing the order of a child element within the parent container. For example, it can be used to move an important component to the visible area when switching from desktop to a mobile screen.

NOTE Child directives expect to be inside an HTML element with a container directive attached.

Let's take a look at how to use the Flex Layout library to align two `<div>` elements next to each other in a row. First, you need to add the Flex Layout library and its peer dependency, `@angular/cdk`, to your project:

```
npm i @angular/flex-layout @angular/cdk
```

The next step is to add the `FlexLayoutModule` to the root `@NgModule()` decorator, as shown in the following listing.

Listing 7.1 Adding the `FlexLayoutModule`

```
import {FlexLayoutModule} from '@angular/flex-layout';

@NgModule({
  imports: [
    FlexLayoutModule
    //...
  ]
})
export class AppModule {}
```

The next listing creates a component that displays the `<div>` elements next to each other from left to right.

Listing 7.2 flex-layout/app.component.ts

```
@Component({
  selector: 'app-root',
  styles: [`
    .parent {height: 100px;}
    .left   {background-color: cyan;}
    .right  {background-color: yellow;}
  `],
  template: `
    <div class="parent" fxLayout="row" >
       <div fxFlex class="left">Left</div>
       <div fxFlex class="right">Right</div>
     </div>
  `
})
export class AppComponent {}
```

The fxLayout directive turns the <div> into a flex-layout container where children are allocated horizontally (in a row).

The fxFlex directive instructs each child element to take equal space within the parent container.

To see this application in action, run the following command:

```
ng serve --app flex-layout -o
```

Figure 7.1 shows how the browser renders the child elements. Each child takes 50% of container's available width.

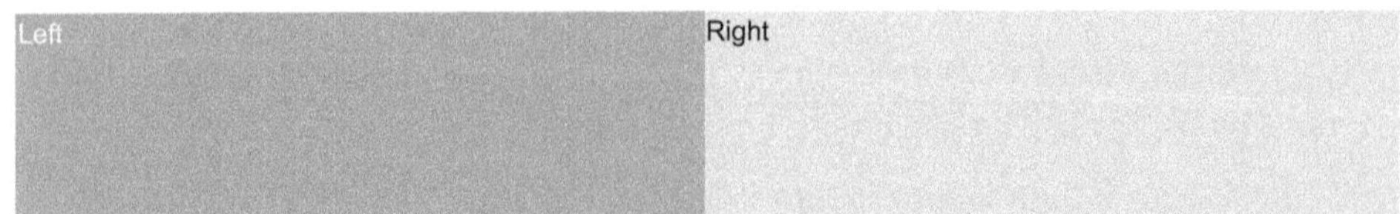

Figure 7.1 Two elements aligned in a row

To make the right div take more space than the left one, you can assign the required space values to the child `fxFlex` directives. The following template uses the child-level directive `fxFlex` to allocate 30% of the available width to the left child and 70% to the right one:

```
<div fxLayout="row" class="parent">
  <div fxFlex="30%" class="left">Left</div>
  <div fxFlex="70%" class="right">Right</div>
</div>
```

Now the UI is rendered as shown in figure 7.2.

Figure 7.2 The right element takes more space than the left one.

To lay out the container's children vertically, change the direction of the container's layout from rows to columns, as in `fxLayout="column"`:

```
<div fxLayout="column" class="parent">
  <div fxFlex="30%" class="left">Left</div>
  <div fxFlex="70%" class="right">Right</div>
</div>
```

Figure 7.3 shows how the child elements are rendered vertically.

Figure 7.3 Column layout of the container element

Say that on a wide screen you have enough room to render your left and right components horizontally next to each other, but if the user opens the same app on a smaller screen, you want to automatically change the layout to vertical so the right component is shown under the left one.

Each directive in the Flex Layout library can optionally have a *suffix* (an alias to the media query rule) that specifies which screen size it has to apply. For example, the `flexLayout.sm` directive has the suffix `.sm`, which means it should be applied only when the screen width is small. These aliases correspond to the width breakpoints defined in the Material Design guidelines (see http://mng.bz/RmLN):

- xs—Extra small (less than 599 px)
- sm—Small (560–959 px)
- md—Medium (960–1279 px)
- lg—Large (1280–1919 px)
- xl—Extra large (1920–5000 px)

The next listing changes your app so its parent container lays out its children horizontally on medium and large screens, and vertically on small devices.

Listing 7.3 Adding the .sm suffix

```
<div class="parent"
        fxLayout="row"                    <- Child elements are aligned in a row by default.
         fxLayout.sm="column" >           <- On small screen sizes, child elements are aligned vertically.
      <div fxFlex="30%" class="left">Left</div>
    <div fxFlex="70%" class="right">Right</div>
  </div>
```

To illustrate how this will change the layout, you'll use Chrome Dev Tools, which has an icon on the left side of its toolbar that allows you to toggle devices. For desktops, the small size means that the width of the window is between 600 and 959 pixels. Figure 7.4 shows how the UI is rendered if the width is 960 (still the medium size).

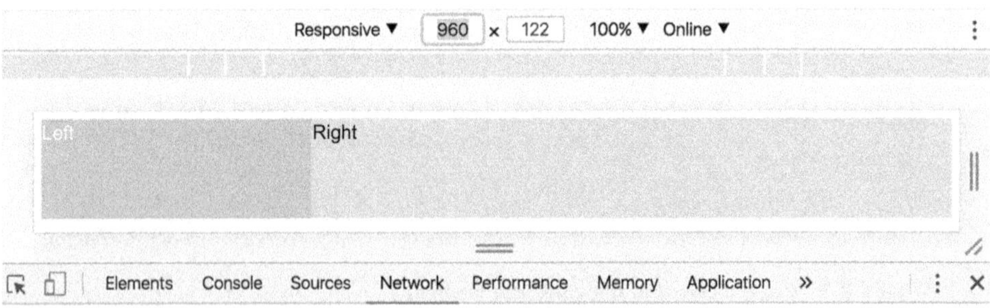

Figure 7.4 Rendering on a medium device with a width of 960 pixels

Let's cross the breakpoint and change the width to 959 to emulate a small device. Figure 7.5 shows that the layout has changed from horizontal to vertical.

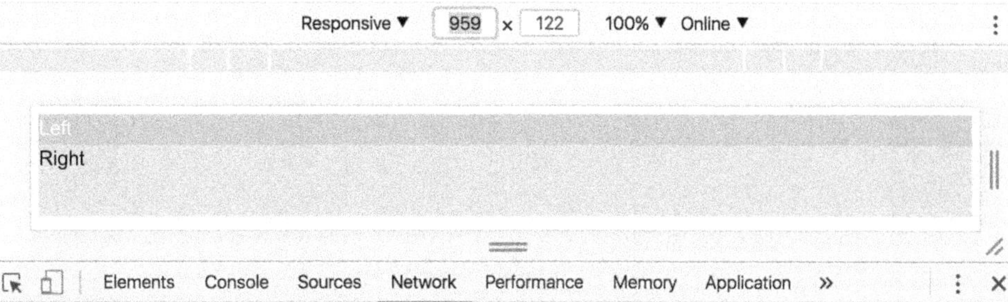

Figure 7.5 Rendering on a small device with a width of 959 pixels

Changing the width to anything smaller than 600 will cause a switch back to the horizontal layout, because you haven't specified that for extra-small devices (the `.xs` suffix), the layout should remain vertical. You can add the vertical layout for extra small (`xs`) devices:

```
<div fxLayout="row" class="parent"
     fxLayout.sm="column"
     fxLayout.xs="column">
```

You can also apply less-than (`lt-`) and greater-than (`>-`) suffixes to the media query aliases. For example, if you use the `lt-md` alias, the respective layout will be applied to the small and extra-small screens. In your app, you can specify that on any screen with a width less than medium, the column layout should be applied:

```
<div fxLayout="row" class="parent"
     fxLayout.lt-md="column">
```

Using breakpoints, you can statically define how your UI should be laid out in the component's template. What if you want not only to change the layout inside the container, but also to conditionally show or hide certain children, depending on the screen size? To dynamically decide what and how the browser should render depending on the screen size, you'll use the `ObservableMedia` service, which comes with the Flex Layout library.

7.1.2 *ObservableMedia service*

The `ObservableMedia` service enables subscribing to screen-size changes and programmatically changing the look and feel of your app. For example, on large screens, you may decide to display additional information. To avoid rendering unnecessary components on small screens, you may subscribe to events emitted by `ObservableMedia`, and if the screen size becomes larger, you can render more components.

To implement this functionality, import the `ObservableMedia` service and subscribe to its `Observable` object. The following listing shows how to subscribe to notifications about screen-size changes with the `async` pipe and print the current size on the console.

Listing 7.4 observable-media/app.component.ts

```
import {Component} from '@angular/core';
import {ObservableMedia} from '@angular/flex-layout';
import {Observable} from 'rxjs';
import {map} from 'rxjs/operators';

@Component({
  selector: 'app-root',
  template: `<h3>Watch the breakpoint activation messages in the console.
  </h3>
  <span *ngIf="showExtras$ | async">        <- Shows/hides text based on the value of showExtras$; the async pipe subscribes to showExtras$
   Showing extra info on medium screens</span>
   `
})
export class AppComponent {
  showExtras$: Observable<boolean>;

  constructor(private media: ObservableMedia) {        <- Injects the ObservableMedia service
     this.showExtras$ = this.media.asObservable()        <- Subscribes to the Observable that emits values when the screen size changes
       .pipe(map(mediaChange => {
           console.log(mediaChange.mqAlias);
           return mediaChange.mqAlias === 'md'? true: false;        <- showExtras$ emits true if the screen is medium.
           })
       );
  }
}
```

NOTE Note the use of the `*ngIf` structural directive. If the `showExtras$` observable emits `true`, the span is added to the DOM. If it emits `false`, the span is removed from the DOM.

The values emitted by `media.asObservable()` have the type `MediaChange` that includes the `mqAlias` property, which holds the value representing the current width—`lg` for large or `md` for medium.

To see listing 7.4 in action, run the following command, and open the browser's console:

```
ng serve --app observable-media -o
```

You'll see the text "Showing extra info on medium screens" when the screen size is `md` (medium). Reduce the width of the browser window to the `sm` size, and this text will be hidden. To see the current CSS media query and other properties of the `mediaChange` class, change the log statement to `console.log(mediaChange);`.

In listing 7.4, you explicitly declared a `showExtras$` observable and subscribed to it because you wanted to monitor `MediaChange`. But this code can be simplified by using the `ObservableMedia.isActive()` API, as shown in the following listing.

Listing 7.5 Using the `ObservableMedia.isActive()` API

```
import {Component} from '@angular/core';
import {ObservableMedia} from '@angular/flex-layout';
```

```
@Component({
  selector: 'app-root',
  template: `<h3>Using the ObservableMedia.isActive() API</h3>
  <span *ngIf="this.media.isActive('md')">         <-- Shows text only if the
    Showing extra info on medium screens</span>        current viewport
  `                                                    width is md
})
export class AppComponent {
  constructor(public media: ObservableMedia) {}
}
```

In the hands-on section later in this chapter, you'll create the new version of ngAuction that will implement RWD using the Flex Layout library and `ObservableMedia`.

> **Other options for implementing RWD**
>
> The Flex Layout library may be appealing to beginners because it's simple to use. But it's not the only solution for creating responsive layouts in Angular apps. Here are some other options:
>
> - The Angular CDK (component development kit) package includes the layout module. After installing the `@angular/cdk` package, you can use the `LayoutModule` and `BreakpointObserver` or `MediaMatcher` classes that monitor changes in the viewport size. Besides, because Angular CDK is a peer dependency of Flex Layout, by working directly with Angular CDK, you'll use one library instead of two.
> - At the time of writing, the Flex Layout library remains in beta, and its creators often introduce breaking changes with new beta releases. If you're not using the latest version of Angular, Flex Layout may not support the version of Angular you use. For example, the Flex Layout library doesn't support Angular 4.
>
> To minimize the number of libraries used in your app, consider implementing RWD by using CSS Flexbox and CSS Grid. Also, using CSS that's natively supported by the browser will always be more performant than using any JavaScript library. We recommend the free CSS Grid video course by Wes Bos, available at https://cssgrid.io.

7.2 Hands-on: Rewriting ngAuction

Starting in this chapter, you'll rewrite ngAuction from scratch. The new ngAuction will be written using Angular Material from the get-go and will include images, not just the grey rectangles. The search component will be represented by a small icon on the toolbar, and you'll add shopping cart functionality. Users will be able to bid on products and buy them if they place winning bids.

7.2.1 Why rewrite the ngAuction app from scratch?

You may be thinking, "We already worked on ngAuction in chapters 2, 3, and 5. Why not just continue building the same app?" In the first chapters, the goal was to gently introduce you to the main artifacts of the Angular framework without overloading you with information on application architecture, implementing RWD, and customizing themes.

The ngAuction app developed in the previous chapters served that goal well. This rewrite will showcase the best development practices for real-world Angular applications. You want to accomplish the following:

- Create a modularized app where each view is a lazy-loaded module.
- Use Angular Material for the UI, illustrating theme customization with SaaS.
- Use the Flex Layout library.
- Remove the dependency on the Bootstrap and JQuery libraries.
- Remove the search box from the landing page to make better use of screen space.
- Keep shared components and services in a separate folder.
- Illustrate state management using injectable services and then reimplement it using the NgRx library.
- Create scripts for unit and end-to-end testing.

You're not going to implement all of that in this chapter, but you'll get started.

In this app, you'll implement RWD using the Flex Layout library and its `ObservableMedia` service, introduced earlier. On large screens, the landing page of ngAuction will display four products per row, as shown in figure 7.6.

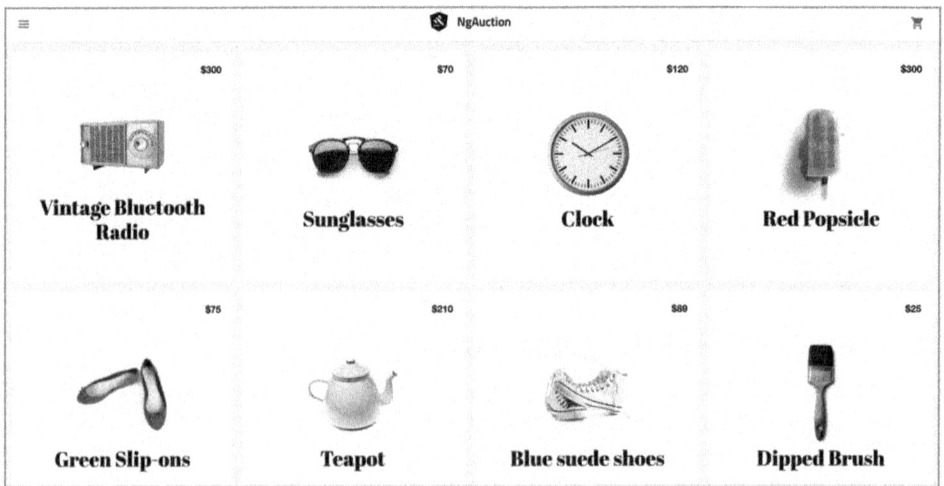

Figure 7.6 Rendering ngAuction on large screens

NOTE We borrowed the data and images from the Google app illustrating the Polymer library (see http://mng.bz/Y5d9).

The app will be subscribed to the `ObservableMedia` service using the `async` pipe and will automatically change the layout to three products per row as soon as the width of the window changes to a medium size, as shown in figure 7.7.

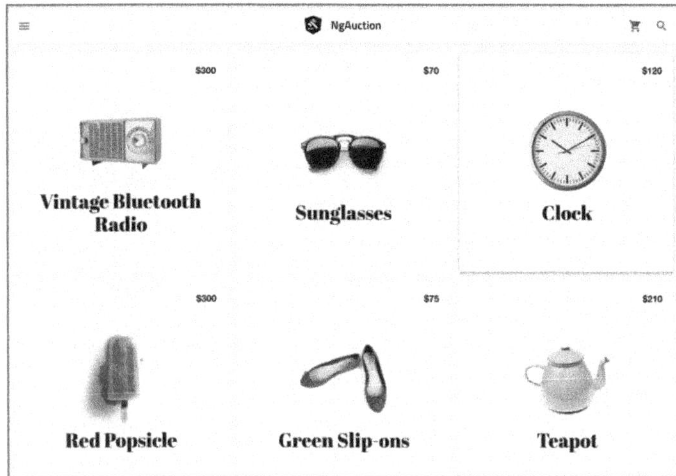

Figure 7.7 Rendering ngAuction on medium screens

On small screens, the app will change to the two-column layout, as shown in figure 7.8.

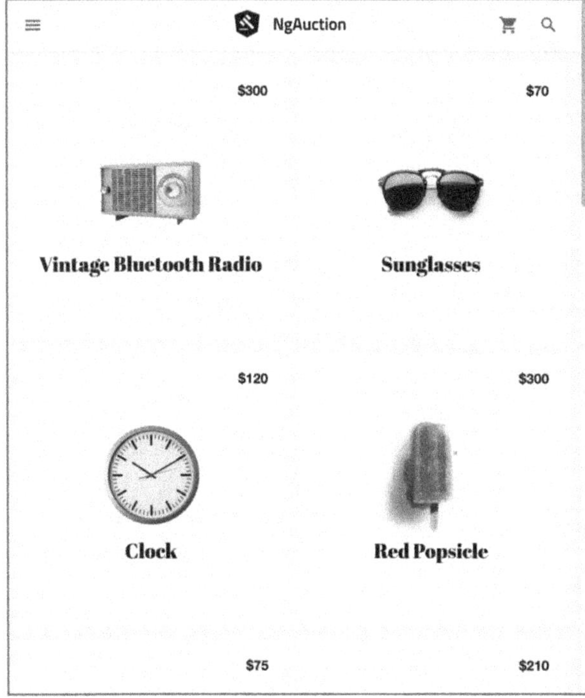

Figure 7.8 Rendering ngAuction on small screens

The app will also change its layout when rendered on extra-small (one-column layout) and extra-large screens (five-column layout).

7.2.2 Generating a new ngAuction app

NOTE Source code for this chapter can be found at https://github.com/Farata/angulartypescript and www.manning.com/books/angular-development-with-typescript-second-edition.

This time, you'll generate the project using the Angular CLI `new` command with options. The new ngAuction will use the Sass preprocessor for styles with the SCSS syntax. You also want to specify the `nga-` prefix, so each newly generated component will have this prefix in its selector:

```
ng new ng-auction --prefix nga --style scss
```

NOTE We discuss the benefits of using SCSS in the next section, "Creating a custom Angular Material theme with Sass."

Change to the ng-auction directory and run the following commands to add Angular Material and Flex Layout libraries to the project:

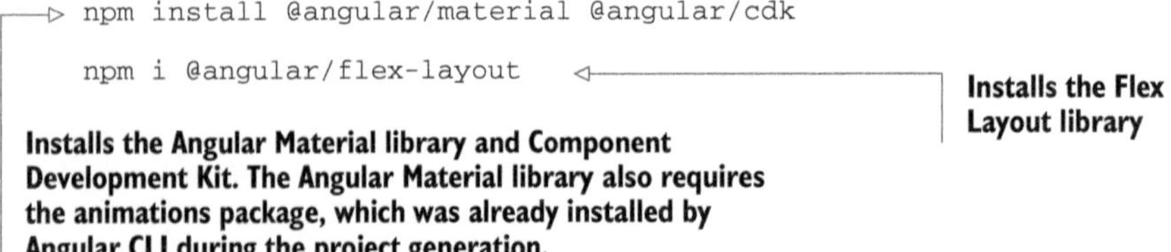

```
npm install @angular/material @angular/cdk

npm i @angular/flex-layout
```

Installs the Angular Material library and Component Development Kit. The Angular Material library also requires the animations package, which was already installed by Angular CLI during the project generation.
Installs the Flex Layout library

The Angular Material library comes with four prebuilt themes, and you had a chance to try one of them in section 5.6.1 in chapter 5. But what if none of the prebuilt themes fits your UI requirements?

7.2.3 Creating a custom Angular Material theme with Sass

If you want to create a custom Angular Material theme for your app, read the Theming Guide at https://material.angular.io/guide/theming. In this section, we'll just give you a code review of the .scss files that we created to customize the theme for ngAuction.

When you generated the ngAuction app, you used the option `--style scss`. By doing so, you informed Angular CLI that you're not going to use CSS files, but instead will use the Syntactically Awesome Style Sheets, also known as Sass (see http://sass-lang.com). Sass is an extension to CSS with its own preprocessor. Some Sass benefits include the following:

- *Variables*—Assigning styles to variables and reusing them in multiple stylesheets
- *Nesting*—An easy-to-write and -read syntax for nested CSS selectors
- *Mixins*—Blocks of styles that can include variables

Sass provides two syntaxes, Sass and SCSS, and you'll use the latter in this book. If you were installing SaaS separately, you'd need to run your .scss files through the preprocessor to compile them into regular .css files before deployment. But Angular CLI supports Sass out of the box, so the preprocessor does its job during bundling.

SCSS syntax

Here's a quick introduction to SCSS syntax:

- *Variables*—A variable name starts with the dollar sign. The following code snippet declares and uses the variable `$font-stack`:

  ```
  $font-stack: Helvetica, sans-serif;

  body {
    font: 100% $font-stack;
  }
  ```

  This variable can be used in multiple places, and if you decide to change the Helvetica font to another one, you do it in one place instead of making changes in each and every .css file where you used it.
- *Nesting*—It's an easy-to-read syntax for writing nested CSS selectors. The following sample shows how to nest the `ul` and `a` style selectors inside the `div` selector:

  ```
  div {
    ul {
      margin: 0;
    }
    a {
      display: block;
    }
  }
  ```
- *Mixins*—A mixin is a block of Sass style. A mixin can be added to your styles with `@include`. Mixins can also use variables and can be invoked as functions with arguments, as in `mat-palette($mat-red);`.
- *Partials*—Partials are just files with code fragments meant to be imported by other Sass files. Partials must have names that start with an underscore, such as _theme.scss. When you import a partial, the underscore isn't needed, as in `@import './theme';` Partials aren't compiled into separate CSS files—their content is compiled only as a part of .scss files that import them.
- *Imports*—The `@import` statement allows you to import styles located in other files. Although CSS also has an `@import` keyword, it makes an additional HTTP request for each file. With Sass, all imports are combined into a single CSS file during preprocessing, so only one HTTP request is needed to load the CSS.

In your ngAuction app, you'll create the styles directory, move the generated styles.scss file there, and add one more partial, _theme.scss. The content of _theme.scss is shown in the following listing. You use the `$mat-cyan` palette defined in the imported file _theming.scss.

Listing 7.6 _theme.scss

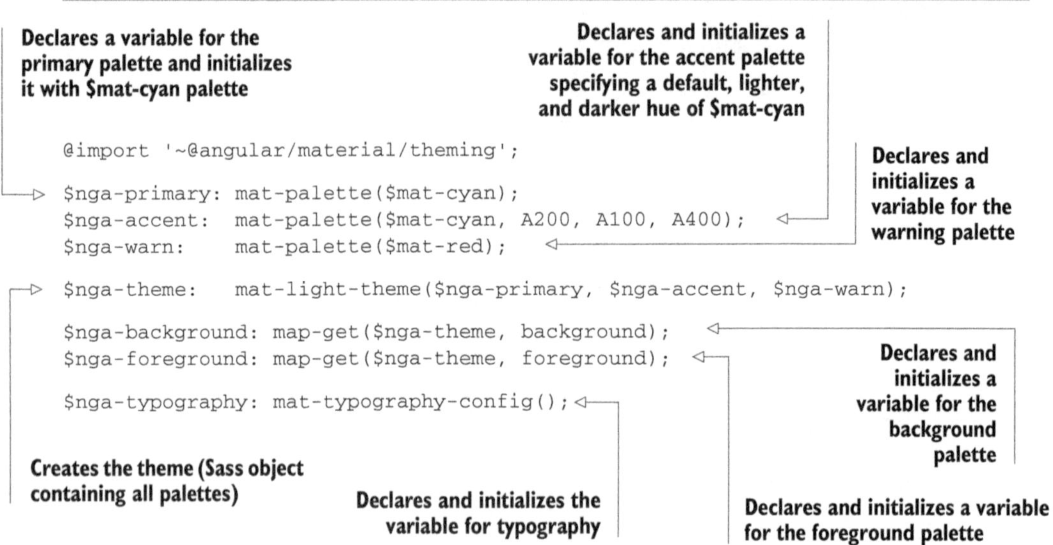
Declares a variable for the primary palette and initializes it with $mat-cyan palette
Declares and initializes a variable for the accent palette specifying a default, lighter, and darker hue of $mat-cyan
Declares and initializes a variable for the warning palette
Declares and initializes a variable for the background palette
Creates the theme (Sass object containing all palettes)
Declares and initializes the variable for typography
Declares and initializes a variable for the foreground palette

```
@import '~@angular/material/theming';

$nga-primary: mat-palette($mat-cyan);
$nga-accent:  mat-palette($mat-cyan, A200, A100, A400);
$nga-warn:    mat-palette($mat-red);

$nga-theme:   mat-light-theme($nga-primary, $nga-accent, $nga-warn);

$nga-background: map-get($nga-theme, background);
$nga-foreground: map-get($nga-theme, foreground);

$nga-typography: mat-typography-config();
```

In the _theme.scss file, you used the cyan color for the primary and accent palettes. You can find their definitions in node_modules/@angular/material/_theming.scss.

In the following listing, you add styles in styles.scss, starting from importing the preceding _theme.scss.

Listing 7.7 styles.scss

```
@import './theme';

@import url('https://fonts.googleapis.com/icon?family=Material+Icons');   ①
 @import url('https://fonts.googleapis.com/css?family=Titillium+Web:600');   ②
 @import url('https://fonts.googleapis.com/css?family=Abril+Fatface');   ③

// Be sure that you only ever include this mixin once!
@include mat-core();   ④

@include angular-material-theme($nga-theme);   ⑤

// Global styles.
html {
  -moz-osx-font-smoothing: grayscale;
  -webkit-font-smoothing: antialiased;
  -webkit-box-sizing: border-box;
  -moz-box-sizing: border-box;
```

① Imports Google Material icons

② Imports the Titillium Web fonts (you'll use it for the toolbar title and later for bid values)

③ Imports the Abril Fatface fonts (you'll use it for product titles)

④ Imports Angular Material core styles that aren't theme-dependent

⑤ Loads your custom theme configured in _theme.scss

```
  box-sizing: border-box;
  height: 100%;
}

body {
  color: #212121;
  background-color: #f3f3f3;
  font-family: mat-font-family($nga-typography);
  line-height: mat-line-height($nga-typography, body-1);
  font-size: mat-font-size($nga-typography, body-1);
  height: 100%;
  margin: 0;
}
```

The styles.scss and _theme.scss files define your global styles for the entire app, and you'll specify them in the `styles` property in the .angular-cli.json file. In ngAuction, you'll also be styling individual components, and _theme.scss will be reused in each component. We've intentionally broken the style definition into two files so you can reuse _theme.scss (just the variables definitions) in components without duplicating the core styles, images, and fonts used in styles.scss.

Now your custom theme is configured, and you can start working on the UI of the landing page of ngAuction.

7.2.4 Adding a toolbar to the top-level component

Figure 7.6 shows the landing page of ngAuction, which includes the Material toolbar and the `HomeComponent`. To be more precise, it includes the toolbar and a `<router-outlet>` tag where you render the `HomeComponent`. Let's start with creating the first version of the toolbar. This toolbar will include the menu icon on the left, the logo of ngAuction in the middle, and the shopping cart icon on the right. It won't include the Search button (you'll add that in section 11.8 in chapter 11) and will look like figure 7.9.

Figure 7.9 The toolbar

On the left, you use the Google Material icon `menu`, and on the right, `shopping_cart`. For the logo, you place the Google Material `gavel` icon on top of the shape resembling the Angular logo, and save it in the logo.svg file, included with the book's source code.

As you learned in the hands-on section of chapter 5, to use Angular Material components, you should include the corresponding modules in the `imports` section of the root module of your app. In your toolbar, you'll need `MatToolbarModule`, `MatButtonModule`, and `MatIconModule`. Since you're going to use the Flex Layout library, you'll also need to add `FlexLayoutModule` to the root module. Later in this section, you'll use `HttpClient` to read the product data, so you need to add the `HttpClientModule` to the root module.

Update the CLI-generated app.module.ts to include the modules in the following listing.

Listing 7.8 app.module.ts

```
import {BrowserModule} from '@angular/platform-browser';
import {NgModule} from '@angular/core';
import {MatButtonModule} from '@angular/material/button';
import {MatIconModule} from '@angular/material/icon';
import {MatToolbarModule} from '@angular/material/toolbar';
import {FlexLayoutModule} from '@angular/flex-layout';
import {HttpClientModule} from '@angular/common/http';
import {AppComponent} from './app.component';

@NgModule({
  declarations: [
    AppComponent
  ],
  imports: [
    BrowserModule,
    MatButtonModule,
     MatIconModule,
     MatToolbarModule,
     FlexLayoutModule,
     HttpClientModule
   ],
  providers: [],
  bootstrap: [AppComponent]
})
export class AppModule {}
```

- Adds the required modules from the Angular Material library (MatButtonModule, MatIconModule, MatToolbarModule)
- Adds the Flex Layout module (FlexLayoutModule)
- Adds HttpClientModule—you'll use HttpClient for getting the product data (HttpClientModule)

Replace the generated app.component.html with the following listing.

Listing 7.9 app.component.html

```
<mat-toolbar class="toolbar">
  <button class="toolbar__icon-button" mat-icon-button>
     <mat-icon>menu</mat-icon>
  </button>

  <div class="toolbar__logo-title-group"
       fxLayout
       fxLayoutAlign="center center">
    <a routerLink="/"
       fxLayout>
     <img class="toolbar__logo"
          src="/assets/logo.svg"
          alt="NgAuction Logo">
   </a>
   <a class="toolbar__title"
       routerLink="/">NgAuction</a>
  </div>
```

- The menu button with the icon (`<button class="toolbar__icon-button" mat-icon-button>`)
- Displays the logo in the center of the toolbar (`<div class="toolbar__logo-title-group" …>`)
- Turns the logo into a clickable link that will display HomeComponent after you configure routes (`<a routerLink="/" …>`)
- Turns the text ngAuction into a clickable link (`<a class="toolbar__title" …>`)

```
<div fxFlex></div>

<button mat-icon-button class="toolbar__icon-button
                  toolbar__shopping-cart-button">
  <mat-icon>shopping_cart</mat-icon>
</button>

</mat-toolbar>

<!--<router-outlet></router-outlet>-->
```

A filler to push the shopping cart icon to the right

The shopping cart button with an icon

You'll keep the router outlet commented out until you configure routes.

To make the toolbar look like figure 7.9, you need to add the following listing's styling to the app.component.scss file.

Listing 7.10 app.component.scss

```
@import '../styles/theme';

:host {
   display: block;
  height: 100%;
}

.toolbar {
   background-color: mat-color($nga-background, card);
  position: relative;
  box-shadow: 0 1px mat-color($nga-foreground, divider);
}

.toolbar__logo-title-group {
   position: absolute;
  right: 50%;
  left: 50%;
}

.toolbar__logo {
   height: 32px;
  margin-right: 16px;
}

.toolbar__title {
   color: mat-color($nga-foreground, text);
  font-family: 'Titillium Web', sans-serif;
  font-weight: 600;
  text-decoration: none;
}

.toolbar__icon-button {
   color: mat-color($nga-foreground, icon);
}

.toolbar__shopping-cart-button {
   margin-right: 8px;
}
```

Imports your custom theme

Uses Angular pseudo selector :host to style the component that hosts the AppComponent

Applies the same background as in the Material card component in this theme (it's white in your theme)

Styles the logo name

Styles the logo image

Styles the toolbar title

Styles the icon foreground

Styles the shopping cart button

Running the `ng serve` command will render the ngAuction app that looks like figure 7.9.

You have a toolbar UI rendered, and now you need to show products under the toolbar. First, you need to create the `ProductService` that will provide the product data, and then you'll create the `HomeComponent` that will render the data. Let's start with the `ProductService`.

7.2.5 Creating the product service

The product service needs data. In real-world apps, the data would be supplied by the server, and you'll do that in chapter 12. For now, you'll just use the JSON file that contains the information about the product. The product images will be located on the client side as well. The code samples that come with the book include the src/data/products.json file, of which a fragment is shown in the following listing.

Listing 7.11 A fragment from src/data/products.json

```
[
  {
    "id": 1,
    "description" : "Isn't it cool when things look old, but they're not...",
    "imageUrl" : "data/img/radio.png",
    "price" : 300,
    "title" : "Vintage Bluetooth Radio"
  },
  {
    "id": 2,
    "description" : "Be an optimist. Carry Sunglasses with you at all times..
    .",
    "featured" : true,
    "imageUrl" : "data/img/sunnies.png",
    "price" : 70,
    "title" : "Sunglasses"
  }
  ...
  ]
```

This file includes URLs of the product images located in the data/img folder. If you're following along and are trying to build ngAuction by yourself, copy the src/data directory into your project from the code that comes with the book and add the line `"data"` to the app property `assets` in the .angular-cli.json file.

You'll use the `ProductService` class in more than one component; you'll generate it in the folder src/app/shared/services. You'll be adding other reusable services in this folder later on (such as `SearchService`). You'll generate `ProductService` using the following Angular CLI command:

```
ng generate service shared/services/product
```

Then you'll add the provider for this service to the app.module:

```
...
import {ProductService} from './shared/services/product.service';

@NgModule({
  ...
  providers: [ProductService]
})
export class AppModule {}
```

Best practice

The import statement for `ProductService` is rather long, and it points at the file where this service is implemented. As your application grows, the number of services as well as the number of import statements in your module increases, polluting the module code.

Create the file named index.ts in the services folder like so:

```
import {Product, ProductService} from './product.service';

export {Product, ProductService} from './product.service';
```

You import the `Product` and `ProductService` classes and reexport them right away. Now the import statement in the app.module can be simplified to look like this:

```
import {Product, ProductService} from './shared/services';
```

If you have just one reexported class, this may look like overkill. But if you have multiple classes in the services folder, you can write just one import statement for all classes, functions, or variables that you want to import—for example:

```
import { ProductService, Product, SearchService } from './shared/services';
```

Keep in mind, this will work only if the file with such reexports is called index.ts.

The product.service.ts file includes the `Product` interface and the `ProductService` class. The `Product` interface defines the type of objects returned by the methods of the `ProductService` class: `getAll ()` and `getById ()`. The code for your `ProductService` is shown in the following listing.

Listing 7.12 product.service.ts

```
import {Injectable} from '@angular/core';
import {HttpClient} from '@angular/common/http';
import {Observable} from 'rxjs';
import {map} from 'rxjs/operators';

export interface Product {        <-- Defines the Product type
   id: number;
  title: string;
  price: number;
  imageUrl: string;
```

```
  description: string;
}

@Injectable()
export class ProductService {
  constructor(private http: HttpClient) {}     // Injects the HttpClient object

  getAll(): Observable<Product[]> {     // This function declares an Observable that can return all Product objects.
     return this.http.get<Product[]>('/data/products.json');
  }

  getById(productId: number): Observable<Product> {     // This function declares an Observable that can return products by ID.
     return this.http.get<Product[]>('/data/products.json')
  .pipe(
    map(products => <Product>products.find(p => p.id === productId)); // map() finds the product ID that matches the function argument.
   )
  }
}
```

Because you don't have a real data server, both methods read the entire products.json file, and the `getById()` method also applies `find ()` to the array of products to find the one with a matching ID.

> **Best practice**
>
> You defined the type `Product` as an interface and not a class. Because JavaScript doesn't support interfaces, the compiled code won't include `Product`. If you were to define `Product` as a class, the TypeScript compiler would turn the `Product` class into either a JavaScript function or a class and would include it in the executable code. Defining types as TypeScript interfaces instead of classes reduces the size of the runnable code.

In the next section, you'll create the feature module that will include `HomeComponent`—the first consumer of the `ProductService`.

7.2.6 Creating the home module

You want to create each view as a feature module. This will allow you to lazy load them, and the code of each view will be built as a separate bundle. Generate a feature home module as follows:

```
ng generate module home
```

This command will create a src/app/home directory containing the home.module.ts file with the content shown in the following listing.

Listing 7.13 home.module.ts

```
import {NgModule} from '@angular/core';
import {CommonModule} from '@angular/common';

@NgModule({
  imports: [
    CommonModule
  ],
  declarations: []
})
export class HomeModule {}
```

You can generate the home component with the following command:

```
ng generate component home
```

After running this command, Angular CLI will print the message that four files were generated (the home component) and one file was updated (the home module)—the `HomeComponent` was added to the `declarations` section in the `@NgModule` decorator of the module:

```
create src/app/home/home.component.scss (0 bytes)
create src/app/home/home.component.html (23 bytes)
create src/app/home/home.component.spec.ts (614 bytes)
create src/app/home/home.component.ts (262 bytes)
update src/app/home/home.module.ts (251 bytes)
```

You'll use the Flex Layout library in this module, so you want to configure the default route so that it renders `HomeComponent`. Also, you're going to display products using the `<mat-grid-list>` component from the Angular Material library. Add the required code to home.module.ts so it looks like the following listing.

Listing 7.14 modified home.module.ts

```
import {NgModule} from '@angular/core';
import {CommonModule} from '@angular/common';
import {RouterModule} from '@angular/router';
import {FlexLayoutModule} from '@angular/flex-layout';
import {MatGridListModule} from '@angular/material/grid-list';
import {HomeComponent} from './home.component';

@NgModule({
  imports: [
    CommonModule,
    RouterModule.forChild([          <- Adds the route configuration for your feature module
       {path: '', component: HomeComponent}
    ]),
    FlexLayoutModule,                <- Adds the Flex Layout library
     MatGridListModule               <- Adds the Angular Material module required by <mat-grid-list>
   ],
  declarations: [HomeComponent]
})
export class HomeModule {}
```

The next step is to update the `HomeComponent` in the generated home.component.ts file. You'll inject two services into this component: `ProductService` and `ObservableMedia`. You'll invoke the `getAll()` method on `ProductService` to get product data. `ObservableMedia` will be watching the viewport width to change the UI layout accordingly. To be more specific, the product data will be shown in a grid, and the `ObservableMedia` service will change the number of columns in the grid from one to five, based on the current viewport width. The code of the `HomeComponent` is shown in the next listing.

Listing 7.15 home.component.ts

```
import {Observable} from 'rxjs';
import {map} from 'rxjs/operators';

import {Component} from '@angular/core';
import {ObservableMedia} from '@angular/flex-layout';
import {Product, ProductService} from '../shared/services';

@Component({
  selector: 'nga-home',
  styleUrls: [ './home.component.scss' ],
  templateUrl: './home.component.html'
})
export class HomeComponent {
  readonly columns$: Observable<number>;
   readonly products$: Observable<Product[]>;

  readonly breakpointsToColumnsNumber = new Map([
    [ 'xs', 1 ],
    [ 'sm', 2 ],
    [ 'md', 3 ],
    [ 'lg', 4 ],
    [ 'xl', 5 ],
  ]);

  constructor(private media: ObservableMedia,
              private productService: ProductService) {
     this.products$ = this.productService.getAll();

    this.columns$ = this.media.asObservable()
      .pipe(
       map(mc => <number>this.breakpointsToColumnsNumber.get(mc.mqAlias))
      );
  }
}
```

- An observable to supply the number of columns in the grid
- An observable of products
- Maps the media query alias to the number of columns in the grid
- Injects ObservableMedia and ProductService
- Gets data about all products
- Turns the ObservableMedia object into an Observable
- Gets the number of the grid column based on the emitted media query alias; <number> means casting from object to number

The `getAll()` method on `ProductService` initializes the `product$` variable of type `Observable`. You don't see the invocation of the `subscribe()` method here, because you'll use the async pipe in the template of the home component.

The role of `ObservableMedia` is to send the media query alias to the component, indicating the current width of the user's device viewport. This width may be changing if the viewport is a window in the browser and the user resizes it. If the user runs this app on a smartphone, the width of the viewport won't change, but `HomeComponent` needs to know it anyway to render the grid of products.

Now you need to replace the generated template in home.component.html with the markup to display products in a grid of rows and columns. For the grid, you'll use the `<mat-grid-list>` component from the Angular Material library. The content of each grid cell will be rendered in a `<mat-grid-tile>` component.

In this template, you'll use the `async` pipe twice. The first `async` pipe will subscribe to the observable that emits the number of columns in a grid, and the second pipe will subscribe to the observable that emits product data. The code of the home.component .html file is shown in the following listing.

Listing 7.16 home.component.html

```
<div class="grid-list-container">
  <mat-grid-list [cols]="columns$ | async"
                 gutterSize="16">
    <mat-grid-tile class="tile" *ngFor="let product of products$ | async">
      <a class="tile__content"
         fxLayout="column"
        fxLayoutAlign="center center"
        [routerLink]="['/products', product.id]">

        <span class="tile__price-tag"
              ngClass.xs="tile__price-tag--xs">
          {{ product.price | currency:'USD':'symbol':'.0' }}
        </span>

        <div class="tile__thumbnail"
             [ngStyle]="{'background-
    image': 'url(' + product.imageUrl + ')'}"></div>

        <div class="tile__title"
             ngClass.xs="tile__title--xs"
             ngClass.sm="tile__title--sm">{{ product.title }}</div>
      </a>
    </mat-grid-tile>
  </mat-grid-list>
</div>
```

Subscribes to the number of columns and binds it to the cols property of <mat-grid-list>

Renders a <mat-grid-tile> for each product using the data from the products$ observable

Wraps the content of each tile in the <a> tag to turn the tile into a clickable link

Clicking on the tile will navigate to the path /products, passing the selected product's id as a parameter.

For extra-small viewports, adds the styles defined in tile__price-tag--xs

NOTE Navigation to the product-detail screen isn't implemented in this version of ngAuction. Clicking the product tile will result in an error in the browser console.

We'd like to explain the last annotation in listing 7.16 a bit more. That `<span>` element is styled as defined in `tile__price-tag`, but if the size of the viewport becomes extra small (`xs`), the Flex Layout `ngClass.xs` directive will add the styles defined in `tile__price-tag--xs`. If you compare the definitions of the `tile__price-tag` and `tile__price-tag--xs` styles in listing 7.17, you see that merging these two styles would mean changing the font size from 16 px to 14 px.

TIP We use the symbols __ and -- in naming some styles, as recommended by the block, element, modifier (BEM) methodology (see http://getbem.com).

To complete the `HomeComponent`, you need to add some styles in home.component .scss.

Listing 7.17 home.component.scss

```
@import '../../styles/theme';        <-- Imports your customized theme

:host {
  display: block;
}

.grid-list-container {
  margin: 16px;
}

.tile {
  background-color: mat-color($nga-background, card);   <-- Makes the tile background color the same as the Angular Material card (white)

  &:hover {
    @include mat-elevation(4);    <-- If the user hovers over the tile, elevates the tile to level 4 by adding the shadow effect (returned by the mat-elevation mixin)
     transition: .3s;
  }
}

.tile__content {
  display: block;
  height: 100%;
  width: 100%;
  padding: 16px;
  position: relative;
  text-align: center;
  text-decoration: none;
}

.tile__price-tag {    <-- Default style for the product price tag
   color: mat-color($nga-foreground, text);
  font-size: 16px;
  font-weight: 700;
  position: absolute;
  right: 20px;
  top: 20px;
}

.tile__price-tag--xs {    <-- Style for the product price tag for extra-small viewports
   font-size: 14px;
```

```
}

.tile__thumbnail {
  background: no-repeat 50% 50%;
  background-size: contain;
  height: 50%;
  width: 50%;
}

.tile__title {                          <-- Default style for the product title
   color: mat-color($nga-foreground, text);
  font-family: 'Abril Fatface', cursive;
  font-size: mat-font-size($nga-typography, display-1);   <-- As per Material Design spec, uses Display 1 for font styles instead of specifying the hardcoded size
   line-height: mat-line-height($nga-typography, display-1);
}

.tile__title--
     sm {                               <-- Style for the product title for small viewports
   font-size: mat-font-size($nga-typography, headline);
  line-height: mat-line-height($nga-typography, headline);
}

.tile__title--xs {                      <-- Style for the product title for extra-small viewports
   font-size: mat-font-size($nga-typography, title);
  line-height: mat-line-height($nga-typography, title);
}
```

The `HomeComponent` is ready. What do you need to do to render it under the toolbar?

7.2.7 Configuring routes

In the beginning of this hands-on exercise, we stated that each view on ngAuction will be a separate module, and you created the `HomeComponent` as a module. Now you need to configure the route for this module. Create an src/app/app.routing.ts file with the following content:

```
import {Route} from '@angular/router';

export const routes: Route[] = [
  {
    path: '',
    loadChildren: './home/home.module#HomeModule'
  }
];
```

As you see, you use the syntax for lazy-loaded modules, as explained in section 4.3 in chapter 4. You to load this configuration in app.module.ts by invoking `Router .forRoot()`:

```
...
import {RouterModule} from '@angular/router';
import {routes} from './app.routing';

@NgModule({
  ...
  imports: [
```

```
    ...
    RouterModule.forRoot(routes)
  ]
  ...
})
export class AppModule { }
```

The last step is to uncomment the last line in app.component.html that has the `<router-outlet>` tag, so the app component template is laid out as follows:

```
<mat-toolbar>...</mat-toolbar>

<router-outlet></router-outlet>
```

The coding part of the landing page is done.

7.2.8 Running ngAuction

The first version of the new ngAuction is ready, so let's build the dev bundles and see how it looks in the browser. Running `ng serve` produces the output shown in figure 7.10.

```
chunk {home.module} home.module.chunk.js, home.module.chunk.js.map () 46.7 kB {main}  [rendered]
chunk {inline} inline.bundle.js, inline.bundle.js.map (inline) 5.83 kB [entry] [rendered]
chunk {main} main.bundle.js, main.bundle.js.map (main) 15 kB {vendor} [initial] [rendered]
chunk {polyfills} polyfills.bundle.js, polyfills.bundle.js.map (polyfills) 217 kB {inline} [initial] [rendered]
chunk {styles} styles.bundle.js, styles.bundle.js.map (styles) 68.4 kB {inline} [initial] [rendered]
chunk {vendor} vendor.bundle.js, vendor.bundle.js.map (vendor) 3.37 MB [initial] [rendered]
```

Figure 7.10 Bundling ngAuction with `ng serve`

Note the first line: Angular CLI placed the home module in a separate bundle. It did that because in configuring routes, you used the syntax for lazy-loaded modules, but when you open the browser at http://localhost:4200, you'll see that the home module was loaded, as shown in figure 7.11.

The home module was eagerly loaded because it was configured as a default route (mapped to an empty path). The landing page of ngAuction is ready, except it doesn't have the Search button on the toolbar. You'll add it in section 11.8 in chapter 11.

> **TIP** If you click on any of the product tiles, the browser console shows an error, as in "Cannot match any routes. URL Segment: 'products/2'." This error will disappear in chapter 9's version of ngAuction, after you develop the product-detail page.

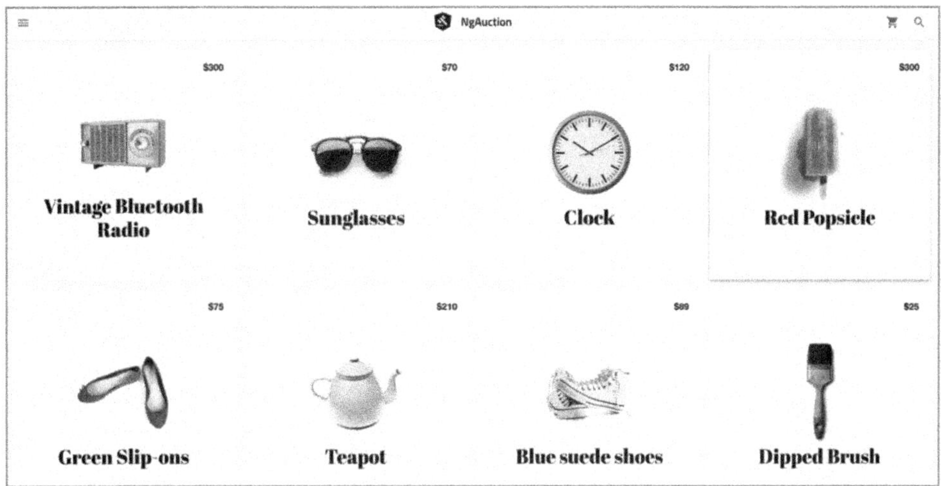

Figure 7.11 Running ngAuction

Summary

- You can keep a single code base of the web app that will adopt its UI based on the available width of the user device.
- The Flex Layout library allows you to subscribe to notifications about viewport width changes and apply the respective UI layout.
- The Flex Layout library includes the `ObservableMedia` class, which can notify you about the current width of the viewport, sparing you from writing CSS for this purpose.

8 Implementing component communications

This chapter covers

- Creating loosely coupled components
- How a parent component should pass data to its child, and vice versa
- Implementing the Mediator design pattern for component communication

An Angular application is a tree of views represented by components. While designing components, you need to ensure that they're self-contained and at the same time have some means of communicating with each other. In this chapter, we'll focus on how components can pass data to each other in a loosely coupled manner.

First, we'll show you how a parent component can pass data to its children by binding to their input properties. Then, you'll see how a child component can send data to its parent by emitting events via its output properties.

We'll continue with an example that applies the Mediator design pattern to arrange data exchange between components that don't have parent-child relationships. Mediator is probably the most important design pattern in any component-based framework.

8.1 Intercomponent communication

Figure 8.1 shows a view that consists of components that are numbered and have different shapes for easier reference. Some of the components contain other components (let's call the outer ones *containers*), and others are peers. To abstract this from any particular UI framework, we've avoided using HTML elements like input fields, drop-downs, and buttons, but you can extrapolate this into a view of your real-world application.

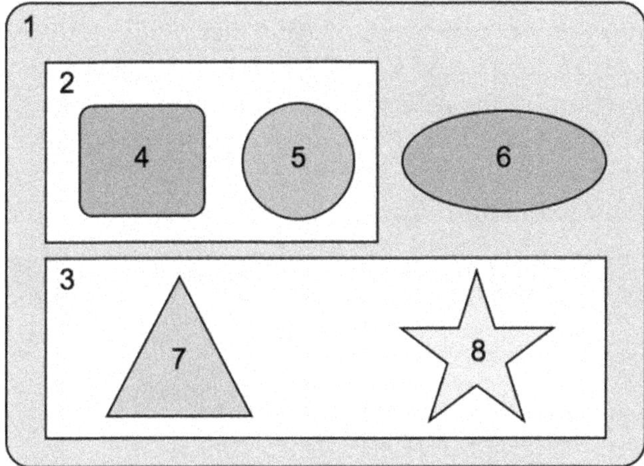

Figure 8.1 A view consists of components.

When you design a view that consists of multiple components, the less they know about each other, the better. Say a user clicks the button in component 4, which has to initiate some actions in component 5. Is it possible to implement this scenario without component 4 knowing that component 5 exists? Yes, it is.

You've seen already examples of loosely coupling components by using dependency injection. Now we'll show you a different technique for achieving the same goal by using bindings and events.

8.2 Input and output properties

Think of an Angular component as a black box with outlets. Some of them are marked as `@Input()`,and others are marked as `@Output()`. You can create a component with as many inputs and outputs as you want.

If an Angular component needs to receive values from the outside world, you can bind the producers of these values to the corresponding inputs of the component. Who are they received from? The component doesn't have to know. The component just needs to know what to do with these values when they're provided.

If a component needs to communicate values to the outside world, it can *emit events* through its output properties. Whom are they emitted to? The component doesn't have to know. Whoever is interested can subscribe to the events that a component emits.

Let's implement these loosely coupled principles. First, you'll create an `OrderProcessorComponent` that can receive order requests from its parent component.

8.2.1 Input properties

The input properties of a component annotated with the `@Input()` decorator are used to get data from the parent component. Imagine that you want to create a UI component for placing orders to buy stocks. It will know how to connect to the stock exchange, but that's irrelevant in the context of this discussion of input properties. You want to ensure that `OrderProcessorComponent` receives data from other components via its properties marked with `@Input()` decorators. Your `OrderProcessorComponent` will look like the following listing.

Listing 8.1 order.component.ts

```
@Component({
    selector: 'order-processor',
    template: `
    <span *ngIf="!!stockSymbol">                    ◁ Doesn't show the text unless the stockSymbol is truthy
        Buying {{quantity}} shares of {{stockSymbol}}
    </span>
  `,
    styles:[`:host {background: cyan;}`]
})
export class OrderProcessorComponent {
    @Input() stockSymbol: string;                   ◁ Declares the input property to receive the stock symbol
     @Input() quantity: number;                     ◁ Declares the input property to receive the quantity
 }
```

The `OrderProcessorComponent` doesn't know who will provide the values for these properties, which makes this component completely reusable.

Next, we'll look at the `AppComponent`, which in your app is the parent of `OrderComponent`. `AppComponent` allows users to enter a stock symbol in the input field, and the entered value is passed to the `OrderProcessorComponent` via property binding. The following listing shows the code of the `AppComponent`.

Listing 8.2 input/app.component.ts

```
@Component({
  selector: 'app-root',
  template: `
    <input type="text" placeholder="Enter stock (e.g. AAPL)"
             (change)="onChangeEvent($event)">      ◁ When the user moves the focus from the input field (change event), invokes the event handler passing the event object to it
```

Binds the input property stockSymbol of the child component to the value of the property stock

Binds the value of the property quantity of the child component to the value of the property numberOfShares

```
<order-processor [stockSymbol]="stock"
                 [quantity]="numberOfShares">
  </order-processor>
`
})
export class AppComponent {
  stock: string;
  readonly numberOfShares = 100;

  onChangeEvent({target}): void {
     this.stock = target.value;
   }
}
```

You can't use the keyword const with class properties; use readonly.

Extracts the value of the property target from the event object given as an argument

Assigns the value entered in the input field to the property stock

Both properties of the `<order-processor>` component are surrounded with square brackets to denote property binding. If you change the value of `stockSymbol` or `quantity` inside the `OrderProcessorComponent`, the change won't affect the property values of the parent component. Property binding is unidirectional: from parent to child.

To see this app in action, run `npm install` in the chapter8/inter-component folder, and run the following command:

```
ng serve --app input -o
```

Best practice

Though we praised TypeScript for allowing specification of variable types, we didn't declare the type for the `numberOfShares` property. Because we initialized it with a numeric value, TypeScript compiler will use *type inference* to guess the type of `NumberOfShares` when it gets initialized. Explicitly declare types in a public API, for example, public class properties, function parameters and return types, and so on.

Figure 8.2 shows the browser window after the user types `IBM` in the input field. The `OrderProcessorComponent` received the input values `100` and `IBM`.

IBM Buying 100 shares of IBM

Figure 8.2 The `OrderProcessorComponent` receives values.

How can a component intercept the moment when the value of the input property `stockSymbol` changes to perform some additional processing? A simple way is to turn `stockSymbol` into a setter. If you want to use `stockSymbol` in the template of the component, create a getter as well, as shown in the following listing.

Listing 8.3 Adding the setter and getter

```
...
private _stockSymbol: string;       <-- This private variable isn't accessible from the template.

@Input() set stockSymbol(value: string)   <-- Defines an input property as a setter

  if (value !== undefined) {
    this._stockSymbol = value;
    console.log(`Buying ${this.quantity} shares of ${value}`);
  }
}

get stockSymbol(): string {       <-- Defines a getter so stockSymbol is accessible from the template
   return this._stockSymbol;
}
```

When this application starts, the change detection mechanism qualifies the initialization as a change of the bound variable `stockSymbol`. The setter is invoked, and, to avoid sending an order for the undefined `stockSymbol`, you check its value in the setter.

> **NOTE** In section 9.2.1 in chapter 9, we'll show you how to intercept the changes in input properties without using setters.

8.2.2 *Output properties and custom events*

Angular components can dispatch custom events using the `EventEmitter` object. These events are to be consumed by the component's parent. `EventEmitter` is a subclass of `Subject` (explained in appendix D) that can serve as both observable and observer, but typically you use `EventEmitter` just for emitting custom events that are handled in the template of the parent component.

> **Best practice**
>
> If you need to have an object that's both an observable and an observer, use the RxJS `BehaviorSubject`. You'll see how to do that in section 8.3.2. In future releases, the internal implementation of `EventEmitter` may change, so it's better to use it only for emitting custom events.

Let's say you need to write a UI component that's connected to a stock exchange and displays changing stock prices. In addition to displaying prices, the component should also send events with the latest prices so its parent component can handle it and apply business logic to the changing prices. Let's create a `PriceQuoterComponent` that implements such functionality. In this component, you won't connect to any financial servers but will rather emulate the changing prices using a random number generator.

Displaying changing prices inside `PriceQuoterComponent` is pretty straightforward—you'll bind the `stockSymbol` and `lastPrice` properties to the component's template.

You'll notify the parent about the latest prices by emitting custom events via the `@Output` property of the component. Not only will you fire an event as soon as the price changes, but this event will also carry a payload: an object with the stock symbol and its latest price. The type of the payload will be defined as `PriceQuote` interface, as shown in the following listing.

Listing 8.4 iprice.quote.ts

```
export interface PriceQuote {
  stockSymbol: string;
  lastPrice: number;
}
```

The `PriceQuoterComponent` will generate random quotes and will emit them every two seconds.

Listing 8.5 price.quoter.component.ts

```
@Component({
  selector: 'price-quoter',
  template: `<strong>Inside PriceQuoterComponent:
              {{priceQuote?.stockSymbol}}
               {{priceQuote?.lastPrice | currency: 'USD'}}</strong>`,
  styles: [`:host {background: pink;}`]
})
export class PriceQuoterComponent {
  @Output() lastPrice = new EventEmitter<PriceQuote>();

  priceQuote : PriceQuote;

  constructor() {
    Observable.interval(2000)
        .subscribe(data =>{
         this.priceQuote = {
           stockSymbol: "IBM",
           lastPrice: 100 * Math.random()
         };

         this.lastPrice.emit(this.priceQuote);}
        )
  }
}
```

The question mark represents the safe navigation operator.

The output property lastPrice is represented by the EventEmitter object, which emits lastPrice events to the parent.

Emulates changing prices by invoking a function that generates a random number every two seconds and populates the priceQuote object

Emits new price via the output property; the lastPrice event carries the PriceQuote object as a payload

The safe navigation operator in `priceQuote?` ensures that if the `priceQuote` object isn't available yet, the code in the template won't try to access properties of an uninitialized `priceQuote`.

TIP We used the `Observable.interval()` instead of `setInterval()` because the latter is the browser-only API. Starting from Angular 6, use `interval()` instead of `Observable.interval()`.

The next listing shows how the parent component will receive and handle the `lastPrice` from the <price-quoter> component.

Listing 8.6 app.component.ts

```
@Component({
  selector: 'app-root',
  template: `
    AppComponent received: {{priceQuote?.stockSymbol}}
                           {{priceQuote?.lastPrice | currency:'USD'}}
   <price-quoter (lastPrice)="priceQuoteHandler($event)">
</price-quoter>
     `
})
export class AppComponent {
  priceQuote : IPriceQuote;

  priceQuoteHandler(event: IPriceQuote) {
     this.priceQuote = event;
  }
}
```

The AppComponent receives the lastPrice event and invokes the priceQuoteHandler, passing the received object as an argument.

Receives the IPriceQuote object and uses its properties to populate the respective properties of the AppComponent

Run this example, and you'll see the prices update every two seconds in both `PriceQuoterComponent` (on a pink background) as well as in `AppComponent` (white background), as shown in figure 8.3.

AppComponent received: IBM $21.00 **Inside PriceQuoterComponent: IBM $21.00**

Figure 8.3 Running the output properties example

To see this app in action, run the following command:

```
ng serve --app output -o
```

Event bubbling

Angular doesn't offer an API to support event bubbling. If you try to listen to the `lastPrice` event not on the <price-quoter> element but on its parent, the event won't bubble up there. In the following code snippet, the `lastPrice` event won't reach the <div>, because it's the parent of <price-quoter>:

```
<div (lastPrice)="priceQuoteHandler($event)">
  <price-quoter></price-quoter>
</div>
```

If event bubbling is important to your app, don't use `EventEmitter`; use native DOM events instead. The following code snippet shows how the `PriceQuoterComponent` uses a `CustomEvent` (from Web API) that supports bubbling:

```
@Component(...)
class PriceQuoterComponent {
  stockSymbol = "IBM";
  price;

  constructor(element: ElementRef) {
    setInterval(() => {
       let priceQuote: IPriceQuote = {
        stockSymbol: this.stockSymbol,
        lastPrice: 100 * Math.random()
      };

      this.price = priceQuote.lastPrice;

      element.nativeElement
          .dispatchEvent(new CustomEvent('lastPrice', {
            detail: priceQuote,
            bubbles: true
          }));
    }, 1000);
  }
}
```

Angular injects an `ElementRef` object, which has a reference to the DOM element that represents `<price-quoter>`, and then a `CustomEvent` is dispatched by invoking `element.nativeElement.dispatchEvent()`. Event bubbling will work here, but using `ElementRef` works only in browser-based apps and won't work with non-HTML renderers.

The `AppComponent` shown next handles the `lastPrice` event in the `<div>`, which is a parent of the `<price-quoter>` component. Note that the type of the argument of the `priceQuoteHandler()` is `CustomEvent`, and you can access its payload via the `detail` property:

```
@Component({
  selector: 'app',
  template: `
    <div (lastPrice)="priceQuoteHandler($event)">
      <price-quoter></price-quoter>
    </div>
    <br>
    AppComponent received: {{stockSymbol}}
                           {{price | currency: 'USD'}}
  `
})
class AppComponent {

  stockSymbol: string;
  price: number;
```

(continued)

```
  priceQuoteHandler(event: CustomEvent) {
    this.stockSymbol = event.detail.stockSymbol;
    this.price = event.detail.lastPrice;
  }}
```

We established that each UI component should be self-contained and shouldn't rely on the existence of other UI components, and using `@Input()` and `@Output()` decorators allows you to create reusable components. But how do you arrange communication between two components if they don't know about each other?

8.3 Implementing the Mediator design pattern

Communication between loosely coupled components can be implemented using the Mediator design pattern, which, according to Wikipedia, "defines how a set of objects interact" (https://en.wikipedia.org/wiki/Mediator_pattern). We'll explain what this means by analogy with interconnecting toy bricks.

Imagine a child playing with building bricks (think *components*) that "don't know" about each other. Today this child (the *mediator*) can use some blocks to build a house, and tomorrow they'll construct a boat from the same components.

NOTE The role of the mediator is to ensure that components properly fit together according to the task at hand while remaining loosely coupled.

Coming back to the web UI realm, we'll consider two cases:

- Arranging communication when components have a common parent
- Arranging communication when components don't have a common parent

8.3.1 Using a common parent as a mediator

Let's revisit the first figure of this chapter, shown again in figure 8.4. Each component except 1 has a parent (a container) that can play the role of mediator. The top-level mediator is container 1, which is responsible for making sure its direct children 2, 3, and 6 can communicate if need be. On the other hand, component 2 is a mediator for 4 and 5. Component 3 is a mediator for 7 and 8.

The mediator needs to receive data from one component and pass it to another. Let's go back to examples of monitoring stock prices.

Imagine a trader monitoring the prices of several stocks. At some point, the trader clicks the Buy button next to a stock symbol to place a purchase order with the stock exchange. You can easily add a Buy button to the `PriceQuoterComponent` from the previous section, but this component doesn't know how to place orders to buy stocks. `PriceQuoterComponent` will notify the mediator (`AppComponent`) that the trader wants to purchase a particular stock at that moment.

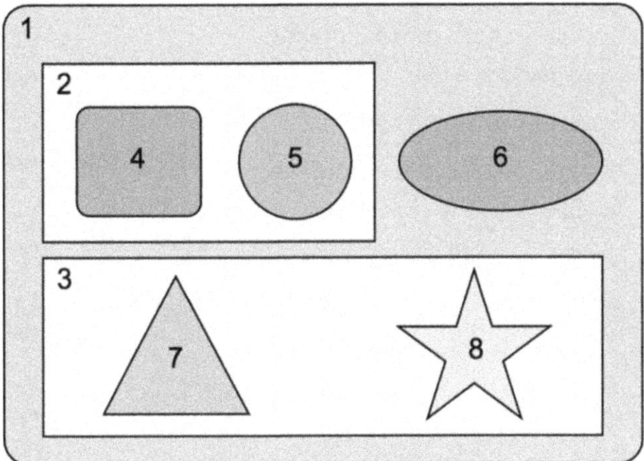

Figure 8.4 A view consists of components.

The mediator should know which component can place purchase orders and how to pass the stock symbol and quantity to it. Figure 8.5 shows how an `AppComponent` can mediate the communication between `PriceQuoterComponent` and `OrderComponent`.

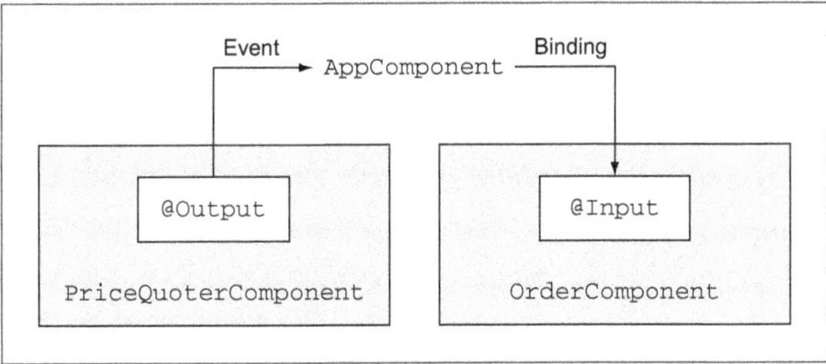

Figure 8.5 Mediating communications

> **NOTE** Emitting events works like broadcasting. `PriceQuoterComponent` emits events via the `@Output()` property without knowing who will receive them. `OrderComponent` waits for the value of its `@Input()` property to change as a signal for placing an order.

To demonstrate the Mediator pattern in action, let's write a small app that consists of the two components shown in figure 8.5. You can find this application in the mediator-parent directory, which has the following files:

- *istock.ts*—The `Stock` interface defining a value object that represents a stock
- *price.quoter.component.ts*—`PriceQuoterComponent`
- *order.component.ts*—`OrderComponent`

- *app.component.ts*—A parent component (the mediator) that contains `<price-quoter>` and `<order-processor>` in its template
- *app.module.ts*—The `AppModule` class

You'll use the `Stock` interface in two scenarios:

- To represent the payload of the event emitted by the `PriceQuoterComponent`
- To represent the data given to the `OrderComponent` via binding

The content of the istock.ts file is shown in the following listing.

Listing 8.7 istock.ts

```
export interface Stock {
  stockSymbol: string;
  bidPrice: number;
}
```

The `PriceQuoterComponent`, shown in the next listing, has a Buy button and the `buy` output property. It emits the `buy` event only when the user clicks the Buy button.

Listing 8.8 price.quoter.component.ts

```
@Component({
  selector: 'price-quoter',
  template: `<strong>
               <button (click)="buyStocks()">Buy</button>
               {{stockSymbol}} {{lastPrice | currency: "USD"}}
             </strong>
            `,
  styles:[`:host {background: pink; padding: 5px 15px 15px 15px;}`]
})
export class PriceQuoterComponent {
  @Output() buy: EventEmitter<Stock> = new EventEmitter();    ◁—— The buy output property will be used as a custom buy event.

  stockSymbol = "IBM";
  lastPrice: number;

  constructor() {
    Observable.interval(2000)
      .subscribe(data =>
      this.lastPrice = 100 * Math.random());
  }

  buyStocks(): void {

    let stockToBuy: Stock = {
      stockSymbol: this.stockSymbol,
      bidPrice: this.lastPrice
    };

    this.buy.emit(stockToBuy);  ◁—— Emits the custom buy event
   }
}
```

When the mediator (AppComponent) receives the buy event from <price-quoter>, it extracts the payload from this event and assigns it to the stock variable, which is bound to the input parameter of <order-processor>, as shown in the following listing.

Listing 8.9 app.component.ts

```
@Component({
  selector: 'app-root',
  template: `
    <price-
     quoter (buy) = "priceQuoteHandler($event)">      <-- When the mediator receives the buy event, it invokes the event handler.
     </price-quoter>

    <order-processor
           [stock] = "receivedStock">      <-- The stock received from <price-quoter> is passed to <order-processor>.
     </order-processor>
  `
})
export class AppComponent {
  receivedStock: Stock;

  priceQuoteHandler(event: Stock) {
    this.receivedStock = event;
  }
}
```

When the value of the buy input property on OrderComponent changes, its setter displays the message "Placed order ...," showing the stockSymbol and the bidPrice.

Listing 8.10 order.component.ts

```
@Component({
  selector: 'order-processor',
  template: `{{message}}`,
  styles:[`:host {background: cyan;}`]
})
export class OrderComponent {

  message = "Waiting for orders...";

  @Input() set stock(value: Stock) {      <-- Receives the stock object through this setter
     if (value && value.bidPrice != undefined) {
      this.message = `Placed order to buy 100 shares      <-- Prepares a message to be displayed in the template
                       of ${value.stockSymbol} at
                      \$${value.bidPrice.toFixed(2)}`;
    }
  }
}
```

Figure 8.6 shows what happens after the user clicked the Buy button when the price of the IBM stock was $36.53. PriceQuoterComponent is rendered on the left, and OrderComponent is on the right. They're self-contained, loosely coupled, and still can communicate with each other via the AppComponent mediator.

Buy IBM $36.53 Placed order to buy 100 shares of IBM at $36.53

Figure 8.6 Running the mediator example

To see this app in action, run the following command:

```
ng serve --app mediator-parent -o
```

The Mediator design pattern is a good fit for ngAuction as well. Imagine the last minutes of a bidding war for a hot product. Users monitor frequently updated bids and click a button to increase their bids.

A real-world example of a multicomponent UI

You can find many UIs that consist of multiple components in real-world web apps. We'll show you a UI taken from the publicly available site www.forex.com that offers a web platform for trading currencies. A trader can monitor the prices of multiple currency pairs (for example, US dollars and euros) in real time and place orders to buy the currencies when the price is right.

Here's a snapshot of a trader's screen that you can find at http://mng.bz/M9Af.

A sample trader's screen from forex.com

We don't know which JavaScript framework (if any) was used for creating this UI, but we can clearly see that it consists of multiple components. If we needed to develop such an app in Angular, we'd create, say, a `CurrencyPairComponent` and would place four of its instances at the top. Below, we'd use other components, such as `PopularMarketComponent`, `WatchListComponent`, and so on.

Within the `CurrencyPairComponent`, we'd create two child components: `SellComponent` and `BuyComponent`. Their Sell and Buy buttons would emit a custom event that would be received by the parent `CurrencyPairComponent`, which in turn would need to communicate with an `OrderComponent` to place a sell or buy order. But what if `CurrencyPairComponent` and `OrderComponent` don't have a common parent? Who will mediate their communications?

8.3.2 Using an injectable service as a mediator

In the last section, you saw how sibling components use their parent as a mediator. If components don't have the same parent or aren't displayed at the same time (the router may not display the required component at the moment), you can use an injectable service as a mediator. Whenever the component is created, the mediator service is injected, and the component can subscribe to events emitted by the service (as opposed to using `@Input()` parameters like `OrderComponent` did).

Figure 8.7 shows a diagram representing a scenario when component 5 needs to send data to components 6 and 8. As you see, they don't have a common parent, so you use an injectable service as a mediator.

The same instance of the service will be injected into components 5, 6, and 8. Component 5 can use the API of the service to provide some data, and components 6

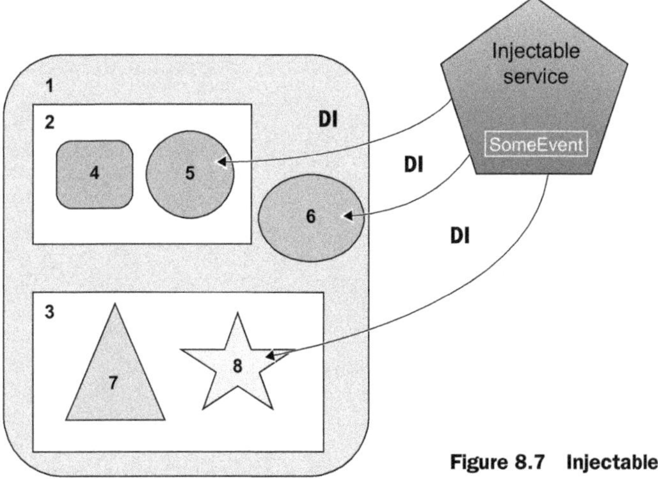

Figure 8.7 Injectable service as mediator

and 8 will subscribe to the data as soon as they're instantiated. By creating a subscription in the constructors of components 6 and 8, you ensure that no matter when these components are created, they'll start getting data from the service right away.

Let's consider a practical example to illustrate how this works. Imagine you have a UI with which you can search for products by typing a product name in an input box of a component. You want to offer searching for products either on eBay or Amazon. Initially, you'll render the eBay component, but if users aren't satisfied with the deal offered on eBay, they'll try to find the same product on Amazon. Figure 8.8 shows the UI of this app after the user enters `aaa` as a product name in the search field. Initially, the eBay component is rendered and receives aaa as a product to search for.

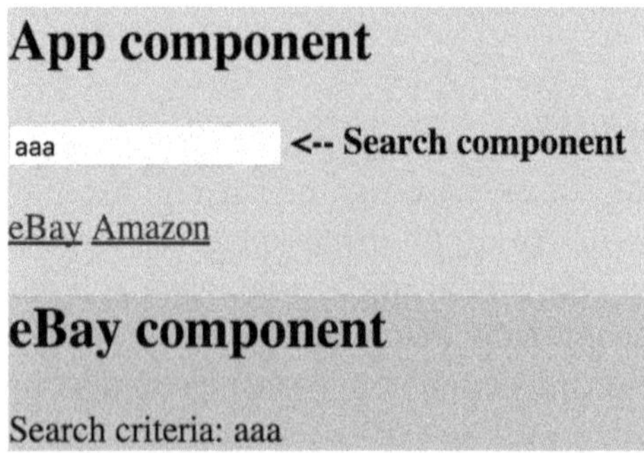

Figure 8.8 Searching for product aaa on eBay

Say eBay provides details and pricing for aaa, but the user isn't happy and clicks the link to find the same product on Amazon. Your UI has two links, one for eBay and another for Amazon. When the user clicks the Amazon link, the router destroys the eBay component and creates the Amazon one. You want to maintain the application state so the user doesn't need to reenter the product name, and the Amazon component has to be rendered showing aaa—the saved search criteria, as shown in figure 8.9.

If the user changes their mind and decides to search for a different product on Amazon, and then returns back to eBay, the new search criteria has to be shown in the eBay component.

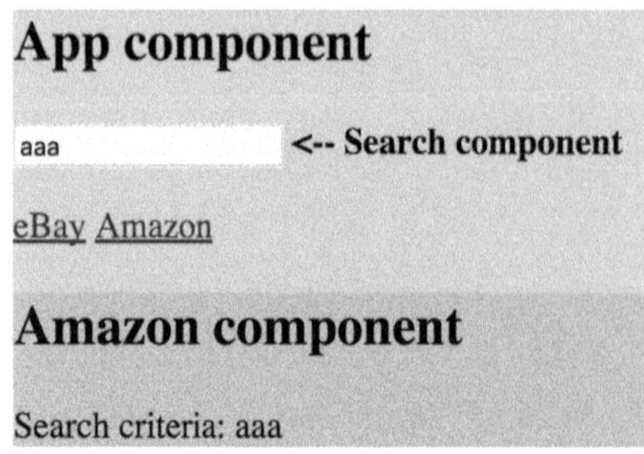

Figure 8.9 Searching for product aaa on Amazon

So you need to implement two features:

- Communication between the search, eBay, and Amazon components.
- State management so the latest search criteria is preserved while the user navigates between eBay and Amazon.

The code for this app is located in the mediator-service-subject folder and contains the following files:

- *app.component.ts*—The top-level component `AppComponent`
- *app.module.ts*—The `AppModule` that includes routes configuration
- *state.service.ts*—The injectable service that also stores the app state
- *search.component.ts*—The `SearchComponent` with an `<input>` field
- *amazon.component.ts*—The `AmazonComponent`
- *ebay.component.ts*—The `EbayComponent`

`AppComponent` serves as a parent for `SearchComponent`, provides two links to eBay and Amazon components, and includes `<router-outlet>`, as shown in the following listing.

Listing 8.11 app.component.ts

```
@Component({
  selector: 'app-root',
  template: ` <div class="main">
               <h2>App component</h2>

               <search></search>  <b><-- Search component</b>
                <p>

               <a [routerLink]="['/']">eBay</a>
                <a [routerLink]="['/amazon']">Amazon</a>
                <router-outlet></router-outlet>
               </div>`,
  styles: ['.main {background: yellow}']
})
export class AppComponent {}
```

The user enters the product name here.

A link used for navigation

The eBay or Amazon component is rendered under the links.

`AppModule` loads the routes configuration as follows:

```
RouterModule.forRoot([
    {path: '',        component: EbayComponent},
    {path: 'amazon', component: AmazonComponent}])
]
```

You want to create an injectable `StateService` that would accept the search criteria from the `SearchComponent` and emit it to its subscribers (eBay or Amazon components). In appendix D, we explain how the RxJS `Subject` works. It contains both observable and observer and would fit your needs except it wouldn't remember the emitted value (the search criteria). You could create a separate variable to store the value provided by the `SearchComponent`, but there's a better solution.

The RxJS library includes `BehaviorSubject`, which supports the functionality of `Subject`—plus it reemits the latest emitted value. Let's see how it'll work in your app:

1. The user enters aaa, and the `SearchComponent` invokes the API on the `StateService` to emit aaa to the subscriber, which is initially an eBay component. The `BehaviorSubject` emits aaa and remembers it (stores the app state).
2. The user navigates to the Amazon component, which immediately subscribes to the same `BehaviorSubject`, which reemits aaa.

The code of the `StateService` is shown in the next listing.

Listing 8.12 state.service.ts

```
@Injectable()
export class StateService {

  private stateSubject: BehaviorSubject<string> = new BehaviorSubject('');

  set searchCriteria(value: string) {

    this.stateSubject.next(value);
  }

  getState(): Observable<string> {
     return this.stateSubject.asObservable();
  }
}
```

- **Creates an instance of BehaviorSubject to reemit the last emitted value to new subscribers**
- **SearchComponent will invoke this method.**
- **Emits the search criteria to subscriber(s)**
- **Returns the reference to Observable of the Subject**

The `getState()` method returns the observable portion of `BehaviorSubject` so the eBay or Amazon components can subscribe to it. Technically, these components could subscribe to the subject directly, but if they had a reference to your `BehaviorSubject`, they could use the `next()` API to emit data on the subject's observers. You want to allow eBay or Amazon components to only use the `subscribe()` API—that's why you'll give them only the reference to the observable property from the `BehaviorSubject`.

> **NOTE** We used the `Injectable()` decorator, but it's optional here because we don't inject other services into `StateService`. If we injected into this service the `HttpClient` or any other service, using `Injectable()` would be required.

The code of the `SearchComponent` is shown next. You use the Forms API to subscribe to the `valueChanges` observable, as explained in chapter 6. Note that you inject the `StateService` into this component, and as the user types in the input field, you assign the values to the `searchCriteria` property on the `StateService`. The `searchCriteria` property is implemented as a setter, which emits the values entered by the user to the subscriber(s) of the `stateSubject`, as shown in the following listing.

Listing 8.13 search.component.ts

```
@Component({
  selector: "search",
  template: `
      <input type="text" placeholder="Enter product"
             [formControl]="searchInput">
    `
})
export class SearchComponent {

  searchInput: FormControl;

  constructor(private state: StateService) {

    this.searchInput = new FormControl('');

    this.searchInput.valueChanges                         <-- An observable that emits the content of the input field
      .pipe(debounceTime(300))
      .subscribe(searchValue =>
                  this.state.searchCriteria = searchValue);   <-- Passes the entered value to StateService
  }
}
```

The following listing shows the code of `EbayComponent`, which gets `StateService` injected and subscribes to the observable of `stateSubject`.

Listing 8.14 ebay.component.ts

```
@Component({
  selector: 'product',
  template: `<div class="ebay">
              <h2>eBay component</h2>
             Search criteria: {{searchFor$ | async}}    <-- The async pipe autosubscribes to the observable searchFor$.
              </div>`,
  styles: ['.ebay {background: cyan}']
})
export class EbayComponent {

  searchFor$: Observable<string>;

  constructor(private state: StateService){    <-- Injects the StateService

      this.searchFor$ = state.getState();    <-- Stores the observable in the class variable
  }
}
```

NOTE The code in the `AmazonComponent` should be identical, but in the source code that comes with this chapter, we keep a more verbose version that uses `subscribe()` and `unsubscribe` so you can compare and appreciate the benefits of the async pipe.

When the eBay (or Amazon) component is created, it gets the existing state of the `stateSubject` and displays it. Figure 8.10 shows how the components of the sample app communicate.

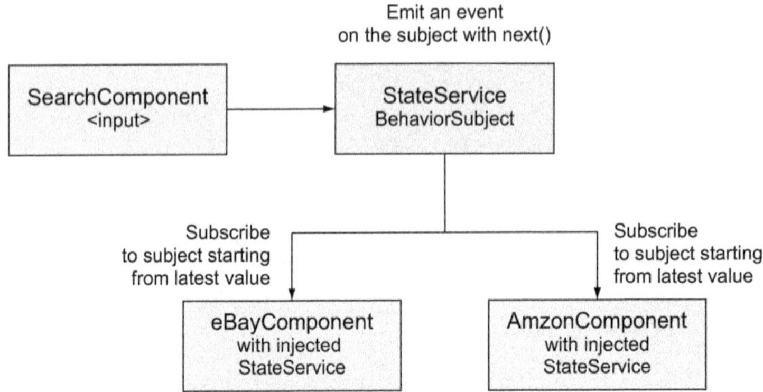

Figure 8.10 The application's workflows

> **NOTE** This sample app not only illustrates how you can arrange intercomponent communication using an injectable service as a mediator, it also shows how you can keep track of the app state in small and mid-size applications. If your application is large, consider implementing app state using the NgRx library, as explained in chapter 15.

To see this application in action, run the following command:

```
ng serve --app mediator-service -o
```

You can also watch a short video that explains how this app works at http://mng.bz/oE0s.

> **TIP** Don't start implementing the UI components of your application until you've identified your mediators, the reusable components, and the means of communication between them.

Now you know that a parent component can pass data to other components without knowing either their content or existence. But what if a parent component knows that it has a child that implements a certain API; can the parent invoke this API on the child directly?

8.4 Exposing a child component's API

You've learned how a parent component can pass data to its child using bindings to input properties. But there are other cases when the parent just needs to use the API exposed by the child. We'll show you an example that illustrates how a parent component can invoke the child's API from both the template and the TypeScript code of the parent.

Let's create a simple application in which a child component has a `greet()` method that will be invoked by the parent. In particular, the parent component includes the following lines in its template:

```
<child name= "John" #child1></child>
<button (click) = "child1.greet()">Invoke greet() on child 1</button>
```

Local template variables are meant to be used within the template. In the preceding code, the parent's template invokes the `greet()` method on the child component, `#child1`.

You can also invoke the child's API from TypeScript. Let's create two instances of the same child component to illustrate how to do this:

```
<child name= "John" #child1></child>
<child name= "Mary" #child2></child>
```

The DOM references to these instances will be stored in template variables `#child1` and `#child2`, respectively. Now you can declare a property in your TypeScript class, decorated with `@ViewChild()` so you can use these objects from your TypeScript code. The `@ViewChild()` decorator is handy when you need a reference to a child component.

Here's how you can pass a reference to the child component from the template variable `#child1` to the TypeScript variable `firstChild`:

```
@ViewChild('child1')
firstChild: ChildComponent;
...
this.firstChild.greet();
```

The `@ViewChildren()` decorator would give you references to several children of the same type. Let's write a small app that will illustrate the use of these decorators. The code of the child component is located in the childapi/child.component.ts file and is shown in the following listing.

Listing 8.15 child.component.ts

```
@Component({
  selector: 'child',
  template: `<h3>Child {{name}}</h3>`

})
export class ChildComponent {

  @Input() name: string;

  greet() {
    console.log(`Hello from ${this.name}`);
  }
}
```

The parent will include two instances of the child and will use both `@ViewChild()` and `@ViewChildren()` decorators. The full code of the parent component that uses both decorators is shown in the following listing.

Listing 8.16 app.component.ts

```
@Component({
  selector: 'app-root',
  template: `
    <h1>Parent</h1>
    <child name = "John" #child1></child>
    <child name = "Mary" #child2></child>

    <button (click) = "child2.greet()">
            Invoke greet() on child 2
    </button>
    <button (click) = "greetAllChildren()">
            Invoke greet() on both children
    </button>
    `
})
export class AppComponent implements AfterViewInit {
  @ViewChild('child1')
  firstChild: ChildComponent;

  @ViewChildren(ChildComponent)
  allChildren: QueryList<ChildComponent>;

  ngAfterViewInit() {
     this.firstChild.greet();
   }

  greetAllChildren() {
     this.allChildren.forEach(child => child.greet());
   }
}
```

- **Obtains the reference to the first child instance**
- **Obtains the references to both children (returns a list of children)**
- **Uses the lifecycle hook ngAfterViewInit()**
- **Invokes the greet() method on the first child**
- **Invokes the greet() method on both children**

NOTE In this class, you use the component lifecycle hook `ngAfterViewInit()` to ensure that you use the child's API after the child is rendered. See section 9.2 in chapter 9 for more details.

If you run this app, the browser renders the window shown in figure 8.11.

You'll also see following line on the browser console:

```
Hello from John
```

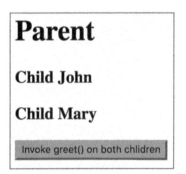

Figure 8.11 Accessing the children API

On app startup, John is greeted, but to be fair, both children should be greeted. Clicking the button will use the reference to the entire list of children and produce the following output:

```
Hello from John
Hello from Mary
```

To see this app in action, run the following command:

```
ng serve --app childapi -o
```

You used different techniques for component communications to send data or invoke the API, but can you send an HTML fragment from one component to be used in another?

8.5 Projecting templates at runtime with ngContent

In some cases, a parent component needs to render arbitrary markup within a child at runtime, and you can do that in Angular using *projection*. You can project a fragment of the parent component's template onto its child's template by using the `ngContent` directive. This is a two-step process:

1. In the child component's template, include the tags `<ng-content></ng-content>` (the *insertion point*).
2. In the parent component, include the HTML fragment that you want to project into the child's insertion point between tags representing the child component (for example, `<my-child>`):

```
template: `
  ...
  <my-child>
    <div>Passing this div to the child</div>
  </my-child>
  ...
```

In this example, the parent component won't render the content placed between `<my-child>` and `</my-child>`. Listings 8.17 and 8.18 illustrate this technique. Notice that both components declare a CSS style selector with the same name, `.wrapper`, but each of them defines a different background color. This illustrates what Angular has to offer in terms of style encapsulation, described in the next section.

Consider an example with two components—parent and child. The parent component will pass an HTML fragment to the child for rendering. The code of the child component is shown in the following listing.

Listing 8.17 child.component.ts

```
import {Component, ViewEncapsulation} from "@angular/core";

@Component({
  selector: 'child',
  styles: ['.wrapper {background: lightgreen;}'],    <-- The class selector to render the UI on the light green background
```

```
    template: `
     <div class="wrapper">
      <h2>Child</h2>
       <div>This content is defined in child</div>
       <p>
       <ng-content></ng-content>
      </div>
   `,
  encapsulation: ViewEncapsulation.Native
 })
export class ChildComponent {}
```

The content that comes from the parent is displayed here.

For styles, use the ViewEncapsulation.Native mode (we explain view encapsulation modes in the next section).

The parent component is shown in the next listing.

Listing 8.18 app.component.ts

```
@Component({
  selector: 'app-root',
  styles: ['.wrapper {background: deeppink;}'],
   template: `
    <div class="wrapper">
     <h2>Parent</h2>
      <div>This div is defined in the Parent's template</div>
      <child>
        <div ><i>Child got this line from parent </i></div>
       </child>
    </div>
  `,
  encapsulation:ViewEncapsulation.Native
})
export class AppComponent {}
```

The class selector to render the UI on the light green background

The content will be projected onto the child's template.

Run this app with the following command in the Chrome browser:

```
ng serve --app projection1 -o
```

The Chrome browser will render the UI shown in figure 8.12.

The text "Child got this line from parent" was projected from the `AppComponent` onto the `Child-Component`. You may ask why you would want to run this app in the Chrome browser: because you specified `ViewEncapsulation.Native`, assuming that the browser supports Shadow DOM, and Chrome supports this feature. The next section provides more details.

Figure 8.12 Running the projection1 app with `ViewEncapsulation.Native`

NOTE `ViewEncapsulation` modes aren't related to projection and can be used in any component, but we wanted to use the app that has a differently styled parent and child components to introduce this feature.

8.5.1 *View encapsulation modes*

JavaScript modules allow you to introduce scope to your scripts so they don't pollute the global space in the browser or any other execution environment. What about CSS? Imagine a parent and child components that coincidentally declare a style with the same CSS class selector name, but define different background colors. Will the browser render components using different backgrounds or will both of them have the same background?

In short, Shadow DOM introduces scopes for CSS styles and encapsulation of DOM nodes in the browser. Shadow DOM allows you to hide the internals of a selected component from the global DOM tree. Shadow DOM is well explained in the article "Shadow DOM v1: Self-Contained Web Components" by Eric Bidelman, available at http://mng.bz/6VV6.

We'll use the app from the previous section to illustrate how Shadow DOM and Angular's `ViewEncapsulation` mode works. The `encapsulation` property of the `@Component()` decorator can have one of three values:

- `ViewEncapsulation.Native` —This can be used with browsers that support Shadow DOM.
- `ViewEncapsulation.Emulated` —By default, Angular emulates Shadow DOM support.
- `ViewEncapsulation.None` —If the styles have the same selectors, the last one wins.

TIP Read about CSS specificity at https://css-tricks.com/specifics-on-css-specificity.

As mentioned earlier, both parent and child components use the `.wrapper` style. In a regular HTML page, this would mean that the CSS rules of the child's `.wrapper` would override the parent's. Let's see if you can encapsulate styles in child components so they don't clash with parent styles, even if their names are the same.

Figure 8.13 shows the running application in `ViewEncapsulation.Native` mode with the Developer Tools panel open. The browser creates `#shadow-root` nodes for parent and child (see the two `#shadow-root` nodes on the right). If you're reading this book in color (the e-book), you'll see that the `.wrapper` style paints the background of the `<app-root>` a deep pink color. The fact that the child also has the `.wrapper` style that uses a light green color doesn't affect the parent. Styles are encapsulated. The child's `#shadow-root` acts like a wall preventing the child's styles from overriding the parent's styles. You can use `ViewEncapsulation.Native` only if you're sure that the users of your app will use browsers that support Shadow DOM.

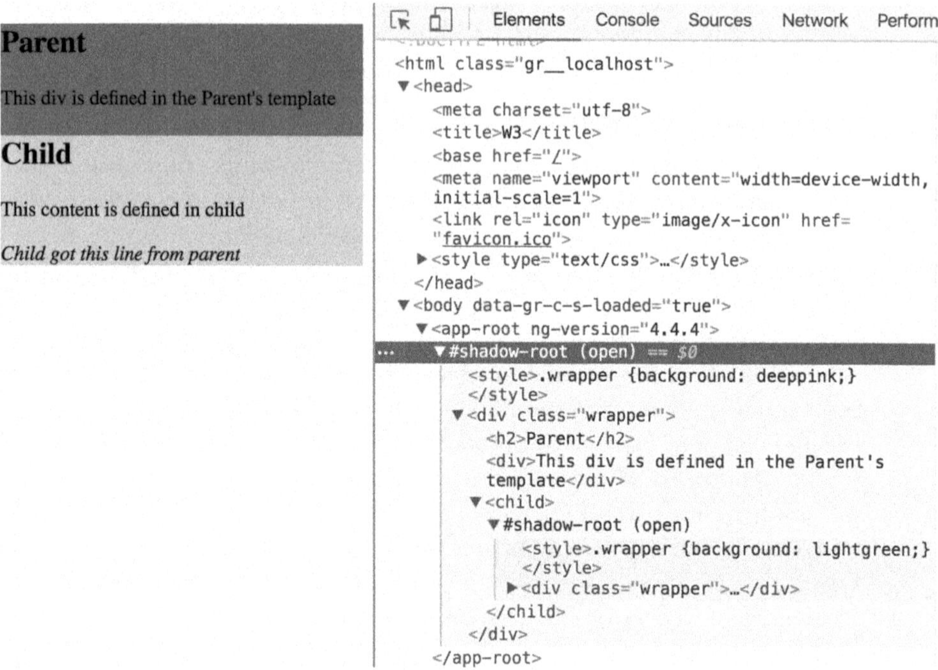
Parent
This div is defined in the Parent's template
Child
This content is defined in child
Child got this line from parent
Elements Console Sources Network Perform
<html class="gr__localhost">
<head>
<meta charset="utf-8">
<title>W3</title>
<base href="/">
<meta name="viewport" content="width=device-width, initial-scale=1">
<link rel="icon" type="image/x-icon" href= "favicon.ico">
<style type="text/css">…</style>
</head>
<body data-gr-c-s-loaded="true">
<app-root ng-version="4.4.4">
#shadow-root (open) == $0
<style>.wrapper {background: deeppink;}
</style>
<div class="wrapper">
<h2>Parent</h2>
<div>This div is defined in the Parent's template</div>
<child>
#shadow-root (open)
<style>.wrapper {background: lightgreen;}
</style>
<div class="wrapper">…</div>
</child>
</div>
</app-root>

Figure 8.13 Browser creating two `#shadow-root` nodes

Figure 8.13 shows what happens after changing the value of the `encapsulation` property to `ViewEncapsulation.Emulated`. Angular uses this mode by default, so the effect is the same as if you didn't add the `encapsulation` property to the `@Component()` decorator. The DOM doesn't have any `#shadow-root` nodes inside the `<app-root>` element, but Angular generates additional attributes for the parent and child elements to differentiate styles in parent and child. Angular modifies all CSS selectors in component styles to incorporate generated attributes:

```
<div _ngcontent-c0="" class="wrapper">   <-- The styles in the <app-root> component
 ...
<div _ngcontent-c1="" class="wrapper">   <-- The styles in the <child> component
```

The UI is rendered the same way, using different background colors for these components as in figure 8.14, but the underlying code is not the same compared to figure 8.13.

Figure 8.15 shows the same example running with encapsulation set to `ViewEncapsulation.None`. In this case, the child's `wrapper` wins, and the entire window is shown with the child's light green background.

Parent
This div is defined in the Parent's template
Child
This content is defined in child
Child got this line from parent
Elements
Console
Sources
Network
Performance
<!DOCTYPE html>
<html class="gr__localhost">
▶<head>…</head>
▼<body data-gr-c-s-loaded="true">
▼<app-root _nghost-c0 ng-version="4.4.4">
▼<div _ngcontent-c0 class="wrapper"> == $0
<h2 _ngcontent-c0>Parent</h2>
<div _ngcontent-c0>This div is defined in the Parent's
▼<child _ngcontent-c0 _nghost-c1>
▼<div _ngcontent-c1 class="wrapper">
<h2 _ngcontent-c1>Child</h2>
<div _ngcontent-c1>This content is defined in chil
▶<p _ngcontent-c1>…</p>
</div>
</child>
</div>
</app-root>

Figure 8.14 Running the projection1 app with `ViewEncapsulation.Emulated`

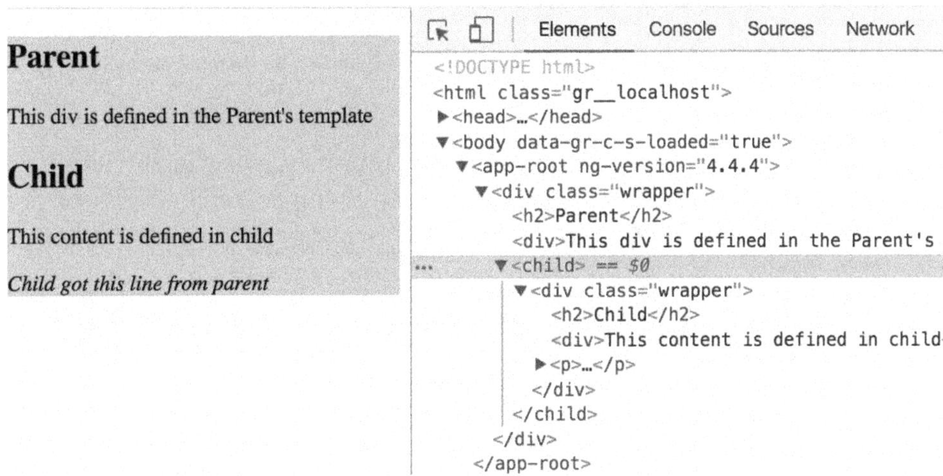
Parent
This div is defined in the Parent's template
Child
This content is defined in child
Child got this line from parent
Elements
Console
Sources
Network
<!DOCTYPE html>
<html class="gr__localhost">
▶<head>…</head>
▼<body data-gr-c-s-loaded="true">
▼<app-root ng-version="4.4.4">
▼<div class="wrapper">
<h2>Parent</h2>
<div>This div is defined in the Parent's
▼<child> == $0
▼<div class="wrapper">
<h2>Child</h2>
<div>This content is defined in child
▶<p>…</p>
</div>
</child>
</div>
</app-root>

Figure 8.15 Running the projection1 app with `ViewEncapsulation.None`

Now that you understand encapsulation modes and basic projection, you may be wondering whether it's possible to project content into multiple areas of the component template.

8.5.2 *Projecting onto multiple areas*

A component can have more than one `<ng-content>` tag in its template. Let's consider an example where a child component's template is split into three areas: header, content, and footer, as in figure 8.16. The HTML markup for the header and footer could be projected by the parent component, and the content area could be defined in the child component. To implement this, the child component needs to include two separate pairs of <ng-content></ng-content>s populated by the parent (header and footer).

To ensure that the header and footer content will be rendered in the proper <ng-content> areas, you'll use the select attribute, which can be any valid CSS selector (a CSS class, tag name, and so on). The child's template could look like this:

```
<ng-content select=".header"></ng-content>
<div>This content is defined in child</div>
<ng-content select=".footer"></ng-content>
```

Parent
This div is defined in the Parent's template
Child
This content is defined in child
Child got this line from parent

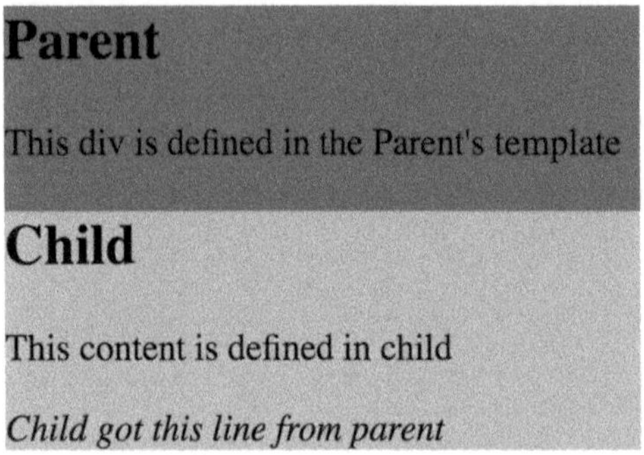

Figure 8.16 Running the projection2 app

The content that arrives from the parent will be matched by the selector and rendered in the corresponding area. We created a separate app in the folder projection2 to illustrate projection onto multiple areas. The following listing shows the child component.

Listing 8.19 child.component.ts

```
@Component({
  selector: 'child',
  styles: ['.wrapper {background: lightgreen;}'],
  template: `
    <div class="wrapper">
     <h2>Child</h2>
      <ng-content select=".header"></ng-content><p>

      <div>This content is defined in child</div><p>

      <ng-content select=".footer"></ng-content>
    </div>
  `
})
export class ChildComponent {}
```

Note that you have two <ng-content> slots now—one with the selector .header and another with .footer. The parent component will project different content into each slot. To make this example more dynamic, you use binding to display today's date in the header, as shown in the following listing.

Listing 8.20 app.component.ts

```
@Component({
  selector: 'app-root',
  styles: ['.wrapper {background: deeppink;}'],
  template: `
  <div class="wrapper">
    <h2>Parent</h2>
    <div>This div is defined in the Parent's template</div>
    <child>

      <div class="header">                      <-- Projects this div onto the child's element with the header selector
         <i>Child got this header from parent {{todaysDate}}</i>   <-- Binds the current date to the projected content
       </div>

      <div class="footer">                     <-- Projects this div onto the child's element with the footer selector
          <i>Child got this footer from parent</i>
      </div>
    </child>
  </div>
`
})
export class AppComponent {
  todaysDate = new Date().toLocaleDateString();
}
```

NOTE The projected HTML can only bind the properties visible in the parent's scope, so you can't use the child's properties in the parent's binding expression.

To see this example in action, run the following command:

```
ng serve --app projection2 -o
```

Running this app will render the page shown earlier in figure 8.16.

Using `<ng-content>` with the `select` attribute allows you to create a universal component with a view divided into several areas that get their markup from the parent.

Projection vs. direct binding to innerHTML

Alternatively, you can programmatically change the HTML content of a component by binding a component to `innerHTML`:

```
<p [innerHTML]="myComponentProperty"></p>
```

But using `<ng-content>` is preferable to binding to `innerHTML` for these reasons:

- `innerHTML` is a browser-specific API, whereas `<ng-content>` is platform independent.
- With `<ng-content>`, you can define multiple slots where the HTML fragments will be inserted.
- `<ng-content>` allows you to bind the parent component's properties into projected HTML.

Summary

- Parent and child components should avoid direct access to each other's internals but should communicate via input and output properties.
- A component can emit custom events via its output properties, and these events can carry an application-specific payload.
- Communications between unrelated components should be arranged using the Mediator design pattern. Either a common parent component or an injectable service can serve as a mediator.

9 Change detection and component lifecycle

This chapter covers

- How Angular knows that a UI update is needed
- Reviewing the milestones in the life of a component
- Writing code in component lifecycle hooks

All the apps you've developed so far have been properly updating the UI when the user or program updates the properties of your components. How does Angular know when to update the UI? In this chapter, we'll discuss the change detection (CD) mechanism that monitors the asynchronous events of your app and decides whether the UI should be updated or not.

We'll also discuss the lifecycle of an Angular component and the callback method hooks you can use to provide application-specific code that intercepts important events during a component's creation, lifespan, and destruction.

Finally, we'll continue working on ngAuction. This time, you'll add the view that displays product details.

9.1 A high-level overview of change detection

As the user works with your app, things change and the values of component properties (the model) get modified. Most of the changes happen asynchronously—for example, the user clicks a button, data is received from a server, an observable starts emitting values, a script invokes the `setTimeout()` function, and so on. Angular needs to know when the result of an asynchronous operation becomes available, to update the UI accordingly.

For automatic CD, Angular uses the library zone.js (the Zone). Angular subscribes to Zone events to trigger CD, which keeps the component's model and UI in sync. The CD cycle is initiated by any asynchronous event that happens in the browser. The change detector keeps track of all async calls made in components, services, and so forth; and when they complete, it makes a single pass from top to bottom of the component tree to see whether the UI of any component has to be updated.

> **NOTE** The CD mechanism applies changes in the component's properties to its UI. CD never changes the value of the component's property.

The zone.js library is one of the dependencies in your Angular project. It spares you from manually writing code to update UI, but starting with Angular 5, using the Zone is optional. To illustrate the role of zone.js, let's do an experiment: you'll create a simple project managed by the Zone first, and then you'll turn the Zone off. This project includes the `AppComponent` shown in the following listing.

Listing 9.1 The Zone is on

```
@Component({
  selector: 'app-root',
  template: `<h1>Welcome to {{title}}!</h1>`
})
export class AppComponent {

  title = 'app';

  constructor() {
    setTimeout(() => {this.title = 'Angular 5'}, 5000);
  }
}
```

Invokes the code asynchronously so the Zone will update the UI in five seconds

Running this app renders "Welcome to app!" Five seconds later, the message changes to "Welcome to Angular 5!" Let's change the app bootstrap code in the main.ts file to use the empty Zone object noop, introduced in Angular 5:

```
platformBrowserDynamic().bootstrapModule(AppModule, {ngZone: 'noop'});
```

Now running the same app will render "Welcome to app!" and this message will never change. You just turned off the Zone, and the app didn't update the UI.

> **NOTE** You can still initiate CD by injecting the `ApplicationRef` servicer in the app constructor and invoking its `tick()` method after updating the value of the `title` property.

An Angular application is structured as a tree of views (components), with the root component at the top of the tree. When Angular compiles component templates, each component gets its own change detector. When CD is initiated by the Zone, it makes a single pass, starting from the root down to the leaf components, checking to see whether the UI of each component needs to be updated (see the sidebar "Lifecycle hooks, change detection, and production mode" at the end of section 9.2 about CD in dev versus production). Is there a way to instruct the change detector not to visit each and every component upon every async property change?

9.1.1 Change detection strategies

For UI updates, Angular offers two CD strategies: `Default` and `OnPush`. If all components use the `Default` strategy, the Zone checks the entire component tree, regardless of where the change happened.

If a particular component declares the `OnPush` strategy, the Zone checks this component and its children only if the bindings to the component's input properties have changed, or if the component uses `AsyncPipe`, and the corresponding observable started emitting values.

If a component that has the `OnPush` strategy changes a value of one of its properties bound to its template, the change detection cycle won't be initiated. To declare the `OnPush` strategy, add the following line to the `@Component()` decorator:

```
changeDetection: ChangeDetectionStrategy.OnPush
```

Figure 9.1 illustrates the effect of the `OnPush` strategy using three components: the parent, a child, and a grandchild. Let's say a property of the parent was modified. CD will begin checking the component and all of its descendants.

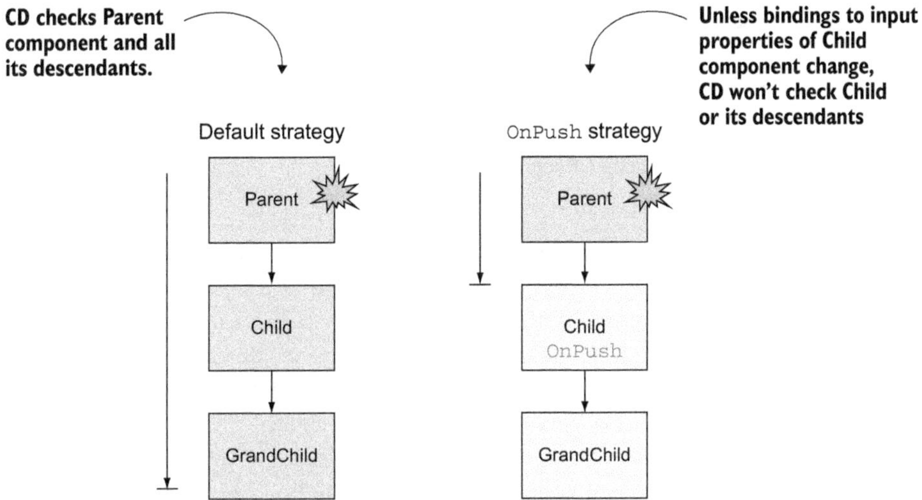

Figure 9.1 Change detection strategies

The left side of figure 9.1 illustrates the default CD strategy: all three components are checked for changes. The right side of figure 9.1 illustrates what happens when the child component has the `OnPush` CD strategy. CD starts from the top, but it sees that the child component has declared the `OnPush` strategy. If no bindings to the input properties have changed and no observable with `AsyncPipe` emits values (for example, via the `ActivatedRoute` parameters), CD doesn't check either the child or the grandchild.

Figure 9.1 shows a small application with only three components, but real-world apps can have hundreds of components. With the `OnPush` strategy, you can opt out of CD for specific branches of the tree.

Figure 9.2 shows a CD cycle caused by an event in the GrandChild1 component. Even though this event happened in the bottom-left leaf component, the CD cycle starts from the top; it's performed on each branch except the branches that originate from a component with the `OnPush` CD strategy and have no changes in the bindings to this component's input properties. Components excluded from this CD cycle are shown on a white background.

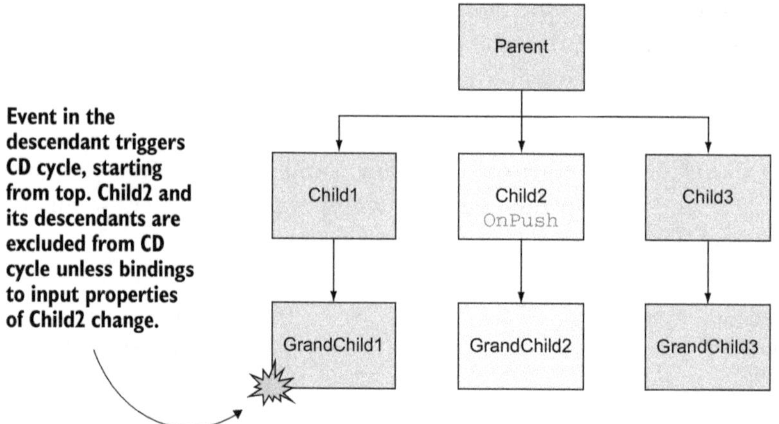
Event in the descendant triggers CD cycle, starting from top. Child2 and its descendants are excluded from CD cycle unless bindings to input properties of Child2 change.
Parent
Child1
Child2
OnPush
Child3
GrandChild1
GrandChild2
GrandChild3

Figure 9.2 Excluding a branch from a CD cycle

This has been a brief overview of the CD mechanism. You should learn about CD in depth if you need to work on performance tuning of a UI-intensive application, such as a data grid containing hundreds of cells with constantly changing values. For in-depth coverage of change detection, see the article "Everything you need to know about change detection in Angular" by Maxim Koretskyi at http://mng.bz/0YqE.

In general, it's a good idea to make `OnPush` a default CD strategy for each component. If you see that the UI of a component doesn't get updated as expected, review the code and either switch back to the `Default` change detection strategy or manually initiate the CD pass by injecting the `ChangeDetectorRef` object and using its API (see https://angular.io/api/core/ChangeDetectorRef).

What if you have a slow-running component with lots of changing template elements? Could multiple passes of the change detector contribute to this slowness?

9.1.2 Profiling change detection

Listing 9.2 shows you how to profile change detection by enabling Angular debug tools. Change the app bootstrap code in main.ts to look like the following.

Listing 9.2 Enabling Angular debug tools

```
import {platformBrowserDynamic} from '@angular/platform-browser-dynamic';
import {AppModule} from './app/app.module';
import {ApplicationRef} from '@angular/core';
import {enableDebugTools} from '@angular/platform-browser';

platformBrowserDynamic().bootstrapModule(AppModule).then((module) => {
  const applicationRef = module.injector.get(ApplicationRef);   // Gets a reference to the bootstrapped app
    const appComponent = applicationRef.components[0];   // Gets a reference to the app's top-level component
    enableDebugTools(appComponent);   // Enables Angular debug tools
 });
```

Launch your app, and in the browser console, enter the following command:

```
ng.profiler.timeChangeDetection({record: true})
```

Now your app will start reporting the time spent on each CD cycle, as shown in figure 9.3.

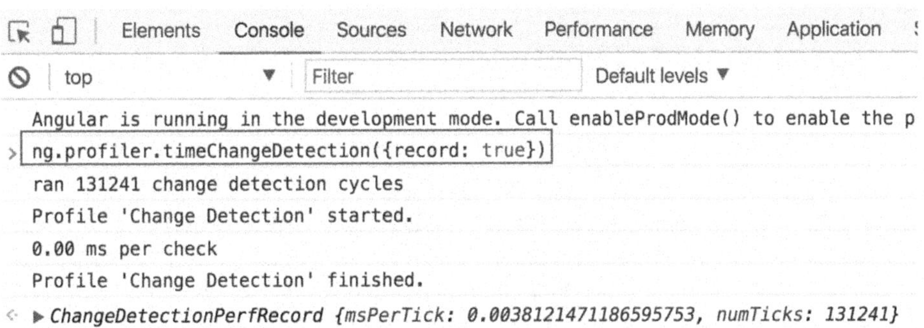

Figure 9.3 Profiling change detection

We've covered change detection, so now let's get familiar with the private life of a component.

9.2 Component lifecycle

Various events happen during the lifecycle of an Angular component: it gets created, reacts to different events, and gets destroyed. As explained in the last section, when a component is created, the CD mechanism begins monitoring it. The component is initialized, added to the DOM, and rendered by the browser. After that, the state of the component (the values of its properties) may change, causing rerendering of the UI, and, finally, the component is destroyed.

Figure 9.4 shows the lifecycle hooks (methods) where you can add custom code to intercept the lifecycle event and add your code there. If Angular sees any of these methods implemented in your app, it'll invoke them.

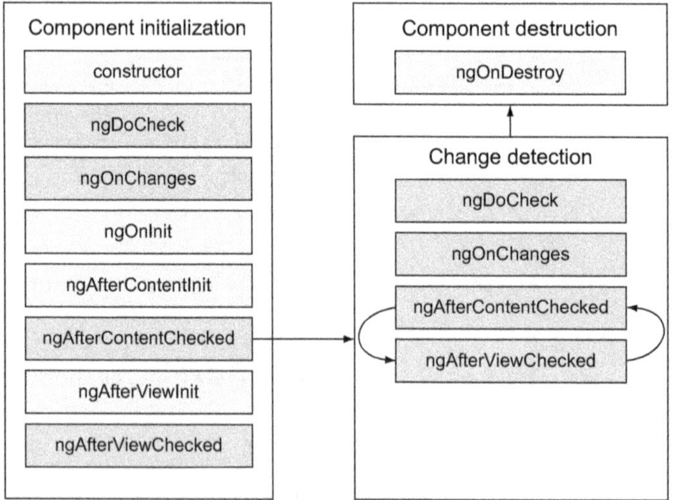

Figure 9.4 A component's lifecycle hooks

The callbacks shown on the light-gray background will be invoked only once, and those on the darker background can be invoked multiple times during the component life span. The user sees the component after the initialization phase is complete. Then the change detection mechanism ensures that the component's properties stay in sync with its UI. If the component is removed from the DOM tree as a result of the router's navigation or a structural directive (such as `*ngIf`), Angular initiates the destroy phase.

The constructor is invoked first when the instance of the component is being created, but the component's properties aren't initialized yet in the constructor. After the constructor's code is complete, Angular will invoke the following callbacks *if you implemented them*:

- `ngOnChanges()`—Called when a parent component modifies (or initializes) the values bound to the input properties of a child. If the component has no input properties, `ngOnChanges()` isn't invoked.

- `ngOnInit()`—Invoked after the first invocation of `ngOnChanges()`, if any. Although you might initialize some component variables in the constructor, the properties of the component aren't ready yet. By the time `ngOnInit()` is invoked, the component properties will have been initialized, which is why this method is mainly used for the initial data fetch.
- `ngDoCheck()`—Called on each pass of the change detector. If you want to implement a custom change detection algorithm or add some debug code, write it in `ngDoCheck()`. But keep in mind that placing any code in the `ngDoCheck()` method can affect the performance of your app because this method is invoked on each and every pass of the change detection cycle.
- `ngAfterContentInit()`—Invoked when the child component's state is initialized and the projection completes. This method is called only if you used `<ng-content>` in your component's template.
- `ngAfterContentChecked()`—During the change detection cycle, this method is invoked on the component that has `<ng-content>` after it gets the updated content from the parent if the bindings used in the projected content change.
- `ngAfterViewInit()`—Invoked after a component's view has been fully initialized. We used it in section 8.4 in chapter 8.
- `ngAfterViewChecked()`—Invoked when the change detection mechanism checks whether there are any changes in the component template's bindings. This callback may be called more than once as the result of modifications in this or other components.
- `ngOnDestroy()`—Invoked when the component is being destroyed. Use this callback to clean unneeded resources, for example, to unsubscribe from explicitly created subscriptions or remove timers.

Each lifecycle callback is declared in the interface with a name that matches the name of the callback without the prefix `ng`. For example, if you're planning to implement functionality in the `ngOnChanges()` callback, add `implements OnChanges` to your class declaration.

Let's consider some code samples illustrating the use of lifecycle hooks. The following code listing illustrates the use of `ngOnInit()`.

Listing 9.3 Fetching data in `ngOnInit()`

```
@Input() productId: number;    // Declares an input property

constructor(private productService: ProductService) { }    // Injects a service, but doesn't use it in the constructor

ngOnInit() {

   this.product = this.productService.getProductById(this.productId);    // Uses the service in ngOnInit() to ensure that the productId is already initialized
   }
```

This code uses the value of the input property `productId` as an argument of the `getProductById()` method. If you'd invoked `getProductById()` in the constructor, the `productId` property wouldn't be initialized yet. By the time `ngOnInit()` is invoked, `productId` is initialized, and you can safely invoke `getProductById()`.

The `ngOnDestroy()` hook is invoked when a component gets destroyed. For example, when you use the router to navigate from component A to component B, component A gets destroyed, and component B is created. If you created an explicit subscription in component A, don't forget to unsubscribe in `ngOnDestroy()`. This hook is also supported by Angular services.

9.2.1 Catching changes in the ngOnChanges hook

Now let's write a small app that uses `ngOnChanges()` and illustrates the different effects of bindings on primitive values versus object values. This app will include parent and child components, and the latter will have two input properties: `greeting` and `user`. The first property is a `string`, and the second is an `Object` with one property: `name`. To understand why the `ngOnChanges()` callback may or may not be invoked, you need to become familiar with the concept of mutable versus immutable values.

Mutable vs. immutable values

JavaScript strings are primitives, which are *immutable*—when a string value is created at a certain location in memory, you can't change it there. Consider the following code snippet:

```
let greeting = "Hello";
greeting = "Hello Mary";
```

The first line creates the value `Hello` in memory. The second line doesn't change the value at that address but creates the new string `Hello Mary` at a different memory location. Now you have two strings in memory, and each of them is immutable.

If the `greeting` variable was bound to an input property of a component, then its binding changed, because the value of this variable was initially at one memory location, and then the address changed.

JavaScript objects (as well as functions and arrays) are *mutable* and are stored in heap memory, and only references to objects are stored on the stack. After the object instance is created at a certain memory location, the reference to this object on the stack doesn't change when the values of the object's properties change in the heap memory. Consider the following code:

```
var user = {name: "John"};
user.name = "Mary";
```

After the first line, the object is created, and the reference to the instance of the `user` object is stored in stack memory and points at a certain memory location. The string `"John"` has been created at another memory location, and the `user.name` variable knows where it's located in memory.

After the second line of the preceding code snippet is executed, the new string "Mary" is created at another location. But the reference variable user is still stored in the same location on the stack. In other words, you mutated the content of the object but didn't change the value of the reference variable that points at this object. To make an object immutable, you need to create a new instance of the object whenever any of its properties changes.

TIP You can read more about JavaScript data types and data structures at http://mng.bz/bzL4.

Let's add the ngOnChanges() hook to the child component to demonstrate how it intercepts modifications of the input properties. This application has parent and child components. The child has two input properties (greeting and user). The parent component has two input fields, and the user can modify their values, which are bound to the input properties of the child. Let's see if ngOnChanges() will be invoked and which values it's going to get. The code of the parent component is shown in the following listing.

Listing 9.4 app.component.ts

```
@Component({
  selector: 'app-root',
  styles: ['.parent {background: deeppink}'],
  template: `
     <div class="parent">
       <h2>Parent</h2>
       <div>Greeting: <input type="text" [(ngModel)]="myGreeting">
        </div>
       <div>User name: <input type="text" [(ngModel)]="myUser.name">
        </div>
       <child [greeting]="myGreeting"
              [user]="myUser">
        </child>
     </div>
  `
})
export class AppComponent {
  myGreeting = 'Hello';
  myUser: {name: string} = {name: 'John'};
}
```

Uses two-way binding to synchronize entered greeting and myGreeting

Uses two-way binding to synchronize entered username and myUser.name

Binds myGreeting to child's input property greeting

Binds myUser to child's input property user

The child component receives the values from the parent component via its input variables. This component implements the OnChanges interface. In the ngOnChanges() method , you print the received data as soon as the binding to any of the input variable changes, as shown in the following listing.

Listing 9.5 child.component.ts

```
@Component({
  selector: 'child',
  styles: ['.child {background: lightgreen}'],
  template: `
    <div class="child">
      <h2>Child</h2>
      <div>Greeting: {{greeting}}</div>
      <div>User name: {{user.name}}</div>
    </div>
  `
})
export class ChildComponent implements OnChanges {    ◁ Implements the OnChanges interface
   @Input() greeting: string;
  @Input() user: {name: string};

  ngOnChanges(changes: {[key: string]: SimpleChange}) {    ◁ Angular invokes ngOnChanges() when the bindings to input properties change.

    console.log(JSON.stringify(changes, null, 2));
  }
}
```

When Angular invokes `ngOnChanges()`, it provides a `SimpleChange` object containing the old and new values of the modified input property and the flag indicating whether this is the first binding change. You use `JSON.stringify()` to pretty-print the received values.

Let's see if changing `greeting` and `user.name` in the UI results in the invocation of `ngOnChanges()` on the child component. We ran this app, deleted the last letter in the word *Hello,* and changed the name of the user from John to John Smith, as shown in figure 9.5.

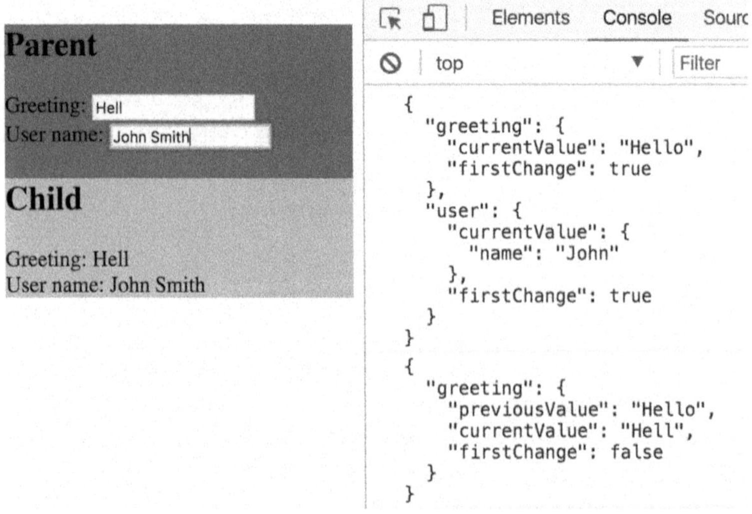

Figure 9.5 `ngOnChanges()` **is invoked after the greeting change**

Initially, `ngOnChanges()` was invoked for both properties. Note the `"firstChange": true`—this was the very first change in bindings. After we deleted the letter *o* in the greeting *Hello,* `ngOnChanges()` was invoked again, and the `firstChange` flag became `false`. But changing the username from *John* to *John Smith* didn't invoke `ngOnChanges()`, because the binding of the mutable object `myUser` didn't change.

To see this app in action, run `npm install` in the project lifecycle, and then run the following command:

```
ng serve --app lifecycle -o
```

Angular doesn't update bindings to input properties if only the object properties change, and that's why the `ngOnChanges()` on the child wasn't invoked. But the change detection mechanism still catches the change. That's why `"John Smith"`, the new value of the property `user.name`, has been rendered in the child component.

> **TIP** Add `changeDetection: ChangeDetectionStrategy.OnPush` to the template of `ChildComponent`, and its UI won't reflect changes in the parent's username. The binding to the child's `user` property doesn't change; hence, the change detector won't even visit the child for UI updates.

You probably appreciate the change detector for properly updating the UI, but what if you still need to programmatically catch the moment when the username changes and implement some code that handles this change?

9.2.2 Catching changes in the ngDoCheck hook

Suppose you want to catch the moment when a JavaScript object gets mutated. Let's rewrite the child component from the preceding section to use the `ngDoCheck()` callback instead of `ngOnChanges()`. The goals are as follows:

- Catch the moment when the object bound to an `Input()` property mutates.
- Find out which property of the bound object changed.
- Get the previous value of the changed property.
- Get the new value of this property.

To achieve these goals, you'll implement the `DoCheck` interface and use Angular's `KeyValueDiffers`, `KeyValueChangeRecord`, and `KeyValueDiffer`. You want to monitor the `user` object and its properties.

First, you'll inject the `KeyValueDiffers` service, which implements diffing strategies for various Angular artifacts. Second, you need to create an object of type `KeyValueDiffer` that will specifically monitor `user` object changes. When a change happens, you'll get an object of type `KeyValueChangeRecord` containing the properties `key`, `previousValue`, and `currentValue`. The code of the new child component is shown in the following listing.

Listing 9.6 child.component-docheck.ts

```
import {
  DoCheck, Input, SimpleChange, Component, KeyValueDiffers,
  ➥KeyValueChangeRecord, KeyValueDiffer} from "@angular/core";

@Component({
  selector: 'child',
  styles: ['.child {background: lightgreen}'],
  template: `
    <div class="child">
      <h2>Child</h2>
      <div>Greeting: {{greeting}}</div>
      <div>User name: {{user.name}}</div>
    </div>
  `
})
export class ChildComponent implements DoCheck {
  @Input() greeting: string;
  @Input() user: {name: string};

  differ: KeyValueDiffer<string, string>;       ⟵ Declares a variable for storing differences

  constructor(private _differs: KeyValueDiffers) { }       ⟵ Injects the service for monitoring changes

  ngOnInit() {
   this.differ = this._differs.find(this.user).create();       ⟵ Initializes the differ variable for storing differences in the user object
   }

  ngDoCheck() {       ⟵ Implements the callback ngDoCheck()

    if (this.user && this.differ) {

      const changes = this.differ.diff(this.user);       ⟵ Checks whether the properties of the user object changed

      if (changes) {
        changes.forEachChangedItem(       ⟵ Gets the record of changes for each user property
           (record: KeyValueChangeRecord<string, string>) =>
            console.log(`Got changes in property ${record.key}       ⟵ Prints the changes on the console
                before: ${record.previousValue} after: ${record.currentValue}
      `));
      }
    }
  }
}
```

The diff() method returns a KeyValueChanges object that includes the record about the change and offers such methods as forEachAddedItem(), forEachChangedItem(), forEachRemovedItem(), and more. In your component, you're interested only in catching changes, so you use forEachChangedItem(), which returns the KeyValueChangeRecord for each changed property.

The KeyValueChangeRecord interface defines the properties key, currentValue, and previousValue, which you print on the console. Figure 9.6 shows what happens after you delete the letter *n* in the User name input field, which was *John* originally.

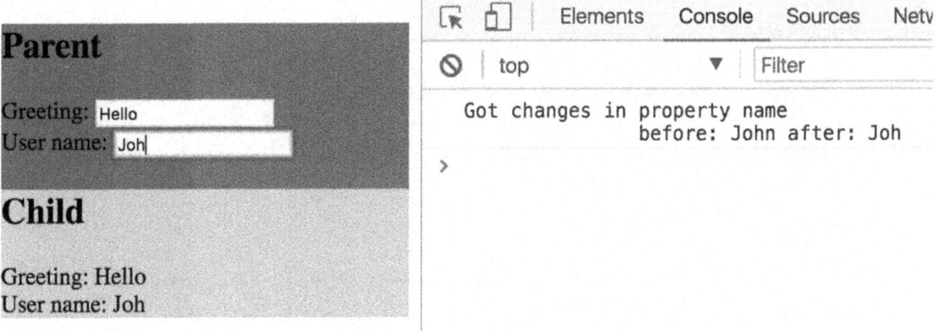

Figure 9.6 `ngDoCheck()` **is invoked after each pass of the change detector.**

Catching the username changes doesn't seem to be a practical use case, but some applications do need to invoke specific business logic whenever the value of a property changes. For example, financial applications may need to log each of a trader's steps. If a trader places a buy order at $101 and then immediately changes the price to $100, that must be tracked in a log file. This may be a good use case for catching such a change and adding logging in the `DoCheck()` callback.

To see this app in action, in the lifecycle/app.module.ts file, modify the import statement for the child component to `import {ChildComponent} from "./child.component-docheck";` and run the following command:

```
ng serve --app lifecycle -o
```

CAUTION We want to warn you once again: use `ngDoCheck()` only if you can't find another way of intercepting data changes, because it may affect the performance of your app.

Lifecycle hooks, change detection, and production mode

At the beginning of the chapter, we stated that the change detector makes one pass from top to bottom of the components tree to see if the component's UI should be updated. This is correct if your app runs in production mode, but in development mode (default), change detector makes two passes.

If you open the browser's console while running most of the apps from this book, you'll see a message stating that Angular is running in development mode, which performs assertions and other checks within the framework. One such assertion verifies that a change detection pass doesn't result in additional changes to any bindings (for example, your code doesn't modify the UI in the component lifecycle callbacks during the CD cycle). If your code tries to change the UI from one of the lifecycle callbacks, Angular will throw an exception.

> **(continued)**
> When you're ready to make a production build, turn on production mode so the change detector will make only one pass and won't perform the additional bindings check. To enable production mode, invoke `enableProdMode()` in your app before invoking the `bootstrap()` method. Enabling production mode will also result in better app performance.

Now that we've covered all the important parts of the component's life, let's continue working on ngAuction.

9.3 Hands-on: Adding the product view to ngAuction

In chapter 7, you created the home page of ngAuction. In this section, you'll create the product view, which will be rendered when the user clicks one of the product tiles in the home view. Figure 9.7 shows how the product view will look if the user selects Vintage Bluetooth Radio.

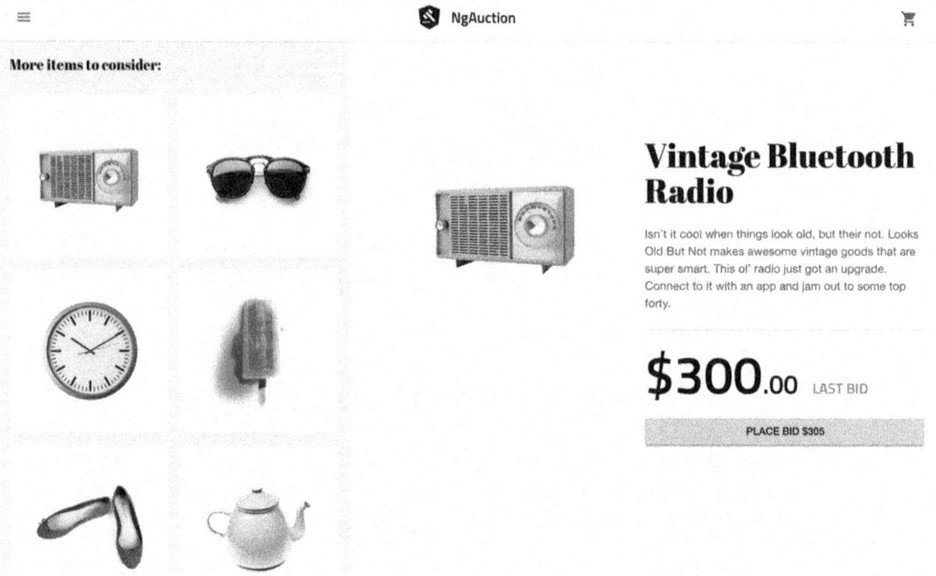

Figure 9.7 The product view

Besides information about the radio on the right, on the left are other suggested products that you want the user to consider. Amazon uses the same marketing technique while showing a product description. You've probably seen "More items to consider" or "Frequently bought together" sections on Amazon's product pages.

Depending on the viewport size, suggested products can be rendered either on the left or at the bottom of the product view.

The view shown in figure 9.7 will be implemented as `ProductComponent`, which will include two child components: `ProductDetailComponent` and `ProductSuggestionComponent`. In the product view, you'll use the Flex Layout library so that the UI layout will adjust to the available width of the viewport on the user's device.

One more thing: your product view will be implemented as a lazy-loaded feature module, explained in section 4.3 in chapter 4. Let's begin.

> **NOTE** If you created this version of ngAuction by following the explanations and instructions from the hands-on section in chapter 7, you can continue working on this app. You'll find the completed version of ngAuction with the implemented product view in the folder chapter9/ng-auction.

9.3.1 Creating product components and the module

You'll start with generating a `ProductModule` feature module by running the following command:

```
ng g m product
```

The command will create the product folder with the product.module.ts file. Because you'll use the Flex Layout library on the product view, add `FlexLayoutModule` to the `imports` property of the `@NgModule()` decorator, as shown in the following listing.

Listing 9.7 product.module.ts

```
import {NgModule} from '@angular/core';
import {CommonModule} from '@angular/common';
import {FlexLayoutModule} from '@angular/flex-layout';

@NgModule({
  imports: [
    CommonModule,
    FlexLayoutModule
  ],
  declarations: []
})
export class ProductModule { }
```

This feature module will contain three components: `ProductComponent`, `ProductDetailComponent`, and `ProductSuggestionComponent`. The latter two will be subcomponents, and you want them to be located in separate subfolder under the product folder. You generate these components with the following commands:

```
ng g c product
ng g c product/product-detail
ng g c product/product-suggestion
```

These commands will generate three components and will add their names to the `declarations` property of the product module. You're going to lazy load the

ProductModule when the user clicks a particular product tile in the home component. To do that, you'll configure an additional route for the products/:productId path, so the app.component.ts file will look like the following listing.

Listing 9.8 app.routing.ts

```
import {Route} from '@angular/router';

export const routes: Route[] = [
  {
    path: '',
    loadChildren: './home/home.module#HomeModule'
  },
  {
    path: 'products/:productId',
    loadChildren: './product/product.module#ProductModule'
  }
];
```

Now you can proceed with implementing the components supporting the product view.

9.3.2 *Implementing the product component*

Your ProductComponent will serve as a wrapper for two child components: Product-DetailComponent and ProductSuggestionComponent. The product component implements the following functionality:

- It should be a default route of the product module.
- It should receive the product ID passed from the home component.
- It should get a reference to the ProductService object to receive product details.
- It should manage the layout of its children based on the viewport width.

To render the ProductComponent when the user navigates to the product view, you need to add the following listing to the ProductModule.

Listing 9.9 product.module.ts

```
...
import {RouterModule} from '@angular/router';

@NgModule({
  imports: [
   ...
    RouterModule.forChild([
      {path: '', component: ProductComponent}
    ])
  ],
  ...
})
export class ProductModule {}
```

In the preceding section, you configured the route for the path `'products/:productId'` in the root module, which means `ProductComponent` has to receive the requested product ID. You also need to inject `ProductService` in the constructor of `Product-Component`, as shown in the following listing.

Listing 9.10 product.component.ts

```
import { filter, map, switchMap} from 'rxjs/operators';
import { Component } from '@angular/core';
import { ActivatedRoute } from '@angular/router';
import { Observable } from 'rxjs';
import { Product, ProductService } from '../shared/services';

@Component({
  selector: 'nga-product',
  styleUrls: [ './product.component.scss' ],
  templateUrl: './product.component.html'
})
export class ProductComponent {
  product$: Observable<Product>;
  suggestedProducts$: Observable<Product[]>;

  constructor(
    private route: ActivatedRoute,
    private productService: ProductService
  ) {
    this.product$ = this.route.paramMap
      .pipe(
        map(params => parseInt(params.get('productId') || '', 10)),   // Gets the product ID
        filter(productId => !!productId),   // Ensures that product ID is a valid number
        switchMap(productId => this.productService.getById(productId))   // Switches to the observable that retrieves details for the specified product
      );

    this.suggestedProducts$ = this.productService.getAll();   // Initializes the observable for populating the suggested products
  }
}
```

This component receives the product ID from the `ActivatedRoute` object. In section 6.6 of chapter 6, you saw the code that directly subscribes to the `paramMap`. In this case, you don't explicitly invoke the `subscribe()` method but will use the `async` pipe in the template. That's why you convert the given parameter from a string to a number with `parseInt()` in the `map` operator.

What if the user enters alpha characters in the URL instead of the product ID, such as http://localhost:4200/products/abc? In this case, `parseInt()` returns `NaN`, which you'll catch in the `filter` operator using double-bang syntax: `!!productId`. Non-alpha characters won't get through the `filter` operator.

The numeric product IDs will be given to the `switchMap` operator that switches over to the observable returned by the `getById()` method. To get the suggested products, you invoke the `getAll()` method .

NOTE Earlier, we stated that `ngOnInit()` is the right place for fetching data, but in this code sample, you do it in the constructor. Would it cause problems? Not in this case, because neither `getById()` nor `getAll()` uses component properties that would be initialized in the constructor.

Homework

The code for `ProductComponent` could use a couple of improvements, and we want you to implement them on your own.

Your product component invokes `productService.getAll()` to retrieve suggested products. This isn't exactly right. Say you select sunglasses. The product-detail component will show the description of the sunglasses, and the sunglasses will be also included as a suggested product. See if you can modify the implementation of the product component so it won't suggest the product that is already selected by the user.

If you enter an invalid product ID in the browser (such as http:// localhost:4200/ products/abc) on the product page, you won't see any errors because the `filter()` operator will ignore this request, but the page will render only suggested products. To handle this scenario in a user-friendly manner, create a resolve guard, which will cancel the navigation if the service doesn't find the product with the provided ID and notify the user about it. For example, you can use the Angular Material snack-bar component for notifications (see http://mng.bz/1hx1).

The template of the product component will be implemented in the product .component .html file. It'll host `<nga-product-detail>` and `<nga-product-suggestion>` components and pass them the product(s) data to render, as shown in the following listing.

Listing 9.11 product.component.html

```
<div class="wrapper"
     fxLayout="column"
     fxLayout.>-md="row-reverse">

  <nga-product-detail
      fxFlex="auto"
       fxFlex.>-md="65%"
      *ngIf="product$ | async as product"
       [product]="product">
   </nga-product-detail>

  <nga-product-suggestion
      fxFlex="auto"
      fxFlex.>-md="35%"
      *ngIf="suggestedProducts$ | async as products"
       [products]="products">
   </nga-product-suggestion>
</div>
```

- On larger than medium viewports, shows product detail on the right and suggested products on the left
- Takes enough space to render this component but not more
- If product$ emitted a value, puts it in the local template variable product
- Passes the product object to <nga-product-detail> for rendering
- If suggestedProducts$ emitted a value, puts it in the local template variable products
- Passes products to <nga-product-suggestion> for rendering.

Best practice

Listing 9.11 uses the `async as` syntax for subscription. `async as product` means "define the local template variable `product`, and store the emitted value there." This syntax is useful when you need to reference the emitted object multiple times. Without the `async as` syntax, it could be written like this:

```
*ngIf = "product$ | async"
[product] = "product$ | async"
```

That would create two subscriptions instead of one, which you want to avoid, especially if a subscription triggers side effects like an HTTP request or some additional processing like filtering or sorting a large set of data.

NOTE From now on, to save space in this book, we won't include the content of the .scss files that contain styles of the ngAuction components. Please refer to the code samples that come with the book, found at https://github.com/Farata/angulartypescript and www.manning.com/books/angular-development-with-typescript-second-edition.

9.3.3 Implementing the product-detail component

The `ProductDetailComponent` is a presentation component that contains no business logic and renders the product provided via its input property. It's a child of the `ProductComponent`, as shown in the following listing.

Listing 9.12 product-detail.component.ts

```
@Component({
  selector: 'nga-product-detail',
  styleUrls: ['./product-detail.component.scss'],
  templateUrl: './product-detail.component.html'
})
export class ProductDetailComponent {
  @Input() product: Product;
}
```

The template of this component is shown in the next listing. It supports responsive web design (RWD) using the directives from the Flex Layout library.

Listing 9.13 product-detail.component.html

```
<div class="wrapper"
     ngClass.lt-md="wrapper--lt-md"
     ngClass.>-md="wrapper-->-md"
     fxLayout="row"
     fxLayoutAlign="center"
     fxLayout.xs="column"
     fxLayoutAlign.xs="center center">    <-- Centers the content of the children both horizontally and vertically
```

```
<div fxFlex="50%">                    <-- Half of the viewport is given
   <img class="thumbnail"                 to the product image.
       [attr.alt]="product.title"
       [attr.src]="product.imageUrl">
</div>                                     Half of the viewport is given
                                           to the title, description, and
<div fxFlex="50%">                    <-- bidding controls.
   <div class="info">
    <h1 class="info__title">{{product?.title}}</h1>
    <div class="info__description">{{product?.description}}</div>
    <div class="info__bid">
      <span>
The last bid --> <span class="info__bid-value"
amount                 ngClass.lt-md="info__bid-value--lt-md">
                 {{product?.price | currency: 'USD': 'symbol': '.0'}}</span>
        <span class="info__bid-value-decimal"
              ngClass.lt-md="info__bid-value-decimal--lt-md">.00</span>
      </span>
      <span class="info__bid-label">LAST BID</span>
    </div>

    <button class="info__bid-button"          Uses the button from
            mat-raised-button            <-- Angular Material
             color="accent">
      PLACE BID {{(product?.price + 5) | currency: 'USD': 'symbol': '.0'}} <--
     </button>
   </div>                                          The user can place
  </div>                                       bids in $5 increments.
</div>
```

In this version of the auction, you don't implement the bidding functionality. You'll do that in the hands-on section in chapter 13.

Because you use `mat-raised-button` from the Angular Material library, add the `MatButtonModule` to the product module

Listing 9.14 product.module.ts

```
....
import {MatButtonModule} from '@angular/material/button';
@NgModule({
  imports: [
    ...
    MatButtonModule
  ]
  ...
})
export class ProductModule {}
```

9.3.4 *Implementing the product-suggestion component*

In real-world online stores or auctions, the product-suggestion component shows similar products from the same category that the user may consider buying. In this version of ngAuction, you'll show all your products (you have only a dozen of them) under the caption "More items to consider," as you saw on the left in figure 9.7.

ProductSuggestionComponent is the second child of ProductComponent, and the content of the product-suggestion.component.ts file is shown in the following listing.

Listing 9.15 product-suggestion.component.ts

```
import { map, startWith } from 'rxjs/operators';
import { Component, Input } from '@angular/core';
import { ObservableMedia } from '@angular/flex-layout';
import { Observable } from 'rxjs';
import { Product } from '../../shared/services';

@Component({
  selector: 'nga-product-suggestion',
  styleUrls: [ './product-suggestion.component.scss' ],
  templateUrl: './product-suggestion.component.html'
})
export class ProductSuggestionComponent {
  @Input() products: Product[];
  readonly columns$: Observable<number>;
  readonly breakpointsToColumnsNumber = new Map([      <-- Sets the number of grid columns for different viewport sizes
    [ 'xs', 2 ],
    [ 'sm', 3 ],
    [ 'md', 5 ],
    [ 'lg', 2 ],
    [ 'xl', 3 ],
  ]);

  constructor(private media: ObservableMedia) {      <-- Injects the ObservableMedia service from the Flex Layout library
     this.columns$ = this.media.asObservable()
      .pipe(
        map(mc => <number>this.breakpointsToColumnsNumber.get(mc.mqAlias)),
        startWith(3) // bug workaround      <-- Gets the number of grid columns based on the media query alias
      );
  }
}
```

The code for ProductSuggestionComponent is similar to the code for the HomeComponent developed for ngAuction in the hands-on section in chapter 7. In this case, you use different numbers of grid columns based on the viewport size, taking into account that a large portion of the screen will be occupied by the ProductDetailComponent. The template of the product suggestions component is shown in the following listing.

Listing 9.16 product-suggestion.component.html

```
<div class="info__title" fxLayout="row">
   More items to consider:
</div>

<mat-grid-list [cols]="columns$ | async" gutterSize="16px">      <-- Subscribes to columns$ using the async pipe

  <mat-grid-tile class="tile" *ngFor="let product of products">      <-- For each product, renders a tile that wraps product info in the anchor tag
     <a class="tile__content"
       fxLayout
       fxLayoutAlign="center center"
```

```
      [routerLink]="['/products', product.id]">       <— Shows another product info if the user clicks the tile

      <div class="tile__thumbnail"
           [ngStyle]="{'background-image':
➥ 'url(' + product.imageUrl + ')'}"></div>
    </a>
  </mat-grid-tile>
</mat-grid-list>
```

Because you use `<mat-grid-list>` from the Angular Material library, add the `MatGridListModule` to the product module.

Listing 9.17 product.module.ts

```
....
import { MatGridListModule } from '@angular/material/grid-list';
@NgModule({
  imports: [
    ...
    MatGridListModule
  ]
  ...
})
export class ProductModule {}
```

To run this version of ngAuction that implements routing and the product view, use the following command:

```
ng serve -o
```

Open the Network tab in Chrome Dev Tools and click one of the products. You'll see that the code and resources of the product module were lazy loaded.

In the hands-on section of chapter 11, you'll add search functionality and category tabs for easily filtering products by category.

Summary

- The change detection mechanism automatically monitors changes to components' properties and updates the UI accordingly.
- You can mark selected branches of your app component tree to be excluded from the change detection process.
- Writing the application code in the component lifecycle hook ensures that this code is executed in sync with UI updates.

10 Introducing the Forms API

This chapter covers

- Understanding the Angular Forms API
- Working with template-driven forms
- Working with reactive forms

HTML provides basic features for displaying forms, validating entered values, and submitting data to the server. But HTML forms may not be good enough for real-world applications, which need a way to programmatically process the entered data, apply custom validation rules, display user-friendly error messages, transform the format of the entered data, and choose the way data is submitted to the server. For business applications, one of the most important considerations when choosing a web framework is how well it handles forms.

Angular offers rich support for handling forms. It goes beyond regular data binding by treating form fields as first-class citizens and providing fine-grained control over form data. In this chapter, we'll introduce you two Forms APIs: template-driven and reactive.

10.1 Two Forms APIs

Every Angular-powered form has an underlying model object that stores the form's data. There are two approaches to working with forms in Angular: *template-driven* and *reactive*. These two approaches are exposed as two different APIs (sets of directives and TypeScript classes).

With the *template-driven* API, forms are fully programmed in the component's template using directives, and the model object is created implicitly by Angular. The template defines the structure of the form, the format of its fields, and the validation rules. Because you're limited to HTML syntax while defining the form, the template-driven approach suits only simple forms.

With the reactive API, you explicitly create the model object in TypeScript code and then link the HTML template elements to that model's properties using special directives. You construct the form model object explicitly using the `FormControl`, `FormGroup`, and `FormArray` classes. In the template-driven approach, you don't access these classes directly, whereas in the reactive approach, you explicitly create instances of these classes. For non-trivial forms, the reactive approach is a better option.

Both template-driven and reactive APIs need to be explicitly enabled before you start using them. To enable reactive forms, add `ReactiveFormsModule` from `@angular/forms` to the `imports` list of `NgModule`. For template-driven forms, import `FormsModule`, as shown in the following listing.

Listing 10.1 Preparing to use the template-driven Forms API

```
...
import { FormsModule} from '@angular/forms';

@NgModule({
  imports: [ BrowserModule,
             FormsModule]        <-- Adds support for the template-driven Forms API
    ...
})
class AppModule {}
```

It's time to discuss both APIs in greater detail.

10.2 Template-driven forms

With the template-driven API, you can use only directives in a component's templates. These directives are included in the `FormsModule`: `NgModel`, `NgModelGroup`, and `NgForm`. We'll briefly look at these directives and then apply the template-driven approach to the sample registration form.

10.2.1 Forms directives

This section briefly describes the three main directives from `FormsModule`: `NgModel`, `NgModelGroup`, and `NgForm`. We'll show you how they can be used in the template and highlight their most important features.

NgForm

NgForm is the directive that represents the entire form. It's automatically attached to every <form> element. NgForm implicitly creates an instance of the FormGroup class that represents the model and stores the form's data (more on FormGroup later in this chapter). NgForm automatically discovers all child HTML elements marked with the NgModel directive and adds their values to the form model object.

You can bind an implicitly created NgForm object to a local template variable so you can access values of the NgForm object inside the template, as shown in the following listing.

Listing 10.2 Binding NgForm to a template variable

```
<form #f="ngForm"></form>            <- Declares a local template variable
                                        f and binds it to ngForm
<pre>{{ f.value | json }}</pre>       <- Displays the values
                                        of the form model
```

The local template variable f points at the instance of NgForm attached to the <form>. Then you can use the f variable to access instance members of the NgForm object. One of them is value, which represents a JavaScript object containing current values of all form fields. You can pass it through the standard json pipe to display the form's value on the page.

NgForm intercepts the standard HTML form's submit event and prevents automatic form submission. Instead, it emits the custom ngSubmit event:

```
<form #f="ngForm" (ngSubmit)="onSubmit(f.value)"></form>
```

This subscribes to the ngSubmit event using event-binding syntax. The onSubmit handler is a method with an arbitrary name defined in the component, and it's invoked when the ngSubmit event is emitted. To pass all the form's values as an argument to this method, use a local template variable (for example, f) to access NgForm's value property.

NgModel

Section 2.6.2 of chapter 2 discusses how the NgModel directive can be used for two-way data binding. But in the Forms API, NgModel plays a different role: it marks the HTML element that should become a part of the form model.

In the context of the Forms API, NgModel represents a single field on the form. If an HTML element includes ngModel, Angular implicitly creates an instance of the FormControl class that represents the model and stores the fields' data (more on FormControl later in this chapter). Note that the Forms API doesn't require a value assigned to ngModel, nor any kind of brackets around this attribute, as you can see in the following listing.

Listing 10.3 Adding the `NgModel` directive to an HTML element

```
<form #f="ngForm">
  <input type="text"
         name="username"
          ngModel>
 </form>
```

The name attribute is required so you can access its value in the code.

Ensures that this <input> field is included in the form model object

The `NgForm.value` property points at the JavaScript object that holds the values of all form fields. The value of the field's name attribute becomes the property name of the corresponding property in the JavaScript object in `NgForm.value`.

> **NOTE** Although the names of the classes that implement form directives are capitalized, their names should start with a lowercase letter in templates (for example, `NgForm` versus `ngForm`).

NgModelGroup

`NgModelGroup` represents a part of the form and allows you to group form fields together. Like `NgForm`, it implicitly creates an instance of the `FormGroup` class. `NgModelGroup` creates a nested object inside the object stored in `NgForm.value`. All the child fields of `NgModelGroup` become properties of the nested object, as you can see in the following listing.

Listing 10.4 A form with a nested form

```
<form #f="ngForm">
  <div ngModelGroup="passwords">
     <input type="text" name="password" ngModel>
    <input type="text" name="pconfirm" ngModel>
  </div>
</form>

<!-- Access the values from the nested object-->
<pre>Password: {{ f.value.passwords.password }}</pre>
 <pre>Password confirmation: {{ f.value.passwords.pconfirm }}</pre>
```

The ngModelGroup attribute requires a string value, which becomes a property name representing the nested form.

Accesses the values of the password and pconfirm form controls, using the nested object passwords for reference

Table 10.1 contains a summary of directives used in template-driven forms.

Table 10.1 Template-driven forms directives

Directive	Description
`NgForm`	Implicitly created directive that represents the entire form
`ngForm`	Used in templates to bind the template element (for example, `<form>`) to `NgForm`, typically assigned to a local template variable

Table 10.1 Template-driven forms directives *(continued)*

Directive	Description
`NgModel`	Implicitly created directive that marks the HTML element to be included in the form model
`ngForm`	Used in templates in form elements (for example, `<input>`) to be included in the form model
`name`	Used in templates in form elements to specify its name in the form model
`NgModelGroup`	Implicitly created directive that represents a part of the form, for example, password and confirm password fields
`ngModelGroup`	Used in templates to name a part of the form for future reference
`ngSubmit`	Intercepts the HTML form's submit event

10.2.2 Applying the template-driven API to HTML forms

Let's create a simple user registration form, applying the template-driven Forms API. You'll also add validation logic and enable programmatic handling of the `ngSubmit` event. You'll start by creating the template, and then you'll work on the TypeScript part. First, modify the standard HTML `<form>` element to match the following listing.

Listing 10.5 Angular-aware form

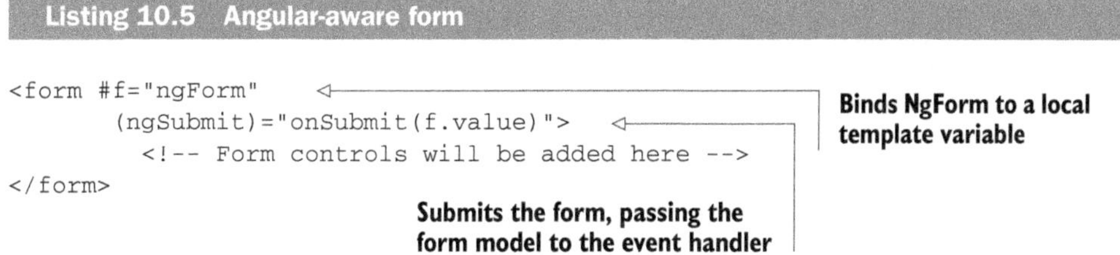

```
<form #f="ngForm"
        (ngSubmit)="onSubmit(f.value)">
          <!-- Form controls will be added here -->
</form>
```

Binds NgForm to a local template variable
Submits the form, passing the form model to the event handler

A local template variable `f` points at the `NgForm` object attached to the `<form>` element in the DOM. You need this variable to access the form's properties (such as `value` and `valid`), and to check whether the form has errors in a specific field.

The `ngSubmit` event is emitted by `NgForm`. You don't want to listen to the standard submit event because `NgForm` intercepts the submit event and stops its propagation. This prevents the form from being automatically submitted to the server, resulting in a page reload. Instead, `NgForm` emits its own `ngSubmit` event.

The `onSubmit()` method will handle the `ngSubmit` event, and you'll add this method to the component's class. It takes one argument—the form's value—which is a plain JavaScript object that keeps the values of all the fields on the form. Next, add the `username` and `ssn` fields (SSN is a unique ID that every US resident has).

Listing 10.6 The username and ssn fields

```
<div>Username: <input type="text" name="username" ngModel></div>
<div>SSN:      <input type="text" name="ssn"      ngModel></div>
```

The ngModel attribute makes this <input> element a part of the NgForm. You also add the name attribute with the value username.

Makes similar changes to the ssn field

Now you'll add the fields to enter and confirm the password. Because these fields are related and represent the same value, it's natural to combine them into a group. Wrapping both passwords into a single object is useful for implementing a validator that checks whether both passwords are the same, as you can see in the following listing (you'll see how to do it in section 11.3.1 in chapter 11).

Listing 10.7 The password fields

```
<div ngModelGroup="passwordsGroup">
   <div>Password: <input type="password"
                  name="password" ngModel></div>
   <div>Confirm password: <input type="password"
                  name="pconfirm" ngModel></div>
 </div>
```

The ngModelGroup directive instructs NgForm to create a nested object within the form's value object that keeps the child fields.

Changes for the password and pconfirm fields are similar to those for ngModelGroup, but the values of the name attributes differ.

The Submit button remains the same as in the plain HTML version of the form:

```
<button type="submit">Submit</button>
```

Now that you're done with the template, you'll use it in a component, as shown in the following listing.

Listing 10.8 A component that uses the template-driven Forms API

```
@Component({
  selector: 'app-root',
  template: `
    <form #f="ngForm" (ngSubmit)="onSubmit(f.value)">
      <div>Username:        <input type="text"     name="username" ngModel>
      </div>
     <div>SSN:            <input type="text"      name="ssn"       ngModel>
     </div>
     <div ngModelGroup="passwordsGroup"> 2((CO8-2))
        <div>Password:        <input type="password" name="password" ngModel>
        </div>
        <div>Confirm password: <input type="password" name="pconfirm"  ngModel>
        </div>
     </div>
```

Binds NgForm to a local template variable and submits the form

Creates a nested group for passwords

```
    <button type="submit">Submit</button>
  </form>
  `
})
export class AppComponent {
  onSubmit(formData) {        <-- The method handler for
    console.log(formData);        the onSubmit event
  }
}
```

The `onSubmit()` event handler takes a single argument: the form model's value, an object containing the field's values. As you can see, the handler doesn't use an Angular-specific API. Depending on the validity flag on the model, you can decide whether to post the `formData` to the server. In this example, you print it to the console.

To see this app in action, run `npm install` in the directory form-samples, and then run the following command:

```
ng serve --app template -o
```

Fill out the form and click the Submit button. The value of the model object will be printed in the browser's console, as shown in figure 10.1.

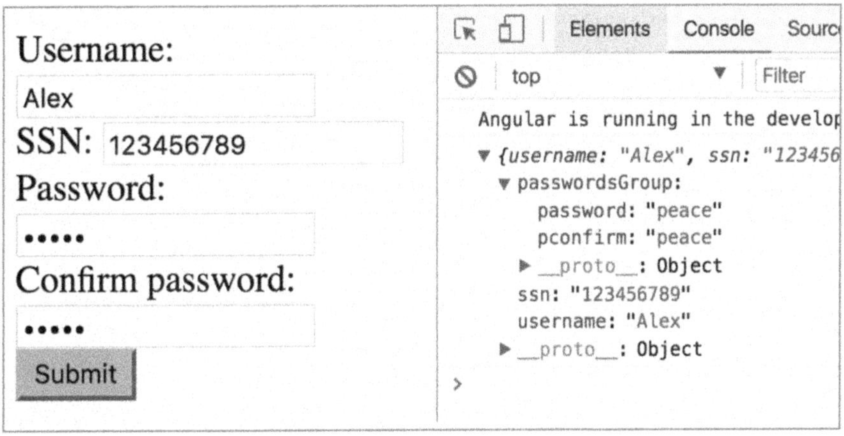

Figure 10.1 Running a template-driven registration form

Figure 10.2 displays a sample registration form with the form directives applied to it. Each form directive is circled so you can see what makes up the form. The complete running application that illustrates how to use form directives is located in the template-driven directory.

> **NOTE** Source code for this chapter can be found at https://github.com/Farata/angulartypescript and www.manning.com/books/angular-development-with-typescript-second-edition.

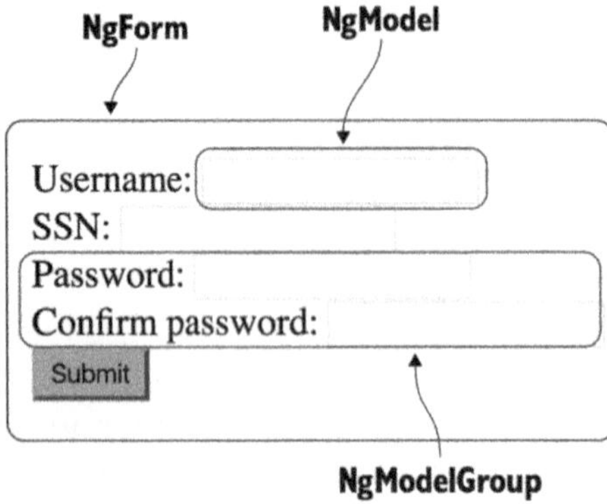

Figure 10.2 Form directives on the registration form

10.3 Reactive forms

Creating a reactive form requires more steps than creating a template-driven one. In short, you need to perform the following steps:

1. Import `ReactiveFormsModule` in the `NgModule()` where your component is declared.
2. In your TypeScript code, create an instance of the model object `FormGroup` to store the form's values.
3. Create an HTML form template, adding reactive directives.
4. Use the instance of the `FormGroup` to access the form's values.

Adding `ReactiveFormsModule` to the `@NgModule()` decorator is a trivial operation.

Listing 10.9 Adding support for reactive forms

```
import { ReactiveFormsModule } from '@angular/forms';

@NgModule({
  ...
  imports: [
    ...
    ReactiveFormsModule          <-- Imports the module that supports reactive forms
  ],
  ...
})
```

Now let's talk about how to create a form model.

10.3.1 Form model

The form model is a data structure that holds the form's data. It can be constructed from `FormControl`, `FormGroup`, and `FormArray` classes. For example, the following listing declares a class property of type `FormGroup` and initializes it with a new object that will contain instances of the form controls for your form.

Listing 10.10 Creating a form model object

```
myFormModel: FormGroup;

  constructor() {
    this.myFormModel = new FormGroup({     <-- Creates an instance of a form model
       username: new FormControl(''),      Adds form controls
       ssn: new FormControl('')            to the form model
     });
  }
```

FormControl

`FormControl` is an atomic form unit. Most often, it corresponds to a single `<input>` element, but it can also represent a more complex UI component like a calendar or a slider. A `FormControl` instance stores the current value of the HTML element it corresponds to, the element's validity status, and whether it's been modified. Here's how you can create a control passing its initial value as the first argument of the constructor:

```
let city = new FormControl('New York');
```

You can also create a `FormControl` attaching one or more built-in or custom validators. Chapter 11 covers form validation, but the following code listing shows how to attach two built-in Angular validators to a form control.

Listing 10.11 Adding validators to a form control

```
let city = new FormControl('New York',           <-- Creates a form control with the initial value New York
                  [Validators.required,          <-- Adds a required validator to a form control
                   Validators.minLength(2)]);    <-- Adds a minLength validator to a form control
```

NOTE You can add a `formControl` directive to a template without wrapping it inside an `NgForm` directive—for example, it can be used with a standalone `<input>` element. You can find such an example in chapter 6 in section 6.3.

FormGroup

`FormGroup` is a collection of `FormControl` objects and represents either the entire form or its part. `FormGroup` aggregates the values and validity of each `FormControl` in the group. If one of the controls in a group is invalid, the entire group becomes invalid. The following listing shows the use of `FormGroup` to represent the form or part of it.

Listing 10.12 Creating a form model by instantiating a `FormGroup`

```
myFormModel: FormGroup;

  constructor() {
    this.myFormModel = new FormGroup({     <-- This FormGroup instance represents the entire form.
```

```
      username: new FormControl(''),
     ssn: new FormControl(''),
     passwordsGroup: new FormGroup({
        password: new FormControl(''),
        pconfirm: new FormControl('')
     })
   });
 }
```

This FormGroup instance represents a part of the form, grouping two password controls together.

Declares and initializes the password form control

Declares and initializes the pconfirm control for password confirmation

In section 10.3.6, you'll see a simplified syntax for creating form models with nesting.

FORMARRAY

When you need to programmatically add (or remove) controls to a form, use `FormArray`. It's similar to `FormGroup` but has a `length` variable. Whereas `FormGroup` represents an entire form or a fixed subset of a form's fields, `FormArray` usually represents a collection of form controls that can grow or shrink. For example, you could use `FormArray` to allow users to enter an arbitrary number of emails. The following listing shows a model that would back such a form.

Listing 10.13 Adding a `FormArray` to a `FormGroup`

```
let myFormModel = new FormGroup({
   emails: new FormArray([
     new FormControl()
   ])
});
```

The FormGroup instance represents the entire form.

This FormArray initially contains a single email control.

Adds an instance of FormControl to the emails array

In section 10.3.4, we'll show you an app that allows the user add more email controls during runtime, to allow users to enter multiple emails.

10.3.2 Reactive directives

The reactive approach also requires you to use directives in component templates, but these directives are different compared to ones from the template-driven API. The reactive directives come with `ReactiveFormsModule` and are prefixed with `form`—for example, `formGroup` (note the small `f`).

You can't create a local template variable in the template that binds to a reactive directive, and it's not needed. In template-driven forms, the model is created implicitly, and local template variables would give you access to the model or its properties. In reactive forms, you explicitly create a model in TypeScript and don't need to access the model in the component template.

The reactive directives formGroup and formControl bind a DOM element to the model object using property-binding syntax with square brackets. The directives that link a DOM element to a TypeScript model's properties by name are formGroupName, formControlName, and formArrayName. They can only be used inside the HTML element marked with the formGroup directive. Let's look at the form directives.

FORMGROUP

The formGroup directive binds an instance of the FormGroup class that represents the entire form model to a top-level form's DOM element, usually a <form>. In the component template, use formGroup with a lowercase f, and in TypeScript, create an instance of the FormGroup class with a capital F. All directives attached to the child DOM elements will be in the scope of formGroup and can link model instances by name. To use the formGroup directive in a template, you need to first create an instance of FormGroup in the TypeScript code of a component, as shown in the following listing.

Listing 10.14 Binding FormGroup to an HTML form

```
@Component({
  selector: 'app-root',
  template: `
    <form [formGroup]="myFormModel">      <-- Binds the instance of the form model to the formGroup directive
     </form>
  `
})
class AppComponent {
  myFormModel = new FormGroup({      <-- Creates an instance of the form model
                // form controls are created here });
}
```

FORMGROUPNAME

The formGroupName directive can be used to link nested groups in a form within templates. Use formGroupName in the scope of a parent formGroup directive to link its child FormGroup instances. The next listing shows how you'd define a form model that uses formGroupName.

Listing 10.15 Using formGroupName

```
@Component({
  ...      <-- Binds the FormGroup that represents the entire form
  template: `<form [formGroup]="myFormModel">
               <div formGroupName="dateRange">...</div>      <-- Links this <div> to the FormGroup called dateRange, defined in myFormModel
             </form>`
})
class FormComponent {
  myFormModel = new FormGroup({      <-- This FormGroup is bound to a DOM element using the formGroup directive in the template.
```

```
    dateRange: new FormGroup({
      from: new FormControl(),
      to  : new FormControl()
    })
  })
}
```

A child FormGroup named dateRange is bound to a DOM element using the formGroupName directive in the template.

FORMCONTROLNAME

`formControlName` must be used in the scope of the `formGroup` directive. It links an individual `FormControl` instance to a DOM element. Let's continue adding code to the example of the `dateRange` model from the previous section. The component and form model remain the same. You only need to add HTML elements with the `formControlName` directive to complete the template.

Listing 10.16 Completed form template

```
<form [formGroup]="myFormModel">
  <div formGroupName="dateRange">
    <input type="date" formControlName="from">
    <input type="date" formControlName="to">
  </div>
</form>
```

from is a property name in the model's nested group dateRange.

to is a property name in the model's nested group dateRange.

As in the `formGroupName` directive, you specify the name of a `FormControl` you want to link to the DOM element. Again, these are the names you chose when defining the form model.

FORMCONTROL

The `formControl` directive is used with individual form controls or single-control forms, when you don't want to create a form model with `FormGroup` but still want to use Forms API features like validation and the reactive behavior provided by the `FormControl.valueChanges` property. You saw it in the weather app in section 6.4 of chapter 6. The following listing shows the essence of that example from the Forms API perspective.

Listing 10.17 `FormControl`

With a standalone FormControl that's not a part of a FormGroup, you can't use the formControlName directive. Use formControl with the property binding.

Instead of defining a form model with FormGroup, create a standalone instance of a FormControl.

```
@Component({
  ...
  template: `<input type="text" [formControl]="weatherControl">`
})
class FormComponent {
  weatherControl: FormControl = new FormControl();
```

```
  constructor() {
    this.weatherControl.valueChanges
        .pipe(
          debounceTime(500),
          switchMap(city => this.getWeather(city))
        )
        .subscribe(weather => console.log(weather));
  }
}
```

Use the valueChanges observable to get the value from the form.

You could use ngModel (as section 2.6.2 of chapter 2) to sync the value entered by the user with the component's property; but because you're using the Forms API, you can use its reactive features. In listing 10.18, you apply two RxJS operators to the observable returned by the valueChanges property to improve the user experience.

10.3.3 Applying the reactive API to HTML forms

Let's refactor the user registration form from section 10.2.2 to use the reactive Forms API. The following listing uses the reactive Forms API, starting by creating a model object in TypeScript.

Listing 10.18 Creating a form model with the reactive API

```
@Component(...)
class AppComponent {
  myFormModel: FormGroup;

  constructor() {
    this.myFormModel = new FormGroup({
       username: new FormControl(),
      ssn: new FormControl(),
      passwordsGroup: new FormGroup({
         password: new FormControl(),
        pconfirm: new FormControl()
      })
    });
  }

  onSubmit() {
    console.log(this.myFormModel.value);
   }
}
```

Declares a component property myFormModel to hold a reference to the form model

Creates an instance of the form model

Creates a nested group for password fields

Prints the form model's values

The myFormModel property holds a reference to the FormGroup instance. You'll bind this property to the formGroup directive in the component template. The myFormModel property is initialized by instantiating a model class. The names you give to form controls in the parent FormGroup will be used in the component's template to link the model to the DOM elements with the formControlName and formGroupName directives.

The passwordsGroup property represents a nested FormGroup that encapsulates the password and confirm password fields. It will be convenient to manage their values as a single object for validation.

NOTE In the reactive API, the `onSubmit()` method doesn't need arguments because you access the form values using your component's `myFormModel` property.

Now that the model is defined, you can write the HTML markup that binds to your model object.

Listing 10.19 HTML binding to the model

```
<form [formGroup]="myFormModel"
      (ngSubmit)="onSubmit()">
  <div>Username: <input type="text" formControlName="username"></div>
  <div>SSN:      <input type="text" formControlName="ssn"></div>

  <div formGroupName="passwordsGroup">
    <div>Password: <input type="password"
                          formControlName="password"></div>

    <div>Confirm password: <input type="password"
                          formControlName="pconfirm"></div>
  </div>
  <button type="submit">Submit</button>
</form>
```

- Binds the <form> element to myFormModel using the formGroup directive
- formControlName links input fields to the corresponding FormControl instances defined in the model.
- Links the model's nested FormGroup to the DOM element using formGroupName
- Links the password input field and pconfirm using the formControlName directive

The behavior of this reactive version of the registration form is identical to the template-driven version, but the internal implementation differs. To see this app in action, open the form-samples directory in your IDE, and run the following command:

```
ng serve --app reactive -o
```

Fill out the form, and click Submit. The object with the entered values will be printed in the browser's console, as shown in figure 10.3.

This was a rather simple form with predefined controls, but what if you want to be able to dynamically add form controls during runtime?

10.3.4 Dynamically adding controls to a form

When you know in advance all the controls in a particular form, you can associate each template form element with a corresponding property of the `FormGroup` instance using the `formControlName` directive. But if you want to be able to dynamically add/remove controls, you need a different way to link the control names with the model properties. By using `FormArray` instead of `FormGroup`, you can specify an array index as a name of the corresponding template element.

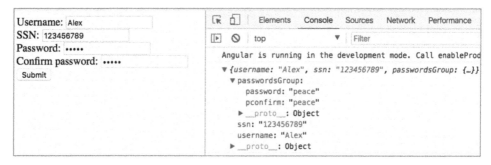

Figure 10.3 Running reactive registration form

Let's look at an example that allows users to have a form with an arbitrary number of email controls. First, you'll define the model that will include a `FormArray` called `emails`, which will initially have just one form control for entering an email.

Listing 10.20 Using `FormArray` in the form model

```
@Component(...)
class AppComponent {
  formModel: FormGroup = new FormGroup({     ◁── Creates a FormGroup that will represent the form
     emails: new FormArray([     ◁── Creates a FormArray for the emails form controls
       new FormControl()     ◁── Adds a single form control to the emails array
     ])
  });
  ...
```

In the template, you'll create a `<ul>` HTML element and will link it to the `emails` array of the model using the `formArrayName` directive. Then, you'll iterate through this array with `*ngFor`, rendering an `<li>` element for each form control from this array. Your template will also have an Add Email button, and if the user clicks it, you'll add a new `FormControl` to the `emails` array, as shown in the next listing.

Listing 10.21 Iterating through the `FormArray` in a template

```
<ul formArrayName="emails">     ◁── Links the emails array to the <ul> element
   <li *ngFor="let e of formModel.get('emails').controls; let i = index">     ◁── Iterates through the emails array and creates a <li> with an <input> field for each array element

     <input [formControlName]="i">     ◁── Uses an emails array element index as a name of the corresponding <input> element
   </li>
</ul>
<button type="button" (click)="addEmail()">Add Email</button>     ◁── Defines the click event handler
```

In Angular templates, the `*ngFor` directive gives you access to a special `index` variable that stores the current index while iterating through a collection. The `let i` notation in the `*ngFor` loop allows you to automatically bind the value `index` to the local template variable `i` available within the loop.

The `formControlName` directive links the `FormControl` in `FormArray` to the currently rendered DOM element; but instead of specifying a name, it uses the current value of the variable `i`. When the user clicks the Add Email button, your component adds a new `FormControl` instance to the `FormArray`:

```
this.formModel.get('emails').push(new FormControl());
```

In the dynamic-form-controls directory, you can find the complete code for the app that dynamically adds email form controls on each click of the Add Email button. To see this example in action, run the following command:

```
ng serve --app dynamic -o
```

Figure 10.4 shows what this form will look like after the user clicks Add Email. The second email field was added dynamically by adding a new `FormControl` instance to the `FormArray` named `emails`, and each control from this array was rendered on the page.

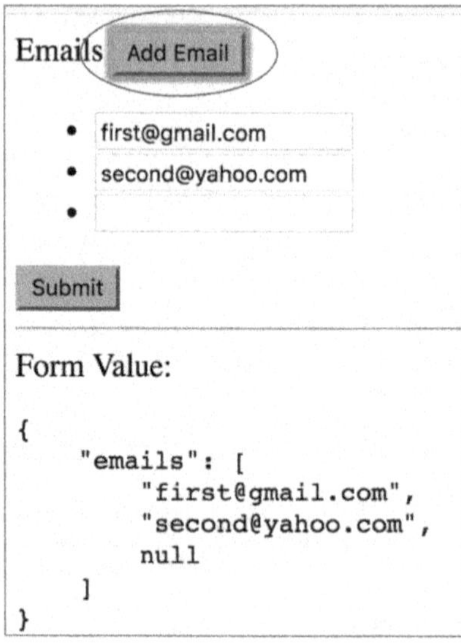

Figure 10.4 Form with growable email controls

10.4 Forms API directives summary

You've used+ many different Forms API directives in both template-driven and reactive forms. Table 10.2 lists what they are for.

Table 10.2 Forms API directives

Directive	Description
Directives for reactive forms	
`FormGroup`	A class that represents the entire form or a subform; create its instance in the TypeScript code of the component. Its API is described at https://angular.io/api/forms/FormGroup.
`formGroup`	Used in templates to bind the template element (for example, `<form>`) to the explicitly created `FormGroup`; typically it's assigned to a variable declared in the component.
`formGroupName`	Used in templates to bind a group of the template elements (for example, `<div>`) to the explicitly created `FormGroup`.
`FormControl`	Represents the value, validators, and validity status of an individual form control; create its instance in the TypeScript code of the component. Its API is described at https://angular.io/api/forms/FormControl.
`formControl`	Used in a template to bind an individual HTML element to the instance of `FormControl`.
`formControlName`	Used in templates in form elements to link an individual `FormControl` instance to an HTML element.
`FormArray`	Allows you to create a group of form controls dynamically and use the array indexes as control names. You create an instance of `FormArray` in TypeScript code. Its API is described at https://angular.io/api/forms/FormArray.
`formArrayName`	Used in a template as a reference to the instance of `FormArray`.
Directives for template-driven forms	
`NgForm`	Implicitly created directive that represents the entire form; it creates an instance of `FormGroup`. Its API is described at https://angular.io/api/forms/NgForm.
`ngForm`	Used in templates to bind the template element (for example, `<form>`) to `NgForm`; typically, it's assigned to a local template variable.
`NgModel`	Implicitly created directive that marks the HTML element to be included in the form model. Its API is described at https://angular.io/api/forms/NgModel.
`ngModel`	Used in templates in form elements (for example, `<input>`) to be included in the form model.

Table 10.2 Forms API directives *(continued)*

Directive	Description
Directives for template-driven forms (continued)	
`name`	Used in templates in form elements to specify its name in the form model.
`NgModelGroup`	Implicitly created directive that represents a part of the form, such as password and confirm password fields. Its API is described at https://angular.io/api/forms/NgModelGroup.
`ngModelGroup`	Used in templates to name a part of the form for future reference.
Both template-driven and reactive forms	
`ngSubmit`	Intercepts the HTML form's submit event.

Note that the name of any directive used in the component template starts with a lowercase letter. The name of the underlying class that implements the directive starts with a capital letter. In template-driven forms, you don't need to explicitly create instances of these classes, but in reactive forms, you instantiate them in the TypeScript code as needed.

All the code samples in this chapter illustrate use cases of the user entering the data in a form, but often you need to populate a form with existing data.

10.5 Updating form data

In some scenarios, a form needs to be populated without the user's interaction. For example, you may need to create a form for editing product data retrieved from the server or another source. Another example is implementing a master-detail relationship—for example, selecting a product in a list should show its details in a form.

The Angular Forms API offers several functions for updating a form model including `reset()`, `setValue()`, and `patchValue()`. The `reset()` function reinitializes the form model and resets the flags on the model, like `touched`, `dirty`, and others. The `setValue()` function is used for updating all values in a form model. The `patchValue()` function is used when you need to update the selected properties of a form model. Let's create a simple app that will have a form with the model shown in the following listing.

Listing 10.22 Creating a form model

```
this.myFormModel = new FormGroup({
      id: new FormControl(''),
      description: new FormControl(''),
      seller: new FormControl('')
    });
```

Your app will also have three buttons: Populate, Update Description, and Reset. Accordingly, the Populate button uses `setValue()` to populate the object that has values for each control defined in the form model.

Listing 10.23 The data for populating the form

```
{
  id: 123,
  description: 'A great product',
  seller: 'XYZ Corp'
}
```

The Update Description button uses `patchValue()` for the partial form update (just the description) from the object in the next listing.

Listing 10.24 The data for updating the description

```
{
  description: 'The best product'
}
```

The Reset button removes all data from the form and resets all flags on the form model. The code of your app is shown in the following listing.

Listing 10.25 The AppComponent

```
@Component({
  selector: 'app-root',
  template: `
    <form [formGroup]="myFormModel">                        <- Binds the form model to formGroup
       <div>Product ID: <input type="text" formControlName="id"></div>
      <div>Description: <input type="text" formControlName="description"></div>
      <div>Seller:      <input type="text" formControlName="seller"></div>
    </form>
    <button (click)="updateEntireForm()">Populate</button>                 <- A button to invoke setValue()
     <button (click)="updatePartOfTheForm()">Update Description</button>   <- A button to invoke patchValue()
     <button (click)="myFormModel.reset()">Reset</button>                  <- A button to invoke reset()
  `
})
export class AppComponent {
  myFormModel: FormGroup;

  constructor() {
    this.myFormModel = new FormGroup({                     <- Creates a form model object
       id: new FormControl(''),
      description: new FormControl(''),
      seller: new FormControl('')
    });
  }

  updateEntireForm() {
```

```
    this.myFormModel.setValue({          <-- Invokes setValue()
       id: 123,                              on the form model
      description: 'A great product',
      seller: 'XYZ Corp'
    });
  }
  updatePartOfTheForm() {
    this.myFormModel.patchValue({        <-- Invokes
       description: 'The best product'       patchValue() on
    });                                      the form model
  }
}
```

The code of this app is located in the populate directory. To see it in action, run the following command:

```
ng serve --app populate -o
```

> **NOTE** You can't use `setValue()` in a form that uses `FormArray`. For such forms, you need to use `patchValue()` and then invoke the `setControl()` method on the form model to reset `FormArray`.

If a form has multiple controls, your code may contain lots of `new` operators creating new instances of form elements. Is there a way to avoid polluting your code with `new` statements?

10.6 Using FormBuilder

The injectable service `FormBuilder` simplifies the creation of form models. It doesn't provide any unique features compared to the direct use of the `FormControl`, `FormGroup`, and `FormArray` classes, but its API is terser and saves you from the repetitive instantiation of objects.

Let's refactor the code in the user registration form from section 10.3.3. The template will remain exactly the same, but the following listing uses `FormBuilder` to construct the form model.

Listing 10.26 Creating a `formModel` with `FormBuilder`

```
Injects the
FormBuilder service.
--> constructor(fb: FormBuilder) {
      this.myFormModel = fb.group({        <-- FormBuilder.group() creates a FormGroup using a configuration object passed to it.
        username: [''],                    <-- Each FormControl is instantiated using the array that may contain an initial control's value and its validators.
        ssn: [''],
       passwordsGroup: fb.group({          <-- Like FormGroup, FormBuilder allows you to create nested groups.
          password: [''],
         pconfirm': ['']
       })
     });
   }
```

The `FormBuilder.group()` method accepts an object with extra configuration parameters as the last argument. You can use it to specify group-level validators there if needed.

As you can see, configuring a form model with `FormBuilder` is less verbose and is based on the configuration object rather than requiring explicit instantiation of the control's classes.

To see this app in action, run the command `ng serve --app formbuilder -o`. Now that you know how to work with form models and templates, you may be wondering how to ensure that the values entered in the form are valid. That's subject of the next chapter.

Summary

- Angular offers two APIs for working with forms: template-driven and reactive.
- The template-driven approach is easier and quicker to configure, but it has limited features.
- The reactive approach gives you more control over forms, which can be created or modified during runtime.

11 Validating forms

This chapter covers

- Using built-in form validators
- Creating custom validators
- Handling sync and async validation

The user fills out a form and clicks Submit, expecting that the app will process the data in some way. In web applications, the data is usually sent to the server. Often, the user receives some data back (for example, search results), but sometimes, the data is just saved in the server's storage (for example, creating a new order). In any case, the data should be valid so the server's software can do its job properly.

For example, an app can't log in a user unless they've provided a user ID and a password in the login form. Both fields are required—otherwise, the form isn't valid. You shouldn't even allow submitting this form until the user has filled out all required fields. A user registration form may be considered invalid if the password doesn't contain at least 8 characters, including a number, an uppercase letter, and a special character.

In this chapter, we'll show you how to validate forms in Angular using built-in validators and how to create custom forms. At the end of the chapter, you'll develop a new version of ngAuction that will include three fields. The entered values will be validated first, and only afterward will they be submitted for finding products that meet entered criteria.

We'll start exploring built-in validators by using a reactive form and then move to a template-driven one.

11.1 Using built-in validators

The Angular Forms API includes the `Validators` class , with static functions such as `required()`, `minLength()`, `maxLength()`, `pattern()`, `email()`, and others. These built-in validators can be used in templates by specifying the directives `required`, `minLength`, `maxLength`, `pattern`, and `email`, respectively. The `pattern` validator enables you to specify a regular expression.

Validators are functions that conform to the interface in the following listing.

Listing 11.1 The `ValidatorFn` interface

```
interface ValidatorFn {
  (c: AbstractControl): ValidationErrors | null;
}
```

If a validator function returns null, that means no errors. Otherwise, it'll return a `ValidationErrors` object of type `{[key: string]: any}`, where the property names (error names) are strings, and values (error descriptions) can be of any type.

A validator function should declare a single argument of type `AbstractControl` (or its descendants) and return an object literal or null. There, you implement business logic for validating user input. `AbstractControl` is the superclass for `FormControl`, `FormGroup`, and `FormArray`; hence, validators can be created for all model classes.

With the reactive Forms API, you can either provide validators while creating a form or form control or attach validators dynamically during runtime. The next listing shows an example that attaches the `required` validator to the form control represented by the variable `username`.

Listing 11.2 Attaching the `required` validator

```
import { FormControl, Validators } from '@angular/forms';
...
let username = new FormControl('', Validators.required);
```

Attaches the required validator to a FormControl

Here, the first parameter of the constructor is the initial value of the control, and the second is the validator function. You can also attach more than one validator to a form control.

Listing 11.3 Attaching two validators

```
let username = new FormControl('',
           [Validators.required, Validators.minLength(5)]);
```

Attaches required and minLength validators to a FormControl

To query the form or form control's validity, use the `valid` property , which can have one of two values, `true` or `false`:

```
let isValid: boolean = username.valid;
```

The preceding line checks whether the value entered in the form control passes or fails all the validation rules attached to this control. If any of the rules fails, you'll get error objects generated by the validator functions, as in the next listing.

Listing 11.4 Getting validators' errors

```
let errors: {[key: string]: any} = username.errors;
```

Gets all errors reported by validators

With the method `hasError ()`, you can check whether a form or control has specific errors and conditionally show or hide corresponding error messages.

Now let's see how to apply built-in validators in a template-driven form. You'll create an app that illustrates how to show or hide error messages for `required`, `minLength`, and `pattern` validators. The UI of this app may look like figure 11.1 if the user enters an invalid phone number.

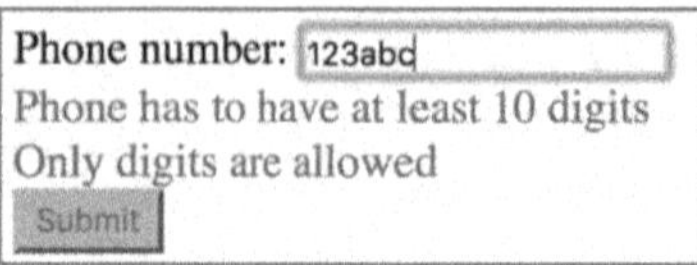

Figure 11.1 Showing validation errors

The app component's template will include the <div> element with error messages located under the <input>, and the <div> will be hidden if the phone number is valid or if its value wasn't entered (*pristine*), as shown in the following listing. The Submit button will stay disabled until the user enters a value that passes all validators.

Listing 11.5 Conditionally showing and hiding errors

```
@Component({
  selector: 'app-root',
  template: `
    <form #f="ngForm" (ngSubmit)="onSubmit(f.value)" >
      <div>
        Phone Number:
        <input type="text" name="telephone" ngModel
               required
                pattern="[0-9]*"
                minlength="10"
                #phone="ngModel">
```

Adds the required validator

Adds the pattern validator to allow only digits

Adds the minlength validator

The local variable #phone gives access to the value of this control's model.

```
        <div [hidden]="phone.valid || phone.pristine">
          <div class="error" [hidden]="!phone.hasError('required')">
               Phone is required</div>
          <div class="error" [hidden]="!phone.hasError('minlength')">
               Phone has to have at least 10 digits</div>
          <div class="error" [hidden]="!phone.hasError('pattern')">
               Only digits are allowed</div>
        </div>
      </div>
      <button type="submit" [disabled]="f.invalid">Submit</button>
    </form>
  `,
  styles: ['.error {color: red}']
})
export class AppComponent {
  onSubmit(formData) {
    console.log(formData);
  }
}
```

Hides the errors section if the form control is valid or pristine

Shows the error message if the value was entered and then erased

Shows the error message if the value violates the minlength requirement

Shows the error message if the value doesn't match the regular expression

Disables the Submit button until the form is valid

To see this app in action, run `npm install` in the project folder named form-validation, and then run the following command:

```
ng serve --app threevalidators -o
```

The ValidationErrors object

The error returned by a validator is represented by a JavaScript object that has a property whose name briefly describes an error. The property value can be of any type and may provide additional error details. For example, the standard `Validators.minLength()` validator returns an error object as shown here:

```
{
  minlength: {
    requiredLength: 7,
    actualLength: 5
  }
}
```

This object has a property named `minlength`, which means that the minimum length is invalid. The value of this property is also an object with two fields: `requiredLength` and `actualLength`. These error details can be used to display a user-friendly error message. Not all validators provide error details. Sometimes, the property just indicates that an error has occurred. In this case, the property is initialized with the value `true`.

> ***(continued)***
> The following snippet shows an example of the built-in `Validators.required()` error object:
>
> ```
> {
>   required: true
> }
> ```
>
> In section 11.6, you'll find an example of how to extract the error description from the `ValidationErrors` object.

Table 11.1 provides a brief description of Angular built-in validators offered by the `Validators` class.

Table 11.1 Built-in validators

Validator	Description
`min`	A value can't be less than the specified number; it can be used only with reactive forms.
`max`	A value can't be greater than the specified number; it can be used only with reactive forms.
`required`	The form control must have a non-empty value.
`requiredTrue`	The form control must have the value `true`.
`email`	The form control value must be a valid email.
`minLength`	The form control must have a value of a minimum length.
`maxLength`	The form control can't have more than the specified number of characters.
`pattern`	The form control's value must match the specified regular expression.

In the code sample that validated the phone number, the validators were checking the value after each character entered by the user. Is it possible to control when validation starts?

11.2 Controlling when validation starts

Prior to Angular 5, the validators performed their work each time a value in the form control changed. Now, you can use the `updateOn` property, which gives you better control over the validation process. When you attach a validator, you can specify when validation should start. The `updateOn` property can take one of these values:

- change—This is the default mode, with validators checking a value as soon as it changes. You saw this behavior in the previous section when validating a phone number.
- blur—Checks validity of a value when the control loses focus.
- submit—Checks validity when the user submits the form.

To try out these options with a template-driven form, add `[ngModelOptions]="{updateOn:'blur'}"` to the telephone input field in listing 11.5, and the user's input will be validated only when you move the focus from this control. To start validation when the Submit button is clicked or the Enter key is pressed, use the option `[ngModelOptions]="{updateOn:'submit'}"`.

NOTE If you use the sample from listing 11.5 with the option `updateOn: 'submit'`, remove the code that conditionally disables the Submit button or use the Enter key to test the validation.

In case of the reactive API, you would set the update mode for a form as follows.

Listing 11.6 Applying validators on blur using the reactive API

```
let telephone = new FormControl('',
        [{validators: Validators.minLength(10),
          updateOn:'blur'});
```

Attaches the minLength validator to a FormControl

Validates the value when focus moves out of the FormControl

You can also specify the update mode on the form level using the property `ngFormOptions`, as shown in the following listing.

Listing 11.7 Applying validators on blur using template-driven API

```
<form #f="ngForm"
      (ngSubmit)="onSubmit(f.value)"
      [ngFormOptions]="{updateOn: 'blur'}">
   ...
</form>
```

Each form control is validated when focus moves out of it.

Built-in validators are good for basic validation, but what if you need to apply application-specific logic to decide whether the entered value is valid?

11.3 Custom validators in reactive forms

You can create custom validators in Angular. Similar to built-in validators, custom validators should comply with the interface in the following listing.

Listing 11.8 The interface custom validators must conform to

```
interface ValidatorFn {
  (c: AbstractControl): ValidationErrors | null;
}
```

In case of errors, returns the ValidationErrors object; otherwise, null

You need to declare a function that accepts an instance of one of the control types—`FormControl`, `FormGroup`, or `FormArray`—and returns the `ValidationErrors` object or null. The next listing shows an example of a custom validator that checks whether the control's value is a valid social security number (SSN).

Listing 11.9 A sample custom validator

```
function ssnValidator(control: FormControl): ValidationErrors | null {
    const value = control.value || '';
    const valid = value.match(/^\d{9}$/);
    return valid ? null : { ssn: true };
}
```

- Validates the FormControl and returns either an error object or null
- Gets the control's value if available, or uses an empty string otherwise
- Matches the value against a regular expression that represents the SSN nine-digit format
- If the value is an invalid SSN, returns the error object; the error name is ssn

You can attach custom validators to form controls the same way you attach the built-in ones, as you can see in the following listing.

Listing 11.10 Attaching custom validators to form controls

```
@Component({
  selector: 'app-root',
  template: `
    <form [formGroup]="myForm">
      SSN: <input type="text" formControlName="socialSecurity">
         <span [hidden]="!myForm.hasError('ssn', 'socialSecurity')">
             SSN is invalid
         </span>
    </form>
  `
})
export class AppComponent {
  myForm: FormGroup;

  constructor() {
    this.myForm = new FormGroup({
      socialSecurity: new FormControl('', ssnValidator)
    });
  }
}
```

- Shows an error message if the socialSecurity form control has the error named ssn
- Attaches your custom ssnValidator

You'll see a window with an input field that requires you to enter nine digits to make the error message go away.

Your ssnValidator returns an error object that indicates there's something wrong with the SSN value: `{ ssn: true }`. You added the error text "SSN is invalid" to the HTML template. The ValidationErrors object can contain a more specific description of the error, for example `{ssn: {description: 'SSN is invalid'}}`, and you can get the error description using the `getError()` method . The following listing shows a modified version of ssnValidator and the template.

Listing 11.11 Adding the error description in a custom validator

```
function ssnValidator(control: FormControl): {[key: string]: any} {
  const value: string = control.value || '';
  const valid = value.match(/^\d{9}$/);
  return valid ? null : {ssn: {description: 'SSN is invalid'}};
 }

@Component({
  selector: 'app',
  template: `
    <form [formGroup]="myForm">
      SSN: <input type="text" formControlName="socialSecurity">
           <span [hidden]="!myForm.hasError('ssn', 'socialSecurity')">
              {{myForm.getError('ssn', 'socialSecurity')?.description}}
            </span>
    </form>
  `
})
class AppComponent {
  myForm: FormGroup;

  constructor() {
    this.form = new FormGroup({
      'socialSecurity': new FormControl('', ssnValidator)
    });
  }
}
```

Creates a specific object with the description property that contains the description of the error

Shows an error message if the socialSecurity form control got the error named ssn

Gets the error message from the description property of the error

NOTE In listing 11.10, you use Angular's *safe navigation operator*, which is represented by a question mark and can be used in the component template. The question mark after the invocation of `getError()` means "Don't try to access the property `description` if the object returned by `getError()` is undefined or null," meaning when the entered value is valid. If you didn't use the safe navigation operator, this code would produce the runtime error "cannot read property `description` of null" for valid SSN values.

If you run this app, the browser shows an empty input field and the message "SSN is invalid," but the user didn't have the chance to enter any value. Before showing a validation error message, always check whether the form control is `dirty` (has been modified). The <span> element should look like the following listing.

Listing 11.12 Using the dirty flag

```
<span [hidden]="!(myForm.get('socialSecurity').dirty        <-- Checks whether the form control has been modified
                    && myForm.hasError('ssn', 'socialSecurity'))">
      {{myForm.getError('ssn', 'socialSecurity')?.description}}
 </span>
```

Now let's add some styling to this form. Angular's Forms API offers a number of CSS classes that work hand in hand with their respective flags on the form: .ng-valid, .ng-invalid, .ng-pending, .ng-pristine, .ng-dirty, .ng-untouched, and .ng-touched. In the code sample, if the value is invalid and dirty, you want to change the background of the input field to be light pink, as shown in the following listing.

Listing 11.13 Adding styles to the input field

```
@Component({
  selector: 'app-root',
  template: `
    <form [formGroup]="myForm">
      SSN: <input type="text" formControlName="socialSecurity"
                  class="social">                <-- Adds the CSS selector social
       <span [hidden]="!(myForm.get('socialSecurity').dirty
                        && myForm.hasError('ssn', 'socialSecurity'))">
             {{myForm.getError('ssn', 'socialSecurity')?.description}}
      </span>
    </form>
  `,
  styles:[`.social.ng-dirty.ng-invalid {       <-- Is the field dirty and invalid?
                background-color: lightpink;     <-- Changes the background to light pink
             }`]
})
```

The application that illustrates the use of ssnValidator in a reactive form is located in the reactive-validator directory, and you can run it as follows:

```
ng serve --app reactive-validator -o
```

Figure 11.2 shows how the browser will render this app if the value isn't valid.

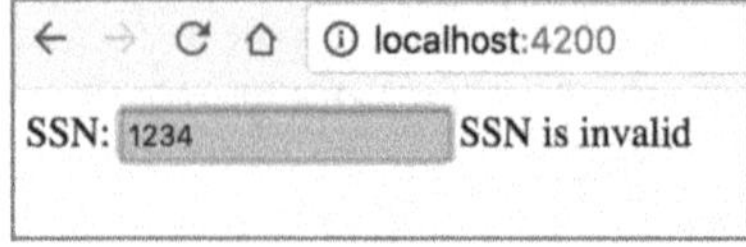

Figure 11.2 Showing the validation error and changing the background color

Now that you know how to create a custom validator for a single form control, let's consider another scenario: validating a group of form controls.

11.4 Validating a group of controls

You can validate a group of form controls by attaching validator functions to a `FormGroup` instead of an individual `FormControl`. The following listing creates an `equalValidator` that ensures that the password and password confirmation fields on the sample user registration form have the same value.

Listing 11.14 A sample validator for a FormGroup

```
function equalValidator({value}: FormGroup): {[key: string]: any} {
  const [first, ...rest] = Object.keys(value || {});
    const valid = rest.every(v => value[v] === value[first]);
    return valid ? null : {equal: true};
  }
```

Using rest parameters, gets the names of all properties of FormGroup.value

If equal, returns null; otherwise, returns an error object with the error named equal

Iterates through the properties' values to check if they're equal

The signature of the preceding function conforms to the `ValidatorFn` interface : the first parameter is of type `FormGroup`, a subclass of `AbstractControl`, and the return type is an object literal. Note that you use object destructuring in the function argument to extract the value property from the instance of the `FormGroup` object.

You also use array destructuring combined with rest parameters in the first line of the function so you can iterate through the properties of `FormGroup.value`. You get the names of all properties in the value object and save them in two variables, `first` and `rest`. `first` is the name of a property that will be used as the reference value—values of all other properties must be equal to it to make validation pass. `rest` holds the names of all the other properties.

Finally, the validator function returns either `null`, if the values in the group are the same, or an error object, otherwise. Let's apply the `ssnValidator` and `equalValidator` in the sample user registration form. The following listing shows the code of the modified `AppComponent` class.

Listing 11.15 A modified form model for a user registration form

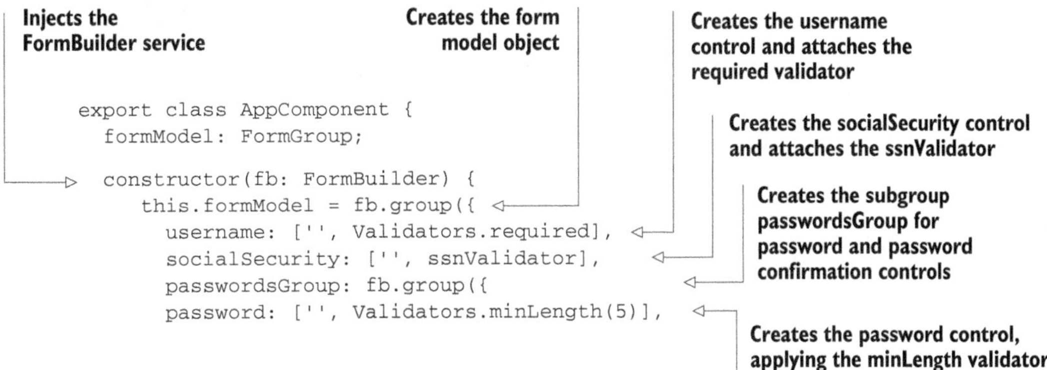
Injects the FormBuilder service
Creates the form model object
Creates the username control and attaches the required validator
Creates the socialSecurity control and attaches the ssnValidator
Creates the subgroup passwordsGroup for password and password confirmation controls
Creates the password control, applying the minLength validator

```
export class AppComponent {
  formModel: FormGroup;

  constructor(fb: FormBuilder) {
     this.formModel = fb.group({
       username: ['', Validators.required],
       socialSecurity: ['', ssnValidator],
       passwordsGroup: fb.group({
       password: ['', Validators.minLength(5)],
```

```
        pconfirm: ['']                           <-- Creates the pconfirm control
      }, {validator: equalValidator})        <--     for confirming the password
    });
  }

  onSubmit() {                                   Attaches the equalValidator
      console.log(this.formModel.value);         to passwordsGroup to
  }                                              ensure that both entered
}                                                passwords are the same
```

To display validation errors when the user enters invalid values, you'll add a <span> element next to each form control in the template. Depending on the return of the `hasError()` method , the error text will be either shown or hidden, as in the following listing.

Listing 11.16 The template and styles of the user registration component

```
template: `
    <form [formGroup]="formModel" (ngSubmit)="onSubmit()">
      <div>
        Username: <input type="text" formControlName="username">
        <span class="error"
              [hidden]="!formModel.hasError('required', 'username')">    <--
               Username is required</span>
      </div>                                If the value of the username control is
                                                invalid, shows the error message
      <div>
        SSN: <input type="text" formControlName="socialSecurity">
        <span class="error"
              [hidden]="!formModel.hasError('ssn', 'socialSecurity')">    <--
               SSN is invalid</span>
      </div>                               If the value of the socialSecurity control
                                               is invalid, shows the error message
      <div formGroupName="passwordsGroup">
        <div>
          Password: <input type="password" formControlName="password">
          <span class="error"
                [hidden]="!formModel.hasError('minlength',
                ➥ ['passwordsGroup', 'password'])">  <--  If the value of the
                 Password is too short</span>              password control is
        </div>                                             invalid, shows the
                                                           error message
        <div>
          Confirm password: <input type="password" formControlName="pconfirm">
          <span class="error"
                [hidden]="!formModel.hasError('equal', 'passwordsGroup')">  <--
                 Passwords must be the same</span>
        </div>                                 If passwords are not the same,
      </div>                                        shows the error message

      <button type="submit" [disabled]="formModel.invalid">Submit</button>
    </form>
  `,
  styles: ['.error {color: red;} ']
```

Note how you access the form model's `hasError()` method. It takes two parameters: the name of the validation error you want to check and the control name from the form model. In the case of `username`, it's a direct child of the top-level `FormGroup` that represents the form model, so you specify the name of the control. But the `password` field is a child of the nested `FormGroup`, so the path to the control is specified as an array of strings: `['passwordsGroup', 'password']`. The first element is the name of the nested group, and the second is the name of the `password` field itself.

You can find the code for this app in the group-validators directory. To see this app in action, run the following command:

```
ng serve --app groupvalidators -o
```

Figure 11.3 illustrates the error messages produced by invalid values in the individual fields Username, SSN, and Password, as well as invalid values in the form group—provided passwords don't match.

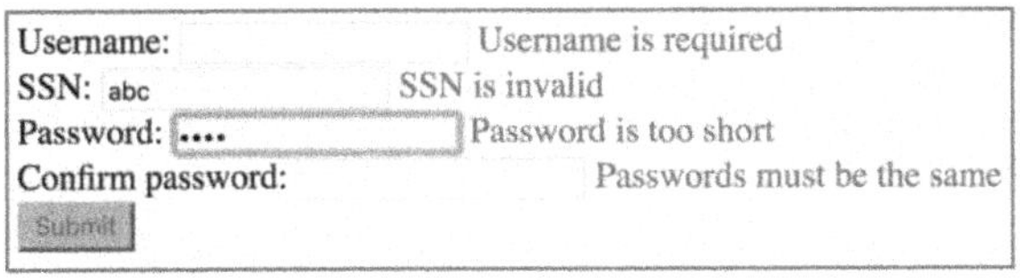

Figure 11.3 Showing multiple validation errors

11.5 Checking a form control's status and validity

You already used such control properties as `valid`, `invalid`, and `errors` for checking field status. In this section, we'll look at a number of other properties that help improve the user experience.

11.5.1 touched and untouched form controls

In addition to checking a control's validity, you can also use the `touched` and `untouched` properties to check whether a form control was visited by the user. If the user puts the focus into a form control using the keyboard or mouse and then moves the focus out, this control becomes `touched`; while the focus remains in the control, it's still `untouched`. This can be useful when displaying error messages—if the value in a form control is invalid, but it was never visited by the user, you can choose not to highlight it with red, because the user didn't even try to enter a value. The following listing shows an example.

Listing 11.17 Using the touched property

Defines a CSS selector that highlights the border of the invalid form control with red

Adds the required validator for the username field

```
<style>.hasError {border: 1px solid red;}</style>
<input type="text" required
```

```
name="username" ngModel #c="ngModel"
[class.hasError]="c.invalid && c.touched">
```

Enables Forms API support for the field and saves a reference to the NgModel directive instance in the local template variable c

Conditionally applies the hasError CSS selector to the <input> element

NOTE All the properties discussed in section 11.5.1 are available for the model classes `FormControl`, `FormGroup`, and `FormArray` as well as for the template-driven directives `NgModel`, `NgModelGroup`, and `NgForm`.

Note the CSS class binding example on the last line. It conditionally applies the `hasError` CSS class to the element if the expression on the right side is `true`. If you used only `c.invalid`, the border would be highlighted as soon as the page was rendered; but that can confuse users, especially if the page has a lot of fields. Instead, you add one more condition: the field must be touched. Now the field is highlighted only after a user visits and leaves this field.

11.5.2 pristine and dirty fields

Another useful pair of properties are `pristine` and `dirty`. `pristine` means the user never interacted with the form control. `dirty` indicates that the initial value of the form control was modified, regardless of where the focus is. These properties can be used to display or hide validation errors.

NOTE All the properties in section 11.5.2 have corresponding CSS classes (`ng-touched` and `ng-untouched`, `ng-dirty` and `ng-pristine`, `ng-valid` and `ng-invalid`) that are automatically added to HTML elements when the respective property is `true`. These can be useful to style elements in a certain state.

11.5.3 Pending fields

If you have async validators configured for a control, the `pending` property may come in handy. It indicates whether the validity status is currently unknown. This happens when an async validator is still in progress and you need to wait for the results. This property can be used for displaying a progress indicator.

For reactive forms, the type of the `statusChanges` property is `Observable`, and it emits one of three values: `VALID`, `INVALID`, and `PENDING`.

11.6 Changing validators dynamically in reactive forms

Using the reactive Forms API, you can change the validators attached to a form or one of its controls during runtime. You may need to implement a scenario where, depending on user input in one control, validation rules for another control should be changed. You can do that using the `setValidators ()` and `updateValueAndValidity()` functions .

Imagine a form that has two controls: country and phone. If the user enters `USA` in the country field, you want to allow entering the phone number without the country code, and the phone has to have at least 10 characters. For other countries, the country code is required, and the phone has to have at least 11 characters. In other words, you need to dynamically set the validator for the phone based on the input in the `country` field. The following listing shows how to implement this: you subscribe to the `valueChanges` property of the `country` field and assign the validator to the `phone` field based on the selected country.

Listing 11.18 Dynamically changing validators

```
@Component({
  selector: 'app-root',
  template: `
    <form [formGroup]="myFormModel">
      Country: <input type="text" formControlName="country">
      <br>
      Phone: <input type="text" formControlName="phone">

      <span class="error" *ngIf="myFormModel.controls['phone'].invalid &&
                             myFormModel.controls['phone'].dirty">    ◁ Displays the error message only if the phone was modified and is invalid
             Min length: {{this.myFormModel.controls['phone']
            ➥.getError('minlength')?.requiredLength}}
           </span>
    </form>
  `,
  styles: ['.error {color: red;}']
})
export class AppComponent implements OnInit{
  myFormModel: FormGroup;

  countryCtrl: FormControl;
  phoneCtrl: FormControl;

    constructor(fb: FormBuilder) {
      this.myFormModel = fb.group({     ◁ Creates the form model using FormBuilder
         country: [''],
       phone: ['']
      });
  }

    ngOnInit(){
      this.countryCtrl = this.myFormModel.get('country') as FormControl;    ◁ Gets the reference to the instance of the country control
       this.phoneCtrl = this.myFormModel.get('phone') as FormControl;    ◁ Gets the reference to the instance of the phone control

      this.countryCtrl.valueChanges.subscribe( country => {    ◁ Subscribes to the changes in the country control
           if ('USA' === country){
            this.phoneCtrl.setValidators([Validators.minLength(10)]);    ◁ Sets the phone validator for the USA
           }else{
            this.phoneCtrl.setValidators([Validators.minLength(11)]);    ◁ Sets the phone validator for other countries
           }
          this.phoneCtrl.updateValueAndValidity();    ◁ Emits the updated validator to the subscribers of valueChanges
        }
      );
  }
}
```

To see this app in action, run the following command:

```
ng serve --app dynamicvalidator -o
```

So far, you've been performing validation on the client side, but what if you want to do server-side validation of form values?

11.7 Asynchronous validators

Asynchronous validators can be used to check form values by making requests to a remote server. Like synchronous validators, async validators are functions. The main difference is that async validators should return either an `Observable` or a `Promise` object. Figure 11.4 compares the interfaces that synchronous and asynchronous validators should implement. It shows the validators for a `formControl`, but the same applies to any subclass of the `AbstractControl`.

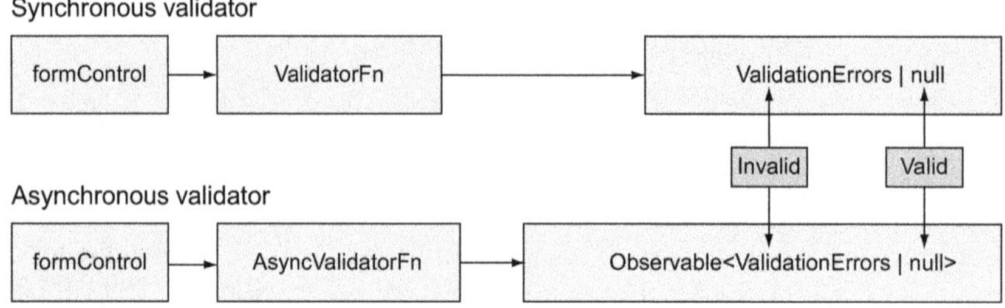

Figure 11.4 Comparing sync and async validators

> **TIP** If a form control has both sync and async validators, the latter will be invoked only after the value(s) pass all synchronous validators.

The code that comes with this chapter includes a directory called async-validator that uses both sync and async validators to validate the SSN. For synchronous validation, you'll reuse the `ssnValidator()` function that you created in section 11.3. That validator checked that the user entered nine digits in the form control.

Now you also want to invoke a service that will check whether the entered SSN authorizes the user to work in the USA. By your rules, if a person's SSN has a sequence 123 in it, they can work in the USA. The following listing creates an Angular service that includes such an asynchronous validator.

Listing 11.19 A service with an async validator

```
@Injectable()
export class SsnValidatorService {

  checkWorkAuthorization(field: AbstractControl):
                           Observable<ValidationErrors | null> {

    // In the real-world app you'd make an HTTP call to server
```

This function properly implements the async validator interface.

```
    // to check if the value is valid

    return Observable.of(field.value.indexOf('123') >=0 ? null
              : {work: " You're not authorized to work"});
  }
}
```

Returns an observable of null—the validation passed

Returns an observable of the ValidationErrors object—the validation failed

The following listing creates a component that, in addition to the synchronous ssn-Validator(), attaches to the form control the async validator, checkWorkAuthorization().

Listing 11.20 async-validator/app.component.ts

```
function ssnValidator(control: FormControl): {[key: string]: any} {
   const value: string = control.value || '';
  const valid = value.match(/^\d{9}$/);
  return valid ? null : {ssn: true};
}

@Component({
  selector: 'app-root',
  template: `
    <form [formGroup]="myForm">
      <h2>Sync and async validation demo </h2>

      Enter your SSN: <input type="text" formControlName="ssnControl">
       <span *ngIf ="myForm.hasError('ssn', 'ssnControl');
       else validSSN"> SSN is invalid.</span>

       <ng-template #validSSN> SSN is valid</ng-template>

       <span *ngIf ="myForm.hasError('work', 'ssnControl')">
       {{myForm.get('ssnControl').errors.work}}</span>
     </form>
  `
})
export class AppComponent{

  myForm: FormGroup;

  constructor(private ssnValidatorService: SsnValidatorService) {
    this.myForm = new FormGroup({
      ssnControl: new FormControl('',
                    ssnValidator,
                    ssnValidatorService.checkWorkAuthorization.bind
                    (ssnValidatorService))
    });
  }
}
```

Synchronous validator

In case of an error, shows the text from <span>; otherwise, from the template validSSN

Defines the template validSSN

Extracts the description of the error named work

Attaches the sync validator to ssnControl

Attaches the async validator to ssnControl

Async validators are passed as the third argument to constructors of model classes. If you need to have several synchronous or asynchronous validators, specify an array as the second and/or third argument.

In general, the HTML <template> element is used to specify the content that's not rendered by the browser on page load but can be rendered by JavaScript later on. The Angular <ng-template> directive serves the same purpose. In your component, the content of <ng-template> is "SSN is valid," and it's not rendered on page load. The Angular directive *ngIf will render it if the entered SSN is valid, using the template variable validSSN as a reference.

When assigning the asynchronous validator checkWorkAuthorization(), you want to make sure that this method runs in the context of the service ssnValidatorService. That's why you used the JavaScript function bind (). To see this application in action, run the following command:

```
ng serve --app async-validator -o
```

Try entering the SSN with and without the 123 sequence to see different validation messages.

NOTE The source code for this example includes one more async validator, checkWorkAuthorizationV2(), that can't be attached to the form control because it doesn't conform to the interface shown in figure 11.4. We added that validator just to show that you can invoke any function for validating the form values.

11.8 Custom validators in template-driven forms

With template-driven forms, you can use only directives to specify validators, so wrapping validator functions into directives is required. The following listing creates a directive that wraps the synchronous SSN validator from section 11.3.

Listing 11.21 SsnValidatorDirective

```
@Directive({
   selector: '[ssn]',
   providers: [{
    provide: NG_VALIDATORS,
     useValue: ssnValidator,
    multi: true
  }]
})
class SsnValidatorDirective {}
```

- Declares a directive using the @Directive decorator
- Defines the directive's selector to be used as an HTML attribute
- Registers ssnValidator as an NG_VALIDATORS provider

The square brackets around the ssn selector denote that the directive can be used as an attribute. This is convenient, because you can add this attribute to any <input> element or to an Angular component represented as a custom HTML element.

In listing 11.20, you register the validator function using the predefined NG_VALIDATORS Angular token. This token is, in turn, injected by the NgModel directive, and NgModel gets the list of all validators attached to the HTML element. Then,

`NgModel` passes validators to the `FormControl` instance it implicitly creates. The same mechanism is responsible for running validators; directives are just a different way to configure them. The `multi` property lets you associate multiple values with the same token. When the token is injected into the `NgModel` directive, `NgModel` gets a list of values instead of a single value. This enables you to pass multiple validators.

Here's how you can use the `SsnValidatorDirective`:

```
<input type="text" name="my-ssn" ngModel ssn>
```

You can find the complete running application that illustrates directive validators in the template-validator directory. To see this app in action, run the following command:

```
ng serve --app template-validator -o
```

Chapter 10 covered the basics of the Forms API. In this chapter, we've explained how to validate form data. Now it's time to modify ngAuction and add a search form so users can search for products.

> **NOTE** Source code for this chapter can be found at https://github.com/Farata/angulartypescript and www.manning.com/books/angular-development-with-typescript-second-edition.

11.9 Adding a search form to ngAuction

You made quite a few changes to the new version of ngAuction. The main addition is the new search component where you use the Angular Forms API. You'll also add tabs with product categories, so the top portion of ngAuction will look like figure 11.5.

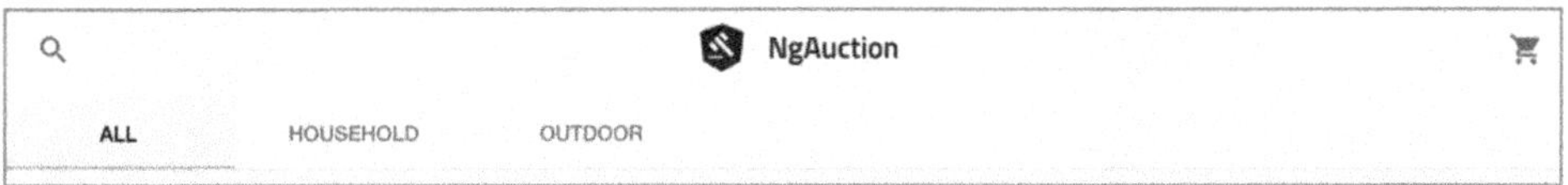

Figure 11.5 The new search icon and product category tabs

To return to the landing page from any other app view, the user should click the ngAuction logo. When the user clicks the search icon, the search-form component will slide from the left, where the user can enter search criteria, as shown in figure 11.6.

After the user clicks the Search button, the app will invoke `ProductService.search()`; the search-form component will slide back off the screen; and the user will see the products that meet the search criteria rendered by the search-results component. Note that there are no tabs with categories in the search result view displayed in

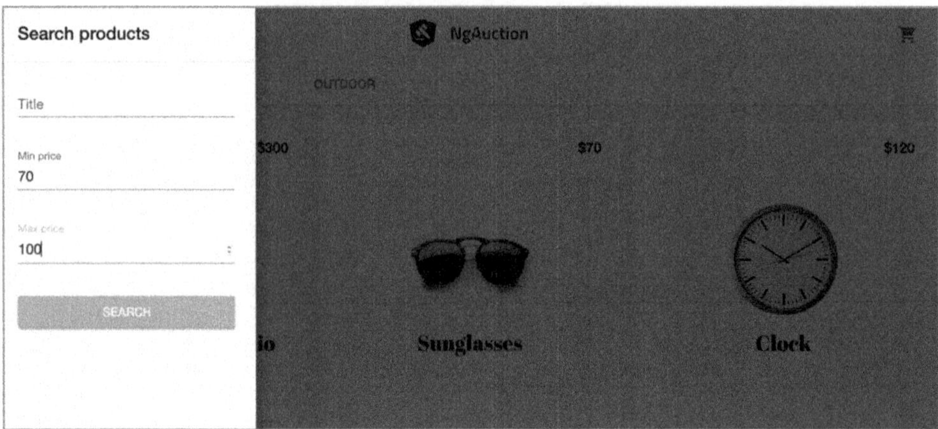

Figure 11.6 The search-form component

figure 11.7. That's because products from different categories can meet the search criteria—for example, a price between $70 and $100.

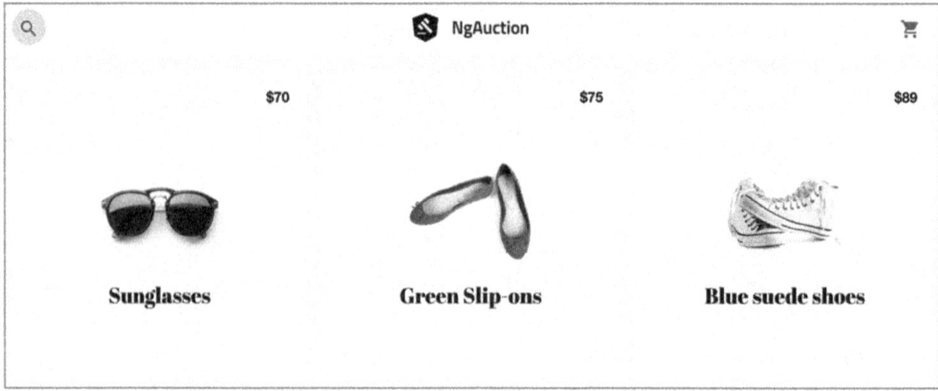

Figure 11.7 The search results view

In this section, we won't be providing detailed instructions for implementing all the code changes, because that would take lots of pages to describe. We'll do a code review of the new search-form component and search-results component. Then we'll highlight other important changes made throughout the code of ngAuction.

11.9.1 The search-form component

You created the search-form component in the shared directory of the project just in case the search functionality will be required in other parts of this app. The template of the search-form component contains a form with three input fields: `Title`, `Min price`, and `Max price`.

Each of these fields, along with corresponding validation error messages (`<mat-error>`), is wrapped into an Angular Material `<mat-form-field>`, and the value in the placeholder attribute (or the field label, if present) becomes a floating label, as you can see in the following listing.

Listing 11.22 search-form.component.html

```
<h1 class="title">Search products</h1>

<form class="form" [formGroup]="searchForm" (ngSubmit)="onSearch()">
  <mat-form-field class="form__field">
    <input matInput type="text" placeholder="Title"          ◁— Title form control
           formControlName="title">
    <mat-error>Title is too short</mat-error>                ◁— Validation error message for Title
  </mat-form-field>

  <mat-form-field class="form__field">
    <input matInput type="number" placeholder="Min price"    ◁— Min price control
                    formControlName="minPrice">
    <mat-error>Cannot be less than 0</mat-error>             ◁— Validation error message for negative values
  </mat-form-field>

  <mat-form-field class="form__field">
    <input matInput type="number" placeholder="Max price"    ◁— Max price control
           formControlName="maxPrice" [errorStateMatcher]="matcher">
     <mat-error *ngIf="searchForm.controls['maxPrice'].hasError('min')">
                 Cannot be less than 0</mat-error>
     <mat-error *ngIf="searchForm.controls['maxPrice'].hasError('max')">
                 Cannot be more than 10000</mat-error>
    <mat-error *ngIf="searchForm.hasError('minLessThanMax')">
                 Should be larger than min price</mat-error>
  </mat-form-field>

  <button class="form__submit" color="primary"
          mat-raised-button>SEARCH</button>
</form>
```

Annotations:
- The matcher controls when to display validation errors.
- Shows an error message if the value is negative. (hasError('min'))
- Shows an error message if the value is greater than max price. (hasError('max'))
- Shows an error message if the entered max price is less than the min price. (hasError('minLessThanMax'))

In the TypeScript code, you'll attach a validator to require at least two characters in the `Title` field. The `<mat-error>` will display the error message if the entered value won't pass the validator. The `Min price` field has a validator that doesn't allow negative numbers.

But the `Max price` field has three validators and three corresponding error messages: the first one is shown if the value is negative, the second is shown if the entered price is greater than 10,000, and the third one is shown if the entered `Max value` is less than the `Min value`.

You'll create a custom validator named minLessThanMaxValidator in the TypeScript code of the search-form component. Because this validator needs the values from two fields, you'll attach it to the entire form and not to the individual form control. Accordingly, for this validator in <mat-error>, you invoke hasError() not in the form control but in the form.

By default, validation errors are shown when the value is invalid and the user interacts with the control. The Max price field is special because one of its validators should kick in when the value in the Min price field is also entered. To specify *when* this validator should check the values, you'll implement the ErrorStateMatcher interface in the TypeScript code of the search-form component. If the entered value doesn't pass one or more validators, the respective error messages will be displayed, as shown in figure 11.8.

Figure 11.8 Showing two validation errors

The search-form.component.ts file includes the decorated class SearchFormComponent and the custom validator minLessThanMaxValidator. The form model is created using FormBuilder.

When the user clicks the Search button, the router navigates to the search-results component, passing the search criteria as query parameters (see section 3.5.2 in chapter 3). The search-results component implements the search functionality. You also emit a custom search event, which notifies the AppComponent that the search panel can be closed, as shown in the following listing.

Listing 11.23 search-form.component.ts

```
@Component({
  selector: 'nga-search-form',
  styleUrls: [ './search-form.component.scss' ],
  templateUrl: './search-form.component.html',
  changeDetection: ChangeDetectionStrategy.OnPush
})
export class SearchFormComponent {
  @Output() search = new EventEmitter();
  readonly matcher = new ShowOnFormInvalidStateMatcher();    // The object that controls when to show the validation error for Max price
   readonly searchForm: FormGroup;

  constructor(fb: FormBuilder, private router: Router) {
    this.searchForm = fb.group({    // Creates a form model with validators
       title   : [, Validators.minLength(2)],
      minPrice: [, Validators.min(0)],
      maxPrice: [, [Validators.min(0), Validators.max(10000)]]
    }, {
      validator: [ minLessThanMaxValidator ]
    });
  }

  onSearch(): void {    // The user clicked the Search button.
     if (this.searchForm.valid) {
      this.search.emit();    // Sends an event to app component to close the search-form component
       this.router.navigate([ '/search-results' ], {    // Navigates to search-results, passing the search criteria
         queryParams: withoutEmptyValues(this.searchForm.value)    // Doesn't send empty values in query parameters
       });
    }
  }
}

export class ShowOnFormInvalidStateMatcher implements
➥ErrorStateMatcher {    // Reports an error when either the form or a control is invalid
  isErrorState(control: FormControl | null,
  ➥form: FormGroupDirective | null): boolean {
    return !!((control && control.invalid) ||
    ➥(form && form.hasError('minLessThanMax')));
  }
}

function withoutEmptyValues(object: any): any {    // Creates a queryParams object that contains only the properties with values
   return Object.keys(object).reduce((queryParams: any, key) => {
    if (object[key]) { queryParams[key] = object[key]; }
    return queryParams;
  }, {});
}

function minLessThanMaxValidator(group: FormGroup):    // A custom validator for comparing min and max prices
                                  ValidationErrors | null {
  const minPrice = group.controls['minPrice'].value;
  const maxPrice = group.controls['maxPrice'].value;

  if (minPrice && maxPrice) {
    return minPrice <= maxPrice ? null : { minLessThanMax: true };
  } else {
```

```
    return null;
  }
}
```

The `matInput` directive has the `errorStateMatcher` property , which takes an instance of the `ErrorStateMatcher` object. This object must implement the `isErrorState()` method that takes the form control and the form and has the app logic to decide whether the error message has to be shown. In this case, this function returns `true` (show the error) if the control's value is invalid or if the `minLessThanMax` validator returned an error.

While searching for products, keep an eye on the URL, which will contain the search parameters. For example, if you enter `red` in the title field and click Search, you'll invoke `Router.navigate()`, and the URL will change to localhost:4200/search-results?title=red. The function `withoutEmptyValues ()` ensures that if some search parameters weren't used (for example, min and max price), they won't be used in the query parameters.

> **NOTE** In ngAuction from chapter 10, the home component included `<mat-grid-list>` for rendering the list of products. In this version of ngAuction, we extracted the grid list into a separate product-grid component that now is reused by two components: categories and search-results (both belong to the home module).

11.9.2 The search-results component

The search-results component receives the query parameters via the observable property `queryParams` of the `ActivatedRoute` object. Using the `switchMap` operator, you pass the value emitted by the `queryParams` observable to another observable, the `search()` method on `ProductService`, as shown in the following listing.

Listing 11.24 search-results.component.ts

```
@Component({
  selector: 'nga-search',
  styleUrls: [ './search-results.component.scss' ],
  templateUrl: './search-results.component.html',
  changeDetection: ChangeDetectionStrategy.OnPush
})
export class SearchResultsComponent {
  readonly products$: Observable<Product[]>;      // Declares an observable for products

  constructor(
    private productService: ProductService,
    private route: ActivatedRoute
  ) {
    this.products$ = this.route.queryParams.pipe(      // Wraps the RxJS pipeable operator into the pipe() function
      switchMap(queryParams => this.productService.search(queryParams))      // Passes the received parameters to the search() method
    );
  }
}
```

If you need a refresher on the `switchMap` operator, see section D.8 of appendix D. You can read about pipeable operators in section D.4.1.

The template of the search-results component incorporates the product-grid component and uses the async pipe to unwrap the observable `products$`, as shown in the next listing.

Listing 11.25 search-results.component.html

```
<div class="grid-list-container">
  <nga-product-grid [products]="products$ | async"></nga-product-grid>
</div>
```

The product-grid component receives the products via its input parameter as follows:

```
@Input() products: Product[];
```

Then it renders the grid with products as described in section 9.3.4 in chapter 9.

11.9.3 Other code refactoring

We won't be providing complete code listings of other ngAuction components that underwent refactoring but rather will highlight the changes. You're encouraged to go through the code of ngAuction that comes with this chapter. If you have specific questions about the code, post them on the book forum at https://forums.manning.com/forums/angular-development-with-typescript-second-edition.

SHOWING AND HIDING THE SEARCH-FORM COMPONENT

In the ngAuction from chapters 2, 3, and 4, the search component was always present on the UI, occupying 25% of the screen width. Why does it take so much space even when the user isn't searching for products? In this version of the app, the search-form component is represented by a small search icon, which is a part of the app toolbar, as shown in figure 11.9.

Figure 11.9 The search icon in a toolbar

Angular Material offers components for side navigation with which you can add collapsible side content to a full-screen app. You use the `<mat-sidenav-container>` component, which acts as a structural container for both the side-navigation panel (the search-form component) and the toolbar of ngAuction. `<mat-sidenav>` represents the added side content—the search-form component, in your case—as shown in the following listing.

Listing 11.26 A fragment of app.component.html

```
<mat-sidenav-container>                                    ◁ Wraps the sidenav and the toolbar into <mat-sidenav-container>
  <mat-sidenav #sidenav>                                   ◁ Wraps the search-form component into <mat-sidenav>
    <nga-search-form (search)="sidenav.close()"></nga-search-form>   ◁ On search event, closes the sidenav with the search-form component
  </mat-sidenav>

  <mat-toolbar class="toolbar">
    <button mat-icon-button                                ◁ Declares a button with an icon
            class="toolbar__icon-button"
            (click)="sidenav.toggle()">                    ◁ Clicking the icon button toggles the sidenav (opening it, in this case).
      <mat-icon>search</mat-icon>                          ◁ Uses the icon named search, offered by Google Material icons
    </button>

    <!-- The markup for the logo and shopping cart is omitted -->

  </mat-toolbar>

  <router-outlet></router-outlet>
</mat-sidenav-container>
```

REFACTORING THE HOME MODULE

In chapter 9, ngAuction had a home module with a home component. The home module still exists, but there's no home component anymore. You split its functionality into three components: categories, search-results, and product-grid components. The categories component is rendered below the navbar. Below the categories component, the browser renders the product-grid component that encapsulates the search-results component.

The routing has also changed, and the route configuration looks like the following listing now.

Listing 11.27 The modified configuration of the routes

```
const routes: Route[] = [
  { path: '', pathMatch: 'full', redirectTo: 'categories' },    ◁ By default, redirects to the componentless categories route
  { path: 'search-results', component: SearchResultsComponent },   ◁ Adds the routing for the search-results component
  { path: 'categories',
    children: [
      { path: '', pathMatch: 'full', redirectTo: 'all' },       ◁ By default, redirects to the categories/all route
       { path: ':category', component: CategoriesComponent },   ◁ Adds the routing for the categories component with a parameter
    ]
  }
];
```

In this code, you use the so-called *componentless route* `categories`, which doesn't have a specific component mapped to the path. It consumes the URL fragment, providing it to its children. By default, the fragment *categories* and *all* will be combined into categories/all.

The parameters passed to the componentless route are passed further down to the child routes. In your case, if there were a parameter after the URL fragment *categories*, it would be passed to the `CategoriesComponent` via the `:category` path.

THE CATEGORIES COMPONENT

The categories component is a part of the home module. It uses the standard HTML <nav> element that's meant to hold a set of links for navigation. To make these links fancy, you add the Angular Material `mat-tab-nav-bar` directive to the <nav> element. In chapter 9, the home component rendered the grid of products, but now the user will see tabs with product category names. The user can click tabs to select all products or those that belong to a particular category, and the product-grid component will render them. The template of the categories component is shown in the following listing.

Listing 11.28 categories.component.html

```
<nav class="tabs" mat-tab-nav-bar>
  <a mat-tab-link
     *ngFor="let category of categoriesNames$ | async"
     #rla="routerLinkActive" routerLinkActive
     [active]="rla.isActive"
    [routerLink]="['/categories', category]">
     {{ category | uppercase }}
  </a>
</nav>

<div class="grid-list-container">
  <nga-product-grid [products]="products$ | async"></nga-product-grid>
 </div>
```

Annotations:
- Adds the mat-tab-nav-bar to the standard HTML <nav> tag
- Each tab title is a link.
- Iterates through the category names to create an <a> tag for each one
- routerLinkActive shows the user which link is active now.
- Navigates to the route categories, passing the category name as param
- The link text (the tab title) is in uppercase.
- The product-grid component gets the array of products to render.

The TypeScript code of the categories component comes next. It uses `ProductService` to retrieve the distinct names of categories to be used as tab titles. It also uses the same service to retrieve the products of all categories or from the selected one.

Listing 11.29 categories.component.ts

```
@Component({
  selector: 'nga-categories',
  styleUrls: [ './categories.component.scss' ],
  templateUrl: './categories.component.html',
  changeDetection: ChangeDetectionStrategy.OnPush
```

```
})
export class CategoriesComponent {
  readonly categoriesNames$: Observable<string[]>;
   readonly products$: Observable<Product[]>;

  constructor(
    private productService: ProductService,
    private route: ActivatedRoute
  ) {
    this.categoriesNames$ =
         this.productService.getDistinctCategories().pipe(
             map(categories => ['all', ...categories]));

    this.products$ = this.route.params.pipe(
      switchMap(({ category }) => this.getCategory(category)));
    }

  private getCategory(category: string): Observable<Product[]> {
    return category.toLowerCase() === 'all'
      ? this.productService.getAll()
       : this.productService.getByCategory(category.toLowerCase());
    }
}
```

Category names to be used as tab titles

Creates an array of category names where the first one is "all"

Gets all products because the user clicked All

Gets corresponding products because the user clicked a tab with a specific category name

Gets products that belong to the selected category

This concludes the code review of ngAuction. To see it in action, run `npm install` in the project directory, and then run `ng serve -o`.

Summary

- Angular comes with several built-in validators, and you can create as many custom ones as you like.
- You can validate user input with synchronous and asynchronous validators.
- You can control when validation happens.

12 Interacting with servers using HTTP

This chapter covers

- Working with the HttpClient service
- Creating a simple web server using the Node and Express frameworks
- Developing an Angular client that communicates with the Node server
- Intercepting HTTP requests and responses

Angular applications can communicate with any web server supporting HTTP, regardless of what server-side platform is used. In this chapter, we'll show you how to use the `HttpClient` service offered by Angular. You'll see how to make HTTP GET and POST methods with `HttpClient`. And you'll learn how to intercept HTTP requests to implement cross-cutting concerns, such as global error handling.

This chapter starts with a brief overview of Angular's `HttpClient` service, and then you'll create a web server using the Node.js and Express.js frameworks. The server will serve the data required for most code samples in this chapter.

Finally, you'll see how to implement HTTP interceptors and report progress while transferring large assets.

12.1 Overview of the HttpClient service

Browser-based web apps run HTTP requests asynchronously, so the UI remains responsive, and the user can continue working with the application while HTTP requests are being processed by the server. Asynchronous HTTP requests can be implemented using callbacks, promises, or observables. Although promises allow you to move away from callback hell (see section A.12.2 in appendix A), they have the following shortcomings:

- There's no way to cancel a pending request made with a promise.
- When a promise resolves or rejects, the client receives either data or an error message, but in both cases it'll be a single piece of data. A JavaScript promise doesn't offer a way to handle a continuous stream of data chunks delivered over time.

Observables don't have these shortcomings. In section 6.4 in chapter 6, we demonstrated how you can cancel HTTP requests made with observables, and in chapter 13, you'll see how a server can push a stream of data to the client using WebSockets.

Angular supports HTTP communications via the `HttpClient` service from the `@angular/common/http` package. If your app requires HTTP communications, you need to add `HttpClientModule` to the `imports` section of the `@NgModule()` decorator.

If you peek inside the type definition file @angular/common/http/src/client.d.ts, you'll see that `get()`, `post()`, `put()`, `delete()`, and many other methods return an `Observable`, and an app needs to subscribe to get the data. To use the `HttpClient` service, you need to inject it into a service or component.

> **NOTE** As explained in chapter 5, every injectable service requires a provider declaration. The providers for `HttpClient` are declared in `HttpClientModule`, so you don't need to declare them in your app.

The following listing illustrates one way of invoking the `get()` method of the `HttpClient` service, passing a URL as a `string`. You retrieve products of type `Product` here.

Listing 12.1 Making an HTTP GET request

```
interface Product {       <-- Defines the type Product
     id: number,
    title: string
}
...
constructor(private httpClient: HttpClient) { }  <-- Injects the HttpClient service

ngOnInit() {
  this.httpClient.get<Product>('/product/123')  <-- Declares a get() request
       .subscribe(
```

```
        data => console.log(`id: ${data.id} title: ${data.title}`),
        (err: HttpErrorResponse) => console.log(`Got error: ${err}`)
      );
}
```

Subscribes to the result of get()

Logs an error, if any

In the `get()` method, you haven't specified the full URL (such as http://localhost:8000/product) assuming that the Angular app makes a request to the same server where it was deployed, so the base portion of the URL can be omitted. Note that in `get<Product>()`, you use TypeScript generics (see section B.9 in appendix B) to specify the type of data expected in the body of the HTTP response. The type annotation doesn't enforce or validate the shape of the data returned by the server; it just makes the other code aware of the expected server response. By default, the response type is `any`, and the TypeScript compiler won't be able to type-check the properties you access on the returned object.

Your `subscribe()` method receives and prints the data on the browser's console. By default, `HttpClient` expects the data in JSON format, and the data is automatically converted into JavaScript objects. If you expect non-JSON data, use the `responseType` option. For example, you can read arbitrary text from a file as shown in the following listing.

Listing 12.2 Specifying string as a returned data type

```
let someData: string;

this.httpClient
    .get<string>('/my_data_file.txt', {responseType: 'text'})
     .subscribe(
        data => someData = data,
        (err: HttpErrorResponse) => console.log(`Got error: ${err}`)
     );
```

Specifies string as a response body type

Logs errors, if any

Assigns the received data to a variable

TIP The `post()`, `put()`, and `delete()` methods are used in a fashion similar to listing 12.2 by invoking one of these methods and subscribing to the results.

Now let's create an app that reads some data from a JSON file.

12.2 Reading a JSON file with HttpClient

To illustrate `HttpClient.get()`, your app will read a file containing JSON-formatted product data. Create a new folder that contains the products.json file shown in the following listing.

Listing 12.3 The file data/products.json

```
[
  { "id": 0, "title": "First Product", "price": 24.99 },
  { "id": 1, "title": "Second Product", "price": 64.99 },
  { "id": 2, "title": "Third Product", "price": 74.99}
]
```

The folder data and the products.json file become assets of your app that need to be included in the project bundles, so you'll add this folder to the app's `assets` property in the .angular-cli.json file (or angular.json, starting from Angular 6), as shown in the next listing.

Listing 12.4 A fragment from .angular-cli.json

```
"assets": [
  "assets",     <-- The name of the default assets folder generated by Angular CLI
   "data"       <-- The name of the folder with assets you add to the project
 ],
```

Let's create an app that will show the product data, as shown in figure 12.1.

Your app component will use `HttpClient.get()` to issue an HTTP GET request, and you'll declare a `Product` interface defining the structure of the expected product data. The observable returned by `get()` will be unwrapped in the template by the async pipe. The app.component.ts file is located in the readfile folder and has the content shown in the following listing.

Figure 12.1 Rendering the content of products.json

Listing 12.5 app.component.ts

```
interface Product {   <-- Declares a product type
   id: string;
  title: string;
  price: number;
}

@Component({
  selector: 'app-root',
  template: `<h1>Products</h1>
  <ul>
    <li *ngFor="let product of products$ | async">   <-- Iterates through the observable products and autosubscribes to them with the async pipe
       {{product.title }}: {{product.price | currency}}   <-- Renders the product title and the price formatted as currency
     </li>
  </ul>
  `})
```

```
export class AppComponent{

  products$: Observable<Product[]>;      <-- Declares a typed observable for products

  constructor(private httpClient: HttpClient) {      <-- Injects the HttpClient service
     this.products$ = this.httpClient
                        .get<Product[]>('/data/products.json');      <-- Makes an HTTP GET request specifying the type of the expected data
    }
}
```

NOTE In this app, you don't use the lifecycle hook `ngOnInit()` for fetching data. That's not a crime, because this code doesn't use any component properties that may not have been initialized during component construction. This data fetch will be executed asynchronously after the constructor when the `async` pipe subscribes to the `products$` observable.

To see this app in action, run `npm install` in the client directory, and then run the following command:

```
ng serve --app readfile -o
```

It wasn't too difficult, was it? Open Chrome Dev tools, and you'll see the HTTP request and response and their headers, as shown in figure 12.2.

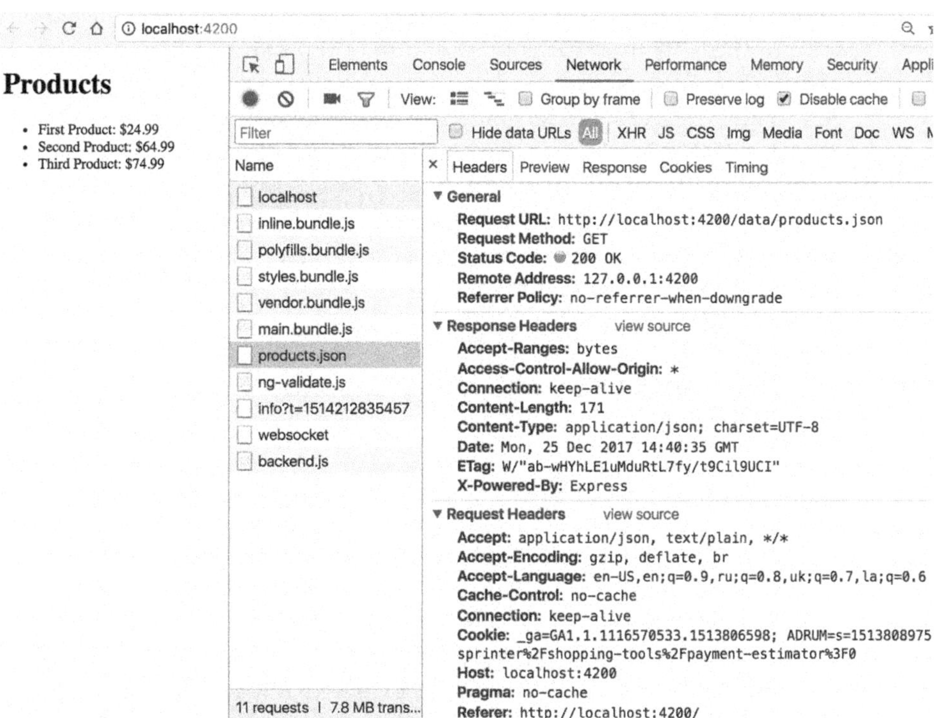

Figure 12.2 Monitoring HTTP request and response

This app illustrates how to make an HTTP GET request that has no parameters and uses default HTTP request headers. If you want to add additional headers and query parameters, use an overloaded version of the `get()` method that offers an extra parameter where you can specify additional options. The following listing shows how to request data from the same products.json file, passing additional headers and query parameters, using the classes `HttpHeaders` and `HttpParams`.

Listing 12.6 Adding HTTP headers and query parameters to the GET request

```
constructor(private httpClient: HttpClient) {

  let httpHeaders = new HttpHeaders()      // Creates the HttpHeaders object with two additional headers
     .set('Content-Type', 'application/json')
     .set('Authorization', 'Basic QWxhZGRpb');

  let httpParams = new HttpParams()      // Creates the object with one query parameter (it can be any object literal)
     .set('title', "First");

  this.products$ = this.httpClient.get<Product[]>('/data/products.json',
    {                                    // Passes the headers and query parameters as a second argument of get()
     headers: httpHeaders,
    params: httpParams
  });
```

Since you simply read a file, passing query parameters doesn't make much sense, but if you needed to make a similar request to a server's endpoint that knows how to search products by title, the code would look the same. Using the chainable `set()` method, you can add as many headers or query parameters as needed.

Running listing 12.7 renders the same data from products.json, but the URL of the request and HTTP headers will look different. Figure 12.3 uses arrows to highlight the differences compared to figure 12.2.

You may be wondering how to send data (for example, using HTTP POST) to the server. To write such an app, you need a server that can accept your data. In section 12.4.2, you'll create an app that uses `HttpClient.post()`, but first let's create a web server using the Node.js and Express.js frameworks.

12.3 Creating a web server with Node, Express, and TypeScript

Angular can communicate with web servers running on any platform, but we decided to create and use a Node.js server in this book for the following reasons:

- There's no need to learn a new programming language to understand the code.
- Node allows you to create standalone applications (such as servers).
- Using Node lets you continue writing code in TypeScript, so we don't have to explain how to create a web server in Java, .NET, or any other language.

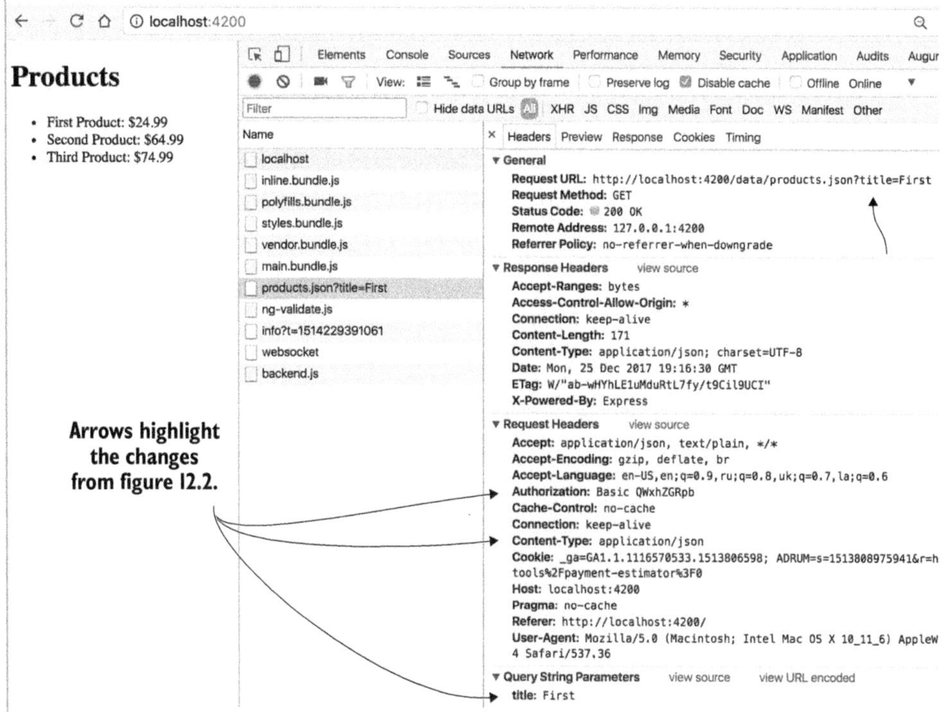

Figure 12.3 Monitoring the modified HTTP request

You'll start with writing a basic web server using Node and Express frameworks. Then, you'll write another web server that can serve JSON data using the HTTP protocol. After this server's ready, you'll create an Angular client that can consume its data.

> **NOTE** Source code for this chapter can be found at https://github.com/Farata/angulartypescript and www.manning.com/books/angular-development-with-typescript-second-edition.

12.3.1 *Creating a simple web server*

In this section, you'll create a web server using Node and Express (http://expressjs.com) frameworks and TypeScript. The code that comes with this chapter has a directory called server, containing a separate project with its own package .json file, which doesn't include any Angular dependencies. The sections for `dependencies` and `devDependencies` of this file look like the following listing.

Listing 12.7 The server's dependencies in package.json

```
"dependencies": {
    "express": "^4.16.2",      <— Express.js framework
    "body-parser": "^1.18.2"   <— Request body parser for Express.js
  },
```

```
"devDependencies": {
  "@types/express": "^4.0.39",     <-- Type definition files for Express.js
  "@types/node": "^6.0.57",        <-- Type definition files for Node.js
  "typescript": "^2.6.2"           <-- Local version of the TypeScript compiler
}
```

You can read about type definition files in section B.12 in appendix B. You'll use the body-parser package for extracting the data from a request object in section 12.4.

NOTE You install the local version of the TypeScript compiler just in case you need to keep a different version of the `tsc` compiler installed globally. Also, you shouldn't expect that a continuous integration server has a global `tsc` executable. To use the local `tsc` version, you can add a custom npm script command in the `scripts` section of package.json (`"tsc": "tsc"`) and start the compiler by running the `npm run tsc` command .

Because you'll write the server code in TypeScript, it needs to be transpiled, so the following listing adds the tsconfig.json file with the compiler's options for `tsc`.

Listing 12.8 tsconfig.json for the server

```
{
  "compilerOptions": {
    "module": "commonjs",    <-- Transpiles modules according to the CommonJS spec
    "outDir": "build",       <-- Saves .js files into the build directory
    "target": "es6"          <-- Transpiles into .js files using ES6 syntax
  },
  "exclude": [
    "node_modules"           <-- Doesn't transpile the code located in the node_modules directory
  ]
}
```

By specifying the CommonJS syntax for modules, you ensure that `tsc` transpiles statements like `import * as express from "express";` into `const express = require ("express");`, as required by Node.

The following listing shows the code of a simple web server from the file my-express-server.ts. This server implements the server-side routing for HTTP `GET` requests by mapping three paths—/, /products, and /reviews—to the corresponding callback functions.

Listing 12.9 my-express-server.ts

```
import * as express from "express";
const app = express();    <-- Instantiates Express.js

app.get('/', (req, res) => res.send('Hello from Express'));    <-- Matches GET requests to the root route

app.get('/products', (req, res) => res.send('Got a request for products'));    <-- Matches GET requests to the /products route
```

```
app.get('/reviews', (req, res) => res.send('Got a request for reviews'));

const server = app.listen(8000, "localhost", () => {

   console.log(`Listening on localhost:8000`);
});
```

Matches GET requests to the /reviews route

Starts listening on localhost:8000 and executes the code from the fat-arrow function

Run npm install; transpile all code samples, including my-express-server.ts, by running tsc; and start this server by running the following command:

```
node build/my-express-server
```

NOTE If you don't have the TypeScript compiler installed globally, you can either run its local version, ./node_modules/typescript/bin/tsc, or add the line `"tsc: "tsc"` to the `scripts` section of package.json, and run it like this: `npm run tsc`.

You'll see the message "Listening on localhost:8000" on the console, and now you can request either products or reviews, depending on which URL you enter in the browser, as shown in figure 12.4.

Figure 12.4 Server-side routing with Express

NOTE To debug Node applications, refer to the documentation of your IDE. If you want to debug the TypeScript code, don't forget to set the option `"sourceMap": true` in the tsconfig.json file of your Node project.

This server responds with simple text messages, but how do you create a server that can respond with data in JSON format?

12.3.2 Serving JSON

To send JavaScript objects (such as products) to the browser in JSON format, you'll use the Express function `json()` on the response object. Your REST server is located in the rest-server.ts file, and it can serve either all products or a specific one (by ID). In this server, you'll create three endpoints: / for the root path, /api/products for all products, and /api/products/:id for the paths that include product IDs. The `products` array will contain three hardcoded objects of type `Product`, which will be turned into JSON format by invoking `res.json ()`, offered by the Express framework.

Listing 12.10 rest-server.ts

```
import * as express from "express";
const app = express();

interface Product {    <- Defines the Product type
     id: number,
    title: string,
    price: number
}

const products: Product[] = [    <- Creates an array of three JavaScript objects with products data
    {id: 0, title: "First Product", price: 24.99},
    {id: 1, title: "Second Product", price: 64.99},
    {id: 2, title: "Third Product", price: 74.99}
];

function getProducts(): Product[] {    <- Returns all products
     return products;
}

app.get('/', (req, res) => {    <- Returns the text prompt as a response to the base URL GET request
     res.send('The URL for products is http://localhost:8000/api/products');
});

app.get('/api/products', (req, res) => {    <- When the GET request contains /api/products in the URL, invokes getProducts()
     res.json(getProducts());    <- Converts products to JSON and returns them to the browser
});

function getProductById(productId: number): Product {    <- Returns the product by ID. Here, you use the array's find() method.
     return products.find(p => p.id === productId);
}

app.get('/api/products/:id', (req, res) => {    <- The GET request came with a parameter. Its values are stored in the params property of the request object.
     res.json(getProductById(parseInt(req.params.id)));    <- Converts the product ID from a string to an integer, invokes getProductById(), and sends the JSON back
 });

const server = app.listen(8000, "localhost", () => {
    console.log(`Listening on localhost:8000`);
});
```

Stop the my-express-server from the previous section if it's running (Ctrl-C), and start the rest-server with the following command:

```
node build/rest-server
```

Enter `http://localhost:8000/api/products` in the browser, and you should see the data in JSON format, as shown in figure 12.5.

```
← → C ⌂ ⓘ localhost:8000/api/products

[{"id":0,"title":"First Product","price":24.99},{"id":1,"title":"Second Product","price":64.99},{"id":2,"title":"Third Product","price":74.99}]
```

Figure 12.5 The server's response to http://localhost:8000/api/products

Figure 12.6 shows the browser window after you enter the URL http://localhost:8000/api/products/1. This time, the server returns only data about the product that has an `id` with the value of `1`.

```
← → C ⌂ ⓘ localhost:8000/api/products/1

{"id":1,"title":"Second Product","price":64.99}
```

Figure 12.6 The server's response to http://localhost:8000/api/products/1

Your REST server is ready. Now let's see how to initiate HTTP GET requests and handle responses in Angular applications.

12.4 Bringing Angular and Node together

In the preceding section, you created the rest-server.ts file, which responds to HTTP GET requests with product details regardless of whether the client was written using a framework or the user simply entered the URL in a browser. In this section, you'll write an Angular client that will issue HTTP GET requests and treat the product data as an `Observable` data stream returned by your server.

> **NOTE** Just a reminder: the Angular app and the Node server are two separate projects. The server code is located in the directory called server, and the Angular app is located in a separate project in the client directory.

12.4.1 Static assets on the server

A typical web app deployed on the server includes static assets (for example, HTML, images, CSS, and JavaScript code) that have to be loaded by the browser when the user enters the URL of the app. From the server's perspective, the Angular portion of a web app is considered *static assets*. The Express framework allows you to specify the directory where the static assets are located.

Let's create a new server: rest-server-angular.ts. In the rest-server.ts file from the previous section, you didn't specify the directory with static assets, because no client app was deployed on the server. In the new server, you add the lines shown in the following listing.

Listing 12.11 Specifying the directory with static resources

```
import * as path from "path";

app.use('/', express.static(path.join(__dirname, 'public')));
```

Adds the Node path module for working with the directory and paths

Assigns the public subdirectory as the location of the static resources

Unlike in rest-server.ts, you just map the base URL (/) to the public directory, and Node will send index.html from there by default. The browser loads index.html, which in turn loads the rest of the bundles defined in the `<script>` tags.

> **NOTE** The original index.html file generated by Angular CLI doesn't contain `<script>` tags, but when you run the `ng build` or `ng serve` commands, they create a new version of index.html that includes the `<script>` tags with all the bundles and other assets.

When the browser requests static assets, Node will look for them in the public subdirectory of the current one (`__dirname`)—the build directory from which you started this server. Here, you use Node's `path.join()` API to ensure that the absolute file path is created in a cross-platform way. In the next section, we'll introduce the Angular client and deploy its bundles in the public directory. The REST endpoints in rest-server-angular.ts remain the same as in rest-server.ts:

- / serves index.html, which contains the code to load the Angular app.
- /api/products serves all products.
- /api/products/:id serves one product by its ID.

The complete code of the rest-server-angular.ts file is shown in the next listing.

Listing 12.12 rest-server-angular.ts

```
import * as express from "express";
import * as path from "path";

const app = express();

app.use('/', express.static(path.join(__dirname, 'public')));

interface Product {
    id: number,
    title: string,
    price: number
}

const products: Product[] = [
    {id: 0, title: "First Product", price: 24.99},
```

Adds the path module that provides utilities for working with file and directory paths

For the root path, specifies the directory from which to serve static assets

```
    {id: 1, title: "Second Product", price: 64.99},
    {id: 2, title: "Third Product", price: 74.99}
];

function getProducts(): Product[] {
    return products;
}
                                                        Configures the endpoint
app.get('/api/products', (req, res) => {          <---  for HTTP GET requests
     res.json(getProducts());
});

function getProductById(productId: number): Product {
    return products.find(p => p.id === productId);
}                                                       Configures another
                                                        endpoint for HTTP
app.get('/api/products/:id', (req, res) => {      <---  GET requests
     res.json(getProductById(parseInt(req.params.id)));
});

const server = app.listen(8000, "localhost", () => {   <--- Starts the server
     console.log(`Listening on localhost:8000`);
});
```

The new server is ready to serve JSON data to the Angular client, so let's start it:

```
node build/rest-server-angular
```

Trying to make a request to this server using the base URL http:// localhost:8000 will return a 404 error, because the directory with static assets doesn't contain the index.html file: you haven't deployed your Angular app there yet. Your next task is to create and deploy the Angular app that will consume JSON-formatted data.

12.4.2 Consuming JSON in Angular apps

Your Angular app will be located in a directory called client. In previous chapters, you were starting all Angular apps building bundles in memory with `ng serve`, but this time you'll also use the `ng build` command to generate bundles in files. Then you'll use npm scripts to automate the deployment of these bundles in the Node server created in section 12.4.1.

In dev mode, you'll keep serving Angular apps using the dev server from Angular CLI that runs on port 4200. But the data will be coming from another web server, powered by Node and Express, that will run on port 8000. Figure 12.7 illustrates this two-server setup.

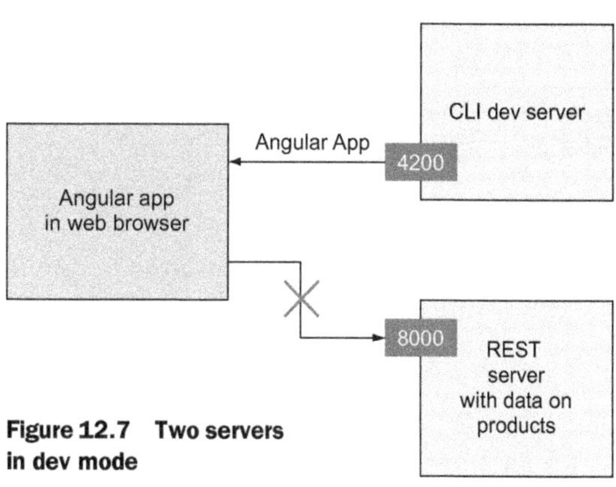

Figure 12.7 Two servers in dev mode

NOTE *Spoiler alert:* We'll run into an issue when the client app served from one server tries to directly access another one. We'll cross that bridge when we get to it.

When the Angular `HttpClient` object makes a request to a URL, the response comes back as `Observable`, and the client's code can handle it either by using the `subscribe()` method or with the `async` pipe introduced in section 6.5 in chapter 6. Using the `async` pipe is preferable, but we'll show you both methods so you can appreciate the advantages of `async`.

Let's start with an app that retrieves all products from the rest-server-angular server and renders them using an HTML unordered list (`<ul>`). You can find this app in the app.component.ts file located in the client/src/app/restclient directory.

Listing 12.13 restclient/app.component.ts

```
// import statements omitted for brevity
interface Product {                          <- Declares the type for products
   id: number,
  title: string,
  price: number
}

@Component({
  selector: 'app-root',
  template: `<h1>All Products</h1>
  <ul>
    <li *ngFor="let product of products">
       {{product.title}}: {{product.price | currency}}   <- Uses the currency pipe for rendering the price
     </li>
  </ul>
  {{error}}
  `})
export class AppComponent implements OnInit {

  products: Product[] = [];
  theDataSource$: Observable<Product[]>;     <- Declares an observable for data returned by HttpClient
   productSubscription: Subscription;        <- Declares the subscription property—you'll need to unsubscribe from observable
   error: string;    <- The HTTP requests errors (if any) are displayed here.

  constructor(private httpClient: HttpClient) {     <- Injects HttpClient
     this.theDataSource$ = this.httpClient
            .get<Product[]>('http://localhost:8000/api/products');   <- Declares the intention to issue HTTP GET for products
   }
  ngOnInit() {
    this.productSubscription = this.theDataSource$
     .subscribe(                             <- Makes an HTTP GET request for products
        data => this.products = data,        <- Adds the received products to the array
        (err: HttpErrorResponse) =>
         this.error = `Can't get products. Got ${err.message}`   <- Sets the value of an error message to a variable for rendering on the UI
     );
  }
}
```

NOTE You didn't use `ngOnDestroy()` to explicitly unsubscribe from the observable because once `HttpClient` gets the response (or an error), the underlying `Observable` completes, so the observer is unsubscribed automatically.

You already started the server in the previous section. Now, start the client by running the following command:

```
ng serve --app restclient -o
```

No products are rendered by the browser, and the console shows a 404 error, but if you used the full URL in the `AppComponent` (for example, http://localhost:8000/api/products), the browser's console would show the following error:

```
Failed to load http://localhost:8000/api/products:
  ➥No 'Access-Control-Allow-
    Origin' header is present on the requested resource.
  ➥Origin 'http://localhost:4200' is therefore not allowed access.
```

That's because you violated the same-origin policy (see http://mng.bz/2tSb). This restriction is set for clients that run in a browser as a security mechanism. Say you visited and logged in to bank.com, and then opened another tab and opened badguys.com. The same-origin policy ensures that scripts from badguys.com can't access your account at bank.com.

Your Angular app was loaded from http://localhost:4200 but tries to access the URL http://localhost:8000. Browsers aren't allowed to do this unless the server that runs on port 8000 is configured to allow access to the clients with the origin http://localhost:4200. When your client app is deployed in the Node server, you won't have this error, because the client app will be loaded from the server that runs on port 8000, and this client will be making data requests to the same server.

In the hands-on section in chapter 13, you'll use the Node.js CORS package (see https://github.com/expressjs/cors) to allow requests from clients with other origins, but this may not be an option if you need to make requests to third-party servers. In dev mode, there's a simpler solution to the same-origin restriction. You'll use the server that runs on port 4200 as a proxy for client requests to the server that runs on port 8000. The same-origin policy doesn't apply to server-to-server communications. In the next section, you'll see how to configure such a proxy on the client.

12.4.3 Configuring the client proxy

In dev mode, you'd like to continue using the server that comes with Angular CLI with its hot reload features and fast rebuilding of application bundles in memory. On the other hand, you want to be able to make requests to other servers.

Under the hood, the Angular CLI dev server uses the Webpack dev server, which can serve as a proxy mediating browser communications with other servers. You just need to create a proxy-conf.json file in the root directory of the Angular project, where you'd configure a URL fragment(s) that the dev server should redirect to another server. In your case, you want to redirect any request that has the URL fragment /api to the server that runs on port 8000, as shown in the following listing.

Listing 12.14 proxy-conf.json

```
{
  "/api": {                                   <-- Hijacks all requests that have /api in the URL
     "target": "http://localhost:8000",       <-- Redirects these requests to this URL
     "secure": false    <-- The target connection doesn't need SSL certificates.
  }
}
```

NOTE Using a proxy file allows you to easily switch between local and remote servers. Just change the value of the `target` property to have your local app retrieve data from a remote server. You can read more about Angular CLI proxying support at http://mng.bz/fLgf.

You need to make a small change in the app from the preceding section. You should replace the full URL of the backend server (http://localhost:8000/api/products) with the path of the endpoint (/api/products). The code that makes a request for products will look as if you try to access the /api/products endpoint on the Angular CLI dev server where the app was downloaded from:

```
this.theDataSource = this.httpClient
              .get<Product[]>('/api/products');
```

But the dev server will recognize the /api fragment in the URL and will redirect this request to another server that runs on port 8000, as shown in figure 12.8 (compare it to figure 12.7).

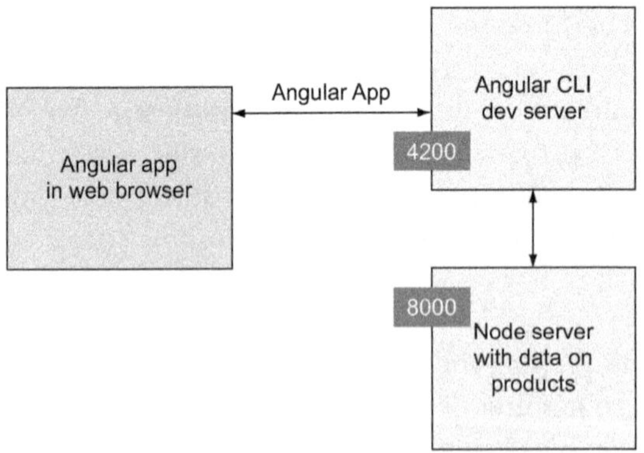

Figure 12.8 Two servers with a proxy

To see the modified app in action, you need to use the `--proxy-config` option, providing the name of the file where you configured the proxy parameters:

```
ng serve --app restclient --proxy-config proxy-conf.json -o
```

NOTE If you forget to provide the name of the proxy file when configuring proxy parameters, you'll get a 404 error, because the /api/products request won't be redirected, and there's no such endpoint in the server that runs on port 4200.

Open your browser to http://localhost:4200, and you'll see the Angular app shown in figure 12.9.

Figure 12.9 Retrieving all products from the Node server via proxy

Note that data arrives from the server that runs on port 4200, which got it from the server that runs on port 8000. Figure 12.8 illustrates this data flow.

In dev mode, using Angular CLI proxying allows you to kill two birds with one stone: have the hot reload of your app on any code change and access data from another server without the need to deploy the app there.

Now let's see how to replace the explicit subscription for products with the `async` pipe.

12.4.4 Subscribing to observables with the async pipe

We introduced `AsyncPipe` (or `async`, when used in templates) in section 6.5 of chapter 6. `async` can receive an `Observable` as input, autosubscribe to it, and discard the subscription when the component gets destroyed. To see this in action, make the following changes in listing 12.13:

- Change the type of the `products` variable from `Array` to `Observable`.
- Remove the declaration of the variable `theDataSource$`.
- Remove the invocation of `subscribe()` in the code. You'll assign the `Observable` returned by the `get()` method to `products`.
- Add the `async` pipe to the `*ngFor` loop in the template.

The following listing implements these changes (see the file restclient/app.component.asyncpipe.ts).

Listing 12.15 app.component.asyncpipe.ts

```
import { HttpClient} from '@angular/common/http';
import {Observable, EMPTY} from 'rxjs';
import {catchError} from 'rxjs/operators';
import {Component} from "@angular/core";

interface Product {
  id: number,
  title: string,
  price: number
}

@Component({
  selector: 'app-root',
  template: `<h1>All Products</h1>
```

```
  <ul>
    <li *ngFor="let product of products$ | async">    ◁── The async pipe
       {{product.title }} {{product.price | currency}}    subscribes and unwraps
    </li>                                                  products from
  </ul>                                                    observable products$.
  {{error}}
  `})
export class AppComponentAsync{
                                                     Initializes the observable
  products$: Observable<Product[]>;                    with HttpClient.get()
  error: string;
  constructor(private httpClient: HttpClient) {
    this.products$ = this.httpClient.get<Product[]>('/api/products')   ◁──
       .pipe(
   ──▷  catchError( err => {
          this.error = `Can't get products. Got ${err.status} from ${err.url}`; ◁──
          return EMPTY;
         });          ◁──                                 Handles the error, if any
  }
}                          Returns an empty observable
                           so the subscriber won't get
Intercepts an error before it   destroyed
reaches the async pipe
```

Running this application will produce the same output shown in figure 12.9.

So far, you've been injecting `HttpClient` instances directly into components, but more often you inject `HttpClient` into a service. Let's see how to do this.

12.4.5 Injecting HttpClient into a service

Angular offers an easy way for separating the business logic implementation from rendering the UI. Business logic should be implemented in services, and the UI in components, and you usually implement all HTTP communications in one or more services that are injected into components. For example, your ngAuction app that comes with chapter 11 has the `ProductService` class with the injected `HttpClient` service. You inject a service into another service.

`ProductService` reads the products.json file using `HttpClient`, but it could get the product data from a remote server the same way you did in the previous section. `ProductService` is injected into components of ngAuction. Check the source code of `ProductService` and `CategoriesComponent` in ngAuction that comes with chapter 11, and you'll recognize the pattern shown in figure 12.10.

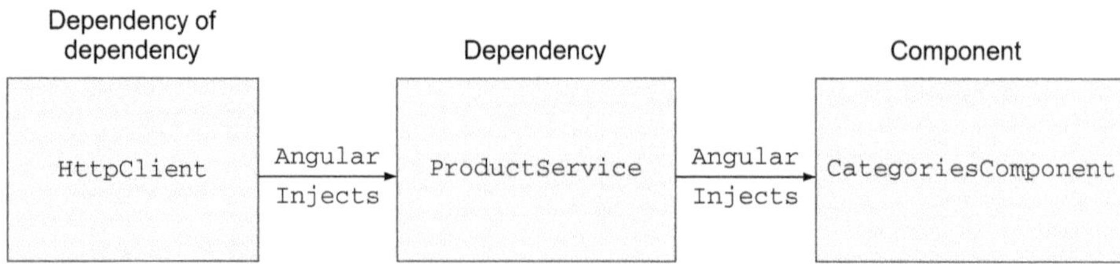

Figure 12.10 Injecting into a service and a component

The following listing from ngAuction's `ProductService` is an example of encapsulating business logic and HTTP communications inside a service.

Listing 12.16 A fragment from ngAuction's `ProductService`

```
@Injectable()
export class ProductService {
  constructor(private http: HttpClient) {}      <-- Injects HttpClient into ProductService

  getAll(): Observable<Product[]> {
    return this.http.get<Product[]>('/data/products.json');      <-- Invokes HttpClient.get()
   }

  getById(productId: number): Observable<Product> {
    return this.http.get<Product[]>('/data/products.json')
      .pipe(
       map(products => products.find(p => p.id === productId))
     );
  }

  getByCategory(category: string): Observable<Product[]> {
    return this.http.get<Product[]>('/data/products.json').pipe(
      map(products => products.filter(p => p.categories.includes(category)))
    );
  }

  getDistinctCategories(): Observable<string[]> {
   return this.http.get<Product[]>('/data/products.json')
     .pipe(
      map(this.reduceCategories),
      map(categories => Array.from(new Set(categories))),
    );
  }
  // Other code is omitted for brevity
}
```

NOTE In the preceding listing 12.19, you use RxJS pipeable operators inside the `pipe()` method (see section D.4.1 in appendix D).

The next listing from `CategoriesComponent` is an example of using the preceding service in the component.

Listing 12.17 A fragment from the ngAuction's `CategoriesComponent`

```
@Component({
  selector: 'nga-categories',
  styleUrls: [ './categories.component.scss' ],
  templateUrl: './categories.component.html'
})
export class CategoriesComponent {
  readonly categoriesNames$: Observable<string[]>;
  readonly products$: Observable<Product[]>;

  constructor(
    private productService: ProductService,      <-- Injects ProductService
```

```
    private route: ActivatedRoute
  ) {
    this.categoriesNames$ = this.productService.getDistinctCategories()
        .pipe(map(categories => ['all', ...categories]));

    this.products$ = this.route.params.pipe(
      switchMap(({ category }) => this.getCategory(category)));
  }

  private getCategory(category: string): Observable<Product[]> {
    return category.toLowerCase() === 'all'
      ? this.productService.getAll()
       : this.productService.getByCategory(category.toLowerCase());
   }
}
```

Uses ProductService

The provider for `ProductService` is declared on the app level in the `@NgModule()` decorator of the root module of ngAuction. In the hands-on section in chapter 13, you'll split ngAuction into two projects, client and server, and the web server will be written using Node and Express frameworks. How can an Angular app (bundles and assets) be deployed in a web server?

12.4.6 Deploying Angular apps on the server with npm scripts

The process of deploying the code of a web client in a server should be automated. At the very minimum, deploying an Angular app includes running several commands for building bundles and replacing previously deployed code (index.html, JavaScript bundles, and other assets) with new code. The deployment may also include running test scripts and other steps.

JavaScript developers use various tools for automating running deployment tasks such as Grunt, gulp, npm scripts, and others. In this section we'll show you how to use npm scripts for deployment. We like using npm scripts, because they're simple to use and offer an easy way to automate running command sequences in a predefined order. Besides, you already have npm installed, so there's no need to install additional software for automating your deployment workflow.

To illustrate the deployment process, you'll use the rest-server-angular server from section 12.3.1, where you'll deploy the Angular app from section 12.3.4. After deployment, you won't need to configure the proxy anymore, because both the server and the client code will be deployed at the same server running http:// localhost:8000. After entering this URL in the browser, the user will see the product data, as shown earlier in figure 12.9.

npm allows you to add the `scripts` property in package.json, where you can define aliases for terminal commands. For example, instead of typing the long command `ng serve --app restclient --proxy-config proxy-conf.json`, you can define a start command in the scripts section of package.json as follows:

```
"scripts": {
  "start": "ng serve --app restclient --proxy-config proxy-conf.json"
}
```

Now, instead of typing that long command, you'll just enter `npm start` in the console. npm supports more than a dozen script commands right out of the box (see the npm-scripts documentation for details, https://docs.npmjs.com/misc/scripts). You can also add new custom commands specific to your development and deployment workflow.

Some of these scripts need to be run manually (such as `npm start`), and some are invoked automatically if they have the `post` and `pre` prefixes (for example, `postinstall`). If any command in the `scripts` section starts with the `post` prefix, it'll run automatically after the corresponding command specified after this prefix.

For example, if you define the command `"postinstall": "myCustomInstall.js"`, each time you run `npm install`, the script myCustomInstall.js will automatically run right after. Similarly, if a command has a `pre` prefix, such a command will run before the command named after this prefix.

If you define custom commands that aren't known by npm scripts, you'll need to use an additional option: `run`. Say you defined a custom command `startDev` like this:

```
"scripts": {
  "startDev": "ng serve --app restclient --proxy-config proxy-conf.json"
}
```

To run that command, you need to enter the following in your terminal window: `npm run startDev`. To automate running some of your custom commands, use the same prefixes: `post` and `pre`.

Let's see how to create a sequence of runnable commands for deploying an Angular app on the Node server. Open package.json from the client directory, and you'll find four custom commands there: `build`, `postbuild`, `predeploy`, and `deploy`. The following listing shows what will happen if you run a single command: `npm run build`.

Listing 12.18 A fragment from client/package.json

```
"scripts": {
  "build": "ng build --prod --app restclient",
  "postbuild": "npm run deploy",
  "predeploy": "rimraf ../server/build/public && mkdirp ../server/build/public",
  "deploy": "copyfiles -f dist/** ../server/build/public"
}
```

The command ng build will create a production build of the restclient app in the default directory dist.

Since there's a postbuild command, it starts automatically and will try to run the deploy command.

Since there's also a predeploy command there, it'll run after the postbuild and before deploy.

Finally, the deploy command is executed.

We'll explain what the commands `predeploy` and `deploy` do in a minute, but our main message here is that starting a single command resulted in running four commands in the specified order. Creating a sequence of deployment commands is easy.

TIP If you build the bundles with AOT compilation and use only standard Angular decorators (no custom ones), you can further optimize the size of the JavaScript in your app by commenting out the line `import 'core-js/es7/reflect';` in the polyfills.ts file. This will reduce the size of the generated polyfill bundle.

Typically, the deployment process removes the directory with previously deployed files, creates a new empty directory, and copies the new files into this directory. In your deployment scripts, you use three npm packages that know how to do these operations, regardless of the platform you use (Windows, Unix, or macOS):

- `rimraf`—Removes the specified directory and its subdirectories
- `mkdirp`—Creates a new directory
- `copyfiles`—Copies files from source to destination

Check the devDependencies section in package.json, and you'll see `rimraf`, `mkdirp`, and `copyfiles` there.

TIP Currently, Angular CLI uses Webpack to build bundles. Angular CLI 7 will come with new build tools. In particular, it'll include Closure Compiler, which produces smaller bundles.

The code that comes with this chapter is located in two sibling directories: client and server. Your `predeploy` command removes the content of the server/build/public directory (this is where you'll deploy the Angular app) and then creates a new empty public directory. The `&&` sign allows you to define commands that run more than one script.

The `deploy` command copies the content of the client/dist directory (the app's bundles and assets) into server/build/public.

In the real world, you may need to deploy an Angular app on a remote server, so using the package copyfiles won't work. Consider using an SCP utility (see https://en.wikipedia.org/wiki/Secure_copy) that performs secure file transfer from a local computer to a remote one.

If you can manually run a utility from the terminal window, you can run it using npm scripts as well. In chapter 14, you'll learn how to write test scripts. Including a test runner into your build process could be as simple as adding `&& ng test` to your `predeploy` command. If you find some useful gulp plugins, create the npm script for it, for example, `"myGulpCommand" : "gulp SomeUsefulTask"`.

To see that your deployment scripts work, perform the following steps:

1. Start the server by running the following command in the server directory:

   ```
   node build/rest-server-angular
   ```

2. In the client directory, run the build and deployment scripts:

   ```
   npm run build
   ```

   Check the server/build/public directory—the client's bundles should be there.

3 Open your browser to http://localhost:8000, and your Angular app will be loaded from your Node server showing three products, as shown in figure 12.9.

We've described the entire process of creating and running a web server, as well as creating and running Angular apps in dev mode and deploying in the server. Your Angular app was using the `HttpClient` service to issue HTTP GET requests to retrieve data from the server. Now let's see how to issue HTTP POST requests to post data to the server.

12.5 Posting data to the server

HTTP POST requests are used for sending new data to the server. With `HttpClient`, making POST requests is similar to making GET requests. Invoking the `HttpClient.post()` method declares your intention to post data to the specified URL, but the request is made when you invoke `subscribe()`.

NOTE For updating existing data on the server, use `HttpClient.put()`; and for deleting data, use `HttpClient.delete()`.

12.5.1 Creating a server for handling post requests

You need a web server with an endpoint that knows how to handle POST requests issued by the client. The code that comes with this chapter includes a server with an /api/product endpoint for adding new products, located in the rest-server-angular-post.ts file. Because your goal isn't to have a fully functional server for adding and saving products, the /api/product endpoint will simply log the posted data on the console and send a confirmation message to the client.

The posted data will arrive in the request body, and you need to be able to parse it to extract the data. The npm package body-parser knows how to do this in Express servers. If you open package.json in the server directory, you'll find body-parser in the dependencies section. The entire code of your server is shown in the following listing.

Listing 12.19 rest-server-angular-post.ts

```
import * as express from "express";
import * as path from "path";
import * as bodyParser from "body-parser";

const app = express();

app.use('/', express.static(path.join(__dirname, 'public')));

app.use(bodyParser.json());

app.post("/api/product", (req, res) => {

  console.log(`Received new product
              ${req.body.title} ${req.body.price}`);
```

- Adds the body-parser package (import of body-parser)
- Creates the parser to turn the payload of req.body into JSON (app.use(bodyParser.json()))
- Creates an endpoint for handling POST requests (app.post)
- Logs the payload of the POST request (console.log)

```
  res.json({'message':`Server responded: added ${req.body.title}`});
 });

const server = app.listen(8000, "localhost", () => {
  const {address, port} = server.address();
  console.log(`Listening on ${address}: ${port}`);
});
```

Sends the confirmation message to the client

Your server expects the payload in a JSON format, and it'll send the response back as a JSON object with one property: message. Start this server by running the following command in the server directory (don't forget to run tsc to compile it):

```
node build/rest-server-angular-post
```

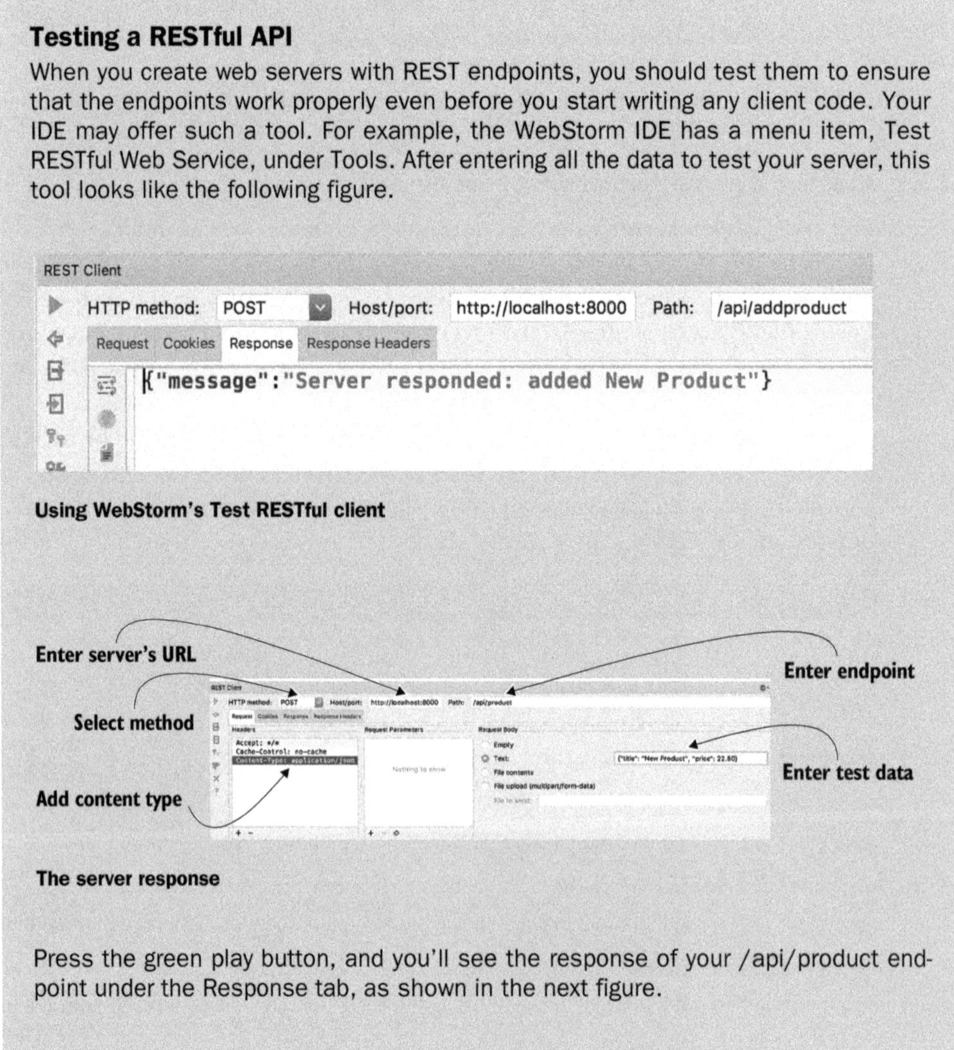

Testing a RESTful API

When you create web servers with REST endpoints, you should test them to ensure that the endpoints work properly even before you start writing any client code. Your IDE may offer such a tool. For example, the WebStorm IDE has a menu item, Test RESTful Web Service, under Tools. After entering all the data to test your server, this tool looks like the following figure.

Using WebStorm's Test RESTful client

The server response

Press the green play button, and you'll see the response of your /api/product endpoint under the Response tab, as shown in the next figure.

REST Client

HTTP method: POST Host/port: http://localhost:8000 Path: /api/addproduct

Request Cookies Response Response Headers

{"message":"Server responded: added New Product"}

The server response

If your IDE doesn't offer such a testing tool, use the Chrome extension called Advanced REST Client (https://install.advancedrestclient.com/#/install) or a tool called Postman (www.getpostman.com).

Now that you've created, started, and tested the web server, let's write the Angular client that will post new products to this server.

12.5.2 Creating a client for making post requests

Your Angular app will render a simple form where the user can enter the product title and price, as shown in figure 12.11.

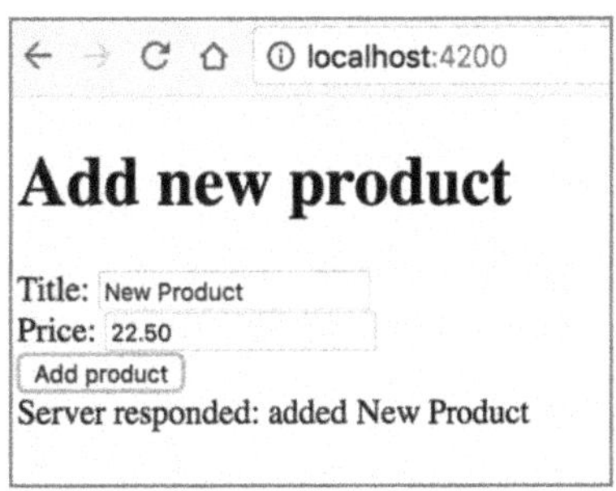

Figure 12.11 UI for adding new products

After filling out the form and clicking the Add Product button, the server will respond with the confirmation message shown under the button.

In this app, you'll use the template-driven Forms API, and your form will require the user to enter the new product's title and price. On the button click, you'll invoke the method `HttpClient.post()`, followed by `subscribe()`.

The code of this Angular app is located in the client directory under the restclient-post subdirectory. It's shown in the following listing.

Listing 12.20 app.component.ts

```
import {Component} from "@angular/core";
import {HttpClient, HttpErrorResponse} from "@angular/common/http";

@Component({
  selector: 'app-root',
  template: `<h1>Add new product</h1>
     <form #f="ngForm" (ngSubmit) = "addProduct(f.value)" >
       Title: <input id="productTitle" name="title" ngModel>
```

```
        <br>
        Price: <input id="productPrice" name="price" ngModel>
        <br>
        <button type="submit">Add product</button>
      </form>
      {{response}}
   `})
export class AppComponent {

  response: string;

  constructor(private httpClient: HttpClient) {}

  addProduct(formValue) {

    this.response='';

    this.httpClient.post<string>("/api/product",
                                 formValue)
      .subscribe(
        data =>  this.response = data['message'],
        (err: HttpErrorResponse) =>
            this.response = `Can't add product. Error code:
             ${err.message} ${err.error.message}`
      );
  }
}
```

Declares the intention to make a POST request

Makes the HTTP POST request

Provides the POST payload

Gets the server's response

Handles errors

When the user clicks Add Product, the app makes a POST request and subscribes to the server response. `formValue` contains a JavaScript object with the data entered in the form, and `HttpClient` automatically turns it into a JSON object. If the data was posted successfully, the server returns a JSON object with the `message` property, which is rendered using data binding.

If the server responds with an error, you display it in the UI. Note that you use `err.message` and `err.error.message` to extract the error description. The second property may contain additional error details. Modify the code of the server to return a string instead of JSON, and the UI will show a detailed error message.

To see this app in action, run the following command in the project client:

```
ng serve --app restclientpost --proxy-config proxy-conf.json -o
```

You now know how to send HTTP requests and handle responses, and there could be lots of them in your app. Is there a way to intercept all of them to provide some additional processing, like showing/hiding the progress bar, or logging requests?

12.6 HTTP interceptors

Angular allows you to create HTTP interceptors for pre- and post-processing of all HTTP requests and responses of your app. They can be useful for implementing such cross-cutting concerns as logging, global error handling, authentication, and others. We'd like to stress that the interceptors work *before* the request goes out or before a response is rendered on the UI. This gives you a chance to implement the fallback scenarios for certain errors or prevent attempts of unauthorized access.

To create an interceptor, you need to write a service that implements the `Http-Interceptor` interface, which requires you to implement one method: `intercept()`. Angular will provide two arguments to this callback: `HttpRequest` and `HttpHandler`. The first one contains the request object being intercepted, which you can clone and modify. The second argument is used to forward the modified request to the backend or another interceptor in the chain (if any) by invoking the `handle()` method.

NOTE The `HttpRequest` and `HttpResponse` objects are immutable, and the word *modify* means creating and passing through the new instances of these objects.

The interceptor service shown in the following listing doesn't modify the outgoing `HttpRequest` but simply prints its content on the console and passes it through as is.

Listing 12.21 A simple interceptor

```
@Injectable()
export class MyFirstInterceptor implements HttpInterceptor {

  intercept(req: HttpRequest<any>, next: HttpHandler): Observable<HttpEvent<any>> {
    // Clone and modify your HTTPRequest using req.clone()
    // or perform other actions here

    console.log("I've intercepted your HTTP request! ${JSON.stringify(req)}`);

    return next.handle(req);
  }
}
```

In listing 12.21, you forward the `HttpRequest`, but you could modify its headers or parameters and return the modified request. The `next.handle()` method returns an observable when the request is complete, and if you want to modify the HTTP response as well, apply additional RxJS operators on the stream returned by `next.handle()`.

The `intercept()` method receives the `HttpRequest` object and returns, not the `HttpResponse` object, but the observable of `HttpEvent`, because Angular implements `HttpResponse` as a stream of `HttpEvent` values.

Both `HttpRequest` and `HttpResponse` are immutable, and if you want to modify their properties, you need to clone them first, as in the following listing.

Listing 12.22 Modifying `HTTPRequest`

```
intercept(req: HttpRequest<any>, next: HttpHandler): Observable<HttpEvent<any
     >> {
    const modifiedRequest = req.clone({
      setHeaders: { ('Authorization', 'Basic QWxhZGRpb') }
    });
    return next.handle(modifiedRequest);
  }
```

Because an interceptor is an injectable service, don't forget to declare its provider for the `HTTP_INTERCEPTORS` token in the `@NgModule()` decorator:

```
providers: [{provide: HTTP_INTERCEPTORS,
             useClass: MyFirstInterceptor, multi: true}]
```

The `multi: true` option tells you that `HTTP_INTERCEPTORS` is a multiprovider token—an array of services can represent the same token. You can register more than one interceptor, and Angular will inject all of them:

```
providers: [{provide: HTTP_INTERCEPTORS,
               useClass: MyFirstInterceptor, multi: true},
            {provide: HTTP_INTERCEPTORS,
               useClass: MySecondInterceptor, multi: true}]
```

NOTE If you have more than one interceptor, they'll be invoked in the order they're defined.

To illustrate how interceptors work, let's create an app with an `HttpInterceptor` that will intercept and log all errors returned by the server. For the client, you'll reuse the app from section 12.5.2 shown in figure 12.11, adding the logging service and the interceptor to log errors on the console.

You'll slightly modify the server from the previous section to randomly generate errors. You can find the complete code of the server in the rest-server-angular-post-errors.ts file. Now, instead of just responding with success messages, it'll randomly return an error, as shown in the following listing.

Listing 12.23 Emulating server errors

```
if (Math.random() < 0.5) {
     res.status(500);
    res.send({'message': `Server responded: error adding product
                         ${req.body.title}`});
} else {
     res.send({'message': `Server responded: added ${req.body.title}`);
}
```

Returns an HTTP response with the status 500

Returns a successful HTTP response

Start this server as follows:

```
node build/rest-server-angular-post-errors
```

Your Angular app is located in the interceptor directory and includes a logging service implemented as two classes: `LoggingService` and `ConsoleLoggingService`. `LoggingService` is an abstract class that declares one method, `log()`.

Listing 12.24 logging.service.ts

```
@Injectable()
export abstract class LoggingService {

  abstract log(message: string): void;
}
```

Because this class is abstract, it can't be instantiated, and you'll create the class `ConsoleLoggingService` shown in the following listing.

Listing 12.25 console.logging.service.ts

```
@Injectable()
export class ConsoleLoggingService implements LoggingService{

   log(message:string): void {
        console.log(message);
   }
}
```

You may be wondering why you create the abstract class for such a simple logging service. It's because in real-world apps, you may want to introduce logging, not only on the browser's console, but also on the server. Having an abstract class would allow you to use it as a token for declaring a provider:

```
providers: [{provide: LoggingService, useClass: ConsoleLoggingService}]
```

Later on, you can create a class called `ServerLoggingService` that implements `LoggingService`, and to switch from console to server logging, you'll need to change the provider without having to modify components that use it:

```
providers: [{provide: LoggingService, useClass: ServerLoggingService}]
```

If your interceptor receives an error, you'll do the following:

1. Log it on the console.
2. Replace the `HttpErrorResponse` with a new instance of `HttpResponse` that will contain the error message.
3. Return the new `HttpResponse` so the client can show it to the user.

The interceptor class will use the `catchError` operator on the observable returned by `HttpHandler.next()`, where you'll implement these steps. Your interceptor is implemented in the logging.interceptor.service.ts file.

Listing 12.26 logging.interceptor.service.ts

```
import {Injectable} from "@angular/core";
import {HttpErrorResponse, HttpEvent, HttpHandler,
      HttpInterceptor, HttpRequest, HttpResponse} from "@angular/common/http";
import {Observable, of} from "rxjs";
```

```
import {catchError} from 'rxjs/operators';
import {LoggingService} from "./logging.service";

@Injectable()
export class LoggingInterceptor implements HttpInterceptor {

  constructor(private loggingService: LoggingService) {}

  intercept(req: HttpRequest<any>, next: HttpHandler):
➥Observable<HttpEvent<any>> {
    return next.handle(req)
        .pipe(
         catchError((err: HttpErrorResponse) =>
            this.loggingService.log(`Logging Interceptor: ${err.error.message}`);
            return of(new HttpResponse(
                {body:{message: err.error.message}}));
           })
        );
  }
}
```

Injects the console logging service

Forwards requests to the server and responses to the client

The new HttpResponse will contain the error message.

Logs the error message on the console

Replaces HttpErrorResponse with HttpResponse

Catches the response errors returned by the server

The code for the application component has no references to the interceptor class, as you'll see in the following listing. It'll be always receiving `HttpResponse` objects that contain either a message that the server successfully added a new product, or an error message.

Listing 12.27 app.component.ts

```
import {Component} from "@angular/core";
import {HttpClient} from "@angular/common/http";
import {Observable} from "rxjs";
import {map} from "rxjs/operators";

@Component({
  selector: 'app-root',
  template: `<h1>Add new product</h1>
  <form #f="ngForm" (ngSubmit) = "addProduct(f.value)" >
    Title: <input id="productTitle" name="title" ngModel>
    <br>
    Price: <input id="productPrice" name="price" ngModel>
    <br>
    <button type="submit">Add product</button>
  </form>
  {{response$ | async}}
   `})
export class AppComponent {

  response$: Observable<string>;

  constructor(private httpClient: HttpClient) {}
```

Renders any messages received from the server (including errors)

This observable is for the interceptor's responses.

```
  addProduct(formValue){
    this.response$=this.httpClient.post<{message: string}>("/api/product",
       formValue)
      .pipe(
        map (data=> data.message)
      );
  }
}
```

Expects the server's responses to HTTP POST as {message: string}

Extracts the text of the message property

When you compare this app with the one from the previous section, note that you don't handle errors in the component, which renders the messages to the UI. Now the `LoggingInterceptor` will handle all HTTP errors.

To see this app in action, run the following command and monitor the browser console for logging messages.

```
ng serve --app interceptor --proxy-config proxy-conf.json -o
```

This app should give you an idea of how to implement a cross-cutting concern like a global error-logging service for all HTTP responses without the need to modify any application components or services that use the `HttpClient` service.

An HTTP request runs asynchronously and can generate a number of progress events that you might want to intercept and handle. Let's look at how you'd do that.

12.7 Progress events

Sometimes uploading or downloading certain assets (like large data files or images) takes time, and you should keep the user informed about the progress. `HttpClient` offers progress events that contain information like total size of the asset, current number of bytes that are already uploaded or downloaded, and more.

To enable progress events tracking, make your requests using the `HttpRequest` object with the option `{reportProgress: true}`. For example, you can make an HTTP GET request that reads the my_large_file.json file.

Listing 12.28 Making a GET request with events tracking

```
const req = new HttpRequest('GET',
                        './my_large_file.json',
                        { reportProgress: true });
 httpClient.request(req).subscribe(
       // Handle progress events here);
```

Declares an intention to make a GET request

Specifies the file to read

Enables progress event

Makes a request

In the `subscribe()` method , check whether the emitted value is an event of the type you're interested in, for example, `HttpEventType.DownloadProgress` or `HttpEventType.UploadProgress`. These events have the `loaded` property for the current number of transferred bytes and the `total` property, which knows the total size of the transfer.

The next app shows how to handle a progress event for calculating and showing the percentage of the file download. This app comes with a large 48 MB JSON file. The content of the file is irrelevant in this case. Figure 12.12 shows the app when the download of the file is complete. The percentage on the left is changing as this file is being loaded by `HttpClient`. This app also reports the progress on the browser's console.

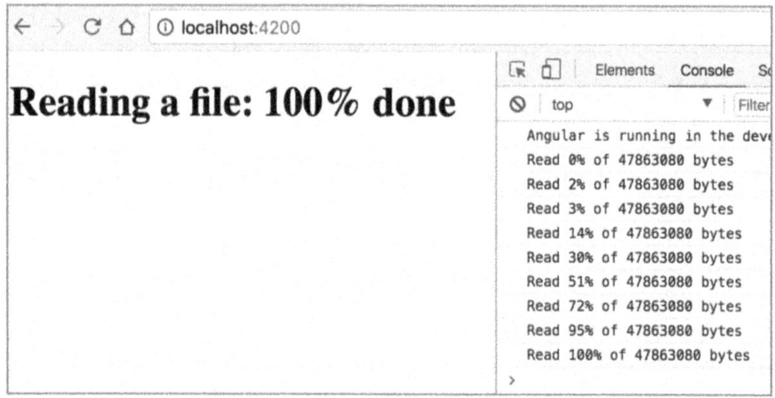

Figure 12.12 Reporting progress while reading a file

This app is located in the progressevents directory, and the content of app.component .ts is shown in the next listing.

Listing 12.29 app.component.ts

```
import {HttpClient, HttpEventType, HttpRequest} from '@angular/common/http';
import {Component} from "@angular/core";

@Component({
  selector: 'app-root',
  template: `<h1>Reading a file: {{percentDone}}% done</h1>
   `})
export class AppComponent{

  mydata: any;
  percentDone: number;

  constructor(private httpClient: HttpClient) {

    const req = new HttpRequest('GET',
                             './data/48MB_DATA.json',
                             {reportProgress: true});

    httpClient.request(req)
    .subscribe(data => {
      if (data.type === HttpEventType.DownloadProgress) {
         this.percentDone = Math.round(100 * data.loaded / data.total);))
         console.log(`Read ${this.percentDone}% of ${data.total} bytes`);
      } else {
```

- Renders the current percentage
- Declares an intention to make a GET request
- Specifies the file to read
- Enables the progress event tracking
- Checks the type of the progress event
- Calculates the current percentage

```
            this.mydata = data          <-- Emitted value is not
          }                                 a progress event
      });
    }
  }
```

To see this app in action, run the following command:

```
ng serve --app progressevents -o
```

This app concludes our coverage of communicating with web servers using HTTP. In the next chapter, you'll see how an Angular client can communicate with web servers using WebSockets.

Summary

- Angular comes with the `HttpClient` service, which supports HTTP communications with web servers.
- Public methods of `HttpClient` return an `Observable` object, and only when the client subscribes to it is the request to the server made.
- An Angular client can communicate with web servers implemented in different technologies.
- You can intercept and replace HTTP requests and responses with modified ones to implement cross-cutting concerns.

13 Interacting with servers using the WebSocket protocol

This chapter covers

- Implementing a server data push to Angular clients
- Broadcasting data from the server to multiple clients
- Splitting ngAuction into two projects
- Implementing bidding in ngAuction

WebSocket is a low-overhead binary protocol supported by all modern web browsers (see https://en.wikipedia.org/wiki/WebSocket). It allows bidirectional message-oriented streaming of text and binary data between browsers and web servers. In contrast to HTTP, WebSocket is not a request/response-based protocol, and both server apps and client apps can initiate data push to the other party as soon as the data becomes available, in real time. This makes the WebSocket protocol a good fit for the following types of applications:

- Live trading/auctions/sports notifications
- Controlling medical equipment over the web
- Chat applications

- Multiplayer online games
- Real-time updates in social streams
- Live charts

All of these apps have one thing in common: there's a server (or a device) that may need to send an immediate notification to the user because some important event happened elsewhere. This is different from the use case when the user decides to send a request to the server for fresh data. For example, if a stock trade happens on the stock exchange, the notification has to be immediately sent to all users.

Another example is an online auction. If user Joe is considering bidding on a certain product, and user Mary (located 1,000 miles away) decides to increase the bid on the same product, you'd better push the notification to Joe right away as opposed to waiting until Joe refreshes the window.

We'll start this chapter with a brief comparison of HTTP and WebSocket protocols, and then we'll show you how a Node server can push data to a plain web page and to an Angular app.

In the hands-on section, you'll continue working on ngAuction. You'll start by splitting ngAuction into two projects: client and server. The server app will start two servers: the HTTP server will serve data, and the WebSocket server can receive user bids and push real-time bid notifications, emulating a scenario in which multiple users can bid on auctioned products. The Angular client interacts with both servers.

13.1 Comparing HTTP and WebSockets

With the request-based HTTP protocol, a client sends a request over a connection and waits for a response to come back, as shown in figure 13.1. Both the request and the response use the same browser-server connection. First, the request goes out, and then the response comes back via the same "wire." Think of a narrow bridge over a river where cars from both sides have to take turns crossing the bridge. In the web realm, this type of communications is called *half-duplex*.

The WebSocket protocol allows data to travel in both directions simultaneously (*full-duplex*) over the same connection, as shown in figure 13.2, and any party can initiate the data exchange. It's like a two-lane road. Another analogy is a phone conversation where two callers can speak and be heard at the same time. The WebSocket

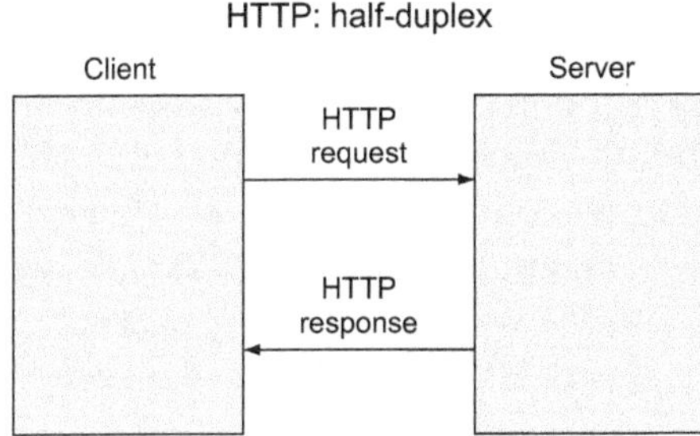

Figure 13.1 Half-duplex communication

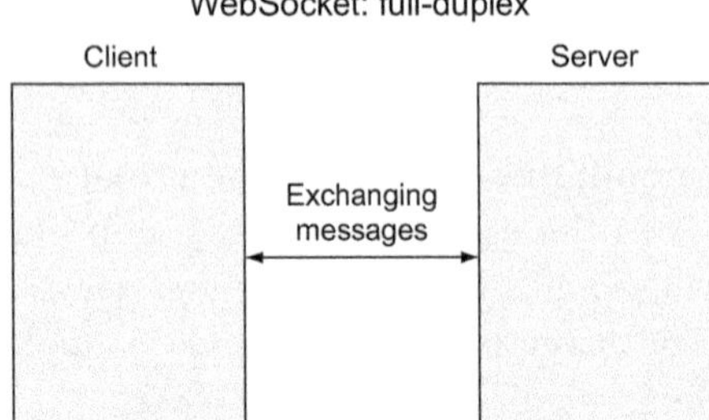

Figure 13.2 Full-duplex communication

connection is kept alive, which has an additional benefit: low latency in the interaction between the server and the client.

A typical HTTP request/response adds several hundred bytes (HTTP headers) to the application data. Say you want to write a web app that reports the latest stock prices every second. With HTTP, such an app would need to send an HTTP request (about 300 bytes) and receive a stock price that would arrive with an additional 300 bytes of an HTTP response object.

With WebSockets, the overhead is as low as a couple of bytes. Besides, there's no need to keep sending requests for the new price quote every second—this stock may not be traded for a while. Only when the stock price changes will the server push the new value to the client. Note the following observation (see goo.gl/zjj7Es):

> *Reducing kilobytes of data to 2 bytes is more than "a little more byte efficient," and reducing latency from 150 ms (TCP round trip to set up the connection plus a packet for the message) to 50 ms (just the packet for the message) is far more than marginal. In fact, these two factors alone are enough to make WebSocket seriously interesting to Google.*
>
> —Ian Hickson

NOTE Although most browsers support the binary protocol HTTP/2 (see https://http2.github.io)—which is more efficient than HTTP and also allows data push from the servers—it's not a replacement for the WebSocket protocol. The WebSocket protocol offers an API that allows pushing *data* to the client's app running in the browser, whereas HTTP/2 pushes *static resources* to the browser and is mainly for faster app delivery.

Every browser supports a `WebSocket` object for creating and managing a socket connection to the server (see http://mng.bz/1j4g). Initially, the browser establishes a regular HTTP connection with the server, but then your app requests a connection upgrade specifying the server's URL that supports the WebSocket connection. After that, the communication succeeds without the need of HTTP. The URLs of the WebSocket endpoints start with ws instead of http—for instance, ws://localhost:8085.

The WebSocket protocol is based on events and callbacks. For example, when your browser app establishes a connection with the server, it receives the `connection` event, and your app invokes a callback to handle this event. To handle the data that the server may send over this connection, expect the `message` event providing the corresponding callback. If the connection is closed, the `close` event is dispatched so your app can react accordingly. In case of an error, the `WebSocket` object gets the `error` event.

On the server side, you'll have to process similar events. Their names may be different depending on the WebSocket software you use on the server. Let's write some code where a Node server will send data to the Angular app over WebSockets.

13.2 Pushing data from a Node server to a plain client

WebSockets are supported by most server-side platforms (Java, .NET, Python, and others). In chapter 12, you started working with Node servers, and you'll continue using Node for implementing your WebSocket server. In this section, you'll implement one particular use case: the server pushes data to a browser client as soon as the client connects to the socket. Since either party can start sending data over the WebSocket connection, you'll see that WebSockets aren't about request/response communication. Your simple client won't need to send a request for data—the server will initiate the communications.

Several Node packages implement the WebSocket protocol, and you'll use the npm package called `ws` (www.npmjs.com/package/ws). You can install this package and its type definitions by entering the following commands in your project directory:

```
npm install ws
npm install @types/ws --save-dev
```

The type definitions are needed so the TypeScript compiler won't complain when you use the API from the `ws` package. Besides, this file is handy for seeing the APIs and types available.

> **NOTE** The code that comes with this chapter has a directory called server, which contains the file package.json that lists both `ws` and `@types/ws` as dependencies. You just need to run the `npm install` command. Source code can be found at https://github.com/Farata/angulartypescript and www.manning .com/books/angular-development-with-typescript-second-edition.

Your first WebSocket server will be pretty simple: it'll push the text "This message was pushed by the WebSocket server" to an HTML/JavaScript client (no Angular) as soon as the socket connection is established. We purposely don't want the client to send any requests to the server so we can illustrate that a socket is a two-way street and that the server can push data without any request ceremony.

Your app creates two servers. The HTTP server runs on port 8000 and is responsible for sending an HTML page to the browser. When this page is loaded, it immediately connects to the WebSocket server that runs on port 8085. This server will push the message with the greeting as soon as the connection is established. The code of this app is located in the server/simple-websocket-server.ts file and is shown in the following listing.

Listing 13.1 simple-websocket-server.ts

```
import * as express from "express";
import * as path from "path";
import {Server} from "ws";          <-- You'll use Server from the ws module to instantiate a WebSocket server.

const app = express();

// HTTP Server
app.get('/', (req, res) => res.sendFile(path.join(__dirname,
                        '../simple-websocket-client.html')));   <-- When the HTTP client connects with the root path, the HTTP server will send back this HTML file.

const httpServer = app.listen(8000, "localhost", () => {        <-- Starts the HTTP server on port 8000
    console.log(`HTTP server is listening on localhost:8000`);
});

// WebSocket Server
const wsServer = new Server({port: 8085});     <-- Starts the WebSocket server on port 8085
 console.log('WebSocket server is listening on localhost:8085');

wsServer.on('connection',                      <-- Listens to connection event from clients
          wsClient => {
            wsClient.send('This message was pushed by the WebSocket server');   <-- Pushes the message to the newly connected client

            wsClient.onerror = (error) =>      <-- Handles connection errors
                console.log(`The server received: ${error['code']}`);
          }
);
```

As soon as any client connects to your WebSocket server via port 8085, the connection event is dispatched on the server, and it'll also receive a reference to the object that represent this particular client's connection. Using the `send()` method, the server sends the greeting to this client. If another client connects to the same socket on port 8085, it'll also receive the same greeting.

> **NOTE** As soon as the new client connects to the server, the reference to this connection is added to the `wsServer.clients` array so you can broadcast messages to all connected clients if needed: `wsServer.clients.forEach (client => client.send('…'));`.

In your app, the HTTP and WebSocket servers run on different ports, but you could reuse the same port by providing the newly created `httpServer` instance to the constructor of the WebSocket server, as shown in the following listing.

Listing 13.2 Reusing the same port for both servers

```
const httpServer = app.listen(8000, "localhost", () => {...});   <-- Creates an instance of the HTTP server on port 8000

const wsServer = new Server({server: httpServer});   <-- Creates an instance of the WebSocket server based on the existing HTTP server
```

NOTE In the hands-on section, you'll reuse port 8000 for both HTTP and WebSocket communications (see the ng-auction/server/ws-auction.ts file).

The content of the server/simple-websocket-client.html file is shown in the next listing. This is a plain HTML/JavaScript client that doesn't use any frameworks.

Listing 13.3 simple-websocket-client.html

```
<!DOCTYPE html>
<html>
<head>
    <meta charset="UTF-8">
</head>
<body>
<span id="messageGoesHere"></span>

<script type="text/javascript">
    var ws = new WebSocket("ws://localhost:8085");      ◁ Establishes the socket connection

    ws.onmessage = function(event) {      ◁ When the message arrives from the socket, displays its content in the <span> element
        var mySpan = document.getElementById("messageGoesHere");
       mySpan.innerHTML = event.data;
    };

    ws.onerror = function(event) {      ◁ In case of an error, the browser logs the error message on the console.
        console.log(`Error ${event}`);
    }
</script>
</body>
</html>
```

When the browser downloads this file, its script connects to your WebSocket server at ws://localhost:8085. At this point, the server upgrades the protocol from HTTP to WebSocket. Note that the protocol is `ws` and not `http`. For a secure socket connection, use the `wss` protocol.

To see this sample in action, run `npm install` in the server directory, compile the code by running the `tsc` command , and then start the server as follows:

```
node build/simple-websocket-server
```

You'll see the following messages on the console:

```
WebSocket server is listening on port 8085
HTTP server is listening on 8000
```

Open the Chrome browser and its Dev Tools at http:// localhost:8000. You'll see the message, as shown on the left in figure 13.3. Under the Network tab on the right, you see two requests made to the server at localhost. The first one loads the simple-websocket-client.html file, and the second makes a request to the WebSocket that's open on port 8085 on your server.

In this example, the HTTP protocol is used only to initially load the HTML file. Then the client requests the protocol upgrade to WebSocket (status code 101), and

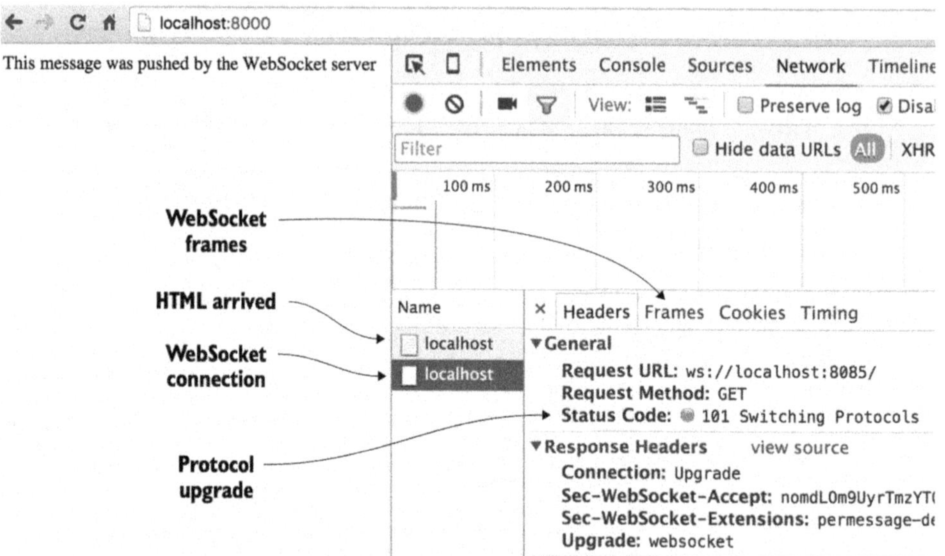

Figure 13.3 Getting the message from the socket

from then on this web page won't use HTTP. You can monitor data going over the socket using the Frames tab in Chrome Developer Tools. In this demo, you wrote a WebSocket client in JavaScript using the browser's native `WebSocket` object, but how can an Angular app consume or send messages to the server over WebSockets?

13.3 Using WebSockets in Angular clients

In Angular, you usually wrap all communications with servers into injectable services. In several apps in chapter 12, you did it with `HttpClient`, and you'll do it with the `WebSocket` object. But these two objects differ in that `HttpClient` is already an Angular injectable service that you'd *inject* into a service class of your app, whereas `WebSocket` is a native browser object, and you'll *create* it inside a service class.

There's another major difference between `HttpClient` and `WebSocket`. If making HTTP requests using `HttpClient` would return an observable with a single value, the `WebSocket` object offers an API that's easy to turn into an observable stream of multiple values like changing stock prices or bids on products.

Think of a WebSocket as a data producer that can emit values, and an `Observable` object can relay these values to subscribers (for example, Angular components). In Angular, you can either manually create a service producing an observable stream from a WebSocket connection or use the `WebSocketSubject` offered by RxJS. In this chapter, you'll see both ways of handling WebSocket messages in Angular clients.

But first, let's see how to wrap any `Observable` emitting values into an Angular service.

13.3.1 Wrapping an observable stream into a service

In this section, you'll create an observable service that emits hardcoded values without connecting to any server. In section D.5 in appendix D, we explain how to use the `Observable.create()` method, providing an observer as an argument. If you haven't read appendix D yet, do it now.

The following listing creates a service with a method that takes an observer as an argument and emits the current time every second.

Listing 13.4 observable.service.ts

```
import {Observable} from 'rxjs';

export class ObservableService {

  createObservableService(): Observable<Date> {    <-- Returns an observable stream of dates

      return new Observable(          <-- Creates an observable
          observer => {      <-- Provides an observer
              setInterval(() =>
                 observer.next(new Date())      <-- Emits the new date every second
              , 1000);
          }
      );
  }
}
```

In this service, you create an instance of the `Observable` object, assuming that the subscriber will provide an `Observer` that knows what to do with the emitted data. Whenever the observable invokes the `next(new Date())` method on the observer, the subscriber will receive the current date and time. Your data stream never throws an error and never completes.

You'll inject the `ObservableService` into the `AppComponent`, which invokes the `createObservableService()` method and subscribes to its stream of values, creating an observer that knows what to do with data. The observer just assigns the received time to the `currentTime` variable that renders the time on the UI, as shown in the following listing.

Listing 13.5 observableservice/app.component.ts

```
import {Component} from "@angular/core";
import {ObservableService} from "./observable.service";

@Component({
  selector: 'app-root',
  providers: [ObservableService],
  template: `<h1>Custom observable service</h1>
       Current time: {{currentTime | date: 'mediumTime'}}    <-- Displays the time using the date pipe
   `})
export class AppComponent {

  currentTime: Date;
```

```
constructor(private observableService: ObservableService) {     // Injects the service that wraps the observable

    this.observableService.createObservableService()     // Creates the observable and starts emitting dates
      .subscribe(data => this.currentTime = data);     // Subscribes to the stream of dates
  }
}
```

This app doesn't use any servers, and you can see it in action here. Run it by entering the following command in the client directory (after `npm install`):

```
ng serve --app observableservice -o
```

In the browser window, the current time will be updated every second. You use the `DatePipe` here with the format `'mediumTime'`, which displays only hours, minutes, and seconds (all date formats are described in the Angular `DatePipe` documentation at http://mng.bz/78lD).

This simple example demonstrates a basic technique for creating an injectable service that wraps an observable stream so components or user services can subscribe to it. In this case, you use `setInterval()`, but you could replace it with any application-specific code that generates one or more values and emits them as a stream.

Don't forget about error handling and completing the stream if need be. The following listing shows an observable that sends one element to the observer, may throw an error, and notifies the observer that streaming is complete.

Listing 13.6 Sending errors and completion events

```
return new Observable(
    observer => {
      try {
        observer.next('Hello from observable');     // Sends the text value to the observer

        // throw("Got an error");     // Emulates an error situation
         // some other code can be here
      } catch(err) {
         observer.error(err);     // Sends the error to the observer
       } finally {
         observer.complete();     // Always let the observer know that the data streaming is over.
       }
    }
);
```

If you uncomment the line with `throw`, the preceding program will jump over "some other code" and continue in the `catch` section, where you invoke `observer.error()`. This will result in the invocation of the error handler on the subscriber, if there is one.

The data producer for your observable stream was the time generator, but it could be a WebSocket server generating some useful values. Let's create an Angular service that communicates with a WebSocket server.

13.3.2 *Angular talking to a WebSocket server*

In the hands-on section, you'll implement a real-world use case of an Angular client communicating with a server over WebSockets. This is how users of ngAuction will place bids and receive notifications of bids made by other users.

In this section, we'll show you a very basic way to wrap a `WebSocket` into an Angular client. This is going to be a rather simple wrapper for the `WebSocket` object, but in the hands-on section, you'll use a more robust `WebSocketSubject` that comes with RxJS.

Your next Angular app will include a service that interacts with the Node WebSocket server. The server-side tier can be implemented with any technology that supports WebSockets. Figure 13.4 illustrates the architecture of such an application (think of bidding messages going between the client and server over the socket connection).

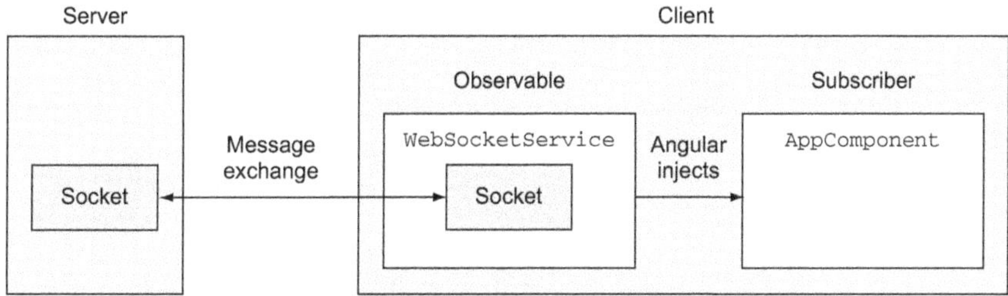

Figure 13.4 Angular interacting with a server via a socket

The code in listing 13.7 wraps the browser's `WebSocket` object into an observable stream. This service creates an instance of the `WebSocket` object that's connected to the WebSocket server based on the provided URL, and the client instance handles messages received from the server.

Your `WebSocketService` also has a `sendMessage()` method so the client can send messages to the server as well. Prior to sending the message, the service checks whether the connection is still open (the `WebSocket.readyState === 1`), as shown in the following listing.

Listing 13.7 wsservice/websocket.service.ts

```
import {Observable } from 'rxjs';

export class WebSocketService {

  ws: WebSocket;
  socketIsOpen = 1;                    // The WebSocket is open.

  createObservableSocket(url: string): Observable<any> {   // This method emits messages received from the specified URL.
     this.ws = new WebSocket(url);                         // Connects to the WebSocket server

    return new Observable(        // Creates an Observable object
       observer => {
```

```
        this.ws.onmessage = (event) =>
          observer.next(event.data);

        this.ws.onerror = (event) => observer.error(event);

        this.ws.onclose = (event) => observer.complete();

        return () =>
            this.ws.close(1000, "The user disconnected");
      }
    );
  }

  sendMessage(message: string): string {
    if (this.ws.readyState === this.socketIsOpen) {
       this.ws.send(message);
       return `Sent to server ${message}`;
    } else {
      return 'Message was not sent - the socket is closed';
     }
  }
}
```

Sends the message received from the server to the subscriber

Sends an error received from the server to the subscriber

If the server closes the socket, notifies the subscriber

Returns a callback so the caller can unsubscribe

Checks if the connection is open

Sends the message to the server

Notifies the caller that the connection was closed

Note that your observer returns a callback, so if the caller invokes the `unsubscribe()` method, this callback will be invoked. It'll close the connection, sending a 1000 status code and the message explaining the reason for closing. You can see all allowed codes for closing the connection at http://mng.bz/5V07.

Now let's write the `AppComponent` that subscribes to the `WebSocketService`, which is injected into the `AppComponent` shown in figure 13.4. This component, shown in the following listing, can also send messages to the server when the user clicks the Send Message to Server button.

Listing 13.8 wsservice/app.component.ts

```
import {Component, OnDestroy} from "@angular/core";
import {WebSocketService} from "./websocket.service";
import {Subscription} from "rxjs";

@Component({
  selector: 'app-root',
  providers: [ WebSocketService ],
  template: `<h1>Angular client for a WebSocket server</h1>
  {{messageFromServer}}<br>
  <button (click)="sendMessageToServer()">Send Message to Server</button>
  <button (click)="closeSocket()">Disconnect</button>
  <div>{{status}}</div>
  `})
export class AppComponent implements OnDestroy {

  messageFromServer: string;
  wsSubscription: Subscription;
   status;
```

This property will hold the reference to the subscription.

```
  constructor(private wsService: WebSocketService) {    <-- Injects the service

    this.wsSubscription =
      this.wsService.createObservableSocket("ws://localhost:8085")    <-- Connects to the server
       .subscribe(
        data => this.messageFromServer = data,    <-- Handles the data received from the server
          err => console.log( 'err'),
        () =>  console.log( 'The observable stream is complete')
      );
  }

  sendMessageToServer(){
    this.status = this.wsService.sendMessage("Hello from client");    <-- Sends the message to the server
   }

  closeSocket(){
    this.wsSubscription.unsubscribe();    <-- Closes the WebSocket connection
     this.status = 'The socket is closed';
  }

  ngOnDestroy() {
    this.closeSocket();
  }
}
```

Note that you store the reference to the subscription in the `wsSubscription` property, and when the user clicks the Disconnect button, this component unsubscribes from the observable. That invokes the callback defined in the observer, closing the connection to the WebSocket.

The client is ready. Now we'll show you the code for the server that will communicate with this client. The callback function that's invoked on the connection event sends the greeting to the client and adds two more event handler functions to the object that represents this particular client.

One function handles messages received from the client, and another handles errors (you'll log the error code). This server is implemented in the two-way-websocket-server.ts file.

Listing 13.9 server/two-way-websocket-server.ts

```
import {Server} from "ws";

let wsServer = new Server({port:8085});    <-- Starts the WebSocket serve

console.log('WebSocket server is listening on port 8085');

wsServer.on('connection',    <-- A new client connected
    websocket => {

     websocket.send('Hello from the two-way WebSocket server');    <-- Greets the newly connected client

     websocket.onmessage = (message) =>    <-- Listens to the message from this client
              console.log(`The server received: ${message['data']}`);
```

```
    websocket.onerror = (error) =>
        console.log(`The server received: ${error['code']}`);

    websocket.onclose = (why) =>
        console.log(`The server received: ${why.code} ${why.reason}`);
});
```

Logs the error from this connection, if any

The client disconnected, so you log the reason.

To see this app in action, start the server by running the following command from the server directory:

```
node build/two-way-websocket-server
```

Then build and start the Angular app from the client directory as follows:

```
ng serve --app wsservice
```

To emulate a scenario where more than one client is connected to the same WebSocket server, open two browsers at http://localhost:4200. Each of the apps will receive a greeting from the server, and you'll be able to send messages to the server by clicking the Send Message to Server button.

We took the screenshot in figure 13.5 after the button is clicked once (Chrome Developer Tools has the WS and Frames tabs opened under Network). On the right, you see the greeting message that arrived from the server and the message that the client sent to the server.

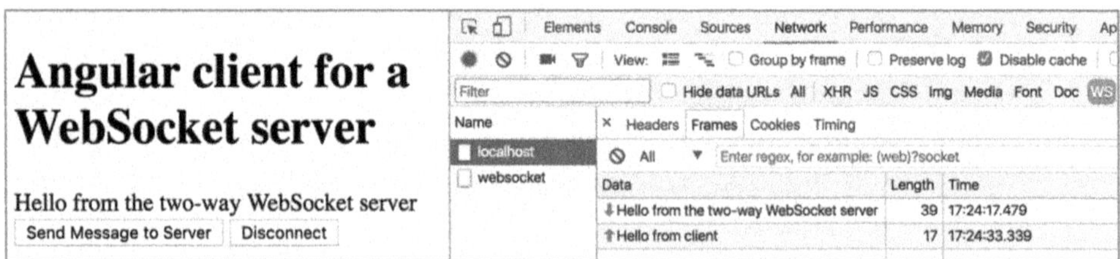

Figure 13.5 Getting the message in Angular from Node

Figure 13.6 shows the screenshot taken after the client clicks the Send Message to Server button, then Disconnect, and then Send Message to Server again.

NOTE Browsers don't enforce the same-origin policy on WebSocket connections. That's why you're able to exchange data between the client originating from port 4200 and the server running on port 8085. Refer to the documentation of whatever server-side technology you use to see what protection is available for WebSockets.

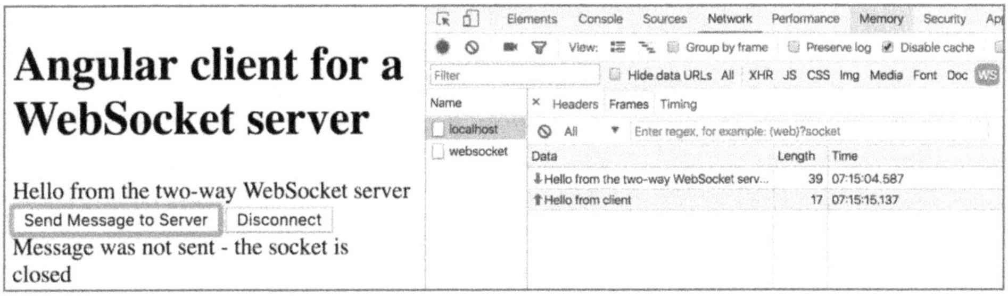

Figure 13.6 Send, disconnect, and send again

Integrating WebSockets with server-side messaging systems

Imagine your server uses a messaging system; let's use ActiveMQ as an example. Say you'd like to enable your JavaScript client to exchange data with ActiveMQ over WebSockets. If you decide to program such data exchange from scratch, you need to come up with a way to notify the server's endpoint that the data sent by the client should be redirected into an ActiveMQ queue with a specific name. Then the server-side code needs to format the client's message to be accepted by ActiveMQ according to its internal protocol. Also, the server-side app needs to keep track of all connected clients, and possibly implement some heartbeats to monitor the health of the socket connection. That's a lot of coding.

The good news is that WebSockets can use subprotocols to integrate with server-side messaging systems. For example, server-side code can map the WebSocket endpoint to an existing queue in ActiveMQ. This way, when a server's software places a message into a queue, it's automatically pushed to the client. Similarly, when a client sends a message to a WebSocket endpoint, it's placed in the queue on the server. Implementing heartbeats comes down to providing a configuration option.

STOMP is one of the popular subprotocols used for sending text messages over WebSockets (see http://mng.bz/PPsy). It describes a client-side message broker that communicates with its server-side peer. For client STOMP support, we use ng2-stompjs, available at http://mng.bz/KdIM.

The server-side admin should install a STOMP connector for their messaging server (ActiveMQ has native STOMP support). In such a setup, client-server communication is more robust and requires less coding on the application level.

In chapter 12, you learned how to communicate with a web server via HTTP. In this chapter, we introduced the WebSocket protocol. The next version of ngAuction will use both communication protocols, but first let's see how the materials covered in this chapter apply to the new functionality of ngAuction that you're about to implement.

The WebSocket protocol isn't based on the request/response model, and the WebSocket server can initiate the communication with the client without any additional ceremony. This is a valuable feature for ngAuction, because the server knows first when any users place a bid on each auctioned product in this multi-user app. Because the server doesn't need to wait for the client's requests for data, it can push the newly placed bids to all users that are connected to this WebSocket server. That means the server can push the latest bids to all users in real time.

13.4 Hands-on: Node server with WebSockets support

In this section, we'll review the refactored version of ngAuction that comes with this chapter. In real auctions, multiple users can bid on products. When the server receives a bid from a user, the bid server should broadcast the latest bid to all users who are watching selected products. This version of ngAuction accomplishes the following main tasks:

- Split ngAuction into two separate projects, client and server, and store the product data and images on the server.
- Modify the client so it'll use the `HttpClient` service to make requests to the server to get products data.
- On the server side, implement HTTP and WebSocket servers. The HTTP server will serve product data.
- The WebSocket server will accept user bids on selected products, and all other users can see the latest bids pushed by the server.

Figure 13.7 shows the rendered `ProductDetailComponent` with the button that will allow a user to place bids in $5 increments. If a user clicks this button once, the price will change to $75 on their UI, as well as for all other users having the product-detail view open for the same product. The server will broadcast (via a WebSocket connection) the latest bid amounts to all users who are looking at this product.

To implement this functionality, you'll add WebSocket support to the server and create a new `BidService` on the client. Figure 13.8 shows the main players involved in client-server communications in this version of ngAuction.

The *DI* in figure 13.8 stands for *dependency injection*. Angular injects the `HttpClient` service into `ProductService`, which in turn is injected into three components: `CategoriesComponent`, `SearchComponent`, and `ProductComponent`. `ProductService` is responsible for all HTTP-based communications with the server.

The `BidService` wraps all WebSocket-based communications with the server. It's injected into the `ProductDetailComponent`. When a user opens the product-detail view, the new bids (if any) will be displayed. When a user places a new bid, the `BidService` will push the message to the server. When the WebSocket server pushes a new bid, the `BidService` receives the bid, and the `ProductDetailComponent` renders it.

Figure 13.8 shows two more injectable values: `API_BASE_URL` and `WS_URL`. The former will contain the URL of the HTTP server, and the latter, the URL of the

Figure 13.7 The `ProductDetailComponent` with a bid button

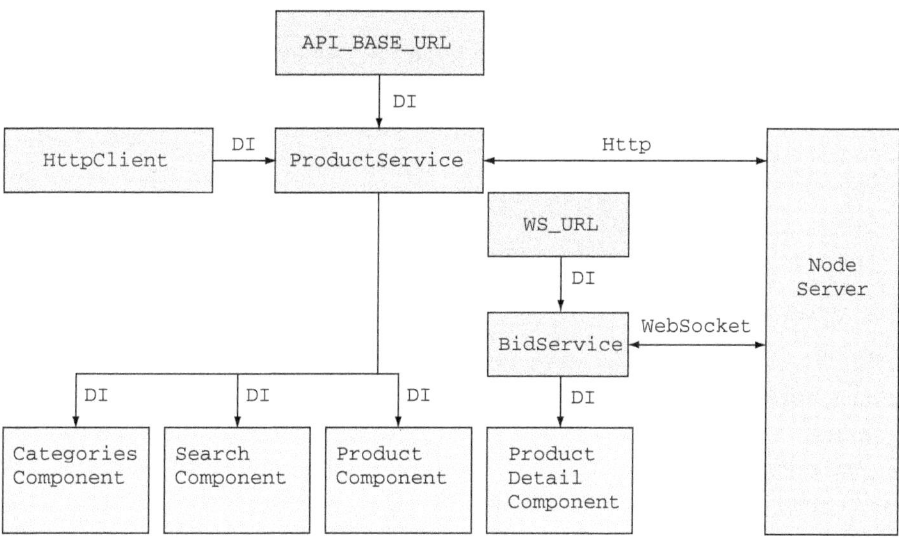

Figure 13.8 Client-server communications in ngAuction

WebSocket server. To inject these values, you'll use `InjectionToken`. Both URLs are configurable, and their values are stored in the Angular project in the environments/environment.ts and environments/environment.prod.ts files.

The environment.ts file is used in dev mode and is shown in the following listing.

Listing 13.10 environment.ts

```
export const environment = {
  production: false,
  apiBaseUrl: 'http://localhost:9090/api',
  wsUrl: 'ws://localhost:9090'
};
```

The environment.prod.ts file is used in production mode, and because the Angular app is expected to be deployed on the same server that serves data, there's no need to specify the full URL for HTTP communications, as shown in the following listing.

Listing 13.11 environment.prod.ts

```
export const environment = {
  production: true,
  apiBaseUrl: '/api',
  wsUrl: 'ws://localhost:9090'
};
```

13.4.1 Running ngAuction in dev mode

ngAuction consists of two projects now, so you need to run `npm install` in each project, and then start the server and the client separately. To start the server, change to the server directory, compile all the TypeScript code into JavaScript by running `tsc`, and start the server as follows:

```
node build/main
```

To start the Angular app, go to the client directory and run the following command:

```
ng serve
```

You'll see the same UI of ngAuction that you created in chapter 11, but now product data and images come from the server via the HTTP connection. Open your Chrome browser at http://localhost:4200, select a product, and click the bid button. You'll see how the price increases by $5. Now open another browser (such as Firefox) at http://localhost:4200, select the same product, and you'll see the latest price. Place a new bid in that second browser, and the new bid is shown in both browsers. The server pushes the new bid to all connected clients.

After reading in chapter 12 about the same-origin restriction and proxying client requests, you may be wondering how the app loaded from port 4200 can access data on the HTTP server running on port 9090 without configuring the proxy on the client. It's because this time, you used a special CORS package on the Node server for unrestricted access from any client. You'll see how to do this in the next section.

13.4.2 Reviewing the ngAuction server code

By now, you know how to create and start HTTP and WebSocket servers using Node.js, Express, and the `ws` package, and you won't repeat that part. In this section, we'll review the code fragments of the server that are relevant to the new functionality of ngAuction. You'll split the server code into four TypeScript files. Figure 13.9 shows the structure of the ngAuction server directory that comes with this chapter.

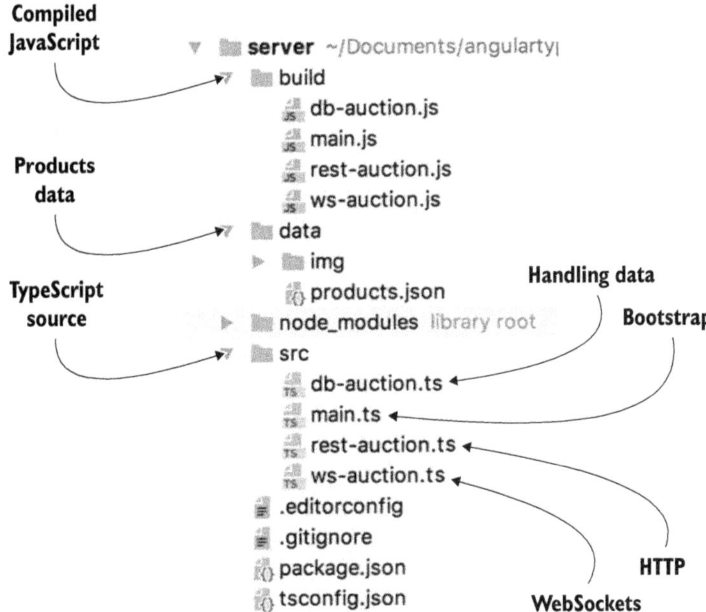

Figure 13.9 ngAuction server structure

In ngAuction from chapter 11, the data folder was located in the Angular project; now, you move the data to the server. In chapter 11, the code that read products.json and the functions to get all the products or products by ID was located in the product .service.ts file, and now is located in the db-auction.ts file. The main.ts file contains the code to launch both HTTP and WebSocket servers. The ws-auction.ts file has the code supporting WebSocket communication with ngAuction clients.

Launching the HTTP and WebSocket servers

Let's start the code review from the main.ts file that's used to launch the servers. The code in this file is similar to simple-websocket-server.ts from section 13.2, but this time you don't start HTTP and WebSocket servers on different ports—they both use port 9090. Another difference is that you create an instance of the HTTP server using the `createServer()` function, one of Node's interfaces (see https://nodejs.org/api/http.html), as shown in the following listing.

Listing 13.12 main.ts

```
import * as express from 'express';
import {createServer} from 'http';
import {createBidServer} from './ws-auction';
import {router} from './rest-auction';

const app = express();
app.use('/api', router);    <-- Forwards requests containing /api to the Express router

const server = createServer(app);    <-- Creates an instance of the http.Server object
 createBidServer(server);    <-- Creates an instance of BidServer using its HTTP peer

server.listen(9090, "localhost", () => {    <-- Launches both servers
   const {address, port} = server.address();
  console.log(`Listening on  ${address} ${port}`);
});
```

This code creates an instance of the HTTP server with Node's `createServer()`, and you pass Express as a callback function to handle all HTTP requests. To start your WebSocket server, you invoke the `createBidServer()` function from ws-auction.ts. But first, let's review your RESTful HTTP server.

THE HTTP SERVER

In chapter 12, section 12.2.2, you created a simple Node/Express server that handles requests for products. In this section, you'll see a more advanced version of such a server. Here, you'll use the Express `Router` to route HTTP requests. You'll also use the CORS module to allow requests from all browsers to ignore the same-origin restriction. That's why you can start the client using `ng serve` without the need to configure a proxy.

Finally, the product data won't be hardcoded—you moved the data-handling part into the db-auction.ts script. Your HTTP REST server is implemented in the rest-auction.ts file, shown in the following listing.

Listing 13.13 rest-auction.ts

```
import * as cors from 'cors';    <-- Imports the CORS module
 import * as express from 'express';
import {
  getAllCategories,
  getProducts,
  getProductById,
  getProductsByCategory
} from './db-auction';    <-- Imports the data-handling functions

export const router = express.Router();    <-- Creates and exports the Express Router instance

router.use(cors());    <-- Uses CORS to allow requests from all clients

router.get('/products',
  async (req: express.Request, res: express.Response) => {    <-- Uses the async keyword to mark the function as asynchronous
   res.json(await getProducts(req.query));    <-- Uses the await keyword to avoid nesting code in then() callbacks
 });
```

```
router.get('/products/:productId', async (req: express.Request,
➥ res: express.Response) => {
  const productId = parseInt(req.params.productId, 10) || -1;
  res.json(await getProductById(productId));
});

router.get('/categories', async (_, res: express.Response) => {
  res.json(await getAllCategories());
});

router.get('/categories/:category', async (req: express.Request,
➥ res: express.Response) => {
  res.json(await getProductsByCategory(req.params.category));
});
```

In section 13.4.1, we stated that the dev server on the client will run on port 4200, and the REST server will run on port 9090. To overcome the same-origin restriction, you use the Express package CORS to enable access from all origins (see http://mng.bz/aNxM). If you open package.json in the server directory, you'll find the dependency `"cors": "^2.8.4"` there.

In this server, you create an instance of the Express `Router` object and use it to route HTTP GET requests based on the provided path.

Note the use of the `async` and `await` keywords. You didn't use them for product retrieval in chapter 12, section 12.2.2, because product data was stored in an array, and functions like `getProducts()` were synchronous there. Now you use the data-handling functions from db-auction.ts, and they read data from a file, which is an asynchronous operation.

Using the `async` and `await` keywords makes the async code look as if it's synchronous (see section A.12.4 in appendix A for more details).

THE DATA-HANDLING SCRIPT

Your HTTP server uses the db-auction.ts script for all data-handling operations. This script has methods to read products from the products.json file as well as search products based on provided search criteria. We won't be reviewing the entire code of the db-auction.ts script, but we will discuss the code changes compared to product .service.ts from the version of ngAuction included with chapter 11, as shown in the following listing.

Listing 13.14 db-auction.ts (partial listing)

```
import * as fs from 'fs';
import * as util from 'util';

type DB = Product[];                                    // Defines a new type to store an array of products

const readFile = util.promisify(fs.readFile);           // Makes fs.readFile to return a promise
 const db$: Promise<DB> =                               // Declares a promise for reading products.json
    readFile('./data/products.json', 'utf8')            // Reads products.json
   .then(JSON.parse, console.error);
```

```
export async function getAllCategories(): Promise<string[]> {
  const allCategories = (await db$)                      <-- This function gets category names for each product.
    .map(p => p.categories)
    .reduce((all, current) => all.concat(current), []);

  return [...new Set(allCategories)];   <-- Gets rid of duplicate categories
 }
...

export async function updateProductBidAmount(productId: number,   <-- This function updates the product price based on the latest bid.
                                             price: number): Promise<any> {
  const products = await db$;
  const product = products.find(p => p.id === productId);
  if (product) {
    product.price = price;
  }
}
```

In chapter 11, the products.json file was located on the client side, and `Product-Service` read this file using the `HttpClient` service, as follows:

```
http.get<Product[]>('/data/products.json');
```

Now this file is located on the server, and you read it using Node's `fs` module, which includes functions for working with the filesystem (see https://nodejs.org/api/fs.html). You also use another Node module, `util`, that includes a number of useful utilities, and you use `util.promisify()` to read the file returning the data as a promise (see http://mng.bz/Z009) instead of providing a callback to `fs.readFile`.

In several places in db-auction.ts, you see `await db$`, which means "execute the `db$` promise and wait until it resolves or rejects." The `db$` promise knows how to read the products.json file.

Now that we've discussed how your RESTful server works, let's get familiar with the code of the WebSocket server.

THE WEBSOCKET SERVER

The ws-auction.ts script implements your WebSocket server that can receive bids from users and notify users about new bids. A bid is represented by a `BidMessage` type containing the product ID and the bid amount (price), as shown in the following listing.

Listing 13.15 `BidMessage` from ws-auction.ts

```
interface BidMessage {
  productId: number;
  price: number;
}
```

The `createBidServer()` function creates an instance of the class `BidServer`, using the provided instance of `http.Server`, as shown in the next listing.

Listing 13.16 `createBidServer()` from ws-auction.ts

```
export function createBidServer(httpServer: http.Server): BidServer {
  return new BidServer(httpServer);
}
```

The `BidServer` class contains the standard WebSocket callbacks `onConnection()`, `onMessage()`, `onClose()`, and `onError()`. The constructor of this class creates an instance of `ws.Server` (you use the `ws` package there) and defines the `onConnection()` callback method to the WebSocket `connection` event. The outline of the `BidServer` class is shown in the following listing.

Listing 13.17 The structure of `BidServer`

```
export class BidServer {
  private readonly wsServer: ws.Server;

  constructor(server: http.Server) {}

  private onConnection(ws: ws): void {...}     <-- Handler for the WebSocket connection event

  private onMessage(message: string): void {...}     <-- Handler for the message event

  private onClose(): void {...}     <-- Handler for the close event

  private onError(error: Error): void {...}     <-- Handler for the error event
}
```

Now let's review the implementation of each method, starting with `constructor()`

Listing 13.18 The constructor

```
constructor(server: http.Server) {
  this.wsServer = new ws.Server({ server });     <-- Instantiates the WebSocket server using the HTTP server instance
   this.wsServer.on('connection',     <-- Defines the handler of the connection event
      (userSocket: ws) => this.onConnection(userSocket));
}
```

When your ngAuction client connects to `BidServer`, the `onConnection()` callback is invoked. The argument of this callback is the `WebSocket` object representing a single client's connection. When the client makes the initial request to switch the protocol from HTTP to `WebSocket`, it'll invoke the `onConnection()` callback, shown in the following listing.

Listing 13.19 Handling the connection event

```
private onConnection(ws: ws): void {
  ws.on('message', (message: string) => this.onMessage(message));     <-- Listens to message events
   ws.on('error', (error: Error) => this.onError(error));     <-- Listens to error events
```

```
    ws.on('close', () => this.onClose());    <—— Listens to close events

  console.log(`Connections count: ${this.wsServer.clients.size}`);   <——
}
                                          Reports the number of
                                          connected clients
```

The `onConnection()` method assigns the callback methods for the WebSocket events `message`, `close`, and `error`. When the `ws` module creates an instance of the WebSocket server, it stores the references to connected clients in the `wsServer.clients` property. On every connection, you print on the console the number of connected clients. The next listing reviews the callback methods one by one, starting from `onMessage()`.

Listing 13.20 Handling the client messages

```
import { updateProductBidAmount} from './db-auction';
...
  private onMessage(message: string): void {                Parses the client's
    const bid: BidMessage = JSON.parse(message);       <——  BidMessage
  ——> updateProductBidAmount(bid.productId, bid.price);

    // Broadcast the new bid
    this.wsServer.clients.forEach(ws => ws.send(JSON.stringify(bid)));   <——

    console.log(`Bid ${bid.price} is placed on product ${bid.productId}`);
  }
                                                        Sends new product bid
Updates the bid amount in                        information to all subscribers
your in-memory database
```

The `onMessage()` callback gets the user's bid on the product and updates the amount in your simple in-memory database implemented in the db-auction.ts script. If a user opens the product-detail view, they become a subscriber to notifications about all users bids, so you push the new bid over the socket to each subscriber.

Next, we'll review the callback for the `close` event. When a user closes the product-detail view, the WebSocket connection is closed as well. In this case, the closed connection is removed from `wsServer.clients`, so no bid notifications will be sent to a nonexistent connection, as shown in the following listing.

Listing 13.21 Handling closed connections

```
private onClose(): void {
  console.log(`Connections count: ${this.wsServer.clients.size}`);
}
```

In the `onError()` callback, you extract the error message from the provided `Error` object and log the error on the console.

Listing 13.22 Handling WebSocket errors

```
private onError(error: Error): void {
    console.error(`WebSocket error: "${error.message}"`);
  }
}
```

Figure 13.10 shows the same product-detail view open in Chrome and Firefox browsers. The latest bid is synchronized in both views as soon as the user clicks the bid button in any of the browsers.

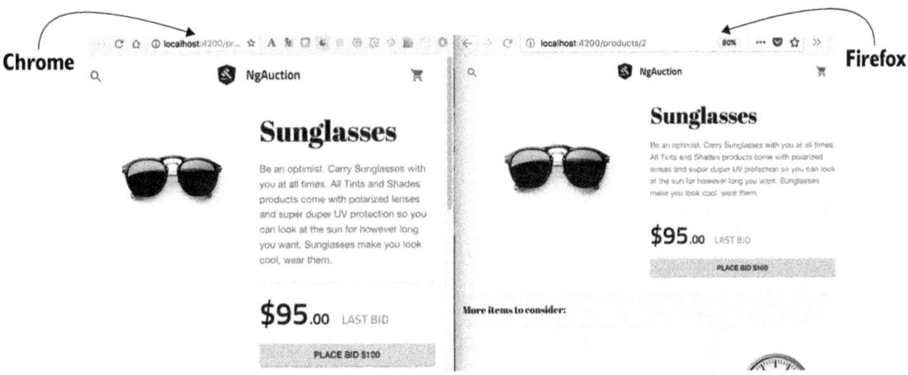

Figure 13.10 Synchronized bids in two browsers

> **Homework**
>
> Your ngAuction isn't a production-grade auction, and you may find some edge cases that aren't properly handled. We'll describe one of them in case you want to improve this app.
>
> Imagine that the current bid of the product is $70, and Joe clicks the bid button to make a $75 bid. At the same time, Mary, who was also shown $70 as the latest product bid, also clicks the bid button. There could be a situation when Joe's request will change the bid to $75 on the server, and some milliseconds later, Mary's $75 bid arrives to the server. Currently, the `BidServer` will just replace Joe's $75 with Mary's $75, and each of them will assume that he or she placed a $75 bid.
>
> To prevent this from happening, modify the code in the `BidServer` to reject the bid unless the bid amount is greater than the existing one. In such scenarios, send the losing user a message containing the new minimum bid amount.

We've covered the server-side code of ngAuction; let's see what changed on the client side compared to the version in chapter 11.

13.4.3 What changed in the ngAuction client code

As stated in the previous section, the main change in the Angular code of ngAuction is that you moved to the server the file with product data and images, and the code that reads these files. Accordingly, you added the code to `ProductService` to interact with the HTTP server using the `HttpClient` service covered in chapter 12.

Remember that the `ProductComponent` is responsible for rendering the product view that includes `ProductDetailComponent` and `ProductSuggestionComponent` with the grid of suggested products, and you modified the code of both components.

Also, you added the bid.service.ts file to communicate with the WebSocket service and modified the code in product-detail.component.ts so the user can place bids on a product and see other user bids. Let's review the changes related to the product view.

TWO OBSERVABLES IN THE PRODUCTCOMPONENT

First, the product view would change if the user looks at the details of one product and then selects another one from the suggested products grid. The route doesn't change (the user is still looking at the product view), and `ProductComponent` subscribes to an observable from `ActivatedRoute` that emits the newly selected `productId` and retrieves the corresponding product details, as shown in the following listing.

Listing 13.23 Handling changed parameters from `ActivatedRoute`

```
this.product$ = this.route.paramMap
  .pipe(
    map(params => parseInt(params.get('productId') || '', 10)),
    filter(productId => Boolean(productId)),
    switchMap(productId => this.productService.getById(productId))
  );
```

Gets the new productId

Handles the possibly invalid productId.

Retrieves the selected product details

In listing 13.23, you retrieve `productId` from `ActivatedRoute` and pass it over to the `ProductService`, using the `switchMap` operator. The `filter` operator is just a precaution to weed out the falsy product IDs. For example, a user can manually enter an erroneous URL like http://localhost:4200/products/A23, and you don't want to request the details for a nonexistent product.

The template of the product component includes the `<nga-product-detail>` component, which gets a selected product via its input property `product`, as shown in the following listing.

Listing 13.24 Passing a selected product to `ProductDetailComponent`

```
<nga-product-detail
    fxFlex="auto"
    fxFlex.>-md="65%"
    *ngIf="product$ | async as product"
     [product]="product">
 </nga-product-detail>
```

Extracts the Product object with async pipe

Passes the selected Product to the ProductDetailComponent

You place the code that unwraps product data inside the `*ngIf` directive because the product data is retrieved asynchronously, and you want to make sure that the `product$` observable emitted the data that you bind to the input property of the `ProductDetail-Component`. Let's see how the `ProductDetailComponent` handles the received product.

PLACING AND MONITORING BIDS IN PRODUCTDETAILCOMPONENT

The UI of the `ProductDetailComponent` is shown in figure 13.10. This component gets the product to display via its input property `product`. If a user clicks the bid button, the new bid ($5 more than the current one) is sent over the WebSocket connection using `BidService`, which implements all communications with the `BidServer`. If another user connected to the `BidServer` bids on the same product, the bid amount on the product-detail view will be immediately updated.

The `ProductDetailComponent` class has the private RxJS subject `productChange$` and the observable `latestBids$`, which merges the data of two observables:

- `productChange$` handles the case when a user opens the product-detail view and then selects another product from the list "More items to consider." When the binding to the input parameter `product` changes, the lifecycle hook `ngOnChanges()` intercepts the change, and `productChange$` emits the product data.
- `latestBids$` emits the new value when either `productChange$` or `BidService` pushes the new bid received from the server.

You have two data sources that can emit values, and on any emission you need to update the view. That's why you combine two observables with the RxJS operator `combineLatest`. The code of the product-detail.component.ts file is shown in the following listing.

Listing 13.25 product-detail.component.ts

```
// imports are omitted for brevity
@Component({
  selector: 'nga-product-detail',
  styleUrls: [ './product-detail.component.scss' ],
  templateUrl: './product-detail.component.html',
  changeDetection: ChangeDetectionStrategy.OnPush
})
export class ProductDetailComponent implements OnInit, OnChanges {
  private readonly productChange$ = new Subject<Product>();
  latestBids$: Observable<number>;
  @Input() product: Product;

  constructor(private bidService: BidService) {}

  ngOnInit() {
    this.latestBids$ = combineLatest(
        this.productChange$.pipe(startWith(this.product)),
        this.bidService.priceUpdates$.pipe(startWith<BidMessage | null>(null)),
```

Injects the BidService

Combines the values of two observables

The first observable starts emission with the currently displayed product.

The second observable emits bids.

```
    (product, bid) =>  bid && bid.productId === product.id ?
                       bid.price: product.price
    );
  }

  ngOnChanges({ product }: { product: SimpleChange }) {
    this.productChange$.next(product.currentValue);
  }

  placeBid(price: number) {
    this.bidService.placeBid(this.product.id, price);
  }
}
```

Checks whether the arrived bid was made on the current product

If new bid was placed, uses its value; otherwise, uses the product price

Emits the newly selected product

Places the bid on this product

The RxJS operator `combineLatest` (see http://mng.bz/Y28Y) subscribes to the values emitted by two observables and invokes the merge function when either of the observables emits the value. In this case, it's either the value emitted by `productChange$` or by `bidService.priceUpdates$` (the `BidService` code is included in the next section). Here's your merge function:

```
(product, bid) =>  bid && bid.productId === product.id ?
                   bid.price: product.price
```

The values emitted by these two observables are represented as the arguments `(product, bid)`, and this function returns either `product.price` or `bid.price`, depending on which observable emitted the value. This value will be used for rendering on the product-detail view.

Because the `combineLatest` operator requires both observables to emit a value to initially invoke the merge function, you apply the `startWith` operator (see http://mng.bz/OL9z) to ensure that there's an initial emission of the provided value before the observable will start making its regular emissions. For the initial values, you use the `product` for one observable, and either `BidMessage` or null for the other. When the `ProductDetailComponent` is initially rendered, the observable `bidService.priceUpdates$` emits null.

Your combined observable is declared in the `ngOnInit()` lifecycle hook, and its values are rendered in the template using the `async` pipe. You do it inside the `*ngIf` directive so the falsy values aren't rendered:

```
*ngIf="latestBids$ | async as price"
```

When the user clicks the bid button, you invoke `bidService.placeBid()`, which internally checks whether the connection to `BidServer` has to be opened or is already opened. The next listing from product-detail.component.html shows how the bid button is implemented in the template.

Listing 13.26 The bid button in the template

```
<button class="info__bid-button"
        mat-raised-button
        color="accent"
```

```
    (click)="placeBid(price + 5)">
  PLACE BID {{ (price + 5) | currency:'USD':'symbol':'.0' }}
</button>
```

Places the bid that's $5 higher than the latest bid/price

Shows the next bid amount on the button

Now let's see how the BidService class communicates with the server, using the WebSocket protocol.

Using RxJS to communicate with the WebSocket server

In section 13.3.2, we showed a very basic way of writing the client code communicating with a WebSocket server. In ngAuction, you'll use a more robust WebSocket service included with RxJS, which means you can use it in any Angular project.

RxJS offers an implementation of the WebSocket service based on the Subject explained in section D.6 in appendix D. The RxJS Subject is both an observer and observable. In other words, it can receive and emit data, which makes it a good fit for handling WebSocket data streams. The RxJS WebSocketSubject is a wrapper around the standard browser WebSocket object and is located in the rxjs/websocket file.

> **TIP** Prior to RxJS 6, the WebSocketSubject class was located in the rxjs/observable/dom/WebSocketSubject file.

In its simplest form, WebSocketSubject can accept a string with the URL of the WebSocket endpoint or an instance of the WebSocketSubjectConfig object, where you can provide additional configuration. When your code subscribes to WebSocketSubject, it either uses the existing connection or creates a new one. Unsubscribing from WebSocketSubject closes the connection if there are no other subscribers listening to the same WebSocket endpoint.

When the server pushes data to the socket, WebSocketSubject emits the data as an observable value. In case of an error, WebSocketSubject emits the error like any other observable. If the server pushes data but there are no subscribers, the values will be buffered and emitted as soon as a new client subscribes.

> **NOTE** There's a difference in handling messages by a regular RxJS Subject and the WebSocketSubject, though. If you call next() on Subject, it emits data to all subscribers, but if you call next() on WebSocketSubject, it won't. Remember that there's a server between an observable and subscribers, and it's up to the server to decide when to emit values.

The ngAuction client that comes with this chapter includes the file shared/services/bid.service.ts, which uses WebSocketSubject. BidService is a singleton that's used only by ProductDetailComponent, which subscribes to it using the async pipe. When a user closes the product-detail view, the component gets destroyed, and the async pipe unsubscribes, closing the WebSocket connection. Let's review the code of script bid.service.ts.

Listing 13.27 bid.service.ts

```
import { WebSocketSubject } from 'rxjs/websocket';
...

export interface BidMessage {
  productId: number;
  price: number;
}

@Injectable()
export class BidService {
  private _wsSubject: WebSocketSubject<any>;
  private get wsSubject(): WebSocketSubject<any> {    // A getter for the private property _wsSubject

    const closed = !this._wsSubject || this._wsSubject.closed;    // The WebSocketSubject was never created or is already disconnected.
     if (closed) {
      this._wsSubject = new WebSocketSubject(this.wsUrl);    // Connects to BidServer
     }
    return this._wsSubject;
  }

  get priceUpdates$(): Observable<BidMessage> {
    return this.wsSubject.asObservable();    // Gets a reference to the subject's observable
   }

  constructor(@Inject(WS_URL) private readonly wsUrl: string) {}    // Injects the URL of the WebSocket server

  placeBid(productId: number, price: number): void {
    this.wsSubject.next(JSON.stringify({ productId, price }));    // Pushes the new bid to BidServer
   }
}
```

The `BidService` singleton includes the `priceUpdates$` getter, which returns the observable. `ProductDetailComponent` uses this getter in `ngOnInit()`. That means `priceUpdates$` opens a WebSocket connection (through `this.wsSubject` getter) as soon as `ProductDetailComponent` is rendered, and the `async` pipe is a subscriber in the template of this component.

`BidService` also has a private property, `_wsSubject`, and the getter `wsSubject`, used internally. When the getter is accessed the very first time from `priceUpdates$`, the `_wsSubject` variable doesn't exist, and a new instance of `WebSocketSubject` is created, establishing a connection with the WebSocket server.

If a user navigates away from the product-detail view, the connection is closed. Because `BidService` is a singleton, if a user closes and reopens the product-detail view, the instance of `BidService` won't be re-created, but because the connection status is closed (`_wsSubject.closed`), it will be reestablished.

The URL of the WebSocket server (`WS_URL`) is stored in environment.ts for the dev environment and in environment.prod.ts for production. This value is injected into the `wsUrl` variable using the `@Inject` directive.

This concludes the code review of the ngAuction updates that implement communication between the Angular client and two servers. Run ngAuction as described in section 13.4.1, and ngAuction becomes operational.

Summary

- The WebSocket protocol offers unique features that aren't available with HTTP, which makes it a better choice for certain use cases. Both the client and the server can initiate communication.
- The WebSocket protocol doesn't use the request/response model.
- You can create an Angular service that turns WebSocket events into an observable stream.
- The RxJS library includes a `Subject`-based implementation of WebSocket support in the `WebSocketSubject` class, and you can use it in any Angular app.

14 Testing Angular applications

This chapter covers

- Using the Jasmine framework for unit testing
- Identifying the main artifacts from the Angular testing library
- Testing services, components, and the router
- Running unit tests against web browsers with the Karma test runner
- End-to-end testing with the Protractor framework

To ensure that your software has no bugs, you need to test it. Even if your application has no bugs today, it may have them tomorrow, after you modify the existing code or introduce new code. Even if you don't change the code in a particular module, it may stop working properly as a result of changes in another module or in the runtime environment. Your application code has to be retested regularly, and that process should be automated. You should prepare test scripts and start running them as early as possible in your development cycle.

This chapter covers two main types of testing for the frontend of web apps:

- *Unit testing*—Asserts that a small unit of code accepts the expected input data and returns the expected result. Unit testing is about testing isolated pieces of code, especially public interfaces.
- *End-to-end testing*— Asserts that the entire application works as end users expect and that all application parts properly interact with each other.

Unit tests are for testing the business logic of small, isolated units of code. They run reasonably fast, and you'll be running unit tests a lot more often than end-to-end tests. End-to-end (e2e) testing simulates user actions (such as button clicks) and checks that the application behaves as expected. During end-to-end testing, you shouldn't run unit-testing scripts.

> **NOTE** There are also integration tests that check that more that one app member can communicate. Whereas unit tests mock dependencies (for example, HTTP responses), integration tests use the real ones. To turn a unit test into an integration test, don't use mocks.

We'll start by covering the basics of unit testing with Jasmine, and then we'll show you how the Angular testing library is used with Jasmine. After that, you'll see how to use Protractor, the library for e2e tests. Toward the end of the chapter, we'll show you how to write and run e2e scripts to test the product-search workflow of ngAuction.

14.1 Unit testing

The authors of this book work as consultants on large projects for various clients. Pretty often these projects were written without unit tests in place. We're going to describe a typical situation that we've run into on multiple occasions.

A large app evolves over several years. Some of the developers who started writing the app are gone. A new developer joins the project and has to quickly learn the code and get up to speed.

A new business requirement comes in, and the new team member starts working on it. They implement this requirement in the existing function `doSomething()`, but the QA team opens another issue, reporting that the app is broken in a seemingly unrelated area. After additional research, it becomes obvious that the app is broken because of the code change made in `doSomething()`. The new developer doesn't know about a certain business condition and can't account for it.

This wouldn't have happened if unit (or e2e) tests were written with the original version of `doSomething()` and run as a part of each build. Besides, the original unit test would serve as documentation for `doSomething()`. Although writing unit tests seems like an additional, time-consuming task, it may save you a lot more time in the long run.

We like the definition given by Google engineer Elliotte Rusty Harold during one of his presentations—that a unit test should verify that a known, fixed input produces a known, fixed output. If you provide a fixed input for a function that internally uses other dependencies, those dependencies should be mocked out, so a single unit test script tests an isolated unit of code.

Several frameworks have been created specifically for writing unit tests, and Angular documentation recommends Jasmine for this purpose (see the Angular documentation at http://mng.bz/0nv3). We'll start with a brief overview of Jasmine.

14.1.1 Getting to know Jasmine

Jasmine (https://jasmine.github.io/) enables you to implement a *behavior-driven development* (BDD) process, which suggests that tests of any unit of software should be specified in terms of the desired behavior of the unit. With BDD, you use natural language constructs to describe what you think your code should be doing. You write unit test specifications (specs) in the form of short sentences, such as "StarsComponent emits the rating change event."

Because it's so easy to understand the meaning of tests, they can serve as your program documentation. If other developers need to become familiar with your code, they can start by reading the code for the unit tests to understand your intentions. Using natural language to describe tests has another advantage: it's easy to reason about the test results, as shown in figure 14.1.

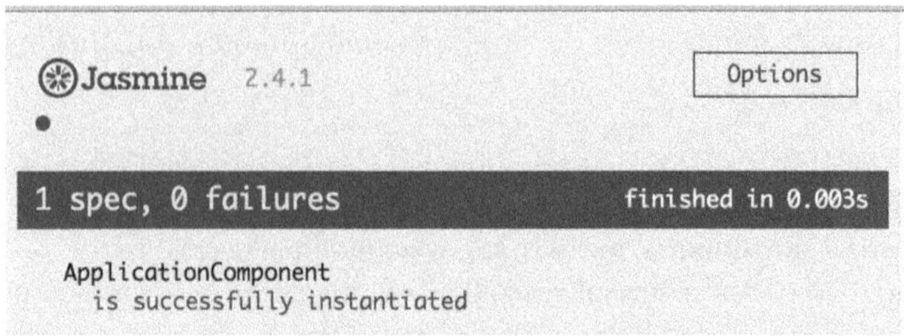

Figure 14.1 Running tests using Jasmine's test runner

> **TIP** Even though Jasmine comes with its own browser-based test runner, you'll be using a command-line-based test runner called Karma that can be easily integrated into the automated build process of your apps.

In BDD frameworks, a test is called a *spec*, and a combination of one or more specs is called a *suite*. A test suite is defined with the `describe()` function —this is where you describe what you're testing. Each spec in a suite is programmed as an `it()` function , which defines the expected behavior of the code under test and how to test it. The following listing shows an example.

Listing 14.1 A simple Jasmine test suite

```
describe('MyCalculator', () => {   ◁── A suite description and a function implementing the suite
   it('should know how to multiply', () => {   ◁── A spec to test multiplication
     // The code that tests multiplication goes here
  });
  it('should not divide by zero', () => {   ◁── A spec to test division
     // The code that tests division by zero goes here
  });
});
```

Testing frameworks have the notion of an *assertion*, which is a way of questioning whether an expression under test is true or false. If the assertion returns `false`, the framework throws an error. In Jasmine, assertions are specified using the `expect()` function, followed by *matchers*:`toBe()`, `toEqual()`, and so on. It's as if you're writing a sentence, "I expect 2 plus 2 to equal 4":

```
expect(2 + 2).toEqual(4);
```

Matchers implement a Boolean comparison between the actual and expected values. If the matcher returns `true`, the spec passes. If you expect a test result not to have a certain value, just add the keyword `not` before the matcher:

```
expect(2 + 2).not.toEqual(5);
```

> **NOTE** You can find the complete list of matchers in the type definition file @types/jasmine/index.d.ts, located in the directory node_modules. The Angular testing library adds more matchers, listed at http://mng.bz/hx5u.

In Angular, test suites have the same names as the files under test, adding the suffix .spec to the name. For example, the file application.spec.ts contains the test script for application.ts. Figure 14.2 shows a minimalistic test suite that can be located in the app.component.spec.ts file; it makes an *assertion* that the variable `app` is an instance of `AppComponent`. An assertion is the expectation plus the matcher.

Figure 14.2 shows a test suite containing a single spec. If you extract the texts from `describe()` and `it()` and put them together, you'll get a sentence that clearly

Figure 14.2 A minimalistic test suite

indicates what you're testing here: "ApplicationComponent is successfully instantiated." If other developers need to know what your spec tests, they can read the texts in `describe()` and `it()`. Each test should be self-descriptive so it can serve as program documentation.

> **TIP** Although the test shown in figure 14.2 was generated by Angular CLI, it's pretty useless because the chances that the `AppComponent` won't be successfully instantiated are close to zero.

The code in figure 14.2 instantiates `AppComponent` and expects the expression `app instanceof AppComponent` to evaluate to `true`. From the `import` statement, you can guess that this test script is located in the same directory as `AppComponent`.

> **NOTE** In Angular applications, you keep each test script in the same directory as the component (or service) under test, so if you need to reuse a component in another app, all related files are located together. If you use Angular CLI for generating a component or service, the boilerplate code for tests (the .spec.ts file) will be generated in the same directory.

If you want some code to be executed before each test (such as to prepare test dependencies), you can specify it in the *setup* functions `beforeAll()` and `beforeEach()`, which will run before the suite or each spec, respectively. If you want to execute some code right after the suite or each spec is finished, use the *teardown* functions `afterAll()` and `afterEach()`.

Let's see how to apply Jasmine API while unit-testing a TypeScript class.

14.1.2 Writing test scripts for a class

Imagine you have a `Counter` class with one `counter` property and two methods that allow incrementing or decrementing the value of this property.

Listing 14.2 counter.ts

```
export class Counter {

  counter = 0;           <---- A class property

  increment() {          <---- A method to increment the value
     this.counter++;
  }

  decrement() {          <---- A method to decrement the value
     this.counter--;
  }
}
```

What do you want to unit-test here? You want to make sure that the `increment()` method increments the value of `counter` by one, and that the `decrement()` method decrements this value by one. Applying Jasmine terminology, you want to write a test suite with two specs.

Remember that a spec should test an isolated piece of functionality, so each spec should create an instance of the `Counter` class and invoke *only one* of its methods. The first version of the counter.spec.ts file is shown in the following listing.

Listing 14.3 counter.spec.ts

```
import {Counter} from './counter';

describe("Counter", ()=> {                                  ⊲ The test suite declaration states that you'll test the Counter.
   it("should increment the counter by 1", () => {       ⊲ The first spec tests if increment works.
        let cnt = new Counter();                          ⊲ The setup phase creates a new instance of the Counter.
        cnt.increment();                                  ⊲ Invokes the function under test
        expect(cnt.counter).toBe(1);                      ⊲ Declares the expectation, assertion, and matcher
     });

  it("should decrement the counter by 1", () => {
       let cnt = new Counter();
       cnt.decrement();
       expect(cnt.counter).toBe(-1);
    });
});
```

Each of your specs has similar functionality. The setup phase creates a fresh instance of the `Counter` class, then it invokes the method to be tested, and finally it declares the expectation with the `expect()` method . In one spec, you expect the `counter` to be `1`, and in another `-1`.

This suite of tests will work, but you have some code duplication here: each of the specs repeats the instantiation of `Counter`. In the refactored version of your test script, you'll remove the `Counter` instantiation from the specs and do it before the specs. Take a look at the new test version in the following listing. Is it correct?

Listing 14.4 Refactored counter.spec.ts

```
import {Counter} from './counter';

describe("Counter", () => {

  let cnt = new Counter();     ⊲ Instantiates Counter before the specs

  it("should increment the counter by 1", () => {
        cnt.increment();
        expect(cnt.counter).toBe(1);
    }
  );

  it("should decrement the counter by 1", () => {
       cnt.decrement();
       expect(cnt.counter).toBe(-1);
    }
  );
});
```

This test is not correct. Your test suite will create an instance of `Counter`, and the first spec will increase the `counter` value to `1` as expected. But when the second spec decrements the `counter`, its value becomes `0`, though the matcher expects it to be `-1`.

The final version of your test script, shown in the nest listing, fixes this mistake by creating the instance of `Counter` inside Jasmine's `beforeEach()` function.

Listing 14.5 The final version of counter.spec.ts

```
import {Counter} from './counter';

describe("Counter", () => {

  let cnt: Counter;??

  beforeEach(() => cnt = new Counter())?;     <-- Instantiates Counter inside beforeEach()

  it("should increment the counter by 1", () => {
        cnt.increment();
        expect(cnt.counter).toBe(1);
    }
  );

  it("should decrement the counter by 1", () => {
      cnt.decrement();
      expect(cnt.counter).toBe(-1);
    }
  );
});
```

Now this script properly instructs Jasmine to create a new instance of `Counter` before running each spec of your suite. Let's see how to run it.

14.2 Running Jasmine scripts with Karma

For projects that don't use Angular CLI, you need to do lots of manual configurations to run Jasmine tests. Without Angular CLI, you start with installing Jasmine and its type definition files as follows:

```
npm install jasmine-core @types/jasmine --save-dev
```

Then you need to create a test.html file that includes script tags to load Jasmine and your specs (the TypeScript code needs to be precompiled into JavaScript). Finally, you need to manually load test.html in each browser you care about and watch whether your tests fail or pass.

But running unit tests from the command line is a better option, because that way you can integrate tests into the project build process. This is one of the main reasons for using a command-line test runner called Karma (see https://karma-runner.github.io). Along with that benefit, Karma has multiple useful plugins and can be used with many JavaScript testing libraries for testing against all major browsers.

Karma is used for testing JavaScript code written with or without frameworks. Karma can run tests to check whether your application works properly in multiple browsers (Chrome, Firefox, Internet Explorer, and so on). In non-Angular CLI projects, you can install Karma and the plugins for Jasmine, Chrome, and Firefox, as shown in the following listing.

Listing 14.6 Installing Karma

```
npm install karma karma-jasmine --save-dev
npm install karma-chrome-launcher --save-dev
npm install karma-firefox-launcher --save-dev
```

Installs Karma and its Jasmine plugin

Installs the plugin to test in Chrome

Installs the plugin to test in Firefox

Then you need to prepare a configuration file, karma.conf.js, for your project—but you're spoiled by Angular CLI, which installs and configures everything you need for testing Angular apps, including Jasmine and Karma. We've generated a new project with Angular CLI and added the code described in the previous section to test the `Counter` class there. You'll find this project in the hello-jasmine directory. Figure 14.3 shows the structure of this project, marking all test-related files and directories.

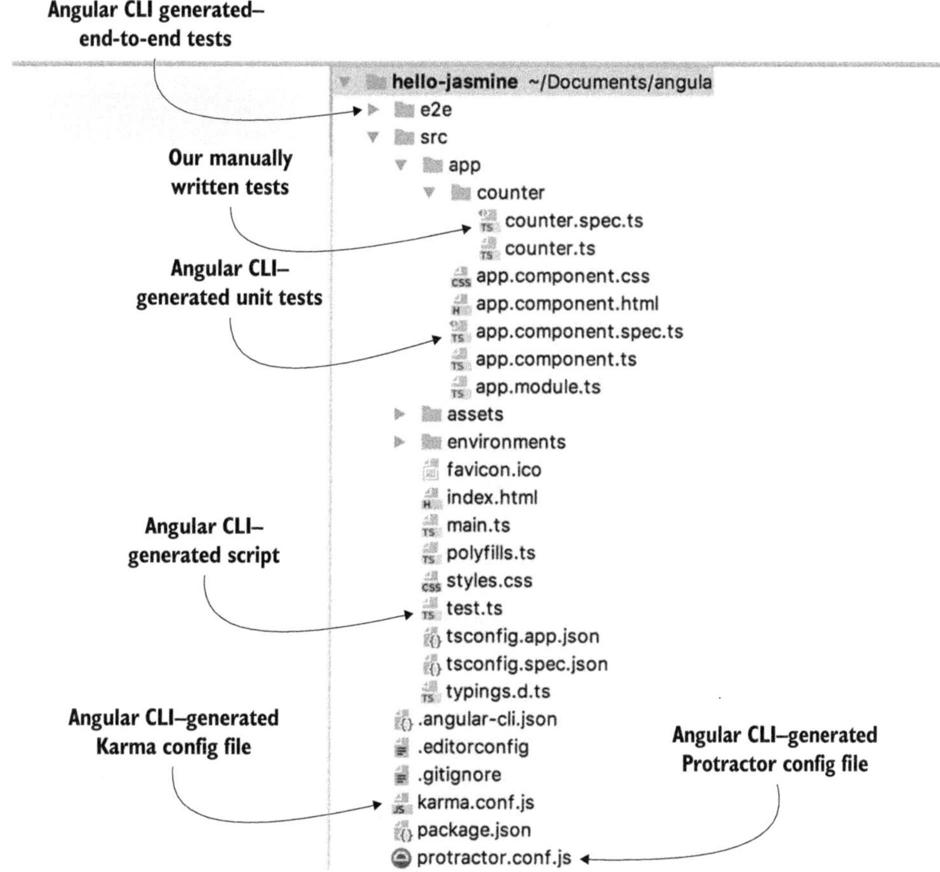

Figure 14.3 The hello-jasmine project

At the very top, you see the e2e directory, and at the bottom, the protractor.conf.js file, which were generated for end-to-end testing, described in section 14.4.

The counter.spec.ts file is the manually written test script described in the previous section. The app.component.spec.ts file was generated by Angular CLI for testing the `AppComponent`, and you'll see its content in section 14.3.1.

The generated file test.ts is the main testing script that loads all test scripts. The karma.conf.js file is used by the Karma runner as soon as you run the `ng test` command, which compiles and runs unit tests. After the tests are compiled, `ng test` uses the compiled script test.js to load the Angular testing library and all the .spec.ts files, and start the Karma runner. Figure 14.4. shows the output of the `ng test` command that in the hello-jasmine project.

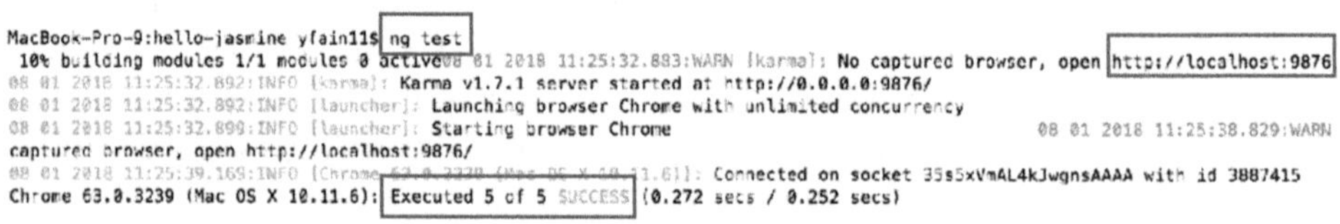

Figure 14.4 Running `ng test` in the hello-jasmine project

To run the tests, Karma starts the Chrome browser (the only one configured by Angular CLI) and runs five tests that end successfully. Why five? You wrote only two tests in the `counter.spec.ts` file, right? Angular CLI also generates the app.component .spec.ts file, which includes the test suite with three `it()` functions defined. Karma executes all files that have an extension .spec.ts.

NOTE Angular CLI projects include the karma-jasmine-html-reporter package, and if you want to see the test results in the browser, open the URL http://localhost:9876.

You don't want to run tests from app.component.spec.ts at this point, so let's turn them off. If you want the test runner to skip some tests, rename their spec function from `it()` to `xit()`. Here, *x* is for *exclude*. If you want to skip the entire test suite, rename `describe()` to `xdescribe()`.

If you exclude the test suite in app.component.spec.ts, the tests will be automatically rerun, reporting that two tests ran successfully (those that you wrote for `Counter`), and three specs were skipped (those that were generated by Angular CLI):

```
Chrome 63.0.3239 (Mac OS X 10.11.6): Executed 2 of 5 (skipped 3)
 SUCCESS (0.03 secs / 0.002 secs)
```

As the number of specs grows, you may want to execute just some of them to see the results faster. Renaming a spec function from `it()` to `fit()` (*f* is for *force*) will execute only these tests while skipping the rest.

You know how to test, but why is still not clear

Let's say you know how to test the methods of your `Counter` class, but you still may have a million-dollar question: Why test such simple functions like `increment()` and `decrement()`? Isn't it obvious that they'll always work fine? In the real world, things change, and what used to be simple becomes not so simple anymore.

Say the business logic for the `decrement()` function changes, and the new requirement is not to allow `counter` to be less than `2`. The developer changes the `decrement()` code to look like this the following.

```
decrement(){
    this.counter >2 ? this.counter--: this.counter;
  }
```

Suddenly, you have two possible *execution paths*:

- The current counter value is greater than `2`.
- The current counter value is equal to `2`.

If you had the unit test for `decrement()`, the next time you run `ng test` it would fail, as follows:

```
Chrome 63.0.3239 (Mac OS X 10.11.6)
    ➥ Counter should decrement the counter by 1
 FAILED
 Expected 0 to be -1.
     at Object.<anonymous> chapter14/hello-jasmine/
    ➥ src/app/counter/counter.spec.ts:18:27)
    ...
```

The text describes the spec that failed.

The assertion failed because the code under test didn't decrement the counter that was equal to zero.

The fact that your unit test failed is a good thing, because it tells you that something changed in the application logic—in `decrement()`. Now the developer should see what changed and add another spec to the test suite so you have two `it()` blocks testing both execution paths of `decrement()` to ensure that it always works properly.

In the real world, business requirements change pretty often, and if developers implement them without providing unit tests for the new functionality, your app can become unreliable and will keep you (or production support engineers) awake at night.

TIP The output of the failed test may not be easy to read because it can include multiple lines of error stack trace. Consider using the continuous testing tool called Wallaby (see https://wallabyjs.com/docs), which shows you a short error message in your IDE right next to the code of the spec that failed.

NOTE In chapter 12, section 12.3.6, we explained how to automate the build process by running a sequence of npm scripts. If you add `ng test` to your build command, the build will be aborted if any of the unit tests fail. For example, the build script can look like this: `"build": "ng test && ng build"`.

It's great that Angular CLI generates a Karma config file that works, but sometimes you may want to modify it based on your project needs.

14.2.1 Karma configuration file

When Angular CLI generates a new project, it includes karma.conf.js preconfigured to run Jasmine unit tests in the Chrome browser. You can read about all available configuration options at http://mng.bz/82cQ, but we'll just highlight some of them that you may want to modify in your projects. The generated karma.conf.js file is shown in the following listing.

Listing 14.7 Angular CLI-generated karma.conf.js file

```
module.exports = function (config) {
  config.set({
    basePath: '',
    frameworks: ['jasmine', '@angular/cli'],
    plugins: [
      require('karma-jasmine'),
      require('karma-chrome-launcher')     <-- Includes the plugin for testing in Chrome
       require('karma-jasmine-html-reporter'),
      require('karma-coverage-istanbul-reporter'),   <-- Includes the code coverage reporter
       require('@angular/cli/plugins/karma')   <-- Includes the Angular CLI plugin for Karma
    ],
    client:{
      clearContext: false // leave Jasmine Spec Runner
                          // output visible in browser
    },
    coverageIstanbulReporter: {
      reports: [ 'html', 'lcovonly' ],
      fixWebpackSourcePaths: true
    },
    angularCli: {
      environment: 'dev'
    },
    reporters: ['progress',     <-- Reports test progress on the console
                'kjhtml'],     <-- Uses karma-jasmine-html-reporter
     port: 9876,     <-- Runs the HTML reporter on this port
     colors: true,
    logLevel: config.LOG_INFO,
    autoWatch: true,
    browsers: ['Chrome'],     <-- Lists the browsers to be used in tests
     singleRun: false     <-- Runs in a watch mode
  });
};
```

NOTE If you want Karma to print a message about each completed spec on the console, add karma-mocha-reporter as `devDependency` in package.json, add the line `require('karma-mocha-reporter')` to karma.conf.js, and replace the progress reporter with `mocha`. If you run tests in continuous integration (CI) servers, use the karma-junit-reporter that can write test results into a file in JUnit XML format.

This configuration file uses only the Chrome plugin, but in real-world apps, you want to run tests in several browsers. The next section shows you how to add Firefox to the list of browsers to be used in tests.

Karma can report how well your code is covered with tests using the Istanbul reporter, and you can run the following command to generate the coverage report:

```
ng test --code-coverage
```

This will create a directory called coverage that will include an index.html file that loads the coverage report. For example, your hello-jasmine project includes one `AppComponent` and the `Counter` class, which are completely covered with unit tests. The generated report is shown in figure 14.5.

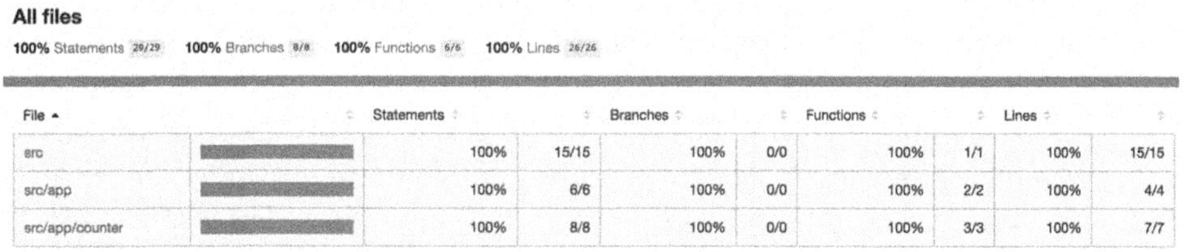

All files

100% Statements 29/29 **100%** Branches 8/8 **100%** Functions 6/6 **100%** Lines 26/26

File ▲		Statements		Branches		Functions		Lines	
src		100%	15/15	100%	0/0	100%	1/1	100%	15/15
src/app		100%	6/6	100%	0/0	100%	2/2	100%	4/4
src/app/counter		100%	8/8	100%	0/0	100%	3/3	100%	7/7

Figure 14.5 Test coverage report for the hello-jasmine project

NOTE Some organizations impose strict rules for code coverage, such as that at least 90% of the code must be covered with unit tests or the build must fail. To enforce such coverage, install the npm package karma-istanbul-threshold and add the `istanbulThresholdReporter` section to karma.conf.js. For more details, see http://mng.bz/544u.

14.2.2 Testing in multiple browsers

Typically, a developer doesn't manually test each and every code change in multiple browsers. Chrome is a preferred browser for dev mode, and you may be unpleasantly surprised when the tester reports that your app works well in Chrome, but produces errors in Safari, Firefox, or Internet Explorer. To eliminate these surprises, you should run unit tests in all browsers that matter to your users.

Luckily, that's pretty easy to set up with Karma. Let's say you want Karma to run tests not only in Chrome, but in Firefox as well (you have to have Firefox installed on your computer). First, install the karma-firefox-launcher plugin:

```
npm i karma-firefox-launcher --save-dev
```

Then, add the following line in the `plugins` section of karma.conf.js:

```
require('karma-firefox-launcher'),
```

Finally, add Firefox to the browsers list in karma.conf.js, so that it looks as follows:

```
browsers: ['Chrome', 'Firefox'],
```

TIP If you need to set up a CI environment on a Linux server, you can either install Xvfb (a virtual display server) or use a *headless* browser (a browser without a UI). For example, you can specify ChromeHeadless to use the headless Chrome browser.

Now if you run the ng test command, it'll run the tests in both Chrome and Firefox. Install Karma plugins for each browser you care about, and this will eliminate surprises like "But it worked fine in Chrome!"

We've gone over the basics of writing and running unit tests. Let's see how to unit-test Angular components, services, and the router.

14.3 Using the Angular testing library

Angular comes with a testing library that includes the wrappers for some Jasmine functions and adds such functions as inject(), async(), fakeAsync(), and others.

To test Angular artifacts, you need to create and configure an Angular module for the class under test using the configureTestingModule() method of the TestBed utility, which allows you to declare modules, components, providers, and so on. For example, the syntax for configuring a testing module looks similar to configuring @NgModule(), as you can see in the following listing.

Listing 14.8 Configuring the testing module for your app

```
beforeEach(async(() => {                    // Runs this code asynchronously before each spec
   TestBed.configureTestingModule({          // Configures the testing module
     declarations: [
      AppComponent                           // Lists components under test
     ],
  }).compileComponents();                    // Compiles components
 }));
```

The beforeEach() function is used in test suites during the setup phase. With it you can specify the required modules, components, and providers that may be needed by each test. The async() function runs in the Zone and may be used with asynchronous code. The async() function doesn't complete until all of its asynchronous operations have been completed or the specified timeout has passed.

In an Angular app, the components are "magically" created and services are injected, but in test scripts, you'll need to explicitly instantiate components and invoke the inject() function or the TestBed.get() function to inject services. If a function under test invokes asynchronous functions, you should wrap such it into async() or fakeAsync().

async() will run the function(s) under test in the Zone. If your test code uses timeouts, observables, or promises, wrap it into async() to ensure that the expect()

function is invoked after all the asynchronous functions are complete. If you don't do this, `expect()` may be executed before the results of async functions are in, and the test will fail. The `async()` function waits for async code to be finished, which is a good thing. On the other hand, such a wait may slow down the tests, and the `fakeAsync()` function allows you to eliminate the wait.

`fakeAsync()`identifies the timers in the code under test and replaces the code inside `setTimeout()`, `setInterval()`, or the `debounceTime()` with immediately executed functions as if they're synchronous, and executes them in order. It also gives you more-precise time control with the `tick()` and `flush()` functions, which allow you to fast-forward the time.

You can optionally provide the time value in milliseconds for fast-forwarding, so there's no need to wait, even if the async function uses `setTimeout()` or `Observable.interval()`. For example, if you have an input field that uses the RxJS operator `myInputField.valueChanges.debounceTime(500).subscribe()`, you can write `tick(499)` to fast-forward the time by 499 milliseconds and then assert that the subscriber didn't get the data entered in the input field.

You can use the `tick()` function only inside `fakeAsync()`. Calling `tick()` without the argument means that you want the code that follows to be executed after all pending asynchronous activities finish.

To see the tests from this section in action, open the unit-testing-samples project that comes with this chapter, run `npm install`, and then run `ng test`.

Let's see some of the APIs of the Angular testing library, starting with reviewing the code of the app.component.spec.ts file generated by Angular CLI.

14.3.1 Testing components

Components are classes with templates. If a component's class contains methods implementing some application logic, you can test them as you would any other function. But more often, you'll be testing the UI to see that the bindings work properly and that the component template displays expected data.

Under the hood, an Angular component consists of two parts: an instance of the class and the DOM element. Technically, when you write a unit test for a component, it's more of an integration test, because it has to check that the instance of the component class and the DOM object work in sync.

The Angular testing library offers the `TestBed.createComponent()` method,which returns a `ComponentFixture` object that gives you access to both the component and the native DOM object of the rendered template.

To access the component instance, you can use the `ComponentFixture.componentInstance` property, and to access the DOM element, use `ComponentFixture.nativeElement`. If you want to get access to the fixture's API (for example, to access the component's injector, run CSS query selectors, find styles or child nodes, or trigger an event handler), use its `DebugElement`, as in `ComponentFixture.debugElement.componentInstance` and `ComponentFixture.debugElement.nativeElement`, respectively. Figure 14.6 illustrates some of the properties of the `ComponentFixture` object, which also exist in `debugElement`.

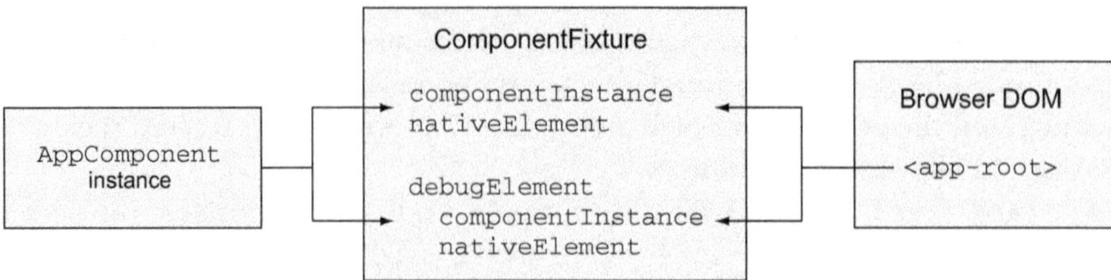

Figure 14.6 Properties of `ComponentFixture`

To update the bindings, you can trigger the change detection cycle on the component by invoking the `detectChanges()` method on the fixture. After change detection has updated the UI, you can run the `expect()` function to check the rendered values.

After configuring the test module, you usually perform the following steps to test a component:

1. Invoke `TestBed.createComponent()` to create a component.
2. Use a reference to `componentInstance` to invoke the component's methods.
3. Invoke `ComponentFixture.detectChanges()` to trigger change detection.
4. Use a reference to `nativeElement` to access the DOM object and check whether it has the expected value.

NOTE If you want change detection to be triggered automatically, you can configure the testing module with the provider for the `ComponentFixtureAutoDetect` service. Although this seems to be a better choice than manually invoking `detectChanges()`, this service only notices the asynchronous activities and won't react to synchronous updates of component properties.

Let's examine the code of the generated app.component.spec.ts file and see how it performs these steps. This Angular CLI–generated script declares a test suite containing three specs:

1. Check that the component instance is created.
2. Check that this component has a `title` property with the value `app`.
3. Check that the UI has an <h1> element with the text "Welcome to app!"

The code is shown in the following listing.

Listing 14.9 app.component.spec.ts

```
import { TestBed, async } from '@angular/core/testing';
import { AppComponent } from './app.component';

describe('AppComponent', () => {
  beforeEach(async(() => {
    TestBed.configureTestingModule({
      declarations: [
        AppComponent
      ],
```

Imports the required modules from the Angular testing library

Wraps component compilation into async()

In setup phase, configures the testing module asynchronously in the Zone

```
    }).compileComponents();
  }));
  it('should create the app', async(() => {
    const fixture = TestBed.createComponent(AppComponent);
     const app = fixture.debugElement.componentInstance;
     expect(app).toBeTruthy();
  }));
  it(`should have as title 'app'`, async(() => {
    const fixture = TestBed.createComponent(AppComponent);
    const app = fixture.debugElement.componentInstance;
    expect(app.title).toEqual('app');
  }));
  it('should render title in a h1 tag', async(() => {
    const fixture = TestBed.createComponent(AppComponent);
    fixture.detectChanges();
     const compiled = fixture.debugElement.nativeElement;
     expect(compiled.querySelector('h1').textContent)
                    .toContain('Welcome to app!');
  }));
});
```

Compiles component(s) to inline styles and templates

Instantiates the AppComponent

Gets a reference to the component's instance

Checks that the coercion of the app to a Boolean yields true

Triggers change detection to update the component's DOM object

Gets a reference to the DOM object

Checks that the DOM object has the <h1> element containing this text

Note that the functions that instantiate the component are wrapped into `async()`. That's because a component can have a template and styles in separate files, and reading files is an asynchronous operation.

Invoking `detectChanges()` triggers change detection that updates the bindings on the DOM elements. After this is done, you can query the content of the DOM elements to assure that the UI shows the expected values.

> **NOTE** Currently, Angular CLI generates the test with repeating `createComponent()` invocations. A better solution would be to write another `beforeEach()` function and create the fixture there.

Running `ng test` in a newly generated project will report that all tests passed. The browser opens at http://localhost:9876, and you'll see the testing report shown in figure 14.7.

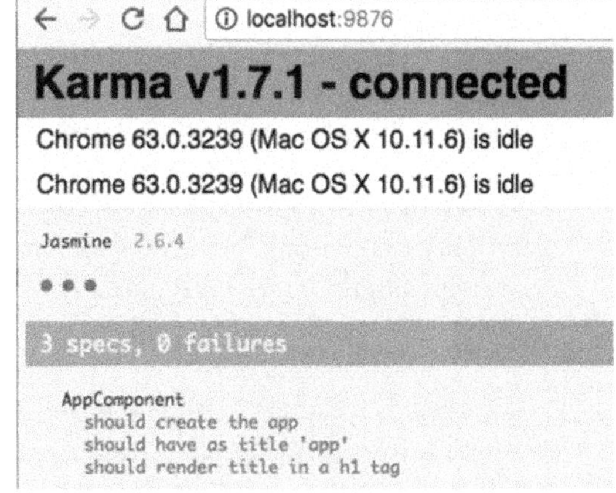

Figure 14.7 A successful run of `ng test`

Let's see what happens if you change the value of the `title` property in the `AppComponent` from app to `my app`. Because `ng test` runs in watch mode, the tests will automatically rerun, you'll see the messages about two failed specs on the console, and the list of specs will look like figure 14.8 (the failed specs are shown in red if you have the e-book).

The first failed spec message reads “AppComponent should have as title 'app',” and the second message is “AppComponent should render title in a h1 tag.” These are the messages provided in the it() functions. Clicking any of the failed specs will open another page, providing more details and the stack trace.

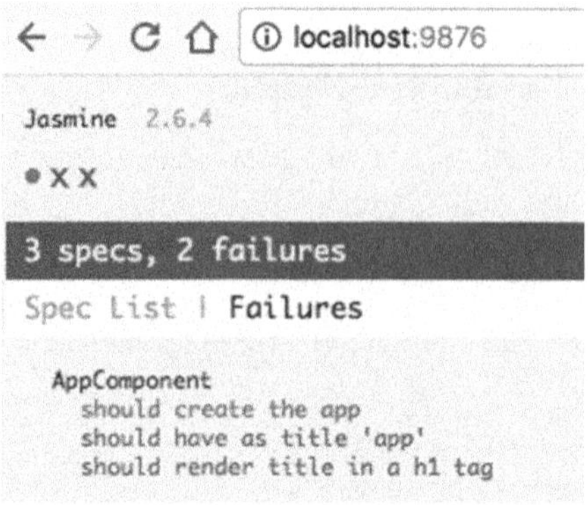

Figure 14.8 Spec list with failures

> **TIP** Keep in mind that if your component uses lifecycle hooks, they won't be called automatically. You need to call them explicitly, as in app.ngOnInit().

Let's add another spec in the next listing to ensure that if the title property changes in the AppComponent class, it'll be properly rendered in the UI.

Listing 14.10 A spec for the title update

```
it('should render updated title', async(() => {
  const fixture = TestBed.createComponent(AppComponent);
  const app = fixture.debugElement.componentInstance;
  app.title = 'updated app!';                          <-- Updates the title property
   fixture.detectChanges();                            <-- Forces change detection
   const compiled = fixture.debugElement.nativeElement;
  expect(compiled.querySelector('h1').textContent)
          .toContain('Welcome to updated app!');     <-- Checks that the UI reflects
 }));                                                     the updated title
```

Now ng test will run this extra spec and will report that it successfully finished. In this section, you used the generated test for AppComponent, but you'll see another script that tests a component in the hands-on section.

A typical component uses services for data manipulation, and you create mock services that return hardcoded (and the same) values to concentrate on testing the component's functionality. The specs for components should test only components; services should be tested separately.

14.3.2 Testing services

A service is a class with one or more methods, and you unit-test only the public ones, which in turn may invoke private methods. In Angular apps, you specify providers for services in @Component or @NgModule, so Angular can properly instantiate and inject them. In test scripts, you also declare providers for services under test, but you do this inside `TestBed.configureTestingModule()` in the setup phase.

Also, if in Angular apps you can use the provider's token in the class constructor to inject a service, in tests, the injection is done differently. For example, you can explicitly invoke the `inject()` function. The other option to instantiate and inject a service is to use the `TestBed.get()` method, which uses the root injector, as shown in figure 14.9. This will work if the service provider is specified in the root testing module.

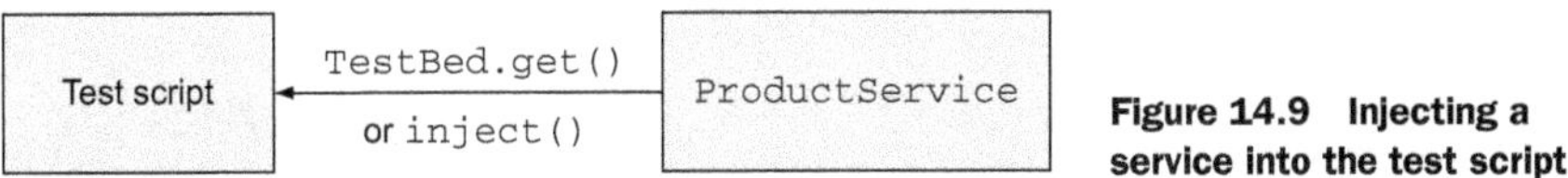

Figure 14.9 Injecting a service into the test script

Component-level injectors can be used as follows:

```
fixture.debugElement.injector.get(ProductService);
```

Let's generate a product service by running the following Angular CLI command:

```
ng g s product
```

This command will generate the files product.service.ts and product.service.spec.ts. The latter will contain the boilerplate code shown in the following listing.

Listing 14.11 product.service.spec.ts

```
import { TestBed, inject } from '@angular/core/testing';
import { ProductService } from './product.service';

describe('ProductService', () => {
  beforeEach(() => {
    TestBed.configureTestingModule({
      providers: [ProductService]     <-- Configures the provider
     });
  });

  it('should be created',
     inject([ProductService],         <-- Injects the service
             (service: ProductService) => {
               expect(service).toBeTruthy();} <-- Implements the testing logic
     )
  );
});
```

If you needed to inject more than one service, the `inject()` function would list an array of DI tokens followed by the function with the argument list corresponding to the names of tokens:

```
inject([ProductService, OtherService],
    (prodService: ProductService, otherService: OtherService) => {...})
```

As you add methods to the `ProductService` class, you could test them similarly to testing methods in the `Counter` class, as you did earlier, but you need to consider a special case when a service relies on another service, such as on `HttpClient`. Making HTTP requests to a server during unit tests would slow them down. Besides, you don't want your unit tests to fail if the server's down. Remember, unit tests are for testing isolated pieces of code.

The code that comes with this chapter includes the unit-testing-samples project and the app called readfile. It includes `ProductService`, which uses `HttpClient` to read the data/products.json file, as shown in the following listing.

Listing 14.12 Reading data/products.json in a service

```
export class ProductService {

  constructor(private httpClient: HttpClient ) {}        <-- Injects HttpClient

  getProducts(): Observable<Product[]> {                  <-- Reads the file
     return this.httpClient.get<Product[]>('/data/products.json');
  }
}
```

Let's write a unit test for the `getProducts()` method . You don't want your test to fail if someone removes the data/products.json file, because that wouldn't mean there's an issue in `getProducts()`. You'll mock the `HttpClient` with the help of `HttpTestingController` from `HttpClientTestingModule`. `HttpTestingController` doesn't make an HTTP request but allows you to emulate it using hardcoded data.

To add the hardcoded data to the response body, you'll use the `HttpTestingController.flush()` method, and to emulate an error, you'll use `HttpTestingController.error()`, as shown in the following listing.

Listing 14.13 product.service.spec.ts

```
import {TestBed, async} from '@angular/core/testing';
import {HttpClientTestingModule, HttpTestingController }
➥ from '@angular/common/http/testing';
import {ProductService} from './product.service';
import {Product} from './product';

describe('ProductService', () => {
  let productService: ProductService;
  let httpMock: HttpTestingController;

  beforeEach(() => {
    TestBed.configureTestingModule({
      imports: [HttpClientTestingModule],     <-- Includes HttpClientTestingModule to the testing module
       providers: [ProductService]
    });

    productService = TestBed.get(ProductService);    <-- Injects ProductService
     httpMock = TestBed.get(HttpTestingController);  <-- Injects HttpTestingController
   });
```

```
it('should successfully get products', async(() => {      ← Subscribes to the response and asserts the result
  const productData: Product[] =                           ← Prepares hardcoded product data
    [{ "id": "0", "title": "First Product", "price": 24.99 }];
   productService.getProducts()
        .subscribe(res => expect(res).toEqual(productData));

  let productsRequest = httpMock.expectOne('/data/products.json');
  productsRequest.flush(productData);     ← Sends the product data to the client
 }));

it('should return error if request for products failed', async( () => {
  const errorType = 'CANNOT_LOAD_PRODUCTS' ;     ← Prepares the error message
   productService.getProducts()
    .subscribe(() => {},                 ← Doesn't handle product data
          errorResponse =>
               expect(errorResponse.error.type).toEqual(errorType));   ← Asserts that the expected error was received

  let productsRequest = httpMock.expectOne('/data/products.json');

  productsRequest.error(new ErrorEvent (errorType));   ← Sends the error to the client
 }));

 afterEach(() => httpMock.verify());    ← Asserts that there are no outstanding requests
});
```

In the first spec, you hardcode the data for one product and then invoke `getProducts()` and subscribe to the response.

> **NOTE** Jasmine offers a `spyOn()` function that could intercept the specified function (for example, `getProducts()`), where you could just return a stub object with the expected data. But using such a spy wouldn't make an HTTP request. Because you use `HttpTestingController`, the HTTP request is made and will be intercepted by `HttpTestingController`, which won't be making a real HTTP request to read products.json but will take the hardcoded product data and send it through the HTTP machinery.

You expect the `getProducts()` method to make a single request to /data/products .json and return its mock, and this is what `expectOne()` is for. If no such request has been made, or if more than one such request has been made, the spec will fail.

With the real `HttpClient` service, invoking the `subscribe()` method would result in receiving either the data or an error, but with `HttpTestingController`, the subscriber won't get any data until you invoke `flush()` or `error()`. Here, you provide hardcoded data in the response body.

When Karma opens the browser with the test results, you can open Chrome Dev Tools in the Sources tab, find the source code for your spec file, and add breakpoints to debug your test code just as you'd do with any TypeScript code. In particular, if you place a breakpoint in the line that invokes `flush()` in listing 14.13, you'll see that it's invoked before the code in `subscribe()`.

The `verify()` method tested all HTTP requests, and there are no outstanding ones. You assert this in the teardown phase after running each spec.

Note that the code in each spec is wrapped into the `async()` function. This ensures that your `expect()` calls will be made after all asynchronous calls from the spec are complete.

> **TIP** You can read about other techniques for replacing real services with mocks, stubs, and spies in the Angular testing documentation at https://angular.io/guide/testing.

Now let's see how to test the router.

14.3.3 Testing components that use routing

If a component includes routing, you may want to test different navigation functionality. For example, you may want to test that the router properly navigates where it's supposed to, that parameters are properly passed to the destination component, and that the guards don't let unauthorized users visit certain routes.

To test router-related functionality, Angular offers the `RouterTestingModule`, which intercepts navigation but doesn't load the destination component. For the test, you need the router configuration; you can either use the same one that's used in the application or create a separate configuration just for testing. The latter could be a better option if your route configuration includes many components.

A user can navigate the app either by interacting with the application or by entering a URL directly in the browser's address bar. The `Router` object is responsible for navigation implemented in your app code, and the `Location` object represents the URL in the address bar. These two objects work in sync.

To test if the router properly navigates your app, invoke `navigate()` and `navigateByUrl()` in your specs, and pass parameters, if needed. The `navigate()` method takes an array of routes and parameters as an argument, whereas `navigateByUrl()` takes a string representing the segment of the URL you want to navigate to.

If you use `navigate()`, you specify the configured path and route params, if any. If the router is properly configured, it should update the URL in the address bar of the browser. To illustrate this, you'll reuse the code of one of the apps from chapter 3, but you'll add the spec file. In that app, the router configuration for the `AppComponent` includes the path /product/:id, as shown in the following listing.

Listing 14.14 A fragment from app.routing.ts

```
export const routes: Routes = [
  {path: '',             component: HomeComponent},              // A default route
   {path: 'product/:id', component: ProductDetailComponent}      // A route with a parameter
 ];
```

When the user clicks the Product Details link, the app navigates to the `ProductDetailComponent`, as shown in the following listing.

Listing 14.15 app.component.ts

```
@Component({
  selector: 'app-root',
  template: `
        <a [routerLink]="['/']">Home</a>
        <a id="product" [routerLink]="['/product', productId]">
            Product Detail</a>
        <router-outlet></router-outlet>
    `
})
export class AppComponent {
  productId = 1234;
 }
```

A link to navigate to the product-detail view

The value to be passed to the product-detail view

In the app.component.spec.ts file, you'll test that when the user clicks the Product Details link, the URL includes the segment /product/1234. The `Router` and `Location` objects will be injected by using the `TestBed.get()` API. To emulate the click on the Product Details link, you need to get access to the corresponding DOM object, which you do by using the `By.css()` API. The utility class `By` has the `css()` method, which matches elements using the provided CSS selector. Because your app component has two links, you assign `id=product` to the product-details link so you can get ahold of it by invoking `By.css('#product')`.

To emulate the click on the link, you use the `triggerEventHandler()` method with two arguments. The first argument has the value `click` that represents the click event. The second argument has the value `{button: 0}` that represents the event object. The `RouterLink` directive expects the value to include the property `button` with the number that represents the mouse button, and zero is for the left mouse button, as shown in the following listing.

Listing 14.16 app.component.spec.ts

```
// imports omitted for brevity
describe('AppComponent', () => {
  let fixture;
  let router: Router;
  let location: Location;

    beforeEach(async(() => {
      TestBed.configureTestingModule({
        imports: [RouterTestingModule.withRoutes(routes)],
         declarations: [
          AppComponent, ProductDetailComponent, HomeComponent
        ]}).compileComponents();
    }));

  beforeEach(fakeAsync(() => {
    router = TestBed.get(Router);
```

Loads the routes configuration

Injects the Router object

```
      location = TestBed.get(Location);      <---- Injects the Location object
      fixture = TestBed.createComponent(AppComponent);
    router.navigateByUrl('/');
    tick();
    fixture.detectChanges();     <---- Triggers change detection
  }));

  it('can navigate and pass params to the product detail view',
   fakeAsync(() => {
    const productLink = fixture.debugElement.query(By.css('#product'));   <---- Get access to the product-details link
Clicks the link --> productLink.triggerEventHandler('click', {button: 0});
     tick();
    fixture.detectChanges();
    expect(location.path()).toEqual('/product/1234');  <---- Checks the assertion
  }));
});
```

The fakeAsync() function wraps the navigation code (the asynchronous operation), and the tick() function ensures that the asynchronous navigation finishes before you run the assertion.

Figure 14.10 shows the sequence of actions performed by the preceding script.

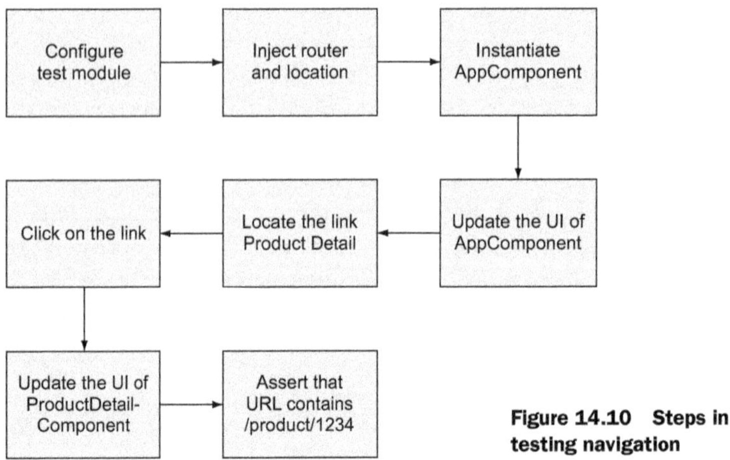

Figure 14.10 Steps in testing navigation

The ng test command will run all unit tests in the unit-testing-samples project, which has three apps. All eight specs should successfully complete. The eighth spec will report "AppComponent can navigate and pass params to the product detail view."

NOTE To make unit testing a part of your automated build process, integrate the ng test command into the build process by adding && ng test to the npm build script described in section 12.3.6 in chapter 12.

Unit testing the functionality implemented in the route guards is another practical use case. In chapter 4, we covered such guards as CanActivate, CanDeactivate, and

`Resolve`. Because guards are services, you can test them separately, as explained in the preceding section.

This concludes our coverage of unit-testing basics. Unit tests assert that each artifact of your Angular app works as expected in isolation. But how can you ensure that several components, services, and other artifacts play well together without the need to manually test each workflow?

14.4 End-to-end testing with Protractor

End-to-end (E2E) testing is for testing the entire app workflow by simulating user interaction with the app. For example, the process of placing an order may use multiple components and services. You can create an E2E test to ensure that this workflow behaves as expected. Also, if in unit tests you're mocking dependencies, E2E tests will use the real ones.

To manually test a specific workflow like the login functionality, a QA engineer prepares an ID/password that works, opens the login page, enters the ID/password, and clicks the Login button. After that, QA wants to assert that the landing page of your app is successfully rendered. The tester can also run another test to ensure that if the wrong ID/password is entered, the landing page won't be rendered. This is a manual way of E2E testing of the login workflow.

Protractor is a testing library that allows you to test app workflows *simulating* user actions without the need to perform them manually. You still need to prepare test data and script the test logic, but the tests will run without human interaction.

By default, Protractor uses the Jasmine syntax for tests, unless you manually configure another supported framework (see http://mng.bz/d64d). So your E2E test scripts will use already familiar `describe()` and `it()` blocks plus an additional API.

14.4.1 Protractor basics

While manually testing app workflows, a user "drives" the web browser by entering data, selecting options, and clicking buttons. Protractor is based on Selenium WebDriver (see http://www.seleniumhq.org/docs/03_webdriver.jsp) that can automatically drive the browser, based on the provided scripts. Protractor also includes an Angular-specific API for locating UI elements.

In your setup, Protractor will run the web browser and tests on the same machine, so you need Selenium WebDriver for the browser(s) you want to run the tests in. The other option would be to set up a separate machine for testing and run Selenium Server there. Selenium offers implementations of WebDriver for different programming languages, and Protractor uses the one called WebDriverJS.

When you generate a new project with Angular CLI, it includes Protractor and its configuration files as well as the e2e directory with sample test scripts. Prior to Angular 6, the e2e directory included three files, as shown in figure 14.11. Starting from Angular 6, the generated e2e directory includes the configuration file protractor .conf.js.

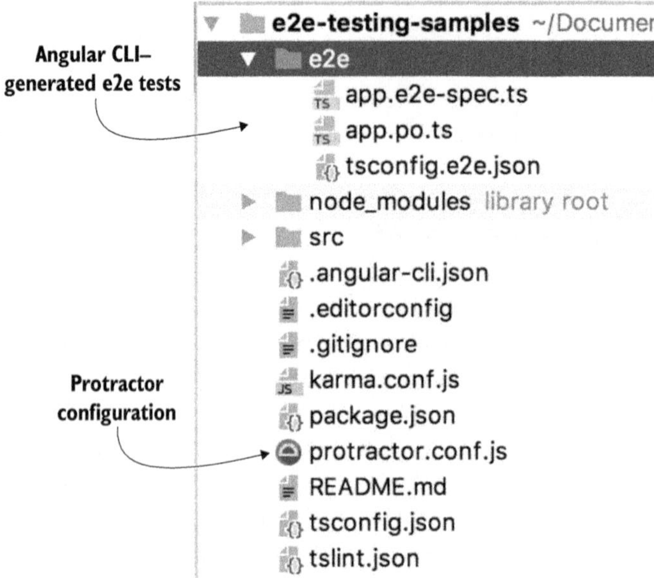

Figure 14.11 Angular CLI-generated E2E code

TIP Starting from Angular CLI 6, when you generate a new project, it includes two apps: one is a project for your app, and another app contains the basic E2E tests.

You run the E2E tests by entering the `ng e2e` command , which loads the test scripts based on the configuration in the protractor.conf.js file. That file by default assumes that all E2E test scripts are located in the e2e directory, and the app has to be launched in Chrome.

Listing 14.17 A fragment from protractor.conf.js

```
specs: [
  './e2e/**/*.e2e-spec.ts'   <-- Where the test scripts are
 ],
capabilities: {
  'browserName': 'chrome'  <-- Which browser to run your app in
 },
directConnect: true   <-- Connects to the browser directly without the server
```

The `ng e2e` command builds the app bundles, starts the Node instance, and loads the test scripts, Protractor, and Selenium WebDriver. Protractor launches your app in the browser(s), and your test scripts communicate with the browser using the API of Protractor and WebDriverJS. Figure 14.12 shows the E2E test players used in this chapter's examples.

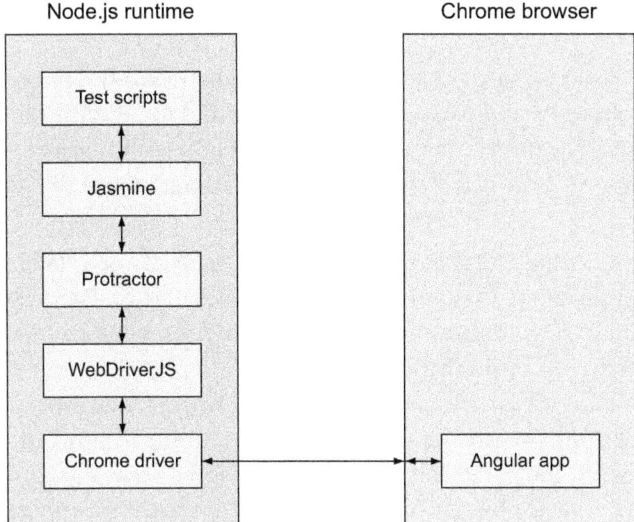

Figure 14.12 Angular CLI-generated E2E code

Prior to running your test scripts, Protractor unzips the browser-specific driver (for example, ChromeDriver) into the node_modules/webdriver-manager/selenium folder so Selenium WebDriver can properly communicate with the browser. During the tests, Protractor will launch the browser, and after the tests finish, Protractor will close it.

Protractor can use scripts created in different unit-testing frameworks (Jasmine is a default one), and each of them may have a different API for locating and representing page elements. To spare you from changing E2E scripts if you decide to switch to another unit-testing framework, Protractor comes with an API (see www.protractortest.org/#/api) that works with all supported frameworks:

- `browser` provides an API to control the browser, for example `getCurrentUrl()`, `wait()`, and so on.
- `by` is a locator for finding elements in Angular applications by ID, CSS, button or link text, and so forth.
- `element` offers an API for finding and working with a single element on a web page.
- `element.all` is used for finding and working with collections of elements, for example, iterating over the elements of an HTML list or table.

TIP `$("selector")` is an alias for `element(by.css("selector"))`, and `$$("selector")` is an alias for `element.all(by.css("selector"))`.

Although in Angular apps you can use the structural directive `*ngFor` for rendering a collection of UI elements, in tests you should use `element.all` for referring to and finding elements in a collection.

> **TIP** Though Protractor defines its own API, it also exposes the WebDriver API, as in `browser.takeScreenshot()`.

The E2E tests load the real app in the browser, locate elements on the page, and can programmatically click buttons and links, fill out forms with data, submit them to the server, and then again locate the elements on the resulting page to ensure that they have the expected content. You can write an E2E test using one of the following approaches:

- In the same script, locate DOM elements by using their IDs or CSS classes and assert that the application logic works correctly. The IDs or CSS classes may change over time, so if you have several scripts testing the same page, you need to update each script accordingly.
- Implement the *Page Object* design pattern (see https://martinfowler.com/bliki/PageObject.html) by writing the expectations and assertions in one file, and in another, write the code that interacts with the UI elements and invokes the app's API. The page object can implement UI interaction with either the entire page or its part (for example, the toolbar), and can be reused by multiple tests. Should the CSS of the HTML elements change, you'll need to modify a single page object script.

Tests written using the first approach are difficult to read because they don't provide an easy way of understanding which workflows are implemented on the page. You'll use the second approach, where all UI interactions are implemented in the page objects (.po.ts files), and the specs with assertions are in the scripts (.e2e-spec.ts files). This approach reduces code duplication because you don't need to copy-paste the element locators if multiple specs need to access the same HTML element. A page object can serve as a single place for simulating user activity for important workflows, such as `login()` or `getProducts()`, rather than having these activities scattered throughout the tests.

Let's look at the E2E test generated by Angular CLI for the new projects.

14.4.2 Angular CLI–generated tests

When you generate a new project with Angular CLI, it creates a directory, e2e, that contains three files:

- *app.po.ts*—The page object for `AppComponent`
- *app.e2e-spec.ts*—The E2E test for the generated `AppComponent`
- *tsconfig.e2e.json*—The TypeScript compiler options

The app.po.ts file contains a simple `AppPage` class with just two methods, as shown in listing 14.18. The first one contains the code to navigate to the root page of the component, and the second has code to locate the HTML element by CSS and get its text. This page object is the only place that contains code locating elements by CSS.

Listing 14.18 The generated app.po.ts file

```
import {browser, by, element} from 'protractor';

export class AppPage {
  navigateTo() {
    return browser.get('/');    <-- Navigates to the default route
  }

  getParagraphText() {
    return element(by.css('app-root h1')).getText();    <-- Gets the text from the <h1> element
  }
}
```

The code for the app.e2e-spec.ts file is shown in listing 14.19. This test looks very similar to the unit tests shown in the last section. Note that this file doesn't include the code that directly interacts with the HTML page; it uses the API of the page object instead.

Listing 14.19 The generated app.e2e-spec.ts file

```
import {AppPage} from './app.po';

describe('e2e-testing-samples App', () => {
  let page: AppPage;

  beforeEach(() => {
    page = new AppPage();    <-- Creates an instance of the page
  });

  it('should display welcome message', () => {
    page.navigateTo();    <-- Navigates to the default route
     expect(page.getParagraphText()).toEqual('Welcome to app!');    <-- Asserts that the text returned by getParagraphText() is correct
  });
});
```

Because app.e2e-spec.ts doesn't contain any element locators, it's easy to follow the test logic: you navigate to the landing page and retrieve the content of a paragraph. You can run the preceding E2E test using the command `ng e2e`.

> **NOTE** E2E tests run slower that unit tests, and you don't want to run them each time you save a file, as you did with `ng test` in the last section. Besides, instead of creating E2E tests for each and every workflow, you may want to identify the most important ones and run tests just for them.

Now that you've seen how generated tests work, you can write your own E2E test.

14.4.3 Testing a login page

The E2E test from the preceding section didn't include a workflow that would require data entry and navigation. In this section, you'll write a test for an app that uses a form and routing. The code that comes with this chapter includes a project called e2e-testing-samples with a simple app that has a login page and a home page. The routes in this app are configured in the following listing.

Listing 14.20 Route configurations

```
[{path: '', redirectTo: 'login', pathMatch: 'full'},      <- Redirects the base URL to the login page
  {path: 'login', component: LoginComponent},             <- Renders the login component
  {path: 'home', component: HomeComponent}]                <- Renders the home component
```

The template of the `HomeComponent` has just one line:

```
<h1>Home Component</h1>
```

The login component in the following listing has a Login button and a form with two fields for entering ID and password. If a user enters `Joe` as the ID and `password` as the password, your app navigates to the home page; otherwise, it stays on the login page and shows the message "Invalid ID or password."

Listing 14.21 login.component.ts

```
@Component({
  selector: 'app-home',
  template: `<h1 class="home">Login Component</h1>
  <form #f="ngForm" (ngSubmit)="login(f.value)">        <- A login form
     ID: <input name="id" ngModel/><br>
    PWD: <input type="password" name="pwd" ngModel=""/><br>
    <button type="submit">Login</button>
    <span id="errMessage"
          *ngIf="wrongCredentials">Invalid ID or password</span>     <- The invalid login message
  </form>
  `
})
export class LoginComponent {
  wrongCredentials = false;
  constructor(private router: Router) {}       <- Router injection

  login(formValue) {
    if ('Joe' === formValue.id && 'password' === formValue.pwd) {
      this.router.navigate(['/home']);        <- Navigation to the home page
       this.wrongCredentials = false;
    } else {
      this.router.navigate(['/login']);       <- Navigation to the login page
       this.wrongCredentials = true;
    }
  }
}
```

Your tests are located in the e2e directory and include two page objects, login.po.ts and home.po.ts, and one spec, login.e2e-spec.ts. The page object for the home page contains a method to return the header's text. The following listing shows home.po.ts.

Listing 14.22 home.po.ts

```
import {by, element} from 'protractor';

export class HomePage {
  getHeaderText() {
    return element(by.css('h1')).getText();
  }
}
```

The login page object uses locators to get references to the form fields and the button. The `login()` method simulates user actions: entering the ID and password and clicking the Login button. The `navigateToLogin()` method instructs the browser to visit the URL configured to the login component—for example, http://localhost:4200/login. The `getErrorMessage()` method returns the login error message that may or may not be present on the page. login.po.ts is shown in the following listing.

Listing 14.23 login.po.ts

```
import {browser, by, element, $} from 'protractor';

export class LoginPage {

  id = $('input[name="id"]');                              // Locates the page elements
  pwd = $('input[name="pwd"]');                            // using $ as an alias for
  submit = element(by.buttonText('Login'));                // element(by.css())
  errMessage = element(by.id('errMessage'));

  login(id: string, password: string): void {
    this.id.sendKeys(id);                                  // Enters the provided
    this.pwd.sendKeys(password);                           // ID and password
    this.submit.click();      // Clicks the Login button
  }

  navigateToLogin() {
    return browser.get('/login');     // Navigates to the login page
  }

  getErrorMessage() {
    return this.errMessage;     // Returns the login error message
  }
}
```

This page object makes the login procedure easy to understand. The `sendKey()` method is used for simulating data entry, and `click()` simulates a button click.

Now let's review the test suite for the login workflow. It instantiates the login page object and includes two specs: one for testing a successful login and another for a failed one.

The first spec instructs Protractor to navigate to the login page and log in the user with the hardcoded data `Joe` and `password`. If the login was successful, the app navigates to the home page, and you assert this by checking that the URL in the browser contains /home. You also assert that the rendered page contains the header "Home Component."

The spec for the failed login asserts that the app stays on the login page and the error message is displayed. Note in the following listing that this script has no code directly interacting with the UI.

Listing 14.24 login.e2e-spec.ts

```
import {LoginPage} from './login.po';
import {HomePage} from './home.po';
import {browser} from 'protractor';

describe('Login page', () => {
  let loginPage: LoginPage;
  let homePage: HomePage;

  beforeEach(() => {
    loginPage = new LoginPage();        // Instantiates the login page object
  });

  it('should navigate to login page and log in', () => {    // A spec for a successful login
     loginPage.navigateToLogin();       // Navigates to the login page
     loginPage.login('Joe', 'password');    // Logs in with proper credentials

    const url = browser.getCurrentUrl();    // Gets the browser's URL
     expect(url).toContain('/home');        // Asserts that the URL contains /home

    homePage = new HomePage();          // Instantiates the home page object
     expect(homePage.getHeaderText()).toEqual('Home Component');   // Asserts that the page header is correct
   });

  it('should stay on login page if wrong credentials entered',
   () => {                              // A spec for a failed login
     loginPage.navigateToLogin();
    loginPage.login('Joe', 'wrongpassword');     // Executes the failed login

    const url = browser.getCurrentUrl();
    expect(url).toContain('/login');    // Asserts that the app still shows the login page
     expect(loginPage.getErrorMessage().isPresent()).toBe(true);   // Asserts that the error message is shown
   });
});
```

The LoginComponent uses the *ngIf structural directive to conditionally show or hide the login error message, and your failed login spec asserts that the error message is present on the page.

Sometimes you need to wait for certain operations to complete before making assertions. For example, the login() method in your page object ends with the button click, and the spec for the successful login contains the assertion that the URL contains /home.

This assertion will always be true because your login process completes in no time as it doesn't connect to an authentication server to check user credentials. In the real world, the authentication could take a couple of seconds, and the assertion for /home could run sooner than the URL changes to /home, causing the test to fail.

In such cases, you can invoke the `browser.wait()` command , where you can specify the condition to wait for. In the hands-on section, you'll write a test that clicks the Search button that makes an HTTP request for products, which needs some time to finish. There, you'll use a helper function that waits for the URL to change before making assertions.

Run this test with the `ng e2e` command, and you'll see how Protractor opens the Chrome browser for a short time, fills out the form, and clicks the Login button. The Terminal window shows the output, which you can see in figure 14.13.

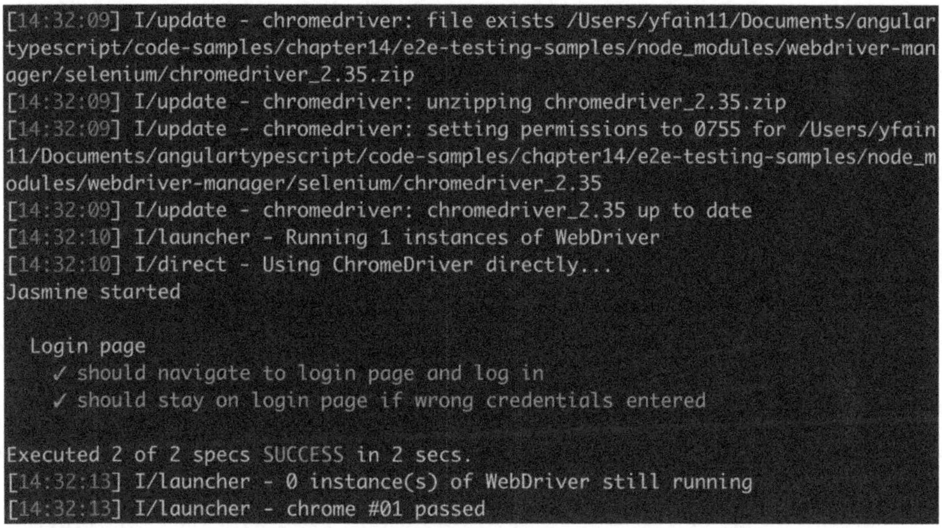

```
[14:32:09] I/update - chromedriver: file exists /Users/yfain11/Documents/angular
typescript/code-samples/chapter14/e2e-testing-samples/node_modules/webdriver-man
ager/selenium/chromedriver_2.35.zip
[14:32:09] I/update - chromedriver: unzipping chromedriver_2.35.zip
[14:32:09] I/update - chromedriver: setting permissions to 0755 for /Users/yfain
11/Documents/angulartypescript/code-samples/chapter14/e2e-testing-samples/node_m
odules/webdriver-manager/selenium/chromedriver_2.35
[14:32:09] I/update - chromedriver: chromedriver_2.35 up to date
[14:32:10] I/launcher - Running 1 instances of WebDriver
[14:32:10] I/direct - Using ChromeDriver directly...
Jasmine started

  Login page
    ✓ should navigate to login page and log in
    ✓ should stay on login page if wrong credentials entered

Executed 2 of 2 specs SUCCESS in 2 secs.
[14:32:13] I/launcher - 0 instance(s) of WebDriver still running
[14:32:13] I/launcher - chrome #01 passed
```

Figure 14.13 Running E2E tests for the login app

Both specs from your E2E test passed. If you want to see the tests fail, remove the <h1> tags in the template of the `HomeComponent` or modify the valid credentials to anything other than `Joe` and `password` in the `LoginComponent`. Changing the names of the form fields in the template of `LoginComponent` will also cause the test to fail because the WebDriver locators won't find these elements on the login page.

> **Using async and await in E2E tests**
>
> Protractor uses WebDriverJS. Its API is entirely asynchronous, and its functions return promises. All asynchronous operations (for example, `sendKey()` and `click()`) are placed in the queue of pending promises called *control-flow queue* using the WebDriver promise manager to ensure that assertions (such as `expect()` functions) run after asynchronous operations.

(continued)

Because the WebDriver promise manager doesn't execute async functions right away but places them in a queue instead, it's hard to debug this code. That's why WebDriver's promise manager is being deprecated, and you can use the `async` and `await` keywords to ensure that flow is properly synchronized (see http://mng.bz/f72u for details).

For example, the following code declares a `login()` method.

```
async login(id: string, password: string) {    // Declares that the function returns a promise
   await this.id.sendKeys(id);
   await this.pwd.sendKeys(password);
   await this.submit.click();                   // Waits for the promise to be resolved or rejected
 }
```

You can't use the `async/await` keywords with WebDriver's promise manager, so you need to turn if off by adding the following option in protractor.conf.js:

```
SELENIUM_PROMISE_MANAGER: false
```

This chapter has enough material to get you started with unit and E2E testing of Angular apps. Both Jasmine and (especially) Protractor offer more APIs that can be used in tests. For more detailed coverage, check out the book *Testing Angular Applications* (Jesse Palmer et al., Manning, 2018), with details at www.manning.com/books/testing-angular-applications.

If after getting familiar with the combination of Protractor and the Selenium ecosystem you'd like to find a simpler solution for E2E testing of your apps, take a look at the Cypress framework available at https://www.cypress.io. It's a new but very promising kid on the block. Meanwhile, let's add some Protractor E2E tests to ngAuction.

14.5 Hands-on: Adding an E2E test to ngAuction

The goal of this exercise is to add one E2E test to the ngAuction app, which you can find in the ng-auction folder in the source code that comes with this chapter. We took the ngAuction project from chapter 13 and added to it the E2E test for the product-search workflow. This test will use the price range from \$10 to \$100 to assert that matching products are retrieved from the server and rendered in the browser.

NOTE Source code for this chapter can be found at https://github.com/Farata/angulartypescript and www.manning.com/books/angular-development-with-typescript-second-edition.

Prior to running this E2E test, you need to run `npm install` in the server directory, compile the code with the `tsc` command, and start the server by running the following command:

```
node build/main
```

Now you're ready to review and run the tests located in the client directory of ngAuction.

14.5.1 E2E testing of the product-search workflow

To perform product search, a real user would need to fulfill the following steps:

1. Open the landing page of ngAuction.
2. Click the Search button in the top-left corner so the search panel will show up.
3. Enter search criteria for products.
4. Click the Search button to see the search results.
5. Browse the products that meet the search criteria.

Your E2E test will consist of two files located in the e2e directory: the page object in the search.po.ts file and the test suite in search.e2e-spec.ts. All assertions will be programmed in the search.e2e-spec.ts file, but the page object will implement the following logical steps:

1. Find the Search button and click it.
2. Fill out the search form with data.
3. Click the Search button.
4. Wait until the server returns and renders products in the browser.
5. Check to see that the browser rendered products.

To ensure that your search will return some products, your test will use a wide range of prices from $10 to $100 as the search criteria.

In several cases, you'll be checking that the browser URL is what you expect it to be, so we'll remind you how the routes are configured in the home.module.ts in ngAuction, as shown in the following listing.

Listing 14.25 Routes configuration from the home module

```
[
  {path: '', pathMatch: 'full', redirectTo: 'categories'},
  {path: 'search', component: SearchComponent},
  {path: 'categories',
    children: [
      { path: '', pathMatch: 'full', redirectTo: 'all'},
      { path: ':category', component: CategoriesComponent},
    ]
  }
]
```

Let's start by identifying the HTML elements that will participate in our test. The file app.component.html includes the markup in the following listing for the Search button.

Listing 14.26 The Search button on the toolbar

```
<button mat-icon-button
        id="search"
         class="toolbar__icon-button"
        (click)="sidenav.toggle()">
  <mat-icon>search</mat-icon>
</button>
```

The added ID simplifies the code for locating this button.

Your page object will contain the lines in the following listing to locate the button and click it.

Listing 14.27 The beginning of the `SearchPage` class

```
export class SearchPage {

  performSearch(minimalPrice: number, maximumPrice: number) {
      const searchOnToolbar = element(by.id('search'));
      searchOnToolbar.click();
     ...
  }
}
```

A method for searching products by price range

Locating the Search button

The button click to display the search form

After the button is clicked, the search form is displayed, and you locate the fields for the minimum and maximum prices and fill them with the provided prices, as shown in the following listing.

Listing 14.28 Entering the search criteria

```
const minPrice = $('input[formControlName="minPrice"]');
 const maxPrice = $('input[formControlName="maxPrice"]');
 minPrice.sendKeys(minimalPrice);
 maxPrice.sendKeys(maximumPrice);
```

Locates the form fields for prices

Fills out some of the form fields

If the user did this manually, the search form would look like figure 14.14.

Now that the search criteria is entered, you need to locate and click the form's Search button to perform the product search. If you run ngAuction and enter the min and max prices as $10 and $100, and then click the Search button, the resulting view will show the products, and the browser URL will look like this: http:// localhost:4200/ search?minPrice=10&maxPrice=100.

But it'll take a second before the HTTP request is complete and the URL changes. The real user would be patiently waiting until the search results appeared. But in your test script, if you try to assert that the URL contains the search segment right after the button click, the assertion may or may not be true depending on how fast your server responds.

Figure 14.14 The form with search criteria

You didn't need to worry about delays in login.po.ts from section 14.4.3, because no server requests were made there, and the URL changed instantaneously. This time, you want to wait until the URL changes before returning from the method `performSearch()`.

You'll use the `ExpectedConditions` class , where you can define the condition to wait for. Then, by invoking `browser.wait()`, you can wait for the expected condition to become true—otherwise, the test has to fail by timeout. The following code listing locates and clicks the Search button and then waits until the URL changes to contain the /search segment.

Listing 14.29 Clicking the form's Search button

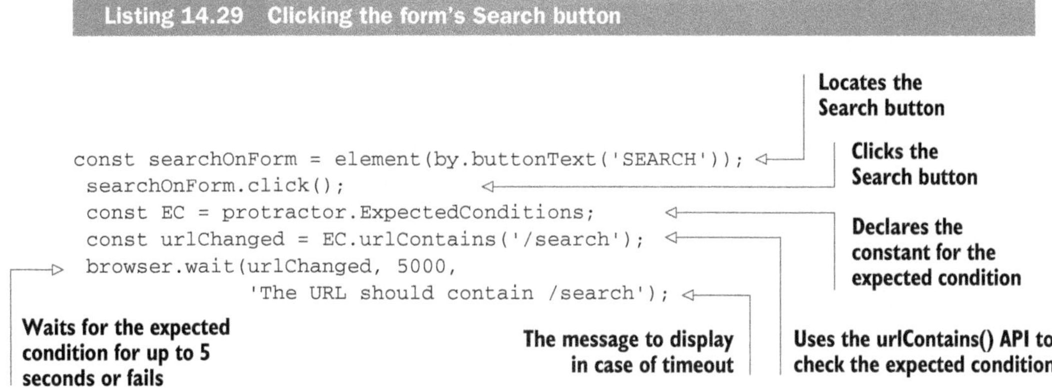

```
const searchOnForm = element(by.buttonText('SEARCH'));
 searchOnForm.click();
 const EC = protractor.ExpectedConditions;
 const urlChanged = EC.urlContains('/search');
 browser.wait(urlChanged, 5000,
              'The URL should contain /search');
```

Locates the Search button
Clicks the Search button
Declares the constant for the expected condition
Waits for the expected condition for up to 5 seconds or fails
The message to display in case of timeout
Uses the urlContains() API to check the expected condition

This code waits for up to 5 seconds, and if the URL doesn't change, it fails, printing the message shown in figure 14.15. You may need to increase the timeout value depending on how fast the product search is performed on your computer.

```
1) ngAuction search should perform the search for products that cost from $10 to $100
  - Failed: The URL should contain /search
  Wait timed out after 5001ms

Executed 1 of 1 spec (1 FAILED) in 4 secs.
```

Figure 14.15 The test fails on timeout.

If the user manually searched for products in the price range between $10 and $100, the resulting view could look like figure 14.16.

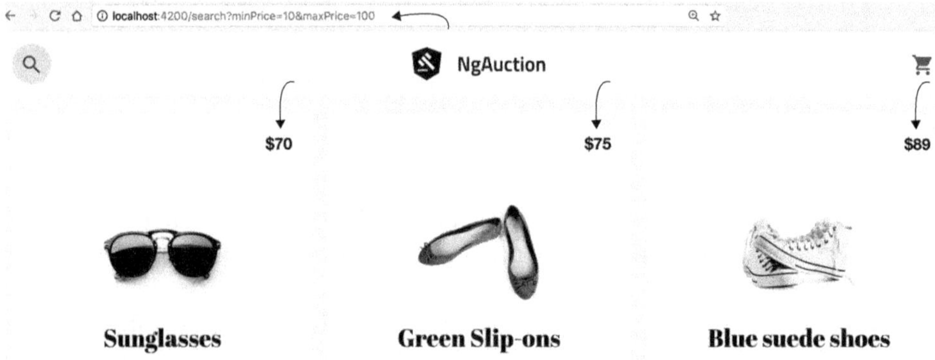

Figure 14.16 The search-result view

If the search operation initiated by the test script returns products, you extract the price of the first product, so later on (in the spec) you can assert that the product price meets the search criteria. Because the search may return a collection of products, you'll access them using the alias `$$` for the `element.all` API.

Each of the products has the `tile__price-tag` style, as shown in figure 14.17, taken from the Element tab in the Chrome Dev Tools panel while the products grid was shown. You'll use the `tile__price-tag` style to locate products.

```
▼<nga-search _nghost-c13 class="ng-star-inserted">
 ▼<div _ngcontent-c13 class="grid-list-container">
  ▼<nga-product-grid _ngcontent-c13 _nghost-c10 ng-reflect-products="[object Object],[object Object">
   ▼<mat-grid-list _ngcontent-c10 class="mat-grid-list" guttersize="16" ng-reflect-cols="3" ng-reflect-gutter-size="16"
   style="padding-bottom: calc(((4 * ((33.3333% - 10.6667px) * 1)) + 0px) + 48px);">
    ▼<div>
      <!--bindings={
        "ng-reflect-ng-for-of": "[object Object],[object Object"
      }-->
     ▼<mat-grid-tile _ngcontent-c10 class="tile mat-grid-tile ng-star-inserted" style="left: 0px; width: calc(((33.3333% -
     10.6667px) * 1) + 0px); margin-top: 0px; padding-top: calc(((33.3333% - 10.6667px) * 1) + 0px);">
      ▼<figure class="mat-figure">
       ▼<a _ngcontent-c10 class="tile__content" fxlayout="column" fxlayoutalign="center center" ng-reflect-router-link="/
       products,2" ng-reflect-layout="column" ng-reflect-align="center center" href="/products/2" style="flex-direction:
       column; box-sizing: border-box; display: flex; max-width: 100%; place-content: center; align-items: center;">
         <span _ngcontent-c10 class="tile__price-tag" ngclass.xs="tile__price-tag--xs" ng-reflect-klazz="tile__price-tag"
         ng-reflect-ng-class-xs="tile__price-tag--xs">
           $70
         </span>
```

Figure 14.17 CSS selector for the price

When the product price is extracted, you need to convert it to a number. In ngAuction, the product price is rendered as a string with the dollar sign, such as "$70" in figure 14.17. But you need its numeric representation so the spec can assert that the price falls within the specified range. The `getFirstProductPrice()` method includes the code that removes the dollar sign from the string and converts it to an integer value, as you can see in the next listing.

Listing 14.30 Getting the price of the first product

```
getFirstProductPrice() {
  return $$('span[class="tile__price-tag"]')      // Uses element.all for finding products
     .first().getText()                           // Gets the text of the first product
     .then((value) => {                           // Protractor's API returns promises, so applies then()
        return parseInt(value.replace('$', ''), 10);   // Converts the product price to a number and returns it
     });
}
```

The complete code of your page object is shown in the following listing.

Listing 14.31 search.po.ts

```
import {protractor, browser, by, element, $, $$} from 'protractor';

export class SearchPage {

  performSearch(minimalPrice: number, maximumPrice: number) {
     const searchOnToolbar = element(by.id('search'));
     searchOnToolbar.click();                      // Clicks the Search icon in the toolbar

     const minPrice = $('input[formControlName="minPrice"]');
     const maxPrice = $('input[formControlName="maxPrice"]');
     minPrice.sendKeys(minimalPrice);              // Fills out min and max prices
     maxPrice.sendKeys(maximumPrice);              // on the search form

     const searchOnForm = element(by.buttonText('SEARCH'));
     searchOnForm.click();                         // Clicks the Search button on the form
     const EC = protractor.ExpectedConditions;
     const urlChanged = EC.urlContains('/search');   // Declares an expected condition
      browser.wait(urlChanged, 5000, 'The URL should contain "/search"');   // Waits for the expected condition for up to 5 seconds
  }

   navigateToLandingPage() {                       // Declares a method for navigating to the landing page
     return browser.get('/');
  }

  getFirstProductPrice() {
    return $$('span[class="tile__price-tag"]')      // Locates all price elements
       .first().getText()                           // Singles out the first product price
       .then((value) => {return parseInt(value.replace('$', ''), 10);});   // Converts the price into a number
  }
}
```

Now let's review the code of the test suite located in the search.e2e-spec.ts file.

The test suite for the search workflow contains one spec, which uses the page object and adds assertions to each step of the workflow. The spec starts by navigating to the landing page of ngAuction and then asserts that the URL of the page contains the segment /categories/all.

Then the spec performs the test by invoking the `performSearch()` method on the page object, passing `10` and `100` as a price range for the search. After this method completes, it performs three assertions to check that the URL of the resulting page contains the segment /search?minPrice=10&maxPrice=100 and the price of the first product is greater than $10 and less than $100. The code of this test suite is shown in the following listing.

Listing 14.32 search.e2e-spec.ts

```
import {SearchPage} from './search.po';
import {browser} from 'protractor';

describe('ngAuction search', () => {
  let searchPage: SearchPage;

  beforeEach(() => {
    searchPage = new SearchPage();          // Instantiates the page object
  });

  it('should perform the search for products that cost from $10 to $100',  ()
      => {
    searchPage.navigateToLandingPage();
    let url =  browser.getCurrentUrl();
    expect(url).toContain('/categories/all');     // Asserts the URL of the landing page

    searchPage.performSearch(10, 100);          // Searches for products
     url =  browser.getCurrentUrl();
    expect(url).toContain('/search?minPrice=10&maxPrice=100');   // Asserts the URL of the page with the search results

    const firstProductPrice = searchPage.getFirstProductPrice();   // Gets the price of the first product
     expect(firstProductPrice).toBeGreaterThan(10);   // Asserts that the price is greater than 10
     expect(firstProductPrice).toBeLessThan(100);     // Asserts that the price is less than 100
   });
});
```

In the Terminal window, switch to the client directory, run `npm install`, and run the test with the `ng e2e` command. The test will successfully complete, and you'll see the message shown in figure 14.18.

```
  ngAuction search
    ✓ should perform the search for products that cost from $10 to $100

Executed 1 of 1 spec SUCCESS in 2 secs.
```

Figure 14.18 The product-search test succeeded.

To make the test fail, modify the spec to test the case when no products are returned by using a price range between $1 and $5,000,000. Your ngAuction isn't created for Sotheby's, and you don't carry expensive items.

Summary

- Unit tests run quickly, but most application business logic should be tested with E2E tests.
- While you're writing tests, make them fail to see that their failure report is easy to understand.
- Running unit tests should be part of your automated build process, but E2E tests shouldn't.

15 Maintaining app state with ngrx

This chapter covers

- A brief introduction to the Redux data flow
- Maintaining your app state using the ngrx library
- Exploring another implementation of the Mediator design pattern
- Implementing state management in ngAuction with ngrx

You've made it to the last chapter, and you're almost ready to join an Angular project. The previous chapter was easy reading, but this chapter will require your full attention; the material we're about to present has many moving parts, and you'll need to have a good understanding of how they play together.

ngrx is a library that can be used for managing state in Angular apps (see https://github.com/ngrx). It's built using the principles of Redux (another popular library for managing state), but the notification layer is implemented using RxJS. Although Angular has other means for managing app state, ngrx is gaining traction in mid- and large-size apps.

Is it worth using the ngrx library for managing state in your app? It certainly has benefits, but they don't come free. The complexity of your app can increase, and the code will become more difficult to understand by any new person who joins the project. In this chapter, we cover the ngrx library so you'll be able to decide whether it's the right choice for managing the state of your app. In the hands-on section, we do a detailed code overview of yet another version of ngAuction that uses ngrx for state management.

15.1 From a convenience store to Redux architecture

Imagine that you're a proud owner of a convenience store that sells various products. Remember how you started? You rented an empty place (the store was in its *initial state*). Then you purchased shelves and ordered products. After that, multiple vendors started delivering those products. You hired employees who arranged these products on the shelves in a certain order, changing the state of the store. Then you put out the Grand Opening sign and festooned the place with lots of colorful balloons. Customers started visiting your store to buy products.

When the store is open, some products lay on the shelves, and some are in shopping carts of customers. Some customers are waiting in lines at cash registers, where there are store employees. You can say that at any given moment, your store has the *current state.*

If a customer takes an *action*, such as buying five bottles of water, the cashier scans the barcode, and this *reduces* the number of bottles in the inventory—it updates the state. If a vendor delivers new products, your clerk updates the inventory (state) accordingly.

Your web app can also maintain a store that holds the state of your app. Like a real store, at any given time your app's *store* has a current *state.* Some data collections have specific data retrieved from the server and possibly modified by a user. Some radio buttons are checked, and a user selects some products and navigates to some routes represented by a specific URL.

If a user interacts with the UI, or the server sends new data, these *actions* should ask the store object to update the state. To keep track of state changes, the current state object is never updated, but a new instance of the state object is created.

15.1.1 What's Redux?

Redux is an open source JavaScript library that offers a state container for JavaScript apps (see http://mng.bz/005X). It was created at Facebook as an implementation of the Flux architecture (see http://mng.bz/jrXy). Initially, the developers working with the React framework made Redux popular, but as it's a JavaScript library, it can be used in any JavaScript app.

Redux is based on the following three principles:

- *There's a single source of truth.* There's a single store where your app contains the state that can be represented by an object tree.

- *State is read-only.* When an action is emitted, the reducer function doesn't update but clones the current state and updates the cloned object based on the action.
- *State changes are made with pure functions.* You write the reducer function(s) that take an action and the current state object and return a new state.

In Redux, the data flow is unidirectional:

1. The app component dispatches the action on the store.
2. The reducer (a pure function) takes the current state object and then clones, updates, and returns it.
3. The app component subscribes to the store, receives the new state object, and updates the UI accordingly.

Figure 15.1 shows the unidirectional Redux data flow.

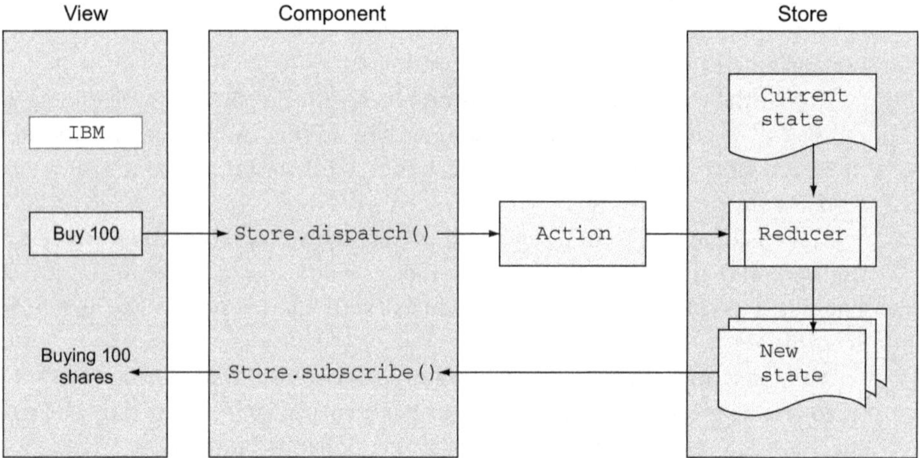

Figure 15.1 The Redux data flow

An *action* is a JavaScript object that has a `type` property describing what happens in your app, such as a user wants to buy IBM stock. Besides the `type` property, an action object can optionally have another property with a payload of data that should change the app state in some fashion. An example is shown in the following listing.

Listing 15.1 An action to buy IBM stock

```
{
  type: 'BUY_STOCK',                                   // The type of action
   stock: {symbol: 'IBM', quantity: 100}               // The action payload
 }
```

This object only describes the action and provides the payload. It doesn't know how the state should be changed. Who does? The reducer.

A *reducer* is a *pure function* that specifies how the state should be changed. The reducer never changes the current state, but creates a new (and updated) version of it. The state object is immutable. The reducer creates a copy of the state object and returns a new reference to it. From an Angular perspective, it's a binding change event, and all interested parties will immediately know that the state has changed without requiring expensive value checking in the entire state tree.

> **NOTE** Your state object can contain dozens of properties and nested objects. Cloning the state object creates a shallow copy without copying each unmodified state property in memory, so memory consumption is minimal and it doesn't take much time. You can read about the rationale for creating shallow state copies at http://mng.bz/3271.

A reducer function has the signature shown in the following listing.

Listing 15.2 A reducer signature

```
function (previousState, action): State {...}
```

A reducer function returns a new state.

Should the reducer function implement app functionality like placing an order, which requires work with external services? No, because reducers are meant for updating and returning the app state—for example, the stock to buy is `"IBM"`. Implementing app logic would require interaction with the environment external to the reducer; it would cause *side effects*, and pure functions can't have side effects.

The reducer can implement minimal app logic related to state change. For example, suppose a user decides to cancel an order, which requires a reset of certain fields on the state object. The main app logic remains in your application code (for example, in services) unless a concrete implementation of the Redux-inspired library offers a special place meant for code with side effects. In this chapter, we use the ngrx library, which suggests using Angular services combined with so-called *effects* that live outside of the store and that can aggregate Angular services working as a bridge between the store and services.

15.1.2 Why storing app state in a single place is important

Recently, one of the authors of this book worked on a web project for a large car manufacturer. This was a web app that allowed a prospective buyer to configure a car by selecting from more than a thousand packages and options (such as model, interior and exterior colors, length of chassis, and so on). The app was developed over many years. The software modules were written using JavaScript, jQuery, Angular, React, and Handlebars, as well as the HTML templating engine Thymeleaf on the server.

From a user perspective, this was one workflow that consisted of several steps resulting in configuring and pricing the car based on selected options. But internally, the process was switching from one module to another, and each module needed to know what was selected in the previous step to show the available options.

In other words, each module needed to know the current state of the app. Depending on the software used in any particular module, the current user selections were stored using one of the following:

- URL parameters
- HTML `data*` attributes
- The browser's local and session storage
- Angular services
- The React store

New requirements came in, new JIRA tickets were created and assigned, and implementation would begin. Time and time again, implementing a seemingly simple new requirement would turn into a time-consuming and expensive task. Good luck explaining to the manager why showing the price in page B would take a half day even though this price was already known in page A, or that the state object used in page B didn't expect to have the price property, and if in page A the price was a part of the URL, page B expected to get the current state from local storage. Rewriting it from scratch was not an option. It would have been so much easier if app state had been implemented in a uniform way and stored in a single place!

TIP If you're starting to develop a new project, pay special attention on how app state is implemented, and it will help you greatly in the long run.

15.2 Introducing ngrx

ngrx is a library inspired by Redux. You can think of it as an implementation of the Redux pattern for managing app state in Angular apps. Similarly to Redux, it implements a unidirectional data flow and has a store, actions, and reducers. It also uses RxJS's ability to send notifications and subscribe to them.

Large enterprise apps often implement messaging architecture on the server side, where one piece of software sends a message to another via some messaging server or a message bus. You can think of ngrx as a client-side messaging system. The user clicks a button, and the app sends a message (for example, dispatches an action). The app state changed because of this button click, and the ngrx `Store` sends a message to the subscriber(s), emitting the next value into an observable stream.

In section 15.1, we described three Redux principles:

- A single source of truth.
- State is read-only.
- State changes are made with pure functions.

In ngrx, app state is accessed with the `Store` service, which is an observable of state and an observer of actions. The declaration of the class `Store` in the store.d.ts file looks like this:

```
class Store<T> extends Observable<T> implements Observer<Action>
```

Besides declaring a new principle, the ngrx architecture includes *effects*, which are meant for the code that communicates with other parts of the app, such as making HTTP requests. With ngrx selectors, you can subscribe to changes in a particular branch of the state object. There's also support for routing and collections of entities, which can be useful in CRUD operations.

We'll start our ngrx introduction with its main players: a store, actions, and reducers.

15.2.1 Getting familiar with a store, actions, and reducers

Let's see how to use ngrx in a simple app that has two buttons that can either increment or decrement the value of the counter. The first version of this app doesn't manage state and looks like the following listing.

Listing 15.3 The counter app without ngrx

```
import {Component} from '@angular/core';

@Component({
  selector: 'app-root',
  template: `
     <button (click)="increment()">Increment</button>
     <button (click)="decrement()">Decrement</button>
     <p>The counter: {{counter}}</p>          ⇽ Shows the counter value
    `
})
export class AppComponent {
  counter = 0;

  increment() {
    this.counter++;          ⇽ Increments the counter
  }

  decrement() {
    this.counter--;          ⇽ Decrements the counter
  }
}
```

You want to change this app so that the ngrx store manages the state of the `counter` variable, but first you need to install the ngrx store in your project:

```
npm i @ngrx/store
```

The `Store` serves as a container of the state, and dispatching actions is the only way to update the state. The plan is to instantiate the `Store` object and remove the app logic (incrementing and decrementing the counter) from the component. Your `decrement()` and `increment()` methods will be dispatching actions on the `Store` instead.

Actions are handled by the ngrx reducer, which will update the state of the counter. The type of your `counter` variable will change from `number` to `Observable`, and to get and render its emitted values in the UI, you'll subscribe to the `Store`.

The only required property in the `Action` object is `type`, and for your app, you'll declare the action types as follows:

```
const INCREMENT = 'INCREMENT';
const DECREMENT = 'DECREMENT';
```

The next step is to create a reducer function for each piece of data you want to keep in the store. In your case, it's just the value of the counter, so you'll create a reducer with the `switch` statement for updating state based on the received action type, as shown in the following listing. Remember, the reducer function takes two arguments: state and action.

Listing 15.4 reducer.ts

```
import { Action } from '@ngrx/store';

export const INCREMENT = 'INCREMENT';
export const DECREMENT = 'DECREMENT';

export function counterReducer(state = 0, action: Action) {   // The initial value of the counter (state) is zero.
     switch (action.type) {        // Checks the action type
         case INCREMENT:
            return state + 1;      // Updates state by incrementing the counter

        case DECREMENT:
            return state - 1;      // Updates state by decrementing the counter

        default:
            return state;          // Returns the existing state if an unknown action is provided
     }
}
```

It's important to note that the reducer function doesn't modify the provided state, but returns a new value. The state remains immutable.

Now you need to inform the root module that you're going to use the `counterReducer()` function as a reducer for your store, as shown in the following listing.

Listing 15.5 app.module.ts

```
import {BrowserModule} from '@angular/platform-browser';
import {NgModule} from '@angular/core';
import {AppComponent} from './app.component';
import {counterReducer} from "./reducer";
import {StoreModule} from "@ngrx/store";

@NgModule({
  declarations: [
    AppComponent
  ],
  imports: [
    BrowserModule,
    StoreModule.forRoot({counterState: counterReducer})   // Lets the store know about the reducer for the app
   ],
  providers: [],
  bootstrap: [AppComponent]
})
export class AppModule {}
```

In this code, you configure the app-level store to provide the object that specifies `counterReducer` as the name of the reducer function, and `counterState` as the property where this reducer should keep the state.

Finally, you need to change the code of your component to dispatch either the action of type `INCREMENT` or `DECREMENT`, depending on which button a user clicks. You'll also inject the `Store` into your component and subscribe to its observable that will emit a value each time the counter changes, as shown in the following listing.

Listing 15.6 app.component.ts

```
import {Component} from '@angular/core';
import {Observable} from "rxjs";
import {select, Store} from "@ngrx/store";
import {INCREMENT, DECREMENT} from "./reducer";

@Component({
  selector: 'app-root',
  template: `
     <button (click)="increment()">Increment</button>
     <button (click)="decrement()">Decrement</button>
     <p>The counter: {{counter$ | async}}</p>          <-- Subscribes to the observable with the async pipe
  `
})
export class AppComponent {
  counter$: Observable<number>;                        <-- Declares the reference variable for the store observable

  constructor(private store: Store<any>) {
    this.counter$ = store.select('counterState');      <-- select() emits changes in the counterState.
  }

  increment() {
    this.store.dispatch({type: INCREMENT});            <-- Dispatches the INCREMENT action
  }

  decrement() {
    this.store.dispatch({type: DECREMENT});            <-- Dispatches the DECREMENT action
  }
}
```

Note that an action is an object (for example, `{type: INCREMENT}`), and in this app, action objects have no payload. You can also think of an action as a message or a command. In the next section, you'll be defining each action as a class with two properties: type and payload.

In this component, you use the `select` operator (defined in the ngrx `Store`), which allows you to observe the state object. The name of its argument must match the name of the state object property used in the `StoreModule.forRoot()` function .

NOTE The `counterReducer` was assigned to the store by invoking the method `StoreModule.forRoot({counterState: counterReducer})` in the module. The `AppComponent` communicated with the `counterReducer` either by dispatching an action on the store or by using the `select` operator on the store.

The app with the ngrx store will have the same behavior as the original one and will increment and decrement the counter depending on the user's action.

Now let's check whether your store is really a single source of truth. You'll add a child component in the next listing that will display the current value of the counter received from the store, and 10 seconds after app launch, the child will dispatch the INCREMENT action.

Listing 15.7 child.component.ts

```
import {Component} from '@angular/core';
import {select, Store} from "@ngrx/store";
import {Observable} from "rxjs";
import {INCREMENT} from "../reducer";

@Component({
  selector: 'app-child',
  template: `
    <h3> Child component </h3>
    <p>
      The counter in child is {{childCounter$ | async}}
    </p>
  `,
  styles: []
})
export class ChildComponent {

    childCounter$: Observable<number>;

    constructor(private store: Store<any>) {            // Injects the store
         this.childCounter$ = store.pipe(select('counterState'));   // Subscribes to the store

        setTimeout(() => this.store.dispatch({type: INCREMENT}),   // In 10 seconds, dispatches the INCREMENT action
             10000);
    }
}
```

The only thing left is adding the <app-child> tag to the template of AppComponent. Figure 15.2 shows the app after the user clicks the Increment button three times. Both parent and child components show the same value of the counter taken from the store (single source of truth). Ten seconds after the app starts, the ChildComponent dispatches the INCREMENT action, and both components will show the incremented counter.

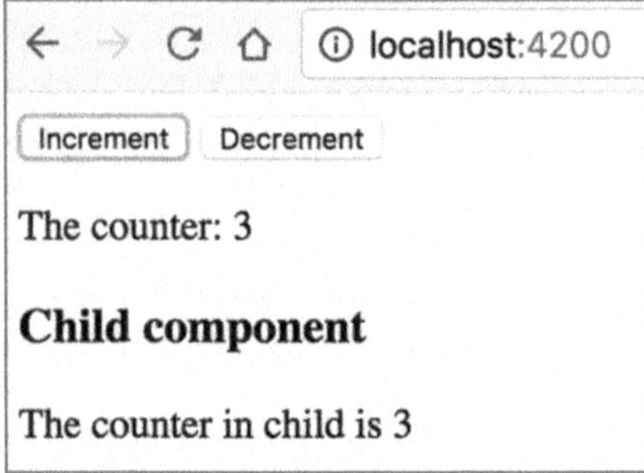

Figure 15.2 Running the counter app

To see this app in action, open the project counter, run `npm install`, and then run `ng serve -o`.

NOTE The ngrx library includes the example app (see http://mng.bz/7F9x), which allows you to maintain a book collection using Google Books API. The ngAuction app that comes with this chapter can also serve as an ngrx demo, although neither of these apps uses every API offered by ngrx.

The counter app is a pretty basic example, with a single reducer function. In practice, a store may have several reducers where each of them would be responsible for a portion of the state object. In the hands-on section, the new version of ngAuction will have several reducers.

Eliminating the need for event bubbling

Here's a diagram you saw in chapter 8 in section 8.3.1.

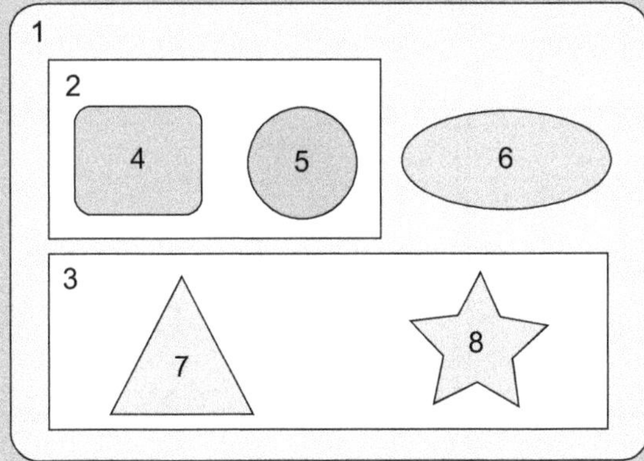

A view consists of components

Say component 7 can emit some data that's needed in component 6. If you use the common parents for intercomponent communication, you need to emit an event via the `@Output` property of component 7; parent component 3 would subscribe to this event and reemit it through its `@Output` property; and component 1 would subscribe to this event and, via binding, pass the payload to component 6.

Using the ngrx store eliminates the need to program this series of unfortunate events. Component 7 emits an action of the store, and component 6 uses a selector to receive it. The same, simple model of intercomponent communication works regardless of how many levels of component nesting exist in any particular view. The only thing that both components 7 and 6 need is the reference to the store object.

This figure doesn't give any details about what these eight components do, but you can assume that 1, 2, and 3 are *container components*, which include other components and implement app logic for interacting with their children, parents, and services. The rest are *presentational components* that can get data in, send data out, and present data on the UI. Some authors suggest that only container components should manage state and communicate with the store. We don't agree with this, because state is not only about storing and sharing data—it's also about storing the state of the UI, which is a part of any type of component.

In the counter example, the store managed app state represented by a number, but did you notice the store played yet another role? In section 8.3.2 in chapter 8, we showed you how an injectable service can play the role of mediator. In the counter app, the main goal of the ngrx store is to manage app state, but it also plays another role: serving as a mediator between parent and child components.

In chapter 8, the mediator was a service with an RxJS `BehaviorSubject`, and you used components for sending and receiving data. With ngrx, you don't need to manually create `BehaviorSubject`, because the `Store` object can be used for emitting values as well as subscribing to them.

To notify `BehaviorSubject` about the new value, you use `next()`, and to notify the store about the new state, you use `dispatch()`. To get the new state, subscribe to the observable in both cases. Figure 15.3 compares the code of `EbayComponent` from listing 8.13 in chapter 8 (on the left) with `ChildComponent` that uses ngrx (on the right). They look similar, don't they?

```
@Component({
  selector: 'product',
  template: `<div>
              <h2 >eBay component</h2>
              Search criteria: {{searchFor$ | async}}
              </div>`
})
export class EbayComponent {

  searchFor$: Observable<string>;

  constructor(private state: StateService) {

      this.searchFor$ = state.getState();
  }
}
```

```
@Component({
  selector: 'app-child',
  template: `
    <h3> Child component </h3>
    <p>The counter in child is {{childCounter$ | async}}
    </p>`
})
export class ChildComponent {

  childCounter$: Observable<number>;

  constructor(private store: Store<any>) {

      this.childCounter$ = store.pipe(select('counterState'));
  }
}
```

Figure 15.3 `EbayComponent` compared to `ChildComponent`

We can say that the `StateService` (left) and the `Store` (right) each serve as a single source of truth. But large non-ngrx apps with multiple injectable services that store different slices of state would have multiple sources of truth. In ngrx apps, the `Store` service always remains a single source of truth, which may have multiple slices of state.

Now take another look at the reducer in listing 15.4, which was a pure function that didn't need to use any external resource to update the state. What if the value for a counter was provided by a server? The reducer can use external resources because it would make the reducer *impure*, wouldn't it? This is where ngrx effects come in, and we'll discuss them next.

15.2.2 Getting familiar with effects and selectors

Reducers are *pure functions* that perform simple operations: take the state and action and create a new state. But you need to implement business logic somewhere, such as reaching out to services, making requests to servers, and so on. You need to implement *functions with side effects*, which is done in effect classes.

Effects are injectable classes that live outside of the store and are used for implementing functionality that has side effects, without breaking unidirectional data flow. ngrx effects come in a separate package, and you need to run the following command to add them to your project:

```
npm i @ngrx/effects
```

If a component dispatches an action that requires communication with external resources, the action can be picked up by the `Effects` object, which will handle this action and dispatch another one on the reducer. For example, an effect can receive a `LOAD_PRODUCTS` action from the store, invoke `loadProducts ()`, and, when the data is loaded, dispatch either of the `LOAD_PRODUCTS_SUCCESS` or `LOAD_PRODUCTS_FAILURE` actions. The reducer will pick it up and update state accordingly. Figure 15.4 shows the ngrx flow that uses effects.

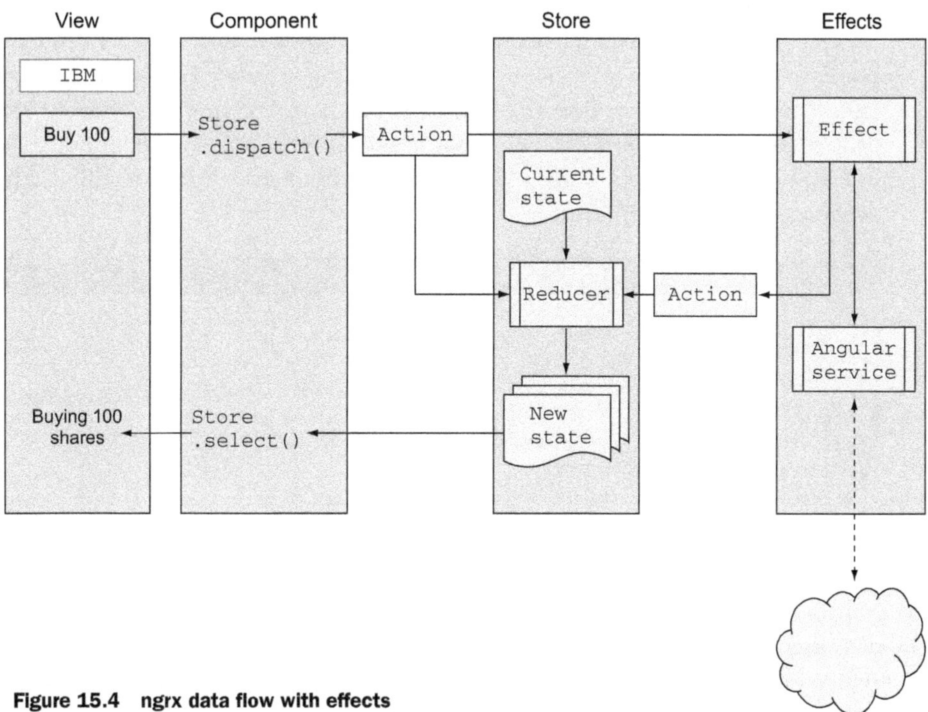

Figure 15.4 ngrx data flow with effects

To understand this diagram, imagine that a user clicks the Buy 100 button. The component would dispatch an action on the store, which can be handled by a reducer, an effect, or both. An effect can access external services and dispatch another action. In any case, a reducer is ultimately responsible for creating a new state, and a component can get it using a selector and update the UI accordingly (such as by rendering the message "Buying 100 shares").

NOTE We'd like to stress that even though actions can be handled in both a reducer and an effect, only a reducer can change the state of an app.

If you compare the Redux and ngrx data flows shown in figures 15.4 and 15.1 respectively, you'll notice that the effects live outside the store. They can communicate with other Angular services, which in turn can communicate with external servers, if need be. Another difference in figure 15.1 is that the view would use `subscribe()` to receive the latest state; 15.4 shows the `select()` method that can use a selector function to retrieve either the entire state object or its part.

In both Redux and ngrx, a component dispatches actions on the store. Redux actions are handled only in reducers, but in ngrx, some actions are handled in reducers, some in effects, and some in both. For example, if a component dispatches `LOAD_PRODUCTS`, a reducer can pick it up to set the state property `loading` to true, which will result in displaying a progress indicator. An effect can receive the same `LOAD_PRODUCTS` action and make an HTTP request for products.

You know that to dispatch an action that should be handled by the reducer, a component invokes `Store.dispatch()`, but how can an effect dispatch an action? An effect returns an observable that wraps some payload. In your effects class, you'll declare one or more class variables annotated with the `@Effect` decorator. Each effect will apply the `ofType` operator to ensure that it reacts to only the specified action type, as shown in the following listing.

Listing 15.8 A fragment of a class with effects

```
@Injectable()
export class MyEffects {
...
@Effect()
loadProducts$ = this.actions$
.pipe(ofType(LOAD_PRODUCTS),
.switchMap(this.productService.getProducts()))
...
}
```

In this example, the `@Effect` decorator marks the observable property `loadProducts$` as a handler for the actions of type `LOAD_PRODUCTS` and invokes `getProducts()`, which returns an `Observable`. Then, based on the emitted value, the effect will dispatch another action (for example, success or failure). You'll see how to do this in the next section. In general, you can think of an effect as middleware between the original action and the reducer, as shown in figure 15.5.

In your app module class, you need to add to the `@NgModule` decorator `EffectsModule.forRoot()` for the root module, or `EffectsModule.forFeature()` for a feature module.

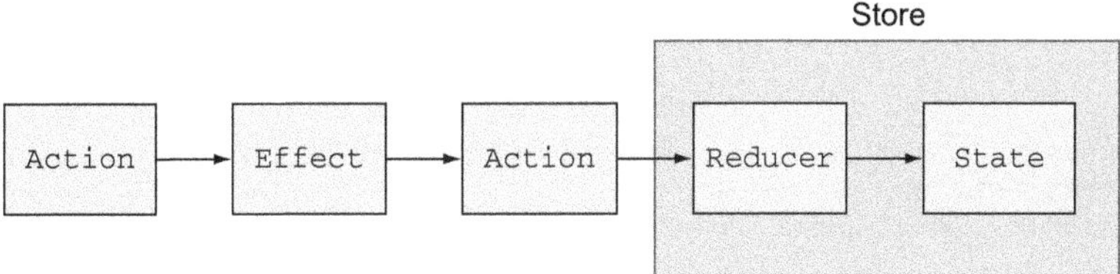

Figure 15.5 Effects in the data flow

We don't want to overwhelm you with the theory behind ngrx, so let's continue developing an app that uses an ngrx store, actions with payloads, reducers, effects, and selectors.

15.2.3 *Refactoring the mediator app with ngrx*

In this section, you'll refactor the app created in section 8.3.2 in chapter 8. That app had a search field and two links, eBay and Amazon. You'll refactor it by replacing the `SearchService` injectable that was maintaining app state with an ngrx store. To illustrate communication between effects and services, you'll add `ProductService`, which will generate the search results: the products containing the entered search criterion in their names.

The new version of the app is located in the mediator folder. It will use the following ngrx building blocks:

- A store for storing and retrieving app state, search query, and results
- A reducer for handing actions of type `SEARCH` and `SEARCH_SUCCESS`
- Effects for handling actions of type `SEARCH` and `SEARCH_SUCCESS`
- Selectors for retrieving the entire state object, search query, or search results

Figure 15.6 The results of an `aaa` search on eBay

Figure 15.6 shows the mediator app after a user enters `aaa` in the search field of the `SearchComponent`.

THE STORE STATE

The state object of this app will contain two properties: search query (for example, `aaa`) and search results (for example, five products). You'll declare the type in the following listing to represent the state of your app.

Listing 15.9 The state of the mediator app

```
export interface State {
  searchQuery: string;          <- Payload of the SEARCH action dispatched by SearchComponent
   searchResults: string[];     <- Payload of SEARCH_SUCCESS dispatched by the effect after invoking ProductService.getProducts()
 }
```

ACTIONS

In the counter app, actions don't contain payloads; they increment or decrement the counter. This time it's different. The `SEARCH` action can have a payload (such as `aaa`), and `SEARCH_SUCCESS` can have a payload as well (such as five products). That's why declaring constants representing the action type isn't enough, and you'll wrap each action into a class with a constructor that has a payload as an argument. The actions will be declared in the file actions.ts, shown in the following listing.

Listing 15.10 actions.ts

```
import {Action} from '@ngrx/store';

export const SEARCH = '[Product] search';                           // Declares action types
 export const SEARCH_SUCCESS = '[Product] search success';

export class SearchAction implements Action {       <- The class representing the search action with a payload
   readonly type = SEARCH;

  constructor(public payload: {searchQuery: string}) {}
}

export class SearchSuccessAction implements Action {     <- The class representing the search-success action with a payload
   readonly type = SEARCH_SUCCESS;

  constructor(public payload: {searchResults: string[]}) {}
}

export type SearchActions = SearchAction | SearchSuccessAction;    <- Declares the union SearchAction type
```

Note the text `[Product]` in the action definitions. In real-world apps, you may have more than one `SEARCH` action—one for products, one for orders, and so on. By prepending the action description with `[Product]`, you create a namespace to make the code more readable. Having namespaced actions helps in understanding which actions were dispatched at any given moment.

The last line of actions.ts uses the TypeScript union operator described in section B.11 in appendix B. Here, you define the `SearchActions` type that will be used in the reducer's signature, so the TypeScript compiler knows which actions are allowed in the reducer's `switch` statement.

THE SEARCHCOMPONENT AS ACTION CREATOR

The actions are declared, but someone has to create and dispatch them. In your app, the `SearchComponent` shown in the following listing will be creating and dispatching the action of type `SEARCH` after the user enters the search criterion.

Listing 15.11 search.component.ts

```
@Component({
  selector: 'app-search',
  template: `
    <h2>Search component</h2>
    <input type="text" placeholder="Enter product"
                 [formControl]="searchInput">`,
  styles: ['.main {background: yellow}']
})
export class SearchComponent {

  searchInput: FormControl;

  constructor(private store: Store<any>) {
    this.searchInput = new FormControl('');

    this.searchInput.valueChanges                    // Subscribes to the form control's observable
      .pipe(debounceTime(300),
            tap(value => console.log(`The user entered ${value}`)))
      .subscribe(searchValue => {
          this.store.dispatch(new SearchAction({ searchQuery: searchValue }))   // Instantiates and dispatches an action of type SEARCH with the payload
    });
  }
}
```

The dispatched action will be picked up by the reducer, which will update the `searchQuery` property on the state object.

> **NOTE** We'll talk about another action creator, the `SearchEffects` class, later in this section.

THE REDUCER

In the reducer shown in listing 15.12, you declare the interface describing the structure of your app state and create an object that represents an initial state. The `reducer()` function will take the initial or current immutable state and, using a `switch` statement, will create and return a new state based on the action type.

Listing 15.12 reducers.ts

```
import {SearchActions, SEARCH, SEARCH_SUCCESS} from './actions';

export interface State {          // Declares the structure of the state object
   searchQuery: string;
  searchResults: string[];
}

const initialState: State = {     // Creates an object representing the initial state
```

```
    searchQuery: '',
    searchResults: []
};

export function reducer(state = initialState, action: SearchActions): State {
  switch (action.type) {
    case SEARCH: {
      return {
        ...state,
        searchQuery: action.payload.searchQuery,
        searchResults: []
      }
    }

    case SEARCH_SUCCESS: {
      return {
        ...state,
        searchResults: action.payload.searchResults
      }
    }

    default: {
      return state;
    }
  }
}
```

This action is dispatched by the component.

Copies the existing state values into the new state object

Updates two state properties with the new values

This action will be dispatched by the effect.

Copies the existing state values into the new state object

Updates one state property with the new value

Returns the current state if an unexpected action was dispatched

TIP If, in a case clause, you use the action type that wasn't declared in the union type `SearchActions` (for example, `SEARCH22`), the TypeScript compiler returns an error.

The more precise name for TypeScript union types is *discriminated unions*. If all the types in a union have a common type property, the TypeScript compiler can discriminate types by this property. It knows which particular type from the union was referred to within the `case` statement and suggests the correct type for the payload property.

For cloning the state object and updating some of its properties, you use the spread operator described in section A.7 in appendix A. Note that state properties will be updated with the value of the action payload.

EFFECTS

In this app, you'll have one effect that will use a `ProductService` injectable to obtain products. To simplify the explanation, you don't load products from an external server or file. Your `ProductService`, shown in the following listing, will generate and return an observable of five products. It uses the RxJS `delay` operator to emulate a one-second delay as if the products are coming from a remote computer.

Listing 15.13 product.service.ts

```
@Injectable()
export class ProductService {

  static counter = 0;
```

The counter concatenated to the search query is a product name.

```
  getProducts(searchQuery: string): Observable<string[]> {

    const productGenerator = () =>
                    `Product ${searchQuery}${ProductService.counter++}`;
     const products = Array.from({length: 5}, productGenerator);

    return Observable.of(products).pipe(delay(1000));
  }
}
```

A function to generate a product name

Returns the observable of products after a one-second delay

Creates a five-element array using productGenerator()

Your SearchEffects class will declare one effect, loadProducts$, that will dispatch the SEARCH_RESULTS effect having an array of products as its payload. You want to ensure that this effect will obtain products only if the store dispatched the SEARCH effect, so you use the ngrx operator ofType(SEARCH).

This effect extracts the payload of the action of type SEARCH (the search query) emitted by the actions$ observable, and, using switchMap, will pass it over to the inner observable (the getProducts() method). Finally, the effect will dispatch the action of type SEARCH_RESULTS with the payload, all of which you can see in the following listing.

Listing 15.14 effects.ts

```
@Injectable()
export class SearchEffects {

  @Effect()
  loadProducts$ = this.actions$
     .ofType(SEARCH)
     .pipe(
      map((action: SearchAction) => action.payload),
       switchMap(({searchQuery})
                    => this.productService.getProducts(searchQuery)),
       map(searchResults => new SearchSuccessAction({searchResults}))
     );

  constructor(private actions$: Actions,
              private productService: ProductService) {}
}
```

Initializes the loadProducts$ effect with the stream/ observable

Executes a search only if the store dispatched the SEARCH action

Extracts the payload from the action of type SEARCH

Obtains the product based on the specified search query

Dispatches the action of type SEARCH_SUCCESS with its payload

Injects the ngrx Actions observable

Injects the ProductService

In this example, you assume that getProducts() will always emit products, but you could add the catchError() function to the observer, where you'd emit the action that reports an error. You'll see the use of catchError() in listing 15.31.

TIP Although it's okay to abandon unwanted results with `switchMap` while reading data, if you write an effect that performs the add, update, or delete operations, use `concatMap` instead. This will prevent possible race conditions when one request is in the middle of updating a record and another one comes in. With `concatMap`, all requests will arrive at the service one after another.

In some cases, you may want to create an effect that handles an action but doesn't need to dispatch another one. For example, you may want to create an effect that merely logs the action. In such cases, you need to pass a `{dispatch: false}` object to the `@Effect` decorator:

```
@Effect({ dispatch: false })
logAction$ = this.actions$
    .pipe(
      tap( action => console.log(action))
    );
```

SELECTORS

In real-world apps, the state object can be represented by a tree of nested properties, and you may want to obtain specific slices of the store state rather than obtain the entire state object and manually traverse its content. Let's see how app components can get the value of a specific state property by using selectors.

First, get the selector of the top-level feature state using the `createFeatureSelector()` method . Then, use this selector as a starting point for other more specific selectors using the `createSelector()` method , which returns a callback function for selecting a slice of state. The selectors of your app are declared in the file selectors.ts.

Listing 15.15 selectors.ts

```
import {createFeatureSelector, createSelector} from '@ngrx/store';
import {State} from './reducers';

export const getState = createFeatureSelector<State>('myReducer');
export const getSearchQuery = createSelector(getState,
                              state => state.searchQuery);
export const getSearchResults = createSelector(getState,
                              state => state.searchResults);
```

- Creates a top-level selector of the top-level state
- Creates a selector for the state property searchQuery
- Creates a selector for the state property searchResults

The argument of the `createFeatureSelector()` method is the name of the reducer specified in the module. In the `@NgModule` decorator, you'll have the following line:

```
StoreModule.forRoot({myReducer: reducer})
```

That's why, to obtain the reference to this reducer, you write `createFeatureSelector('myReducer');`.

Let's recap what you've accomplished so far:

1. You declared classes to represent the actions of types `SEARCH` and `SEARCH_RESULTS`.
2. The `SearchComponent` can dispatch the action of type `SEARCH`.
3. The reducer can handle both action types.
4. You declared the effect that can obtain products and dispatch the action of type `SEARCH_RESULTS`.
5. You declared selectors to obtain slices of the app state.

To close the loop, you'll use the selectors in eBay and Amazon components to render the search criterion and the retrieved products. The following listing shows only the code of the `EbayComponent` (the code of the `AmazonComponent` looks identical).

Listing 15.16 ebay.component.ts

```
@Component({
  selector: 'app-ebay',
  template: `
    <div class="ebay">
      <h2>eBay component</h2>
      Search criteria: {{searchFor$ | async}}          ◁ Subscribes to the observable that emits the search criteria and renders it

      <ul>
        <li *ngFor="let p of searchResults$ | async ">{{ p }}</li>          ◁ Subscribes to the observable that emits products and renders them
       </ul>
    </div>`,
  styles: ['.ebay {background: cyan}']
})
export class EbayComponent {

  searchFor$ = this.store.select(getSearchQuery);          ◁ Invokes the getSearchQuery() selector on the store

  searchResults$ = this.store.select(getSearchResults);          ◁ Invokes the getSearchResults() selector on the store

  constructor(private store: Store<State>) {}          ◁ Injects the store
 }
```

The code of `EBayComponent` is concise and doesn't contain any app logic. With ngrx, you need to write more code, but each method in your Angular component becomes either a command that sends an action or a selector that retrieves the data, and each command changes the state of your app.

There's one more step to complete the app-ngrx communication. You need to register the store and effects in the app module. Your module, shown in the next listing, also includes route configuration, so a user can navigate between the eBay and Amazon components.

Listing 15.17 app.module.ts

```
@NgModule({
  imports: [BrowserModule, CommonModule, ReactiveFormsModule,
    RouterModule.forRoot([
      {path: '',        component: EbayComponent},
       {path: 'amazon', component: AmazonComponent}]),
    StoreModule.forRoot({myReducer: reducer}),
     EffectsModule.forRoot([SearchEffects]),
         StoreDevtoolsModule.instrument({
                   logOnly: environment.production}),
   ],
  declarations: [AppComponent, EbayComponent, AmazonComponent, SearchComponent],
  providers: [
    ProductService,
    {provide: LocationStrategy, useClass: HashLocationStrategy}
  ],
  bootstrap:[AppComponent]
})
export class AppModule {}
```

Annotations: **Configures the routes** (RouterModule.forRoot); **Registers the store and links it to the reducer** (StoreModule.forRoot); **Registers the effects** (EffectsModule.forRoot); **Enables the use of Redux DevTools** (StoreDevtoolsModule.instrument).

In the next section, we'll show you how to monitor state with the Chrome extension Redux DevTools and what the `instrument()` method is for.

The app component in the following listing remains the same as in the mediator example from chapter 8. Listing 8.10 contains annotations, so we won't describe it here.

Listing 15.18 app.component.ts

```
@Component({
  selector: 'app-root',
  template: ` <div class="main">
              <app-search></app-search>
              <p>
              <a [routerLink]="['/']">eBay</a>
              <a [routerLink]="['/amazon']">Amazon</a>
              <router-outlet></router-outlet>
              </div>`,
  styles: ['.main {background: yellow}']
})
export class AppComponent {}
```

To see this app in action, run `npm install` in the project mediator, and then run `ng serve -o`.

What else ngrx has to offer

Your mediator app utilizes the packages `@ngrx/store` and `@ngrx/effects`, which can address most of your state-management needs. In the hands-on section, you'll also use `@ngrx/router-store`, which offers bindings for connecting and monitoring Angular `Router`. There are other packages as well:

- `@ngrx/entity` is an entity state adapter for managing record collections.
- `@ngrx/schematics` is a scaffolding library that provides blueprints for generating ngrx-related code.

Consider exploring these packages on your own. The API of all ngrx packages is described at http://mng.bz/362y.

Now let's see how to monitor app state with Redux DevTools.

15.2.4 Monitoring state with ngrx store DevTools

Because you delegate state-management operations to ngrx, you need a tool to monitor state changes during runtime. The browser extension Redux DevTools along with the `@ngrx/store-devtools` package are used for the instrumentation of the app state. First, install `@ngrx/store-devtools`:

```
npm install @ngrx/store-devtools
```

Second, add the Chrome extension Redux DevTools (there is such an add-on for Firefox as well).

Third, add the instrumentation code to the app module. For example, for instrumentation with the default configuration, you can add the following line to the imports section of the `@NgModule` decorator:

```
StoreDevtoolsModule.instrument()
```

`StoreDevtoolsModule` must be added after `StoreModule`. If you want to add instrumentation minimizing its overhead in the production environment, you can use the `environment` variable as follows:

```
StoreDevtoolsModule.instrument({
  logOnly: environment.production
})
```

In production, set the `logOnly` flag to `true`, which doesn't include tools like dispatching and reordering actions, persisting state and actions history between page reloads that introduces noticeable performance overhead. You can find the complete list of features that `logOnly: true` turns off at http://mng.bz/cOwC.

The `instrument()` method can accept the argument of type `StoreDevtoolsConfig` defined in the node_modules/@ngrx/store-devtools/src/config.d.ts file. The next code listing shows how to add instrumentation that will allow monitoring of up to 25 recent actions and work in log-only mode in the production environment.

Listing 15.19 Adding instrumentation with two configuration options

```
StoreDevtoolsModule.instrument({
    maxAge: 25,                                  <-- Retains the last 25 states in the browser extension
     logOnly: environment.production            <-- Restricts the browser extension to logOnly mode in production
 })
```

You can also restrict some of the features of the Chrome Redux extension by providing the `features` argument to the `instrument()` method. For more details on configuring ngrx instrumentation and supported API, see http://mng.bz/3AXe, but here we'll show you some Chrome Redux extension screenshots to illustrate some of the features of ngrx store DevTools.

> **TIP** If you run your app, but the Chrome Redux panel shows you a black window with the message "No store found," refresh the page in the browser.

Launching the app creates the initial state in the store. Figure 15.7 shows the screen after you launch the mediator app and enter `aaa` in the input field. The sequence of actions starts with two `init` actions that are dispatched internally by the packages `@ngrx/store` and `@ngrx/effects`, and you select the `@ngrx/store/init` action on the left and the State button at the top right. The state properties `searchQuery` and `searchResults` are empty. To see the app state after one of the search actions is dispatched, click this action.

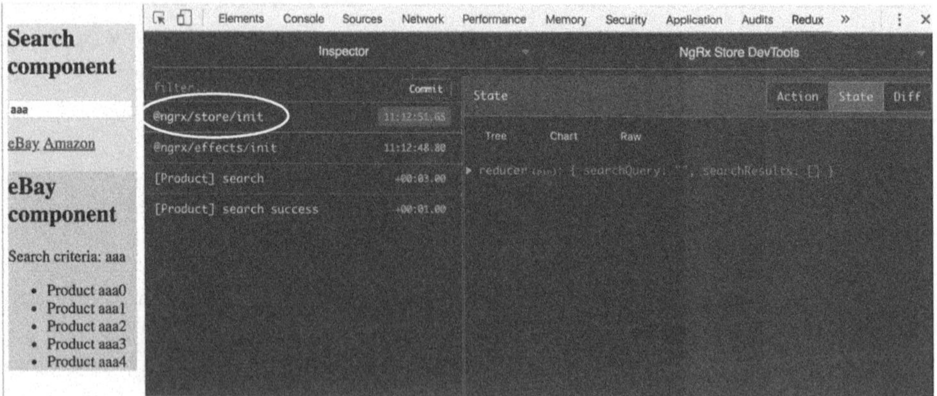

Figure 15.7 The store `init` action is selected.

Think of `init` actions as hooks that your app can subscribe to and implement some logic upon app launch—for example, you can check whether the user is logged in. If your app uses lazy-loaded modules that have their own reducers, you may also see the `@ngrx/store/update-reducer` action for each newly loaded module, and its reducer will be added to the collection of store reducers.

Figure 15.8 shows the screen after clicking the Action button at the top right, and shows the type and payload of the latest action:

1. The latest action is `"[Product] search success"`.
2. The Action tab is selected.
3. The action payload is stored in the state property `searchResults`.
4. The action type is `"[Product] search success"`.

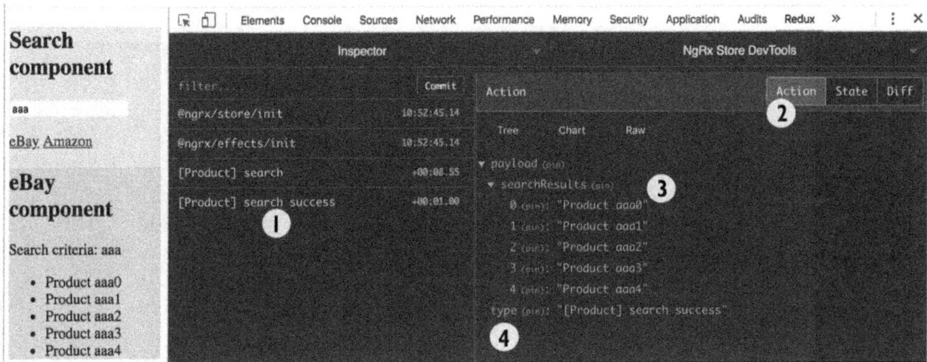

Figure 15.8 The Action tab view

> **TIP** If your state object has many branches, by clicking `(pin)`, you can pin a certain slice of the state to the top while browsing actions.

As shown in figure 15.9, after clicking the State button, you can see the current values of your state variables `searchQuery` and `searchResults`:

1. The latest action is `"[Product] search success"`.
2. The State tab is selected.
3. The search criterion is stored in the state property `searchQuery`.
4. The search results are stored in the state property `searchResults`.

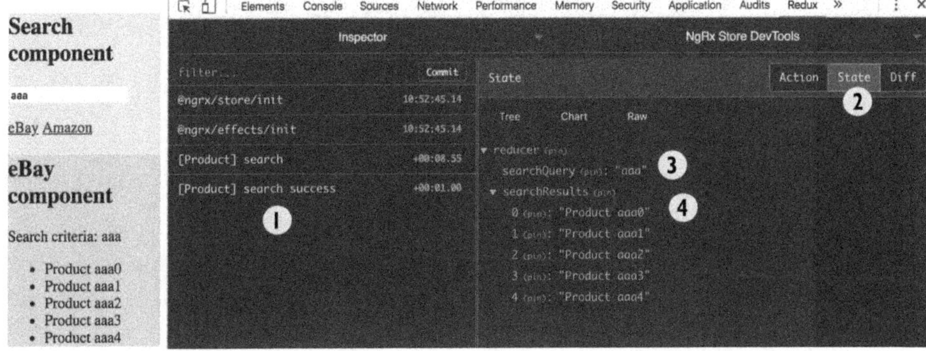

Figure 15.9 The State tab view

If the State tab shows the entire state object, clicking the Diff button shows what has changed as the result of the specific action. As shown in figure 15.10, if no action is selected, the Diff tab shows the state changes made by the latest action:

1 The latest action is `"[Product] search success"`.
2 The Diff tab is selected.
3 The content of the state property `searchResults` is different.

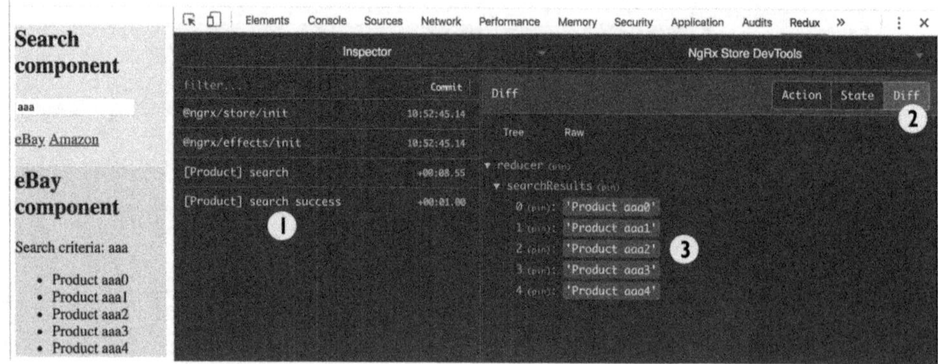

Figure 15.10 The Diff tab is selected.

While debugging an app, developers often need to re-create a certain state of the app, and one way to do that is to refresh the page and repeat user actions by clicking buttons, selecting list items, and so on. With Redux DevTools, you can travel back in time and re-create a certain state without refreshing the page—you can jump back to the state after a certain action occurred, or you can skip an action.

When you select an action, as shown in figure 15.11, you'll see the Jump and Skip buttons, and then clicking Skip will strike through the selected action, and your running app will reflect this change. The Sweep button will be displayed at the top, and clicking it removes this action from the list. The Jump button jumps you to a specific state of the app for a selected action. Redux DevTools will show you the state properties at the moment, and the UI of the app will be rerendered accordingly:

1 The Skip button for this action has been clicked.
2 The State tab is selected.
3 The search query is `aaabbb`.
4 The state property `searchResults` shows no results for the `aaabbb` products.
5 The Sweep button was not clicked.

We've shown you the main features of the ngrx store DevTools, but to understand this tool better, we encourage you to spend some time playing with it on your own.

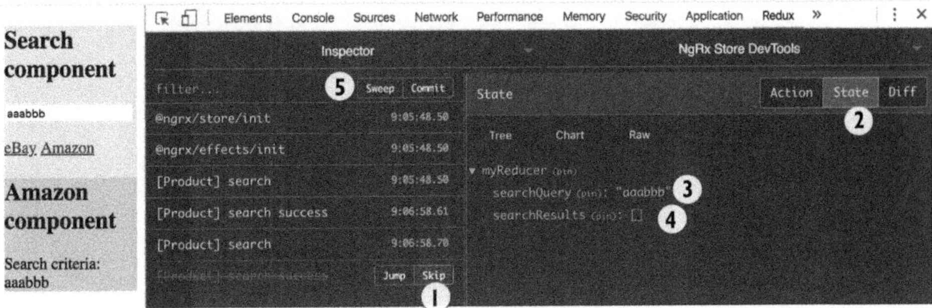

Figure 15.11 The [Product] search-success action is skipped

15.2.5 Monitoring the router state

When a user navigates an app, the router renders components, updates the URL, and passes parameters or query strings if need be. Behind the scenes, the router object represents the current state of the router, and the `@ngrx/router-store` package allows you to keep track of the router state in the ngrx store.

This package doesn't change the behavior of Angular `Router`, and you can continue using the `Router` API in components, but because the store should be a single source of truth, you may want to consider representing the router state there as well. At any given time, the ngrx store can give you access to such route properties as `url`, `params`, `queryParams`, and many others.

As with any other state properties, you'll need to add a reducer to the ngrx store, and the good news is that you don't need to implement it in your app because the `routerReducer` is defined in `@ngrx/router-store`. To add router state support, install this package first:

```
npm i @ngrx/router-store
```

After that, add `StoreRouterConnectingModule` to the `NgModule` decorator and add `routerReducer` to the list of reducers. `StoreRouterConnectingModule` holds the current router state. During navigation, before the route guards are invoked, the router store dispatches the action of type `ROUTER_NAVIGATION` that carries the `RouterStateSnapshot` object as its payload.

To get access to the `routerReducer` in your app, you need to perform two steps:

1 Give it a name by assigning a value to the property `StoreRouterConnectingModule.stateKey`.
2 Use the value from the previous step as the name of the `routerReducer`.

The following listing shows how the `StoreRouterConnectingModule` can be added to the app module. Here, you use `myRouterReducer` as the name of the `routerReducer`.

Listing 15.20 An app module fragment

```
import {StoreRouterConnectingModule, routerReducer}
  ➥ from '@ngrx/router-store';
...
@NgModule({
  imports: [
   ...
      StoreModule.forRoot({myReducer: reducer, ?
                          myRouterReducer: routerReducer}),    <- Adds routerReducer to the StoreModule
     StoreRouterConnectingModule.forRoot({
      stateKey: 'myRouterReducer'    <- Stores the name of the reducer in the stateKey property
     })
  ]
   ...
})
export class AppModule { }
```

Now the state property `myRouterReducer` can be used to access the router state. The value of this property will be updated on each router navigation.

The app from section 15.2.3 didn't include router state monitoring, but the source code that comes with this chapter has another app called mediator-router, which does monitor router state. Run this app and open the Redux DevTools panel. Then navigate to the Amazon route and you'll see the `ROUTER_NAVIGATION` action and the `myRouterReducer` property in the app state object, as shown in figure 15.12.

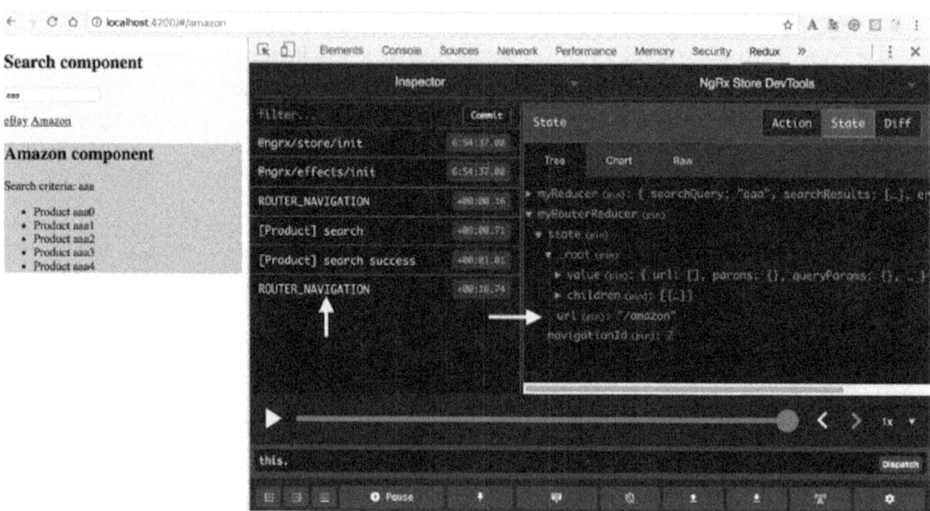

Figure 15.12 The `RouterStateSnapshot` object in Redux DevTools

TIP By clicking the down arrow on the bottom toolbar, a QA engineer can save the current state of the app and send it to a developer, who can load it into the Redux extension (up arrow) to reproduce the scenario reported as a bug.

Expand the nodes of `RouterStateSnapshot`; it has lots and lots of properties. This object is so big that it may even crash Redux DevTools. Typically, you need to monitor just a small number of router state properties, and this is where the router state serializer comes in handy.

To implement the serializer, define a type that will include only those properties of `RouterStateSnapshot` that you want to monitor. Then write a class that implements the `RouterStateSerializer` interface, and `@ngrx/router-store` will start using it. This interface requires you to implement the `serialize()` callback, where you should destructure the provided `RouterStateSnapshot` to extract only those properties you care about.

Some of the properties, like `url`, are available at the top level, and others, such as `queryParams`, are sitting under the `RouterStateSnapshot.root` property. The mediator-router project implements a router state serializer in the serializer.ts file, as shown in the following listing.

Listing 15.21 serializer.ts

```
import { RouterStateSerializer } from '@ngrx/router-store';
import {Params, RouterStateSnapshot} from '@angular/router';

interface MyRouterState {            <-- Defines the router state properties you want to monitor
   url: string;
  queryParams: Params;
}

export class MyRouterSerializer
        implements RouterStateSerializer<MyRouterState> {   <-- Creates a class that implements RouterStateSerializer

  serialize(routerState: RouterStateSnapshot): MyRouterState {

    const {url, root: {queryParams}} = routerState;   <-- Uses destructuring to get only the properties you need

    return {url, queryParams};    <-- Returns an object with the properties url and queryParams
   }
}
```

Now Redux DevTools will show only the values of `url` and `queryParams`. To get the value of the router state object, use the `select()` operator. The next listing shows how you do it in the mediator-router project.

Listing 15.22 app.component.ts

```
export class AppComponent {

  constructor(store: Store<any>) {
    store
```

```
      .select(state => state.myRouterReducer)
      .subscribe(routerState =>
          console.log('The router state: ', routerState));
  }
}
```

Extracts a router state slice

If you want to handle the router state action in your effects class, create an effect that handles the actions of type ROUTER_NAVIGATION. The following code listing from the effects.ts file from the mediator-router project shows how to do it in the effect.

Listing 15.23 A fragment of effects.ts

```
@Injectable()
export class SearchEffects {

...

  @Effect({ dispatch: false })
   logNavigation$ =
    this.actions$.pipe(
      ofType('ROUTER_NAVIGATION'),
       tap((action: any) => {
        console.log('The router action in effect:', action.payload);
      })
    );

  constructor(private actions$: Actions,
              private productService: ProductService) {}
}
```

This effect doesn't dispatch its own actions.

Listens to the ROUTER_NAVIGATION action

In some cases, you may want to arrange navigation inside the effects class. For this, shown in the following listing, you can keep using the router API without any help from ngrx.

Listing 15.24 Navigating in effects

```
@Effect({ dispatch: false })
navigateToAmazon$ =
  this.actions$.pipe(
    ofType('GOTO_AMAZON')
     tap((action: any) => {
      this.router.navigate('/amazon');
     })
  );
```

Listens to the GOTO_AMAZON action

Navigates to the /amazon route

This concludes our introduction to ngrx, but you'll see how you use it in the ngAuction app in the hands-on section of this chapter.

15.3 To ngrx or not to ngrx

Recently, one of our clients explained their needs for storing state. In their app, state is represented by a large object with nested arrays, and each array stores data rendered as a chart. The app retrieves one of the arrays, performs some calculations, and renders a chart. In the future, they plan to add new charts and arrays.

The client asked whether using a singleton Angular service with `BehaviorSubject` would offer a less scalable solution than ngrx for this use case. He added that in ngrx, they could use separate arrays (state slices) with their reducers, which could make adding new arrays and charts easier because ngrx automatically creates one global state object from individual reducers.

Let's see if ngrx would help. First of all, if they needed lots of data to render the chart that doesn't use the data directly, it could make sense to move computations to the server to avoid keeping huge objects in memory and calculating numbers in the browser. But what if they still wanted to implement all the data crunching on the client?

With the Angular service approach, the object with nested arrays would grow and become less maintainable. In the case of separate reducers/arrays, it would be easier to add them to the state and reason about the state.

But with the ngrx approach, the state object would also grow, and they'd need to add more reducers and selectors to handle the growth. With the Angular service approach, they could either add more methods for getting the state slices or could split the singleton into multiple services—the main one would store the data, and separate services (one per chart) would get and process the data from the main service.

Both ngrx and service approaches can do the job and remain maintainable. If the app doesn't use ngrx yet, it wouldn't make sense to use ngrx just because of charts.

15.3.1 Comparing ngrx with Angular services

Okay, is there a use case where ngrx offers advantages over the Angular service approach? Let compare three main features of state management:

- A single source of truth could mean two things:
  a There's only one copy of each set of data. This is easily achievable with an Angular service with `BehaviorSubject`.
  b There's a single object that keeps all the app data. This is a unique feature of the Redux/ngrx approach that enables Redux DevTools. This can be a valuable feature for large apps with cross-module interaction and lots of shared data. Without a single state object, it would be nearly impossible. DevTools allows exporting/importing the entire state of the app if you need to reproduce a bug found by a user or a QA engineer. But in the real world, state changes trigger side effects and don't restore the app in exactly the same state.
- State can be modified only by a reducer, so you can easily locate and debug an issue related to state. But if you use `BehaviorSubject` to keep data in your Angular services, you can do this as well. Without `BehaviorSubject`, it would be hard to identify all assignments that can modify state, but with `BehaviorSubject`, there's a single place where you can put a breakpoint. Also, by applying the `map` operator to `BehaviorSubject`, you can handle all data modifications just like in a reducer.

- With ngrx and specific selectors, you can produce a derived state that combines data from different parts of the store object, plus it can be memoized. You can easily do this in an Angular service as well. Define a service that injects other services, aggregates their values with `combineLatest` or `withLatestFrom` operators, and then emits the "derived" state.

If you want all these features, it can be easier to start with ngrx because ngrx enforces them. Without enforced discipline, your singleton service that started with 30 lines of code can quickly turn into an unmaintainable monster with hundreds of lines. If you're not sure that best practices can be enforced in your team, go with ngrx, which offers a well-defined structure for your app.

> **TIP** Instead of writing the code for creating a store, effects, actions, and so on, you can generate them using Angular CLI, but first install the ngrx blueprints (a.k.a. schematics). You can read about using `@ngrx/schematics` at http://mng.bz/7W30. If your project was generated by Angular CLI 6 or newer, you can add NGRX artifacts to it by using the following commands:

```
ng add @ngrx/store
ng add @ngrx/effects
```

15.3.2 State mutation problems

These issues do exist, but Angular has all you need to address them. In your projects, all Angular components use the change detection strategy `OnPush`. When you need to modify a component's data, create a new instance of an object bound to the component's `@Input`.

There are cases when using the default change detection strategy makes more sense. For example, you may need to create a dynamic form, and its content changes depending on the values entered in other form controls. Control values are exposed as observables (as `valueChanges`), and if your component uses `OnPush`, and all other component properties are RxJS `Subjects`, it makes the code overly complex to express the logic in terms of RxJS operators.

The code definitely can be complex, but often it doesn't have any benefits over disabling the `OnPush` strategy and mutating a component's state directly. Then don't use `OnPush`. On rare occasions, you can even manually trigger change detection with `ChangeDetectorRef`.

These techniques aren't a replacement for the immutable ngrx state, and they don't provide the same level of control over your data that ngrx does. But they help avoid problems caused by state mutation.

15.3.3 ngrx code is more difficult to read

Actions and reducers introduce indirection and can quickly complicate your code if used without care. A new hire would need to spend more time to become productive with your app since each component can't be understood in isolation. You may say the same is true for any Angular app that doesn't use ngrx, but we would disagree for two reasons.

First, components and services look pretty much the same in every Angular app, but every ngrx project has its own approach for implementing and organizing actions, reducers, store selectors, and effects. Actions can be defined as variables, classes, interfaces, and enums. They can be directly exposed as ES module members or grouped into classes. The same applies to reducers.

Second, supporting actions and reducers requires writing additional code that wouldn't exist in your app otherwise—it's not just moving the existing app code from components to ngrx entities. If your components are already complex, using ngrx could make the code difficult to read.

15.3.4 The learning curve

ngrx considerably steepens the learning curve. You need to learn how the packages `@ngrx/store` and `@ngrx/effects` work. You may also want to learn the `@ngrx/entity` package that helps normalize relational data. If you have experience working with relational databases, you know how easy it is to join data located in related tables. Using `@ngrx/entity` eliminates the need to create nested JavaScript objects (for example, a customer object with nested orders) and write complex reducers.

You also need to be comfortable with the RxJS library. It's not rocket science, but if you're already in the process of learning Angular, TypeScript, and all the tooling, it would be wiser to postpone adding libraries that you can live without.

15.3.5 Conclusion

Good libraries are those that allow you to write less code. Currently, ngrx requires you to write lots of additional code, but we hope that future versions of ngrx will be simpler to implement and understand. Meanwhile, keep an eye on a promising state management library called NGXS (see https://ngxs.gitbooks.io/ngxs), which doesn't require you to write as much code as ngrx and is built on TypeScript decorators. Another new project called ngrx-data (http://mng.bz/h6Nc) promises to support ngrx/Redux workflows with less coding.

Start with managing state using a singleton injectable service with `BehaviorSubject`. This approach may cover all your needs. Watch the video "When ngrx is an overkill" by Yakov Fain (www.youtube.com/watch?v=xLTIDs0CDCM), where he compares two small apps that manage state with and without ngrx. It's never too late to add ngrx to your app, so don't try to prematurely solve a problem you're not facing yet.

Now let's see how ngrx can be used in your ngAuction app.

15.4 Hands-on: Using ngrx in ngAuction

The ngAuction app that comes with this chapter uses ngrx for state management. It's modularized and has the root module `AppModule` and two feature modules, `HomeModule` and `ProductModule`. Since your feature modules are lazy loaded, we've added to each module the directory store, which in turn has its own subdirectories: actions, effects, and reducers, as shown in figure 15.13. Although this project has three directories named store, the running app will have a single store with merged states from each module.

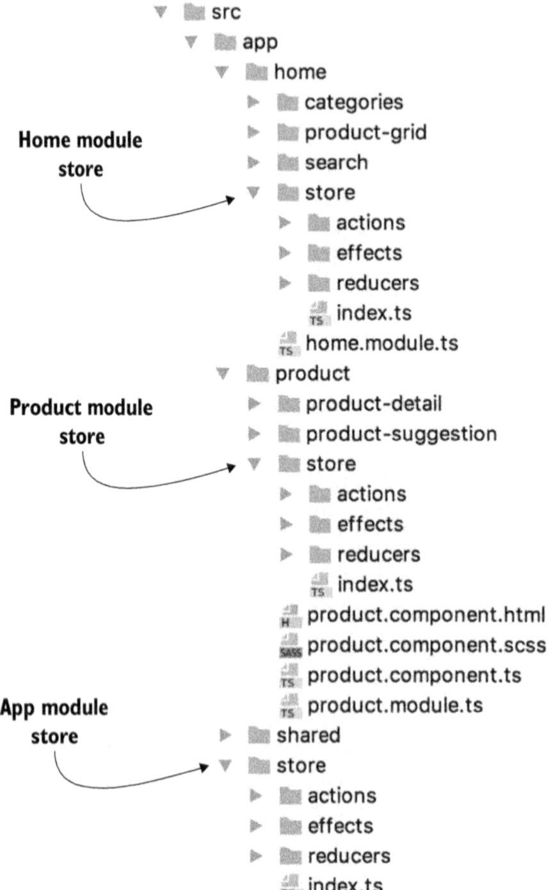

Figure 15.13 The state branches in the app and home modules

Inside of each folder—actions, effects, and reducers—we have separate files related to specific slices of state. For example, you can find a separate search.ts file that implements a respective piece of the search functionality in each of those folders.

App state can represent not only data (such as the latest search query or results), but also the state of the UI (such as the loading indicator is shown or hidden). You may also be interested to know the current state of the router and the URL displayed by the browser.

Figure 15.14 depicts the combined state of the running ngAuction. The names of reducers are shown in bold italic font, and arrows point at the state properties handled by each reducer. In particular, the `loading` property of the `products` reducer could represent the state of the progress indicator. We'll also add router support using the `router` reducer.

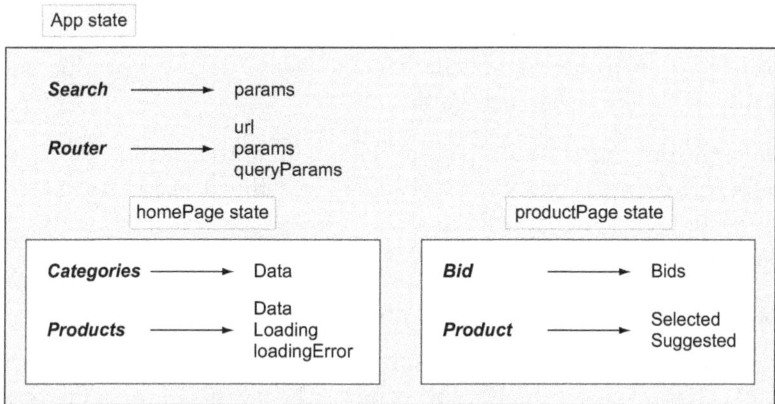

Figure 15.14 The combined state object of ngAuction

The router reducer is special in that you don't need to implement it in your app because it's defined in `@ngrx/router-store`, reviewed in the next section. Your ngAuction has the `@ngrx/router-store` package as a dependency in package.json.

Figure 15.15 shows a screenshot from Redux DevTools after ngAuction has launched and a user navigates to a specific product page. Note the router property there. The app state in figure 15.15 matches the state structure shown in figure 15.14:

- The State tab is selected.
- You see a `search` slice of state, a `router` slice of state, a `homePage` slice of state, and a `productPage` slice of state.

To run the ngAuction that comes with this chapter, you'll need to open two terminal windows, one for the client and one for server. Go to the server directory and run `npm install` there. Then, compile the code with the `tsc` command and start the server with the `node build/main` command. After that, open a separate Terminal window in the client directory and run the `npm install` command, followed by `ng serve`. We recommend you keep Redux DevTools open to monitor app state changes.

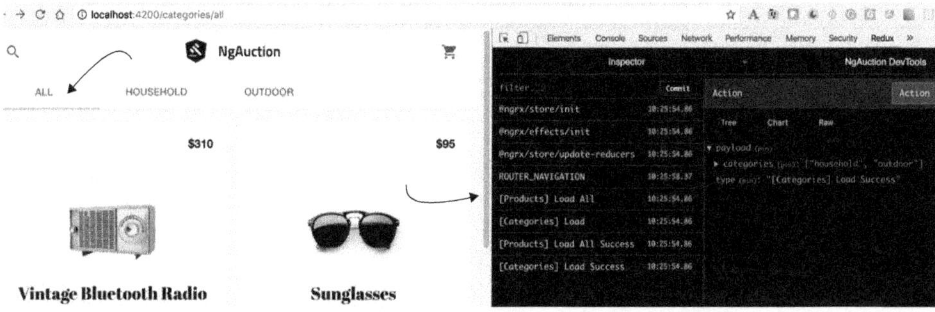

Figure 15.15 The ngAuction state in Redux DevTools

NOTE To keep the length of this section relatively short, we'll review just the code that implements state management in the home module and give you a brief overview of the router state. The state management of the product module is implemented in a similar fashion.

ngAuction uses four ngrx modules: `StoreModule`, `EffectsModule`, `StoreRouterConnectingModule`, and `StoreDevtoolsModule`, and the package for each of these modules is included in the dependencies section of package.json. Let's review the router-related code of the app module.

15.4.1 Adding the router state support to app module

When you select a product, the router navigates to the corresponding product view, and the URL changes accordingly—for example, http://localhost:4200/products/1. Selecting another product will change the router state, and you can bind these types of changes to the app state as well. The next listing shows the code fragments from app.module.ts focusing on the code related to router state support.

Listing 15.25 app.module.ts

```
import {EffectsModule} from '@ngrx/effects';
import {StoreRouterConnectingModule, routerReducer}
                from '@ngrx/router-store';        ◁ Imports the store module and the reducer for the router's state
 import {StoreModule} from '@ngrx/store';
import {StoreDevtoolsModule} from '@ngrx/store-devtools';
import {environment} from '../environments/environment';
import {reducers,
         RouterEffects,        ◁ Imports the router effects
          SearchEffects} from './store';
...
@NgModule({
  imports: [
   ...
    StoreModule.forRoot({...reducers, router: routerReducer}),   ◁ Adds the routerReducer to the collection of app reducers
     StoreRouterConnectingModule.forRoot({   ◁ Adds the router state support
       stateKey: 'router'     ◁ Names the router state property as router
     }),
    StoreDevtoolsModule.instrument({
      name: 'ngAuction DevTools',
      logOnly: environment.production
    }),
    EffectsModule.forRoot([RouterEffects, SearchEffects]),   ◁ RouterEffects listens to router events and dispatches ngrx actions handled by routerReducer.
     ...
  ],
   ...
})
export class AppModule {
```

TIP The next section provides more details about the line that loads reducers, while reviewing the code of the home module's index.ts file.

The name of the router state within the store is defined by the property name (for example, `router`) mapped to the router reducer. In your app, you'll use the default `routerReducer` and add it to the collection of app reducers:

```
StoreModule.forRoot({...reducers, router: routerReducer}),
```

The value of the `stateKey` property is used to find the router state within the store and connect it to Redux DevTools, so that time traveling during debugging works. The value assigned to `stateKey` (the `router`, in your case) must match the property name used in the map of reducers provided to the `forRoot()` method. To access a particular property of the router state, you can use the ngrx `select` operator on the object represented by the `router` variable.

Accessing the entire router state may crash Redux DevTools, which is why we created a custom router state serializer to keep in the store only the state properties you need. In the shared/services/router-state-serializer.service.ts file, we've implemented a serializer that returns an object containing only `url`, `params`, and `queryParams`. If we didn't implement this serializer, the router state shown in figure 15.14 would have lots of nested properties.

15.4.2 Managing state in the home module

When the home module is lazy loaded, its reducers are registered with the store, and its state object is merged with the root state. For this to happen, add the lines in the following listing to declare the store, reducer, and effects in the home.module.ts file

Listing 15.26 A fragment from home.module.ts

```
import {CategoriesEffects, ProductsEffects, reducers} from './store';
...
@NgModule({
  imports: [
  ...
   StoreModule.forFeature('homePage', reducers),        <- Registers the reducers for the feature home module
    EffectsModule.forFeature([ CategoriesEffects, ProductsEffects ])   <- Registers the effects for the feature home module
   ]
```

TIP The difference between the methods `forFeature()` and `forRoot()` is that the latter also sets up the required providers for services from the `StoreModule`.

The home module has reducers in the files store/reducers/products.ts and store/reducers/categories.ts. Note that you import reducers not from a specific file, but from the directory store, and you can guess that this directory has a file named index.ts that combines and reexports reducers from several files. You'll see the content of index.ts later in this section.

ACTIONS FOR PRODUCTS

In ngAuction, `CategoriesComponent` serves as a container of the home view, which renders the category tabs and the product grid on the home view. Figure 15.16 shows that `"[Products] Load All"` is the first action dispatched by the app. Then it dispatches `"[Categories] Load"`. When the data is loaded, two more actions are dispatched by the effects: `"[Products] Load All Success"` and `"[Categories] Load Success"`.

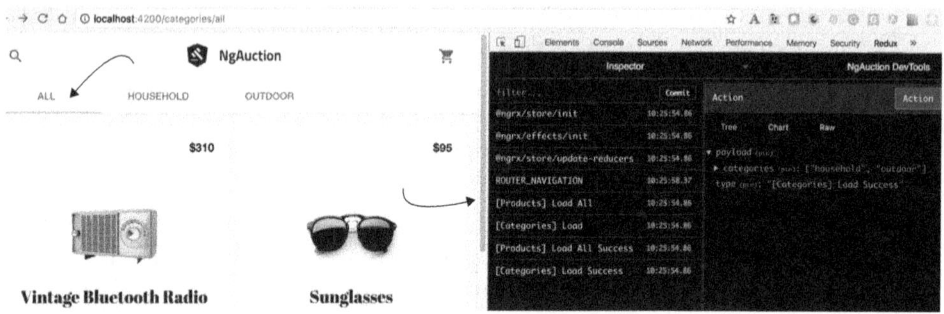

Figure 15.16 Loading products from all categories

Actions for categories are declared in the home/store/actions/categories.ts file, and actions for products in the home/store/actions/products.ts file. We'll review only the content of home/store/actions/products.ts; the categories actions are declared in a similar way.

In ngAuction, each file with actions usually consists of three logical sections:

- The `enum` containing string constants defining the action types. You can read about TypeScript enums at http://mng.bz/sTmp.
- Classes for actions (one class per action) that implement the `Action` interface.
- The union type that combines all action classes. You'll use this type in reducers and effects, so the TypeScript compiler can check that the action types are correct, such as `ProductsActionTypes.Load`.

The next listing shows how actions are declared in the home/store/actions/products.ts file.

Listing 15.27 home/store/actions/products.ts

```
import {Action} from '@ngrx/store';
import {Product} from '../../../shared/services';

export enum ProductsActionTypes {
   Load = '[Products] Load All',
  Search = '[Products] Search',
  LoadFailure = '[Products] Load All Failure',
  LoadSuccess = '[Products] Load All Success',
  LoadProductsByCategory = '[Products] Load Products By Category'
}
```

Declares allowed action types as the enum of string constants

```
export class LoadProducts implements Action {
    readonly type = ProductsActionTypes.Load;
}

export class LoadProductsByCategory implements Action {
    readonly type = ProductsActionTypes.LoadProductsByCategory;
    constructor(public readonly payload: {category: string}) {}
}

export class LoadProductsFailure implements Action {
    readonly type = ProductsActionTypes.LoadFailure;
    constructor(public readonly payload: {error: string}) {}
}

export class LoadProductsSuccess implements Action {
    readonly type = ProductsActionTypes.LoadSuccess;
    constructor(public readonly payload: {products: Product[]}) {}
}

export class SearchProducts implements Action {
    readonly type = ProductsActionTypes.Search;
    constructor(public readonly payload:
                        {params: {[key: string]: any}}) {}
}

export type ProductsActions
    = LoadProducts | LoadProductsByCategory | LoadProductsFailure
   | LoadProductsSuccess | SearchProducts;
```

Declares the class for the action

Declares the action type

Uses the constructor argument to declare the action payload

Declares the union type of allowed actions

As you see, some of the action classes include only the action type, and some include the payload as well.

CategoriesComponent

The code of the `CategoriesComponent` has changed compared to the chapter 14 version. Fragments of the categories.component.ts file related to state management are shown in listing 15.28. In the constructor of the `CategoriesComponent`, you subscribe to the route parameters. When this component receives the category value, it either dispatches the action to load the products of all categories or only the selected one.

Listing 15.28 Fragments from categories.component.ts

```
import {
  getCategoriesData, getProductsData,
   LoadCategories, LoadProducts, LoadProductsByCategory,
   State
} from '../store';


@Component({...})
export class CategoriesComponent implements OnDestroy {
  readonly categories$: Observable<string[]>;
  readonly products$: Observable<Product[]>;
```

Imports ngrx selectors

Imports ngrx actions

```
  constructor(private route: ActivatedRoute,
              private store: Store<State>) {          <-- Injects the Store object
    this.products$ = this.store.pipe(select(getProductsData));
    this.categories$ = this.store.pipe(               <-- Subscribes to the categories to be rendered as tabs
      select(getCategoriesData),
      map(categories => ['all', ...categories])       <-- Adds the all element to the array of category names
    );

    this.productsSubscription = this.route.params.subscribe(
      ({ category }) => this.getCategory(category)    <-- Loads the selected or all categories
    );
    this.store.dispatch(new LoadCategories());        <-- Dispatches the action to load categories
  }

  private getCategory(category: string): void {
    return category.toLowerCase() === 'all'
      ? this.store.dispatch(new LoadProducts())       <-- Dispatches the action to load all products
      : this.store.dispatch(new LoadProductsByCategory(   <-- Dispatches the action to load products by category
                      {category: category.toLowerCase()}));
  }
}
```

THE REDUCER FOR PRODUCTS

The home module has two reducers: one for products and one for categories. The reducers and selectors for products are shown in the following listing.

Listing 15.29 home/store/reducers/products.ts

```
import {Product} from '../../../shared/services';
import {ProductsActions, ProductsActionTypes} from '../actions';

export interface State {          <-- Declares the structure of the products state
   data: Product[];
  loading: boolean;
  loadingError?: string;
}

export const initialState: State = {     <-- The initial state has no products, and the loading flag is false.
   data: [],
  loading: false
};

export function reducer(state = initialState, action: ProductsActions): State
      {
  switch (action.type) {
    case ProductsActionTypes.Load: {     <-- Handles the Load action
       return {
        ...state,
        loading: true,                   <-- Updates the loading flag because the loading begins
         loadingError: null
      };
    }
```

```
    case ProductsActionTypes.LoadSuccess: {      <-- Handles the LoadSuccess action
      return {
        ...state,
        data: action.payload.products,          <-- The products are
         loading: false,                            loaded—updates the
        loadingError: null                          state with data.
      };
    }

    case ProductsActionTypes.LoadFailure: {      <-- Handles the LoadFailure action
      return {
        ...state,
        data: [],          <-- Removes products data, if any
         loading: false,
        loadingError: action.payload.error    <-- Updates the error message
      };
    }

    default: {
      return state;
    }
  }
}

export const getData = (state: State) => state.data;
export const getDataLoading = (state: State) => state.loading;
export const getDataLoadingError = (state: State) => state.loadingError;)
```

The accessors returning state properties

The state object for products has three properties: the array with products, the flag to control the loading indicator, and the text of the loading error, if any. When the reducer receives the action of type `Load`, it creates a new state object with an updated `loading` property that can be used by a component for showing a progress indicator.

If the `LoadSuccess` action has been dispatched, it indicates that the products were retrieved successfully. The reducer extracts them from the action's `payload` property and updates the state's `data` and `loading` properties. The `LoadFailure` action indicates that the products couldn't be retrieved, and the reducer removes the data (if any) from the state object, updates the error message, and turns off the `loading` flag.

At the end of the reducer script for products, you see three lines with the functions that know how to access the data in the products state object. You define these functions here to keep them where the `State` interface is declared. These accessors are used to create selectors defined in index.ts.

> **NOTE** The products reducer has no code that makes requests for data. Remember, the code communicating with external store parties is placed in the effects.

THE ROLE OF INDEX.TS IN HOME REDUCERS

In general, the files named index.ts are used for reexporting multiple members declared in separate files. This way, if another script needs such a member, you import this member from a directory without the need to know the full path to a specific file.

When reexporting members, you can give them new names and combine them into new types.

The home/store/reducers/index.ts file has the line `import * as fromProducts from './products';`, and to access exported members from the products.ts file, you can use the alias `fromProducts` as a reference—for example, `fromProducts.State` or `fromProducts.getData()`. With this in mind, let's review the code of the home/store/reducers/index.ts file in the following listing.

Listing 15.30 home/store/reducers/index.ts

```
import {createFeatureSelector, createSelector} from '@ngrx/store';
import * as fromRoot from '../../../store';
 import * as fromCategories from './categories';
 import * as fromProducts from './products';

export interface HomeState {
   categories: fromCategories.State;
  products: fromProducts.State;
}

export interface State extends fromRoot.State {
   homePage: HomeState;
 }

export const reducers = {
   categories: fromCategories.reducer,
  products: fromProducts.reducer
};

// The selectors for the home module

export const getHomeState =
                createFeatureSelector<HomeState>('homePage');
export const getProductsState =
                createSelector(getHomeState, state => state.products);
export const getProductsData =
                createSelector(getProductsState, fromProducts.getData);
export const getProductsDataLoading =
                createSelector(getProductsState, fromProducts.getDataLoading);
export const getProductsDataLoadingError =
                createSelector(getProductsState, fromProducts.getDataLoadingError);
export const getCategoriesState =
                createSelector(getHomeState, state => state.categories);
export const getCategoriesData =
                createSelector(getCategoriesState, fromCategories.getData);
```

- Imports various exported members and gives them alias names
- Combines states from categories and products
- Declares the State type by extending it from the root State
- Declares a feature named homePage to be used with StoreModule or createFeatureSelector()
- Combines the reducers from categories and products

This script starts with creating descriptive alias names (for example, `fromRoot`), so it's easier to read the code knowing where a particular member is coming from. Then you declare a `HomeState` interface combining all the properties declared in the `State` interfaces in the reducers for both products and categories.

The app store includes one state object that can be a complex object containing multiple branches. Each of these branches is created by a module reducer. When an action is triggered on the store, it goes through each registered reducer and finds the ones that have to handle this action. The reducer creates a new state and updates the corresponding branch of the global app state.

Here, you create a representation of the home module branch by declaring the `State` type that extends the `State` root and adding a new `homePage` property to it. You used this property in `createFeatureSelector()` and in listing 15.26 for registering the state object for the module home. When the combined app store is being formed, ngrx adds the `homePage` object to it.

The exported `reducers` member combines the reducers for products and categories. Now take another look at the app module in listing 15.25 which has the following line:

```
StoreModule.forRoot({...reducers, router: routerReducer})
```

Initially, the store finds and invokes each module reducer, which returns the corresponding state object. This is how the combined app state is created. The following code fragment from index.ts assigns the names `categories` and `products` to the respective slices of state:

```
export const reducers = {
  categories: fromCategories.reducer,
  products: fromProducts.reducer
};
```

At the end of the script, you declare and export all the selectors that can be used for retrieving slices of the home module state. Note that you use the state accessor functions declared in the respective reducer files.

EFFECTS FOR PRODUCTS

In the home module, effects are located in the files home/store/effects/categories.ts and home/store/effects/products.ts, and in the following listing, we review the code of the latter. The `ProductsEffects` class declares three effects: `loadProducts$`, `loadByCategory$`, and `searchProducts$`.

Listing 15.31 home/store/effects/products.ts

```
import {Injectable} from '@angular/core';
import {Actions, Effect, ofType} from '@ngrx/effects';
import {Action} from '@ngrx/store';
import {Observable, of} from 'rxjs';
import {catchError, map, switchMap} from 'rxjs/operators';

import {Product, ProductService} from '../../../shared/services';
import {LoadProductsByCategory, LoadProductsFailure,
     LoadProductsSuccess, ProductsActionTypes, SearchProducts} from '../actions';

@Injectable()
export class ProductsEffects {

  constructor(
    private readonly actions$: Actions,
    private readonly productService: ProductService) {}
```

```
  @Effect()
  loadProducts$: Observable<Action> = this.actions$
    .pipe(
      ofType(ProductsActionTypes.Load),          ⇽ Processes only Load actions
      switchMap(() => this.productService.getAll()),   ⇽ Tries to load all products
      handleLoadedProducts()      ⇽ Dispatches either LoadProductsSuccess
    );                              or LoadProductsFailure

  @Effect()
  loadByCategory$: Observable<Action> = this.actions$
    .pipe(
      ofType<LoadProductsByCategory>(          Processes only
➥ ProductsActionTypes.LoadProductsByCategory),   LoadProductsByCategory actions

      map(action => action.payload.category),   ⇽ Extracts the category from the payload
      switchMap(category => this.productService.getByCategory(category)),  ⇽ Tries to load products by provided category
      handleLoadedProducts()   ⇽ Dispatches either LoadProductsSuccess or LoadProductsFailure
    );

  @Effect()
  searchProducts: Observable<Action> = this.actions$
    .pipe(
      ofType(ProductsActionTypes.Search),   ⇽ Processes only Search actions
      map((action: SearchProducts) => action.payload.params),
      switchMap(params => this.productService.search(params)),
      handleLoadedProducts()
    );
}

const handleLoadedProducts = () =>   ⇽ The function to dispatch either LoadProductsSuccess or LoadProductsFailure
  (source: Observable<Product[]>) => source.pipe(
    map(products => new LoadProductsSuccess({products})),
    catchError(error => of(new LoadProductsFailure({ error })))
  );
```

Note the use of the `<LoadProductsByCategory>` type annotation in the `ofType` operator. This is one way of declaring the type of the action payload. Declaring the type explicitly (as in `map((action: SearchProducts))` is another way to do this.

Figure 15.17 shows the state after the action of type `LoadSuccess` is dispatched:

1. The search state is empty.
2. The router state shows the URL and parameters.
3. The categories state will be populated after the load success for categories is dispatched.
4. The state of products has data retrieved from the server.
5. The `loading` flag is `false`.
6. There are no errors.

As usual, the actions dispatched by effects will be handled by the reducer, which will update the state with the data or error message.

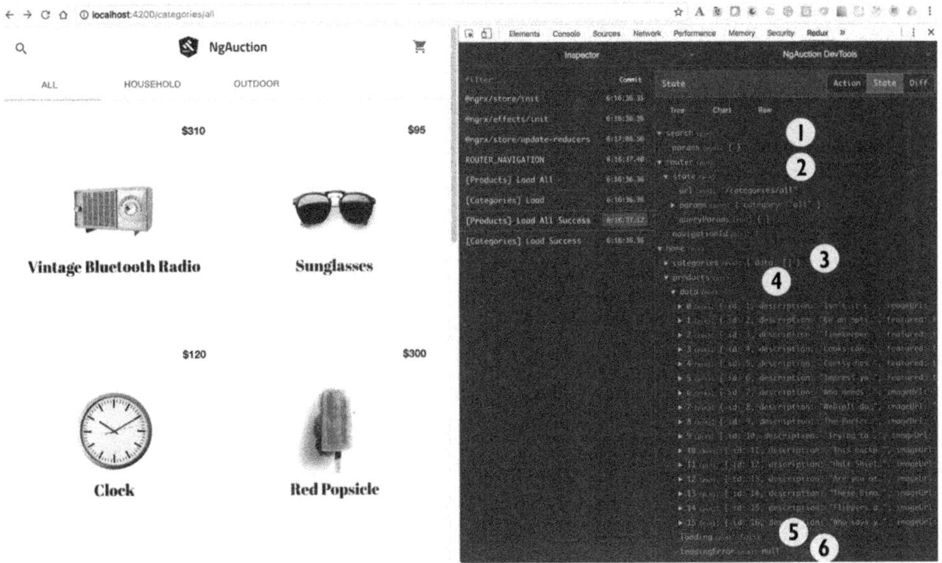

Figure 15.17 The state after the LoadSuccess action

15.4.3 Unit-testing ngrx reducers

Unit-testing state-related functionality is quite simple because only the reducer can change app state. Remember, a reducer is a pure function, which always returns the same output if the provided arguments are the same.

Because every action is represented by a class, you just need to instantiate the action object and invoke the corresponding reducer, providing the state and action objects to the reducer. After that, you assert that the state property under test has the expected value. For example, the home module has a reducer for products that defines the state object in the following listing.

Listing 15.32 The products slice in the home module state

```
export interface State {
  data: Product[];              // Current products are stored here.
    loading: boolean;           // If this flag is true, the UI should show a progress indicator.
    loadingError?: string;      // If loading fails, the error message is stored here.
 }
```

Let's review the code of the home/store/reducers/products.spec.ts file, shown in the following listing, which uses this state object and asserts that the `loading` flag is properly handled by the actions `LoadProducts` and `LoadProductsSuccess`.

Listing 15.33 home/store/reducers/products.spec.ts

```
import {LoadProducts, LoadProductsSuccess} from '../actions';
import {initialState, reducer} from './products';

describe('Home page', () => {
  describe('product reducer', () => {
    it('sets the flag for a progress indicator while loading products',
➥ () => {
      const loadAction = new LoadProducts();
      const loadSuccessAction = new LoadProductsSuccess({products: []});

      const beforeLoadingState = reducer(initialState, {} as any);
       expect(beforeLoadingState.loading).toBe(false);

      const whileLoadingState = reducer(beforeLoadingState, loadAction);
       expect(whileLoadingState.loading).toBe(true);

      const afterLoadingState = reducer(whileLoadingState,
                                        loadSuccessAction);
       expect(afterLoadingState.loading).toBe(false);
    });
  });
});
```

- Instantiates the LoadProducts action
- Instantiates the action of type LoadProductsSuccess that has no products
- Invokes the reducer with the initial state
- Asserts that the initial value of loading is false
- Invokes the reducer providing the current state and Load action
- Asserts that the loading flag is true
- Invokes the reducer providing the current state and LoadSuccess action
- Asserts that the loading flag is false

When you invoke the reducer with the initial state, you provide an empty object and cast it to the type any, so regardless of the provided action, the reducer must return a valid state. Check the code of the reducer and note the `default` case in the `switch` statement there. Run the `ng test` command, and Karma will report that it executed successfully.

The listing 15.33 spec tests whether the reducer properly handles the `loading` property in the state object, without worrying about the action payload. But if you write a test for an action that has a payload, create a stub object with hardcoded data to simulate the payload and invoke the corresponding reducer.

This concludes our review of the ngrx code added to the home module of ngAuction. We encourage you to complete the code review of the product module on your own; its ngrx-related code is similar.

Summary

- The app state should be immutable.
- The app logic can be removed from components and placed in effects and services.
- A component's methods should only send commands (actions) and subscribe to data for further rendering.
- Although the ngrx learning curve is steep, using ngrx may result in better code organization, which is especially important in large apps.

Angular 6, 7, and beyond

The authors started working on the first edition of this book when Angular was in its early alpha versions. Every new Alpha, Beta, and Release Candidate was full of breaking changes. Writing the second edition was easier because Angular became a mature and feature-complete framework. New major releases come twice a year, and switching from one release to another isn't a difficult task. Every new release is tested against roughly 600 Angular apps used internally at Google to ensure backward compatibility.

We'd like to highlight some of the new features introduced in Angular 6 or planned for future releases:

- *Angular Elements*—Angular is a great choice for developing single-page applications, but creating a widget that can be added to an existing web page isn't a simple task. The Angular Elements package will allow you to create a self-bootstrapping Angular component that's hosted by a custom web element (see www.w3.org/TR/custom-elements/) that can be used in any HTML page.

  Simply put, you can define new DOM elements and register them with the browser. At the time of writing, all major browsers except Internet Explorer natively support custom elements; for IE, you should use polyfills.

  Say there's an existing web app built using JavaScript and jQuery. The developers of this app will be able to use Angular components (packaged as custom elements) in the pages of such an app. For example, if you build a price-quoter component, Angular Elements will generate a script that can be added to an HTML page, and your component can be used on an HTML page. Here's an example:

  ```
  <price-quoter stockSymbol="IBM"></price-quoter>
  ```

  As you can guess, the `stockSymbol` is an `@Input` parameter of the Angular price-quoter component. And if this component emits custom events via its `@Output` properties, your web page can listen to them using the standard browser API `addEventListener()`.

  In our opinion, this killer feature will open many enterprise doors to the Angular framework. Angular Elements will be officially released in Angular 7.

- *Ivy renderer*—This is the codename of a new renderer that will make the size of an app smaller and the compilation faster. The size of the Hello World app is only 7 KB minified and 3 KB gzipped. This renderer will eliminate unused code while building bundles, as opposed to optimizing bundles, as is currently done. The Ivy renderer will be introduced in Angular 8.
- *Bazel and Closure Compiler*—Bazel is a fast build system used for nearly all software built at Google, including their 300+ apps written in Angular. Bazel makes it easier to publish Angular code that can be distributed as npm packages. The Closure Compiler is the bundling optimizer used to create JavaScript artifacts for nearly all Google web applications. The Closure Compiler consistently generates smaller bundles and does a better job of dead code elimination compared to Webpack and Rollup bundlers. By default, the Angular CLI project uses Webpack 4, which produces smaller bundles compared to its older versions.
- *Component Dev Kit (CDK)*—This package is already used by the Angular Material library, which offers 30+ UI components. Angular 6 introduces the tree component, which is good for displaying hierarchical data. The new flexible overlay component automatically resizes and positions itself based on viewport size. The badge component can show notification markers.

  What if you don't want to use Angular Material but want to build your own library of UI components and control page layouts? You can do that with CDK. CDK contains multiple subpackages, including overlay, layout, scrolling, table, and tree.

  For example, the CDK table deals with rows and columns but doesn't have its own styling. Although Angular Material adds styles to the CDK table, you can create your own according to your company guidelines. CDK supports responsive web design layout, eliminating the need for using libraries like Flex Layout, or learning CSS Grid. Angular 7 adds virtual scrolling for large lists of elements by rendering only the items that fit onscreen. Angular 7 also adds drag-and-drop support.
- *Angular CLI*—The .angular-cli.json file is renamed to angular.json, and its structure changes. The `ng update @angular/cli` command automatically converts existing .angular-cli.json into angular.json. The `ng update @angular/core` command updates the dependencies in your project's package.json to the latest version of Angular. If you need to upgrade your existing project to Angular 6, read Yakov Fain's blog, "How I migrated a dozen projects to Angular 6 and then 7," at http://mng.bz/qZwC. Upgrades from Angular 6 to 7 should not require code changes.

  The `ng new library <name>` command generates a project for creating a library instead of an app. This command will generate a library project with a build system and test infrastructure.

  The `ng add` command can add a package to your project, but in addition to what `npm install` does, it can also modify certain files in your project so you don't need to do that manually. For example, the following command will install Angular Material, add a prebuilt theme to angular.json, add Material design icons to index.html, and add the `BrowserAnimationsModule` to the `@NgModule()` decorator:

```
ng add @angular/material
```

- *Schematics and* `ng update`—Angular CLI generates artifacts using a technology called *Schematics*, which uses code templates to generate various artifacts for your project. If you decide to create your own templates and have Angular CLI use them, Schematics will help you with this. The `ng update` command automatically updates your project dependencies and makes automated version fixes.

  With Schematics, you'll be able to create your own code transformations, similar to `ng update`. But you'll find some of the new prebuilt templates that come with Angular 6. For example, to generate all files for a `root-nav` component that already include the code of a sample Angular Material navigation bar, you can run the following command:

  ```
  ng generate @angular/material:materialNav --name=root-nav
  ```

We're looking forward to all the new features that will make Angular even better!

With that, we'd like to thank you for reading our book. We hope you liked it and will leave positive feedback so that Manning will ask us to write a new edition in the future.

appendix A
An overview of ECMAScript

ECMAScript is a standard for scripting languages. ECMAScript syntax is implemented in several languages, the most popular implementation being JavaScript. The first edition of the ECMAScript specification was released in 1997, and the sixth edition was finalized in 2015. This edition is known as ES6 or ES2015. Lots of new features were introduced in ES6 compared to its predecessor ES5, and most of the syntax covered in this appendix is about the ES6 syntax. ES7 was finalized in 2016, and ES8 in 2017. ES7 and ES8 didn't introduce many new syntax elements, but we'll cover the async/await syntax from ES8 at the end of this appendix.

At the time of writing, most web browsers fully support the ES6 specification, which introduced the most significant syntax additions. You can visit the ECMAScript compatibility site at http://mng.bz/ao59 to see the current state of ES6 support. Even if the users of your app have older browsers, you can develop in ES6/7/8 today and use transpilers like Traceur, Babel, or TypeScript to turn code that uses the latest syntax into its ES5 version.

We assume you're familiar with the ES5 syntax and APIs, and we'll cover only selected new features introduced in the newer editions of ECMAScript. In this appendix, we'll often compare the code snippets in ES5 with their ES6 equivalents, but ES6 doesn't deprecate any old syntax, so you'll be able to safely run legacy ES5 code in future web browsers or standalone JavaScript engines.

A.1 How to run the code samples

The code samples for this appendix come as JavaScript files with the .js extension. Typically, the code samples produce some output on the console, so you need to open the browser console to see the output. You can create a simple HTML file and include a particular .js file there using the `<script>` tag.

The other option is to use CodePen (see https://codepen.io). This site allows you to quickly write, test, and share apps that use HTML, CSS, and JavaScript. To save you some typing, we'll provide CodePen links to most of the code samples so you can just follow the link, see the selected code sample in action, and modify it if you choose to do so. If a code sample produces output on the console, just click Console at the bottom of the CodePen window to see it.

Let's review some of the relatively new features of ECMAScript as they're implemented in JavaScript.

A.2 Scope of variables and this

The scoping mechanism in ES5 is rather confusing. Regardless of where we declare a variable with the `var` keyword, the declaration is moved to the top of the execution context (for example, a function). This is called *hoisting* (see more on hoisting at http://mng.bz/3x9w). The use of the `this`keyword is also not as straightforward as it is in languages like Java or C#.

ES6 eliminates this hoisting confusion (discussed in the next section) by introducing the `let` keyword, and the `this` confusion is cured by using arrow functions. Let's look closer at the hoisting and `this` problems.

A.2.1 Hoisting of variable declarations

In JavaScript, all variable declarations that use the `var` keyword are moved to the top of the execution context even if a variable is declared inside the code block. Look at the following simple example that declares the variable `i` inside the `for` loop but uses it outside as well:

```
function foo() {

   for (var i=0; i<10; i++) {

   }

  console.log("i=" + i);
}

foo();
```

Running this code will print `i=10`. The variable `i` is still available outside the loop, even though it seems like it was meant to be used only inside the loop. JavaScript automatically hoists the variable declaration to the top.

In the preceding example, hoisting didn't cause any harm, because there was only one variable named `i`. If two variables with the same name are declared inside and outside the function, however, this may result in confusing behavior. Consider listing A.1, which declares the variable `customer` on the global scope. A bit later, we'll introduce another `customer` variable in the local scope, but for now let's keep it commented out.

Listing A.1 Hoisting a variable declaration

```
var customer = "Joe";
(function () {
    console.log("The name of the customer inside the function is "  +
    customer);
   /*  if (true) {
         var customer = "Mary";
     } */
})();
console.log("The name of the customer outside the function is "  + customer);
```

The global variable customer is visible inside and outside the function, and running this code will print the following:

```
The name of the customer inside the function is Joe
The name of the customer outside the function is Joe
```

Uncomment the if statement that declares and initializes the customer variable inside the curly braces. Now we have two variables with the same name—one on the global scope and another on the function scope. The console output is different now:

```
The name of the customer inside the function is undefined
The name of the customer outside the function is Joe
```

The reason is that in ES5, variable declarations are hoisted to the top of the scope (the expression within the topmost parentheses), but variable initializations with values aren't. When a variable is created, its initial value is undefined. The declaration of the second undefined customer variable was hoisted to the top of the expression, and console.log () printed the value of the variable declared inside the function, which has shadowed the value of the global variable customer.[1] Function declarations are hoisted as well, so we can invoke a function before it's declared:

```
doSomething();

function doSomething() {
   console.log("I'm doing something");
}
```

On the other hand, function expressions are considered variable initializations, so they aren't hoisted. The following code snippet will produce undefined for the doSomething variable:

```
doSomething();

var doSomething = function() {
   console.log("I'm doing something");
}
```

Let's see how ES6 can help us with scoping.

[1] See it on CodePen: http://mng.bz/cK9y.

A.2.2 Block scoping with let and const

Declaring variables with the ES6 `let` keyword instead of `var` allows variables to have block scoping. The next listing shows an example.

Listing A.2 Variables with block scoping

```
let customer = "Joe";
  (function () {
      console.log("The name of the customer inside the function is "  +
➥customer);
      if (true) {
       let customer = "Mary";
        console.log("The name of the customer inside the block is "  +
➥customer);
      }
  })();

console.log("The name of the customer in the global scope is "  + customer);
```

Now two `customer` variables have different scopes and values, and this program will print the following:

```
The name of the customer inside the function is Joe
The name of the customer inside the block is Mary
The name of the customer in the global scope is Joe
```

To put it simply, if we're developing a new application, we don't use `var`. We use `let` instead. The `let` keyword allows us to assign and reassign a value to a variable as many times as we want. The only exception to this rule is a `for` loop. Using `let` to declare a loop variable may cause performance issues.

If we want to declare a variable that doesn't change its value after its initialization, we declare it with the `const` keyword for constants. Constants also support block scope.

The only difference between `let` and `const` is that the latter won't allow the assigned value to be changed. The best practice is to start declaring variables with `const`; if we see that this value needs to change, we replace `const` with `let`. Listing A.2 should use `const` instead of `let`, because we never reassigned the values for both `customer` variables.[2]

A.3 Template literals

ES6 introduces a new syntax for working with string literals, which can contain embedded expressions. This feature is known as *string interpolation.*

In ES5 we'd use concatenation to create a string that contains string literals combined with the values of variables:

```
const customerName = "John Smith";
console.log("Hello" + customerName);
```

[2] See it on CodePen: http://mng.bz/fkJd

In ES6, template literals are surrounded with backtick symbols, and we can embed expressions right inside a literal by placing them between the curly braces, prefixed with a dollar sign. In the next code snippet, the value of the variable `customerName` is embedded in the string literal:

```
const customerName = "John Smith";
console.log(`Hello ${customerName}`);

function getCustomer() {
  return "Allan Lou";
}
console.log(`Hello ${getCustomer()}`);
```

The output of this code is shown here:[3]

```
Hello John Smith
Hello Allan Lou
```

In the preceding example, we embed the value of the variable `customerName` into the template literal, and then embed the value returned by the `getCustomer()` function. We can use any valid JavaScript expression between the curly braces.

A.3.1 Multiline strings

Strings can span multiple lines in our code. Using backticks, we can write multiline strings without the need to concatenate them or use the backslash character:

```
const message = `Please enter a password that
               has at least 8 characters and
               includes a capital letter`;

console.log(message);
```

The resulting string will treat all spaces as part of the string, so the output will look like this:[4]

```
Please enter a password that
               has at least 8 characters and
               includes a capital letter
```

A.4 Optional parameters and default values

In ES6, we can specify default values for function parameters (arguments) that will be used if no value is provided during function invocation. Say we're writing a function to calculate tax, that takes two arguments: the annual income and the state where the person lives. If the state value isn't provided, we want to use Florida as a default.

In ES5, we'd need to start the function body by checking whether the state value was provided; otherwise, we'd use Florida:

[3] See it in CodePen at http://mng.bz/Ey30

[4] See it in CodePen: http://mng.bz/1SSP.

```
function calcTaxES5(income, state) {

    state = state || "Florida";

    console.log("ES5. Calculating tax for the resident of " + state +
                                        " with the income " + income);
}

calcTaxES5(50000);
```

Here's what this code prints:

```
"ES5. Calculating tax for the resident of Florida with the income 50000"
```

In ES6, we can specify the default value right in the function signature:

```
function calcTaxES6(income, state = "Florida") {

  console.log("ES6. Calculating tax for the resident of " + state +
                                    " with the income " + income);
}

calcTaxES6(50000);
```

The output looks similar:[5]

```
"ES6. Calculating tax for the resident of Florida with the income 50000"
```

Rather than providing a hardcoded value for an optional parameter, we can invoke a function that returns one:

```
function calcTaxES6(income, state = getDefaultState()) {
console.log("ES6. Calculating tax for the resident of " + state +
            " with the income " + income);
};

function getDefaultState() {
return "Florida";
}

calcTaxES6(50000);
```

Just keep in mind that the `getDefaultState()` function will be invoked each time we invoke `calcTaxES6()`, which may have performance consequences. This new syntax for optional parameters means we write less code and the code is easier to understand.

A.5 Arrow function expressions, this, and that

ES6 introduced arrow function expressions, which provide a shorter notation for anonymous functions and add lexical scope for the `this` variable. In some other programming languages (such as C# and Java) a similar syntax is called *lambda expressions.*

---

[5] See it in CodePen: http://mng.bz/U51z.

The syntax of arrow function expressions consists of arguments, the fat-arrow sign (=>), and the function body. If the function body is just one expression, we don't even need curly braces. If a single-expression function returns a value, there's no need to write the `return` statement—the result is returned implicitly:

```
let sum = (arg1, arg2) => arg1 + arg2;
```

The body of a multiline arrow function expression should be enclosed in curly braces and use the explicit `return` statement:

```
(arg1, arg2) => {
  // do something
  return someResult;
}
```

If an arrow function doesn't have any arguments, use empty parentheses:

```
() => {
  // do something
  return someResult;
}
```

If the function has just one argument, parentheses aren't mandatory:

```
arg1 => {
  // do something
}
```

In the following code snippet, we pass arrow function expressions as arguments to an array's `reduce()` method to calculate a sum, and `filter()` to print even numbers:

```
const myArray = [1, 2, 3, 4, 5];

console.log( "The sum of myArray elements is " +
                myArray.reduce((a,b) => a+b));  // prints 15

console.log( "The even numbers in myArray are " +
                myArray.filter( value => value % 2 === 0)); // prints 2 4
```

Now that you're familiar with the syntax of arrow functions, let's see how they streamline working with the `this` object reference.

In ES5 , figuring out which object is referred to by the `this` keyword isn't always a simple task. Search online for "JavaScript this and that," and you'll find multiple posts where people complain about `this` pointing to the "wrong" object. The `this` reference can have different values depending on how the function is invoked and whether strict mode was used (see the documentation for strict mode on the Mozilla Developer Network at http://mng.bz/VNVL). We'll illustrate the problem first, and then we'll show you the solution offered by ES6.

Consider the code in the following listing that invokes the anonymous function every second. The function prints randomly generated prices for the stock symbol provided to the `StockQuoteGenerator ()` constructor function.

Listing A.3 `this` and `that`

```
function StockQuoteGenerator(symbol) {
    // this.symbol = symbol;
     const that = this;
     that.symbol = symbol;

     setInterval( function () {
         console.log("The price of " + that.symbol
                 + " is " + Math.random());
     }, 1000);
 }
 const stockQuoteGenerator = new StockQuoteGenerator("IBM");
```

The line that's commented out in listing A.3 illustrates the wrong way of using `this` when a value is needed in the anonymous function that seemingly has the same `this` reference but doesn't. If we hadn't saved the value of `this` in `that`, and used `this.symbol` inside the anonymous function, it would print `undefined` instead of `IBM`. You'll see the same behavior not only if a function is invoked inside `setInterval ()`, but if a function is invoked in any callback. Inside the callback, `this` would point at the global object, which is not the same as `this` defined by the `StockQuoteGenerator()` constructor function.[6] The other solution for ensuring that a function runs in a particular `this` object is to use the JavaScript `call()`, `apply()`, or `bind()` functions.

> **NOTE** If you're not familiar with the `this` problem in JavaScript, check out Richard Bovell's article, "Understand JavaScript's 'this' with Clarity, and Master It" at http://mng.bz/ZQfz.

The following listing illustrates an arrow function solution that eliminates the need to store `this` in `that`.

Listing A.4 Fat-arrow function

```
function StockQuoteGenerator(symbol) {
      this.symbol = symbol;
      setInterval( () => {
                 console.log("The price of " + this.symbol
                         + " is " + Math.random());
              }, 1000);
}

const stockQuoteGenerator = new StockQuoteGenerator("IBM");
```

[6] See it in CodePen: http://mng.bz/cK70.

Listing A.4 will properly resolve the `this` reference. An arrow function that's given as an argument to `setInterval ()` uses the `this` value of the enclosing context, so it will recognize `IBM` as the value of `this.symbol`.

A.6 The rest operator

In ES5 , writing a function with a variable number of parameters required using a special `arguments` object. This object is *similar* to an array, and it contains values corresponding to the arguments passed to a function. The implicit `arguments` variable could be treated as a local variable in any function.

The rest operator represents a variable number of arguments in a function, and it has to be the last one in the argument list. If the name of the function argument starts with the three dots, the function will get the rest of the arguments in an array. The ES6 rest operator is represented by three dots (...).

For example, we can pass multiple customers to a function using a single variable name with a rest operator:

```
function processCustomers(...customers) {
  // implementation of the function goes here
}
```

Inside this function, we can handle the `customers` data the same way we'd handle any array. Imagine that we need to write a function to calculate taxes that must be invoked with the first argument, `income`, followed by any number of arguments representing the names of the customers. Listing A.5 shows how we could process a variable number of arguments using first ES5 and then ES6 syntax. The `calcTaxES5()` function uses the object named `arguments`, and the `calcTaxES6()` function uses the ES6 rest operator.

Listing A.5 Rest operator

```
// ES5 and arguments object
  function calcTaxES5() {

      console.log("ES5. Calculating tax for customers with the income ",
                              arguments[0]);   // income is the first element

      // extract an array starting from 2nd element
      var customers = [].slice.call(arguments, 1);

      customers.forEach(function (customer) {
          console.log("Processing ", customer);
      });
  }

  calcTaxES5(50000, "Smith", "Johnson", "McDonald");
  calcTaxES5(750000, "Olson", "Clinton");

// ES6 and rest operator
  function calcTaxES6(income, ...customers) {
      console.log(`ES6. Calculating tax for customers with the income ${income}`);
```

```
    customers.forEach( (customer) => console.log(`Processing ${customer}`));
}

calcTaxES6(50000, "Smith", "Johnson", "McDonald");
calcTaxES6(750000, "Olson", "Clinton");
```

Both functions, `calcTaxES5()` and `calcTaxES6()`, produce the same results:[7]

```
ES5. Calculating tax for customers with the income 50000
Processing Smith
Processing Johnson
Processing McDonald
ES5. Calculating tax for customers with the income 750000
Processing Olson
Processing Clinton
ES6. Calculating tax for customers with the income 50000
Processing Smith
Processing Johnson
Processing McDonald
ES6. Calculating tax for customers with the income 750000
Processing Olson
Processing Clinton
```

There's a difference in handling customers, though. Because the `arguments` object isn't a real array, we had to create an array in the ES5 version by using the `slice ()` and `call()` methods to extract the names of customers starting from the second element in `arguments`. The ES6 version doesn't require us to use these tricks because the rest operator gives us a regular array of customers. Using the rest arguments made the code simpler and more readable.

A.7 The spread operator

The ES6 spread operator is also represented by three dots (...), like the rest operator, but whereas the rest operator can turn a variable number of parameters into an array, the spread operator can do the opposite: turn an array into a list of values or function parameters.

> **TIP** If you see three dots on the right side of the equals sign, it's a spread operator. Three dots on the left of the equals sign represent the rest operator.

Say we have two arrays and we need to add the elements of the second array to the end of the first one. With the spread operator, it's one line of code:

```
let array1= [...array2];
```

Here, the spread operator extracts each element of `myArray` and adds to the new array (here, the square brackets mean "create a new array"). We can also create a copy of an array as follows:

```
array1.push(...array2);
```

[7] See it on CodePen: http://mng.bz/I2zq.

Finding a maximum value in the array is also easy with the spread operator:

```
const maxValue = Math.max(...myArray);
```

In some cases, we want to clone an object. For example, suppose we have an object that stores the state of our app and want to create a new object when one of the state properties changes. We don't want to mutate the original object but want to clone it with modification of one or more properties. One way to implement immutable objects is by using the `Object.assign()` function. The following listing creates a clone of the object first and then creates another clone, changing the `lastName` at the same time.

Listing A.6 Cloning with `assign ()`

```
// Clone with Object.assign()
const myObject = {name: "Mary" , lastName: "Smith"};
const clone = Object.assign({}, myObject);
console.log(clone);

// Clone with modifying the `lastName` property
const cloneModified = Object.assign({}, myObject, {lastName: "Lee"});
console.log(cloneModified);
```

The spread operator offers a more concise syntax for achieving the same goals, as you can see in the following listing.

Listing A.7 Cloning with `spread`

```
// Clone with spread
const myObject = { name: "Mary" , lastName: "Smith"};
const cloneSpread = {...myObject};
console.log(cloneSpread);

// Clone with modifying the `lastName`
const cloneSpreadModified = {...myObject, lastName: "Lee"};
console.log(cloneSpreadModified);
```

Our `myObject` has two properties: `name` and `lastName`. The line that clones `myObject` with modification of the `lastName` will still work even if we or someone else adds more properties to `myObject`.[8]

In chapter 15, we show you how to work with immutable state objects. There, we use the spread operator to clone the state object.

A.8 Generator functions

When a browser executes a JavaScript function, it runs without interrupting its own flow to the end. But the execution of a *generator function* can be paused and resumed multiple times. A generator function can yield control to the calling script, which runs on the same thread.

[8] See it in CodePen: http://mng.bz/X2pL.

As soon as the code in a generator function reaches the `yield` keyword, it gets suspended, and the calling script can resume the function's execution by calling `next ()` on the generator. To turn a regular function into a generator, we need to place an asterisk between the `function` keyword and the function name. Here's an example:

```
function* doSomething() {

  console.log("Started processing");

  yield;

  console.log("Resumed processing");
}
```

When we invoke this function, it doesn't immediately execute the function code but returns a special `Generator` object, which serves as an iterator. The following line won't print anything:

```
var iterator = doSomething();
```

To start executing the body of the function, we need to call the `next()` method on the generator:

```
iterator.next();
```

After the preceding line, the `doSomething()` function will print "Started processing" and will be suspended because of the `yield` operator. Calling `next()` again will print "Resumed processing."

Generator functions are useful when we need to write a function to produce a stream of data, but we want to control *when* to handle the next stream value. Imagine that we need a function to retrieve and produce stock prices for a specified stock symbol (such as IBM). If a stock price falls below a specified value (the limit price), we want to purchase this stock.

The generator function in the next listing, `getStockPrice()`, emulates this scenario by generating random prices with `Math.random()`.

Listing A.8 `getStockPrice()`

```
function* getStockPrice(symbol) {

  while (true) {
    yield Math.random()*100;

    console.log(`resuming for ${symbol}`);
  }
}
```

If there's a value after `yield`, it's returned to the caller, but the function isn't completed yet. Even though the `getStockPrice()` function has an infinite loop, it will yield (return) the price only if the script that invoked `getStockPrice()` calls `next()` on this generator, as in the following listing.

Listing A.9 Invoking `getStockPrice ()`

```
function* getStockPrice(symbol) {

  while (true) {
    yield Math.random()*100;

    console.log(`resuming for ${symbol}`);
  }
}

const priceGenerator = getStockPrice("IBM");

const limitPrice = 15;
 let price = 100;

while (price > limitPrice) {

    price = priceGenerator.next().value;
     console.log (`The generator returned ${price}`);
}

console.log(`buying at ${price} !!!`);
```

- Creates the Generator object but doesn't execute the body of the getStockPrice() function
- Sets the limit price to 15 and the initial price to 100 dollars
- Keeps requesting stock prices until they fall below 15 dollars
- Requests the next price and prints it to the console
- If the price falls below 15 dollars, the loop is over and the program prints a message about buying the stock and its price.

Running listing A.9 will print something like this:

```
The generator returned 61.63144460879266
resuming for IBM
The generator returned 96.60782956052572
resuming for IBM
The generator returned 31.163037824444473
resuming for IBM
The generator returned 18.416578718461096
resuming for IBM
The generator returned 55.80756475683302
resuming for IBM
The generator returned 14.203652134165168
buying at 14.203652134165168 !!!
```

Note the order of the messages. When we call the `next()` method on the `priceGenerator`, the execution of the suspended `getStockPrice()` method resumes at the line below `yield`, which prints `"resuming for IBM"`. Even though the control flow went outside the function and then came back, `getStockPrice()` remembers that the value of `symbol` was `IBM`. When the `yield` operator returns control to the outside script, it creates a snapshot of the stack so it can remember all the values of the local variables. When execution of the generator function is resumed, these values haven't been lost.[9]

With generators, you can separate the implementation of certain operations (such as getting a price quote) and the consumption of the data produced by these

[9] See it on CodePen: http://mng.bz/4d40.

operations. The consumer of the data lazily evaluates the results and decides if requesting more data is necessary.

A.9 Destructuring

Creating instances of objects means constructing them in memory. The term *destructuring* means taking objects apart. In ES5, we could deconstruct any object or a collection by writing a function to do it. ES6 introduces the destructuring assignment syntax that allows us to extract data from an object's properties or an array in a simple expression by specifying a *matching pattern*. It's easier to explain by example, which we'll do next.

A.9.1 Destructuring objects

Let's say that a `getStock()` function returns a `Stock` object that has the attributes `symbol` and `price`. In ES5, if we wanted to assign the values of these attributes to separate variables, we'd need to create a variable to store the `Stock` object first, and then write two statements assigning the object attributes to corresponding variables:

```
var stock = getStock();
var symbol = stock.symbol;
var price = stock.price;
```

Starting in ES6, we just need to write a matching pattern on the left and assign the `Stock` object to it:

```
let {symbol, price} = getStock();
```

It's a little unusual to see curly braces on the left of the equals sign, but this is part of the syntax of a matching expression. When we see curly braces on the left side, we think of them as a block of code and not the object literal. The following listing demonstrates getting the `Stock` object from the `getStock()` function and destructuring it into two variables.

Listing A.10 Destructuring an object

```
function getStock() {

    return {
        symbol: "IBM",
        price: 100.00
    };
}

let {symbol, price} = getStock();

console.log(`The price of ${symbol} is ${price}`);
```

Running that script will print the following:

```
The price of IBM is 100
```

In other words, we bind a set of data (object properties, in this case) to a set of variables (symbol and price) in one assignment expression. Even if the Stock object had more than two properties, the preceding destructuring expression would still work because symbol and price would have matched the pattern. The matching expression lists only the variables for the object attributes we're interested in.[10]

Listing A.10 works because the names of the variables are the same as the names of the Stock attributes. Let's change symbol to sym:

```
let {sym, price} = getStock();
```

Now we'll get an error "symbol is not defined" because JavaScript doesn't know that the object's symbol attribute should be assigned to the variable sym. This is an example of a wrong matching pattern. If we really want to map the variable named sym to the symbol attribute, we introduce an alias name for symbol:

```
let {sym: symbol, price} = getStock();
```

If we provide more variables on the left than the number of attributes the object has, the extra variables will get the value undefined. If we add a stockExchange variable on the left, it will be initialized with undefined, because there's no such attribute in the object returned by getStock():

```
let {symbol, price, stockExchange} = getStock();
console.log(`The price of ${symbol} is ${price} ${stockExchange}`);
```

If we apply the preceding destructuring assignment to the same Stock object, the console output will look like this:

```
The price of IBM is 100 undefined
```

If we want the stockExchange variable to have a default value, such as "NASDAQ", we could rewrite the destructuring expression like this:

```
let {symbol, price, stockExchange = "NASDAQ"} = getStock();
```

We can also destructure nested objects. Listing A.11 creates a nested object that represents Microsoft stock and passes it to the printStockInfo() function, which pulls the stock symbol and name of the stock exchange from this object.

Listing A.11 Destructuring a nested object

```
let msft = {
    symbol: "MSFT",
    lastPrice: 50.00,
    exchange: {       <—— The nested object
        name: "NASDAQ",
       tradingHours: "9:30am-4pm"
```

[10] See in CodePen: http://mng.bz/CI47.

```
    }
};

function printStockInfo(stock) {
    let {symbol, exchange: {name}} = stock;
     console.log(`The ${symbol} stock is traded at ${name}`);
}

printStockInfo(msft);
```

Destructures a nested object to get the name of the stock exchange

Running the preceding script will print the following:[11]

```
The MSFT stock is traded at NASDAQ
```

Say we're writing a function to handle a browser DOM event. In the HTML part, we invoke this function, passing the event object as an argument. The event object has multiple properties, but our handler function only needs the `target` property to identify the component that dispatched this event. The destructuring syntax makes it easy:

```
<button id="myButton">Click me</button>
...
document
  .getElementById("myButton")
  .addEventListener("click", ({target}) =>
                              console.log(target));
```

Note the destructuring syntax `{target}` in the function argument.[12]

A.9.2 Destructuring arrays

Array destructuring works much like object destructuring, but instead of curly brackets, we need to use square ones. Whereas in destructuring objects we need to specify variables that match object properties, with arrays, we specify variables that match arrays' indexes. The following code extracts the values of two array elements into two variables:

```
let [name1, name2] = ["Smith", "Clinton"];
console.log(`name1 = ${name1}, name2 = ${name2}`);
```

The output will look like this:

```
name1 = Smith, name2 = Clinton
```

If we wanted to extract the second element of this array, the matching pattern would look like this:

```
let [, name2] = ["Smith", "Clinton"];
```

---

[11] See it in CodePen: http://mng.bz/Xauq.

[12] See it on CodePen: http://mng.bz/Dj24.

If a function returns an array, the destructuring syntax turns it into a function with a multiple-value return, as shown in the `getCustomers()` function:

```
function getCustomers() {
    return ["Smith", , , "Gonzales"];
}

let [firstCustomer, , , lastCustomer] = getCustomers();
console.log(`The first customer is ${firstCustomer} and the last one is ${las
     tCustomer}`);
```

Now let's combine array destructuring with rest parameters. Let's say we have an array of multiple customers, but we want to process only the first two. The following code snippet shows how to do it:

```
let customers = ["Smith", "Clinton", "Lou", "Gonzales"];

let [firstCust, secondCust, ...otherCust] = customers;

console.log(`The first customer is ${firstCust} and the second one is ${secon
     dCust}`);
console.log(`Other customers are ${otherCust}`);
```

Here's the console output produced by that code:

```
The first customer is Smith and the second one is Clinton
Other customers are Lou, Gonzales
```

On a similar note, we can pass the matching pattern with a rest parameter to a function:

```
var customers = ["Smith", "Clinton", "Lou", "Gonzales"];

function processFirstTwoCustomers([firstCust, secondCust, ...otherCust]) {

  console.log(`The first customer is ${firstCust} and the second one is ${sec
     ondCust}`);
  console.log(`Other customers are ${otherCust}`);

}

processFirstTwoCustomers(customers);
```

The output will be the same:

```
The first customer is Smith and the second one is Clinton
Other customers are Lou,Gonzales
```

To summarize, the benefit of destructuring is that we can write less code when we need to initialize some variables with data that's located in object properties or arrays.

A.10 Iterating with forEach(), for-in, and for-of

We can loop through a collection of objects using different JavaScript keywords and APIs. In this section, we'll show you how to use the `for-of` loop. We'll compare it with `for-in` loops and the `forEach()` function .

A.10.1 Using the forEach() method

Consider the following code, which iterates through an array of four numbers. This array also has an additional `description` property , which is ignored by `forEach()`:

```
var numbersArray = [1, 2, 3, 4];
numbersArray.description = "four numbers";

numbersArray.forEach((n) => console.log(n));
```

The output of the script looks like this:

```
1
2
3
4
```

The `forEach()` method takes a function as an argument and properly prints four numbers from the array, ignoring the `description` property. Another limitation of `forEach()` is that it doesn't allow us to break the loop prematurely. We'd need to use the `every()` method instead of `forEach()` or come up with some other hack to do that. Let's see how the `for-in` loop can help.

A.10.2 Using the for-in loop

The `for-in` loop iterates over the *property names* of objects and data collections. In JavaScript, any object is a collection of key-value pairs, where a *key* is a property name and a *value* is the property value. The array has five properties: four for the numbers, and `description`. Let's iterate through the properties of this array:

```
var numbersArray = [1, 2, 3, 4];
numbersArray.description = "four numbers";

for (let n in numbersArray) {
  console.log(n);
}
```

The output of the preceding code looks like this:

```
0
1
2
3
description
```

Running this code through a debugger shows that each of these properties is a `string`. To see the actual values of the properties, print the array elements using the `numbersArray[n]` notation:

```
var numbersArray = [1, 2, 3, 4];
numbersArray.description = "four numbers";

for (let n in numbersArray) {
    console.log(numbersArray[n]);
}
```

Now the output looks like this:

```
1
2
3
4
four numbers
```

As you can see, the `for-in` loop iterated through all the properties, not only the data, which may not be what you need. Let's try the new `for-of` syntax.

A.10.3 Using for-of

ES6 introduced the `for-of` loop, which allows us to iterate over data regardless of what other properties the data collection has. We can break out of this loop if need be by using the `break` keyword :

```
var numbersArray = [1, 2, 3, 4];
numbersArray.description = "four numbers";

console.log("Running for-of for the entire array");
for (let n of numbersArray) {
  console.log(n);
}

console.log("Running for-of with a break");
for (let n of numbersArray) {
  if (n > 2) break;

  console.log(n);
}
```

This script produces the following output:[13]

```
Running for-of for the entire array
1
2
3
4
Running for-of with a break
1
2
```

[13] See it in CodePen: http://mng.bz/53DO.

The for-of loop works with any iterable object, including Array, Map, Set, and others. Strings are iterable as well. The following code prints the content of the string "John", one character at a time:

```
for (let char of "John") {
  console.log(char);
}
```

A.11 Classes and inheritance

Although ES5 supports object-oriented programming and inheritance, with ES6 classes, the code is easier to read and write.

In ES5, objects can be created either from scratch or by inheriting from other objects. By default, all JavaScript objects are inherited from Object. This object inheritance is implemented via a special property called prototype, which points at this object's ancestor. This is called *prototypal inheritance*. For example, to create an NJTax object that inherits from the object Tax, we can write something like this:

```
function Tax() {
  // The code of the tax object goes here
}

function NJTax() {
  // The code of New Jersey tax object goes here
}

NJTax.prototype = new Tax();       <—— Inherits NJTax from Tax

var njTax = new NJTax();
```

ES6 introduced the keywords class and extends to bring the syntax in line with other object-oriented languages such as Java and C#. The ES6 equivalent of the preceding code is shown next:

```
class Tax {
  // The code of the tax class goes here
}

class NJTax extends Tax {
  // The code of New Jersey tax object goes here
}

let njTax = new NJTax();
```

The Tax class is an ancestor or *superclass*, and NJTax is a descendant or *subclass*. We can also say that the NJTax class has the "is-a" relation with the class Tax. In other words, NJTax is a Tax. You can implement additional functionality in NJTax, but NJTax still "is a" or "is a kind of" Tax. Similarly, if we create an Employee class that inherits from Person, we can say that Employee is a Person.

We can create one or more instances of the objects like this:

```
var tax1 = new Tax();       <-- First instance of the Tax object
 var tax2 = new Tax();      <-- Second instance of the Tax object
```

NOTE Class declarations aren't hoisted. You need to declare the class first and then work with it.

Each of these objects will have properties and methods that exist in the `Tax` class, but they will have different *state*; for example, the first instance could be created for a customer with an annual income of $50,000, and the second for a customer who earns $75,000. Each instance would share the same copy of the methods declared in the `Tax` class, so there's no duplication of code.

In ES5, we can also avoid code duplication by declaring methods, not inside the objects, but on their prototypes:

```
function Tax() {
  // The code of the tax object goes here
}

Tax.prototype = {
  calcTax: function() {
    // code to calculate tax goes here
  }
}
```

JavaScript remains a language with prototypal inheritance, but ES6 allows us to write more elegant code:

```
class Tax() {

  calcTax() {
    // code to calculate tax goes here
  }
}
```

Class member variables aren't supported

The ES6 syntax doesn't allow you to declare class member variables, as you can in Java, C#, or TypeScript. The following syntax is *not* supported:

```
class Tax {
  var income;
}
```

A.11.1 Constructors

During instantiation, classes execute the code placed in special methods called *constructors*. In languages like Java and C#, the name of the constructor must be the same as the name of the class; but in ES6, we specify the class's constructor by using the `constructor` keyword:

```
class Tax {

  constructor(income) {
    this.income = income;
  }
}

var myTax = new Tax(50000);
```

A constructor is a special method that's executed only once: when the object is created. The Tax class doesn't declare a separate class-level income variable, but creates it dynamically on the this object, initializing this.income with the values of the constructor argument. The this variable points at the instance of the current object.

The next example shows how we can create an instance of an NJTax subclass, providing the income of 50,000 to its constructor:

```
class Tax {
    constructor(income) {
       this.income = income;
    }
}

class NJTax extends Tax {
    // The code specific to New Jersey tax goes here
}

let njTax = new NJTax(50000);

console.log(`The income in njTax instance is ${njTax.income}`);
```

The output of this code snippet is as follows:

```
The income in njTax instance is 50000
```

Because the NJTax subclass doesn't define its own constructor, the one from the Tax superclass is automatically invoked during the instantiation of NJTax. This wouldn't be the case if a subclass defined its own constructor. You'll see such an example in the next section.

A.11.2 The super keyword and the super function

The super() function allows a subclass (descendant) to invoke a constructor from a superclass (ancestor). The super keyword is used to call a method defined in a superclass. Listing A.12 illustrates both super() and super. The Tax class has a calculateFederalTax() method, and its NJTax subclass adds the calculateStateTax() method. Both of these classes have their own versions of the calcMinTax() method.

Listing A.12 super() and super

```
class Tax {
    constructor(income) {
       this.income = income;
    }
```

```
    calculateFederalTax() {
        console.log(`Calculating federal tax for income ${this.income}`);
    }

    calcMinTax() {
        console.log("In Tax. Calculating min tax");
        return 123;
    }
}

class NJTax extends Tax {
   constructor(income, stateTaxPercent) {
       super(income);
       this.stateTaxPercent=stateTaxPercent;
   }

   calculateStateTax() {
       console.log(`Calculating state tax for income ${this.income}`);
   }

    calcMinTax() {
        let minTax = super.calcMinTax();
        console.log(`In NJTax. Will adjust min tax of ${minTax}`);
    }
}

const theTax = new NJTax(50000, 6);

theTax.calculateFederalTax();
theTax.calculateStateTax();

theTax.calcMinTax();
```

Running this code produces the following output:[14]

```
Calculating federal tax for income 50000
Calculating state tax for income 50000
In Tax. Calculating min tax
In NJTax. Will adjust min tax of 123
```

The `NJTax` class has its own explicitly defined constructor with two arguments, `income` and `stateTaxPercent`, which we provide while instantiating `NJTax`. To make sure the constructor of `Tax` is invoked (it sets the `income` attribute on the object), we explicitly call it from the subclass's constructor: `super(income)`. Without this line, running listing A.12 would report an error; we must call the constructor of a superclass from the derived constructor by calling the function `super()`.

The other way of invoking code in superclasses is by using the `super` keyword. Both `Tax` and `NJTax` have the `calcMinTax()` methods. The one in the `Tax` superclass calculates the base minimum amount according to federal tax laws, whereas the subclass's version of this method uses the base value and adjusts it. Both methods have the same signature, so we have a case for *method overriding*.

---

[14] See it in CodePen: http://mng.bz/6e9S.

By calling `super.calcMinTax()`, we ensure that the base federal tax is taken into account for calculating state tax. If we didn't call `super.calcMinTax()`, the subclass's version of the `calcMinTax()` method would apply. Method overriding is often used to replace the functionality of the method in the superclass without changing its code.

A warning about classes and inheritance

ES6 classes are just syntactic sugar that increases code readability. Under the hood, JavaScript still uses prototypal inheritance, which allows you to replace the ancestor dynamically at runtime, whereas a class can have only one ancestor. Try to avoid creating deep inheritance hierarchies, because they reduce the flexibility of your code and complicate refactoring if it's needed.

Although using the `super` keyword lets you invoke code in the ancestor, you should try to avoid using it to avoid tight coupling between the descendant and ancestor objects. The less the descendant knows about its ancestor, the better.

A.11.3 *Static variables*

If we need a class property that's shared by multiple class instances, we need to create it outside of the class declaration. In listing A.13, the static variable `counter` is visible from both instances of the object `A` by invoking the `printCounter()` method. But if we try to access the variable `counter` on the instance level, it'll be undefined.

Listing A.13 Sharing a class property

```
class A {
  printCounter(){
    console.log("static counter=" + A.counter);
  };
}

A.counter = 25;

let a1 = new A();
a1.printCounter();
console.log("In the a1 instance counter=" + a1.counter);

let a2 = new A();
a2.printCounter();
console.log("In the a2 instance counter=" + a2.counter);
```

That code produces this output:[15]

```
static counter=25
In the a1 instance counter=undefined
static counter=25"
In the a2 instance counter=undefined
```

[15] See it in CodePen: http://mng.bz/lCXD.

A.11.4 Getters, setters, and method definitions

The syntax for the object's getter and setter methods isn't new in ES6, but let's review it before going on to the new syntax for defining methods. Setters and getters bind functions to object properties. Consider the declaration and the use of the object literal `Tax`:

```
const Tax = {
  taxableIncome: 0,
  get income() {return this.taxableIncome;},
  set income(value) { this.taxableIncome = value}
};

Tax.income=50000;
console.log("Income: " + Tax.income); // prints Income: 50000
```

NOTE Note that you assign and retrieve the value of `income` using dot notation, as if it were a declared property of the `Tax` object.

In ES5, we'd need to use the `function` keyword, such as `calculateTax = function(){…}`. With ES6, we can skip the `function` keyword in any method definition:

```
const Tax = {
    taxableIncome: 0,
    get income() {return this.taxableIncome;},
    set income(value) {this.taxableIncome = value},
    calculateTax() {return this.taxableIncome*0.13}
};

Tax.income = 50000;
console.log(`For the income ${Tax.income} your tax is ${Tax.calculateTax()}`);
```

The output of that code comes next:[16]

```
For the income 50000 your tax is 6500
```

Getters and setters offer a convenient syntax for working with properties. For example, if we decide to add some validation code to the `income` getter, the scripts using the `Tax.income` notation won't need to be changed. The bad part is that ES6 doesn't support private variables in classes, so nothing stops programmers from accessing the variable used in a getter or setter (such as `taxableIncome`) directly. We'll talk about hiding (encapsulating) variables in section A.13.

A.12 Asynchronous processing

To arrange asynchronous processing in previous implementations of ECMAScript, we had to use *callbacks*, functions that are given as arguments to another function for invocation. Callbacks can be called synchronously or asynchronously.

[16] See it in CodePen: http://mng.bz/5729.

Earlier, we passed a callback to the `forEach()` method for synchronous invocation. In making AJAX requests to the server, we pass a callback function to be invoked asynchronously when the result arrives from the server.

A.12.1 A callback hell

Let's consider an example of getting data about some ordered products from the server. It starts with an asynchronous call to the server to get the information about the customers, and then for each customer we'll need to make another call to get the orders. For each order, we need to get products, and the final call will get the product details.

In asynchronous processing, we don't know when each of these operations will complete, so we need to write callback functions that are invoked when the previous one is complete. Let's use the `setTimeout()` function to emulate delays, as if each operation requires one second to complete. Figure A.1 shows what this code may look like.

```
(function getProductDetails() {

    setTimeout(function () {
        console.log('Getting customers');
        setTimeout(function () {
            console.log('Getting orders');
            setTimeout(function () {
                console.log('Getting products');
                setTimeout(function () {
                    console.log('Getting product details')
                }, 1000);
            }, 1000);
        }, 1000);
    }, 1000);
})();
```


Figure A.1 Callback hell or pyramid of doom

> **NOTE** Using callbacks is considered an anti-pattern, also known as Pyramid of Doom, as seen in figure A.1 on the left. In our code sample we had four callbacks, and this level of nesting makes the code hard to read. In real-world apps, the pyramid may quickly grow, making the code very hard to read and debug.

Running the code in figure A.1 will print the following messages with one-second delays:[17]

```
Getting customers
Getting orders
Getting products
Getting product details
```

[17] See it in CodePen: http://mng.bz/DAX5.

A.12.2 ES6 promises

When you press the button on your coffee machine, you don't get a cup of coffee that very second. You get a promise that you'll get a cup of coffee sometime later. If you didn't forget to provide the water and the ground coffee, the promise will be *resolved*, and you can enjoy the coffee in a minute or so. If your coffee machine is out of water or coffee, the promise will be *rejected*. The entire process is asynchronous, and you can do other things while your coffee is being brewed.

JavaScript promises allow us to avoid nested calls and make the async code more readable. The `Promise` object represents an eventual completion or failure of an async operation. After the `Promise` object is created, it waits and listens for the result of an asynchronous operation and lets us know if it succeeded or failed so we can proceed with the next steps accordingly. The `Promise` object represents the future result of an operation, and it can be in one of these states:

- *Fulfilled*—The operation successfully completed.
- *Rejected*—The operation failed and returned an error.
- *Pending*—The operation is in progress, neither fulfilled nor rejected.

We can instantiate a `Promise` object by providing two functions to its constructor: the function to call if the operation is fulfilled, and the function to call if the operation is rejected. Consider a script with a `getCustomers()` function , shown in the following listing.

Listing A.14 Using a promise

```
function getCustomers() {

  return new Promise(
     function (resolve, reject) {

      console.log("Getting customers");
        // Emulate an async server call here
      setTimeout(function() {
        var success = true;
        if (success) {
          resolve("John Smith");          <— Gets the customer
         } else {
          reject("Can't get customers");       <— Invoked if an error occurs
         }
      }, 1000);

     }
  );
}

getCustomers()
  .then((cust) => console.log(cust))     <— Invoked when the promise is fulfilled
   .catch((err) => console.log(err));     <— Invoked if the promise is rejected
 console.log("Invoked getCustomers. Waiting for results");
```

The `getCustomers()` function returns a `Promise` object, which is instantiated with a function that has `resolve` and `reject` as the constructor's arguments. In the code, we invoke `resolve()` if we receive the customer information. For simplicity, `setTimeout()` emulates an asynchronous call that lasts one second. We also hardcode the `success` flag to be `true`. In a real-world scenario, we could make a request with the `XMLHttpRequest` object and invoke `resolve()` if the result was successfully retrieved or `reject()` if an error occurred.

At the bottom of listing A.14, we attach `then()` and `catch()` methods to the `Promise()` instance. Only one of these two will be invoked. When we call `resolve("John Smith")` from inside the function, it results in the invocation of the `then()` that received `"John Smith"` as its argument. If we changed the value of `success` to `false`, the `catch()` method would be called with the argument containing `"Can't get customers"`:

```
Getting customers
Invoked getCustomers. Waiting for results
John Smith
```

Note that the message `"Invoked getCustomers. Waiting for results"` is printed before `"John Smith"`. This proves that the `getCustomers()` function worked asynchronously.[18]

Each promise represents one asynchronous operation, and we can chain them to guarantee a particular order of execution. Let's add a `getOrders()` function in the following listing that can find the orders for a provided customer, and chain `getOrders()` with `getCustomers()`.

Listing A.15 Chaining promises

```
function getCustomers() {

  return new Promise(
     function (resolve, reject) {

      console.log("Getting customers");
        // Emulate an async server call here
      setTimeout(function() {
        const success = true;
        if (success){
          resolve("John Smith");      <-- Invoked when the customer is successfully obtained
         }else{
          reject("Can't get customers");
        }
      }, 1000);

     }
  );
  return promise;
}
```

[18] See it in CodePen: http://mng.bz/5rf3.

```
function getOrders(customer) {

  return new Promise(
     function (resolve, reject) {

        // Emulate an async server call here
       setTimeout(function() {
         const success = true;
         if (success) {
           resolve(`Found the order 123 for ${customer}`);    <-- Invoked when the order for a customer is successful
          } else {
           reject("Can't get orders");
         }
       }, 1000);

     }
  );
}
getCustomers()
  .then((cust) => {
          console.log(cust);
          return cust;
       })
  .then((cust) => getOrders(cust))    <-- Chains with getOrders()
   .then((order) => console.log(order))
  .catch((err) => console.error(err));    <-- Handles errors
 console.log("Chained getCustomers and getOrders. Waiting for results");
```

This code not only declares and chains two functions but also demonstrates how we can print intermediate results on the console. The output of listing A.15 follows (note that the customer returned from `getCustomers()` was properly passed to `getOrders()`):[19]

```
Getting customers
Chained getCustomers and getOrders. Waiting for results
John Smith
Found the order 123 for John Smith
```

We can chain multiple function calls using `then()` and have just one error-handling script for all chained invocations. If an error occurs, it will be propagated through the entire chain of `then`s until it finds an error handler. No `then`s will be invoked after the error.

Changing the value of the `success` variable to `false` in listing A.15 will result in printing the message `"Can't get customers"`, and the `getOrders()` method won't be called. If we remove these console prints, the code that retrieves customers and orders looks clean and is easy to understand:

```
getCustomers()
  .then((cust) => getOrders(cust))
  .catch((err) => console.error(err));
```

[19] See it in CodePen: http://mng.bz/6z5k.

Adding more thens doesn't make this code less readable (compare it with the pyramid of doom shown in figure A.1).

A.12.3 Resolving several promises at once

Another case to consider is asynchronous functions that don't depend on each other. Say we need to invoke two functions in no particular order, but we need to perform some action only after both of them are complete. The Promise object has an all() method that takes an iterable collection of promises and executes (resolves) all of them. Because the all() method returns a Promise object, we can add then() or catch() (or both) to the result.

Imagine a web portal that needs to make several asynchronous calls to get the weather, stock market news, and traffic information. If we want to display the portal page only after all of these calls have completed, Promise.all() is what we need:

```
Promise.all([getWeather(),
             getStockMarketNews(),
             getTraffic()])
.then( (results) => { /* render the portal GUI here */ })
.catch(err => console.error(err)) ;
```

Keep in mind that Promise.all() resolves only after all of the promises resolve. If one of them rejects, the control goes to the catch() handler.

Compared to callback functions, promises make our code more linear and easier to read, and they represent multiple states of an application. On the negative side, promises can't be canceled. Imagine an impatient user who clicks a button several times to get some data from the server. Each click creates a promise and initiates an HTTP request. There's no way to keep only the last request and cancel the uncompleted ones.

The next step in the evolution of a Promise object is an Observable object, which should be introduced in future ECMAScript specifications; in chapter 5, we explain how to use it today.

The JavaScript code with promises is easier to read, but if you look at the then() function carefully, you'll see that you still have to provide a callback function that will be called sometime later. The keywords async and await are the next step in the evolution of the JavaScript syntax for asynchronous programming.

A.12.4 async and await

The keywords async and await were introduced in ES8 (a.k.a. ES2017). They allow us to treat functions returning promises as if they're synchronous. The next line of code is executed only when the previous one completes. It's important to note that the waiting for the asynchronous code to complete happens in the background and doesn't block the execution of other parts of the program:

- async is a keyword that marks a function that returns a promise.
- await is a keyword that we place right before the invocation of the async function. This instructs the JavaScript engine to not proceed to the next line until the asynchronous function either returns the result or throws an error. The JavaScript engine will internally wrap the expression on the right of the await keyword into a promise and the rest of the method into a then() callback.

To illustrate the use of async and await keywords, the following listing reuses the functions getCustomers() and getOrders() that use promises inside to emulate asynchronous processing.

Listing A.16 Declaring two functions that use promises

```
function getCustomers() {

    return new Promise(
        function (resolve, reject) {

            console.log("Getting customers");
            // Emulate an async call that takes 1 second to complete
            setTimeout(function() {
                const success = true;
                if (success){
                    resolve("John Smith");
                } else {
                    reject("Can't get customers");
                }
            }, 1000);
        }
    );
}

function getOrders(customer) {

    return new Promise(
        function (resolve, reject) {

            // Emulate an async call that takes 1 second
            setTimeout(function() {
                const success = true;    // change it to false

                if (success){
                    resolve( `Found the order 123 for ${customer}`);
                } else {
                    reject(`getOrders() has thrown an error for ${customer}`);
                }
            }, 1000);
        }
    );
}
```

We want to chain these function calls, but this time we won't be using the then() calls as we did with promises. We'll create a new function, getCustomersOrders(), that internally invokes getCustomers(), and when it completes, getOrders().

We'll use the `await` keyword in the lines where we invoke `getCustomers()` and `getOrders()` so the code will wait for each of these functions to complete before continuing execution. We'll mark the `getCustomersOrders()` function with the `async` keyword because it'll use `await` inside. The following listing declares and invokes the function `getCustomersOrders()`.

Listing A.17 Declaring and invoking an `async` function

```
(async function getCustomersOrders() {      // Declares the function with the async keyword
   try {
      const customer = await getCustomers();   // Invokes the asynchronous function getCustomers() with await so the code below won't be executed until the function completes
       console.log(`Got customer ${customer}`);
      const orders = await getOrders(customer);   // Invokes the asynchronous function getOrders() with await so the code below won't be executed until the function completes
       console.log(orders);
  } catch(err) {      // Handles errors
       console.log(err);
  }
})();

console.log("This is the last line in the app.
  Chained getCustomers() and getOrders() are still
  running without blocking the rest of the app.");   // This code runs outside of the async function.
```

As you see, this code looks as if it's synchronous. It has no callbacks and is executed line by line. Error processing is done in a standard way using the `try/catch` block.

Running this code will produce the following output:

```
Getting customers
This is the last line in the app.
  Chained getCustomers() and getOrders() are still
  running without blocking the rest of the app.
Got customer John Smith
Found the order 123 for John Smith
```

Note that the message about the last line of code is printed before the name of the customer and the order number. Even though these values are retrieved asynchronously a bit later, the execution of this small app wasn't blocked, and the script reached the last line before the async functions `getCustomers()` and `getOrders()` finished their execution.[20]

A.13 ES6 modules

In any programming language, splitting code into modules helps organize the application into logical and possibly reusable units. Modularized applications allow programming tasks to be split between software developers more efficiently. Developers

---

[20] See it in CodePen: http://mng.bz/pSV8.

get to decide which API should be exposed by the module for external use and which should be used internally.

ES5 doesn't have language constructs for creating modules, so we have to resort to one of these options:

- Manually implement a module design pattern as an immediately initialized function.
- Use third-party implementations of the AMD (http://mng.bz/JKVc) or CommonJS (http://mng.bz/7Lld) standard.

CommonJS was created for modularizing JavaScript applications that run outside the web browser (such as those written in Node.js and deployed under Google's V8 engine). AMD is primarily used for applications that run in a web browser.

You should split your app into modules to make your code more maintainable. Besides that, you should minimize the amount of JavaScript code loaded to the client on app startup. Imagine a typical online store. Do you need to load the code for processing payments when users open the application's home page? What if they never click the Place Order button? It would be nice to modularize the application so the code is loaded on an as-needed basis. RequireJS is probably the most popular third-party library that implements the AMD standard; it lets you define dependencies between modules and load them on the browser on demand.

Starting with ES6, modules have become part of the language, which means developers will stop using third-party libraries to implement various standards. A script becomes a module if it uses `import` and/or `export` keywords.

ES6 modules and global scope

Say we have a multifile project, and one of the files has the following content:

```
class Person {}
```

Because we didn't export anything from this file, it's not an ES6 module, and the instance of the `Person` class would be created in the global scope. If you already have another script in the same project that also declares the `Person` class, the TypeScript compiler will give you an error in the preceding code stating that you're trying to declare a duplicate of what already exists.

Adding the `export` statement to the preceding code changes the situation, and this script becomes a module:

```
export class Person {}
```

Now objects of type `Person` won't be created on the global scope, and their scope will be limited to only those scripts (other ES6 modules) that import `Person`. In chapters 1 and 2, we introduce Angular modules that (in contrast to ES6 modules) serve as registries of Angular artifacts that belong together.

NOTE ES6 modules allow you to avoid polluting the global scope and restrict the visibility of the script and its members (classes, functions, variables, and constants) to those modules that import them.

A.13.1 Import and export

A *module* is just a JavaScript file that implements certain functionality and exports (or imports) a public API so other JavaScript programs can use it. There's no special keyword to declare that the code in a particular file is a module. Just by using the keywords `import` and `export`, you turn a script into an ES6 module.

The `import` keyword enables one script to declare that it needs to use exported members from another script. Similarly, the `export` keyword lets you declare variables, functions, and classes that the module should be exposed to other scripts. Using the `export` keyword, you can make selected APIs available to other modules. A module's functions, variables, and classes that aren't explicitly exported remain private to the module.

ES6 offers two types of `export` usage: named and default. With named exports, you can use the `export` keyword in front of multiple members of the module (such as classes, functions, and variables). The code in the following file (tax.js) exports the `taxCode` variable and the functions `calcTaxes()` and `fileTaxes()`, but the `doSomethingElse()` function remains hidden to external scripts:

```
export let taxCode = 1;

export function calcTaxes() { }

function doSomethingElse() { }

export function fileTaxes() { }
```

When a script imports named, exported module members, their names must be placed in curly braces. The main.js file illustrates this:

```
import {taxCode, calcTaxes} from 'tax';

if (taxCode === 1) { // do something }

calcTaxes();
```

Here, `tax` refers to the filename of the module, minus the file extension. The curly braces represent destructuring. The module from tax.js exports three members, but we're interested in importing only `taxCode` and `calcTaxes`.

One of the exported module members can be marked as `default`, which means this is an anonymous export, and another module can give it any name in its `import` statement. The my_module.js file that exports a function may look like this:

```
export default function() { // do something }      <-- No semicolon

export let taxCode;
```

The main.js file imports both named and default exports while assigning the name `coolFunction` to the default one:

```
import coolFunction, {taxCode} from 'my_module';

coolFunction();
```

Note that you don't use curly braces around `coolFunction` (default export) but you do around `taxCode` (named export). A script that imports a class, variable, or function that was exported with the `default` keyword can give them new names without using any special keywords:

```
import aVeryCoolFunction, {taxCode} from 'my_module';

aVeryCoolFunction();
```

But to give an alias name to a named export, we need to write something like this:

```
import coolFunction, {taxCode as taxCode2016} from 'my_module';
```

`import` module statements don't result in copying the exported code. Imports serve as references. A script that imports modules or members can't modify them, and if the values in imported modules change, the new values are immediately reflected in all places where they were imported. We use the import statement in each chapter of this book, so you'll have a chance to get a good feeling for how to use ES6 modules.

> **TIP** Don't use default exports in Angular apps because you'll get errors during ahead-of-time (AoT) compilation.

appendix B TypeScript essentials

TypeScript was released in 2012 by Microsoft, and its core developer was Anders Hejlsberg. He's also one of the authors of Turbo Pascal and Delphi, and is a lead architect of C#. In this appendix, we'll cover main elements of the TypeScript syntax.

We'll also show you how to turn TypeScript code into JavaScript (ES5) so it can be executed by any web browser or a standalone JavaScript engine. This appendix doesn't offer a complete coverage of TypeScript. Refer to the TypeScript documentation at www.typescriptlang.org/docs/home.html for complete coverage. Also, TypeScript supports all syntax constructs described in appendix A, so we don't repeat those here.

B.1 The role of transpilers

Web browsers don't understand any language but JavaScript. If the source code is written in TypeScript, it has to be *transpiled* into JavaScript before you can run it in a JavaScript engine, whether browser or standalone.

Transpiling means converting the source code of a program in one language into source code in another language. Many developers prefer to use the word *compiling*, so phrases like "TypeScript compiler" and "compile TypeScript into JavaScript" are also valid.

Figure B.1 shows TypeScript code on the left and its equivalent in an ES5 version of JavaScript generated by the TypeScript transpiler on the right. In TypeScript, we declared a variable `foo` of type `string`, but the transpiled version doesn't have the type information. In TypeScript, we declared a class `Bar`, which was transpiled in a class-like pattern in the ES5 syntax.

You can try it for yourself by visiting the TypeScript playground at www.typescriptlang.org/play. If we had specified ES6 as a target for transpiling, the generated JavaScript code would look different; you'd see the `let` and `class` keywords on the right side as well.

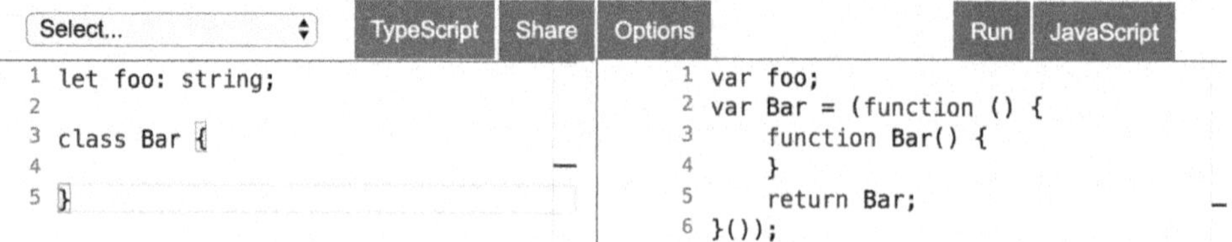

Figure B.1 Transpiling TypeScript into ES5

A combination of Angular with statically typed TypeScript simplifies the development of web applications. Good tooling and a static type analyzer substantially decrease the number of runtime errors and shorten the time to market. When complete, your Angular application will have lots of JavaScript code; and although developing in TypeScript may require you to write a little more code, you'll reap benefits by saving time on testing and refactoring and minimizing the number of runtime errors.

B.2 Getting started with TypeScript

Microsoft has open sourced TypeScript and hosts the TypeScript repository on GitHub at https://github.com/Microsoft/TypeScript/wiki/Roadmap. You can install the TypeScript compiler using npm. The TypeScript site www.typescriptlang.org has the language documentation and has a web-hosted TypeScript compiler (under the Playground menu), where you can enter TypeScript code and compile it to JavaScript interactively, as shown in figure B.1. Enter TypeScript code on the left, and its JavaScript version (ES5) is displayed on the right. Click the Run button to execute the transpiled code (open the browser console to see the output produced by your code, if any).

Such interactive tools will suffice for learning the language syntax, but for real-world development, you'll need better tooling to be productive. You may decide to use an IDE or a text editor, but having the TypeScript compiler installed locally is a must for development. We'll show you how to install the TypeScript compiler and run code samples in this appendix, using the Node JavaScript engine.

We assume that you have Node.js and npm installed on your computer. If you don't have them yet, refer to appendix C.

B.2.1 Installing and using the TypeScript compiler

We'll use Node.js's npm package manager to install the TypeScript compiler. To install it globally, run the following npm command in the Terminal window:

```
npm install -g typescript
```

The `-g` option installs the TypeScript compiler globally on your computer, so it's available from the Terminal window in all your projects. To check the version of your TypeScript compiler, run the following command:

```
tsc
 --version
```

As mentioned earlier, code written in TypeScript has to be transpiled into JavaScript so web browsers can execute it. TypeScript code is saved in files with the .ts extension. Say you write a script and save it in the main.ts file. The following command will transpile main.ts into main.js:

```
tsc main.ts
```

You can also generate source map files that map lines in the TypeScript program to corresponding lines in the generated JavaScript. With source maps, you can place breakpoints in your TypeScript code while running it in the browser, even though it executes JavaScript. To compile main.ts into main.js while also generating the source map file main.js.map, run the following command:

```
tsc --sourcemap main.ts
```

If a browser has the Developer Tools panel open, it loads the source map file along with the JavaScript file, and you can debug your TypeScript code there as if the browser runs TypeScript.

During compilation, TypeScript's compiler removes from the generated code all TypeScript types, interfaces, and keywords not supported by JavaScript. By providing compiler options, you can generate JavaScript compliant with ES3, ES5, ES6, or newer syntax.

Here's how to transpile the code to ES5-compatible syntax (the `--t` option specifies the target syntax):

```
tsc --t ES5 main.ts
```

You can start your TypeScript compiler in watch mode by providing the `-w` option. In this mode, whenever you modify and save your code, it's automatically transpiled into corresponding JavaScript files. To compile and watch all .ts files from the current directory, run the following command:

```
tsc -w *.ts
```

The compiler will compile all the TypeScript files, print error messages (if any) on the console, and continue watching the files for changes. As soon as a file changes, `tsc` will immediately recompile it.

> **NOTE** Typically, we turn off TypeScript autocompilation in the IDE. With Angular apps, we use Angular CLI to compile and bundle the entire project. The IDEs use the TypeScript code analyzer to highlight errors even without compilation.

`tsc` offers dozens of compilation options described at http://mng.bz/rf14. You can preconfigure the process of compilation (specifying the source and destination directories, source map generation, and so on). The presence of the tsconfig.json file in the project directory means you can enter tsc on the command line, and the compiler will read all the options from tsconfig.json. A sample tsconfig.json file from one of the Angular projects is shown in the following listing.

Listing B.1 tsconfig.json

```
{
    "compilerOptions": {
        "baseUrl": "src",
         "outDir": "./dist",
         "sourceMap": true,
         "moduleResolution": "node",
         "noEmitOnError": true,
         "target": "es5",
         "experimentalDecorators": true
    }
}
```

- "baseUrl": Transpiles .ts files located in the src directory
- "outDir": Saves the generated .js files in the dist directory
- "sourceMap": Generates sourcemaps
- "moduleResolution": Looks for modules according to the structure of Node-based projects
- "noEmitOnError": If any of the files has compilation errors, doesn't generate JavaScript files
- "target": Transpiles the .ts file into ES5 syntax
- "experimentalDecorators": Required to support decorators

Every Angular/TypeScript app uses *decorators* with classes or class members (such as `@Component()` and `@Input()`). We'll discuss decorators later in this appendix.

If you want to exclude some of your project files from compilation, add the `exclude` property to tsconfig.json. This is how you can exclude the entire content of the node_modules directory:

```
"exclude": [
    "node_modules"
  ]
```

B.2.2 TypeScript as a superset of JavaScript

TypeScript supports ES5, ES6, and newer ECMAScript syntax. Just change the name extension of a file with JavaScript code from .js to .ts, and it'll become valid TypeScript code. Being a superset of JavaScript, TypeScript adds a number of useful features to JavaScript. We'll review them next.

B.3 How to run the code samples

To run the code samples from this appendix locally on your computer, perform the following steps:

1. Install Node.js from https://nodejs.org/en/download/ (use the current version).
2. Clone or download the https://github.com/Farata/angulartypescript repository into any directory.
3. In the command window, change into this directory, and then go to the code-samples/appendixB subdirectory.

4. Install the project dependencies (the TypeScript compiler) *locally* by running `npm install`.
5. Use the locally installed TypeScript compiler to compile all code samples into the dist directory by running `npm run tsc`, which will transpile all code samples from the src directory into the dist directory.
6. To run a particular code sample (such as fatArrow.js) use the following command: `node dist/fatArrow`.

B.4 Optional types

You can declare variables and provide types for all or some of them. The following two lines are valid TypeScript syntax:

```
let name1 = 'John Smith';

let name2: string = 'John Smith';
```

> **TIP** In the second line, specifying the type `string` is unnecessary. Since the variable is initialized with the string, TypeScript will guess (infer) that the type of `name2` is `string`.

If you use types, TypeScript's transpiler can detect mismatched types during development, and IDEs will offer code completion and refactoring support. This will increase your productivity on any decent-sized project. Even if you don't use types in declarations, TypeScript will guess the type based on the assigned value and will still do type checking afterward. This is called type *inference*.

The following fragment of TypeScript code shows that you can't assign a numeric value to a `name1` variable that was meant to be a `string`, even though it was initially declared without a type (JavaScript syntax). After initializing this variable with a `string` value, the inferred typing won't let you assign the numeric value to `name1`:

```
let name1 = 'John Smith';
name1 = 123;
```

Assigning a value of a different type to a variable is valid in JavaScript but invalid in TypeScript because of the inferred type.

In TypeScript, you can declare typed variables, function parameters, and return values. There are four keywords for declaring basic types: `number`, `boolean`, `string`, and `void`. The last one indicates the absence of a return value in a function declaration. A variable can have a value of type `null` or `undefined`, similar to JavaScript.

Here are some examples of variables declared with explicit types:

```
let salary: number;
let isValid: boolean;
let customerName: string = null;
```

> **NOTE** Starting from TypeScript 2.7, you need to either initialize variables during declaration or initialize (member variables) in the constructor.

All of these types are subtypes of the any type. You may as well explicitly declare a variable, specifying any as its type. In this case, inferred typing isn't applied. Both of these declarations are valid:

```
let name2: any = 'John Smith';
name2 = 123;
```

If variables are declared with explicit types, the compiler will check their values to ensure that they match the declarations. TypeScript includes other types that are used in interactions with the web browser, such as HTMLElement and Document. If you define a class or an interface, it can be used as a custom type in variable declarations. We'll introduce classes and interfaces later, but first let's get familiar with TypeScript functions, which are the most-used constructs in JavaScript.

B.5 Functions

TypeScript functions and function expressions are similar to JavaScript functions, but you can explicitly declare parameter types and return values. Let's write a JavaScript function that calculates tax. It'll have three parameters and will calculate tax based on the state, income, and number of dependents. For each dependent, the person is entitled to a $500 or $300 tax deduction, depending on the state the person lives in. The function is shown in the following listing.

Listing B.2 Calculating tax in JavaScript

```
function calcTax(state, income, dependents) {
    if (state === 'NY') {
        return income * 0.06 - dependents * 500;
    } else if (state === 'NJ') {
        return income * 0.05 - dependents * 300;
    }
}
```

Say a person with an income of $50,000 lives in the state of New Jersey and has two dependents. Let's invoke calcTax():

```
let tax = calcTax('NJ', 50000, 2);
```

The tax variable gets the value of 1,900, which is correct. Even though calcTax() doesn't declare any types for the function parameters, you can guess them based on the parameter names. Now let's invoke it the wrong way, passing a string value for a number of dependents:

```
var tax = calcTax('NJ', 50000, 'two');
```

You won't know there's a problem until you invoke this function. The tax variable will have a NaN value (not a number). A bug sneaked in just because you didn't have a chance to explicitly specify the types of the parameters. The next listing rewrites this function in TypeScript, declaring types for parameters and the return value.

Listing B.3 Calculating tax in TypeScript

```
function calcTax(state: string, income: number, dependents: number): number {

    if (state === 'NY'){
        return income * 0.06 - dependents * 500;
    } else if (state ==='NJ'){
        return income * 0.05 - dependents * 300;
    }
}
```

Now there's no way to make the same mistake and pass a `string` value for the number of dependents:

```
let tax: number = calcTax('NJ', 50000, 'two');
```

The TypeScript compiler will display an error saying, "Argument of type `string` is not assignable to parameter of type `number`." Moreover, the return value of the function is declared as `number`, which stops you from making another mistake and assigning the result of the tax calculations to a non-numeric variable:

```
let tax: string = calcTax('NJ', 50000, 'two');
```

The compiler will catch this, producing the error "The type 'number' is not assignable to type 'string': var tax: string." This kind of type checking during compilation can save you a lot of time on any project.

B.5.1 Default parameters

While declaring a function, you can specify default parameter values. For example:

```
function calcTax(income: number, dependents: number, state: string = 'NY'): n
     umber{
    // the code goes here
}
```

There's no need to change even one line of code in the body of `calcTax()`. You now have the freedom to invoke it with either two or three parameters:

```
let tax: number = calcTax(50000, 2);
// or
let tax: number = calcTax(50000, 2, 'NY');
```

The results of both invocations will be the same.

B.5.2 Optional parameters

In TypeScript, you can easily mark function parameters as optional by appending a question mark to the parameter name. The only restriction is that optional parameters must come last in the function declaration. When you write code for functions with optional parameters, you need to provide application logic that handles the cases when the optional parameters aren't provided.

Let's modify the tax-calculation function in the following listing: if no dependents are specified, it won't apply any deduction to the calculated tax.

Listing B.4 Calculating tax in TypeScript, modified

```
function calcTax(income: number, state: string = 'NY', dependents?: number):
     number{

    let deduction: number;

    if (dependents) {
        deduction = dependents * 500;
    }else {
      deduction = 0;
    }

    if (state === 'NY') {
        return income * 0.06 - deduction;
    } else if (state === 'NJ') {
        return income * 0.05  - deduction;
    }
}

let tax: number = calcTax(50000, 'NJ', 3);
console.log(`Your tax is ${tax}`);

tax = calcTax(50000);
console.log(`Your tax is ${tax}`);
```

Note the question mark in `dependents?: number`. Now the function checks whether the value for dependents was provided. If it wasn't, you assign 0 to the `deduction` variable ; otherwise, you deduct 500 for each dependent.

Running the preceding script will produce the following output:

```
Your tax is 1000
Your tax is 3000
```

NOTE TypeScript supports the syntax of fat-arrow expressions described in section A.5 in appendix A.

Function overloading

JavaScript doesn't support function overloading, so having several functions with the same name but different lists of arguments isn't possible. TypeScript supports function overloading, but because the code has to be transpiled into a single JavaScript function, the syntax for overloading isn't elegant.

You can declare several signatures of a function with one and only one body, where you need to check the number and types of the arguments and execute the appropriate portion of the code:

```
function attr(name: string): string;
function attr(name: string, value: string): void;
```

```
function attr(map: any): void;
function attr(nameOrMap: any, value?: string): any {
  if (nameOrMap && typeof nameOrMap === "string") {
      // handle string case
  } else {
      // handle map case
  }

  // handle value here
}
```

B.6 Classes

If you have Java or C# experience, you'll be familiar with the concepts of classes and inheritance in their classical form. In those languages, the definition of a class is loaded in memory as a separate entity (like a blueprint) and is shared by all instances of this class. If a class is inherited from another one, the object is instantiated using the combined blueprint of both classes.

TypeScript is a superset of JavaScript, which only supports *prototypal inheritance*, where you can create an inheritance hierarchy by attaching one object to the *prototype* property of another. In this case, an inheritance (or rather, a linkage) of *objects* is created dynamically.

In TypeScript, the `class` keyword is syntactic sugar to simplify coding. In the end, your classes will be transpiled into JavaScript objects with prototypal inheritance. In JavaScript, you can declare a constructor function and instantiate it with the `new` keyword. In TypeScript, you can also declare a class and instantiate it with the `new` operator.

A class can include a constructor, fields (properties), and methods. Declared properties and methods are often referred to as *class members* . We'll illustrate the syntax of TypeScript classes by showing you a series of code samples and comparing them with the equivalent ES5 syntax.

Let's create a simple `Person` class that contains four properties to store the first and last name, age, and Social Security number (a unique identifier assigned to citizens and residents of the United States). At left in figure B.2, you can see the TypeScript code that declares and instantiates the `Person` class; on the right is a JavaScript closure generated by the `tsc` compiler. By creating a closure for the `Person` function, the TypeScript compiler enables the mechanism for exposing and hiding the elements of the `Person` object.

TypeScript also supports class constructors that allow you to initialize object variables while instantiating the object. A class constructor is invoked only once during object creation. The left side of figure B.2 shows the `Person` class, which uses the `constructor` keyword that initializes the fields of the class with the values given to the constructor.

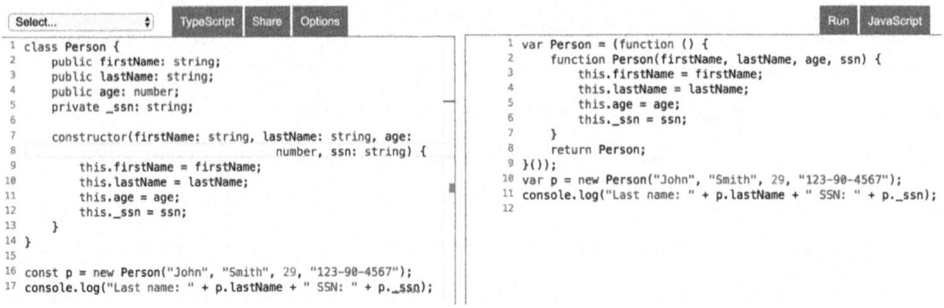

Select... TypeScript Share Options

```
class Person {
    public firstName: string;
    public lastName: string;
    public age: number;
    private _ssn: string;

    constructor(firstName: string, lastName: string, age:
                                    number, ssn: string) {
        this.firstName = firstName;
        this.lastName = lastName;
        this.age = age;
        this._ssn = ssn;
    }
}

const p = new Person("John", "Smith", 29, "123-90-4567");
console.log("Last name: " + p.lastName + " SSN: " + p._ssn);
```

Run JavaScript

```
var Person = (function () {
    function Person(firstName, lastName, age, ssn) {
        this.firstName = firstName;
        this.lastName = lastName;
        this.age = age;
        this._ssn = ssn;
    }
    return Person;
}());
var p = new Person("John", "Smith", 29, "123-90-4567");
console.log("Last name: " + p.lastName + " SSN: " + p._ssn);
```

Figure B.2 Transpiling a TypeScript class into a JavaScript closure

B.6.1 *Access modifiers*

JavaScript doesn't have a way to declare a variable or a method as *private* (hidden from external code). To hide a property (or a method) in an object, you need to create a closure that neither attaches this property to the `this` variable nor `returns` it in the closure's return statement.

TypeScript provides `public`, `protected`, and `private` keywords to help you control access to object members during the development phase. By default, all class members have public access, and they're visible from outside the class. If a member is declared with the `protected` modifier, it's visible in the class and its subclasses. Class members declared as `private` are visible only in the class.

Let's use the `private` keyword to hide the value of the `_ssn` property so it can't be directly accessed from outside of the `Person` object. We'll show you two versions of declaring a class with properties that use access modifiers. The longer version of the class looks like the following listing.

Listing B.5 Using a private property

```
class Person {
    public firstName: string;
    public lastName: string;
    public age: number;
    private _ssn: string;

    constructor(firstName: string, lastName: string, age: number, ssn: string
     ) {
        this.firstName = firstName;
        this.lastName = lastName;
        this.age = age;
        this._ssn = ssn;
    }
}

const p = new Person("John", "Smith", 29, "123-90-4567");
console.log("Last name: " + p.lastName + " SSN: " + p._ssn);
```

Note that the name of the private variable starts with an underscore: `_ssn`. This is a naming convention for private properties.

The last line of listing B.5 attempts to access the `_ssn` private property from outside, so the TypeScript code analyzer will give you a compilation error: "Property '_ssn' is private and is only accessible in class 'Person'." But unless you use the `--noEmitOnError` compiler option, the erroneous code will still be transpiled into JavaScript:

```
const Person = (function () {
    function Person(firstName, lastName, age, _ssn) {
        this.firstName = firstName;
        this.lastName = lastName;
        this.age = age;
        this._ssn = _ssn;
    }
    return Person;
})();

const p = new Person("John", "Smith", 29, "123-90-4567");
console.log("Last name: " + p.lastName + " SSN: " + p._ssn);
```

The `private` keyword only makes it private in the TypeScript code, but the generated JavaScript code will treat all properties and methods of the class as public anyway.

TypeScript also allows you to provide access modifiers with constructor arguments, as shown in the short version of the `Person` class in the following listing.

Listing B.6 Using access modifiers

```
class Person {

    constructor(public firstName: string,
        public lastName: string, public age: number,  private _ssn: string) {
    }
}

const p = new Person("John", "Smith", 29, "123-90-4567");
```

When you use a constructor with access modifiers, the TypeScript compiler takes it as an instruction to create and retain class properties matching the constructor arguments. You don't need to explicitly declare and initialize them. Both the short and long versions of the `Person` class generate the same JavaScript, but we recommend using the shorter syntax as shown in figure B.3.

B.6.2 Methods

When a function is declared in a class, it's called a *method*. In JavaScript, you need to declare methods on the prototype of an object, but with a class, you declare a method by specifying a name followed by parentheses and curly braces, as you would in other object-oriented languages.

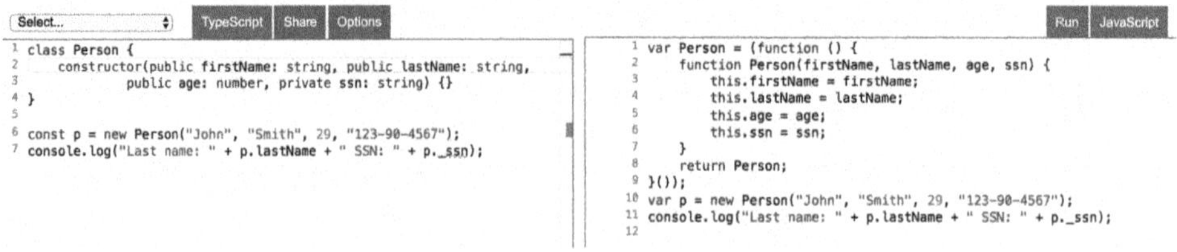

Select... TypeScript Share Options

```
class Person {
    constructor(public firstName: string, public lastName: string,
             public age: number, private ssn: string) {}
}

const p = new Person("John", "Smith", 29, "123-90-4567");
console.log("Last name: " + p.lastName + " SSN: " + p._ssn);
```

Run JavaScript

```
var Person = (function () {
    function Person(firstName, lastName, age, ssn) {
        this.firstName = firstName;
        this.lastName = lastName;
        this.age = age;
        this.ssn = ssn;
    }
    return Person;
}());
var p = new Person("John", "Smith", 29, "123-90-4567");
console.log("Last name: " + p.lastName + " SSN: " + p._ssn);
```

Figure B.3 Transpiling a TypeScript class with `constructor`

The next code listing shows how you can declare and use a `MyClass` class with a `doSomething()` method that has one argument and no return value.

Listing B.7 Creating a method

```
class MyClass {

   doSomething(howManyTimes: number): void {
      // do something here
   }
}

const mc = new MyClass();
mc.doSomething(5);
```

Static and instance members

The code in listing B 7, as well as the class shown in figure B.2, creates an instance of the class first and then accesses its members using a reference variable that points at this instance:

```
mc.doSomething(5);
```

If a class property or method were declared with the `static` keyword, its values would be shared between all instances of the class, and you wouldn't need to create an instance to access static members. Instead of using a reference variable (such as `mc`), you'd use the name of the class:

```
class MyClass{

   static doSomething(howManyTimes: number): void {
      // do something here
   }
}

MyClass.doSomething(5);
```

If you instantiate a class and need to invoke a class method from within another method declared in the same class, don't use the `this` keyword (as in, `this.doSomething(5)`), but still use the class name, as in `MyClass.doSomething(10);`.

B.6.3 Inheritance

JavaScript supports prototypal *object-based* inheritance, where one object can assign another object as its prototype, and this happens during runtime. TypeScript has the `extends` keyword for inheritance of classes, like ES6 and other object-oriented languages. But during transpiling to JavaScript, the generated code uses the syntax of prototypal inheritance.

Figure B.4 shows how to create an `Employee` class (line 9) that extends the `Person` class. On the right, you can see the transpiled JavaScript version, which uses prototypal inheritance. The TypeScript version of the code is more concise and easier to read.

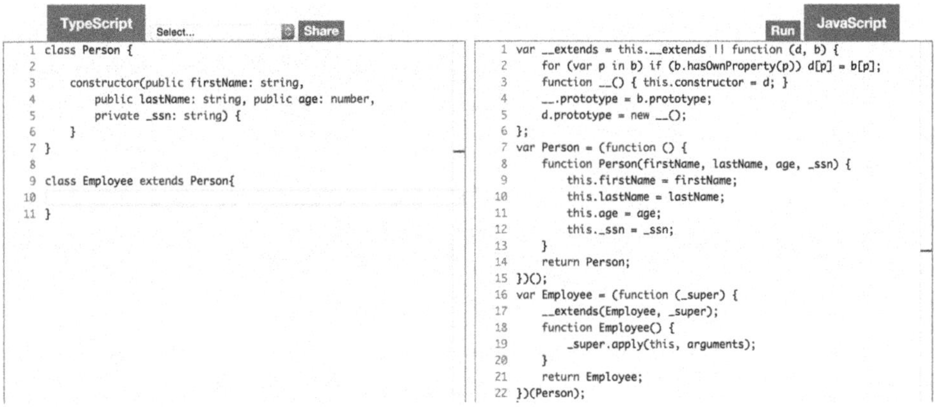

TypeScript Select... Share

```
1 class Person {
2
3     constructor(public firstName: string,
4         public lastName: string, public age: number,
5         private _ssn: string) {
6     }
7 }
8
9 class Employee extends Person{
10
11 }
```

Run JavaScript

```
1 var __extends = this.__extends || function (d, b) {
2     for (var p in b) if (b.hasOwnProperty(p)) d[p] = b[p];
3     function __() { this.constructor = d; }
4     __.prototype = b.prototype;
5     d.prototype = new __();
6 };
7 var Person = (function () {
8     function Person(firstName, lastName, age, _ssn) {
9         this.firstName = firstName;
10        this.lastName = lastName;
11        this.age = age;
12        this._ssn = _ssn;
13    }
14    return Person;
15 })();
16 var Employee = (function (_super) {
17     __extends(Employee, _super);
18     function Employee() {
19         _super.apply(this, arguments);
20     }
21     return Employee;
22 })(Person);
```

Figure B.4 Class inheritance in TypeScript

Let's add a constructor and a `department` property to the `Employee` class in the next listing.

Listing B.8 Using inheritance

```
class Employee extends Person {
    department: string;

    constructor(firstName: string, lastName: string,
            age: number, _ssn: string, department: string) {

        super(firstName, lastName, age, _ssn);

        this.department = department;
    }
}
```

Declares a property department

Creates a constructor that has an additional department argument

A subclass that declares a constructor must invoke the constructor of the superclass using super().

If you invoke a method declared in a superclass on the object of the subclass type, you can use the name of this method as if it were declared in the subclass. But sometimes you want to specifically call the method of the superclass, and that's when you should use the `super` keyword.

The super keyword can be used two ways. In the constructor of a derived class, you invoke it as a method. You can also use the super keyword to specifically call a method of the superclass. It's typically used with method overriding. For example, if both a superclass and its descendant have a doSomething() method, the descendant can reuse the functionality programmed in the superclass and add other functionality as well:

```
doSomething() {
    super.doSomething();

    // Add more functionality here
}
```

B.7 Interfaces

JavaScript doesn't support interfaces, which, in other object-oriented languages, are used to introduce a *code contract* that an API has to abide by. An example of a contract can be class X declaring that it implements interface Y. If class X won't include an implementation of the methods declared in interface Y, it's considered a violation of the contract and won't compile.

TypeScript includes the keywords interface and implements to support interfaces, but interfaces aren't transpiled into JavaScript code. They just help you avoid using the wrong types during development.

In TypeScript, we use interfaces for two reasons:

- Declare an interface that defines a custom type containing a number of properties. Then declare a method that has an argument of such a type. The compiler will check that the object given as an argument includes all the properties declared in the interface.
- Declare an interface that includes abstract (non-implemented) methods. When a class declares that it implements this interface, the class must provide an implementation for all the abstract methods.

Let's apply these two patterns by example.

B.7.1 Declaring custom types with interfaces

When you use JavaScript frameworks, you may run into an API that requires some sort of configuration object as a function parameter. To figure out which properties must be provided in this object, either open the documentation for the API or read the source code of the framework. In TypeScript, you can declare an interface that includes all the properties, and their types, that must be present in a configuration object.

Let's see how to do this in the Person class, which contains a constructor with four arguments: firstName, lastName, age, and ssn. This time, in the following listing, you'll declare an IPerson interface that contains the four members, and you'll modify the constructor of the Person class to use an object of this custom type as an argument.

Listing B.9 Declaring an interface

```
interface IPerson {
    firstName: string;
    lastName: string;
    age: number;
    ssn?: string;
}

class Person  {
    constructor(public config: IPerson) {}
}

let aPerson: IPerson = {
     firstName: "John",
    lastName: "Smith",
    age: 29
}

let p = new Person(aPerson);
 console.log("Last name: " + p.config.lastName );
```

Declares an IPerson interface with ssn as an optional member (note the question mark)

The Person class has a constructor with one argument of type IPerson.

Creates an aPerson object literal with members compatible with IPerson

Instantiates the Person object, providing an object of type IPerson as an argument

TypeScript has a structural type system, which means that if two different types include the same members, the types are considered compatible. In listing B.9, even if you didn't specify the type of the `aPerson` variable, it still would be considered compatible with `IPerson` and could be used as a constructor argument while instantiating the `Person` object. If you change the name or type of one of the members of `IPerson`, the TypeScript compiler will report an error.

The `IPerson` interface didn't define any methods, but TypeScript interfaces can include method signatures without implementations.

B.7.2 Using the implements keyword

The `implements` keyword can be used with a class declaration to announce that the class will implement a particular interface. Say you have an `IPayable` interface declared as follows:

```
interface IPayable {
  increase_cap: number;

  increasePay(percent: number): boolean
}
```

Now the `Employee` class can declare that it implements `IPayable`:

```
class Employee implements IPayable {
    // The implementation goes here
}
```

Before going into details, let's answer this question: why not just write all required code in the class rather than separating a portion of the code into an interface? Let's say you need to write an application that allows increasing salaries for the employees of your organization.

You can create an `Employee` class (that extends `Person`) and include the `increaseSalary()` method there. Then the business analysts may ask you to add the ability to increase pay to contractors who work for your firm. But contractors are represented by their company names and IDs; they have no notion of salary and are paid on an hourly basis.

You can create another class, `Contractor` (not inherited from `Person`), that includes some properties and an `increaseHourlyRate()` method. Now you have two different APIs: one for increasing the salary of employees, and another for increasing the pay for contractors. A better solution is to create a common `IPayable` interface and have `Employee` and `Contractor` classes provide *different implementations* of `IPayable` for these classes, as illustrated in the following listing.

Listing B.10 Using multiple interface implementations

The Person class serves as a base class for Employee.

The IPayable interface includes the signature of the increasePay() method that will be implemented by the Employee and Contractor classes.

The Employee class inherits from Person and implements the IPayable interface. A class can implement multiple interfaces.

The Employee class implements the increasePay() method. The salary of an employee can be increased by any amount, so the method prints the message on the console and returns true (allowing the increase).

The Contractor class includes a property that places a cap of 20% on pay increases.

The implementation of increasePay() in the Contractor class is different, invoking increasePay() with an argument that's more than 20 results in the "Sorry" message and a return value of false.

```
interface IPayable {

  increasePay(percent: number): boolean
}

class Person {
     // properties are omitted for brevity
}

class Employee extends Person implements IPayable {

    increasePay(percent: number): boolean {

        console.log(`Increasing salary by ${percent}`);
        return true;
    }
}

class Contractor implements IPayable {
    increaseCap:number = 20;

    increasePay(percent: number): boolean {
         if (percent < this.increaseCap) {
            console.log(`Increasing hourly rate by ${percent}`);
            return true;
        } else {
            console.log(`Sorry, the increase cap for contractors is
                     ${this.increaseCap}`);
            return false;
        }
    }
}
```

```
const workers: IPayable[] = [];
 workers[0] = new Employee();
workers[1] = new Contractor();

workers.forEach(worker => worker.increasePay(30));
```

Declaring an array of type IPayable lets you place any objects that implement the IPayable type there.

Now you can invoke the increasePay() method on any object in the workers array. Note that you don't use parentheses with the fat-arrow expression that has a single worker argument.

Running the preceding script produces the following output on the browser console:

```
Increasing salary by 30
Sorry, the increase cap for contractors is 20
```

> **Why declare classes with the implements keyword?**
>
> If you remove `implements Payable` from the declaration of either `Employee` or `Contractor`, the code will still work, and the compiler won't complain about lines that add these objects to the `workers` array. The compiler is smart enough to see that even if the class doesn't explicitly declare `implements IPayable`, it implements `increasePay()` properly.
>
> But if you remove `implements IPayable` and try to change the signature of the `increasePay()` method from any of the classes, you won't be able to place such an object into the `workers` array, because that object would no longer be of the `IPayable` type. Also, without the `implements` keyword, IDE support (such as for refactoring) will be broken.

B.8 Generics

TypeScript supports parameterized types, also known as *generics*, which can be used in a variety of scenarios. For example, you can create a function that can take values of any type; but during its invocation, in a particular context, you can explicitly specify a concrete type.

Take another example: an array can hold objects of any type, but you can specify which particular object types (for example, instances of `Person`) are allowed in an array. If you were to try to add an object of a different type, the TypeScript compiler would generate an error.

The following code listing declares a `Person` class and its descendant, `Employee`, and an `Animal` class. Then it instantiates each class and tries to store them in the `workers` array declared with the generic type. Generic types are denoted by placing them in angle brackets (as in `<Person>`).

Listing B.11 Using a generic type

```
class Person {
    name: string;
}

class Employee extends Person {
    department: number;
}

class Animal {
    breed: string;
}

let workers: Array<Person> = [];

workers[0] = new Person();
workers[1] = new Employee();
workers[2] = new Animal();  // compile-time error
```

By declaring the workers array with the generic type <Person>, you announce your plan to store only instances of the Person class or its descendants. An attempt to store an instance of Animal in the same array will result in a compile-time error.

Nominal and structural type systems

If you're familiar with generics in Java or C#, you may get a feeling that you already understand this syntax. There's a caveat, though. Though Java and C# use a *nominal* type system, TypeScript uses a *structural* one. In a nominal system, types are checked against their names, but in a structural system, by their structure.

With a nominal type system, the following line would result in an error:

```
let person: Person = new Animal();
```

With a structural type system, as long as the structures of the type are similar, you may get away with assigning an object of one type to a variable of another. Let's illustrate it by adding the name property to the Animal class.

Select... TypeScript Share Options

```
class Person {
    name: string;
}

class Employee extends Person{
    department: number;
}

class  Animal {
    name: string;
    breed: string;
}

let workers: Array<Person> = [];

workers[0] = new Person();
workers[1] = new Employee();
workers[2]  = new  Animal();  // no errors

let worker: Person = new Animal(); // no errors
```

Structural type system in action

Now the TypeScript compiler doesn't complain about assigning an `Animal` object to a variable of type `Person`. The variable of type `Person` expects an object that has a `name` property, and the `Animal` object has it. This is not to say that `Person` and `Animal` represent the same types, but these types are compatible. On the other hand, trying to assign the `Person` object to a variable of type `Animal` will result in the compilation error "Property breed is missing in type Person":

```
let worker: Animal = new Person(); // compilation error
```

Can you use generic types with any object or function? No. The creator of the object or function has to allow this feature. If you open TypeScript's type definition file (lib.d.ts) on GitHub at http://mng.bz/I3V7 and search for "interface Array," you'll see the declaration of the `Array`, as shown in figure B.5. Type definition files are explained later in this appendix.

The `<T>` in line 1008 serves as a placeholder for the actual type. It means TypeScript allows you to declare a type parameter with `Array`, and the compiler will check for the specific type provided in your program. Earlier in this section, we specified a generic `<T>` parameter as `<Person>` in `let workers: Array<Person>`. But because

```
1004  /////////////////////////////
1005  /// ECMAScript Array API (specially handled by compiler)
1006  /////////////////////////////
1007
1008  interface Array<T> {
1009      /**
1010        * Gets or sets the length of the array. This is a number one higher than the
1011        */
1012      length: number;
1013      /**
1014        * Returns a string representation of an array.
1015        */
1016      toString(): string;
1017      toLocaleString(): string;
1018      /**
1019        * Appends new elements to an array, and returns the new length of the array.
1020        * @param items New elements of the Array.
1021        */
1022      push(...items: T[]): number;
1023      /**
1024        * Removes the last element from an array and returns it.
1025        */
1026      pop(): T;
1027      /**
1028        * Combines two or more arrays.
1029        * @param items Additional items to add to the end of array1.
1030        */
```

Figure B.5 The fragment of lib.d.ts describing the `Array` API

generics aren't supported in JavaScript, you won't see them in the code generated by the transpiler. It's just an additional safety net for developers at compile time.

You can see another `T` in line 1022 in figure B.5. When generic types are specified with function arguments, no angle brackets are needed. But there's no `T` type in TypeScript. The `T` here means the `push` method lets you push objects of a specific type into an array, as in the following example:

```
workers.push(new Person());
```

You can create your own classes and functions that support generics, as well. The next listing defines a `Comparator<T>` interface that declares a `compareTo()` method, expecting the concrete type to be provided during method invocation.

Listing B.12 Creating an interface that uses generics

```
interface Comparator<T> {                          // Declares a Comparator interface with a generic type
     compareTo(value: T): number;
}

class Rectangle implements Comparator<Rectangle> {  // Creates a class that implements Comparator, specifying the concrete type Rectangle

    constructor(private width: number, private height: number) {};

    compareTo(value: Rectangle): number {           // Implements the method for comparing rectangles
         if (this.width * this.height >= value.width * value.height) {
            return 1;
        } else  {
            return -1;
        }
    }
}

let rect1: Rectangle = new Rectangle(2,5);
let rect2: Rectangle = new Rectangle(2,3);

rect1.compareTo(rect2) === 1? console.log("rect1 is bigger"):
                          console.log("rect1 is smaller");   // Compares rectangles (the type T is erased and replaced with Rectangle)

class Programmer implements Comparator<Programmer> {  // Creates a class that implements Comparator, specifying the concrete type Programmer

    constructor(public name: string, private salary: number) {};

    compareTo(value: Programmer): number {          // Implements the method for comparing programmers
         if (this.salary >= value.salary) {
            return 1;
        } else  {
            return -1;
        }
    }
}

let prog1: Programmer = new Programmer("John",20000);
```

```
let prog2: Programmer = new Programmer("Alex",30000);

prog1.compareTo(prog2)===1? console.log(`${prog1.name} is richer`):
                            console.log(`${prog1.name} is poorer`) ;
```

Compares programmers (the type T is erased and replaced with Programmer)

B.9 The readonly modifier

ES6 introduced the const keyword that you can apply to variables, but not to properties of a class or interface. You can't write this:

```
class Person {
    const name: = "Mary";  // compiler error
}

const p = new Person();  // no errors
```

TypeScript adds a readonly keyword that can be applied to class properties:

```
class Person {
    readonly name = "Mary";  // no errors
}
```

You can initialize a readonly property only during its declaration or in the class constructor. Now if you'll try to write the code that modifies the value of the name property, the TypeScript compiler (or static analyzer) will report an error:

```
class Person {
    readonly name = "Mary";

    changeName() {
        this.name = "John";  // compiler error
    }
}
```

But creating an immutable object is a more interesting use case for applying the readonly modifier. In some cases, especially in Angular apps, you may want to ensure that an object is immutable, and you can't mutate the object by mistake. Let's try to apply readonly to an object property:

```
class Person {

    readonly bestFriend: { name: string } = {name: "Mary"};

    changeFriend() {
        this.bestFriend = { name: "John" }; // compiler error
    }

    changeFriendName() {
        this.bestFriend.name = "John";      // no errors
    }
}
```

An attempt to assign another object to the bestFriend variable results in a compilation error, because bestFriend is marked as readonly. But changing the internal property of the object represented by bestFriend is still allowed. To prohibit this, use the readonly modifier with each property of the object:

```
class Person {

    readonly bestFriend: { readonly name: string } = {name: "Mary"};

    changeFriend() {
        this.bestFriend = { name: "John" }; // compiler error
    }

    changeFriendName(newName: string) {
        this.bestFriend.name = "John";      // compiler error
    }
}
```

In Angular apps, you may want to store application state in an immutable object bound to the input property of a component. To enforce the creation of a new object instance whenever its properties change, write a function that creates a copy of the object with modification of the properties (see code samples in section A.7 in appendix A).

If an object has multiple properties, adding the readonly modifier to each of them is a tedious job, and you can use a read-only mapped type instead. The following example uses the type keyword to define a new type and generics to provide a concrete object to the Readonly class:

```
type Friend = Readonly<{ name: string, lastName: string }>;

class Person {

     bestFriend: Friend = {name: "Mary", lastName: "Smith"};

    changeFriend() {
        this.bestFriend = { name: "John" }; // compiler error
    }

    changeFriendName() {
        this.bestFriend.name = "John";     // compiler error
        this.bestFriend.lastName = "Lou";  // compiler error
    }
}
```

B.10 Decorators

There are different definitions of the term *metadata*. The popular definition is that metadata is data about data. We think of metadata as data that describes and enhances code. Internally, TypeScript decorators are special functions that add metadata enhancing the functionality of a class, property, method, or parameter. TypeScript decorators start with an @ sign.

Decorators exist in Typescript, and they are proposed in ECMAScript. To properly transpile them, turn on experimental features in the Typescript transpiler by adding the following line in the tsconfig.json file:

```
"experimentalDecorators": true
```

In this section, we'll show you how to create a simple decorator that will print the information about the class it's attached to.

Imagine that you want to create a decorator, `UIComponent()`, that can accept an HTML fragment as a parameter. The decorator should be able to print the received HTML and understand the properties of the attached artifact—for example, a class. The following listing does this.

Listing B.13 A custom `UIComponent` decorator

```
function UIComponent (html: string) {
    console.log(`The decorator received ${html} \n`);

    return function(target) {
        console.log(`Creating a UI component from \n ${target} ` );
    }
}

@UIComponent('<h1>Hello Shopper!</h1>')
class Shopper {

    constructor(private name: string) {}
}
```

The `UIComponent()` function has one `string` parameter and returns another function that prints the content of the implicit variable `target`, which knows the artifact the decorator is attached to. If you compile this code into ES5 syntax and run it, the output on your console will look as follows:

```
The decorator received <h1>Hello Shopper!</h1>

Creating a UI component from
 function Shopper(name) {
        this.name = name;
    }
```

If you compile the same code into ES6, the output will be different, because ES6 supports classes:

```
The decorator received <h1>Hello Shopper!</h1>

Creating a UI component from
 class Shopper {
    constructor(name) {
        this.name = name;
    }
}
```

Under the hood, TypeScript uses the `reflect-metadata` library to query the structure of the artifact the decorator is attached to. This simple decorator knows what HTML you want to render and that your class has a member variable `name`. If you're a developer of a framework that needs to render UI, the code of this decorator can come in handy. The process of creating custom decorators is described in the TypeScript documentation at http://mng.bz/gz6R.

To turn a TypeScript class into an Angular component, you need to decorate it with the `@Component()` decorator. Angular will internally parse your annotations and generate code that adds the requested behavior to the TypeScript class. To turn a class variable into a component property that can receive values, you use the `@Input()` decorator:

```
@Component({
  selector: 'order-processor',
  template: `
    Buying {{quantity}} shares}
  `
})
export class OrderComponent {

  @Input() quantity: number;

}
```

In this example, the `@Component()` decorator defines the selector and a template (UI) for the `OrderComponent` class. The `@Input()` decorator enables the `quantity` property to receive values from the parent component via binding. When you use decorators, there should be a decorator processor that can parse the decorator content and turn it into code that the runtime (the browser's JavaScript engine) understands. Angular includes the `ngc` compiler that performs the duties of a decorator processor.

To use Angular decorators, import their implementation in your application code. For example, import the `@Component()` decorator as follows:

```
import { Component } from '@angular/core';
```

Angular comes with a set of decorators, but TypeScript allows you to create your own decorators regardless of whether you use Angular or not.

B.11 The union type

In TypeScript, you can declare a new type based on two or more existing types. For example, you can declare a variable that can accept either a string value or a number:

```
let padding: string | number;
```

Although TypeScript supports the `any` type, the preceding declaration provides some benefits compared to the declaration `let padding: any`. In the following listing, we'll review the code of one of the code samples from the TypeScript documentation at http://mng.bz/5742. This function can add left padding to the provided string. The padding can be specified either as a string that has to prepend the provided argument or the number of spaces that should prepend the string.

Listing B.14 union.ts with any type

```
function padLeft(value: string, padding: any ) {      <-- Provides the string and the padding of type any
    if (typeof padding === "number") {                 <-- For a numeric argument, generates spaces
        return Array(padding + 1).join(" ") + value;
    }
    if (typeof padding === "string") {                 <-- For a string, uses concatenation
        return padding + value;
    }
    throw new Error(`Expected string or number, got '${padding}'.`);   <-- If the second argument is neither a string nor a number, throws an error
}
```

The following are examples of invoking `padLeft()`:

```
console.log( padLeft("Hello world", 4));         // returns "    Hello world"
console.log( padLeft("Hello world", "John says "));// returns "John says Hell
    o world"

console.log( padLeft("Hello world", true)); // runtime error
```

But if you change the type of the `padding` to the union of a string or a number, the compiler will report an error if you try to invoke `padLeft()` providing anything other than a string or a number. This will also eliminate the need to throw an exception. The new version of the `padLeft()` function is more bulletproof, as you can see in the following listing.

Listing B.15 union.ts with a union type

```
function padLeft(value: string, padding: string | number ) {     <-- Allows only a string or a number as a second argument
    if (typeof padding === "number") {
        return Array(padding + 1).join(" ") + value;
    }
    if (typeof padding === "string") {
        return padding + value;
    }
}
```

Now invoking `padLeft()` with the wrong type (for example, `true`) of the second argument returns a compilation error:

```
console.log( padLeft("Hello world", true)); // compilation error
```

Another benefit of using a union type is that IDEs have an autocomplete feature that will prompt you with allowed argument types, so you won't even have a chance to make such a mistake. In section 15.2.3 in chapter 15, there's another practical example of using a union type.

B.12 Using type definition files

The purpose of type definition files is to describe an API of a JavaScript library (or a script) providing types offered by this API. Say you want to use the popular JavaScript library Lodash in your Typescript code. If you have a Lodash type definition file in your project, the TypeScript static analyzer will know what types are expected by Lodash functions, and if you provide wrong types, you'll get a compile-time error. Also, an IDE will offer autocomplete for the Lodash API.

Initially, a TypeScript community created a repository of TypeScript definition files called *DefinitelyTyped* at http://definitelytyped.org. In 2016, Microsoft created an organization, `@types`, at npmjs.org, and this is what we use now. This organization has more than 5,000 type definition files for various JavaScript libraries.

The suffix of any type definition filename is *d.ts*, and you install type definition files using npm. For example, to install type definition files for Lodash, run the following command:

```
npm i @types/lodash --save-dev
```

This will download the Lodash definitions in the node_modules/@types directory of your project and will also update the package.json file, so you won't need to run this command again.

When you install Angular, you're getting the definition files in Angular modules in the subfolders of the node_modules/@angular folder after running `npm install`, as explained in chapter 1. All required d.ts files are bundled with Angular npm packages, and there's no need to install them separately. The presence of definition files in your project will allow the TypeScript compiler to ensure that your code uses the correct types while invoking the Angular API.

For example, Angular applications are launched by invoking the `bootstrapModule()` method, giving it the root module for your application as an argument. The application_ref.d.ts file includes the following definition for this function:

```
abstract bootstrapModule<M>(moduleType: Type<M>,
compilerOptions?: CompilerOptions | CompilerOptions[]): Promise<NgModuleRef<M>>;
```

By reading this definition, you (and the `tsc` compiler) know that this function can be invoked with one mandatory module parameter of type `Type<M>` and an optional array of compiler options. If application_ref.d.ts wasn't a part of your project, TypeScript's compiler would let you invoke the `bootstrapModule` function with a wrong parameter type, or without any parameters at all, which would result in a runtime error. But application_ref.d.ts is present, so TypeScript would generate a compile-time error reading "Supplied parameters do not match any signature of call target." Type definition files also allow IDEs to show context-sensitive help when you're writing code that invokes Angular functions or assigns values to object properties.

Specifying type definition files explicitly

To explicitly specify the type definition files located in the node_modules/@types directory, add the required files to the `types` section of tsconfig.json. Here's an example:

```
"compilerOptions": {
   ...
   "types": ["es6-shim", "jasmine"],
}
```

In the past, we used special type definition managers `tsd` and `Typings` to install type definition files, but these managers are no longer needed. If your application uses other third-party JavaScript libraries, install their type definition files with npm to get compiler help and autocomplete in your IDE.

B.13 Controlling code style with TSLint

Linters help to ensure that code complies with the accepted coding style. With TSLint, you can enforce specified rules and coding styles for TypeScript. For example, you can configure TSLint to check that the TypeScript code in your project is properly aligned and indented, that the names of all interfaces start with a capital I, that class names use CamelCase notation, and so on.

You can install TSLint globally using the following command:

```
npm install tslint -g
```

To install the TSLint node module in your project directory, run the following command:

```
npm install tslint
```

The rules you want to apply to your code are specified in a tslint.json configuration file, which is generated by running `tslint init`:

```
{
 "defaultSeverity": "error",
 "extends": [
     "tslint: recommended"
 ],
 "jsRules": {},
 "rules": {},
 "rulesDirectory": []
}
```

A file with recommended rules comes with TSLint, but you can use custom rules of your preference. You can check the recommended rules in the node_modules/tslint/lib/configs/recommended.js file. The core TSLint rules are documented at http://mng.bz/xx6B. Your IDE may support linting with TSLint out of the box. If you generated your project with Angular CLI, it already includes TSLint.

appendix C
Using the npm package manager

This appendix is an overview of the tools we use to install Angular and its dependencies using the npm package manager.

For most of this book, we use Node.js for installing software. Node.js (or simply *Node*) isn't just a framework or a library: it's a JavaScript runtime environment as well. We use the Node runtime for running various utilities like npm or launching JavaScript code without a browser. We also use npm scripts to automate building, testing, and deploying Angular apps.

To get started, download and install the current version of Node.js from https://nodejs.org. After installation is complete, open your terminal or command window and enter the following command:

```
node --version
```

This command should print the version of Node installed, for example, 10.3.0. Node comes with the package manager npm, which we use to install Angular and other packages from the npm registry located at www.npmjs.com. This repository hosts Angular as well as more than 400,000 other JavaScript packages.

The Node.js framework

Node.js is also a framework that can be used to develop JavaScript programs that run outside the browser. You can develop the server-side layer of a web application in JavaScript or Typescript. We write a web server using Node in chapter 12 by using Node.js and Express frameworks. Google developed a high-performance V8 JavaScript engine for the Chrome browser, and it can also be used to run code written using the Node.js API. The Node.js framework includes an API to work with the filesystem, access databases, listen to HTTP requests, and more.

To install a JavaScript library, run the command `npm install`, or `npm i` for short. Say you want to install the TypeScript compiler locally. Open the Terminal in any directory and run the following command:

```
npm i typescript
```

After this command completes, you'll see a new subdirectory named node_modules, where the TypeScript compiler has been installed. npm always installs packages in the node_modules directory. If such a directory doesn't exist, npm will create it.

If you want to install a package globally, add the `-g` option:

```
npm i typescript -g
```

This time the TypeScript compiler will be installed not in the current directory, but globally in the lib/node_modules subdirectory of your Node.js installation.

If you want to install a specific version of the package, add the version number to the package name after the `@` sign. For example, to install Typescript 2.9.0 globally, use the following command:

```
npm i typescript@2.9.0 -g
```

All available options of the `npm install` command are described at https://docs.npmjs.com/cli/install.

In some cases, you may want to have the same package installed both locally and globally. As a example, you may have the TypeScript compiler 2.7 installed locally, and TypeScript 2.9 installed globally. To run the global version of this compiler, you enter the `tsc` command in your terminal or command window, and to run the locally installed compiler, you could use the following command from your project directory:

```
node_modules/.bin/tsc
```

A typical Node-based project may have multiple dependencies, and we don't want to keep running separate `npm i` commands to install each package. Creating a package.json file is a better way to specify all project dependencies.

C.1 Specifying project dependencies in package.json

To start a new Node-based project, create a new directory (for example, my-node-project), open your terminal or command window, and change the current working directory to the newly created one. Then run the `npm init -y` command, which will create the initial version of the package.json configuration file. Normally, `npm init` asks several questions while creating the file, but the `-y` flag makes it accept the default values for all options. The following example shows this command running in the empty my-node-project directory:

```
$ npm init -y
Wrote to /Users/username/my-node-project/package.json:
```

```
{
  "name": "my-node-project",
  "version": "1.0.0",
  "description": "",
  "main": "index.js",
  "scripts": {
    "test": "echo \"Error: no test specified\" && exit 1"
  },
  "keywords": [],
  "author": "",
  "license": "ISC"
}
```

Most of the generated configuration is needed either for publishing the project into the npm registry or while installing the package as a dependency for another project. We'll use npm only for managing project dependencies and automating development and build processes.

Because we're not going to publish it into the npm registry, remove all the properties except `name`, `description`, and `scripts`. Also, add a `"private": true` property, because it's not created by default. That will prevent the package from being accidentally published to the npm registry. The package.json file should look like this:

```
{
  "name": "my-node-project",
  "description": "",
  "private": true,
  "scripts": {
    "test": "echo \"Error: no test specified\" && exit 1"
  }
}
```

The `scripts` configuration allows you to specify command aliases that you can run in your command window. By default, `npm init` creates the `test` alias, which can be run like this: `npm test`. The generated script command include double ampersands, `&&`, which are used as a separator between commands. When you run `npm test`, it runs two commands: `echo \"Error: no test specified\"` and `exit -1`. npm scripts support about a dozen command names like `test`, `start`, and others. A list of these commands is at https://docs.npmjs.com/misc/scripts.

You can create your own command aliases with any names:

```
"scripts": {
    "deploy": "copyfiles -f dist/** ../server/build/public",
  }
```

Because `deploy` is a custom alias name, you need to run this command by adding the keyword `run`:

```
npm run deploy
```

In section 12.3.6 in chapter 12, we discuss how to write npm scripts for building and deploying an app on the web server.

If you generate package.json using the `npm init` command, it'll be missing two important sections: `dependencies` and `devDependencies`. Let's see how dependencies of an Angular project are specified. Figure C.1 shows a fragment from a package.json file of a typical Angular project.

```
"dependencies": {
  "@angular/animations": "^6.0.0",
  "@angular/common": "^6.0.0",
  "@angular/compiler": "^6.0.0",
  "@angular/core": "^6.0.0",
  "@angular/forms": "^6.0.0",
  "@angular/http": "^6.0.0",
  "@angular/platform-browser": "^6.0.0",
  "@angular/platform-browser-dynamic": "^6.0.0",
  "@angular/router": "^6.0.0",
  "core-js": "^2.5.4",
  "rxjs": "^6.0.0",
  "ws": "^5.2.0",
  "zone.js": "^0.8.26"
},
"devDependencies": {
  "@angular/compiler-cli": "^6.0.0",
  "@angular-devkit/build-angular": "~0.6.1",
  "typescript": "~2.7.2",
  "@angular/cli": "~6.0.1",
  "@angular/language-service": "^6.0.0",
  "@types/jasmine": "~2.8.6",
  "@types/jasminewd2": "~2.0.3",
  "@types/node": "~8.9.4",
  "codelyzer": "~4.2.1",
  "jasmine-core": "~2.99.1",
  "jasmine-spec-reporter": "~4.2.1",
  "karma": "~1.7.1",
  "karma-chrome-launcher": "~2.2.0",
  "karma-coverage-istanbul-reporter": "~1.4.2",
  "karma-jasmine": "~1.1.1",
  "karma-jasmine-html-reporter": "^0.2.2",
  "protractor": "~5.3.0",
  "ts-node": "~5.0.1",
  "tslint": "~5.9.1"
}
```

Figure C.1 Angular dependencies in package.json

It looks intimidating, but the good news is that you don't need to remember all these packages and their versions, because you'll be generating projects with Angular CLI, which will create the file package.json with the proper content.

The `dependencies` section lists all the packages required for your application to run. As you can see, the Angular framework comes in several packages with names starting with `@angular`. You may not need to install all of them. If your app doesn't use forms, for example, there's no need to include `@angular/forms` in your package.json.

The `devDependencies` section lists all the packages required to be installed on a developer's computer. It includes several packages, and none of them is needed on the production server. There's no need to have testing frameworks or a TypeScript compiler on the production machine, right?

To install a single package with npm, list the name of this package. For example, to add the Lodash library to your node_modules directory, run the following command:

```
npm i lodash
```

To add the package to node_modules and add the corresponding dependency to the `dependencies` section of your package.json file, you can explicitly specify the `--save-prod` option :

```
npm i lodash --save-prod
```

You can also use the abbreviation `-P` for `--save-prod`. If no options are specified, the `npm i lodash` command updates the `dependencies` section of the package.json file.

To add the package to node_modules and add the corresponding dependency to the `devDependencies` section of your package.json file, use the `--save-dev` option:

```
npm i protractor --save-dev
```

You can also use the abbreviation `-D` for `--save-dev`.

Sometimes the GitHub version of a package has an important bug fix that hasn't been released yet on npmjs.org. If you want install such a package from GitHub, you need to replace the version number in package.json dependencies with its location on GitHub. Changing the dependency to include the name of the GitHub organization and repository should allow you to install the latest builds from GitHub versions of this library. For example:

```
"@angular/flex-layout": "angular/flex-layout-builds"
```

The preceding configuration will work, assuming that the master branch of the Flex Layout library has no code issues preventing npm from installing it.

C.2 Semantic versioning

Numbering of Angular releases uses a set of rules known as *semantic versioning*. The version of a package consists of three digits—for example, 6.1.2. The first digit denotes a major release that includes new features and potentially breaking changes in the API. The second digit represents a minor release, which introduces new backward-compatible APIs but has no breaking changes. The third digit represents backward-compatible patches with bug fixes.

Take another look at figure C.1 in the previous section. Every package has a three-digit version, and many of them have additional symbols: ^ or ~. If the specified version has just the three digits, that means you instruct npm to install exactly that version. For example, the following line in package.json tells npm to install Angular CLI version 6.0.5, ignoring the newer versions even if they're available:

```
"@angular/cli": "6.0.5"
```

Many packages in that package.json file have the hat sign ^ in front of the version. For example:

```
"@angular/core": "^6.0.0"
```

This means you'll allow npm to install the latest minor release of version 6 if available. If the latest version of the Angular Core package is 6.2.1, it will be installed.

The tilde ~ means you want to install the latest patch for the given major and minor version:

```
"jasmine-core": "~2.99.1"
```

There are many other symbols you can use with version numbers with npm—see http://mng.bz/YnyW for details.

C.3 Yarn as an alternative to npm

Yarn (see https://yarnpkg.com) is another package manager that can be used as an alternative to npm. Prior to version 5, npm was slow, which was one reason we started using the faster Yarn.

Now npm is fast too, but Yarn has an additional benefit: it creates the file yarn.lock that keeps track of exact versions of packages that were installed in your project. Let's say your package.json file has a `"@angular/core": "^6.0.0"` dependency, and your project has no yarn.lock file. If version 6.1.0 is available, it'll be installed, and yarn.lock is created with a record about the version 6.1.0. If you run `yarn install` in a month, and if yarn.lock exists in your project, Yarn will use it and install version 6.1.0, even if version 6.2.0 is available.

The following fragment from yarn.lock shows that although the dependency in package.json for the `@angular/core` package was set as `^6.0.0`, version `6.0.2` was installed:

```
"@angular/core@^6.0.0":
  version "6.0.2"
  resolved "https://registry.yarnpkg.com/@angular/core/-/core-
     6.0.2.tgz#d183..."
  dependencies:
    tslib "^1.9.0"
```

In a team setup, you should check the yarn.lock file into the version control repository so every member of your team has the same versions of packages.

npm also creates the package-lock.json file, but npm isn't designed to install exact package version(s) listed in this file if you run `npm install`(see https://github.com/npm/npm/issues/17979). The good news is that starting from version 5.7, npm supports the `npm ci` command, which ignores the versions listed in package.json, but installs the versions listed in the package-lock.json file.

If at some point you decide to upgrade packages, overriding the versions stored in yarn.lock, run the `yarn upgrade-interactive` command, as shown in figure C.2.

```
MacBook-Pro-9:form-validation yfain11$ yarn upgrade-interactive
yarn upgrade-interactive v1.3.2
info Color legend :
 "<red>"    : Major Update backward-incompatible updates
 "<yellow>" : Minor Update backward-compatible features
 "<green>"  : Patch Update backward-compatible bug fixes
? Choose which packages to update. (Press <space> to select, <a> to toggle all, <i> to inverse selection)
 dependencies
   name                                range    from       to      url
)o @angular/animations                 ^5.0.0   5.1.2  >  5.2.0   https://github.com/angular/angular#readme
 o @angular/common                     ^5.0.0   5.1.2  >  5.2.0   https://github.com/angular/angular#readme
 o @angular/compiler                   ^5.0.0   5.1.2  >  5.2.0   https://github.com/angular/angular#readme
 o @angular/core                       ^5.0.0   5.1.2  >  5.2.0   https://github.com/angular/angular#readme
 o @angular/forms                      ^5.0.0   5.1.2  >  5.2.0   https://github.com/angular/angular#readme
```

Figure C.2 Upgrading package versions with Yarn

Yarn works with your project's package.json file, so there's no need for any additional configuration. You can read more about using Yarn at https://yarnpkg.com/ en/docs.

> **TIP** You can ask Angular CLI to use Yarn instead of npm while installing dependencies of the newly generated project. Starting with Angular CLI 6, you can do this by using the following command:
>
> ```
> ng config --global cli.packageManager yarn
> ```
>
> If you use older versions of Angular CLI, use the following command:
>
> ```
> ng set --global packageManager=yarn
> ```

appendix D
RxJS essentials

Synchronous programming is relatively straightforward in that each line of your code is executed after the previous one. If you invoke a function in line 25 that returns a value, you can use the returned value as an argument for the function invoked in line 26.

Asynchronous programming dramatically increases code complexity. In line 37, you can invoke an asynchronous function that will return the value sometime later. Can you invoke a function in line 38 that uses the value returned by the previous function? The short answer is, "It depends."

This appendix is an introduction to the RxJS 6 library, which can be used with any JavaScript-based app. It shines when it comes to writing and composing asynchronous code. Because Angular uses the RxJS library internally, we decided to add a primer to this book.

The first library of reactive extensions (Rx) was created by Erik Meijer in 2009. Rx.NET was meant to be used for apps written with Microsoft .Net technology. Then the Rx extensions were ported to multiple languages, and in the JavaScript world, RxJS 6 is the current version of this library.

> **NOTE** Though Angular depends on RxJS and can't function without it, RxJS itself is an independent library that can be used in any JavaScript app.

Let's see what being reactive means in programming by considering a simple example:

```
let a1 = 2;?
let b1 = 4;??
let c1 = a1 + b1;  // c1 = 6??
```

This code adds the values of the variables `a1` and `b1`, and `c1` is equal to `6`. Now let's add a couple of lines to this code, modifying the values of `a1` and `b1`:

```
let a1 = 2;?
let b1 = 4;??
let c1 = a1 + b1;  // c1 = 6??

a1 = 55;        // c1 = 6 but should be 59 ?
b1 = 20;        // c1 = 6 but should be 75
```

While the values of `a1` and `b1` change, `c1` doesn't react to these changes, and its value is still `6`. You can write a function that adds `a1` and `b1` and invokes it to get the latest value of `c1`, but this would be an *imperative* style of coding, where you dictate when to invoke a function to calculate the sum.

Wouldn't it be nice if `c2` were automatically recalculated upon any `a1` or `b1` changes? Think of a spreadsheet program like Microsoft Excel, where you could put a formula like `=sum(a1, b1)` into the C1 cell, and C1 would react immediately upon changes in A1 and B1. In other words, you don't need to click any button to refresh the value of C1—the data is pushed to this cell.

In the *reactive* style of coding (as opposed to the imperative one), the changes in data drive the invocation of your code. Reactive programming is about creating responsive, event-driven applications, where an observable event stream is pushed to subscribers, who observe and handle the events.

In software engineering, Observer/Observable is a well-known pattern and is a good fit in any asynchronous-processing scenario. But reactive programming is a lot more than just an implementation of the Observer/Observable pattern. Observable streams can be canceled, they can notify about the end of a stream, and the data pushed to the subscriber can be transformed on the way from the data producer to the subscriber by applying one or more composable operators.

D.1 Getting familiar with RxJS terminology

We want to observe data, which means there's a data producer—a server sending data using HTTP or WebSockets, a UI input field where a user enters some data, an accelerometer in a smartphone, and so on. An *observable* is a function (or object) that gets the producer data and pushes it to the subscriber(s). An *observer* is an object (or function) that knows how to handle data elements pushed by the observable, as shown in figure D.1.

The main players of RxJS are as follows:

- *Observable*—Data stream that pushes data over time
- *Observer*—Consumer of an observable stream
- *Subscriber*—Connects observer with observable
- *Operator*—Function for en route data transformation

We'll introduce each of these players by showing multiple examples of their use. For complete coverage, refer to the RxJS documentation available at http://reactivex.io/rxjs.

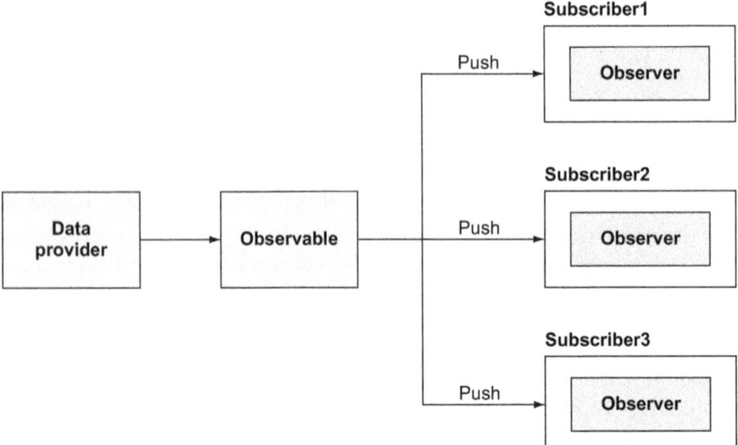

Figure D.1 The data flow from observable to observers

Hot and cold observables

There are two types of observables: hot and cold. The main difference is that a cold observable creates a data producer for each subscriber, whereas a hot observable creates a data producer first, and each subscriber gets the data from one producer, starting from the moment of subscription.

Let's compare watching a movie on Netflix to going into a movie theater. Think of yourself as an observer. Anyone who decides to watch *Mission: Impossible* on Netflix will get the entire movie, regardless of when they hit the play button. Netflix creates a new producer to stream a movie just for you. This is a cold observable.

If you go to a movie theater and the showtime is 4 p.m., the producer is created at 4 p.m., and the streaming begins. If some people (subscribers) are late to the show, they miss the beginning of the movie and can only watch it starting from the moment of arrival. This is a hot observable.

A cold observable starts producing data when some code invokes a `subscribe()` function on it. For example, your app may declare an observable providing a URL on the server to get certain products. The request will be made only when you subscribe to it. If another script makes the same request to the server, it'll get the same set of data.

A hot observable produces data even if no subscribers are interested in the data. For example, an accelerometer in your smartphone produces data about the position of your device, even if no app subscribes to this data. A server can produce the latest stock prices even if no user is interested in this stock.

Most of the examples in this appendix are about cold observables.

D.2 Observable, observer, and subscriber

As stated earlier, an observable gets data from a data source (a socket, an array, UI events) one element at a time. To be precise, an observable knows how to do three things:

- Emit the next element to the observer
- Throw an error on the observer
- Inform the observer that the stream is over

Accordingly, an observer object provides up to three callbacks:

- The function to handle the next element emitted by the observable
- The function to handle errors thrown by the observable
- The function to handle the end of a stream

The subscriber connects an observable and observer by invoking the `subscribe()` method and disconnects them by invoking `unsubscribe()`. A script that subscribes to an observable has to provide the observer object that knows what to do with the produced elements. Let's say you create an observable represented by the variable `someObservable` and an observer represented by the variable `myObserver`. You can subscribe to such an observable as follows:

```
let mySubscription: Subscription = someObservable.subscribe(myObserver);
```

To cancel the subscription, invoke the `unsubscribe()` method:

```
mySubscription.unsubscribe();
```

How can an observable communicate with the provided observer? By invoking the following functions on the observer object:

- `next()`, to push the next data element to the observer
- `error()`, to push the error message to the observer
- `complete()`, to send a signal to the observer about the end of a stream

You'll see an example of using these functions in section D.5.

D.3 Creating observables

RxJS offers several ways of creating an observable, depending on the type of the data producer—for example, a data producer for a DOM event, a data collection, a custom function, a WebSocket, and more.

Here are some examples of the API to create an observable:

- `of(1,2,3)`—Turns the sequence of numbers into an `Observable`
- `Observable.create(myObserver)`—Returns an `Observable` that can invoke methods on `myObserver` that you'll create and supply as an argument
- `from(myArray)`—Converts an array represented by the `myArray` variable into an `Observable`. You can also use any iterable data collection or a generator function as an argument of `from()`.

- `fromEvent(myInput, 'keyup')`—Converts the `keyup` event from an HTML element represented by `myInput` into an `Observable`. Chapter 6 has an example of using the `fromEvent()` API.
- `interval(1000)`—Emits a sequential integer (0,1,2,3...) every second

TIP There's a proposal for introducing `Observable` into future versions of ECMAScript. See https://github.com/tc39/proposal-observable.

Let's create an observable that will emit 1, 2, and 3 and subscribe to this observable.

Listing D.1 Emitting 1,2,3

```
of(1,2,3)
    .subscribe(
        value => console.log(value),
         err => console.error(err),
         () => console.log("Streaming is over")
);
```

Handles the value emitted by the observable

Handles the error

Handles the stream completion message

Note that you pass three fat-arrow functions to `subscribe()`. These three functions combined are the implementation of your observer. The first function will be invoked for each element emitted by the observable. The second function will be invoked in case of an error, providing the object representing the error. The third function takes no arguments and will be invoked when the observable stream is over. Running this code sample will produce the following output on the console:[1]

```
1
2
3
Streaming is over
```

NOTE In appendix A, we discuss using the `Promise` object, which can invoke an event handler specified in the `then()` function only once. Think of a `subscribe()` method as a replacement of the `then()` invocation on a `Promise` object, but the callback for `subscribe()` is invoked not just once, but for each emitted value.

D.4 Getting familiar with RxJS operators

As data elements flow from an observable to an observer, you can apply one or more *operators*, which are functions that can process each element prior to supplying it to the observer. Each operator takes an observable as an input, performs its action, and returns a new observable as an output, as seen in figure D.2.

Because each operator takes in an observable and creates an observable as its output, operators can be chained so that each observable element can go through several transformations prior to being handed to the observer.

[1] See it in CodePen: http://mng.bz/MwTz. Open the console view at the bottom to see the output.

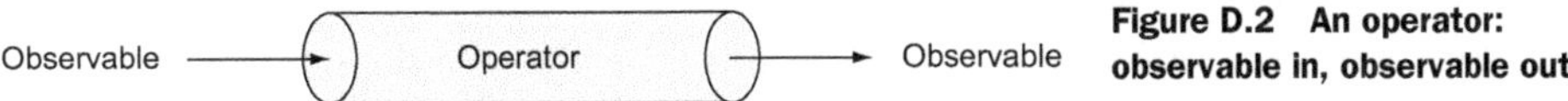

Figure D.2 An operator: observable in, observable out

RxJS offers about 100 various operators, and their documentation may not always be easy to understand. On the positive side, the documentation often illustrates operators with marble diagrams. You can get familiar with the syntax of marble diagrams at http://mng.bz/2534. Figure D.3 shows how the RxJS manual illustrates the `map` operator with a marble diagram (see http://mng.bz/65G7).

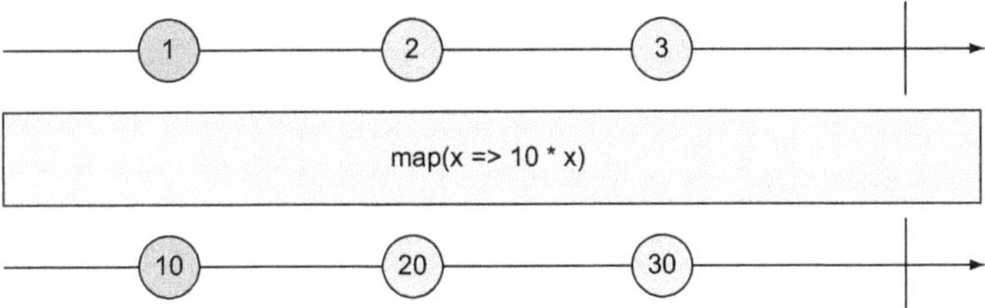

Figure D.3 The map operator

At the top, a marble diagram shows a horizontal line with shapes representing a stream of incoming observable elements. Next, there's the illustration of what a particular operator does. At the bottom, you see another horizontal line depicting the outgoing observable stream after the operator has been applied. The vertical bar represents the end of the stream. When you look at the diagram, think of time as moving from left to right. First, the value 1 was emitted, then time went by, 2 was emitted, then time went by, 3 was emitted, and then the stream ended.

The `map` operator takes a transforming function as an argument and applies it to each incoming element. Figure D.3 shows the `map` operator that takes a value of each incoming element and multiplies it by 10.

Now let's get familiar with the marble diagram of the `filter` operator, shown in figure D.4. The `filter` operator takes a function predicate as an argument, which returns `true` if the emitted value meets the criteria, and `false` otherwise. Only the values that meet the criteria will make it to the subscriber. This particular diagram uses

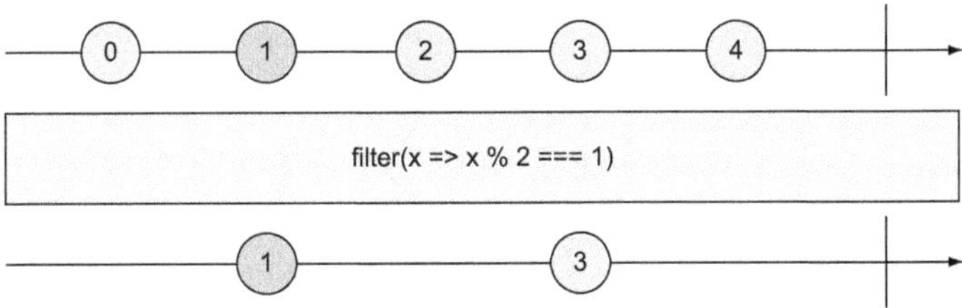

Figure D.4 The filter operator

the fat-arrow function that checks whether the current element is an odd number. Even numbers won't make it further down the chain to the observer.

Operators are composable, and you can chain them so the item emitted by the observable can be processed by a sequence of operators before it reaches the observer.

Deprecated operator chaining

Prior to RxJS 6, you could chain operators using the dot between operators.

Listing D.2 Dot-chainable operators

```
const beers = [
    {name: "Stella", country: "Belgium", price: 9.50},
    {name: "Sam Adams", country: "USA", price: 8.50},
    {name: "Bud Light", country: "USA", price: 6.50}
];

from(beers)
    .filter(beer => beer.price < 8)    // Applies the filter operator
     .map(beer => `${beer.name}: $${beer.price}`)    // Dot-chains the map operator
     .subscribe(
        beer => console.log(beer),
        err => console.error(err)
);

console.log("This is the last line of the script");
```

Starting with RxJS 6, the only way to chain operators is by using the `pipe()` method, passing to it comma-separated operators as arguments. The next section introduces *pipeable* operators.

D.4.1 Pipeable operators

Pipeable operators are those that can be chained using the `pipe()` function. We'll talk about dot-chaining operators first to explain why pipeable operators were introduced in RxJS.

If you have RxJS prior to version 6 installed, you can import dot-chaining operators from the rxjs/add/operator directory. For example:

```
import 'rxjs/add/operator/map';
import 'rxjs/add/operator/filter';
```

These operators patch the code of the `Observable.prototype` and become a part of this object. If you decide later on to remove, say, the `filter` operator from the code that handles the observable stream, but you forget to remove the corresponding import statement, the code that implements `filter` would remain a part of `Observable.prototype`. When bundlers tried to eliminate the unused code (*tree shaking*), they may decide to keep the code of the `filter` operator in the `Observable` even though it's not being used in the app.

RxJS 5.5 introduced pipeable operators, pure functions that don't patch the `Observable`. You can import operators using ES6 import syntax (for example, `import {map} from 'rxjs/operators'`) and then wrap them into a `pipe()` function that takes a variable number of parameters, or chainable operators.

The subscriber in listing D.2 will receive the same data as the one in the sidebar "Deprecated operator chaining," but it's a better version from the tree-shaking perspective, because it uses pipeable operators. This listing includes import statements, assuming that RxJS is locally installed.

Listing D.3 Using pipeable operators

```
import {map, filter} from 'rxjs/operators';
 import {from} from 'rxjs';
 ...
from(beers)
    .pipe(
          filter(beer => beer.price < 8),
         map(beer => `${beer.name}: $${beer.price}`)
      )
    .subscribe(
        beer => console.log(beer),
        err => console.error(err)
);
```

Imports pipeable operators from rxjs/operators instead of rxjs/add/operator

Imports the from() function

Wraps pipeable operators into the pipe() function

Now if you remove the line `filter` from listing D.2, the tree-shaking module of the bundlers (such as Webpack 4) can recognize that the imported function isn't used, and the code of the `filter` operator won't be included in the bundles.[2]

By default, the `from()` function returns a synchronous observable, but if you want an asynchronous one, use a second argument specifying an async scheduler:

```
from(beers, Scheduler.async)
```

Making this change in the preceding code sample will print "This is the last line of the script" first and then will emit the beers info. You can read more about the scheduler at http://mng.bz/744Y.

Now we'd like to introduce the `reduce` operator, which allows you to aggregate values emitted by an observable. A marble diagram of the `reduce` operator is shown in figure D.5. This diagram shows an observable that emits 1, 3, and 5, and the `reduce` operator adds them up, producing the accumulated value of 9.

The `reduce` operator has two arguments: an accumulator function where we specify how to aggregate the values, and the initial (seed) value to be used by the accumulator function. Figure D.5 shows that 0 was used as an initial value, but if we changed it to 10, the accumulated result would be 19.

2 See it in CodePen: http://mng.bz/RqO5.

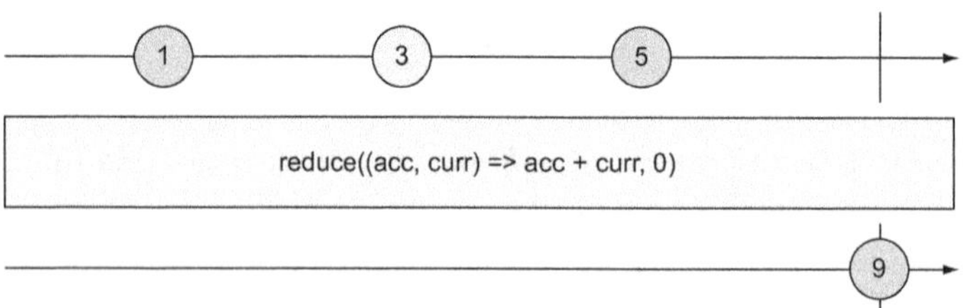

Figure D.5 The reduce operator

As you see in figure D.5, the accumulator function also has two arguments:

- `acc` stores the currently accumulated value, which is available for each emitted element.
- `curr` stores the currently emitted value.

The following listing creates an observable from the `beers` array and applies two operators to each emitted element: `map` and `reduce`. The `map` operator takes a `beer` object and extracts its price, and the `reduce` operator adds the prices.

Listing D.4 Using the `map` and `reduce` operators

```
const beers = [
    {name: "Stella", country: "Belgium", price: 9.50},
    {name: "Sam Adams", country: "USA", price: 8.50},
    {name: "Bud Light", country: "USA", price: 6.50},
    {name: "Brooklyn Lager", country: "USA", price: 8.00},
    {name: "Sapporo", country: "Japan", price: 7.50}
];

from(beers)
    .pipe(
      map(beer =>  beer.price),                    // Transforms the beer object into its price
       reduce( (total, price) => total + price, 0)    // Sums the prices
    )
    .subscribe(
        totalPrice => console.log(`Total price: ${totalPrice}`)   // Prints the total price of all beers
 );
```

Running this script will produce the following output:

```
Total price: 40
```

In this script, we were adding all prices, but we could apply any other calculations to the aggregate value, such as to calculate an average or maximum price.

The `reduce` operator emits the aggregated result when the observable completes. In this example, it happened naturally, because we created an observable from an array with a finite number of elements. In other scenarios, we'd need to invoke the `complete()` method on the observer explicitly; you'll see how to do that in the next section.[3]

Code samples from this section have been turning the array into an observable, and magically pushing the array elements to the observer. In the next section, we'll show you how to push elements by invoking the `next()` function on the observer.

> **Debugging observables**
>
> The `tap` operator can perform a side effect (for example, log some data) for every value emitted by the source observable, but return an observable that's identical to the source. In particular, these operators can be used for debugging purposes.
>
> Say you have a chain of operators and want to see the observable values before and after a certain operator is applied. The `tap` operator will allow you to log the values:

```
import { map, tap } from 'rxjs/operators';

myObservable$
  .pipe(
    tap(beer => console.log(`Before: ${beer}`)),
    map(beer => `${beer.name}, ${beer.country}`),
    tap(beer => console.log(`After: ${beer}`))
  )
  .subscribe(...);
```

> In this example, you print the emitted value before and after the `map` operator is applied. The `tap` operator doesn't change the observable data—it passes it through to the next operator or the `subscribe()` method.

D.5 Using an observer API

An *observer* is an object that implements one or more of these functions: `next()`, `error()`, and `complete()`. Let's use an object literal to illustrate an observer, but later in this section, we'll use a simplified syntax with arrow functions:

```
const beerObserver = {
  next: function(beer) { console.log(`Subscriber got ${beer.name}`)},
  error: function(err) { console.err(error)},
  complete: function() {console.log("The stream is over")}
}
```

We can create an observable with the `create` method, passing an argument that represents an observer. When an observable gets created, it doesn't know yet which concrete object will be provided. That'll be known later, at the time of subscription:

```
const beerObservable$ = Observable.create( observer => observer.next(beer));
```

[3] See it in CodePen: http://mng.bz/68fR.

This particular observable thinks "When someone subscribes to my beers, they'll provide me with a concrete beer consumer, and I'll push one beer object to this guy." At the time of subscription, we'll provide a concrete observer to our observable:

```
beerObservable$.subscribe(beerObserver);
```

The observer will get the beer and will print on the console something like this:

```
Subscriber got Stella
```

The next listing has a complete script that illustrates creation of the observer, the observable, and the subscription. The `getObservableBeer()` function creates and returns an observable that will loop through the array of beers and push each beer to the observer by invoking `next()`. After that, our observable will invoke `complete()` on the observer, indicating that there won't be any more beers.

Listing D.5 Using `Observable.create()`

```
function getObservableBeer(){

    return Observable.create( observer => {        // Creates and returns the observable object

      const beers = [
        {name: "Stella", country: "Belgium", price: 9.50},
        {name: "Sam Adams", country: "USA", price: 8.50},
        {name: "Bud Light", country: "USA", price: 6.50},
        {name: "Brooklyn Lager", country: "USA", price: 8.00},
        {name: "Sapporo", country: "Japan", price: 7.50}
      ];

         beers.forEach( beer => observer.next(beer));   // Pushes each beer to the observer

         observer.complete();   // Pushes the end of the stream message to the observer
         }
    );
}

getObservableBeer()
    .subscribe(        // Subscribes to the observable, providing the observer object in the form of three fat-arrow functions
      beer => console.log(`Subscriber got ${beer.name}`),
     error => console.err(error),
        () => console.log("The stream is over")
);
```

The output of this script is shown next:[4]

```
Subscriber got Stella
Subscriber got Sam Adams
```

[4] See it in CodePen: http://mng.bz/Q7sb.

```
Subscriber got Bud Light
Subscriber got Brooklyn Lager
Subscriber got Sapporo
The stream is over
```

In our code sample, we were invoking `next()` and `complete()` on the observer. But keep in mind that an observable is just a data pusher, and there's always a data producer (the array of beers, in our case) that may generate an error. In that case, we'd invoke `observer.error()`, and the stream would complete. There's a way to intercept an error on the subscriber's side to keep the streaming alive, discussed in section D.9.

It's important to note that our data producer (the array of beers) is created inside the `getObservableBeer()` observable, which makes it a cold observable. A WebSocket could be another example of the producer. Imagine we have a database of beers on the server, and we can request them over a WebSocket connection (we could use HTTP or any other protocol here):

```
Observable.create((observer) => {
  const socket = new WebSocket('ws://beers');
  socket.addEventListener('message', (beer) => observer.next(beer));
  return () => socket.close(); // is invoked on unsubscribe()
});
```

With cold observables, each subscriber will get the same beers, regardless of the time of subscription, if the query criteria (in our case, show all beers) are the same.

D.6 Using RxJS Subject

An RxJS `Subject` is an object that contains an observable and the observer(s). This means you can push the data to its observer(s) using `next()`, as well as subscribe to it. A `Subject` can have multiple observers, which makes it useful when you need to implement for *multicasting*—emitting a value to multiple subscribers, as shown in figure D.6.

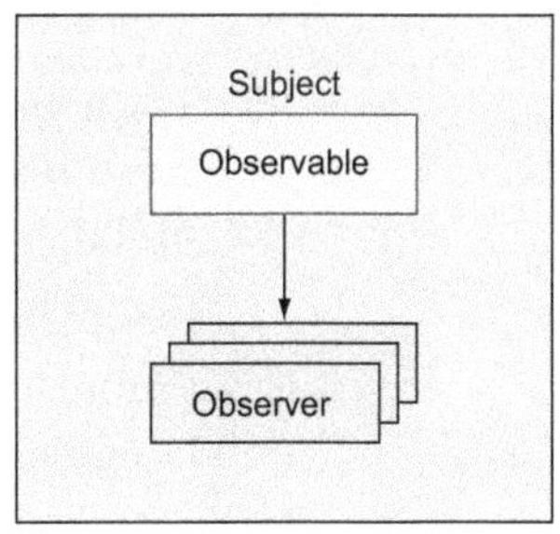

Figure D.6 RxJS `Subject`

Say you have an instance of a `Subject` and two subscribers. If you push a value to the subject, each subscriber will receive it:

```
const mySubject$ = new Subject();

const subscription1 = mySubject$.subscribe(...);?
const subscription2 = mySubject$.subscribe(...);?
...
?mySubject$.next(123); // each subscriber gets 123
```

The following example has one `Subject` with two subscribers. The first value is emitted to both subscribers, and then one of them unsubscribes. The second value is emitted to one active subscriber.

Listing D.6 One subject and two subscribers

```
const mySubject$ = new Subject();

const subscriber1 = mySubject$
    .subscribe( x => console.log(`Subscriber 1 got ${x}`) );

const subscriber2 = mySubject$
    .subscribe( x => console.log(`Subscriber 2 got ${x}`) );

mySubject$.next(123);

subscriber2.unsubscribe();

mySubject$.next(567);
```

Creates the first subscriber

Creates the second subscriber

Pushes the value 123 to subscribers (we have two of them)

Unsubscribes the second subscriber

Pushes the value 567 to subscribers (we have just one now)

Running this script produces the following output on the console:[5]

```
Subscriber 1 got 123
Subscriber 2 got 123
Subscriber 1 got 567
```

> **TIP** There's a naming convention to end the names of variables of type `Observable` or `Subject` with a dollar sign.

Now let's consider a more practical example. A financial firm has traders who can place orders to buy or sell stocks. Whenever the trader places an order, it has to be given to two scripts (subscribers):

- The script that knows how to place orders with a stock exchange
- The script that knows how to report each order to a trade commission that keeps track of all trading activities

The following listing, written in TypeScript, shows how to ensure that both subscribers can receive orders as soon as a trader places them. We create an instance of `Subject` called `orders`, and whenever we invoke `next()` on it, both subscribers will receive the order.

5 See it in CodePen: http://mng.bz/jx16.

Listing D.7 Broadcasting trade orders

```
enum Action{
     Buy = 'BUY',
    Sell = 'SELL'
}

class Order{
     constructor(public orderId: number, public traderId: number,
    ➥public stock: string, public shares: number, public action:Action){}
}

const orders$ = new Subject<Order>();

class Trader {

    constructor(private traderId:number, private traderName:string){}

    placeOrder(order: Order){
        orders$.next(order);
     }
}

const stockExchange = orders$.subscribe(
     ord => console.log(`Sending to stock exchange the order to
    ➥${ord.action} ${ord.shares} shares of ${ord.stock}`));
const tradeCommission = orders$.subscribe(
     ord => console.log(`Reporting to trade commission the order to
    ➥${ord.action} ${ord.shares} shares of ${ord.stock}`));

const trader = new Trader(1, 'Joe');
const order1 = new Order(1, 1,'IBM',100,Action.Buy);
const order2 = new Order(2, 1,'AAPL',100,Action.Sell);

trader.placeOrder( order1);
trader.placeOrder( order2);
```

Annotations:
- Uses enums to declare which actions are allowed for orders
- A class representing an order
- A subject instance that works only with Order objects
- A class representing a trader
- When an order is placed, pushes it to subscribers
- A stock exchange subscriber
- A trade commission subscriber
- Places the first order
- Places the second order

Running listing D.6 produces the following output:[6]

```
Sending to stock exchange the order to BUY 100 shares of IBM
Reporting to trade commission the order to BUY 100 shares of IBM
Sending to stock exchange the order to SELL 100 shares of AAPL
Reporting to trade commission the order to SELL 100 shares of AAPL
```

NOTE In listing D.6, we use TypeScript enums that allow us to define a limited number of constants. Placing the actions to buy or sell inside an `enum` provides additional type checking to ensure that our script uses only the allowed actions. If we used string constants like `"SELL"` or `"BUY"`, the developer could misspell a word (`"BYE"`) while creating an order. By declaring `enum Action`, we restrict possible actions to `Action.Buy` or `Action.Sell`. Trying to use `Action.Bye` results in a compilation error.

[6] See it in CodePen: http://mng.bz/4PIH.

TIP We wrote listing D.6 in TypeScript, but if you want to see its JavaScript version, run `npm install` and the `tsc` commands in the project that comes with this appendix. The original code is located in the subject-trader.ts file, and the compiled version is in subject-trader.js.

Chapter 6 contains an example of using a `BehaviorSubject`—a special flavor of `Subject` that always emits its last or initial value to new subscribers.

D.7 The flatMap operator

In some cases, you need to treat each item emitted by an observable as another observable. The outer observable emits the inner observables. Does that mean you need to write nested `subscribe()` calls (one for the outer observable and another for the inner one)? No, you don't. The `flatMap` operator autosubscribes to each item from the outer observable.

Some operators are not explained well in RxJS documentation, and we recommend you refer to the general ReactiveX (reactive extensions) documentation for clarification. The `flatMap` operator is better explained at http://mng.bz/7RQB, which states that `flatMap` is used to "transform the items emitted by an observable into observables, then flatten the emissions from those into a single observable." This documentation includes the marble diagram shown in figure D.7.

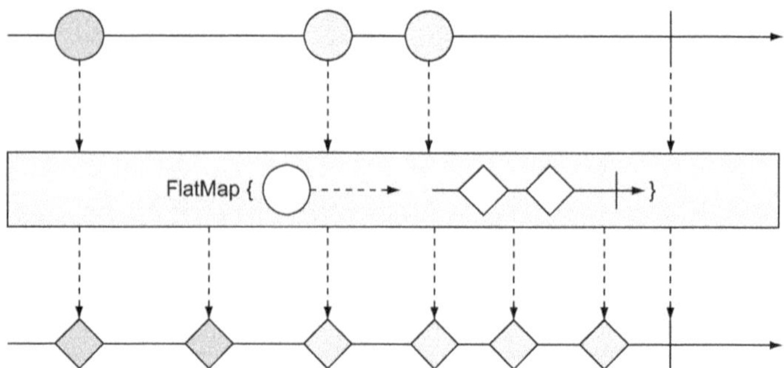

Figure D.7 The `flatMap` operator

As you see, the `flatMap` operator takes an emitted item from the outer observable (the circle) and unwraps its content (the inner observable of diamonds) into the flattened output observable stream. The `flatMap` operator merges the emissions of the inner observables, so their items may interleave.

Listing D.8 has an observable that emits drinks, but this time it emits not individual drinks, but palettes. The first palette has beers, and the second, soft drinks. Each palette is an observable. We want to turn these two palettes into an output stream with individual beverages.

Listing D.8 Unwrapping nested observables with `flatMap`

```
function getDrinks() {

    const beers$ = from([
         {name: "Stella", country: "Belgium", price: 9.50},
        {name: "Sam Adams", country: "USA", price: 8.50},
        {name: "Bud Light", country: "USA", price: 6.50}
    ], Scheduler.async);

    const softDrinks$ = from([
         {name: "Coca Cola", country: "USA", price: 1.50},
        {name: "Fanta", country: "USA", price: 1.50},
        {name: "Lemonade", country: "France", price: 2.50}
    ], Scheduler.async);

    return Observable.create( observer => {
            observer.next(beers$);
             observer.next(softDrinks$);
             observer.complete();
        }
    );
}

// We want to "unload" each palette and print each drink info

getDrinks()
  .pipe(flatMap(drinks => drinks))
   .subscribe(
       drink => console.log(`Subscriber got ${drink.name}: ${drink.price}`),
      error => console.err(error),
      () => console.log("The stream of drinks is over")
  );
```

Creates an async observable from beers

Creates an async observable from soft drinks

Emits the beers observable with next()

Emits the soft drinks observable with next()

Unloads drinks from pallets into a merged observable

Subscribes to the merged observable

This script will produce output that may look as follows:[7]

```
Subscriber got Stella: 9.5
Subscriber got Coca Cola: 1.5
Subscriber got Sam Adams: 8.5
Subscriber got Fanta: 1.5
Subscriber got Bud Light: 6.5
Subscriber got Lemonade: 2.5
The stream of observables is over
```

Are there any other uses of the `flatMap` operator besides unloading palettes of drinks? Another scenario where you'd want to use `flatMap` is when you need to execute more than one HTTP request, in which the result of the first request should be given to the second one, as shown in the following listing. In Angular, HTTP requests return observables, and without `flatMap()`, this could be done (it a bad style) with nested `subscribe` calls.

7 See it in CodePen: http://mng.bz/F38l.

Listing D.9 Subscribing to an HTTP request in Angular

```
this.httpClient.get('/customers/123')
  .subscribe(customer => {
              this.httpClient.get(customer.orderUrl)
              .subscribe(response => this.order = response)
  })
```

The `HttpClient.get()` method returns an `Observable`, and the better way to write the preceding code is by using the `flatMap` operator, which autosubscribes, unwraps the content of the first observable, and makes another HTTP request:

```
import {flatMap} from 'rxjs/operators';
...
httpClient.get('/customers/123')
    .pipe(
        flatMap(customer => this.httpClient.get(customer.orderUrl))
    )
    .subscribe(response => this.order = response);
```

Because a `flatMap` is a special case of `map`, you can specify a transforming function while flattening observables into a common stream. In the preceding example, we transform the value `customer` into a function call `HttpClient.get()`.

Let's consider one more example of using `flatMap`. This one is a modified version of the subject-trader example used earlier. This example is written in TypeScript, and it uses two `Subject` instances:

- `traders$`—This `Subject` keeps track of traders.
- `orders$`—This `Subject` is declared inside the `Trader` class and keeps track of each order placed by a particular trader.

You're the manager who wants to monitor all orders placed by all traders. Without `flatMap`, you'd need to subscribe to `traders$` (the outer observable) and create a nested subscription for `orders$` (the inner observable) that each subject has. Using `flatMap` allows you to write just one `subscribe()` call, which will be receiving the inner observables from each trader in one stream, as shown in the following listing.

Listing D.10 Two subjects and `flatMap`

```
enum Action{                    <-- Uses TypeScript enums
     Buy = 'BUY',                   to define action types
    Sell = 'SELL'
}

class Order{
    constructor(public orderId: number, public traderId: number,
         public stock: string, public shares: number, public action: Action)
      {}
}
```

```
let traders$ = new Subject<Trader>();

class Trader {

    orders$ = new Subject<Order>();

    constructor(private traderId: number,
    ➥public traderName: string) {}
}

let tradersSubscriber = traders$.subscribe
➥(trader => console.log(`Trader ${trader.traderName} arrived`));

let ordersSubscriber = traders$
   .pipe(flatMap(trader => trader.orders$))
   .subscribe(ord =>
        console.log(`Got order from trader ${ord.traderId}
       ➥to ${ord.action} ${ord.shares} shares of ${ord.stock}`));

let firstTrader = new Trader(1, 'Joe');
let secondTrader = new Trader(2, 'Mary');

traders$.next(firstTrader);
traders$.next(secondTrader);

let order1 = new Order(1,1,'IBM',100,Action.Buy);
let order2 = new Order(2,1,'AAPL',200,Action.Sell);
let order3 = new Order(3,2,'MSFT',500,Action.Buy);

// Traders place orders
firstTrader.orders$.next(order1);
firstTrader.orders$.next(order2);
secondTrader.orders$.next(order3);
```

Declares the Subject for traders

Each trader has its own Subject for orders.

Starts with the outer observable traders$

Extracts the inner observable from each Trader instance

The function subscribe() receives a stream of orders.

NOTE The enum containing string constants defines the action types. You can read about TypeScript enums at http://mng.bz/sTmp.

In this version of the program, the `Trader` class doesn't have a `placeOrder()` method. We just have the trader's `orders$` observable push the order to its observer by using the `next()` method . Remember, a `Subject` has both an observable and an observer.

The output of this program is shown next:

```
Trader Joe arrived
Trader Mary arrived
Got order from trader 1 to BUY 100 shares of IBM
Got order from trader 1 to SELL 200 shares of AAPL
Got order from trader 2 to BUY 500 shares of MSFT
```

In our example, the subscriber prints the orders on the console, but in a real-world app, it could invoke another function that would place an order with the stock exchange for execution.[8]

[8] See it in CodePen: http://mng.bz/4qC3.

D.8 The switchMap operator

Whereas `flatMap` unwraps and merges *all the data* from the outer observable values, the `switchMap` operator handles the data from the outer observable but cancels the inner subscription being processed if the outer observable emits a new value. The `switchMap` operator is easier to explain with the help of its marble diagram, shown in figure D.8.

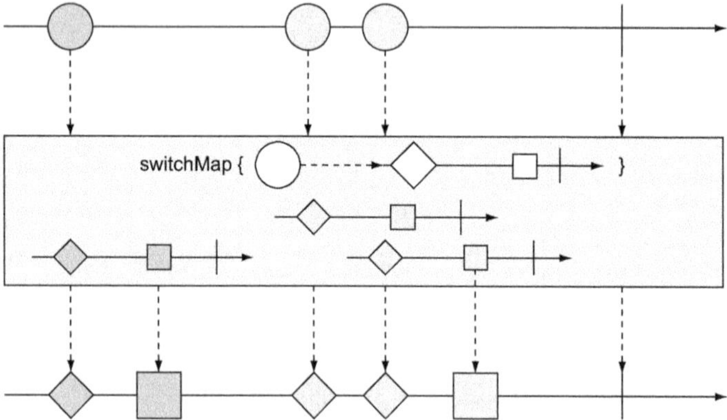
switchMap {
}

Figure D.8 The `switchMap` operator

For those reading the printed edition of this book, we need to say that the circles in the outer observable are red, green, and blue (from left to right). The outer observable emits the red circle, and `switchMap` emits the items from the inner observable (red diamond and square) into the output stream. The red circle was processed without any interruptions because the green circle was emitted after the inner observable finished processing.

The situation is different with the green circle. `switchMap` managed to unwrap and emit the green diamond, but the blue circle arrived *before* the green square was processed. The subscription to the green inner observable was cancelled, and the green square was never emitted into the output stream. The `switchMap` operator *switched* from processing the green inner observable to the blue one.

Listing D.11 has two observables. The outer observable uses the `interval()` function and emits a sequential number every second. With the help of the `take` operator, we limit the emission to two values: `0` and `1`. Each of these values is given to the `switchMap` operator, and the inner observable emits three numbers with an interval of 400 ms.

Listing D.11 Two observables and `switchMap`

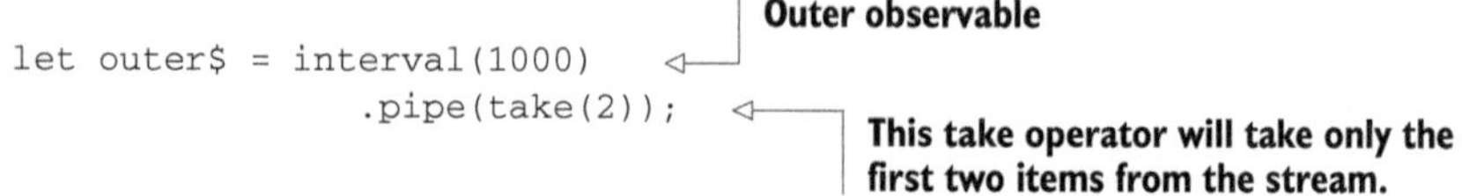

```
let outer$ = interval(1000)
                .pipe(take(2));
```

Outer observable
This take operator will take only the first two items from the stream.

```
let combined$ = outer$
    .pipe(switchMap((x) => {
            return interval(400)        <—— Inner observable
               .pipe(
                 take(3),
                 map(y => `outer ${x}: inner ${y}`)
               )
          })
      );

combined$.subscribe(result => console.log(`${result}`));
```

The output of listing D.10 is shown next:

```
outer 0: inner 0
outer 0: inner 1
outer 1: inner 0
outer 1: inner 1
outer 1: inner 2
```

Note that the first inner observable didn't emit its third value, 2. Here's the timeline:

1. The outer observable emits `0` and the inner emits `0` 400 ms later.
2. 800 ms later, the inner observable emits `1`.
3. In 1000 ms, the outer observable emits `1`, and the inner observable is unsubscribed.
4. The three inner emissions for the second outer value went uninterrupted because it didn't emit any new values.

If you replace `flatMap` with `switchMap`, the inner observable will emit three values for each outer value, as shown here:[9]

```
outer 0: inner 0
outer 0: inner 1
outer 0: inner 2
outer 1: inner 0
outer 1: inner 1
outer 1: inner 2
```

The chances are slim that you'll be writing outer and inner observables emitting integers. Chapter 6 explains a very practical use of the `switchMap` operator.

Just think of a user who types in an input field (the outer observable), and HTTP requests are being made (inner observable) on each `keyup` event. The circles in figure D.8 are the three characters that the user is typing. The inner observables are HTTP requests issued for each character. If the user entered the third character while the HTTP request for the second one is still pending, the inner observable gets cancelled and discarded.

---

[9] See it in CodePen: http://mng.bz/Y9IA.

TIP The `interval()` function is handy if you want to invoke another function periodically based on a specified time interval. For example, `interval(1000).subscribe(n => doSomething())` will result in calling the `doSomething()` function every second.

D.9 Error handling with catchError

The Reactive Manifesto (see www.reactivemanifesto.org) declares that a reactive app should be resilient, which means the app should implement a procedure to keep it alive in case of a failure. An observable can emit an error by invoking the `error()` function on the observer, but when the `error()` method is invoked, the stream completes.

RxJS offers several operators to intercept and handle an error before it reaches the code in the `error()` method on the observer:

- `catchError(error)`—Intercepts an error, and you can implement some business logic to handle it
- `retry(n)`—Retries an erroneous operation up to *n* times
- `retryWhen(fn)`—Retries an erroneous operation as per the provided function

Next, we'll show you an example of using the pipeable `catchError` operator. Inside the `catchError` operator, you can check the error status and react accordingly. Listing D.12 shows how to intercept an error and, if the error status is 500, switch to a different data producer to get the cached data. If the received error status isn't 500, this code will return an empty observable, and the stream of data will complete. In any case, the `error()` method on the observer won't be invoked.

Listing D.12 Intercepting errors with `catchError`

```
.pipe(
   catchError(err => {
    console.error("Got " + err.status + ": " + err.description);

    if (err.status === 500){
        console.error(">>> Retrieving cached data");

        return getCachedData();  // failover
    } else{
      return EMPTY;   // don't handle the error
    }
}))
```

Listing D.13 shows the complete example, where we subscribe to the stream of beers from a primary source—`getData()`—which randomly generates an error with the status 500. The `catchError` operator intercepts this error and switches to an alternate source: `getCachedData()`.

Listing D.13 Implementing failover with `catchError`

```
function getData(){
  const beers = [
      {name: "Sam Adams", country: "USA", price: 8.50},
      {name: "Bud Light", country: "USA", price: 6.50},
      {name: "Brooklyn Lager", country: "USA", price: 8.00},
      {name: "Sapporo", country: "Japan", price: 7.50}
  ];

  return Observable.create( observer => {
      let counter = 0;
      beers.forEach( beer => {
            observer.next(beer);        <-- Emits the next beer from the primary data source
             counter++;

            if (counter > Math.random() * 5) {    <-- Randomly generates the error with the status 500
                 observer.error({
                    status: 500,
                    description: "Beer stream error"
                  });
            }
          }
      );

      observer.complete();}
  );
}

// Subscribing to data from the primary source
getData()
  .pipe(
     catchError(err => {                 <-- Intercepts the error before it reaches the observer
       console.error(`Got ${err.status}: ${err.description}`);
      if (err.status === 500){
          console.error(">>> Retrieving cached data");
          return getCachedData();          <-- Fails over to the alternative data source
       } else{
        return EMPTY;   <-- Doesn't handle the non-500 errors; returns an empty observable to complete the stream
       }
    }),
    map(beer => `${beer.name}, ${beer.country}`)
  )
  .subscribe(
      beer => console.log(`Subscriber got ${beer}`),
      err => console.error(err),
      () => console.log("The stream is over")
  );

function getCachedData(){                <-- The alternate data source for failover
   const beers = [
      {name: "Leffe Blonde", country: "Belgium", price: 9.50},
      {name: "Miller Lite", country: "USA", price: 8.50},
      {name: "Corona", country: "Mexico", price: 8.00},
      {name: "Asahi", country: "Japan", price: 7.50}
  ];
```

```
  return Observable.create( observer => {
      beers.forEach( beer => {
              observer.next(beer);
          }
      );

      observer.complete();}
  );
}
```

The output of this program can look as follows:[10]

```
Subscriber got Sam Adams, USA
Subscriber got Bud Light, USA
Got 500: Beer stream error
>>> Retrieving cached data
Subscriber got Leffe Blonde, Belgium
Subscriber got Miller Lite, USA
Subscriber got Corona, Mexico
Subscriber got Asahi, Japan
The stream is over
```

[10] See it in CodePen: http://mng.bz/QBye.

index

O

P

Q

R

S

T

U

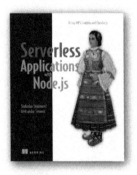